Policy-Making in the European Union

Fifth Edition

Edited by

Helen Wallace,
William Wallace

and

Mark A. Pollack

OXFORD

UNIVERSITY PRESS

OXFORD
UNIVERSITY PRESS

Great Clarendon Street, Oxford OX2 6DP

Oxford University Press is a department of the University of Oxford.
It furthers the University's objective of excellence in research, scholarship,
and education by publishing worldwide in

Oxford New York

Auckland Cape Town Dar es Salaam Hong Kong Karachi
Kuala Lumpur Madrid Melbourne Mexico City Nairobi
New Delhi Shanghai Taipei Toronto

With offices in

Argentina Austria Brazil Chile Czech Republic France Greece
Guatemala Hungary Italy Japan Poland Portugal Singapore
South Korea Switzerland Thailand Turkey Ukraine Vietnam

Oxford is a registered trade mark of Oxford University Press
in the UK and in certain other countries

Published in the United States
by Oxford University Press Inc., New York

© Oxford University Press 2005

British Library Cataloguing in Publication Data
Data available

Library of Congress Cataloging in Publication Data
Data available

Typeset by Newgen Imaging Systems (P) Ltd., Chennai, India
Printed in Great Britain
on acid-free paper by
Ashford Colour Press Ltd, Gosport, Hampshire

ISBN 978-0-19-927612-7

5 7 9 10 8 6 4

Outline contents

Part I Institutions, Process, and Analytical Approaches

Part II Policies

Part III **Conclusions**

Detailed contents

Preface

This is a new book which builds on four previous editions. It follows the pattern established in *Policy-Making in the European Communities* (1977), extended and developed in the second, third, and fourth editions of 1983, 1996, and 2000. All of its chapters have been rewritten, many extensively, with references to the earlier versions as appropriate. Readers who wish to understand the historical development of EU policies and policy-making in more detail are encouraged to refer back to earlier editions, to gain a broader sense of how patterns of policy-making and institutional interaction have changed over the past two decades.

In the five years since the last edition went to press the European Union (EU) has enlarged from fifteen to twenty-five members, with yet more would-be members waiting in the wings. It is early days still to judge the policy impacts of this most recent enlargement. As our policy cases show, so far the story is mainly about the efforts to maintain the *acquis communautaire*. How sustainable this will prove remains for the moment a matter of speculation. In the meantime a good deal of work has been put into reforming the institutional fabric of the EU. In 2000 an Intergovernmental Conference produced an interim reform in the Treaty of Nice, followed by the experiment of a more broadly based Convention on the Future of Europe. Its central result was a Constitutional Treaty signed symbolically in Rome in October 2004. It awaits ratification by the twenty-five members of the EU. In January 2002 the euro was launched, a single European currency with the surprising number of eleven member states participating—Greece joined later—in the experiment of economic and monetary union (EMU). But even as this remarkable experiment was made the member governments of the EU realized that this would not be enough to ensure a prosperous European economy. In March 2000 at the European Council in Lisbon the goal was set of making of the EU the 'most dynamic knowledge-based economy in the world' by 2010. This 'Lisbon strategy' has yet to yield substantive results. Over the past five years Europeans have witnessed profound changes in the global environment and have found themselves struggling to define collective responses. Initially aligned in the immediate response to the 9/11 attack on the twin towers in New York, Europeans from many countries took part in the invasion of Afghanistan. The American decision to invade Iraq provoked much more disagreement in Europe. Nonetheless European foreign and security policy cooperation has proceeded pragmatically to gain momentum and to acquire responsibilities. In parallel and in response to the international turbulence, European policy collaboration on internal security, migration, justice, and home affairs has been among the most active domains within the EU.

This is a study of policy-making, not of European integration as such. We do not therefore plunge into discussions of the broader political processes of the EU. Other dimensions of the EU are well covered in the companion volumes in *The New European Series*. Our aim here is to provide a detailed picture of the diversity of EU policy-making across a range of policy domains, to identify predominant patterns, and characteristic styles and trends over time.

The first edition was produced to fill a gap in what was then a thin academic literature on west European integration. Since then European academic research has mushroomed, contributing to a broadening flow of empirical and theoretical publications. We have included in this edition a new chapter by Mark Pollack setting out some of the theories and conceptual lenses which can be drawn on to help us better understand and explain EU policy-making. This fills a void in the third and fourth editions.

The fifteen case studies have been chosen both to cover the most important fields of EU activity and to illustrate the range of policy domains in which EU institutions now operate. Familiar issues of distribution and redistribution, the single market, agriculture, competition, external trade, north-south relations, monetary integration, and foreign policy have been covered in each of the five editions. The expansion of the EU's policy agenda since the early 1980s is reflected in the inclusion of case studies of environmental regulation, the social dimension, justice, and home affairs, and the response to the journey of the central and east European states from the socialist bloc to full EU membership for eight of them in 2004. Some of the most insightful examples of how European policy is made and managed emerge from examination of developing fields of policy, or of narrowly-defined sectors of established policy. Case studies of the fisheries regime and of the attempts to develop common policies in the biotechnology sector illustrate the blend of entrenched interests, expert communities and encapsulated regimes which characterizes much of EU policy-making. We have added to this edition a case study of employment policy, in part to address the pressing challenge of the Lisbon Agenda.

Ten of the eighteen authors of this volume contributed to the fourth edition, and the other eight are new conscripts, in particular Mark Pollack, who joins as co-editor, a task he cheerfully undertook without fully realizing quite what would be involved, and who in turn extends his thanks to the College of Liberal Arts at Temple University for their research support. The authors come from a spread of nationalities and intellectual traditions. This volume continues to benefit from informal ties and friendships among contributors since the first edition, sustained through exchanges of visits and children as well as through conferences and shared research. Special thanks go to those authors who have succeeded in producing both chapters and babies at the same time.

We would like to thank Sue Dempsey and Ruth Anderson at Oxford University Press for their patience and encouragement, as well as John Peterson, series co-editor, for his constant vigilance and commitment. Children grow up, and thus Edward and Harriet Wallace have not been available to help their parents out in the preparation of this edition. Instead Clare Tame, a freelance editor based in Florence, has brought her excellent skills and experience to steer us through the final stages of putting the volume into order. Tim Oliver carried out work on the graphics, Bastian Giegerich worked as research assistant for the chapter on CFSP, and Wim van Aken compiled data on contested voting in the Council of Ministers. All should be thanked for their help. Angelika Lanfranchi and Jennifer Chapa provided calm secretarial support. Gracia Marin Duran has carefully checked our references to the treaties and legislation. A special debt is owed to Josef Falke and Stephan Leibfried for compiling the remarkable statistics on the case loads of the European Courts, which appear in

Tables 3.4*a*, 3.4*b*, and 3.5. Table 4.1 is reproduced by kind permission of the Royal Institute of International Affairs. Figure 3.3, Box 3.1, and Table 3.3 in Chapter 3 also appear in Chapter 10 of the forthcoming volume on the Council of Ministers by Fiona Hayes-Renshaw and Helen Wallace, and has been reproduced here with the kind permission of the authors. Table 7.4 has been reproduced with the permission of the Institut für Agrarentwicklung in Mittel- und Osteuropa.

MP, HW, WW
Philadelphia, Florence, and London
December 2004

List of Figures

List of Boxes

List of Tables

Abbreviations and Acronyms

ACFM	Advisory Committee on Fishery Management
ACP	African, Caribbean and Pacific countries
AFSJ	area of freedom, security and justice
Agis	framework programme in the area of cooperation against international crime
AGRI	Directorate-General for Agriculture
APEC	Asia Pacific Economic Cooperation
ARGO	action programme for administrative cooperation in the areas of asylum, immigration, visas and external borders
AWACS	Airborne Warning and Control System
Benelux	Belgium, Netherlands and Luxembourg
BEPG	Broad Economic Policy Guidelines
BEUC	European Bureau of Consumer Unions
BKA	Bundeskartellamt
BSE	bovine spongiform encephalopathy
BUDG	Directorate-General for Budget
CAP	common agricultural policy
CARICOM	Caribbean Community and Common Market
CCBG	Committee of Central Bank Governors
CCP	common commercial policy
CCT	Common Commercial Tariff
CEECs	countries of central and eastern Europe
CEEP	European Centre of enterprises with Public Participation and of Enterprises of General Economic Interest
CEFAS	Centre for Environment, Fisheries and Acquaculture Services
CEN	Committee for European Norms (Standards)
CENELEC	Committee for European Electrical Norms (Standards)
CEPOL	European Police College
CFI	Court of First Instance
CFP	common fisheries policy
CFSP	common foreign and security policy
CIREFI	centre for information and exchange on migration
CIS	Commonwealth of Independent States (ex-USSR)
CITES	Convention on International Trade in Endangered Species
CJTF	Combined Joint Task-Forces
CMEA	Council for Mutual Economic Assistance ('Comecon')
CNE	Climate Network Europe
CNPEM	Comité national des pêches maritimes et des élevages marins
COG	chief of government
COPA	Confederation of Professional Agricultural Organizations
CoR	Committee of the Regions

Coreper	Committee of Permanent Representatives
Coreu	Correspondant Européen (European Communications Network of EPC)
COMP	Directorate-General for Competition
COSAC	Conférence des organs spécialisées aux affaires Européennes
CSCE	Conference on Security and Cooperation in Europe
CSF	Community Support Framework
CT	Constitutional Treaty
CTEU	Consolidated Treaty of the European Union
DDA	Doha Development Agenda
DG	Directorate-General (for European Commission, see Table 3.1)
DSU	Dispute Settlement Understanding
EA	Europe Agreement
EAGGF	European Agricultural Guidance and Guarantee Fund
EAP	Environmental Action Programme
EBA	Everything But Arms
EBRD	European Bank for Reconstruction and Development
EC	European Community
EC6	Belgium, France, Federal Republic of Germany, Italy, Luxembourg, and the Netherlands
EC9	EC6 plus Denmark, Ireland, UK
EC10	EC9 plus Greece
EC12	EC10 plus Portugal, Spain
EC/EU15	EC10 plus Austria, Finland, Sweden
EU25	EU15 plus Cyprus, the Czech Republic, Estonia, Hungary, Latvia, Lithuania, Malta, Poland, Slovakia, Slovenia
ECB	European Central Bank
ECHO	European Humanitarian Aid Office
ECN	European Competition Network
ECO	European Cartel Office
ECJ	European Court of Justice
Ecofin	Council of Economic and Financial Affairs
ECOWAS	Economic Community of Western African States
ECR	European Court Reports
ECSC	European Coal and Steel Community
ecu	European currency unit
EDC	European Defence Community
EDF	European Development Fund
EDU	European Drugs Unit
EEA	European Economic Area
EEB	European Environmental Bureau
EEC	European Economic Community
EEG	European Employment Guidelines
EES	European Employment Strategy
EET	European Employment Taskforce
EEZ	exclusive economic zone
EFSA	European Food Safety Authority

EFTA	European Free Trade Association
EIB	European Investment Bank
ELARG	Directorate-General for Enlargement
EMCDDA	European Monitoring Centre on Drugs and Drug Addiction
EMCO	Employment Committee
EMEA	European Medicines Agency, previously the European Agency for the Evaluation of Medicinal Products
EMI	European Monetary Institute
EMPL	Directorate-General for Employment
EMS	European Monetary System
EMU	economic and monetary union
ENV	Directorate-Generate for Environment
ENVIREG	programme combining economic resources and environmental protection
EP	European Parliament
EPC	European political cooperation
EPSCO	Employment, Social Affairs, Health and Consumer Affairs Council
ERDF	European Regional Development Fund
ERM	exchange-rate mechanism
ERT	European Round Table of Industrialists
ESA	European Space Agency
ESC	Economic and Social Committee
EDSI	European Security and Defence Identity
ESCB	European System of Central Banks
ESF	European Social Fund
ETUC	European Trade Union Confederation
EU	European Union
EUMC	European Monitoring Centre on Racism and Xenophobia
Euratom	European Atomic Energy Community
€ euro	name of the single currency for EMU
Eurocorps	multilateral European force, expanded from Franco-German brigade in 1991
Eurodac	European system for collecting fingerprints from asylum-seekers (from French abbrev.)
Eurogroup	European group within Nato from 1970
Eurojust	EU body to coordinate investigation and prosecution of serious cross-border and organized crime
Europol	European Police Office
Falcone	programme to enhance cooperation and exchange between persons and organizations involved in the fight against organized crime
FDA	Food and Drug Administration (US)
FIFG	Financial Instrument for Fisheries Guidance
FISH	Directorate-General for Fisheries
FSC	Foreign Sales Corporation Tax (US)
FTA	Free Trade Agreement
FTAA	Free Trade Agreement of the Americas
FTC	Federal Trade Commission
fYROM	former Yugoslav Republic of Macedonia

G7	Group of 7 (western economic powers): Canada, France, Germany, Italy, Japan, UK, US
G8	G7 plus Russia
G20	Group of Twenty, finance ministers and central banks of Argentina, Australia, Brazil, Canada, China, France, Germany, India, Indonesia, Italy, Japan, Korea, Mexico, Russia, Saudi Arabia, South Africa, Turkey, the UK, the US, and the EU
G24	Group of 24 (member states of OECD)
GAC	General Affairs Council
GAERC	General Affairs and External Relations Council
GATS	General Agreement on Trade in Services
GATT	General Agreement on Tariffs and Trade
GDP	gross domestic product
GDR	German Democratic Republic
GMO	genetically modified organism
GNI	gross national income
GNP	gross national product
Govecor	Economic Governance through Self-Coordination
GSP	Generalized System of Preferences
ha.	hectare
ICCAT	International Commission for the Conservation of the Atlantic Tuna
ICES	International Council for the Exploration of the Sea
IDP	Integrated Development Programme
IEEP	Institute for European Environmental Policy
IEPG	Independent European Programme Group
IFREMER	Institut français de recherche pour l'exploitation de la mer
IGC	Intergovernmental Conference
IMF	International Monetary Fund
IMP	Integrated Mediterranean Programmes
IMPEL	European Network for the Implementation and Enforcement of Environmental Law
IR	international relations
ISO	International Standards Organization
ITQ	individual transferable quotas
JAI	Directorate-General for Justice and Home Affairs
JHA	justice and home affairs
K4	committee of senior officials for JHA (now Article 36 Committee)
LDC	less developed country
LIBE	Committee on Citizens' Freedoms and Rights, Justice and Home Affairs
LIFE	Financial Instrument for the Environment
MAFF	Ministry of Agriculture, Fisheries, and Food (UK)
MAG'92	Mutual Assistance Group (for 1992)
MAGP	Multi-annual Guidance Programme
MAI	Multilateral Agreement on Investment
MEDSPA	Mediterranean Special Programme of Action
MEP	member of the European Parliament

Mercosur	Common Market of the Southern Cone
MFN	most-favoured nation (in GATT)
MLG	multi-level governance
MSC	Marine Stewardship Council
MTR	Mid-Term Review of Uruguay Round
NACC	North Atlantic Consultative Council
NAFTA	North Atlantic Free Trade Area
NAMA	non-agricultural market access
NAP	national action plan
Nato	North Atlantic Treaty Organization
NCA	national competition authority
NEAFC	North Eastern Atlantic Fisheries Commission
NFFO	National Federation of Fishermen's Organizations
NGO	non-governmental organization
NTB	non-tariff barrier
Octopus	programme to tackle corruption in eastern Europe
OECD	Organization for Economic Cooperation and Development
OEEC	Organization for European Economic Cooperation
OFT	Office of Fair Trading (UK)
OISIN	cooperation programme against organized crime
OLAF	European Anti-Fraud Office, Office de la Lutte Anti-Fraude, formerly UCLAF
OMC	open method of coordination
OSCE	Organization for Security and Cooperation in Europe
PCOTF	European Police Chiefs' Task Force
PESC	politique étrangère et de sécurité commune
Phare	Pologne-Hongrie: Actions pour la reconversion économique (extended to other CEECs)
PJCCM	police and judicial cooperation in criminal matters
PO	producers' organization
QMV	qualified majority voting
QR	quantitative restriction
R&D	research and development
rDNA	recombinant DNA
RDP	Regional Development Plans
SAAs	Stabilization and Association Agreements
SAD	Statement of Assurance
SANCO	Directorate-General for Health and Consumer Protection
SBF	'Save Britain's Fish'
SCA	Special Committee on Agriculture
SCIFA	Strategic Committee on Immigration, Frontiers and Asylum
SCIFA+	SCIFA plus heads of national border control authorities
SCV	subsidies and countervailing duties
SEA	Single European Act
SEM	single European market
SFC	Sea Fisheries Committee
SFF	Scottish Fishermen's Federation

SG	Steering Group
SGP	Stability and Growth Pact
SIC	Schengen Implementing Convention
SIRENE	Supplementary Information System of Schengen
SIS	Schengen Information System
SME	small and medium-sized enterprises
SPD	Single Programming Document
STECF	Scientific, Technical and Economic Committee for Fisheries
STOP II	programme to prevent and combat trade in human beings and sexual exploitation
TAC	Total Allowable Catch
TACIS	Technical Assistance for the CIS countries
TAIEX	Technical Assistance Information Exchange Office
TARGET	intra-European large payments clearing-house system
TBR	Trade Barriers Regulation
TBT	technical barriers to trade
TCA	trade and cooperation agreement
TEC	Consolidated Treaty establishing the European Community, Revised Treaty of Rome
T&E	transport and environment
TEN	Trans-European Network
TEU	Treaty on European Union
ToA	Treaty of Amsterdam
ToN	Treaty of Nice
TPA	Trade Promotion Authority
TRADE	Directorate-General for Trade
TREN	Directorate-General for Energy and Transport
Trevi	Terrorism, Radicalism, Extremism, Violence, Information (agreement on internal security cooperation)
TRIMs	Trade-Related Investment Measures
TRIPS	Trade-Related Intellectual Property Rights
troika	grouping of three successive Council presidencies
UAPF	Union des Armateurs à la Pêche de France
UCLAF	Unité de coordination de la lutte anti-fraude, now OLAF
UEAPME	European Association of Craft, Small and Medium-sized Enterprises (union européenne de l'artisan et des petites et moyennes enterprises)
UK	United Kingdom
UN	United Nations
UNHCR	United Nations High Commission for Refugees
UNICE	Union of Industrial and Employers' Confederations of Europe
Unprofor	United Nations Protection Force in Bosnia
UR	Uruguay Round
US	United States
USTR	United States Trade Representative
VAT	value-added tax

VIS	Visa Information System
WEU	Western European Union
WG	working group
WTO	World Trade Organization
WWF	World-Wide Fund for Nature

List of Contributors

DAVID ALLEN, Loughborough University
BRIGID LAFFAN, University College, Dublin
SANDRA LAVENEX, University of Bern
STEPHAN LEIBFRIED, University of Bremen
ANDREA LENSCHOW, University of Osnabrück
CHRISTIAN LEQUESNE, CERI, Paris, CEFRES, Prague
JOHANNES LINDNER, European Central Bank
KATHLEEN R. MCNAMARA, Georgetown University
MARK A. POLLACK, Temple University
MARTIN RHODES, European University Institute
ELMAR RIEGER, University of Bremen
ULRICH SEDELMEIER, Central European University
GREGORY C. SHAFFER, University of Wisconsin
HELEN WALLACE, European University Institute, University of Sussex
WILLIAM WALLACE, London School of Economics and Political Science
STEPHEN WILKS, University of Exeter
STEPHEN WOOLCOCK, London School of Economics and Political Science
ALASDAIR R. YOUNG, University of Glasgow

Table of Cases

European Court of Justice (ECJ) and Court of First Instance (CFI)

Source
Court of Justice of the European Communities website:
www.curia.eu.int/en/content/juris/index.htm

Table of Secondary Legislation

EC Regulations, Directives, and Decisions

Resolution

Sources

- The Official Journal of the European Communities: *http://europa.eu.int/eur-lex/en/oj/*
- European Commission, DG Competition:
  http://europa.eu.int/comm/competition/index_en.html

Editors' Note

A number of problems of dating and numbering and nomenclature should be noted.

Generally in this volume for convenience we use the term European Union (EU) to embrace the family of arrangements under different treaties, even though it was not formally introduced until 1992. Where specifically relevant we refer to individual Communities or the European Community (EC). Pending ratification of the Constitutional Treaty (CT) the EU does not have legal personality, and hence formally speaking it is the EC which is sometimes party to international legal conventions or treaties (see Table 3.1 for the main treaties and treaty reforms).

Treaty reforms are dated to their year of signature by member governments, rather than to the completion of negotiations (often the year before), or ratification (often the year after). The well-intentioned renumbering of treaty articles, agreed as an afterthought to the Treaty of Amsterdam (ToA), has created immense difficulties for all students of European Union. This Consolidated Treaty on European Union (CTEU) agreed in 1997, confusingly contains the Consolidated Treaty establishing the European Community (TEC). We generally quote treaty articles under this new numbering, but special care is needed to follow the two parallel sets of numbering that cover the common foreign and security policy and justice and home affairs. For the new Constitutional Treaty signed in Rome in October 2004 we use the final numbering, not earlier versions or those of the draft text from the preceding Convention.

As regards terminology, readers will notice that we frequently refer to 'member government' rather than 'member state'. Although, strictly speaking, it is 'states' that sign and are parties to treaties and conventions, it is the member 'governments' which negotiate policies and legislation, or implement them at home, acting not only as representatives of states, but as the domestically accountable executive authorities.

Gross domestic product (GDP) is the most commonly used measure of the value of production in the area concerned (a country or a region). Gross national product (GNP) is GDP plus net transfers of factor incomes, i.e. the repatriated profits of member-state multinationals overseas, and less the profits of non-national multinationals operating in the member state. In most countries the difference between the two may be insignificant, but in countries such as Ireland the difference between the two may be as high as 25 per cent. Recently, gross national income (GNI) has become the more commonly used name for GNP.

Until September 1999 Directorates-General (DGs) of the European Commission were generally known by their numbers, e.g. DGVI for Agriculture. Numbers have been replaced by functional names. However, in this volume the numbers have sometimes been retained, since much of the material belongs to the period in which they were relevant. The two nomenclatures are set out in Table 3.2.

The ecu, or European currency unit, referred to in several chapters was the unit of account adopted for certain EU transactions or statistical comparisons. It has been replaced by the euro with the advent of economic and monetary union.

Part I

Institutions, Process, and Analytical Approaches

Chapter 1
An Overview

Helen Wallace, William Wallace and Mark A. Pollack

Contents

Introduction

The European Union (EU) is perhaps the most important agent of change in contemporary government and policy-making in Europe. In 1988 Jacques Delors, then the President of the European Commission, claimed that around 80 per cent of socio-economic legislation in the EU member states was framed by treaty commitments, policy rules, and legislation agreed through the institutions of the EU. Whether or not the percentage is precisely accurate does not matter. What matters is the acknowledgement that EU agreements pervade the policy-making activities of individual European countries, both the member states and their neighbours. Explaining how and why this is so is the key aim of this volume.

More specifically, this book, like its four predecessors, seeks to understand the processes which make EU policies. We do not advance any single theory of EU policy-making, although we do draw extensively on theories of European integration, comparative politics, and contemporary governance in our search for vocabulary to understand and explain our subject. Similarly, we make no effort to identify a single EU policy style, but instead classify and explore empirically the extraordinary and ever-increasing diversity of 'policy modes' whereby the preferences of national governments, sub-national actors, and supranational organizations are changed into common policies.

The volume is organized in three parts. In Part I we sketch the broad contours of the EU policy process, identify some of the different theories and concepts with which the policy process can be analysed, and then explain the institutions through which policies are articulated. We also present a classification of five 'policy modes', drawn from the scholarly literature and empirical practice, which serve as an analytic backdrop for the analysis of policy-making in specific sectors.

Part II consists of a series of fifteen case studies, which cover the main policy domains in which the EU dimension is significant. The cases cover a wide range of long-established and infant regimes, overarching complex policies and specific sectoral concerns, and more and less formally structured policies. One new case on employment policy (Chapter 11) appears in this edition. The case studies carried over from previous editions have been extensively revised to illustrate either different dimensions of their policy domain or major changes that have occurred over the past few years.

Part III offers some conclusions on the character of the process and the directions in which it is evolving. In the remainder of this chapter, we offer preliminary observations about the nature of the EU and the challenge of understanding policy-making in this ever-evolving political system.

The EU and its predecessors

For convenience, we have generally used the term European Union (EU) in this volume. The EU is built out of three originally separate Communities, each with different powers, characteristics, and policy domains, complemented by other 'pillars' of organized cooperation. These various elements of the EU are as follows (note that the dates of treaties are given by year of signature rather than year of ratification):

- The European Coal and Steel Community (ECSC), founded in 1951 by the Treaty of Paris;

- The European Economic Community (EEC), founded in 1957 by the Treaty of Rome;

- The European Atomic Energy Community (Euratom), also founded in 1957 by another Treaty of Rome;

- These three together were generally known as the European Community (EC), and in a loose sense the 'first pillar', once the term EU was introduced by the (Maastricht) Treaty on European Union (TEU) of 1992;

- The 'second pillar' for developing the common foreign and security policy (CFSP), acknowledged in the Single European Act (SEA) of 1986, and put onto a more formal basis in the TEU;

- The 'third pillar' for developing cooperation in justice and home affairs (JHA), also established by the TEU in 1992;

- Further development of the JHA provisions, in particular, was addressed in the Treaty of Amsterdam (ToA) of 1997, which also incorporated the Schengen treaties;

- Subsequently, also in 1997, a Consolidated Treaty of the European Community (TEC) was issued, which confusingly renumbered a good many treaty provisions (we indicate both versions of numbering in the volume for important provisions); the Treaty of Nice (ToN) of 2001 made some rule changes, but did not alter the overall architecture of the EU; and

■ The reform initiatives of 2002–4, based on the work of the Convention on the Future of Europe, which led to the Constitutional Treaty (CT), signed in Rome in October 2004 and thereafter subject to the outcome of ratification processes in all twenty-five member states, and *inter alia* intended to simplify the treaties and to amalgamate the pillars into an overarching framework.

Membership of the EU had expanded from six countries in 1951 to fifteen by 1995, and to twenty-five in May 2004, with further enlargement in prospect, as follows:

1951   Belgium, France, Germany, Luxembourg, Italy, Netherlands

1973   +Denmark, Ireland, the UK

1981   +Greece

1986   +Portugal, Spain

1995   +Austria, Finland, Sweden

2004   +Cyprus, the Czech Republic, Estonia, Hungary, Latvia, Lithuania, Malta, Poland, Slovakia, Slovenia

Current applicants include: Bulgaria, Croatia, Macedonia, Romania, and Turkey, with yet more waiting in the wings (see Chapter 16).

Some preliminary observations

Four broad points need to be made clear at the outset. First, the EU policy process is based on west European experience. Until 2004 the member countries of the EU, and its various precursors, were west European countries with market economies and liberal democratic polities, even though some, notably Greece, Portugal, and Spain, had moved quite swiftly from authoritarian regimes to EU membership in the 1980s, and from 1991 Germany included as new *Länder* what had been the German Democratic Republic under a communist regime. It is not our contention that these countries all neatly fitted into a single political and economic mould, but nonetheless they have some strong shared characteristics which permeate the EU policy process. However, the EU has now enlarged eastwards to embrace already eight central and east European countries, with very different inheritances. One important question which follows is whether this fit between country characteristics and European process will be sustainable in a larger and more diverse Union.

A second preliminary point is that the west European experience, in which the EU is embedded, is one of which dense multilateralism is a strong feature. The EU consti-tutes a particularly intense form of multilateralism, but western Europe constituted a region of countries with an apparent predisposition to engage in cross-border regime-building. In part this relates to specific features of history and geography, but it seems also to be connected to a political culture of investing in institutionalized cooperation with neighbours and partners, at least in the period since the second world war. This is part of the reason why transnational policy development has become more structured and more iterative than in most other regions of the world. This also explains in part some of the nervousness at the challenge of absorbing central and east European countries which had not undergone that same experience.

Thirdly, the EU has, since its inception, been active in a rather wide array of policy domains, and indeed has over the decades extended its policy scope. Most international or transnational regimes are more one-dimensional. Part of our contention in this volume is that this array of policy domains has generated not one, but several, modes of policy-making, as the case studies reveal. Moreover, the same EU institutions, and the same national policy-makers, have different characteristics, exhibit different patterns of behaviour, and produce different kinds of outcome, depending on the policy domain and depending on the period. Thus, as we shall see, there is no single and catch-all way of capturing the essence of EU policy-making. All generalizations need to be nuanced, although, as will be seen in Chapter 3, five main variants of the policy process can be identified.

Fourthly, this volume goes to press at a moment when important systemic changes are taking place in the EU. The EU will be altered by eastern enlargement, a dimension which we have endeavoured to take into account across the volume. The questions hang in the air as to when, and whether, the new Constitutional Treaty will be ratified, and what impacts it would have on the policy-making process of the EU. There are, however, also other major factors of change. Three in particular stand out: efforts to make the European economy more dynamic, with both economic and monetary union (EMU) (Chapter 6), and the objective of economic reform under the Lisbon Strategy (partly covered in Chapter 11); the incorporation of internal security and immigration policies, through the 'area of freedom, security and justice' (Chapter 18); and the moves under way to strengthen European foreign policy and defence autonomy (Chapter 17). As will become clear, both from the individual accounts of these topics and from Part III, the net effect may be to change in rather fundamental ways the nature of EU policy-making.

One striking feature characterizes the patterns of policy-making in these three domains. Each is being constructed to a large extent outside the classical Community framework. Some EU institutions, so far at least, have been on the margins of the main developments. In particular the Commission, the European Court of Justice (ECJ), and the European Parliament (EP) have been less central actors, while the main dynamics have been found in the intensive interactions between national policy-makers, with both new agencies, such as the European Central Bank (ECB) or Europol, and new consultative fora, notably to pursue the Lisbon Strategy. The investments being made in new institutional arrangements in each of these areas have been designed to underpin this structured transgovernmentalism rather than to incorporate them within the traditional Community procedures (communitarization). The case study chapters suggest that this may be a sustained pattern, not a mere staging post in the transition from nationally rooted policy to 'communitarization'. Tempting though it is to interpret this as the triumph of 'intergovernmentalism' (a process in which traditional states predominate) over 'supranationalism' (a process in which new European institutions enjoy political autonomy and authority), we argue that new transnational policy modes are emerging.

Chapter 2 therefore takes a broad and eclectic approach in identifying a deliberately wide range of theories and concepts with which to examine and to explain EU policy-making. We argue that care should be taken to avoid over-sharp dichotomies, between supranationalism, on the one hand, and intergovernmentalism, on the other, or between theoretical templates from comparative politics, on one hand, and international relations, on the other. Instead, we look to a variety of approaches, drawing on diverse theoretical traditions and from both comparative politics and international relations, in order to explicitly 'mainstream' the study of the EU by linking EU policy processes to comparable domestic and international processes, particularly in multi-layered polities. We also point out that policy-making and governance in contemporary societies are subject to many factors of change, and thus some of the shifts within the EU are not unique phenomena.

The EU in context

Most studies of the EU concentrate on describing what happens in and through the special institutions of the EU, located in Brussels, Luxembourg, and Strasbourg: the European Commission; the Council of the EU; the European Council; the European Parliament (EP); and the European Court of Justice (ECJ). Those new to the subject should note the existence of the entirely separate organization—the Council of Europe, created in 1949, based in Strasbourg, originally with only west European members, but now with a continent-wide membership of forty-five countries. It has a classical intergovernmental structure, except for the rather autonomous European Court of Human Rights. However, we should be careful not to regard these EU institutions as existing in a vacuum. Most of the policy-makers who devise and operate EU rules and legislation are from the member states themselves. They are people who spend the greater part of their time as national policy-makers, for whom the European dimension is an extended policy arena, not a separate activity. Indeed, much of EU policy is prepared and carried out by national policy-makers and agents who do not spend much, if any, time in Brussels. Instead, what they do is consider how EU regimes might help or hinder their regular activities, and apply the results of EU agreements on the ground in their normal daily work. If we could calculate the proportions we might well find that in practice something like 80 per cent of that normal daily life was framed by domestic preoccupations and constraints. Much the same is true of the social and economic groups, or political representatives, who seek to influence the development and content of EU policy.

On the face of it, it might appear that it cannot simultaneously be the case that 80 per cent of the member states' socio-economic legislation is shaped by the EU, while 80 per cent of the policy context of national policy-makers is framed by domestic concerns. Yet precisely what distinguishes the EU as a policy arena is that it rests on a kind of amalgam of these two levels of governance. Country-defined policy demands and policy capabilities are set in a shared European framework to generate collective regimes, most of which are then implemented back in the countries concerned. Moreover, as we shall see from several of the case studies in this volume, how those European regimes operate varies a good deal between one EU member state and another. In other words, the EU policy process is one which has differentiated outcomes, with significant variations between countries. Hence it is just as important to understand the national institutional settings as to understand the EU-level institutions in order to get a grip on the EU policy process as a whole (H. Wallace 1973, 1999).

This two-level picture does not, however, describe the whole story. In all EU countries there are other levels of infra-national government, that is local or regional authorities, the responsibilities of which are to varying extents shaped by EU regimes. Many of these authorities have occasional direct contacts with the EU institutions, and in some countries may be the key ones for implementing specific EU policies and legislation. In addition, and increasingly, national policy processes in Europe depend on other kinds of agencies and institutions, which lie between the public and the private spheres and also vary a good deal in character from one country to another. One striking feature of western Europe in the past decade or so, an experience now replicated in central and eastern Europe, has been the proliferation of bodies with public policy functions outside the central governments. This is especially so in the regulatory arena, perhaps the most extensive domain of EU policy activity. The shift towards more autonomous or semi-autonomous agencies, or to forms of 'self-regulation', represents a move away from the inherited heavy state version of government towards a kind of partnership model. What the EU policy process does is to add another layer, making cross-agency coordination one of its key features, as we shall see in various of our case studies.

Even this multi-faceted picture does not encompass the whole story. The EU arena is only part of a wider pattern of making policy beyond the nation-state. In many areas of public policy, including those within which the EU is active, there are broader transnational consultations and regimes. These vary a great deal in their robustness and intensity, but they are part of a continuum of policy-making that spreads from the country level, through the European arena, to the global level. Many of the same policy-makers are active across these different levels, and policy development consists of choices between these levels or the assignment of different segments of a given policy domain to different levels. Several of our policy case studies illustrate this phenomenon, and mostly stress its increased salience. One important question to bear in mind here is whether or not the EU institutions provide the main junction box through which connections are made between the country-level and the global level.

One further preliminary point needs to be made. Most accounts of the EU policy process work from the EU treaties outwards, starting from the policy powers explicitly assigned to them, and then considering extensions of policy powers, or refusals to extend policy powers. Such accounts place the EU at the centre of the picture, and tend to make the EU appear the fulcrum of policy-making. Other European transnational policy regimes—and there are many—tend to be viewed as second-best solutions, or weaker forms of policy cooperation. This volume takes issue with this image. Instead we argue that the EU is only one, even if by far the most invasive, arena for building European policy regimes. Hence we need to compare and contrast the EU with these other policy regimes, both the highly structured (such as the North Atlantic Treaty Organization (Nato) for defence), and the relatively informal (such as in the past have enabled national police forces to develop cross-border cooperation). Then we can consider with more nuance why the EU process is especially important in some policy domains, but not in others, just as we can examine how experiences in other kinds of European policy regime might be changing the character of the EU policy process.

In short, the EU policy process needs to be viewed through several sets of spectacles. Different lenses may be needed depending on the division of powers and influences between these different levels and arenas of policy development. Certainly, we then need to focus squarely on what happens in and through the EU institutions. But we need peripheral vision to take in the country-level processes (both national and infra-national), the global level, and the alternative European frameworks. And we need to be aware that policy-making shifts between these in a fluid and dynamic way.

The EU as a unique arena—or perhaps not

Most accounts of the EU policy process, as we have noted, concentrate on the EU's own institutions. Their main features and characteristics are set out in Chapter 3, and their roles in the policy process will be a recurrent theme in this volume. We shall observe general features that are present in most areas of EU policy, as well as features that are specific to particular sectors, issues, events, and periods.

But how far do the particular features of the EU's institutional system produce a distinctive kind of policy-process? It has been commonplace for commentators on the EU to stress its distinctive features, and indeed often to argue that they result in a unique kind of politics. Whether such an assertion is warranted is a question to keep in mind in reading subsequent chapters. In forming an answer to the question it is important to reflect on what other political arrangements might be appropriately compared with those of the EU. Some would say loose-knit states, such as Canada or Switzerland, mostly confederal in character, or a federal state like the United States of America, Belgium, or Germany. Others would say some multilateral regimes, especially those which focus on the political economy, such as the Organization for Economic Cooperation and Development (OECD), or the various regional customs unions and free trade areas elsewhere in the world. Depending on which comparators are chosen, different 'benchmarks' will be useful for evaluating the EU institutions and their performance.

As we shall see in Chapter 2, this issue has been one of the longest running sources of controversy among political analysts of the EU. On one side of the debate are ranged those who see the EU as one example, perhaps a particularly richly developed example, of a transnational or international organization. On the other side of the debate are those who view the EU as a kind of polity-in-the-making, and, in this sense, state-like. The analyses of the EU's institutions conducted in these two camps differ considerably. A third camp argues that contemporary politics in Europe are changing anyway, with traditional forms of politics and government being transformed in quite radical ways. The net result, it is argued, is that it is more appropriate to talk of 'governance' than of 'government'. The EU has, according to this view, emerged as part of a reconfigured pattern of European governance, with an evolution of institutional arrangements and associated processes that have interestingly novel characteristics.

This volume starts out closer to the third camp than to either of the first two. However, subsequent chapters will reveal some policy sectors in which the EU has powers as extensive as those normally associated with country-level governance, while other chapters will describe much lighter and more fragile European regimes. The institutional patterns vary between these two kinds of cases. Chapter 3 provides an anatomical overview of the institutions together with a broad characterization of five main policy modes that vary across issue areas and across time. Subsequent case studies identify many of the variations of institutional patterns that are observable in specific areas of policy, along with the organic features of the institutional processes. These variations make the EU policy process a challenging one to characterize and hence the subject of lively argument for both practitioners and analysts.

However distinctive and unusual the EU institutions might be argued to be, we should not forget that the people, groups, and organizations which are active within these institutions are for the most part going about their 'normal' business in seeking policy and political outcomes. There is no reason to suppose that their activities have different purposes simply because the institutional arena is different from the others in which they are involved. The politics of the EU are just that—normal politics, with whatever one thinks are the normal features of domestic politics, and by extension policy-making—in European countries. Nonetheless, we need to be alert to differences in behaviour, in opportunities, and in constraints that arise from being involved in a multi-level and multi-layered process. It is around this feature of the EU that much of the most interesting analytical debate takes place, to which we turn in Chapter 2.

Further reading

A good understanding of the recent history of Europe is a valuable starting point. Dinan (2004) provides a straightforward overview of the development of the EU. Milward (2000) offers a robust critique of much of the orthodoxy surrounding interpretations of the EU. Moravcsik (1998) submits the history of the EU to fine-grained political analysis. For insights into the deeper history Mazower (1999) is an excellent and provoking volume, usefully complemented by the more social scientific insights of Stein Rokkan, whose collected writings are drawn together by Flora (1999). Scharpf (1999) draws together very succinctly many of the contemporary challenges to governance in western Europe, some of which are also interestingly surveyed by Kapteyn (1996) and Majone (2005). For an attempt to situate European integration in both its global and its domestic contexts, see Laffan, O'Donnell and Smith (1999). For the link to 'pan-Europe', see also H. Wallace (2001, ch. 1), and Schimmelfennig and Sedelmeier (2005).

Dinan, D. (2004), *Europe Recast: A History of European Union* (London: Palgrave Macmillan).

Flora, P. (1999) (ed.), *State Formation, Nation-Building and Mass Politics in Europe: The Theory of Stein Rokkan* (Oxford: Oxford University Press).

Kapteyn, P. (1996), *The Stateless Market: The European Dilemma of Integration and Civilization* (London: Routledge).

Kohler-Koch, B. (2003) (ed.), *Linking EU and National Governance* (Oxford: Oxford University Press).

Laffan, B., O'Donnell, R., and Smith, M. (1999), *Europe's Experimental Union: Rethinking Integration* (London: Routledge).

Majone, G. (2005), *Dilemmas of European Integration: The Ambiguities and Pitfalls of Integration by Stealth* (Oxford: Oxford University Press).

Mazower, M. (1999), *Dark Continent: Europe's Twentieth Century* (London: Penguin).

Milward, A. S. (2000), *The European Rescue of the Nation-State*, 2nd edn. (London: Routledge).

Moravcsik, A. (1998), *The Choice for Europe: Social Purpose and State Power from Messina to Maastricht* (Ithaca: Cornell University Press).

Scharpf, F. W. (1999), *Governing in Europe: Effective and Democratic?* (Oxford: Oxford University Press).

Schimmelfennig, F., and Sedelmeier, U. (2005) (eds.), *The Europeanisation of Central and Eastern Europe* (Ithaca: Cornell University Press).

Wallace, H. (2001) (ed.), *Interlocking Dimensions of European Integration* (London: Palgrave Macmillan).

Chapter 2
Theorizing EU Policy-Making

Mark A. Pollack

Contents

Summary

Our understanding of EU policy-making and policy processes is shaped largely by the language of theory, and an understanding of the main currents of EU-related theories is therefore a useful starting point for the case studies in this volume. Three primary currents or strands of theory are identified and explored. First, we examine the various theories of European integration, which initially pitted neo-functionalist models of integration through spill-over against intergovernmentalist models emphasizing the continuing dominance of national governments; later, this debate was largely supplanted by a second debate pitting rational-choice theorists against constructivist analyses.

Secondly, we survey the increasing number of studies that approach the EU through the lenses of comparative politics and comparative public policy, focusing on the federal or quasi-federal aspects of the EU and the legislative, executive, and judicial politics of the Union. Thirdly and finally, we examine the 'governance approach' to the EU, which theorizes the Union as an experiment in non-hierarchical, public-private and deliberative governance, and focuses in large part on the normative questions of the EU's democratic legitimacy. Taken together, these theories pose important questions and provide distinctive hypotheses about the key actors and the dominant processes in EU policy-making.

Introduction

This chapter sketches the theoretical background for the book, by surveying theories of European integration, comparative politics, and governance, laying out clearly the analytical concepts that will subsequently be employed by our contributors.[1] The chapter does not seek to come up with a single theory to explain European integration, or even the policy process within the EU, a project beyond the scope of this volume. Indeed, a consistent theme of this book from its first edition onwards has been the need to guard against overgeneralizing about 'the' EU policy process, but instead being open to the prospect that policy-making may differ considerably and systematically across issue areas. Nevertheless, theories of European integration and public policy-making are useful in providing us with the analytical tools with which to chart and explain variation in EU policy-making both across issue areas and over time, and these theories inform the language and the categories of analysis used in the subsequent chapters of the volume.

This chapter is organized in four parts. The first provides a brief overview of the most influential theories of European integration, namely neo-functionalism, intergovernmentalism, institutionalism, and constructivism, paying particular attention to the implications of each theory for our specific focus on EU policy-making. The second section looks beyond the integration literature, drawing on rationalist theories of comparative public policy for a set of analytical categories that can be used to analyse the participants, processes, and policies that we observe in the EU. In doing so, we pay special attention to the concept of the EU as a political system, characterized by a horizontal and a vertical separation of powers, which, we argue, has implications for the nature of policy-making and the key actors in the EU policy process. The third section examines the recent development of a 'governance approach' to the European Union. The governance approach emphasizes a series of interrelated concepts, including: the non-hierarchical or 'network' character of EU policy-making; the emergence of 'multi-level governance' implicating subnational, national, and supranational actors; the challenge to the governance capacity of national governments and the limited governance capacity and legitimacy of the EU; and the prospect for 'deliberative supranationalism' as a partial response to the challenge of democratic legitimacy beyond the nation-state. The fourth section concludes with a brief restatement of the primary theoretical debates in EU studies today, and the questions that they raise for the study of policy-making in the European Union.

Theories of European Integration

For many years, the academic study of the European Communities (EC), as they were then called, was virtually synonymous with the study of European *integration*. The initially modest and largely technocratic achievements of the EC seemed less significant than the potential that they represented for the gradual integration of the countries of western Europe into something else: a supranational polity. When the integration process was going well, as during the 1950s and early 1960s, neo-functionalists and other theorists sought to explain the process whereby European integration proceeded from modest sectoral beginnings to something broader and more ambitious. When things seemed to be going badly, as from the 1960s until the early 1980s, intergovernmental-ists and others sought to explain why the integration process had not proceeded as smoothly as its founders had hoped. Regardless of the differences among these bodies of theory, we can say clearly that the early literature on the EC sought to explain the process of European *integration* (rather than, say, policy-making), and that in doing so it drew largely (but not exclusively) on theories of international relations.

In the first edition of this volume, Carole Webb (1977) surveyed the debate among the then dominant schools of European integration, neo-functionalism, and intergovern-mentalism, drawing from each approach a set of implications and hypotheses about the nature of the EC policy process. Similarly, here we review neo-functionalism and its views about the EU policy process, and then the intergovernmentalist response, as well as the updating of 'liberal intergovernmentalism' by Andrew Moravcsik in the 1990s. In addition, we examine more recent bodies of integration theory—institutionalism and constructivism—which offer very different views of the integration process and very different implications for EU policy-making.

Neo-functionalism

In 1958, on the eve of the establishment of the EEC and Euratom, Ernst Haas pub-lished his seminal work, *The Uniting of Europe*, setting out a 'neo-functionalist' theory of regional integration. As elaborated in subsequent texts by Haas and other scholars (e.g. Haas 1961; Lindberg 1963; Lindberg and Scheingold 1970), neo-functionalism posited a process of 'functional spill-over', in which the initial decision by govern-ments to place a certain sector, such as coal and steel, under the authority of central institutions creates pressures to extend the authority of the institutions into neigh-bouring areas of policy, such as currency exchange rates, taxation, and wages. Thus, neo-functionalists predicted, sectoral integration would produce the unintended and unforeseen consequence of promoting further integration in additional issue areas.

George (1991) identifies a second strand of the spill-over process, which he calls 'political' spill-over, in which both supranational actors (such as the Commission) and subnational actors (interest groups or others within the member states) create addi-tional pressures for further integration. At the subnational level, Haas suggested that interest groups operating in an integrated sector would have to interact with the international organization charged with the management of their sector. Over time, these groups would come to appreciate the benefits from integration, and would thereby transfer their demands, expectations, and even their loyalties from national governments to a new centre, thus becoming an important force for further integration. At the supranational level, moreover, bodies such as the Commission would encourage such a transfer of loyalties, promoting European policies and brokering bargains among the member states so as to 'upgrade the common interest'. As a result of such sectoral and political spill-over, neo-functionalists predicted, sectoral integration would become self-sustaining, leading to the creation of a new political entity with its centre in Brussels.

For our purposes in this book, the most important contribution of neo-functionalists to the study of EU policy-making was their conceptualization of a 'Community method' of policy-making. As Webb pointed out, this ideal-type Community method was based largely on the observation of a few specific sectors (the common agricultural policy (CAP), see Chapter 7, and the customs union, see Chapters 4 and 15) during the formative years of the Community, and presented a distinct picture of EC policy-making as a process driven by an entrepreneurial Commission and featuring supranational deliberation among member-state representatives in the Council. The Community method in this view was not just a legal set of policy-making institutions but a 'procedural code' conditioning the expectations and the behaviour of the participants in the process. The central elements of this original Community method, Webb (1977: 13–14) continued, were four-fold:

1. Governments accept the Commission as a valid bargaining partner and expect it to play an active role in building a policy consensus.
2. Governments deal with each other with a commitment to problem-solving, and negotiate over how to achieve collective decisions, and not whether these are desirable or not.
3. Governments, the Commission, and other participants in the process are responsive to each other, do not make unacceptable demands, and are willing to make short term sacrifices in expectation of longer term gains.
4. Unanimity is the rule, necessitating that negotiations continue until all objections are overcome or losses in one area are compensated for by gains in another. Issues are not seen as separate but related in a continuous process of decision such that 'log-rolling' and 'side payments' are possible.

This Community method, Webb suggested, characterized EEC decision-making during the period from 1958 to 1963, as the original six member states met alongside the Commission to put in place the essential elements of the EEC customs union and the CAP. By 1965, however, Charles de Gaulle, the French President, had precipitated the so-called 'Luxembourg crisis', insisting on the importance of state sovereignty and arguably violating the implicit procedural code of the Community method. The EEC, which had been scheduled to move to extensive qualified majority voting (QMV) in 1966, continued to take most decisions *de facto* by unanimity, the Commission emerged weakened from its confrontation with de Gaulle, and the nation-state appeared to have reasserted itself. These tendencies were reinforced, moreover, by developments in the 1970s, when economic recession led to the rise of new non-tariff barriers to trade among EC member states and when the intergovernmental aspects of the Community were strengthened by the creation in 1974 of the European Council, a regular summit meeting of EU heads of state and government. In addition, the Committee of Permanent Representatives (Coreper), an intergovernmental body of member-state representatives, emerged as a crucial decision-making body preparing legislation for adoption by the Council of Ministers. Similarly, empirical studies showed the importance of national gatekeeping institutions (H. Wallace 1973). Even some of the major advances of this period, such as the creation of the European monetary system (EMS) in 1978 (see Chapter 6), were taken outside the structure of the EEC Treaty, and with no formal role for the Commission or other supranational EC institutions.

Intergovernmentalism

Reflecting these developments, a new 'intergovernmentalist' school of integration theory emerged, beginning with Stanley Hoffmann's (1966) claim that the nation-state, far from being obsolete, had proven 'obstinate'. Most obviously with de Gaulle, but later with the accession of new member states such as the UK, Ireland, and Denmark in 1973, member governments made clear that they would resist the gradual transfer of sovereignty to the Community, and that EC decision-making would reflect the continuing primacy of the nation-state. Under these circumstances, Haas himself (1976) pronounced the 'obsolescence of regional integration theory', while other scholars such as Paul Taylor (1983), and William Wallace (1982) argued that neo-functionalists had underestimated the resilience of the nation-state. At the same time, historical scholarship by Alan Milward and others (Milward 2000; Milward and Lynch 1993) supported the view that EU member governments, rather than supranational organizations, played the central role in the historical development of the EU and were strengthened, rather than weakened, as a result of the integration process.

By contrast with neo-functionalists, the intergovernmentalist image suggested that 'the bargaining and consensus building techniques which have emerged in the Communities are mere refinements of intergovernmental diplomacy' (Webb 1977: 18). And indeed, the early editions of *Policy-Making in the European Communities* found significant evidence of intergovernmental bargaining as the dominant mode of policy-making in many (but not all) issue areas.

Liberal intergovernmentalism

The period from the mid-1960s through the mid-1980s has been characterized as 'the doldrums era', both for the integration process and for scholarship on the EU (Keeler 2004; Jupille 2005). While a dedicated core of EU scholars continued to advance the empirical study of the EU during this period, much of this work either eschewed grand theoretical claims about the integration process or accepted with minor modifications the theoretical language of the neo-functionalist/intergovernmentalist debate. With the 'relaunching' of the integration process in the mid-1980s, however, scholarship on the EU exploded, and the theoretical debate was revived. While some of this scholarship viewed the relaunching of the integration process as a vindication of earlier neo-functionalist models (Tranholm-Mikkelsen 1991; Zysman and Sandholtz 1989), Andrew Moravcsik (1993a, 1998) argued influentially that even these steps forward could be accounted for by a revised intergovernmental model emphasizing the power and preferences of EU member states. In other words, Moravcsik's 'liberal intergovernmentalism' is a three-step model, which combines: (1) a liberal theory of national preference formation with; (2) an intergovernmental model of EU-level bargaining; and (3) a model of institutional choice emphasizing the role of international institutions in providing 'credible commitments' for member governments. In the first or liberal stage of the model, national chiefs of government (COGs) aggregate the interests of their domestic constituencies, as well as their own interests, and articulate their respective national preferences toward the EU. Thus, national preferences are complex, reflecting the distinctive economics, parties, and institutions of each member state, but they are determined *domestically*, not shaped by participation in the EU, as some neo-functionalists had proposed.

In the second or intergovernmental stage, national governments bring their preferences to the bargaining table in Brussels, where agreements reflect the relative power of each member state, and where supranational organizations such as the Commission exert little or no influence over policy outcomes. By contrast with neo-functionalists, who emphasized the entrepreneurial and brokering roles of the Commission and the upgrading of the common interest among member states in the Council, Moravcsik and other intergovernmentalists emphasized the hardball bargaining among member states and the importance of bargaining power, package deals, and 'side payments' as determinants of intergovernmental bargains on the most important EU decisions.

Third and finally, Moravcsik puts forward a rational choice theory of institutional choice, arguing that EU member states adopt particular EU institutions—pooling sovereignty through QMV, or delegating sovereignty to supranational actors like the Commission and the Court—in order to increase the credibility of their mutual commitments. In this view, sovereign states seeking to cooperate among themselves invariably face a strong temptation to cheat or 'defect' from their agreements. Pooling and delegating sovereignty through international organizations, he argues, allows states to commit themselves credibly to their mutual promises, by monitoring state compliance with international agreements and filling in the blanks of broad international treaties, such as those that have constituted the EC/EU.

In empirical terms, Moravcsik argues that the EU's historic intergovernmental agreements, such as the 1957 Treaties of Rome and the 1992 Treaty on European Union (TEU), were not driven primarily by supranational entrepreneurs, unintended spillovers from earlier integration, or transnational coalitions of interest groups, but rather by a gradual process of preference convergence among the most powerful member states, which then struck central bargains among themselves, offered side-payments to smaller member states, and delegated strictly limited powers to supranational organizations that remained more or less obedient servants of the member states.

Overarching the three steps of this model is a 'rationalist framework' of international cooperation. The relevant actors are assumed to have fixed preferences (for wealth, power, etc.), and act systematically to achieve those preferences within the constraints posed by the institutions within which they act. As Moravcsik (1998: 19–20) points out:

The term *framework* (as opposed to *theory* or *model*) is employed here to designate a set of assumptions that permit us to disaggregate a phenomenon we seek to explain—in this case, successive rounds of international negotiations—into elements each of which can be treated separately. More focused theories—each of course consistent with the assumptions of the overall rationalist framework—are employed to explain each element. The elements are then aggregated to create a multicausal explanation of a large complex outcome such as a major multilateral agreement. (emphasis in original)

During the 1990s, liberal intergovernmentalism emerged as arguably the leading theory of European integration, yet its basic theoretical assumptions were questioned by international relations scholars coming from two different directions. A first group of scholars, collected under the rubrics of rational choice and historical institutionalism, accepted Moravcsik's rationalist assumptions, but rejected his spare, institution-free model of intergovernmental bargaining as an accurate description of the EU policy process. By contrast, a second school of thought, drawing from sociological institutionalism and constructivism, raised more fundamental objections to the methodological individualism of rational choice theory in favour of an approach in which national preferences and identities were shaped, at least in part, by EU norms and rules.

The 'new institutionalisms' in rational choice

The rise of institutionalist analysis of the EU did not develop in isolation, but reflected a gradual and widespread re-introduction of institutions into a large body of theories (such as pluralism, Marxism, and neo-realism), in which institutions had been either absent or considered epiphenomenal, reflections of deeper causal factors or processes such as capitalism or the distribution of power in domestic societies or in the international system. By contrast with these institution-free accounts of politics, which dominated much of political science between the 1950s and the 1970s, three primary 'institutionalisms' developed during the course of the 1980s and early 1990s, each with a distinct definition of institutions and a distinct account of how they 'matter' in the study of politics (March and Olsen 1984, 1989; Hall and Taylor 1996).

The first arose within the rational-choice approach to the study of politics, as pioneered by students of American politics. Rational choice institutionalism began with the effort by American political scientists to understand the origins and effects of US Congressional institutions on legislative behaviour and policy outcomes. More specifically, rational choice scholars noted that majoritarian models of Congressional decision-making predicted that policy outcomes would be inherently unstable, since a simple majority of policy-makers could always form a coalition to overturn existing legislation, yet substantive scholars of the US Congress found considerable stability in Congressional policies. In this context, Kenneth Shepsle (1979, 1986) argued that Congressional institutions, and in particular the committee system, could produce 'structure-induced equilibrium', by ruling some alternatives as permissible or impermissible, and by structuring the voting power and the veto power of various actors in the decision-making process. More recently, Shepsle and others have turned their attention to the problem of 'equilibrium institutions', namely, how actors choose or design institutions to secure mutual gains, and how those institutions change or persist over time.

Shepsle's innovation and the subsequent development of the rational choice approach to institutions have produced a number of theoretical offshoots with potential applications to both comparative and international politics. For example, Shepsle and others have examined in some detail the 'agenda-setting' power of Congressional committees, which can send draft legislation to the floor that is often easier to adopt than it is to amend. In another offshoot, students of the US Congress have developed 'principal-agent' models of Congressional delegation to regulatory bureaucracies and to courts, and they have problematized the conditions under which legislative principals are able—or unable—to control their respective agents (Moe 1984; Kiewiet and McCubbins 1991). More recently, Epstein and O'Halloran (1999), and others (Huber and Shipan 2002) have pioneered a 'transaction-cost approach' to the design of political institutions, arguing that legislators deliberately and systematically design political institutions to minimize the transaction costs associated with the making of public policy.

Although originally formulated and applied in the context of American political institutions, rational-choice institutionalist insights 'travel' to other domestic and international contexts, and were quickly taken up by students of the EU. Responding to the increasing importance of EU institutional rules, such as the cooperation and co-decision procedures, these authors argued that purely intergovernmental models of EU decision-making underestimated the causal importance of formal EU rules in shaping policy outcomes. In an early application of rational-choice theory to the EU, for example, Fritz Scharpf (1988) argued that the inefficiency and rigidity of the CAP and other EU policies was due not simply to the EU's intergovernmentalism, but also to specific institutional rules, such as unanimous decision-making and the 'default condition' in the event that the member states failed to agree on a common policy (see Chapter 7). By the mid-1990s, George Tsebelis, Geoffrey Garrett, and many others sought to model the selection—and in particular the functioning—of EU institutions, including the adoption, execution, and adjudication of EU public policies, in terms of rational choice. Many of these studies drew increasingly on relevant literatures from comparative politics, and are therefore reviewed in the second part of this chapter.

By contrast, sociological institutionalism and constructivist approaches in international relations defined institutions much more broadly to include informal norms and conventions as well as informal rules. They argued that such institutions could 'constitute' actors, shaping their identities and hence their preferences in ways that rational-choice approaches could not capture (see next section).

Historical institutionalists took up a position between these two camps, focusing on the effects of institutions *over time*, in particular on the ways in which a given set of institutions, once established, can influence or constrain the behaviour of the actors who established them. In its initial formulations (Hall 1986; Thelen and Steinmo 1992), historical institutionalism was seen as having dual effects, influencing both the constraints on individual actors *and* their preferences, thereby making the theory a 'big tent', encompassing the core insights of the rationalist and constructivist camps. What makes historical institutionalism distinctive, however, is its emphasis on the effects of institutions on politics *over time*. In perhaps the most sophisticated presentation of this thinking, Paul Pierson (2000) has argued that political institutions are characterized by what economists call 'increasing returns', insofar as they create incentives for actors to stick with and not abandon existing institutions, adapting them only incrementally in response to changing circumstances. Thus, politics should be characterized by certain interrelated phenomena, including: *inertia*, or 'lock-ins', whereby existing institutions may remain in equilibrium for extended periods despite considerable political change; a critical role for *timing and sequencing*, in which relatively small and contingent events at critical junctures early in a sequence shape events that occur later; and *path-dependence*, in which early decisions provide incentives for actors to perpetuate institutional and policy choices inherited from the past, even when the resulting outcomes are manifestly inefficient.

Understood in this light, historical institutionalist analyses typically begin with rationalist assumptions about actor preferences, and proceed to examine how institutions can shape the behaviour of rational actors over time through institutional lock-ins and processes of path dependence. In recent years, these insights have been applied increasingly to the development of the EU, with various authors emphasizing the temporal dimension of European integration (Armstrong and Bulmer 1998).

Pierson's (1996*b*) study of path-dependence in the EU, for example, seeks to understand European integration as a process that unfolds over time, and the conditions under which path-dependent processes are most likely to occur. Working from essentially rationalist assumptions, Pierson argues that, despite the initial primacy of member governments in the design of EU institutions and policies, 'gaps' may occur in the ability of member governments to control the subsequent development of institutions and policies, for four reasons. First, member governments in democratic societies may, because of electoral concerns, apply a high 'discount rate' to the future, agreeing to EU policies that lead to a long-term loss of national control in return for short-term electoral returns. Secondly, even when governments do not heavily discount the future, unintended consequences of institutional choices can create additional gaps, which member governments may or may not be able to close through subsequent action. Thirdly, the preferences of member governments are likely to change over time, most obviously because of electoral turnover, leaving new governments with new preferences to inherit an *acquis communautaire* negotiated by, and according to the preferences of, a previous government. Given the frequent requirement of unanimous voting (or the high hurdle of QMV) to overturn past institutional and policy choices, individual member governments are likely to find themselves 'immobilized by the weight of past initiatives' (Pierson 1996*b*: 137). Finally, EU institutions and policies can become locked-in not only as a result of change-resistant institutions from above, but also through the incremental growth of entrenched support for existing institutions *from below*, as societal actors adapt to and develop a vested interest in the continuation of specific EU policies. In the area of social policy, for example, the European Court of Justice (ECJ) has developed jurisprudence on issues such as gender equity and workplace health and safety that certainly exceeded the initial expectations of the member states; yet these decisions have proven difficult to roll back, both because of the need for unanimous agreement to overturn ECJ decisions and because domestic constituencies have developed a vested interest in their continued application (see Chapter 10).

At their best, historical institutionalist analyses offer not only the banal observation that institutions are 'sticky', but also a tool kit for predicting and explaining *under what conditions* we should expect institutional lock-ins and path-dependent behaviour. More specifically, we should expect that, *ceteris paribus*, institutions and policies will be most resistant to change: where their alteration requires a unanimous agreement among member states, or the consent of supranational actors like the Commission or the Parliament; and where existing EU policies mobilize cross-national bases of support that raise the cost of reversing or significantly revising them. Both factors vary across issue areas, and we should therefore expect variation in the stability and path-dependent character of EU institutions and policies. To take one example, the EU structural funds might at first glance seem to be an ideal candidate for path-dependent behaviour, much like the CAP. By contrast with the CAP, however, the structural funds must be reauthorized at periodic intervals by a unanimous agreement among the member states, giving recalcitrant states periodic opportunities to veto their continuation.[2] Furthermore, because the structural funds are explicitly framed as redistributive, transferring money from rich states and regions to poor ones, we see an uneven pattern of reliance upon and support for the structural funds among member states and their citizens. The practical upshot of these differences is that EU governments have been able to reform the structural funds more readily, and with less incidence of path-dependence, than we find in the CAP, which has indeed resisted all but the most incremental change (see Chapters 7 and 9).

In sum, for both rational-choice and historical institutionalists, EU institutions 'matter', shaping both the policy process and policy outcomes in predictable ways, and indeed shaping the long-term process of European integration. In both cases, however, the effects of EU institutions are assumed to influence only the incentives confronting the various public and private actors—the actors themselves are assumed to remain unchanged in their fundamental preferences and identities. Indeed, despite their differences on substantive issues, liberal intergovernmentalism, rational-choice institutionalism, and most historical institutionalism arguably constitute a shared rationalist research agenda—a community of scholars operating from similar basic assumptions and seeking to test hypotheses about the most important determinants of European integration.

Constructivism, and reshaping European identities and preferences

Constructivist theory did not begin with the study of the EU—indeed, as Thomas Risse (2004) points out in an excellent survey, constructivism came to EU studies relatively late, with the publication of a special issue of the *Journal of European Public Policy* on the 'Social Construction of Europe' in 1999. Yet since then constructivist theorists have been quick to apply their theoretical tools to the EU, promising to shed light on its potentially profound effects on the peoples and governments of Europe.

Constructivism is a notoriously difficult theory to describe succinctly. Indeed, like rational choice, constructivism is not a substantive theory of European integration at all, but a broader 'meta-theoretical' orientation with implications for the study of the EU. As Risse (2004: 161) explains:

[i]t is probably most useful to describe constructivism as based on a social ontology which insists that human agents do not exist independently from their social environment and its collectively shared systems of meanings ('culture' in a broad sense). This is in contrast to the methodological individualism of rational choice according to which '[t]he elementary unit of social life is the individual human action'. The fundamental insight of the agency-structure debate, which lies at the heart of many social constructivist works, is not only that structures and agents are mutually co-determined. The crucial point is that constructivists insist on the *constitutiveness* of (social) structures and agents. The social environment in which we find ourselves, 'constitutes' who we are, our identities as social beings. (references removed)

For constructivists, institutions are understood broadly to include not only formal rules but also informal norms, and these rules and norms are expected to 'constitute' actors, i.e. to shape their identities and their preferences. Actor preferences, therefore, are not exogenously given and fixed, as in rationalist models, but *endogenous* to institutions, and individuals' identities shaped and re-shaped by their social environment. Taking this argument to its logical conclusion, constructivists generally reject the rationalist conception of actors as utility-maximizers operating according to a 'logic of consequentiality', in favour of March and Olsen's (1989: 160–2) conception of a 'logic of appropriateness'. In this view, actors confronting a given situation do not consult a fixed set of preferences and calculate their actions in order to maximize their expected utility, but look to socially constructed roles and institutional rules and ask what sort of behaviour is appropriate in that situation. Constructivism, therefore, offers a fundamentally different view of human agency from rational-choice approaches, and it suggests that institutions influence individual identities, preferences, and behaviour in more profound ways than those hypothesized by rational-choice theorists.

A growing number of scholars has argued that EU institutions shape not only the behaviour, but also the preferences and identities of individuals and member governments (Sandholtz 1993; Jørgensen 1997; Lewis 1998). This argument has been put most forcefully by Thomas Christiansen, Knud Erik Jørgensen, and Antje Wiener in their introduction to the special issue of the *Journal of European Public Policy* (1999: 529):

A significant amount of evidence suggests that, as a process, European integration has a transformative impact on the European state system and its constituent units. European integration itself has changed over the years, and it is reasonable to assume that in the process agents' identity and subsequently their interests have equally changed. While this aspect of change can be theorized within constructivist perspectives, it will remain largely invisible in approaches that neglect processes of identity formation and/or assume interests to be given endogenously.

In other words, the authors begin with the claim that the EU is indeed reshaping national identities and preferences, and reject rationalist approaches for their inability to predict and explain these phenomena. Not surprisingly, constructivist accounts of the EU have been forcefully rebutted by rationalist theorists (Moravcsik 1999; Checkel and Moravcsik 2001).

According to Moravcsik (1999: 670) constructivist theorists raise an interesting and important set of questions about the effects of European integration on individuals and states. Yet, he argues, constructivists have failed to make a significant contribution to our empirical understanding of European integration, for two reasons. First, constructivists typically fail to construct 'distinct falsifiable hypotheses', opting instead for broad interpretive frameworks that can make sense of almost any possible outcome, and are therefore not subject to falsification through empirical analysis. Secondly, even if constructivists *do* posit hypotheses that are in principle falsifiable, they generally do not formulate and test those hypotheses so as to distinguish clearly between constructivist predictions and their rationalist counterparts. Until constructivists test their hypotheses, and do so against prevailing and distinct rationalist models, he argues, constructivism will not come down 'from the clouds' (Checkel and Moravcsik 2001).

Constructivists might respond that Moravcsik privileges rational-choice explanations and sets a higher standard for constructivist hypotheses (since rational-choice scholars typically do not attempt to test their own hypotheses against competing constructivist formulations). Many 'post-positivist' scholars, moreover, dispute Moravcsik's image of EU studies as 'science', with its attendant claims of objectivity and of an objective, knowable world. For such scholars, Moravcsik's call for falsifiable hypothesis-testing appears as a power-laden demand that 'non-conformist' theories play according to the rules of a rationalist, and primarily American, social science (Jørgensen 1997: 6–7). To the extent that constructivists do indeed reject positivism and the systematic testing of competing hypotheses, the rationalist/constructivist debate would seem to have reached a 'metatheoretical' impasse—that is to say, constructivists and rationalists fail to agree on a common standard for judging what constitutes support for one or another approach.

In recent years, however, an increasing number of constructivist theorists have embraced positivism—the notion that constructivist hypotheses can, and should, be tested and validated or falsified empirically—and these scholars have produced a spate of constructivist work that attempts rigorously to test hypotheses about social-ization, norm-diffusion, and collective preference formation in the EU (Wendt 1999; Checkel 2003; Risse 2004: 160). Some of these studies, including Liesbet Hooghe's (2002, 2005) extensive analysis of the attitudes of Commission officials, and several studies of national officials participating in EU committees (Beyers and Dierickx 1998; Egeberg 1999), use quantitative methods to test hypotheses about the nature and determinants of officials' attitudes, including socialization in national as well as European institutions. Such studies, undertaken with methodological rigour and with a frank reporting of findings, seem to demonstrate that that EU-level socialization, although not excluded, plays a relatively small role by comparison with national-level socialization, or that EU socialization interacts with other factors in complex ways. Other studies, including Checkel's (1999, 2003) study of citizenship norms in the EU and the Council of Europe, and Lewis's (1998, 2003) analysis of decision-making in the EU's Coreper, utilize qualitative rather than quantitative methods, but are similarly designed to test falsifiable hypotheses about whether, and under what conditions, EU officials are socialized into new norms, preferences, and identities.

As a result, the metatheoretical gulf separating rationalists and constructivists appears to have narrowed considerably, and EU scholars have arguably led the way in confronting and—possibly—reconciling the two theoretical approaches. Three scholars (Jupille, Caporaso, and Checkel 2003) have recently put forward a framework for promoting integration of—or at least a fruitful dialogue between—rationalist and constructivist approaches to international relations. Rationalism and constructivism, the authors argue, are not hopelessly incommensurate, but can engage each other through 'four distinct modes of theoretical conversation', namely:

- competitive testing, in which competing theories are pitted against each other in explaining a single event or class of events;

- a 'domain of application' approach, in which each theory is considered to explain some sub-set of empirical reality, so that, for example, utility-maximizing and strategic bargaining obtain in certain circumstances, while socialization and col-lective preference formation obtain in others;

- a 'sequencing' approach, in which one theory may help explain a particular step in a sequence of actions (e.g. a constructivist explanation of national preferences) while another theory might best explain subsequent developments (e.g. a ration-alist explanation of subsequent bargaining among the actors); and

- 'incorporation' or 'subsumption', in which one theory claims to subsume the other so that, for example, rational choice becomes a sub-set of human behaviour ultimately explicable in terms of the social construction of modern rationality.

Looking at the substantive empirical work in their special issue, Jupille, Caporaso and Checkel (2003) find that most contributions to the rationalist/constructivist debate utilize competitive testing, while only a few (see, for example, Schimmelfennig 2003a) have adopted domain of application, sequencing, or subsumption approaches. Nevertheless, they see substantial progress in the debate, in which both sides generally accept a common standard of empirical testing as the criterion for useful theorizing about EU politics.

Integration theory today

European integration theory is far more complex than it was in 1977 when the first edition of this volume was published. In place of the traditional neo-functionalist/intergovernmentalist debate, the 1990s witnessed the emergence of a new dichotomy in EU studies, pitting rationalist scholars against constructivists. During the late 1990s, it appeared that this debate might well turn into a metatheoretical dialogue of the deaf, with rationalists dismissing constructivists as 'soft', and constructivists denouncing rationalists for their obsessive commitment to parsimony and formal models. The past several years, however, have witnessed the emergence of a more productive dialogue between the two approaches, and a steady stream of empirical studies allowing us to adjudicate between the competing claims of the two approaches. Furthermore, whereas the neo-functionalist/intergovernmentalist debate was limited almost exclusively to the study of European integration,[3] the contemporary rationalist/constructivist debate in EU studies mirrors larger debates among those same schools in the broader field of international relations theory. Indeed, not only are EU studies *relevant* to the wider study of international relations, they are in many ways the *vanguard* of international relations theory, insofar as the EU serves as a laboratory for broader processes such as globalization, institutionalization, and socialization.

Despite these substantial measures of progress, however, the literature on European integration has not produced any consensus on the likely future direction of the integration process. At the risk of overgeneralizing, more optimistic theorists tend to be drawn from the ranks of neo-functionalists and constructivists, who point to the potential for further integration, the former through functional and political spill-overs, and the latter through gradual changes in both élite and mass identities and preferences as a result of prolonged and productive cooperation. In empirical terms, these analysts frequently point to the rapid development of new institutions and policies in the second and third pillars, and the increasing use of the so-called 'open method of coordination' (OMC) to address issues that had been beyond the scope of EU competence. Rationalist and intergovernmentalist critics, on the other hand, tend to be sceptical regarding claims of both spill-over and socialization, pointing to the poor record of Commission entrepreneurship over the past decade and the sparse evidence for socialization of national officials into European preferences or identities, noting that the Commission has proven to be a poor stimulator of political spill-over in recent years. For these scholars, the EU may well represent an 'equilibrium polity', one in which functional pressures for further integration are essentially spent, and in which the current level of institutional and policy integration is unlikely to change substantially for the foreseeable future (Moravcsik 2001: 163). Yet others point to the EU's 'democratic deficit', the strains of enlargement, and the difficulties of ratifying the Constitutional Treaty (CT) as evidence of disintegrative tendencies at the heart of the Union. In sum, while the literature on European integration has advanced substantially over the past decade, a consensus on the causes and the future of the integration process remains as elusive as ever.

EU policy-making in comparative perspective

Thus far we have examined the EU literature as one concerned overwhelmingly with the causes and the direction of European integration as a process, with its theoretical inspiration primarily from the study of international relations, associating the EU with processes of regional integration or international cooperation. However, many scholars have approached the EU very differently, as a polity or political system akin to other *domestic* political systems. This tendency was most pronounced in the work of federalist writers, who explicitly compared the EU to federal and confederal systems in Germany, Switzerland, and the US (Friedrich 1969; Pinder 1968; Burgess 1989; Capelletti, Seccombe, and Weiler 1986; Scharpf 1988; Sbragia 1992, 1993), as well as in the work of systems theorists like Lindberg and Scheingold (1970), who saw the EU as a political system characterized by political demands (inputs), governmental actors, and public policies (outputs). At the same time, an increasing number of EU scholars, not least the editors and authors of the first (1977) edition of *Policy-Making in the European Union*, deliberately sought to bracket the question of integration and the EU's final destination, focusing instead on a better understanding of the EU policy process in all its complexity and diversity.

Notwithstanding these pioneering efforts, most studies of the EU, especially those undertaken in the US, continued to be dominated by scholars of international relations. By the mid-1990s, however, this dominance of international relations came under serious challenge, with a growing number of scholars seeking explicitly to understand the EU as a political system using the theoretical tools developed in the study of domestic polities. This perspective was championed most effectively by Simon Hix (1994, 1999, 2005), who issued a call to arms to comparativists in a series of publications. Previous studies of the EU, Hix argued, had neglected the *politics* of the EU, as well as its characteristics as a political system. The EU, he contended, was clearly less than a Weberian state, lacking in particular a monopoly on the legitimate use of force; yet he echoed Lindberg and Scheingold by suggesting that the EU could be theorized as a political system, with a dense web of legislative, executive, and judicial institutions that adopted binding public policies and hence influenced the 'authoritative allocation of values' in European society. Furthermore, Hix suggested that EU politics takes place in a two-dimensional space, with integration representing one dimension, alongside a second dimension spanning the traditional left-right divide over the extent and nature of government intervention in the economy. Hence the EU could, and should, be studied using 'the tools, methods and cross-systemic theories from the general study of government, politics, and policy-making. In this way, teaching and research on the EU can be part of the political science mainstream' (Hix 1999: 2).

Hix's call to arms among comparativists has not escaped criticism, with a number of authors arguing that his dichotomous formulation of the division of labour between international and comparative politics represented an oversimplification and a disciplinary step backwards from aggregation to fragmentation of subfields within political science. Indeed, 'converging empirical and intellectual trends, especially in the area of political economy, increasingly undermine . . . the distinction between comparative and international' (Jupille, Caporaso, and Checkel 2003: 10; see also Hurrell and Menon 1996). Empirically, the phenomenon of globalization has drawn scholars' attention to the links between international developments and domestic politics, not just in the EU, but globally. An increasing number of theories—Peter Gourevich's (1978) 'second-image reversed', Robert Putnam's (1988) 'two-level games' model, and various models of globalization (Keohane and Milner 1998; Caporaso 1997)—all identified mechanisms linking domestic politics to developments at the international level, suggesting that purely comparative approaches might miss this domestic-international interaction. Furthermore, as was seen earlier, institutionalist theories of politics promised precisely to provide a single overarching theoretical framework, linking together US, comparative, and international politics (Milner 1998; Jupille, Caporaso, and Checkel 2003: 10). Under the circumstances, 'it would be perverse if the erosion of such disciplinary boundaries were to be resisted in EU Studies, the object of study of which seems precisely to fall in the interstices of the two subfields!' (Jupille 2005).

For all of these reasons, the comparative/IR divide did *not* prove to be the important schism in EU studies that many had expected, and much useful work has integrated domestic and international politics within a single theoretical framework (Hix 1998). Nevertheless, comparative political scientists *have* moved increasingly into EU studies, in part because the EU has intruded increasingly into what had previously been seen as exclusively 'domestic' arenas, and in part because an increasing number of scholars accepted Hix's claim that the EU could be theorized as a 'political system'. This movement of comparativists into EU studies is reflected in quantitative data collected by Jupille (2005), demonstrating the rise of EU studies from an almost entirely IR-based initiative to one that features equally in the pages of IR and comparative journals. Although such comparative work on the EU is extraordinarily diverse, comprising numerous 'islands of theory' (Dalton 1991) and empirical research, much of it can fairly be characterized as comparative, rational-choice, and positivist in nature. First, as Hix (1998) argues most starkly, much of the work on EU politics proceeds from the assumption that the EU is not a *sui generis* system of governance, but is a variant on existing political systems. It can therefore be studied and understood with the aid of off-the-shelf models of policy-making in other (primarily national) contexts. In recent years, a growing number of these theories have drawn from American politics, since the EU arguably resembles the US in possessing both a horizontal and a vertical separation of powers.

Secondly, most of the work reviewed in this section is either implicitly or explicitly rationalist, taking the assumption that actors (be they states, individuals, or supranational organizations) have fixed, exogenously determined preferences, and act systematically to maximize those preferences within the constraints of the EU's institutional system. A growing sub-set draws not only on the language of rational choice (i.e. 'soft' rational choice), but also elaborates formal and game-theoretic models of EU decision-making.

Thirdly and finally, much of the work discussed here can be characterized as implicitly or explicitly positivist, adopting and adapting the standards of the natural sciences, seeking to test theory-driven hypotheses systematically, and often (though by no means always) using quantitative as well as qualitative methods. Much of this work has appeared in 'mainstream' American and European journals of political science, such as the *American Journal of Political Science*, the *American Political Science Review*, the *British Journal of Political Science*, and the *European Journal of Political Science*. Its spiritual home, however, is undoubtedly the journal *European Union Politics*, which publishes a steady stream of articles featuring formal models of decision-making and innovative use of new and existing data sets to test hypotheses about political behaviour in the EU. Indeed, the editors of the journal, and many of its contributors, explicitly put forward a model of 'normal science', in which scholars deduce theories of specific aspects of EU politics (e.g. legislative or executive or judicial politics) and seek to test them comparatively with the most precise available data, in particular quantitative or statistical (Gabel, Hix, and Schneider 2002). A complete survey of this literature would take us beyond the remit of this volume; we therefore focus on two dimensions that are most relevant to the study of policy-making, namely the horizontal or 'federal' division of powers between the EU and member-state levels, and the vertical or 'separation-of-powers' division of powers among the legislative, executive, and judicial branches of the Union.

The horizontal separation of powers: the EU as a federal system

The EU did not begin life as a federal union, nor, in the view of most analysts, does it constitute a fully developed federation today. In political terms, the very term 'federal' was contentious and referred to obliquely as 'the f-word'; and in analytical terms some scholars question whether the EU can or should be accurately described as a federal state:

> The contemporary EU is far narrower and weaker a federation than any extant national federation—so weak, indeed, that we might question whether it is a federation at all. . . . The EU was designed as, and remains primarily, a limited international institution to coordinate national regulation of trade in goods and services, and the resulting flows of economic factors. Its substantive scope and institutional prerogatives are limited accordingly. The EU constitutional order is not only barely a federal state; it is barely recognizable as a state at all. (Moravcsik 2001: 163–4)

Nevertheless, federalism was a powerful *normative* ideal motivating many of the founders of the European movement and much of the early scholarship on the EU. Recognizing the strong resistance of national governments to directly federal proposals, Jean Monnet and his colleagues opted instead for a more sectoral and incremental approach, more accurately captured in neo-functionalist theory than in traditional federalist approaches. By the 1980s, however, the EC had developed features with analytical similarities to those of existing federations. Theories of federalism therefore took on greater importance, not just as a normative ideal motivating European integration, but as a positive theoretical framework, capable of explaining and predicting the workings of the EU as a political system.

The term federalism has been the subject of numerous overlapping definitions, but most rely on the three elements emphasized by R. Daniel Kelemen (2003: 185), who defines federalism as 'an institutional arrangement in which: (a) public authority is divided between state governments and a central government; (b) each level of government has some issues on which it makes final decisions; and (c) a federal high court adjudicates disputes concerning federalism'. In most federal systems, moreover, the structure of representation is two-fold, with popular or functional interests represented directly through a directly elected lower house, while territorial units are typically represented in an upper house, whose members may be either directly elected (as in the US Senate) or appointed by state governments (as in the German Bundesrat). In both of these senses, the EU *already* constitutes a federal system, with a constitutionally guaranteed separation of powers between the EU and member-state levels, and a dual system of representation through the European Parliament (EP) and the Council of Ministers. Hence the literature on comparative federalism provides a useful tool-kit for thinking about policy-making in the EU.

Perhaps the most difficult issue, as in other federal systems, is the question of the distribution of powers among the federal and state levels of government. Economic models of 'fiscal federalism', for example, have suggested that the functions of macroeconomic stabilization and distribution are best exercised at the federal level, since these functions would be likely to go unprovided or underprovided if left to the individual states. Indeed, most mature federations feature a strong fiscal role for government, smoothing out asymmetric shocks across states and providing for redistribution of funds from wealthier to poorer states (Börzel and Hosli 2003: 180–1). More generally, Helen Wallace (2000) has pointed out, the choice of a given level of government—federal/EU v. national/state—can be theorized through the metaphor of a pendulum, where the choice of policy arena varies depending on a number of contextual, functional, motivational, and institutional factors.

The scope for oscillation between the state and federal levels, moreover, is considerable. While the division of powers between the two levels may be constitutionally guaranteed, these constitutional assignments of authority are often stated in vague terms, and in practice federal and state governments frequently enjoy concurrent rather than exclusive jurisdiction in most issue areas. Both the US Constitution and the EC/EU treaties feature broad and flexible clauses which authorize the federal legislature to regulate interstate commerce (the interstate commerce clause in the US, or Article 95 TEC (ex Art. 100a EEC as amended by the SEA) in the EU), or indeed to adopt any legislation deemed to be 'necessary and proper' in achieving the fundamental aims of the federation. We often see cycles or rhythms of federalism in which federal governments centralize power and authority, followed periodically by backlashes in which states seek a rebalancing or devolution of power back to the states. In this view, the history of the EU can be viewed as a series of centralizing initiatives (e.g. the founding years of the 1950s, and the relaunching of the integration process in the 1980s), followed by periods of retrenchment or devolution (e.g. the Gaullist-led resistance of the 1960s and the post-Maastricht backlash of the 1990s) (Donahue and Pollack 2001: 98). The struggle over European integration, in this view, is not a *sui generis* process, but is a constitutionally structured process of oscillation between states and central governments familiar from other federal systems.

Students of comparative federalism have also pointed to an exceptional aspect of the EU, namely the absence or at least the weakness of 'fiscal federalism', and the dominance of 'regulatory federalism'. Most federal systems engage in substantial fiscal transfers across state boundaries, but the EU budget has been capped at a relatively small 1.27 per cent of EU GDP, predominantly devoted to agricultural and cohesion spending (see Chapters 7, 8, and 9). The EU is therefore unable to engage in substantial redistribution or macroeconomic stabilization through fiscal policy (see Chapter 6), and only indirectly influences the structure of European welfare states, which remain predominantly national (see Chapter 11). In contrast, the Union has engaged primarily in regulatory activity (see Chapters 4, 10, 11, 12, and 13), earning it the moniker of a 'regulatory state' in the work of Giandomenico Majone (1996) and others (Kelemen 2004; Chapter 3 in this volume). The regulatory output of the Union, in Majone's view, has been driven by both demand and supply factors. On the demand side, the imperative of creating a single internal market has put pressure on EU member states to adopt common or harmonized EU-wide regulations, most notably on products, in order to remove non-tariff barriers to trade and ensure the free movement of goods, services, labour, and capital throughout the Union. On the supply side, an entrepreneurial European Commission has seen regulation as a viable way to enhance its own policy competence despite the financial limits imposed by the EU's strict budgetary ceiling.

In empirical terms, therefore, the Union has engaged in a vast EU-wide project of economic regulation, driven largely by the creation and maintenance of the internal market, and these EU regulations have been adopted according to a 'regulatory mode' of governance within which the Commission plays a vital entrepreneurial role, the Council and the EP a collective role as a bicameral legislature, and the ECJ and national courts a dual role in enforcing EU regulations and challenging national regulations that might impede the free movement of labour (see Chapter 10). As in other federal systems, the adoption of far-reaching central regulations has taken the Union into areas of regulation not originally envisaged by the framers of the treaties, generating significant controversy and increasing demands since the 1990s for adherence to the principle of 'subsidiarity', the notion that the EU should govern as close as possible to the citizen and therefore that the EU should engage in regulation only where necessary to ensure the completion of the internal market and/or other fundamental aims of the treaties. Even in the regulatory field, therefore, the horizontal separation of powers is not fixed but fluid, and the result resembles not so much a layer cake as a marble cake, in which EU and member-state authorities are concurrent, intermixed, and constantly in flux.

The vertical separation of powers

Unlike the parliamentary states of western Europe, but like the US, the EU has a vertical separation of powers in which three distinct branches of government take the leading role in the legislative, executive, and judicial functions of government, respectively. This does not mean that any one institution enjoys sole control of any of these three functions; indeed, as Amie Kreppel (2002: 5) points out, the Madisonian conception of the separation of powers 'requires to a certain extent a co-mingling of powers in all three arenas (executive, legislative, and judicial)'. In the case of the EU, for example, the legislative function is today shared by the Council of Ministers and the EP, with an agenda-setting role for the Commission; the executive function is shared by the Commission, the member states, and (in some areas) independent regulatory agencies; and the judicial function is shared by the ECJ, the Court of First Instance (CFI), and a wide array of national courts bound directly to the ECJ through the preliminary reference procedure (see Chapter 3).

Reflecting this separation of powers, comparative-politics scholars have over the past decade devoted extraordinary attention to theorizing, predicting, and explaining legislative, executive, and judicial behaviour using off-the-shelf theories drawn from the rational-choice study of American and comparative politics. A brief review of the literature will illustrate the application of comparative and rationalist theories to each of these three domains, and the promise and limits of such applications.

Legislative politics: towards bicameralism

A first strand within the rationalist/comparativist literature, most relevant to our concerns with EU policy-making, is the large and growing literature on the EU legislative process. Drawing heavily on theories of legislative behaviour (i.e. the ways in which legislators vote), and legislative organization (the ways in which legislatures organize their business), students of EU legislative politics have adapted, applied, and tested off-the-shelf theories of legislative politics to understand the process of legislative decision-making inside the Council of Ministers and the EP, their respective powers, and their increasing resemblance to a classic bicameral legislature.

A number of authors have, for example, attempted to model the relative voting power of member states in the Council of Ministers and the formation of voting coalitions among the member governments under different decision rules. Under unanimity voting, for example, EU legislative rules provide each member government with equal voting weight and with the opportunity to veto a decision that could leave them worse off than the status quo. Moving to QMV, however, raises the possibility that states can form winning coalitions reflecting their respective interests and the voting weights within the EU's system of QMV. In this context, a number of scholars have used increasingly elaborate formal models of Council voting to establish the relative bargaining power of various member states; and in recent intergovernmental conferences (IGCs) member governments have increasingly lobbied for the voting formulae which they believe would maximize their legislative influence. Moreover, the relative preferences of member governments are also relevant: governments with preferences close to the centre of the distribution on a given issue are thus most likely to be in a winning majority independent of their formal voting weight, while other governments may be 'preference outliers' (in terms of either the integration or the left-right dimension), and therefore more likely to be isolated in EU decision-making, again independent of their formal voting weights.[4] Finally, it is worth noting that the Council tends to operate on an informal norm of reaching consensus whenever possible (see Chapter 3), so that the game-theoretical assumption of minimum-winning-coalitions underlying most rational-choice models may provide a poor guide to understanding day-to-day practice in the Council (Hayes-Renshaw and Wallace 2005).

The EP, similarly, has been the subject of extensive theoretical modelling and empirical study over the past two decades, with a growing number of scholars studying the legislative organization of the EP and the voting behaviour of its members (MEPs) through the lenses of comparative legislative studies. The early studies of the Parliament, in the 1980s and early 1990s, emphasized the striking fact that the best predictor of MEP voting behaviour is not nationality, but an MEP's 'party group', with the centre-left Party of

European Socialists, the centre-right European People's Party, and other smaller party groups demonstrating extraordinarily high measures of cohesion in empirical studies of roll-call votes (see Kreppel 2001). These MEPs, moreover, were shown to contest elections and cast their votes in a two-dimensional 'issue space', including not only the familiar nationalism/supranationalism dimension, but also a more traditional, 'domestic' dimension of left-right contestation (Hix 2001). Many observers of the EP noted the tendency of the two major party groups to form oversized voting coalitions, ostensibly to ensure large majorities and to increase the EP's influence relative to the Council. Recent studies, however, have pointed to a tentative retreat from oversized coalitions toward more 'normal' patterns of minimum-winning coalitions on the left or the right (Kreppel and Hix 2003). Yet other studies have focused on the legislative organization of the EP, including its powerful committees, whose members play an important agenda-setting role in preparing legislation for debate on the floor of Parliament, and therefore have a tangible impact on what policies the EU can adopt (Kreppel 2001; McElroy 2004). Perhaps most fundamentally, these scholars have shown that the EP can increasingly be studied as a 'normal parliament', whose members vote predictably and cohesively within a political space dominated by the familiar contestation between parties of the left and those of the right (Hix, Noury, and Roland 2002).

During the 1980s and the 1990s, the legislative powers of the EP have grown sequentially, from the relatively modest and non-binding 'consultation procedure' of the EEC Treaty through the creation of the 'cooperation' procedure in the 1980s and the creation and reform of a 'co-decision procedure' in the 1990s (see Chapter 3). This expansion of EP legislative power has fostered the development of a burgeoning literature and led to two vigorous debates about the nature and extent of the EP's and the Council's respective influence across the various procedures. The first debate concerns the cooperation procedure. George Tsebelis (1994) argued that this gave the Parliament 'conditional agenda-setting' power, insofar as it would now enjoy the ability to make specific proposals that would be easier for the Council to adopt than to amend. Others disputed this, arguing that the EP's proposed amendments had no special status without the approval of the Commission, which therefore remained the principal agenda setter in the EU legislative process (Moser 1996). Empirical studies appear to confirm the basic predictions of Tsebelis's model, namely that the Parliament enjoyed much greater influence on legislation under cooperation than under the older consultation procedure (Tsebelis 1996; Kreppel 1999; Jacobs, Corbett, and Shackleton 2000: 187–8).

A second controversy concerns the impact of Parliament under the co-decision procedure introduced by the 1993 Maastricht Treaty on European Union (TEU) (co-decision I), and reformed by the 1997 Treaty of Amsterdam (ToA) (co-decision II). In a series of controversial articles, Garrett and Tsebelis argued that the EP had actually *lost* legislative power in the move from cooperation to co-decision I. Other scholars disputed Garrett and Tsebelis's claims, noting that alternative specifications of the model predicted more modest agenda-setting power for the EP under cooperation, and/or a stronger position for the EP in co-decision (Scully 1997a, 1997b, 1997c; Crombez 1997; Moser 1997). In any event, the ToA simplified the co-decision procedure, creating a more symmetrical co-decision II procedure in which 'the Council and the Parliament are now co-equal legislators and the EU's legislative regime is truly bicameral' (Tsebelis and Garrett 2000: 24). Several core studies in this volume illustrate the role of the EP in the legislative, as well as the budgetary, processes of the EU.

Executive politics: delegation and discretion

Throughout the history of the EU, scholars have debated the causal role of supranational actors in the processes of European integration and policy-making, with neofunctionalists generally asserting, and intergovernmentalists generally denying, any important causal role for supranational organizations in the integration process. By and large, however, neither school has generated testable hypotheses regarding the conditions under which, and the ways in which, supranational institutions exert an independent causal influence on the process of European integration. Rational-choice institutionalists have devoted increasing attention over the past decade to the question of delegation to, and agency and agenda-setting by, supranational organizations such as the Commission. These studies generally address two specific sets of questions. First, they ask why and under what conditions a group of (member-state) *principals* might delegate powers to (supranational) *agents*, such as the Commission, the ECB, or the ECJ. With regard to this first question, rationalists such as Moravcsik (1998), Majone (2000), and Pollack (2003) have drawn from the theoretical literature on delegation in American, comparative, and international politics in order to devise and to test hypotheses about the motives of EU governments in delegating specific powers and functions to the Commission and other supranational actors.

Simplifying considerably, such *transaction-cost* accounts of delegation argue that member-state principals, as rational actors, delegate powers to supranational organizations primarily to lower the transaction costs of policy-making, in particular by allowing member governments to commit themselves credibly to international agreements and to benefit from the policy-relevant expertise provided by supranational actors. Despite differences in emphasis, the empirical work of these scholars has collectively demonstrated that EU member governments do indeed delegate powers to the Commission, the ECB, and the ECJ largely to reduce the transaction costs of policy-making, in particular through the monitoring of member-state compliance, the filling-in of framework treaties ('incomplete contracts'), and the swift and efficient adoption of implementing regulations that would otherwise have to be adopted in a time-consuming legislative process by the member governments themselves. By the same token, however, the same studies generally concede that transaction-cost models do a poor job of predicting patterns of delegation to the EP, which appears to have won delegated powers primarily in response to concerns about democratic legitimacy rather than in order to reduce the transaction costs of policy-making.

Rational-choice institutionalists have devoted greater attention to a second question posed by principal-agent models: what occurs if an agent—such as the Commission, the ECJ, or the ECB—behaves in ways that diverge from the preferences of the principals? Their answer lies primarily in the administrative procedures that the principals may establish to define *ex ante* the scope of agency activities, as well as the oversight procedures that allow for *ex post* oversight and sanctioning of errant agents. Applied to the EU, principal-agent analysis therefore leads to the hypothesis that agency autonomy is likely to vary across issue areas and over time, as a function of the preferences of the member states, the distribution of information between principals and agents, and the decision rules governing the application of sanctions or the adoption of new legislation (Pollack 1997, 2003; Tallberg 2000; Tsebelis and Garrett 2000).

Much of this literature focuses on the rather arcane question of 'comitology', the committees of member-state representatives established to supervise the Commission in its implementation of EU law. For rational-choice theorists, comitology committees act as control mechanisms designed by member-state principals to supervise their supranational agent (the Commission) in its executive duties. More specifically, rational-choice analysts have analysed the differences among the three primary types of comitology committees—namely, advisory committees, management committees, and regulatory committees—noting that, in formal models of executive decision-making, the Commission is least constrained under the advisory committee procedure, and most constrained under the regulatory committee procedure, with the management committee procedure occupying a middle ground (Steunenberg, Koboldt, and Schmidtchen 1996, 1997). Under these circumstances, rationalists predict, the influence of the Commission as an agent should vary with the type of committee governing a given issue area, and preliminary research suggests that member governments do indeed design and use comitology committees as instruments of control, and that Commission autonomy and influence vary as a function of the administrative and oversight procedures adopted by the Council (Dogan 1997; Franchino 2001; Pollack 2003).

Finally, students of executive politics in the EU have turned increasingly to the study of a relatively new phenomenon, notably the ECB and a diverse array of independent regulatory agencies at the EU level. The ECB, now the collective central bank of the Eurozone, is without doubt the most spectacular example of supranational delegation in the history of the EU. Indeed, both rational-choice scholars and EU practitioners have referred to the ECB as the most independent central bank in the world, due to the long and non-renewable terms of office of its members and the insulation of the Bank and its mandate, which can be altered only by a unanimous agreement of the member states. For rationalist scholars, the creation of the ECB is a classic case of delegation to increase the credibility of member-state commitments to a stable, non-inflationary common currency (Moravcsik 1998; Majone 2000). Arguing from a sociological institutionalist perspective, however, Kathleen McNamara (2002; and Chapter 6) has argued that the functional advantages of delegation to independent central banks are disputable, and that the creation of the ECB therefore represents a process of 'institutional isomorphism', in which organizational forms considered to be successful and legitimate in one setting diffuse and are copied in other settings 'even if these rules are materially inappropriate to their needs'.

The past decade, finally, has witnessed the growth of a growing number of EU agencies, such as the European Medicines Agency (EMEA) and the European Food Safety Authority (EFSA), among more than a dozen others (see Chapter 13). Although most of these agencies are still in their infancy, early research has catalogued their diverse functions, as well as the wide range of control mechanisms designed by member governments to limit the discretion of these agencies in ways appropriate to their various tasks. This suggests again that EU member governments delegate functions to executive actors for the reasons specified in rationalist theories, and tailor control mechanisms to the functions and expected preferences of the respective agencies (Kreher 1997; Everson et al. 2001).

Judicial politics and the ECJ

Rational-choice institutionalists have also engaged in increasingly sophisticated research into the nature of EU judicial politics and the role of the ECJ in the integration process.

Geoffrey Garrett (1992) first drew on principal-agent analysis to argue that the Court, as an agent of the EU's member governments, was bound to follow the wishes of the most powerful member states. These member states, Garrett claimed, had established the ECJ as a means to solve problems of incomplete contracting and monitoring compliance with EU obligations, and they rationally accepted ECJ jurisprudence, even when rulings went against them, because of their longer term interest in the enforcement of EU law. In such a setting, Garrett and Weingast (1993: 189) argued, the ECJ might identify 'constructed focal points' among multiple equilibrium outcomes, but the Court was unlikely to rule against the preferences of powerful EU member states, as Burley and Mattli (1993) had suggested in a famous article drawing on neo-functionalist theory.

Other scholars have argued forcefully that Garrett's model overestimated the control mechanisms available to powerful member states and the ease of sanctioning an activist Court, which has been far more autonomous than Garrett suggests. Such accounts suggest that the Court has been able to pursue the process of legal integration far beyond the collective preferences of the member governments. This is partly due to the high costs to member states in overruling or failing to comply with ECJ decisions, and in part because the ECJ enjoys powerful allies in the form of national courts and individual litigants which refer hundreds of cases per year to the ECJ via the 'preliminary reference' procedure of Article 234 TEC (ex Art. 177 EEC) (Weiler 1994; Mattli and Slaughter 1995, 1998a; Stone Sweet and Caporaso 1998; Stone Sweet and Brunell 1998a, 1998b; Alter 2001). According to Stone Sweet and Caporaso (1998: 129), 'the move to supremacy and direct effect must be understood as audacious acts of agency' by the Court.

By contrast with traditional principal-agent analyses, however, Stone Sweet and his collaborators suggest that the extraordinary discretion of the Court *vis-à-vis* member governments means that we should also turn our attention to the ECJ's other interlocutors, including notably the national courts that bring the majority of cases before the ECJ, and the individual litigants who use EU law to achieve their aims within national legal systems (Mattli and Slaughter 1998a; Alter 2001; Conant 2002). Such studies have demonstrated the complexities of ECJ legal integration, the interrelationships among supranational, national, and subnational political and legal actors, and the limits of EU law in national legal contexts.

Toward normal science?

Students of the EU have thus approached the study of policy-making employing the theoretical tools of comparative politics, formal and informal models drawn from rational choice, and a positivist commitment to systematic empirical testing. The resulting literature, although sometimes highly abstract and inaccessible to the general reader, has substantially advanced our understanding of EU policy-making, of the respective roles and influence of the Commission, Council, Parliament, and Court, and increasingly of the relationship between EU institutions and their national and subnational interlocutors. Furthermore, with the creation and dissemination of a range of new databases, the scope for systematic testing and falsification of theories is certain to increase in the years to come, making the EU an increasingly promising arena for the practice of 'normal science'.

The governance approach: the EU as a polity

The reader might easily conclude from the chapter so far that the story of theorizing about the EU is a linear progression from international relations theories to comparative-politics theories, with an increasing attention over time to rational-choice approaches and to positivist testing of hypotheses. Such a story, however, would be misleading. International relations scholars continue to pose important questions about the process of European integration, and to theorize about the EU in the context of regional cooperation and regional integration among states in various parts of the world. The comparative-politics approach to the study of the EU has not replaced the international-relations study of regional integration, but now exists alongside it. Just as importantly, these approaches now co-exist with a third approach, typically labelled the 'governance approach', which draws on both IR and comparative politics and considers the EU as neither a traditional international organization *nor* as a domestic 'political system', but rather as a new and emerging system of 'governance without government'.

The governance approach is not a single theory of the EU or of European integration, but rather a cluster of related theories emphasizing common themes (Jachtenfuchs 2001; Jachtenfuchs and Kohler-Koch 2004). Simon Hix (1998) has usefully contrasted the governance school to its rationalist/comparativist/positivist alternative, arguing that the governance approach constitutes a distinctive research agenda across four dimensions. First, the governance approach theorizes EU governance as non-hierarchical, mobilizing networks of private as well as public actors, who engage in deliberation and problem-solving efforts guided as much by informal as by formal institutions. Secondly, the practitioners of the governance approach are suspicious of 'off the shelf' models, advocating the need for a 'new vocabulary' (Schmitter 1996: 133) to capture the distinctive features of EU governance.[5] Thirdly, students of EU governance often (although not always) emphasize the capacity of the EU to foster 'deliberation' and 'persuasion'—a model of policy-making in which actors are open to changing their beliefs and their preferences, and in which good arguments can matter as much as, or more than, bargaining power. Fourthly, governance theorists, like comparativists, frequently express a normative concern with the 'democratic deficit' in the EU; but whereas comparativists emphasize majoritarian or parliamentary models of democracy in their assessments, many governance theorists emphasize the potential for the EU as a 'deliberative democracy' in which collective problem-solving offers a normatively superior alternative form of policy-making in a multinational Union. Finally, one might add, whereas Hix and other comparative scholars are committed to a positivist model of hypothesis-testing and generalization, governance scholars tend to eschew hypothesis-testing in favour of 'thick description' and a normative critique of contemporary EU governance.

The literature on 'governance' thus defined has exploded in the course of the past decade.[6] I focus here on a few key issues: (1) the concept of 'governance' as derived from both the comparative and international relations literatures; (2) early applications to the EU, in the literatures on 'multi-level governance' and policy networks; (3) a substantial literature on the governance capacity of member states and of EU institutions, and the problems of legitimacy faced by the latter; and (4) a new and novel set of claims about the EU as a process of 'deliberative supranationalism' capable of resolving these normative dilemmas.

Governing without government

In Hix's (1998) critique, the governance approach is presented as a *sui generis* approach, treating the EU as fundamentally different from other polities and therefore requiring new—as opposed to 'off the shelf'—theoretical approaches. Nonetheless, the EU governance literature draws heavily on the concept(s) of governance worked out by students of both comparative politics *and* international relations.

Within the field of comparative politics, the term governance has appeared with increasing frequency, but with different definitions and different emphases—indeed, Rod Rhodes (1996) identifies at least six distinct uses of the term in the literature, including familiar concepts such as corporate governance, the 'new public management', and normative conceptions of 'good governance'. At their most far-reaching, however, theorists of governance put forward the radical claim that contemporary governments lack the knowledge and information required to solve complex economic and social problems, and that governance should therefore be conceived more broadly as the negotiated interactions of public and private actors in a given policy arena. In this view, modern society is 'radically decentred', and government features as only one actor among many in the larger process of socioeconomic governance (Kooiman 1993).

Perhaps the most systematic definition of governance has been offered by Rhodes (1996: 660), who defines governance in terms of 'self-organizing, interorganizational networks', and goes on to identify four basic characteristics of 'governance', which distinguish the term from the traditional notion of 'government':

- *Interdependence between organizations.* Insofar as governance is broader than government, covering non-state actors; changing the boundaries of the state meant the boundaries between public, private, and voluntary sectors became shifting and opaque.

- *Continuing interactions between network members*, caused by the need to exchange resources and negotiate shared purposes.

- *Game-like interactions*, rooted in trust and regulated by rules of the game negotiated and agreed by network participants.

- *A significant amount of autonomy from the state.* Insofar as networks are not accountable to the state; they are self-organizing; although the state does not occupy a privileged, sovereign position, it can indirectly and imperfectly steer networks.

In this view, governance through public-private networks complements Williamson's (1985) traditional classification of 'markets' and 'hierarchies' as the two ideal-typical modes of 'authoritatively allocating resources and exercising control and coordination'. In this sense, governance is not new, insofar as governments have always cooperated with public and private actors in the provision of services, but the adoption of neo-liberal policies in Europe and the US has prompted a general move toward governance by such networks, as states reduce the size of their public sectors and attempt to off-load responsibility for service provision to the private and voluntary sectors.

This shift from government to governance, moreover, raises new analytical and normative issues, including the inter-linked issues of fragmentation, steering, and accountability. Fragmentation may occur when centralized state bureaucracies out-source the provision of public services to a broad array of public, quasi-public, and private organizations, reducing central government control over policy outcomes. At best, Rhodes and others argue, governments may 'steer' public policies in a given direction, but in practice policy outcomes will depend on the interactions of multiple actors over whom governments have only imperfect control. Finally, the contracting-out of public functions by governments to independent agencies and private actors raises questions about democratic accountability to the electorate—questions that are also at the heart of the governance literature in international relations.

Within IR theory, the analysis of governance typically begins with the systemic view of states co-existing in a condition of anarchy, rather than public policy-making within states, and the primary question is whether, and under what conditions, states can cooperate to realize joint gains, despite the absence of a global government to enforce agreements among them. In this context, an international order can be main-tained even in the absence of world government, through processes of international governance, which, according to Rosenau (1992: 4),

... is not synonymous with government. Both refer to purposive behavior, to goal-oriented activities, to systems of rule; but government suggests activities rather are backed by formal authority, by police powers to ensure the implementation of duly constituted policies, whereas governance refers to activities back by shared goals that may or may not derive from legal and formally prescribed responsibilities and that do not necessarily rely on police powers to overcome defiance and attain compliance. Governance, in other words, is a more encompassing phenom-enon than government. It embraces governmental institutions, but it also subsumes informal, non-governmental mechanisms whereby persons and organizations within its purview move ahead, satisfy their needs, and fulfill their wants.

Other international relations theorists have examined the workings of various international regimes, defined as 'social institutions that consist of agreed-upon prin-ciples, rules, norms, decision-making procedures and programmes that govern the interactions of actors in specific issue-areas' (Young 1997: 4). Moreover, while tradi-tional regime theories assumed that states were the primary, or sole, actors within international regimes—in essence, the intergovernmental view discussed in the first section of this chapter—an increasing number of IR theorists have argued for the importance of different types of networks, including 'transgovernmental' networks of lower-level government or judicial actors interacting across borders with their for-eign counterparts (Slaughter 2004), and 'transnational' networks of private actors forming a sort of 'global civil society' to lobby states and to influence individual behaviour directly through joint actions such as international campaigns or boycotts (Wapner 1996).[7]

In sum, many of the key themes of the governance approach—the emphasis on non-hierarchical networks, on public-private interactions, and on the prospects for governance without government—draw from the parallel governance traditions in both comparative politics and international relations.

Multi-level governance and EU policy networks

By most accounts (Jachtenfuchs 2001; Bache and Flinders 2004: 3), the governance approach to the EU can be traced, at least in part, to Gary Marks' (1992, 1993) work on the making and implementation of the EU's structural funds. Writing in opposition to intergovernmentalists, such as Moravcsik, he argued that the structural funds of the 1980s and 1990s provided evidence for a very different image of the EU, one in which central governments were losing control both to the European Commission (which played a key part in designing and implementing the funds), and to local and regional governments inside each member state (which were granted a 'partnership' role in planning and implementation by the 1988 reforms of the funds). In making this argument, Bache and Flinders (2004: 3) point out that:

The multi-level governance concept . . . contained both vertical and horizontal dimensions. 'Multi-level' referred to the increased interdependence of governments operating at different territorial levels, while 'governance' signaled the growing interdependence between governments and non-governmental actors at various territorial levels.

More specifically, Marks' multi-level governance (MLG) analysis married the fundamental insights of the policy networks literature, with its emphasis on policy networks and policy communities of public and private actors in given issue areas, with the view of an EU in which supranational and subnational actors were chipping away at the traditional dominance and control of national governments.

Later studies of the EU structural funds questioned Marks' far-reaching empirical claims, noting in particular that EU member governments played central roles in the successive reforms of the funds, and that these member states remained effective 'gatekeepers', containing the inroads of both the Commission and subnational governments into the traditional preserve of state sovereignty (Pollack 1995; Bache 1998; see also Chapter 9). Following these challenges, proponents of the multi-level governance approach have retreated somewhat from the early, and more far-reaching, claims about the transformative effects of EU structural policy, while continuing to explore both the vertical dimension of territorial reform and the horizontal dimension of EU policy networks.

With regard to the vertical aspect, Liesbet Hooghe, Gary Marks and others returned to EU regional policies, seeking to delineate and to explain the substantial variation in the empowerment of supranational and subnational actors in the various member states by the EU's structural funds. In some cases, the authors demonstrate, new and especially existing regional authorities were able to draw upon EU resources and on their place in emerging policy networks to enhance regional autonomy, while in other states, such as the UK and Greece, national governments were indeed able to retain a substantial gatekeeping role between the EU and subnational governments (Hooghe 1996). More broadly, however, the authors describe and purport to explain what they call 'an immense shift of authority' from national governments to the European arena and to subnational, regional governments in a substantial number of states including France, Italy, Spain, Belgium, and the UK. It remains controversial whether such devolution was driven wholly or in part by European integration or by purely national considerations, but it is clear that many regional governments have taken a pro-active stance in European policy-making, establishing permanent offices in Brussels (most often in the German and Belgian cases), sometimes being part of the delegations from their respective member states in the Council of Ministers where EU policies encroach on constitutionally protected regional prerogatives (Marks, Hooghe, and Blank 1996). Like the literature on federalism, then, MLG focuses in large part on the territorial aspects of governance in Europe. By contrast with the federalism literature, however, MLG scholars are concerned not only with the distribution of authority between the nation-state and the EU, but also more broadly with the shift of authority away from national governments and toward both supranational and subnational actors (Hooghe and Marks 2001; Bache and Flinders 2004).

Other scholars have focused on the horizontal or network aspects of European integration, drawing on network theory to describe and explain the workings of transnational and transgovernmental networks that can vary from the relatively closed 'policy communities' of public and private actors in areas such as research and technological development to the more open and porous 'issue networks' prevailing in areas such as environmental regulation. The openness and interdependence of these networks, it is argued, determine both the relative influence of various actors and the substantive content of EU policies (particularly in their early stages, when the Commission drafts policies in consultation with various public and private actors) (Peterson and Bomberg 1999; Peterson 2004). This network form of governance, moreover, has been accentuated further over the past decade by the creation of formal and informal networks of national regulators, in areas such as competition (antitrust) policy, utilities regulation, and financial regulation. By contrast with most students of legislative politics, who emphasize the importance of *formal* rules in shaping actors' behaviour and polity outcomes (Hix 1998; Jupille 2004), students of policy networks emphasize the *informal* politics of the Union, in which such networks of private and public actors substantially determine the broad contours of the policies that are eventually brought before the Council and the European Parliament for their formal adoption.

A final offshoot from the multi-level governance tradition examines the phenomenon of 'Europeanization', the process whereby EU institutions and policies influence national institutions and policies within the various member states. In general terms, such studies date to the 1970s, when a small number of scholars examined how EU membership had influenced national political institutions and public policies (see, for example, H. Wallace 1973; Bulmer and Patterson 1987). During the 1990s, the study of Europeanization became a cottage industry, with a growing number of studies seeking to explain both the process of Europeanization and the significant variation in outcomes observed across both member states and issue areas. In one particularly influential formulation, Cowles, Caporaso, and Risse (2001) suggested that the extent of Europeanization should be the dual product of: (1) adaptational pressures resulting from the varying 'goodness of fit' between EU and national institutions and policies; and (2) domestic intervening variables, including the number of veto points and the organizational and political cultures embedded in existing national institutions. Subsequently, scholars have sketched alternative rationalist and constructivist mechanisms whereby the EU might influence national politics—in the first instance by constraining national choices, in the second case by instilling new norms and reshaping national identities and preferences (Börzel and Risse 2000). More recently, Frank

Schimmelfennig and Ulrich Sedelmeier (2002, 2005) have led teams of researchers who tested alternative rationalist and constructivist hypotheses about the effect of EU membership on the new member states. They find some evidence of EU-led policy learning and socialization, as predicted by constructivist models, but the content and the timing of policy reforms in the new members suggest that the greatest impact of the EU has resulted from explicit EU conditionality, a classic rationalist mechanism.

Globalization, Europeanization, and the question of democratic legitimacy

A second major branch of the governance approach to the EU emerged out of the European political economy literature of the 1980s and 1990s, associated with scholars such as a Wolfgang Streeck (1996) and Fritz Scharpf (1999). Much of this work analyses and undertakes a normative critique of an EU that purportedly undermines the autonomy and domestic governance capacity of the member states through 'negative integration', while failing to establish governance capacity that is both substantial and democratically legitimate at the supranational EU level. This critique is typically made in two stages. First, it is argued, EU internal market regulations and ECJ decisions have increasingly eroded, invalidated, or replaced national social regulations, thereby thwarting the social aims and the democratically expressed preferences of national electorates and their legislatures. Moreover, even where EU legislation and ECJ jurisprudence leave national laws, taxation systems, and welfare programmes untouched, it is often argued that the free movement provisions of the Union may set in train a process of regulatory competition in which national governments face pressures to adjust national regulations in an effort to make them more attractive to mobile capital. This may lead to a 'race to the bottom', in which national governments compete to lower the tax burden and the regulatory burdens on businesses threatening to move to other jurisdictions. The recent adoption of the euro, and the limitations on national budget deficits contained in the EU Stability and Growth Pact, have arguably constrained national autonomy still further, depriving states of fiscal policy tools that have proven effective in the past pursuit of economic and social goals (see Chapter 6). In the words of Claus Offe (2000), the *acquis communautaire* (the body of rules and legislation mandated by the EU) now threatens the *acquis nationale* of strong liberal democracy and well-developed welfare states. The extent and character of this purported race to the bottom remain a matter of dispute, with Scharpf (1999) and others acknowledging that the extent of competitive deregulation appears to vary systematically across issue areas. In addition, some commentators suggest that it may not be so much a 'race to the bottom' as the embedding of predominant and especially neo-liberal policy preferences. But either way, the prospect of the undermining national regulations and welfare states poses important analytic as well as normative challenges, especially to social democrats and to students of democratic theory.

This challenge to national governance raises a second question: whether the race to the bottom might be averted, and democracy regained, at the EU level. On this score, many contributors to the debate are pessimistic, pointing to: the distant and opaque nature of EU decision-making; the strong role of indirectly elected officials in the Council of Ministers and unelected officials in the European Commission; the weakness of the EP and the second-order nature of its elections; and the bias in the treaties in favour of market liberalization over social regulation (Williams 1991; Scharpf 1999;

Greven 2000). Furthermore, even if these institutional flaws in the EU treaties were to be addressed, Joseph Weiler (1995) and others have suggested that Europe lacks a *demos*, a group of people united by a sense of community or 'we-feeling' that could provide the constituent basis for an EU-level democracy. For all these reasons, governance theorists argue, the EU faces a 'democratic deficit' and a profound crisis of legitimacy. Much of the governance literature is given over to proposals for increasing the democratic accountability and the governance capacity of the Union. Whereas in the past EU institutions had relied primarily on 'output legitimacy' (i.e. the efficiency or popularity of EU policy outputs), today there are increased calls for reforms that would increase the 'input legitimacy' (i.e. the democratic accountability of EU institutions to the electorate).

We can identify three distinct reform tracks in the literature: parliamentarization, constitutionalization, and deliberation. Parliamentarization would involve *inter alia* the strengthening of the EP's legislative and budgetary powers; a strengthening of EU party groups; the increased salience of EU (rather than national) issues in European elections; and the subordination of the Commission to the Parliament as in the national parliamentary systems of Europe. Some critics, however, have cast doubt on the parliamentary model, suggesting that such an approach could exacerbate, rather than ameliorate, the EU's crisis of legitimacy by subjecting national communities, or *demoi*, to a long-term minority position in an EU25 (Weiler 1995).

A second and more modest proposal is 'constitutionalization', the creation of overarching rules and procedural controls that would ensure minimum levels of transparency and public participation in EU policy-making. The Commission opened the debate with its White Paper on governance (Commission 2001d), which called for various reforms, including the on-line publication of information on policies and policy proposals, a code of conduct for consultation with civil-society groups, strengthened rules on public access to EU documents, and the establishment of a systematic dialogue with local and regional governments in the member states. Even these reforms, however, would arguably fail to bring the EU on a par with many national governments, which remain far more visible, transparent, and accountable to their citizens than EU institutions.

Hence an increasing number of authors have suggested a third model for the EU, namely a 'deliberative democracy' in which citizens, or at least their representatives, would collectively deliberate in search of the best solution to common problems.

Argument, persuasion, and the 'deliberative turn'

This emphasis on deliberation derives largely from the work of Jürgen Habermas (1985, 1998), whose theory of communicative action has been adapted to the study of international relations and to the study of EU governance. The core claim of the approach, as popularized by Risse (2000) in the field of international relations, is that there are not two but three 'logics of social action', namely: the logic of consequentiality (or utility maximization) emphasized by rational-choice theorists; the logic of appropriateness (or rule-following behaviour) associated with constructivist theory; and a 'logic of arguing' derived largely from Habermas's theory of communicative action.

Habermasian communicative action, or what Risse (2000: 7) calls the logic of arguing:

. . . implies that actors try to challenge the validity claims inherent in any causal or normative statement and seek a communicative consensus about their understanding of a situation as well as justifications for the principles and norms guiding their action. Argumentative rationality also implies that participants in a discourse are open to being persuaded by the better argument and that relationships of power and social hierarchies recede into the background . . . Actors' interests, preferences, and the perceptions of the situation are no longer fixed, but subject to discursive challenges. Where argumentative rationality prevails, actors do not seek to maximize or to satisfy given interests and preferences, but to challenge and to justify the validity claims inherent in them—and they are prepared to change their views of the world or even their interests in light of the better argument.

Put more simply, political actors do not simply bargain based on fixed preferences and relative power, they may also 'argue', questioning their own beliefs and preferences, and being open to persuasion and the power of a better argument. In the view of many democratic theorists, moreover, such processes lead to the promise of a normatively desirable 'deliberative democracy', in which societal actors engage in a sincere collective search for truth and for the best available public policy, and in which even the losers in such debates accept the outcome by virtue of their participation in the deliberative process and their understanding of the principled arguments put forward by their fellow citizens (Elster 1998; Bohman 1998).

Despite the purported benefits of such deliberative democracy, Habermas and his followers concede that genuine communicative action, or argumentative rationality, is likely only under a fairly restrictive set of three preconditions. First, the participants in a deliberation must demonstrate an ability to empathize, to see the world through others' eyes. Secondly, the participants must also share a 'common lifeworld, . . . a supply of collective interpretations of the world and of themselves, as provided by language, a common history, or culture'. Thirdly, an ideal speech situation requires that the discourse be undertaken openly and that all actors have equal access to the discourse (Risse 2000: 10–11). These are demanding preconditions, and all the more so at the international level, where a common lifeworld cannot be taken for granted and where relationships of power are ubiquitous. For this reason, Risse (2000: 19–20) concedes, we should expect international deliberation or arguing only under certain conditions, including notably:

- the existence of a common lifeworld provided by a high degree of international institutionalization in the respective issue area;
- uncertainty of interests and/or lack of knowledge about the situation among the actors; and
- international institutions based on non-hierarchical relations enabling dense interactions in informal, network-like settings.

These conditions are by no means satisfied everywhere in international politics. Where they are present, constructivist scholars predict that international actors will engage in arguing rather than bargaining. Empirical studies of deliberation face significant methodological hurdles in distinguishing between arguing and bargaining, or between genuine communicative action and 'cheap talk' (Checkel 2001; Magnette

2004: 208). Despite these challenges, a growing number of studies have pointed to at least suggestive evidence of deliberation in international institutions such as the UN Security Council (Johnstone 2003).

The promise of deliberation has received extraordinary attention within the study of the EU in recent years, for three reasons. First, the EU has been identified by governance theorists as an environment characterized by 'dense interactions in informal, network-like settings', making the EU a particularly promising place to look for evidence of international deliberation. Secondly, the constructivist nature of the deliberation literature has been attractive to EU scholars dissatisfied with the methodological individualism of rational choice theory (Eriksen and Fossum 2000, 2003). Thirdly, the prospect of what Christian Joerges (2001a) has called 'deliberative supranationalism' offers a potentially compelling solution to the normative challenge of democratic legitimacy within the EU.

In empirical terms, EU scholars have identified the promise of deliberation in three EU-related forums: comitology committees, the Constitutional Convention of 2003–4, and the 'new governance' mechanisms of the EU's 'open method of coordination'. With regard to the first, Christian Joerges and Jürgen Neyer (1997a, 1997b) draw on Habermasian accounts of deliberative democracy as well as constructivist analysis in political science to argue that EU comitology committees provide a forum in which national and supranational experts meet and *deliberate* in a search for the best or most efficient solutions to common policy problems. In this view, comitology is a technocratic version of deliberative democracy in which informal norms, deliberation, good arguments, and consensus matter more than formal voting rules, which are rarely invoked. However, rational-choice scholars argue that EU member states design and utilize comitology committees systematically as instruments of control, and that evidence of deliberation in such committees remains partial and sketchy (Pollack 2003: 114–45). Other critics question the normative value of 'deliberative supranationalism' in comitology committees, noting that such expert deliberation takes place largely outside the public eye (Zürn 2000).

A second EU arena often identified as a promising venue for deliberation was the Convention on the Future of Europe, which met in 2003 to consider changes to the EU treaties and proposed a draft Constitution, although here again the evidence for genuine deliberation, as opposed to bargaining from fixed interests, remains unclear and controversial (Maurer 2003; Closa 2004; Magnette 2004).

Thirdly, the promise of deliberation has also been emphasized by students of the OMC, codified and endorsed by the Lisbon European Council in March 2000. This is a non-binding form of policy coordination, based on the collective establishment of policy guidelines, targets, and benchmarks, coupled with a system of periodic 'peer review' in which member governments present their respective national programmes for consideration and comment by their EU counterparts (see Chapter 3). The OMC remains controversial both politically and in the academic community (see Chapter 11). For many commentators, the OMC offered a flexible means to address common policy issues without encroaching on sensitive areas of national sovereignty, representing a 'third way' between communitarization and purely national governance and a potential test case for Habermasian deliberation (Hodson and Maher 2001; Scott and Trubek 2002). Careful empirical work, however, has at least tempered the more far-reaching claims put forward by the supporters of the OMC. A number of scholars have argued that when it comes to politically sensitive questions, national representatives revert to a presentation of fixed national positions, engaging clearly in bargaining rather than arguing behaviour (see, for example, Jacobsson and Vifell 2003; Jobelius 2003; Borrás and Jacobsson 2004; De la Porte and Nanz 2004; and Chapter 11).[8]

Legitimate governance?

The governance approach to the EU draws on comparative politics as well as international relations and asks analytically and normatively important questions about: the workings of EU policy networks; the transformation of territorial governance at the national, supranational, and subnational levels; the variable Europeanization of national institutions and policies; the limitations that the EU places on the governance capacity of states and the limits of the Union's own governance capacity; the putative democratic deficit and legitimacy crisis of today's EU; and finally the prospects for deliberative policy-making at the EU level. Certainly, the governance approach is not without its flaws or critics, and even its proponents concede that it remains a constellation of interrelated claims rather than a single, coherent theory. In empirical terms, moreover, one can argue that the analytical and normative elaboration of the governance approach has outpaced the empirical work needed to assess the plausibility of its claims. Nevertheless, students of EU governance have made significant progress in formulating a research agenda and in producing more empirical evidence and more nuanced claims about territorial change, Europeanization, and deliberation in an enlarged EU.

Conclusions

In 1972, Donald Puchala likened theorists of EU integration to blind men touching an elephant, each one feeling a different part of the elephant and purporting to describe a very different animal. Today, theories of the EU are even more diverse, comprising three distinct approaches with lively debates both within and across all three. Puchala's metaphor suggested the relative immaturity and weakness of integration theory and the partiality of its insights, yet there is a more optimistic reading of the dizzying array of theories purporting to provide insights into the workings of the EU and the telos of European integration. The 1990s and early 2000s have witnessed at least a partial retreat from grand theorizing about the integration process in favour of a series of mid-range questions about a variety of topics including *inter alia*: the workings of the EU's legislative, executive, and judicial processes; the prospects of socialization or deliberation in EU institutions; the effects of European integration on national institutions and policies; and a wide range of other questions. This diversity of mid-range questions has spawned a corresponding theoretical diversity, with various theories seeking to problematize and explain different aspects of the EU, and a greater dialogue across different theories and different theoretical approaches, and with increasingly careful empirical work in all three traditions.

On a more practical note, the theoretical debates reviewed here also pose a common set of questions about the key actors in EU policy-making and the nature of the policy process. First, with regard to actors, the past several decades have seen an increasingly sophisticated and discriminating set of theoretical claims about the most influential actors in the EU policy process. By contrast with the neo-functionalist/intergovern-mentalist debate, which pitched supranational institutions against EU member governments in a fairly stark fashion, more recent institutionalist approaches generate specific and testable hypotheses about the bargaining power of member governments in the Council, about the legislative powers of the Parliament under different voting procedures, about the agenda-setting and implementing powers of executive actors such as the Commission, and about the ECJ and its various interlocutors. As we shall see in the case studies in this volume, both member states and supranational institutions 'matter' in EU policy-making, but their respective roles and influence remains highly variable across different modes of EU policy-making.

Secondly, with regard to policy processes, the theories reviewed in this chapter put forward a range of hypotheses about the nature of the EU policy process, which we can for the sake of simplicity group under the respective rubrics of rationalism and constructivism. In the first, rationalist, view, the policy process is one of bargaining among the key actors (supranational and/or governmental), with each seeking to max-imize its expected utility on the basis of fixed preferences and within the constraints of the EU's formal institutions. In the second, constructivist view, EU policy-making may be conducive to the socialization of actors into European norms and identities, and/or to the logic of arguing posited by students of deliberative supranationalism. Before tackling such broad questions in our case studies, however, we need to assess the state of our knowledge about EU institutions and about the full range of policy modes in today's EU—a task undertaken by Helen Wallace in Chapter 3.

Notes

1 The author is grateful to Helen Wallace, William Wallace, Orfeo Fioretos, and Daniel Wincott for comments on earlier drafts of this chapter, and to the College of Liberal Arts at Temple University for research support. A longer and more empirically oriented application of the tripartite theoretical framework presented here can be found in Pollack (2005).

2 The Constitutional Treaty (Arts. 1–55) states that the European Council may *unanimously* decide to act by QMV when adopting the multiannual financial framework.

3 Haas (1961) had written of a 'European and universal process', believing the process of functional spill-over to be generalizable to other instances of regional organization. However, he (1976) retreated from these claims, and the neo-functionalist/intergovernmentalist debate was subsequently confined to the study of European integration.

4 For a vigorous debate on the utility of power-index analysis and the importance of considering preferences alongside formal voting weights, see Garrett and Tsebelis 1996, and the 1999

special issue of the *Journal of Theoretical Politics*, 11/3.

5 Far from being a caricature by Hix, this demand for new theories and concepts is widespread within the governance literature. Bache and Flinders (2004: 2), for example, cite with approval Fritz Scharpf's claim that 'the conceptual tools with which the political science subdisciplines of international relations and comparative politics are approaching the study of European institutions are ill suited to deal with multi-level interactions. The argument put is that the EU neither resembles domestic politics nor international organizations, and therefore defies explanation from approaches applied either to politics within states or politics between states. As such, these traditional disciplines must engage in dialogue to facilitate understanding of a complex and unpredictable world'. For a similar and equally strong statement, see Eriksen and Fossum (2000: 2).

6 Seminal statements include Jachtenfuchs 1995; Scharpf 1999; Jachtenfuchs 2001; Hooghe and Marks 2001; and Jachtenfuchs and Kohler-Koch 2004.

7 For a detailed discussion of the comparative politics and international relations literatures on governance, see Pollack and Shaffer (2001a), from which this section has drawn.

8 For a comprehensive bibliography on the OMC, see OMC Research Forum, 'OMC Bibliography', available on-line at *http://eucenter.wisc.edu/OMC/open12.html*.

Further reading

Excellent introductions to European integration theories can be found in Rosamond's (2000) clear and concise text, and in the essays in Wiener and Diez (2004). Keeler (2004) and Jupille (2005) provide illuminating and thorough analyses of trends in the literature, especially the US literature, over the past five decades. Haas (2004 [1958]) remains the *locus classicus* on neo-functionalism, and Hoffmann (1966) the founding text on intergovernmentalism. For more recent developments, see Moravcsik (1998) on liberal intergovernmentalism; Aspinwall and Schneider (1999), Dowding (2000), and Jupille and Caporaso (2000) on institutionalism; and Risse (2004) and Jupille, Caporaso, and Checkel (2003) on constructivism and the EU. Hix (1994) is a fervent manifesto for the comparative study of the EU, and his later (1999, 2005) texts deftly reviews comparative politics approaches to various aspects of EU policy-making. The governance literature remains extremely diverse, but useful overviews are provided by Scharpf (1999), Jachtenfuchs (2001), Hooghe and Marks (2001), and Jachtenfuchs and Kohler-Koch (2004). Pollack (2005) provides an extended version of this chapter.

Aspinwall, M. D., and Schneider, G. (1999), 'Same Menu, Separate Tables: The Institutionalist Turn in Political Science and the Study of European Integration', *European Journal of Political Research*, 38: 1–36.

Dowding, K. (2000), 'Institutionalist Research on the European Union: A Critical Review', *European Union Politics*, 1: 125–44.

Haas, E. B. (2004) [1958], *The Uniting of Europe* (Stanford: Stanford University Press); reprinted in 2004 by Notre Dame University Press.

Hix, S. (1994), 'The Study of the European Community: The Challenge to

Comparative Politics', *West European Politics*, 17/1: 1–30.

Hix, S. (1999), *The Political System of the European Union* (London: Palgrave).

Hix, S. (2005), *The Political System of the European Union*, 2nd edn. (London: Palgrave).

Hoffmann, S. (1966), 'Obstinate or Obsolete? The Fate of the Nation-State and the Case of Western Europe', *Daedalus*, 95/3: 862–915.

Hooghe, L., and Marks, G. (2001), *Multi-Level Governance and European Integration* (Lanham, MD: Rowman & Littlefield).

Jachtenfuchs, M. (2001), 'The Governance Approach to European Integration', *Journal of Common Market Studies*, 39/2: 245–64.

Jachtenfuchs, M., and Kohler-Koch, B. (2004), 'Governance and Institutional Development', in Wiener and Diez (eds.), *European Integration Theory* (Oxford: Oxford University Press), 97–115.

Jupille, J. (2005), 'Knowing Europe: Metatheory and Methodology in EU Studies', in Cini and Bourne (eds.), *Palgrave Guide to European Union Studies* (London: Palgrave), forthcoming.

Jupille, J., and Caporaso, J. A. (1999), 'Institutionalism and the European Union: Beyond International Relations and Comparative Politics', *Annual Review of Political Science*, 2: 429–44.

Jupille, J., Caporaso, J. A., and Checkel, J. (2003), 'Integrating Institutions: Rationalism, Constructivism, and the Study of the European Union', *Comparative Political Studies*, 36/1–2: 7–40.

Moravcsik, A. (1998), *The Choice for Europe: Social Purpose and State Power from Messina to Maastricht* (Ithaca: Cornell University Press).

Pollack, M. A. (2005), 'Theorizing the European Union: International Organization, Domestic Polity, or Experiment in New Governance?', *Annual Review of Political Science*, vol. 7, in press.

Risse, T. (2004), 'Social Constructivism and European Integration', in Wiener and Diez (eds.), *European Integration Theory* (Oxford: Oxford University Press), 159–76.

Rosamond, B. (2000), *Theories of European Integration* (London: Palgrave).

Scharpf, F. W. (1999), *Governing in Europe: Democratic and Effective?* (Oxford: Oxford University Press).

Wiener, A., and Diez, T. (2004) (eds.), *European Integration Theory* (Oxford: Oxford University Press).

Chapter 3

An Institutional Anatomy and Five Policy Modes

Helen Wallace

Contents

Summary

This chapter sets the European Union's (EU) policy process in its institutional context, in a period where enlargement in May 2004 to twenty-five members poses new challenges. Since the EU is part of, and not separate from, the politics and policy processes of the member states, the institutions that are relevant include national (and infranational, i.e. local and regional) institutions, as well as those created by the EU treaties. Features of the national processes pervade the EU, and differences between member states pervade EU policies and the way in which they are applied. The institutional design of the EU is explained, especially the Commission, Council, European Council, European Parliament, and the European Court of Justice. New trends include the emergence of quasi-autonomous agencies, such as the ECB and Europol. EU and national institutions interact differently in different policy domains. Five variants of the EU policy process are identified: a classical Community method; the EU regulatory mode; an EU distributional mode; the policy coordination mode; and intensive transgovernmentalism. The last two of these are particularly strong in the newer areas of active EU policy development.

The institutional design of the European Union

The EU has grown out of three originally separate Communities (ECSC, EEC, and Euratom), each with its own institutions. These were formally merged in 1967. The main elements originally consisted of: a collective executive of sorts—the European Commission; a collective forum for representatives of member governments—the Council (of Ministers); a mechanism for binding arbitration and legal interpretation—the European Court of Justice (ECJ); and a parliamentary chamber—the European Parliament (EP, originally 'Assembly')—with members drawn from the political classes of the member states, and later by direct election. In addition the Economic and Social Committee provided a forum for consulting other sectors of society; later, in the 1990s the Committee of the Regions was created to allow for consultation with local and regional authorities. The powers and responsibilities are set out in the treaties, and have been periodically revised (see Table 3.1).

In the 1990s the EC was turned into what is now generally called the European Union, a term which serves two quite different purposes. One is to imply a stronger binding together of the member states. The other is to embrace within one broad framework the different Communities and also the other arenas of cooperation that have emerged, in particular what came following the TEU to be described as the two 'pillars' of so-called intergovernmental cooperation: the 'second pillar' for common foreign and security policy (CFSP; see Chapter 17); and the 'third pillar' for justice and home affairs (JHA; see Chapter 18). The new Constitutional Treaty (CT), when ratified, would draw these pillars within a more unified institutional and procedural framework. Nonetheless, we note that the institutional design is not stable, but subject to periodic debate, argument, and revision. We summarize here some key elements of the institutional arrangements (see Fig. 3.1 below)—readers already familiar with these can move on to the section dealing with the five policy modes in the EU policy process.

The European Commission

The Commission was designated as both secretariat and proto-executive in the EU's institutional system. In its earliest version, as the High Authority of the European Coal and Steel Community (agreed in 1951), it leaned more towards being executive in nature, with considerable autonomy. It is from this experiment that the term 'supra-national' was coined. When the EEC was created in 1958, some member governments had second thoughts about the consequences of creating a strong autonomous institution. Thereafter the Commission had an ambiguous remit, with strong powers in some fields (notably competition policy; see Chapter 5), and weaker powers in most others. The onus was left to the Commission itself to develop credibility, expertise, and the bases for a political power of its own.

The Commission exercises its responsibilities collectively. The Commissioners, historically two from each of the 'larger' member states and one from each of the others, but from November 2004 one from each of the twenty-five member states, constitute a 'college' of senior officials. Their decisions and proposals to the Council and EP have

Table 3.1 The main treaties and treaty reforms

Year*	Treaty	Outcome
1951	Treaty of Paris	European Coal and Steel Community (ECSC) (signed by Belgium, the Federal Republic of Germany, France, Italy, Luxembourg, and the Netherlands)
1957	Treaty of Rome	European Economic Community (EEC)
1957	Treaty of Rome	European Atomic Energy Community (Euratom)
1965–6	Luxembourg crisis and compromise	Interrupts extension of qualified majority voting (QMV)
1965	Merger Treaty	Combines institutions into single set
1970	Budgetary Treaty	'Own resources' (i.e. revenue) created; some budgetary powers for European Parliament (EP)
1972	Act of Accession	Admits Denmark, Ireland, and UK
1975	Budgetary Treaty	More powers to EP; new Court of Auditors
1978	Treaty revision	For direct elections to EP
1980	Act of Accession	Admits Greece
1985	Act of Accession	Admits Portugal and Spain
1986	Single European Act (SEA)	More QMV in Council; some legislative power for EP; new Court of First Instance; introduces cohesion; expands policy scope
1992	Treaty on European Union (Maastricht) (TEU)	Three-pillar structure of European Union (common foreign and security policy (CFSP) and justice and home affairs (JHA); more QMV in Council; formalizes European Council; some co-decision for EP; new Committee of the Regions; expands policy scope; especially for economic and monetary union (EMU); introduces subsidiarity and citizenship; Social Protocol (UK opt-out)
1994	Act of Accession	Admits Austria, Finland, and Sweden
1997	Treaty of Amsterdam (ToA)	More legislative powers to EP, and stronger requirement for its 'assent' on (e.g.) enlargement and Commission appointments; introduces 'flexibility' (some member states cooperating without others); modest extra QMV in Council; incorporates Schengen; reverses UK social opt-out
1997	Consolidated Treaty on European Union (CTEU)	'Simplifies' the treaties by combining into a single set, and therefore renumbering, the provisions of earlier treaties
2001	Treaty of Nice (ToN)	Intended to streamline the EU institutions for further enlargement
2003	Act of Accession	Admits Cyprus, Czech Republic, Estonia, Hungary, Latvia, Lithuania, Malta, Poland, Slovakia, Slovenia
2004	Constitutional Treaty (CT)	Wide-ranging reorganization of treaties into three parts: I—main 'constitutional' provisions; II—The Charter of Fundamental Rights; III—The Policies and functioning of the Union, and some institutional changes'

*Note: dates of signature.

Figure 3.1 An institutional overview

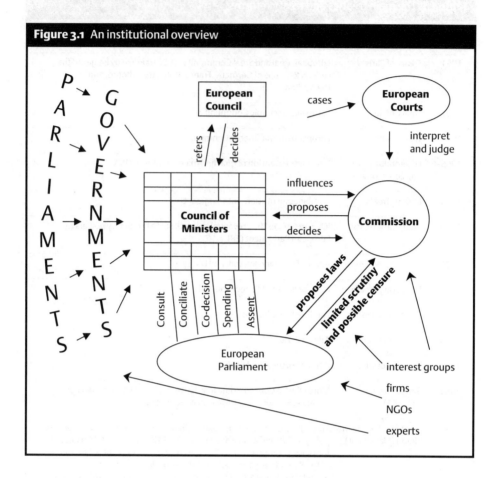

to be agreed by the entire college, voting, if necessary, by simple majority, at its weekly meetings. The Commission is chaired by a President, chosen with other colleagues, historically by 'common accord' in the Council, under the Treaty of Nice (ToN) from 2004 by qualified majority vote (QMV), with two other commissioners as vice-presidents until 2004, and from then on five vice-presidents, each responsible for a strategic area of policy. Those chosen are senior politicians or high officials from member states, but they swear an oath of independence on taking office. Under the Treaty on European Union (TEU) the term-of-office was extended from four to five years, to coincide with that of the EP, and nominations were made subject to consultation with the EP; the Treaty of Amsterdam (ToA) gave the EP the stronger power to confirm in office the college of commissioners. This power was tested in October 2004, when a majority of members of the EP (MEPs) made their disapproval of some members of the Commission so clear that the President-designate, José Manuel Barroso, withdrew his proposed team for reconsideration.

Commissioners are accountable to the EP, which has the power to censure the college with a two-thirds vote. In March 1999 the college, presided over by Jacques Santer, was forced into resignation by the EP on a charge of financial mismanagement. This prompted a decision by the European Council to nominate what they hoped would be a stronger team under the presidency of Romano Prodi, a former Italian prime minister. In November 2004 a new college took office under the presidency of José Manuel Barroso, formerly the Portuguese prime minister.

The Commission as an institution is organized into Directorates-General (DGs), historically known by their numbers, but from 1999 by the name of each main area of policy activity. Table 3.2 illustrates the structure under the Prodi Commission in 1999, which could be subject to further revision by the new Commission, not least because there are more Commissioners. The staff of the DGs make up the European civil service, recruited mostly in competitions across the member states, and supplemented by seconded national experts and temporary staff. The powers and 'personalities' of the DGs vary a good deal, as do their relationships with 'their' commissioners. New DGs have been added as new policy powers have been assigned to the EU, not always tidily. One DG leads on each policy topic, as *chef de file*, but most policy issues require coordination between several DGs, sometimes master-minded by the Secretariat-General under the *aegis* of the Secretary-General. Specialist services provide particular kinds of expertise, most importantly the Legal Service, and the linguistic and statistical services. One indicator of the volume of work done by the Commission is the amount of translation done: in 2003 DG Translation produced an output of 1,416,817 pages, of which almost 60 per cent had been drafted in English (up from just over 35 per cent in 1992), slightly over 28 per cent from French (around 47 per cent in 1992), almost 4 per cent from German, and almost 9 per cent from other languages (*Translating for a Multilingual Community*, DG Translation, May 2004). The commissioners have their own private offices, or *cabinets*, which act as their eyes, ears, and voices, inside the house and *vis-à-vis* other institutions, including those of the member states.

The Commission's powers vary a good deal between policy domains. In competition policy it operates many of the rules directly; in many domains it drafts the proposals for legislation, which then have to be approved by the Council and the EP; it defines, in consultation with the member governments, the way in which spending programmes operate; it monitors national implementation of EU rules and programmes; in external economic relations it generally negotiates on behalf of the EU with third countries or in multilateral negotiations; in some areas one of its key functions is to develop cross-EU expertise, on the basis of which national policies can be compared and coordinated; and in yet other areas the Commission is a more passive observer of cooperation among member governments. In addition it should be noted that though the Commission is supposed to operate collectively, in practice there are debates, and indeed arguments, among commissioners and their DGs, such that contradictory lines of policy can often be observed.

Broadly, within the classical areas of Community cooperation the Commission has a jealously guarded power of initiative, which gives it the opportunity to be the agenda-setter. For this reason it is a target for everyone who wants to influence the content of policy. One of the key questions therefore to be asked about the Commission is how it exploits the opportunities available to it. Its resources include: the capability to build up expertise; the potential for developing policy networks and coalitions; the scope for acquiring grateful or dependent clients; and the chance to help member governments to resolve their own policy predicaments. Versions of all of these are the subject of debate in the theoretical literature, and are addressed throughout the case studies in this volume.

Table 3.2 The organization of the European Commission, 1999–2004

Commissioner area of responsibility with acronym	Old No. where relevant	No. of staff in 2003	Size of budget in 2003
President			
—Cabinets (CA)		352	
—Secretariat General (SG)		484	
—Group of Policy Advisers (GOPA)		32	€174mn
—Legal Service (SJ)		355	
—Press and Communication DG (PRESS)		433	€139mn
Vice-President for Administrative Reform			
—Personnel and Administration DG (ADMIN)	IX	1,331	
—Joint Interpreting and Conference DG (SCIC)		623	
—Translation DG (DGT)		1,779	€615mn
—Informatics DG (DIGIT)		0	
—Infrastructure and Logistics DG Bx(OIB) Lux(OIL)		834	€83mn
—PayMaster Office (PMO)		387	€31mn
—European Personnel Selection Office		118	€21mn
Vice-President for Relations with the European Parliament and for Transport and Energy			
—Transport and Energy DG (TREN)	VII, XVII	995	€1 003mn
includes Euratom Supply Agency	AAE	8	
Commissioner for Competition			
—Competition DG (COMP)	IV	668	€76mn
Commissioner for Agriculture and Fisheries			
—Agriculture DG (AGRI)	VI	939	€47 783mn
—Fisheries DG (FISH)	XIV	288	€883mn
Commissioner for Enterprise and Information Society			
—Enterprise DG (ENTR)	III, XXIII	844	€320mn
—Information Society DG (INFSO)	XIII	1,017	€934mn
Commissioner for Internal Market			
—Internal Market DG (MARKT)	XV	425	€62mn
—Taxation and Customs Union DG (TAXUD)	XXI	403	€74mn
Commissioner for Research			
—Research DG (RTD)	XII	1 617	€2 252mn
—Joint Research Centre (JRC)		1 575	€285mn
Commissioner for Economic and Monetary Affairs			
—Economic and Financial Affairs DG (ECFIN)	II	472	€496mn
—Statistical Office 'Eurostat' (ESTAT)		741	€103mn

Table 3.2 (*Continued*)

Commissioner for External Relations			
—External Relations DG (RELEX)	IA, IB	719 ⎫	
—Delegations in non-member countries		821 ⎬	€3 144mn
—Europe Aid Cooperation Office—part (AIDCO)		1 221 ⎭	
Commissioner for Development and Humanitarian Aid			
—Development DG (DEV)	VIII	287	€1 182mn
—Humanitarian Aid Office (ECHO)		172	€458mn
—also part responsibility for AIDCO (see above)			
Commissioner for Enlargement			
—Enlargement DG (ELARG)		355	€1 826mn
Commissioner for Trade			
—Trade DG (TRADE)	I	464	€69mn
Commissioner for Health and Consumer Protection			
—Health and Consumer Protection DG (SANCO)	XXIV	717	€363mn
Includes Food and Veterinary Office (FVO)		150	
Commissioner for Regional Policy			
—Regional Policy DG (REGIO)	XVI	588	€16 957mn
—*ad personam* dealt with Intergovernmental Conferences			
Commissioner for Education and Culture			
—Education and Culture DG (EAC)	X, XXII	715	€771mn
—Publications Office (OPOCE)		612	€175mn
Commissioner for Budget			
—Budget DG (BUDG)	XIX	486	€66mn
—Financial Control DG (IAS) *	XX	84	€9mn
—European Anti-Fraud Office (OLAF)		364	€44mn
Commissioner for Environment			
—Environment DG (ENV)	XI	542	€262mn
Commissioner for Justice and Home Affairs			
—Justice and Home Affairs DG (JAI)		287	€126mn
Commissioner for Employment and Social Affairs			
—Employment and Social Affairs DG (EMPL)	V	693	€9 059mn
Total:		25 847	€89 845mn

Source: Author with help of Tim Oliver and DG ADMIN, drawn from various Commission publications, including *European Financial Report 2003*, and *General Budget of the European Union for the Financial Year 2004*, vol. 4, Annex 1bis.

Note: *In 2001 as part of a wider reform the Financial Control DG was divided between financial control, which was absorbed into the Budget DG and a new Internal Audit Service.

However, as we shall see, in many areas of policy the Commission has a less entrepreneurial role, either because it is not able to exploit the opportunities available to it, or because the nature of the policy regime allows less room for the Commission to play a central role. In addition we should note that there is a broader problem of capacity. The Commission is a quite small institution, with only some 20,000 or so staff, not very many to develop or implement policies across twenty-five different countries. Hence a great deal depends on how the Commission works with national institutions, which in practice operate most Community rules and programmes. Over the years this feature of the policy process has become more explicit. Indeed, as several of our case studies illustrate (see, for example, Chapters 5, 9, 11, and 14), if anything the balance is tilting towards recognizing much more systematically the role of national (or local) agencies in operating Community policies.

Hence partnership between the national and the European levels of governance has become one of the marked features of EU policy-making. One key mechanism for this is the clumsily-named system of 'comitology'. In essence this is very straightforward. Both to prepare policy proposals and to implement agreed policies the Commission needs regular channels for consultation and cooperation with relevant national officials. Over the years a dense network of advisory, regulatory, and management committees has grown up to provide these channels, much the same as happens in individual countries. In the case of the EU these committees are the subject of procedural, legal, and political debate. Most of the committees are governed by legally specified arrangements, which vary according to the policy, and which strike different balances of influence between national representatives and the Commission. Some insights into the workings of these committees appear in several of our case studies.

The Commission has had several high points of political impact, especially in the early 1960s and the mid-1980s, under the presidencies of respectively Walter Hallstein and Jacques Delors. It has also had low points, after the 1965–6 Luxembourg crisis (when President de Gaulle withdrew French ministers from Council meetings), in the late 1970s, and the late 1990s. In this most recent period the problems have partly been the result of weak internal management and coordination, overstretched staff, and lacklustre leadership. But there also seems to have been an underlying shift of influence away from the Commission towards other EU institutions and the member governments.

The Council of the European Union

The Council of the EU is both an institution with collective EU functions and the crea-ture of the member governments. In principle and in law there is only one Council, empowered to take decisions on any topic. Its members are usually ministers from incumbent governments in the member states, but which ministers attend meetings depends on the subjects being discussed, and on how individual governments choose to be represented. Time and practice have sorted this out by the Council developing specialized configurations according to policy domains. Figure 3.2 summarizes the core pattern of work. Highly specialized groupings have evolved, each with its own policy domain, and each developing its own culture of cooperation.

To the extent that there is a hierarchy among these groupings, the General Affairs Council (GAC), composed of foreign ministers, was supposed to be the senior Council.

Figure 3.2 The structures of the Council

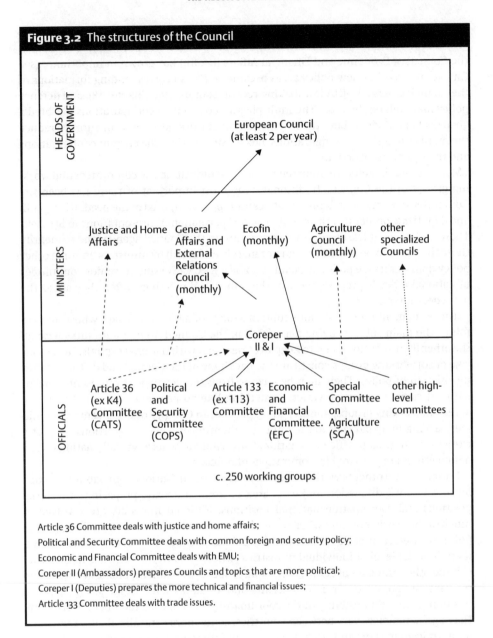

Article 36 Committee deals with justice and home affairs;

Political and Security Committee deals with common foreign and security policy;

Economic and Financial Committee deals with EMU;

Coreper II (Ambassadors) prepares Councils and topics that are more political;

Coreper I (Deputies) prepares the more technical and financial issues;

Article 133 Committee deals with trade issues.

Its seniority rested on the presumption that foreign ministers have an overarching and coordinating role inside the member governments. It is partly because in practice foreign ministers cannot always arbitrate that prime ministers have become more involved through the European Council, but on some cross-cutting issues foreign ministers remain leading decision-makers (see Chapters 8, 9, 15, and 16). The proliferation of foreign policy issues in recent years led to GAC meetings being increasingly dominated by foreign policy and external affairs, leaving less time or inclination to coordinate on other subjects (see Chapter 17). Consequent reforms introduced in 2003 a General

Affairs and External Relations Council (GAERC) with two streams, one to handle coordination and the other to deal with external policies. As EMU has taken shape, so the Council of Economic and Financial Affairs (Ecofin) has grown in importance (see Chapter 6). As other new policy areas became active, so corresponding formations of the Council emerged—JHA is a striking recent example (see Chapter 18), and defence policy may well be the next. The multiplication of Council configurations has bred a good deal of criticism about the fragmentation of work, leading to an effort to reduce the number of distinct configurations. Box 3.1 summarizes the current configurations and their patterns of activity.

Meetings of ministers are prepared by national officials in the committees and working groups of the Council. Traditionally the most important of these has been the Committee of Permanent Representatives (Coreper), composed of the heads (Coreper II) and deputies (Coreper I) of the member states' permanent representations in Brussels. These each meet at least weekly to agree items on the Council agenda, and to identify those that need to be discussed (and not merely endorsed) by ministers. In some other policy domains (trade policy, agriculture, EMU, JHA, CFSP) similar senior committees of national officials prepare many of the ministerial meetings; often they act as the main decision-makers.

The permanent representations contain a range of national officials, whose job is to follow the main subjects being negotiated in the Council, to maintain links with all the other EU institutions, and to keep in close touch with national capitals. Numerous (250 or so) working groups constitute the backbone of the Council and do the detailed negotiation of policy. Their members come from the permanent representations or national capitals—practice varies. Something like 70 per cent of Council texts are agreed in working groups, another 10–15 per cent in Coreper or other senior committees, leaving 10–15 per cent to the ministers themselves. These proportions are pretty close to the normal practice in a national government, where typically national cabinet meetings are prepared by committees of officials.

National governments work in parallel to the Council. National officials follow each level of Council discussion and each area of Council debate, preparing ministerial positions and coordinating national positions. National ministers are involved in much of this work, how and when depends on national practices and on the degree of political interest in each subject within individual countries. Much of this involvement is at the level of individual ministries, where the relevant officials in turn consult the other branches of central, regional, or local government, public agencies, and relevant private-sector or non-governmental organizations. Aggregating national positions is the responsibility of the coordinating units in each member government. Here again, practices vary between countries, some more centralized and some more decentralized in their approaches. Thus, a comprehensive view of how the deliberations of the Council proceeds needs to include that part that emanates from the continuous engagement of national administrations.

What does the Council do in its various configurations? Mostly it negotiates over detailed proposals for EU action, and very often it does so on the basis of a draft from the Commission. Sometimes the Council will have indicated earlier to the Commission that it would welcome a draft on a particular subject. On most of the topics where the Commission has been the primary drafter, the EP is now co-legislator with the Council (see below). In these areas of policy the decision-making outcome depends on the

Box 3.1 Council configurations

The Council is in law a single entity, irrespective of which ministers take part in it. Over time it developed several specialized formations reflecting the development of policy activities and with varying frequencies of meetings. This led to a highly segmented structure, with over twenty formations in the 1990s.

In the period from 2000 onwards efforts were made to streamline the Council into first sixteen, and then—from June 2002—nine, configurations. However, some of these in practice meet in several parts.

As of late 2004 the configurations were as follows, numbers of meetings in brackets:

General Affairs and External Relations (GAERC)
- general affairs, and coordination (2004: 10; 2003: 9)
- external relations (2004: 9; 2003: 11)

Economic and Financial Affairs (Ecofin)
- economics and finance (2004: 9; 2003: 11)
- budget (2004: 2; 2003: 2)

Cooperation in the fields of Justice and Home Affairs (JHA)(2004: 9; 2003: 6)

Competitiveness (2004: 4; 2003: 7)
- internal market
- industry
- research

Transport, Telecommunications and Energy (TTE) (2004: 5; 2003: 7)
- transport
- telecommunications
- energy

Agriculture and Fisheries (2004: 9; 2003: 11)

Environment (2004: 3; 2003: 3)

Education, Youth and Culture (EYC) (2004: 3; 2003: 3)

Employment, Social Policy, Health and Consumer Affairs (EPSCO) (2004: 4; 2003: 5)

The European Council met six times in 2003, and seven times in 2004.

Note: This box also appears in Wallace and Hayes-Renshaw (2005) and has been reproduced here with the kind permission of the authors.

interactions among these three institutions. The dynamics of the process rest on the way in which coalitions emerge within the Council and between the Council members and the other EU institutions.

In some other areas the Commission and the EP play more marginal roles, and the Council itself is more in charge of its own agenda—CFSP and JHA are apt examples. Here more reliance has to be placed on the Council's own General Secretariat. This has not historically been an organ of policy-making, but rather a facilitator of collective decision-making. However, the growth of work related to CFSP and JHA has prompted the considerable expansion of the Council Secretariat over recent years. Successive treaty reforms over the past decade have accepted that the CFSP needs administrative underpinning. Member governments have therefore chosen to expand the relevant sections of the Council Secretariat (see Chapter 17). Following the ToA a section of the Council Secretariat has been strengthened to deal with JHA (see Chapter 18). Following the ToN an important initiative was taken to designate Javier Solana as the Secretary General of the Council and the High Representative of the Union to represent the EU externally and help to develop firmer policies, with the aid of a bigger staff. In parallel a Deputy Secretary General was appointed to oversee the regular work of the Secretariat. As a result we now need to consider the Council Secretariat as much more of an actor in the policy process than hitherto, although these arrangements are due to be further modified after ratification of the CT, when an EU Foreign Minister is to be appointed combining the current High Representative role of Solana with that of the Commission Vice President for external affairs.

The proceedings of the Council are managed by its presidency. This rotates between member governments every six months. The Council presidency chairs meetings at all levels of ministers and officials, except for a small number of committees which have elected chairs. Under the CT, however, the new Foreign Minister is to chair the GAERC when it deals with external affairs. The role of the presidency involves the preparation of agendas, as well as the conduct of meetings. The presidency speaks on behalf of the Council in discussions with other EU institutions and with outside partners on issues other than CFSP. Often the Council and the Commission presidencies have to work closely together, for example in external negotiations where policy powers are divided between the EU and the national levels. In the legislative field it is the Council and EP presidencies that have to work together to reconcile Council and parliamentary views on legislative amendments. A recurrent question is how far individual governments try to impose their national preferences during the presidency or whether the experience pushes them towards identifying with collective EU interests. As EU policy cooperation has developed directly between governments, rather than at the promptings of the Commission and through formal procedures, so it has fallen to successive presidencies to act as the main coordinators. This has historically been a particular feature of CFSP and JHA. There are some doubts as to how well the rotating presidency can continue to function within an EU25, although the Convention that drafted the Constitutional Treaty failed to agree on alternative arrangements, such as 'team' presidencies.

The important point to bear in mind is that the Council is the EU institution that belongs to the member governments. It works the way it does, because that is the way that the member governments prefer to manage their negotiations with each other. Regularity of contact and a pattern of socialization mean that the Council, and especially its specialist formations, develop a kind of insider amity. Sometimes clubs of ministers—in agriculture, or dealing with the environment, and so forth—are able to use agreements in Brussels to force on their own governments commitments that might not otherwise have been accepted at the national level. Nonetheless the ministers and officials who meet in the Council are servants of their governments, affiliated to national political parties, and accountable to national electorates. Thus, generally their first priority is to pursue whatever seems to be the preferred objective of national policy.

The Council spends much of its time acting as the forum for discussion on the member governments' responses to the Commission's proposals. It does so through continuous negotiation, mostly by trying to establish a consensus. The formal rules of decision-making vary according to policy domain and over time—sometimes unanimity, sometimes qualified majority voting (QMV), sometimes (albeit rarely) simple majority. The decisional rules are a subject of controversy and have been altered in successive treaty reforms, in particular under the ToN and the Constitutional Treaty to bring the voting weights more in line with the different population sizes of individual member states. Broadly speaking, QMV has become the formal rule in areas where Community regimes are fairly well established, while unanimity is a requirement either in areas in which EU regimes are embryonic or in those domains where governments have tenaciously retained more control of the process. In an average year some 30 per cent of Council decisions deal with topics subject to the unanimity rule, with 70 per cent subject to the QMV rule, and a tiny number of decisions subject to a simple majority rule (see Fig. 3.3).

There is a great deal of misunderstanding about how the process works in practice. Habits of consensus-seeking are deeply ingrained, and actual votes relatively rare, even when technically possible—votes are explicitly contested on only around 20 per cent of eligible decisions. Under QMV the knowledge that votes may be called often makes doubting governments focus on seeking amendments to meet their concerns, rather than on blocking progress altogether. Under unanimity rules governments are generally much more likely to delay or obstruct agreements, or to exercise blocking power until their views are accommodated, typically on major budgetary and spending decisions (see Chapters 8 and 9). In practice explicitly contested votes at ministerial level are concentrated in a few areas of policy: around half are operational decisions on agriculture and fisheries; and the rest scattered on regulatory issues, especially the single market and public health. Table 3.3 summarizes the recent patterns of 'no' votes and abstentions by the member states. Further details are to be found in Hayes-Renshaw and Wallace (2005).

The Council used to be the main legislator on EU policies. However, as the EP has acquired powers over legislation, the system has become more bicameral. Thus the Council now reaches 'common positions' which have to be frequently reconciled with amendments to legislation proposed by MEPs in a 'conciliation' procedure. This has meant that the Council is now more explicitly required to make a public justification for its collective preferences, which is an important change in the process.

In some policy domains the Council remains the decision-maker of last resort. Interestingly this includes some established areas, such as agriculture, where the EP still has little opportunity to intervene (see Chapter 7), and some new policy domains, where the member governments, through the Council, retain the main control of

Figure 3.3 Percentage share of contested and uncontested votes and of different voting rules, 1999–2003

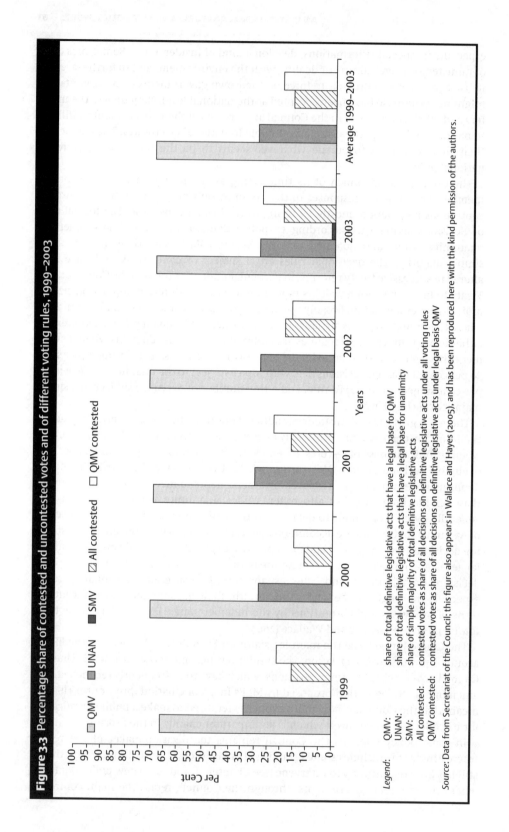

Legend:
QMV: share of total definitive legislative acts that have a legal base for QMV
UNAN: share of total definitive legislative acts that have a legal base for unanimity
SMV: share of simple majority of total definitive legislative acts
All contested: contested votes as share of all decisions on definitive legislative acts under all voting rules
QMV contested: contested votes as share of all decisions on definitive legislative acts under legal basis QMV

Source: Data from Secretariat of the Council; this figure also appears in Wallace and Hayes (2005), and has been reproduced here with the kind permission of the authors.

Table 3.3 Aggregate data on contested votes by member state, 1994–2003

Year	Austria n	Austria a	Belgium n	Belgium a	Denmark n	Denmark a	Finland n	Finland a	France n	France a	Germany n	Germany a	Greece n	Greece a	Ireland n	Ireland a	Italy n	Italy a	Luxembourg n	Luxembourg a	Netherlands n	Netherlands a	Portugal n	Portugal a	Spain n	Spain a	Sweden n	Sweden a	UK n	UK a	TOTAL n	TOTAL a
94			2	0	11	1			2	3	9	6	0	4	1	2	3	3	4	0	10	5	3	3	2	7			7	14	58	44
95	2	0	0	1	5	1	1	1	0	3	8	3	0	1	0	2	4	2	1	0	5	0	2	2	1	2	34	1	10	9	78	26
96	2	1	1	5	2	0	0	1	0	3	14	4	2	0	0	2	6	1	0	2	2	1	1	2	4	0	4	0	7	0	55	14
97	2	1	0	1	6	1	4	0	3	3	9	2	0	4	1	1	6	1	1	1	2	2	2	2	2	1	7	3	7	3	56	17
98	3	0	4	3	7	1	0	0	3	0	11	7	2	2	2	0	8	5	0	2	12	1	2	4	1	7	3	0	2	0	60	34
99	1	0	2	0	4	0	0	0	0	3	2	1	1	0	1	0	1	8	1	2	4	1	1	1	1	2	0	0	0	3	30	9
00	2	0	0	1	3	2	1	1	1	0	4	0	3	0	0	0	2	0	0	0	2	1	0	0	0	0	2	0	2	1	22	12
01	1	0	4	2	3	1	0	3	3	3	3	5	1	0	0	0	2	3	0	2	1	1	0	1	3	2	4	0	2	2	27	25
02	1	0	0	0	2	3	2	2	2	6	2	3	2	0	0	0	0	2	1	1	5	1	1	3	1	1	6	4	4	4	26	29
03	5	2	2	0	6	2	1	0	3	1	5	1	2	1	1	3	3	2	3	0	0	1	6	0	5	2	5	3	4	5	51	25
TOTAL	**19**	**8**	**16**	**16**	**49**	**12**	**11**	**4**	**21**	**22**	**67**	**32**	**21**	**4**	**13**	**4**	**43**	**20**	**12**	**9**	**43**	**13**	**21**	**18**	**20**	**24**	**65**	**8**	**42**	**41**	**463**	**235**

Note: n = negative vote; a = abstention; on issues subject to QMV.

Source: 1994 data released informally from the Council to the authors; 1995 data from Mattila (2001), supported by online database at *www.valt.helsinki.fi/staff/mmattila/julkaisu.htm*; 1996–2003 data from Secretariat of the Council. This table also appears in Wallace and Hayes-Renshaw (2005), and has been reproduced here with the kind permission of the authors.

policy. JHA and CFSP are the main examples. EMU provides a different contrast—here the main control of the single currency has been assigned to the ECB, leaving Ecofin and the new Euro–12 Council (including ministers only from member governments whose currencies are part of EMU) pushing to gain influence over decision-making (see Chapter 6).

The European Council

The European Council began life in the occasional 'summit' meetings of heads of state (France and Finland have presidents with some policy powers who attend meetings), or government (i.e. prime ministers). Two especially important meetings, in The Hague in 1969 and Paris in 1972, were agenda-setters and package-makers for several succeeding years. From 1974 onwards, under the prompting of Giscard d'Estaing, then French President, European Councils were put on a regular footing, meeting at least twice a year. Successive treaty reforms have put the European Council on a more formal basis. It remains, however, the case that the European Council operates to an extent outside the main institutional structure: it is due to be fully incorporated once the Constitutional Treaty is ratified. The European Council will then acquire a more stable presidency, under an individual chosen for a renewable term of two-and-a-half years. The preparation of its meetings, as well as the drafting of its conclusions, depend essentially on the presidency-in-office of the Council, and the agenda of its sessions is much influenced by the preferences of the government in the chair. Historically one meeting of each semester has been held in the country of the presidency but the ToN stated that when the EU reached a membership of eighteen (sic) all sessions would be held in Brussels. By custom and practice national delegations in the room are restricted to the president or prime minister and the foreign ministers, and sometimes finance ministers. Increasingly large cohorts of other ministers and officials have parallel meetings where the topics discussed depend on the preoccupations of the moment.

Over the years the role of the European Council has varied. Conceived of initially as an informal 'fireside chat', it became in the 1970s and 1980s a forum for resolving issues that departmental ministers could not agree, or that were subjects of disagreement within the member governments. By tradition it is the European Council that has been left to resolve the periodic major arguments about EU revenue and expenditure, as Chapter 8 explains in general, and Chapter 9 illustrates in relation to the structural funds. In addition the European Council became, from the negotiations over the SEA in 1985, the key forum for determining treaty reforms. Views have varied as to whether the shifting of decision-making to so senior a political level marked a failure of the 'normal' institutional arrangements, or was a sign of success for the EU, as its agenda has risen up the ladder of political salience.

From the late 1980s and during the 1990s the role and behaviour of the European Council have changed. It has increasingly become the venue for addressing what Peterson (1995) calls the 'history-making decisions' in the EU, namely the big and more strategic questions to do with the core new tasks of the EU and those that define its 'identity' as an arena for collective action. Some of our case studies, especially Chapter 6 on EMU, Chapter 8 on the financial perspectives, Chapter 16 on eastern enlargement, Chapter 17 on CFSP, and Chapter 18 on JHA, record European Council pronouncements as the main staging posts in the development of policy. The level of activity has expanded, with six sessions in 1999, and what seems to be a sharply increasing concern on the part of the most senior national politicians to take control of the direction of the EU, including at the 'Spring' European Councils which chart progress with the Lisbon Strategy. Their offices now have a direct electronic link (Primenet), and within their national settings it seems that they are more strongly engaged in framing national European policies.

The European Parliament

The EP consists since June 2004 of 785 members (MEPs) elected directly on a basis of proportional representation from across the twenty-five member states. Originally it was composed of national parliamentarians, but in 1978 a treaty amendment provided for direct elections, of which the first were in 1979. Its location, for reasons of member-state sensitivities, is divided between Luxembourg, Strasbourg, and Brussels. MEPs vary in their backgrounds, some having been national politicians, other bringing different professional experience, and a few having made the EP their primary career. The EP is organized into party groupings, of which by far the largest and most important are the European People's Party and the European Socialists. These groupings have gained in importance over time. Much of the work of the EP is carried out in its specialist committees, which have become increasingly adept at probing particular policy issues in detail, more so than in many national parliaments.

In the early years of the EU the EP had only a marginal role in the policy process, with only consultative powers, apart from its power to dismiss the Commission in a censure motion. During the 1970s the EP gained important powers *vis-à-vis* the EU budget, and especially over some areas of expenditure (although significantly not over most agricultural expenditure) (see Chapter 8). In the 1980s and 1990s the role of the EP has been transformed, as it has acquired legislative powers in successive treaty reforms. These were rationalized under the ToA into *co-decision* with the Council across a wide range of policy domains; *cooperation* with the Council in some other domains, especially on EMU-related questions; and *consultation* in those areas where member governments have been wary of letting MEPs into the process, including agriculture, and JHA. A further streamlining is envisaged under the CT. In addition the EP must now give its formal *assent* on some issues: these include certain agreements with third countries and enlargement (see Box 3.2).

The net result of these changes is that the EP is now a force to be reckoned with across a wide range of policy domains. It is in important respects a necessary partner for the Council, although one with a contested electoral authority, because of the rather low participation rate in European elections (in many member states). On many areas of detailed rule-setting the EP has a real impact, as some of the case studies in this volume show, and therefore it too is the target of those outside the institutions who seek to influence legislation (see, for example, Chapters 12 and 13). However, there are other areas—JHA, CFSP, and oddly enough, the CAP—where its voice is muted. In 1999 the EP acquired greater political prominence as a result of its role in provoking the resignation of the European Commission on the issue of financial mismanagement. In 2004 the EP delayed the installation of the new Commission, because of criticisms of its composition. This increased political standing of the EP is likely to enable it to influence the policy process as a whole rather more in the future.

Box 3.2 Powers of the European Parliament

Consultation
Commission proposals to Council are passed to EP for an Opinion. EP may suggest alterations, delay passing a resolution to formalize its Opinion, or refer matters back to its relevant committee(s).

Applies to: agriculture, and those (few) JHA topics that fall within the 'Community' framework.

Cooperation (Art. 252 TEC, ex Art. 189c EEC)
Commission proposals passed to Council for a 'common position' and to EP for a first reading, in which it may propose amendments. The EP may at its second reading seek to amend the Council's common position, or by an absolute majority reject it. Council can override the EP's rejection only by unanimity. Alternatively, the EP and Council try to negotiate agreement in a conciliation procedure.

Applies to: limited aspects of economic and monetary union.

Co-decision (Art. 251 TEC, ex Art. 189b EEC)
Council and EP may both agree a proposal at first reading. If they disagree at second reading, the EP may by an absolute majority reject the proposal, which then falls. Or the EP may amend the Council's common position by an absolute majority, in which case conciliation takes place between the Council and the EP. The results of conciliation must be approved in third reading by both Council (QMV) and EP (majority of votes cast). Proposal falls if not agreed.

Applies since Treaty of Amsterdam (ToA) to: most areas of legislation, unless otherwise specified as exempted, or falling under one of the other procedures.

Assent
On certain issues the EP must, in a single vote, give its assent by an absolute majority of its members.

Applies to: certain international agreements, enlargement treaties, and framework agreements on the structural funds.

Budget (Arts. 272–3, ex Arts 203–4 EEC)
EP may try to modify 'compulsory' expenditure, or to amend 'non-compulsory' expenditure. It must approve the budget as a whole, and subsequently 'discharge' the accounts of previous years' actual expenditure (see Box 8.1).

Installation of the College of Commissioners (Art. 214(2) TEC, ex Art. 158(2) EEC)
EP holds individual hearings with nominated commissioners and passes a vote to approve the whole college.

Censure of Commission (Art. 201 TEC, ex Art. 144 EEC)
EP may censure the college of commissioners by a two-thirds majority of its members.
Note: the Constitutional Treaty would extend some of these powers.

The European Court of Justice

Relatively early on it became clear to close observers of the EU that the role and rule of law were going to be critical in anchoring EU policy regimes. If the legal system could ensure a high rate of compliance, a way of giving authoritative interpretation to disputed texts, and a means of redress for those for whom the law was created, then the EU process as a whole would gain a solidity and a predictability that would help it to be sustained. The ECJ was established in the first treaty texts; these have been virtually unchanged since then, except to cater for the increasing workload and successive enlargements of the EU membership.

The ECJ, sited in Luxembourg, is now composed of twenty-five judges, as well as eight advocates-general, who deliver preliminary opinions on cases. The SEA in 1986 established a second court, the Court of First Instance (CFI), composed now of twenty-five judges, to help in handling the heavy flow of cases. The EU is thus something like a supreme court, able to provide an overarching framework of jurisprudence, and to deal with litigation, both in cases referred via the national courts and those brought directly before it. The Courts' sanctions are mostly the force of their own rulings, backed up in some instances by the ability to impose fines on those (usually companies) found to have broken EU law. The TEU gave the ECJ power to fine member governments for non-application of European law. Moreover, as a result of its own rulings (especially one of the *Factortame* cases on fisheries; see Chapter 14), damages can be claimed against governments that fail to implement European law correctly. The Courts hear their cases in public, but reach their judgments in private by, if necessary, majority votes; the results of their votes are not made public, and minority opinions are not issued.

Since the early 1960s a series of key cases has established important principles of European law, such as: the supremacy of EC law over the law of the member states; the direct effect of EC law in national legal orders; a doctrine of proportionality, and another of non-discrimination on the basis of nationality among nationals of EU member states. In so doing the ECJ has gone further in clarifying the rule and the role of law than had specifically been laid down in the treaties. In some policy domains court cases have been one of the key forces in developing EU policy regimes (see Chapters 4, 5, 10, and 14). Tables 3.4*a*, 3.4*b*, and 3.5 summarize the pattern and volume of cases before the two Courts. This very thorough overview, collated specially for this volume, of cases before the ECJ by policy sector gives us a very full picture of the pattern of litigation. The case load is impressive, reaching 400 cases before the ECJ in the 1980s, and rising to over 500 from 1999 onwards, with an impressive CFI caseload as well, though in both cases the volume of EU staff cases should be discounted. There appears to be an increase in the number of cases following each enlargement of the EU. Agriculture is in 'gold medal' position cumulatively, with strong numbers for free movement of persons, of establishment, and of goods which generate many cases, as do taxation issues, although with some variations over time. Competition and state aid cases remain important. Environmental and consumer cases have also become latterly more numerous reflecting a growth of policy activities in these fields. Further commentary on the roles of the Courts follows in our case studies.

Table 3.4a New caseload of the European Court of Justice by subject matter, 1953 [1971]–1991

Subject matter	1953–1971	1972	1973	1974–1975	1976	1977	1978	1979	1980	1981	1972–1981 Σ2–10	1982	1983	1984	1985	1986	1987	1988	1989	1990	1991	1982–1991 Σ12–21	1972–1991 Σ11+22	1953–1991 Σ1+23
	1	2	3	4	5	6	7	8	9	10	11	12	13	14	15	16	17	18	19	20	21	22	23	24
1 Accession of new member states		—																						
2 Agriculture and fisheries	135	36	36	84	47	61	94	48	48	55	509	83	47	47	70	70	81	88	63	155	97	801	1,310	1,445
3 Approximation of laws	—																							
4 Brussels convention	—																							
5 Commercial policy																								
6 Competition (incl. line 19 before 1992)	44	6	26	16	6	10	64	14	13	7	162	42	18	21	34	27	34	16	69	20	30	311	473	517
7 Energy		—																						
8 Environment and consumers		—																						
9 External Relations		—																						
10 Free movement for persons (incl. line 18 before 1992)	48	11	12	27	17	19	20	25	17	26	174	17	31	26	37	24	35	39	40	37	77	363	537	585
11 Freedom of establishment and to provide services, company law	1	—	—	8	3	2	7	2	2	12	36	4	15	10	17	12	12	7	19	27	10	133	169	170
12 Free movement of capital		—																						
13 Free movement of goods and customs	56	3	11	18	16	25	24	41	55	53	246	56	38	68	62	33	45	70	72	39	36	519	765	821
14 Industrial policy		—																						
15 Intellectual property		—																						
16 Law governing the institutions		—																						

No. / Category																								
17 Principles of Community law	—																							
18 Social policy (see line 10 before 1992)	—																							
19 State aid (see line 6 before 1992)	—																							
20 Taxation	27	1	—	4	3	2	9	7	7	20	53	9	13	17	39	18	35	30	19	26	24	230	283	310
21 Transport	3	—	1	1	1	2	6	2	—	13	4	5	5	6	6	5	5	4	16	7		63	76	79
22 Rest (EC)	8	2	2	4[a]	11	16	10	12	12	23	92	21	22	35	68	53	44	48	56	37	44	428	557	565
23 Other (ECSC, EAEC)	282	—	4	3	2	—	12	7	3	33	64	25	40	35	28	27	10	3	1	1		212	276	558
24 Staff of EU institutions	291	23	100	67	19	25	22	117	94	1,163	1,630	85	68	41	65	57	77	59	40	0		492	2,122	2,413
25 **All (officially reported sums)**	895	82	192	238	120	162	268	280	323	1,322	2,987	348	297	312	433	328	395[b]	372	385	—[c]	326[d]	3,196	6,183	7,078
26 **All[e] (mathematical sums)**	895	82	192	232	125	162	268	274	323	1,321	2,979	346	297	312	433	328	395	372	385	358	326	3,552	6,531	7,426

Sources: Fifth to Twenty-fifth General Report of the European Commission, 1972–1992. For 1974 and 1975 (8th and 9th Report) values were not reported but could be calculated as follows: per each category from the total number of cases at the end of 1976 the new 1976 caseload (both 10th Report) and also the total caseload at the end of 1973 (7th Report) could be subtracted to arrive at the added caseload for that two-year period. Compiled by Josef Falke, Centre for European Law and Policy (ZERP) and Research Centre TranState (Transformations of the State), and by Stephan Leibfried, Research Centre TranState and Centre for Social Policy Research (CeS), and tabulated by Monika Sniegs of TranState, all University of Bremen.

Legend:
[a] Under 'Rest (EC)' 1974–75 (line 22) the new 1976-category 'treaties' in the 10th Report could be ignored as no case dated to an earlier year.
[b] Own calculation; no total number reported in the 21st Report.
[c] In 1990 the Court of First Instance was founded which reduced the original 36 competition cases (line 6) by sixteen appeals, left only one EAEC case remaining under 'Other' (line 23), and moved all staff cases (line 24) to the new court. The statistics were adjusted accordingly, leading to a different 1990 total of ECJ cases.
[d] Without 14 appeal cases.
[e] Sums different from line 25 are underlined.

Table 3.4b New caseload of the European Court of Justice by subject matter, [1953–] 1992–2003

Subject matter[a]	until 1971	Distribution (line 1 in %)	1972–1981	Distribution (line 3 in %)	1982–91	Distribution (line 5 in %)	1992	1993	1994	1995	1996	1997	1998	1999	2000	2001	2002	2003	1992–2003 Σ7–18	Distribution (line 19 in %)
	1	2	3	4	5	6	7	8	9	10	11	12	13	14	15	16	17	18	19	20
1 Accession of new member states	—						—	1	—	13	9	6	1	—	2	1	2	1	36	0.65
2 Agriculture and fisheries	135	15.08	509	17.08	801	22.55	197	207	63	64	55	64	38	80	88	55	58	60	1,029	18.45
3 Approximation of laws	—						4	7	27	11	32	38	43	42	26	63	38	50	381	6.83
4 Brussels convention	—						8	9	2	9	3	6	–	2	9	6	10	6	70	1.26
5 Commercial policy	—						6	13	8	4	3	2	7	11	9	5	2	1	71	1.27
6 Competition (included line 19 before 1992)	44	4.92	162	5.43	311	8.76	34	17	13	24	20	24	28	29	22	30	13	21	275	4.93
7 Energy	—						—	—	—	—	3	2	—	2	–	1	2	4	14	0.25
8 Environment and consumers	—						18	16	15	44	36	42	30	41	57	55	71	69	494	8.86
9 External Relations	—						6	14	8	13	10	8	11	12	7	8	10	13	120	2.15
10 Free movement for persons (included line 18 before 1992)	48	5.36	174	5.84	363	10.22	35	45	71	42	69	50	36	69	32	13	21	23	506	9.07
11 Freedom of establishment and to provide services, company law	1	0.11	36	1.21	133	3.74	6	6	10	14	15	17	53	33	43	62	55	57	371	6.65
12 Free movement of capital	—						—	1	4	1	2	2	6	3	6	6	3	5	39	0.70
13 Free movement of goods and customs	56	6.26	246	8.26	519	14.61	33	54	55	62	31	28	32	23	28	20	31	29	426	7.64

No.	Category	1	2	3	4	5	6	1992	1993	1994	1995	1996	1997	1998	1999	2000	2001	2002	2003	Total	%
14	Industrial policy	—						—	—	—	—	—	—	—	5	16	4	10	16	51	0.91
15	Intellectual property	—						—	—	—	—	—	—	—	2	6	15	8	9	40	0.72
16	Law governing the institutions	—						5	8	14	10	13	11	13	11	9	13	15	27	149	2.67
17	Principles of Community law	—						4	4	1	4	16	25	4	4	7	4	1	2	76	1.36
18	Social policy (before 1992 see line 10)	—						20	26	15	25	42	26	33	33	45	35	33	39	372	6.67
19	State aid (before 1992 see line 6)	—						13	12	6	12	7	18	13	15	22	15	18	30	181	3.25
20	Taxation	27	3.02	53	1.78	230	6.48	19	20	22	31	29	36	73	61	30	36	36	33	426	7.64
21	Transport	3	0.34	13	0.44	63	1.77	12	9	7	4	3	9	27	22	22	22	9	23	169	3.03
22	Rest (EC)	8	0.89	92	3.09	428	12.05	2	9	6	5	1	5	4	7	5	4	6	4	58	1.04
23	Other (ECSC, EAEC)	282	31.51	64	2.15	212	5.97	7	—	2	5	4	10	4	18	5	14	8	3	80	1.43
24	Staff of EU institutions	291	32.51	1,630	54.72	492	13.85	12	9	5	11	13	13	19	16	8	16	10	10	142	2.55
25	**All (officially reported sums)**	**895**	**100.00**	**2,987**		**3,196**		**442**	**469**	**354**	**408**	**416**	**443**	**481**	**541**	**500**	**503**	**470**	**555**	**5,576**	**100.00**
26	**All[b] (mathematical sums)**	**895**	**100.00**	**2,979**	**100.00**	**3,552**	**100.00**	**441**	**487**	**354**	**408**	**416**	**442**	**475**	**541**	**504**	**503**	**470**	**535**		**—**

Sources: For columns 1, 3 and 5 see Table 1.1. For columns 7–18 see the *Annual Reports of the Court of Justice and the Court of First Instance of the European Communities*, 1992–2003. Compiled by Josef Falke, Centre for European Law and Policy (ZERP) and Research Centre TranState (Transformations of the State), and by Stephan Leibfried, Research Centre TranState and Centre for Social Policy Research (CeS), and tabulated by Monika Sniegs of TranState, all University of Bremen.

Legend: [a] Over time, and in particular since 1992, the court statistics have had to become more differentiated because increasing caseload required some categories to be subdivided, i.e. 'approximation of laws' which was included in line 22 ('Rest (EC)') is now reported separately (line 3); and because new competencies were created or old ones decisively extended, like 'industrial policy' (line 14) in Articles 157 ff. ToA (1997), such that separate reporting was deemed necessary. [b] Sums different from line 25 are underlined.

Table 3.5 Number of new cases at the Court of First Instance, 1992–2003

Subject matter	1992	1993	1994	1995	1996	1997	1998	1999	2000	2001	2002	2003	1992–2003 Σ1–12	Distribution (column 13 in %)
	1	2	3	4	5	6	7	8	9	10	11	12	13	14
1 Agriculture	—	420	216	46	33	73	19	42	23	17	9	11	909	20.67
2 Commercial policy	—	—	20	11	6	15	12	5	8	4	5	6	92	2.09
3 Competition	36	28	59	74	28	22	23	34	36	39	61	43	483	10.98
4 Customs	—	1	2	2	3	17	—	—	—	2	5	5	37	0.84
5 Environment and consumer policy	—	3	2	3	—	—	4	5	14	2	8	13	54	1.23
6 External Relations	—	—	—	—	—	—	10	5	14	26	11	13	79	1.80
7 Fisheries	—	5	7	3	2	2	—	2	1	3	6	25	56	1.27
8 Free movement for persons and social policy	—	14	2	3	9	4	17	14	15	4	5	9	96	2.18
9 Free movement of goods	—	1	—	—	2	1	7	10	17	1	—	—	39	0.89
10 Freedom of establishment and to provide services, company law	—	1	—	3	1	3	3	3	4	7	3	3	31	0.71

11	Intellectual property	–	–	–	–	–	–	1	18	34	37	83	101	**274**	6.23
12	Law governing the institutions	–	–	–	–	–	–	10	19	29	12	18	26	**114**	2.59
13	State aid	–	13	12	13	25	28	16	100	80	42	51	25	**405**	9.21
14	Taxation	–	–	3	–	–	–	–	–	–	–	1	5	**9**	0.20
15	Transport	–	1	1	–	–	1	3	2	–	2	1	1	**12**	0.27
16	Rest (EC)	–	16	18	9	16	309	4	3	5	12	10	17	**419**	9.53
17	Other (ECSC, EAEC)	–	2	23	6	5	6	12	8	1	4	3	11	**81**	1.84
18	Staff of EU institutions	79	84	85	79	107	155	79	86	106	111	112	124	**1,207**	27.45
19	*All (officially reported sums)*	**115**	**589**	**460**	**249**	**237**	**636**	**215**	**356**	**387**	**327**	**393**	**438**	**4,402**	
20	*All[a] (mathematical sums)*	**115**	**589**	**450**	**252**	**237**	**636**	**220**	**356**	**387**	**325**	**392**	**438**	**4,397**	**100.00**

Source: Annual Reports of the Court of Justice and the Court of First Instance of the European Communities, 1992–2003. Compiled by Josef Falke, Centre for European Law and Policy (ZERP) and Research Centre TranState (Transformations of the State), and by Stephan Leibfried, Research Centre TranState and Centre for Social Policy Research (CeS), and tabulated by Monika Sniegs of TranState, all University of Bremen.

Legend: ᵃ Sums different from line 19 are underlined.

This strong legal dimension has a marked influence on the policy process. Policy-makers pay great attention to the legal meaning of the texts that they devise; policy advocates look for legal rules to achieve their objectives, because they know that these are favoured by the institutional system; policy reformers can sometimes use cases to alter the impact of EU policies; and in general there is a presumption that rules will be more or less obeyed. Hence policy-makers have to choose carefully between treaty articles in determining which legal base to use, and to consider carefully which kind of legislation to make.

The EU makes three main kinds of laws. Regulations are directly applicable within the member states once promulgated by the EU institutions. Directives have to be transposed into national law, which allows some flexibility to member governments, but within limits set by the ECJ. Decisions are more limited legal instruments applied to specific circumstances or specific addressees, as in competition policy (see Chapter 5). All three kinds of law may be made either by the Commission (under delegated powers), or by the Council, or jointly by the Council and EP (under co-decision). And all are subject to challenge through the national and European courts. Under the Constitutional Treaty (Art. I-33), when ratified the categories of legal acts will be redefined as: European laws, regulations renamed; European framework laws, directives renamed; European regulations, non-legislative acts, essentially for implementation, which may be directly binding on all, or, as to the result to be achieved, binding on those member states addressed; and European decisions, non-legislative and binding on either all member states or those to which they are addressed.

The vigour of the European legal system is one of the most distinctive features of the EU. It has helped reinforce the powers and reach of the EU process, although in recent years the ECJ has become a bit more cautious in its judgments. We should note also that in some policy domains member governments have gone to considerable lengths to keep the ECJ out of the picture. Part of the reason for the three-pillar structure of the TEU was to keep both CFSP and JHA well away from the reach of the European legal system. Even though the ToA goes some way towards incorporating parts of JHA and Schengen more fully within the system, it remains contested how far they will be brought within the jurisdiction of the ECJ. The adoption of the Charter of Fundamental Rights, initially on a declaratory basis, but under the Constitutional Treaty to be anchored in the EU legal system, adds an important new dimension. This to some extent draws it together with the other European legal order, based on the European Convention on Human Rights attached to the Council of Europe.

The wider institutional setting

The EU institutional system includes in addition a number of additional organizations that have an impact on, or provide instruments for, EU policies. Some are consultative. Some provide control mechanisms. And some provide autonomous operating arms.

Consultation and lobbying

The founding treaties established the Economic and Social Committee (and the Consultative Committee for the ECSC), as a point of access to the policy process for socio-economic groups. Its creation borrowed from the corporatist traditions in some of the founder member countries. It has not, however, become an influential body in the policy process. Instead socio-economic groups have found their own more direct points of access since the 1960s, both through EU-level federal associations and through sector-specific trade and producer organizations. These became even more active in the period around the development of the single European market. Individual large firms have also taken pains to develop links with the EU institutions, again some since the 1960s, but many more and with more vigour since the early 1980s. A more recent development has been the increased activity of groups and lobbies representing societal interests, consumers, environmentalists, women's groups, and increasingly a range of other advocacy groups and non-governmental organizations (NGOs). Illustrations of the activities of these different kinds of groups can be found in many of our case studies.

The TEU introduced a second consultative body, the Committee of the Regions, in response to the extensive involvement of local and regional authorities in seeking to influence those EU policies that impacted on them. The Committee provides regional and local politicians from the member states with a multilateral forum, and an opportunity to enhance their local political credibility. At least as important, however, is the direct lobbying by infranational (local and regional) authorities, many with their own offices in Brussels. These same infranational authorities also engage in efforts to influence national policy positions and the implementation of Community programmes. Chapters 9 and 14 comment on this in relation to the structural funds and the common fisheries policy.

Control and scrutiny

In the mid-1970s concern started to be voiced that the EU policy process was subject to few external controls. The EP at the time had few powers, and national parliaments paid relatively little attention to EU legislation and programmes. It was the growing scale and scope of the EU budget and spending programmes that spearheaded the arguments about the inadequacy of scrutiny. This led to the creation of the European Court of Auditors by the 1975 Budget Treaty. Since 1978 it has, from its seat in Luxembourg, endeavoured to evaluate systematically both revenue-raising and spending. Both in its Annual Reports and in specific reports it has drawn attention to various weaknesses in the budgetary process, as handled by the Commission and national agencies. Here we should note that around four-fifths of EU budgetary expenditure is disbursed by national agencies. Chapter 8 describes some of the Court of Auditors' activities and impact. We note here that many of its criticisms fell for many years on deaf ears—member governments that were reluctant to face up to some of the issues, an EP that had other preoccupations, and a Commission which repeatedly undervalued the importance of sound financial management. In late 1998 this situation was reversed by the row over alleged financial mismanagement by the Commission.

Another new instrument of *post hoc* control is provided by the European Ombudsman, attached to the EP, under the provisions of the TEU. The aim, borrowed from Nordic practice, is to provide a channel for dealing with cases of maladminstration *vis-à-vis* individuals. Thus far the existence of this office has not had a large impact, although it may have contributed to making the policy process a little more open than hitherto.

Some control and scrutiny of policy depends on national institutions, both parliamentary and financial. National parliaments had no official recognition in the institutional system until the early 1990s. Each member state had developed its own, mostly rather limited, procedures for national parliamentary scrutiny of EU policy. The same discontent that had led to some strengthening of European procedures started to provoke a debate on national scrutiny. Both the TEU and the ToA mention the importance of encouraging this, and the issue was raised without clear resolution in the Convention on the Future of Europe that drafted the CT. However, EU-level policymakers, especially in the Commission, are under increasing pressure to pay increased attention to national parliamentary discussions and appear more readily before national parliamentary committees of inquiry. This heightened sensitivity to country-level preoccupations is becoming a more marked feature of the EU policy process. It may well be emphasized by the establishment of national parliamentary offices in Brussels (as of mid-2004 from Denmark, Finland, France, Italy, Ireland, Latvia, Lithuania, Poland, Slovenia, Sweden, and the UK). Some see more cooperation between the EP and national parliaments as a promising way forward. Others argue that to date experience, for example through COSAC (Conférence des Organes Spécialisées aux Affaires Européennes), has been disappointing. COSAC brings together twice a year representatives from the EC scrutiny committees of national parliaments.

Operations

The longest established autonomous agency is the European Investment Bank (EIB), established by the Treaty of Rome (EEC). Its task was, and is, to generate loans for agreed investments in support of EU objectives, both within the EU and in associated third countries. It operates like a private bank, with triple A credit rating in money markets. Its work is to varying degrees coordinated with programmes directly administered by the Commission, such as the structural funds. It had its potential 'big moment' in the early 1990s after the breakdown of the communist system in central and eastern Europe. However, a decision was taken to establish a new and separate European Bank for Reconstruction and Development (EBRD), with the reforming post-communist countries and other western states as stakeholders.

One other phenomenon should be noted. Especially during the past decade there has been a trend in the EU to contract out some policy implementation activities to a variety of agencies, mirroring practice that was becoming more common in many of the member states. One group of agencies has been set up, or contracted, to administer programmes for which the Commission lacked either the staff or the inclination; for example the Humanitarian Aid Office (ECHO), and the office which administers the Socrates programme for educational interchange. Another group of agencies handles regulatory functions, such as the European Agency for the Evaluation of Medicinal Products. Europol is another example. A third group provides direct services for the EU institutions, such as the translation centre. There has been some discussion on whether this process could be taken even further, for example, by setting up a European Competition Office clearly separate from the Commission (see Chapter 5).

The most important example of a new and autonomous operating agency is the European Central Bank (ECB) in Frankfurt (see Chapter 6). The battle in 1998 over who should be its first president was an indication of the anticipated importance of an agency that was to exercise considerable independence in a crucial policy domain with high political salience. The ECB has made an impressive start in developing its own functional and operational identity. Quite what the extent of the ECB's autonomy will be in the longer term remains to be seen; several finance ministers have already made it clear that they want their own hands on the tiller.

Thus, we note the proliferation of agencies for operating EU policy regimes and programmes. This diffuseness of arrangements for policy operation and programme delivery has increased over the past decade. It seems set to be a persistent feature of the policy process, especially as regards policy implementation, and thus likely to fragment the institutional structures. This should lead us to modify the notion of the Commission as a centralized and centralizing policy executive.

National institutions

We have summarized above some key points about the EU's own institutions and agencies. However, we should stress that those institutions are in a real sense the property of the member states which comprise the EU. In addition, the institutions in the member states are also fundamental elements in the EU institutional architecture and partners in the EU policy process. The European dimension is not just an add-on to the work of national governments; in a real and tangible sense national governments, and other authorities and agencies, provide much of the operating life-blood of the EU. After all in some senses what the EU system does is to extend the policy resources available to the member states. The case studies in this volume illustrate a variety of ways in which this is so. As a result learning how to manage this extra dimension to national public policy has been one of the most important challenges faced by national governments in the past fifty years.

Much of that challenge has had to be faced by the central governments in each member state, and the patterns of response have varied a good deal from one to another. As a broad generalization we note that the experience has been somewhat different from what many commentators had expected. The trend has been not so much a defensive adjustment to the loss of policy-making powers, but rather in most member states an increasingly nuanced approach to incorporating and encapsulating the European dimension. This has not, however, meant that central governments can operate as gatekeepers between the national and the EU levels. The points of cross-border access and opportunities for building cross-national networks and coalitions have steadily proliferated for both public agencies and private actors. National actors play important and influential roles at all stages of the EU policy process.

Opportunities for access and influence are, however, not evenly distributed within member states. Economic agents and NGOs seem the most flexible in operating at both EU and national levels. Infranational authorities have become more adept, though how much influence they exert is still open to question. National parliaments have been much slower to adapt, and indeed are among the national institutions most displaced by the emergence of a strong European dimension to policy-making.

One Community method, or several policy modes?

Central to our approach to policy-making in the EU is the argument that it includes several different policy modes, which are illustrated by the empirical case studies in this volume. These different policy modes—we identify five—are the product of: evolution and experimentation over time in the EU; changes in national policy-making processes; and developments in economic and social behaviour. We can observe important rearrangements in the roles and behaviour of the various key actors, in the approaches to policy dilemmas, and in the instruments used to address these. In the context of the EU a further factor is the continuing debate about where to strike the balance between EU policy powers and those of the member states, increasingly in the shadow of the globalization phenomenon. This issue remains a subject of contestation, both as regards the 'high politics' of the EU, and as regards the 'functional appropriateness' of one or other policy mode. Also of critical importance is the contemporary context of the EU, which has over time evolved from a small membership of only six relatively similar countries (though the degree of similarity can be exaggerated) to a large membership of twenty-five rather more heterogeneous countries with diverse legacies, practices, and socio-economic characteristics.

One further point should be re-emphasized: EU policy-making never takes place in a vacuum, but on the contrary, in a context where there are multiple locations for addressing policy issues, ranging across levels from the local to the global and across processes from formal to informal. Figures 3.4 and 3.5 show two different pictures of policy-making across multiple locations. European policy-makers have to manage the

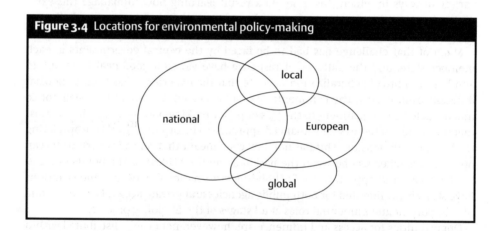

Figure 3.4 Locations for environmental policy-making

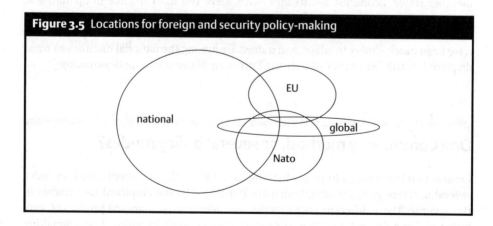

Figure 3.5 Locations for foreign and security policy-making

connections between these different locations, and sometimes make choices as to which is their preferred forum for addressing a particular issue. In the sections that follow we focus on the policy modes within the EU; each of these has interfaces with other policy locations or fora, as most of the case studies in this volume demonstrate.

In this section we set out five variants of the EU policy process:

- a traditional Community method;
- the EU regulatory mode;
- the EU distributional mode;
- policy coordination; and
- intensive transgovernmentalism.

It should be noted that these variants apply to 'day-to-day' policy-making in the EU, and thus wittingly exclude the domain of constitutive politics or system-shaping as regards the overall political and institutional architecture of the EU. The five variants are identified with the deliberate objective of escaping from the either/or dichotomy between 'supranational' and 'intergovernmental' ways of proceeding. Our central argument is that the patterns of policy-making in the EU are much more diverse, not only because of the continuing arguments about which policy powers to transfer from national to European processes, but also because these patterns reflect functional differences between policy domains and changing views about how to develop contemporary government and governance.

A traditional Community method

For a long time much of the literature on west European integration and the EU took as its starting point that a single predominant Community method of policy-making was emerging. Because of its early priority on the agenda of the original EEC, the CAP set the template. This was defined by the late 1960s roughly as follows:

- a strong role delegated to the European Commission in policy design, policy-brokering, policy execution, and managing the interface with 'abroad';
- an empowering role for the Council of Ministers through strategic bargaining and package deals;
- a locking-in of stakeholders, in this case the agricultural interests, through a form of cooption into a European process which offered them better rewards than national politics;
- an engagement of national agencies as the subordinated operating arms of the agreed common regime;
- a distancing from the influence of elected representatives at the national level, and only limited opportunities for the EP to impinge;
- an occasional, but defining, intrusion by the ECJ to reinforce the legal authority of the Community regime; and
- the resourcing of the policy on a collective basis, as an expression of sustained 'solidarity'.

The template constituted a form of 'supranational' policy-making, in which powers were transferred from the national to the EU level. It was structured by a kind of functionalist logic, in which those concerned with a particular policy sector could be encapsulated and build cross-national allegiances, but mediated by a form of politics in which political and economic élites colluded to further their various, and often different, interests. The collusion also generated what Scharpf (1988) called a 'joint-decision trap', which set high obstacles to the revision of common policy once agreed. A similar approach was envisaged in the early years for transport policy and for civil nuclear energy under Euratom, but in neither case was this adopted. On the other hand, EU trade policy has some features of this approach, given the considerable delegation to the Commission for managing trade instruments and trade agreements (see Chapter 15).

How far this template accorded with reality, even in the case of agriculture, is a matter for debate. Chapter 7 suggests that the real story may be different, and one in which national politics determined rather more of the outcomes. Interestingly, the fisheries regime, which was intended to imitate the CAP regime and which included strong delegation of powers to manage quotas, does not fit the template very well either, as Chapter 14 shows. Nonetheless this version of the Community method came to set many of the reference points for both practitioners and commentators. However, by the mid-1980s two successors to this traditional Community method became current: the EU regulatory mode; and the EU distributional mode.

There are strikingly sparse recent examples of new common policies being introduced according to this traditional Community method, with a centralized and hierarchical institutional process, with clear delegation of powers, and aimed at 'positive integration'. The single currency is perhaps the most apt example. However, in this case, as we can see in Chapter 6, the delegated institutional powers are centred on the ECB rather than on the Commission, and they apply only to the monetary strand of EMU and not to the economic strand. This form of delegation to function-specific agencies, rather than to the Commission, may be an emerging trend, for which there is some evidence in the fields of justice and home affairs—the instances of Europol and Eurojust (see Chapter 18), and of common foreign and security policy—the instance of the new European Defence Agency (see Chapter 17).

The EU regulatory mode

As the competition regime took root (see Chapter 5) and the single European market developed (see Chapter 4), so an alternative policy mode emerged. Its roots went back to the ambition of the Treaty of Rome to remove barriers between the national economies of the member states. But much of its driving force came from changes in the international economy, which had made the search for competitiveness in both domestic and international markets critical to the ability of firms to adjust and to prosper. Public policy-makers across the industrialized 'western' world found themselves subject to demands for different kinds of regulation that would facilitate that adjustment. Within the US there were already traditions of both public regulation and private self-regulation that showed an alternative approach to market management. A version of this regulatory approach started to develop in western Europe, although in varied formats in individual countries.

It turned out that the EU arena was especially amenable to the further development of a regulatory mode of policy-making, described by some commentators as a form of 'negative integration'. The strength of the European legal process, the machinery for promoting technical cooperation, and the distance from parliamentary interference were all factors that encouraged this further, namely by removing national barriers to the creation of the single market (see Chapter 4). In addition the bargaining process, in and through the European Commission and Council of Ministers, helped national policy-makers to escape some of the constraints of politics that had built rigidities into national policy-making. The EU was particularly well-fitted for generating an overarching regulatory framework that could combine transnational standards with country differences. Indeed, so successful was its implantation that this European approach has sometimes been promoted as a model for the development of broader global regulation. Examples can be found in Chapters 12, 13, and 15.

This regulatory mode provides the framework for numerous micro-level decisions and rules, for the shape of relationships with member governments and economic actors within the EU, and for those involved in relevant international regimes. It has been characterized by:

- the Commission as the architect and defender of regulatory objectives and rules, increasingly by reference to economic criteria, and often working with the stakeholders and communities of experts;
- the Council as a forum (at both ministerial and official levels) for agreeing minimum standards and the direction of harmonization (mostly upwards towards higher standards), to be complemented by mutual recognition of national preferences and controls, operated differentially in individual countries;
- the ECJ and the CFI as the means of ensuring that the rules are applied reasonably evenly, backed by the national courts for local application, and enabling individual entrepreneurs to have access to redress in case of non-application or discrimination;
- the EP as one of several means for prompting the consideration of non-economic factors (environmental, regional, social, and so forth), with increasing impact as its legislative powers have grown, but little leverage on the implementation of regulation; and
- extensive opportunities for stakeholders, especially economic actors, but sometimes other societal actors, to be consulted about, and to influence, the shape and content of European market rules.

This regulatory mode has been applied most obviously in the development of a single market without internal barriers (Chapter 4), and an evolutionary version of it is developing in EU competition policy (Chapter 5). To the extent that the EU has an industrial policy, it is mostly by using regulatory prompts and the competition regime to lever industrial adjustment. Insofar as the EU has a social policy (see Chapter 10), it is mainly constructed through legal regulation and market-making. Much of what the EU has done in the environmental domain (see Chapter 12) has been by regulating industrial processes. A cognate example—biotechnology and food safety—is explained in Chapter 13. Moreover, the EU's interactions with the rest of the world are an external reflection of its internal approach to regulation and industrial adjustment, and also of preferences emerging from domestic politics, as is made evident in Chapter 13 on biotechnology, Chapter 15 on trade policy, and Chapter 16 in relation to central and eastern Europe. Interestingly, Chapter 7 suggests that the regulatory mode increasingly characterizes the operation of the CAP as reforms are introduced.

The strength of this regulatory mode is considerable. Efforts to analyse it account for a good deal of the literature on west European integration. During the 1990s regulation displaced the CAP as the predominant policy paradigm among many EU policy practitioners. It had the advantage of reflecting an approach focused on a modernization trajectory, through which the rigidities of the 'old' west European political economy would be replaced by more flexible, mainly legal, instruments of market encouragement, and through which a different, and less corporatist, relationship could be struck with socio-economic actors. The literature on this regulatory mode has been marked by an emphasis on the role of interest groups, lobbying, and corporate actors (firms rather than trade associations), by approaches based on the networks, coalitions, and alliances that they form, and by a much increased interest in the rule of law as an instrument of policy-making.

However, over the twenty years of experience in developing the single market we can observe changes in and limits to this regulatory mode. Thus, for example, it appears to have been particularly successful in dealing with product regulation, and less robust in dealing with process standards, where difference either in levels of economic development or in societal preferences intervene, sometimes with sub-national as well as country variations (see Chapters 12 and 13). The mode has also had rather less purchase on the regulation of services, financial markets, and utilities, where instead we see moves towards more decentralized, less hierarchical versions of regulation. Here we see across the member states, and indeed in the global economy, the emergence of more-or-less independent regulatory agencies at arm's length from governments, as well as emerging forms of self-regulation. Within the EU there are experiments with: new quasi-independent regulatory agencies, such as the European Food Safety Authority (see Chapter 13); steered partnerships of national agencies working with the Commission, notably in the case of competition policy (see Chapter 5); transnational consortia of national regulatory bodies, for example in the energy sector; and looser networks of self-regulation, notably as regards the operation of financial markets or corporate governance. It is thus becoming much harder to identify the contours of a single coherent EU regulatory mode. A pending issue is how this regulatory mode will apply to—and be affected by—the new member states with less advanced economies, with more limited legal and administrative capacities, and with their domestic societal preferences as yet less explicit. A further issue is the evidence of friction between EU regulation and some relevant international regimes and partners.

The EU distributional mode

Persistently over the years the EU policy process had been caught up in distributional policy-making, that is, the allocation of resources to different groups, sectors, regions, and countries, sometimes explicitly and intentionally, and sometimes as a by-product of policies designed for other purposes. The framers of the original treaties included some elements of distribution in the policy repertoire to be exploited. The CAP was funded from a collective base and for a long time accounted for the lion's share of the EU budget. Farmers became both the clients of European funding and the beneficiaries of high prices, gaining transfers of resources from both taxpayers and consumers. It is to the early years of the EEC that the language of 'financial solidarity' owes its origins. From the early 1970s, efforts were made to develop a similar common fisheries policy (Chapter 14). In both of these cases the European arena was used to protect social groups that were being marginalized in the domestic economy and rendered uncompetitive by global markets, albeit at a cost to other social groups.

When the arguments came to be joined over the distribution of burdens and benefits of participation in the EU, notably in the period following British accession in 1973, it was on the budget as a measure of the impacts of EU membership that attention was focused. As Laffan and Lindner point out in Chapter 8 (and as previous editions of this volume have shown in more detail), EU policy-makers had to make some difficult choices about how to establish financial arrangements, for both revenue and expenditure, that would be equitable between member states. This persists as a highly contentious issue in the EU, now greatly complicated by the arrival of ten new and less prosperous member states.

When the single market was being pushed forward in the mid-1980s the debate about the distributional impacts of integration was joined again, but this time more explicitly couched in the language of relative wealth and poverty. The term 'cohesion' was added to the policy-makers' vocabulary; it connoted a commitment to pay attention to economic and social divergence, and the needs of the more backward regions and social groups. This appeared to signal a shift from haphazard distribution of resources to a planned redistribution through designed transfers of resources. The main spending mechanism was through the 'structural funds' (see Chapter 9), which involved EU co-financing with national exchequers of programmes and projects for, on the one hand, agencies dealing with training and employment creation, and, on the other hand, regional and local authorities. While most of the spending was concentrated in the main 'cohesion' countries—Greece, Ireland, Portugal, and Spain, and later the eastern *Länder* of Germany—some programmes were also open to some clients in the other member states. Thus, the EU began to acquire some scope for using financial incentives to influence policy developments within the member states. In addition various other spending instruments were introduced in fields such as research, with programmatic rather than redistributional aims.

This distributional mode comprised:

- the Commission as the deviser of programmes, in partnership with local and regional authorities or sectoral stakeholders and agencies, and using financial incentives to gain attention;

- member governments in the Council, under pressure from local and regional authorities or other stakeholders, agreeing to a budget with some redistributive elements;

- an EP in which the MEPs would often constitute an additional source of pressure from territorial politics in the regions;

- local and regional authorities benefiting from policy empowerment as a result of engaging in the European arena, with, from 1993 onwards, a new embryonic institution, the Committee of the Regions, to represent their concerns, and many of them with their own offices in Brussels;

- some scope for other stakeholders to be similarly coopted into the EU policy process; and

- a recasting of the EU budget to spend quite large sums of money on cohesion, and proportionately less on agriculture.

It was this opening for more direct contacts between the European and the infra-national levels of government, and the politics that developed around them, that provoked the term 'multi-level governance' to characterize the EU process more generally (Marks 1993). It rested on two essential points: first, that national central governments could no longer monopolize the contacts between the country and the EU levels of policy-making; and, secondly, that engagement at the European level created an opportunity to reinforce a phenomenon of regionalization. The implication was that the domestic polities of the member states were being partially reshaped as a consequence of EU policy-making, in which financial incentives could apply leverage on new political relationships. The multi-level governance approach inverted much of the discussion on how the EU worked with its emphasis on politics on the ground, and by shifting attention away from the Brussels-centred and entrepreneur-oriented images of, respectively, the Community method and the regulatory mode.

The approach is, however, not without its critics. Chapter 9 suggests that the evidence does not add up to support the argument, in that infranational activity should not be confused with impact. Central governments from the member states have, it is argued, remained in the driving seat of the bargains about EU spending. In current discussions about the future of the EU budget for an enlarged membership the inherited distributional mode is being disturbed, as much sharper focus is put on the net positions of member states, with vying coalitions of net payers, historical beneficiaries, and vocal claimants from the new member states (see Chapter 8). Here the debate is more explicitly about country positions than about regional redistribution. A further shadow cast on this is the constraining impact on public budgets of the Maastricht criteria to govern EMU, which is shifting attention away from spending programmes towards other kinds of policy measures.

The idea of an EU distributional mode focused partially on deliberate redistribution is under attack for two other reasons: a shift towards the idea of collective goods: and pressures for spending on external responsibilities. Two additional areas of spending have increased in salience in recent years. One concerns spending to promote innovation, research and development, and the other measures to support JHA policies. The EU Framework Programme for research and development accounted in 2003 for some 4 per cent of the EU budget, with its spending in principle focused on collective research priorities rather than a cross-country share out of the relevant resources, although historically considerable care was taken by the Commission to distribute grants in an even-handed way among member states. The salience of this policy area has increased considerably since the European Council in March 2000 adopted the Lisbon Strategy, aimed at making Europe 'the most competitive and dynamic economy in the world', including by promoting substantial boosts to R&D spending, both public and private. Concerns about the sluggishness of the European economy have gained cogency with the low growth of recent years, and led to louder calls for more EU investment in R&D, whether through the inherited EU budget mechanisms or through new European agencies (Sapir *et al.* 2004). Meanwhile preoccupations with internal security and the impacts of migration are beginning to generate calls for spending on, for example, collective border control measures (see Chapter 18). These trends suggest that there may be less grounds in the future for applying the multi-level governance approach to EU spending programmes.

The other new budgetary development is the sharp increase in EU spending as a result of its foreign policy activities, which (depending on how one counts) is now running at 8–10 per cent of the EU budget. Here again we can see something with the features of a 'collective good' rather than an intra-EU distribution of costs and benefits. The policy procedures associated with this area of spending differ from those that prevail for internal spending, with different roles for the EP. All in all therefore the distributional mode is subject to interesting changes, which would become different again if agreement were to be forthcoming on developing collective mechanisms for reinforcing European foreign and security policies (see Chapter 17).

Policy coordination

An old contrast in the study of European collaboration has been drawn between the EU policy modes outlined above and what in shorthand might be described as the 'OECD technique'. The Organization for Economic Cooperation and Development, the Paris-based club of western industrialized countries, has since the early 1960s provided a forum within which its members could appraise and compare each other's ways of developing public policies.

In its early years the Commission used this technique to develop light forms of cooperation and coordination in fields adjacent to core EU economic competences in order to make the case for direct policy powers. Thus, for example, in the 1970s the Commission promoted increasingly systematic consultations among member governments on environmental issues, and eventually made a persuasive case for the SEA to give the EU formal legislative powers. Similar efforts were made to develop coordination of macro- and microeconomic policies, as well as in domains such as research and development or aspects of education policy. Policy coordination was intended as a mechanism of transition from nationally rooted policy-making to an EU collective regime. As Chapter 14 shows cogently, this approach has been one of the key elements in the efforts to address the conservation of fish stocks. Chapter 18 provides a different kind of example of policy coordination as a technique to achieve better practice in the absence of centralized policy regimes. For the advocates of a strong EU, policy coordination might be a useful starting point, but it used to be seen as very much a second best resting point.

The approach rests a great deal on expertise, and the accumulation of technical arguments in favour of developing a shared approach and to promote modernization and innovation. The typical features are:

- the Commission as the developer of networks of experts or epistemic communities, and of stakeholders and/or civil society;
- the involvement of 'independent' experts as promoters of ideas and techniques;
- the convening of high-level groups in the Council, in brain-storming or deliberative rather than negotiating mode, often designed to develop forms of peer pressure; and

■ dialogue (sometimes) with specialist committees in the EP, as the advocates of
   particular approaches (drawing on the greater willingness of MEPs, in comparison
   with their national counterparts, to probe some policy predicaments in depth).

Latterly we can see that this approach of coordination, strengthened by the contemporary fashions for 'benchmarking' and systematic policy comparisons, is being
developed not as a transitional mechanism, but as a policy mode in its own right.
Indeed, some would argue normatively (J. Scott and Trubek 2002) that there is a case
for understanding this development as the emergence of new forms of post-modern
governance. When the previous edition of this volume was being prepared there was
very little analytical literature on this policy mode, apart from a scattering of commentary on the Cologne, Cardiff, and Luxembourg processes of policy coordination.
However, three factors then served to emphasize policy coordination as a technique.
One was the move to a form of EMU with a single monetary policy but only a coordinated macroeconomic policy, with an effort being made to move on from the looser
form of pre-EMU policy coordination to forms of more intense and more structured
policy coordination through the Broad Economic Policy Guidelines and so forth (see
Chapter 6). A second impulse came from the Lisbon Strategy adopted in March 2000,
which specifically identified and elevated the 'open method of coordination' (OMC) as
a distinctive policy technique, using 'soft' policy incentives to shape behaviour, rather
than 'hard', often legally binding, methods to require compliance. This was to be used
specifically in those fields of socio-economic (mainly microeconomic) policy-making
where the EU lacked—and was unlikely to gain—strong delegated policy powers.
OMC, it was argued, could be a way of engaging member governments, relevant stakeholders, and civil society in iterative comparison, benchmarking, and continuous
coordination as ends in themselves (Sapir Report 2004; Kok Report 2004). A third factor was the increasing recognition of cross-country variations in policy and economic
performance, which made it harder to argue for uniform policy templates that would
be applicable across the whole of the EU, especially an EU that would become even
more diverse after enlargement.

   The employment policy domain (see Chapter 11) illustrates particularly well the
debates and features that have propelled OMC as a technique. Here the main thrust of
EU involvement is to compare national, local, and sectoral experiences of labour market adaptation. The object is not so much to establish a single common framework,
but rather to share experience and to encourage the spread of best practice. In the
now extensive literature and commentary on OMC we find hugely varying assessments of its effectiveness. These range between considerable scepticism as to the
value of so 'soft' a form of joint policy-making, as argued in Chapter 11, and great
enthusiasm for its success—and further potential—as a mechanism for extending EU
influences into parts of the domestic policy processes of the member states where
there remain deep obstacles to formal transfers of policy competences to the EU.
Judging between these competing assessments is especially hard against the back-
cloth of a sluggish European economy where causality and outputs are particularly
hard to pin down, and where some of the changes being sought are to social behaviour
in the hope of improving economic performance. Here too enlargement impinges,
since the heterogeneity that it adds to the range of comparisons and indicators of socio-
economic reforms makes the notion of common EU-wide policy templates particularly
implausible—and perhaps inappropriate. A complication of these policy coordination

techniques is that they diffuse and disperse political responsibilities among the relevant policy actors, making it harder to pin down where political 'ownership' rests or how to exercise political accountability.

Intensive transgovernmentalism

Throughout the history of the EU there have been examples of policy cooperation which have depended mainly on interaction between the relevant national policy-makers, and with relatively little involvement by the EU institutions. This has been especially so in domains that touch sensitive issues of state sovereignty, and which lie beyond the core competences of the Union for market-making and market-regulating. Generally such cooperation has been described as 'intergovernmentalism'—by both practitioners and commentators. Generally it has been regarded as a weaker and much less constraining form of policy development. In the early 1960s General de Gaulle was instrumental in promoting the controversial Fouchet Plans, which aimed to shift delicate areas of cooperation well away from the then EEC into a firmly intergovernmental framework. This was vigorously resisted by some of the more integration-minded governments. Nonetheless in the early 1970s policy cooperation did develop in two domains in particular—money and foreign policy—largely outside the EU institutional framework. In both domains heads of state or government were important actors, and often their preferences were developed in groupings smaller than the whole EU membership. Franco–German bilateral cooperation was at some moments an important catalyst of policy advancement. In the 1980s, and more intensively in the 1990s, some EU countries chose to develop policy cooperation outside the EU framework so as to establish a common external border with liberalized internal borders through the Schengen Agreements, deliberately excluding some EU partners from the initial regime.

The term 'intergovernmental' does not, however, really capture the character of this policy mode in the EU. It resonates too much of cooperation between governments in many other international organizations, in which the intensity of cooperation is quite limited. We therefore prefer the term 'transgovernmental', to connote the greater intensity and denser structuring of some of our examples, where EU member governments have been prepared cumulatively to commit themselves to rather extensive engagement and disciplines, but have judged the full EU institutional framework to be inappropriate or unacceptable, or not yet ripe for adoption.

Intensive transgovernmentalism is characterized by:

- the active involvement of the European Council in setting the overall direction of policy;
- the predominance of the Council of Ministers (or an equivalent forum of national ministers), in consolidating cooperation;
- the limited or marginal role of the Commission;
- the exclusion of the EP and the ECJ from the circle of involvement;
- the involvement of a distinct circle of key national policy-makers;
- the adoption of special arrangements for managing cooperation, in particular the Council Secretariat;

- the opaqueness of the process, to national parliaments and citizens; but
- the capacity on occasion to deliver substantive joint policy.

It might be tempting to dismiss this intensive transgovernmentalism as simply a weak form of cooperation. However, two factors challenge such a conclusion. First, this is the preferred policy mode in some other strong European regimes. Nato is one obvious example; the European Space Agency is another, and very different, case. In both instances quite extensive and sustained policy collaboration has been achieved, albeit with evident limitations. Secondly, within the EU this mode has in practice been a vehicle for developing extensive and cumulative cooperation, gradually with elements of a treaty foundation, but one which has made arrangements aside from most of the main EU institutions.

In the case of EMU (Chapter 6) over the years since the early 1960s the European Council, national finance ministers and officials, and central bankers between them produced such sustained intensity and dense structuring of cooperation that the idea of managing a single currency became feasible and eventually acceptable. Interestingly the development of EMU then bifurcated between, on the one hand, strong delegation to a collective regime for monetary policy with the ECB as the collective agent (Community method), and, on the other hand processes of policy coordination. Thus, a period of intensive transgovernmentalism can lead to a shift from one policy mode to another. Yet, the arguments in autumn 2003 over whether or not the disciplines of the Stability and Growth Pact could be applied to erring member governments illustrate the forces of resistance to a collective regime, especially from larger member states.

In the sphere of foreign policy (Chapter 17), first European political cooperation (EPC) from 1970, then from 1993 onwards CFSP was built up. Initially defence cooperation was left within two separate frameworks, Nato and Western European Union (WEU), with clear competition between these alternative frameworks. However, since 1998 these frameworks have gradually been drawn together, with the Nato mode of policy cooperation setting many of the parameters of the way in which defence is being pulled into the EU setting. For many reasons the CFSP area continues to illustrate the differences among EU member states of both policy preferences and policy capabilities, differences accentuated by the sharp arguments over especially the intervention in Iraq in 2003. These differences also pervaded the debates about EU treaty reform in 2002–4, where one of the key issues was about whether, and if so how, to enhance the EU's collective institutional capabilities to take forward CFSP and an associated collective defence capability. Interestingly, however, arguments about Iraq and about treaty reform notwithstanding, the process of intensive transgovernmentalism has proved more resilient and less voluntarist than appears at first sight. In practice there is more not less cooperation among EU governments on an array of foreign and defence policy issues, and at both the practical and the discursive level. The evolution of the EU joint military staff and the decision in early 2004 to set up a combined European Defence Agency are both interesting examples of cumulative transgovernmentalism, which coexist with continuing arguments about shifts from transgovernmentalism to 'communitarization'.

In JHA (Chapter 18), two transgovernmental processes have converged. On the one hand, informal policy consultations, both bilateral and multilateral, have bred habits of increasingly intense transgovernmental cooperation since the early 1970s. On the other hand, a wittingly separate treaty framework was constructed with loose *ad hoc* institutions under the Schengen Agreements, at first deliberately apart from the EU, then to be incorporated within the EU under the Treaty of Amsterdam. In addition events—both increased migration flows and increased challenges from terrorism and cross-border crime—have accentuated demand for policy cooperation. On the one hand, these different processes of cooperation are now being drawn together, including the transfer since January 2005 of some JHA issues to a form of Community method; but, on the other hand, there remains a mixed pattern of different policy modes in which transgovernmentalism continues to be a strong feature.

These three domains were among the most dynamic areas of EU policy development at the end of the 1990s and in the early 2000s. In each case the EU framework has become in a broad sense more accepted, but the detailed institutional arrangements are untypical. In the case of EMU, on the one hand, an ECB, a network of national banks, and a privileged Economic and Financial Committee of national finance officials have established a variant of the Community method, while, on the other hand, as regards macroeconomic policy techniques of policy coordination predominate, with lingering elements of transgovernmentalism and European Council oversight. The heart of foreign and defence policy is the European Council, flanked by defence and foreign ministry ministers and officials, working with a secretariat so far located in the Council of Ministers (not the Commission), and a great deal of consultation among national capitals. In the case of JHA, policy is being developed among the relevant national ministries and executive agencies, with a new secretariat in the Council, much more involvement of the Commission, some shared agencies, such as Europol, some legal agreements based on conventions, and others through classical EU law.

These three cases suggest that an important systemic change may be under way within the EU policy process. New areas of sensitive public policy are being assigned by EU member governments to forms of collective or pooled regimes, but using institutional formats over which they retain considerable control. These regimes have 'soft' institutions, though the arrangements for EMU have gone the furthest in hardening the institutional arrangements. Yet, these soft institutions sometimes seem capable of developing 'hard' policy, or at least to be aimed at creating the capacity to deliver 'hard' policy.

As we can see, therefore, the EU operates through a variety of different methods, with different patterns of institutional practice, and changing over time. These have evolved organically, and continue to evolve in response to both internal and external factors, both procedural and functional. These five policy modes provide a typology— a set of ideal-types—for exploring the shifting patterns of EU policy-making. The case studies should be read in the light of these evolutionary and experimental features of EU policy-making, providing examples of policy successes and of policy failures, of innovation, and of atrophy.

Further reading

There is a huge literature on the institutions of the EU and their development. Peterson and Bomberg (1999) provide a dynamic analysis, as well as

detailed illustrations of policy cases, while Peterson and Shackleton (2002) provide an up-to-date overview. Scharpf (1999) offers an excellent and critical overview, linking national and European processes. Hix (2005) stresses the politics of the process. Nugent (2002) gives a thorough catalogue of the EU institutions, while Dinan (2004) sets them into their historical context. Among the many studies of the Commission, Edwards and Spence (1997), and Page (1997) provide valuable explanation and insights. For the Council and European Council, see Hayes-Renshaw and Wallace (1997, 2005), and Westlake and Galloway (2005). Jacobs, Corbett, and Shackleton (2000), provide a comprehensive account of the European Parliament. The ECJ and the European legal system are covered by Dehousse (1998), and Mattli and Slaughter (1998b). On the national dimension, see Maurer and Wessels (2003), Cowles, Caporaso, and Risse (2001), and Bulmer and Lequesne (2005). These academic texts should be supplemented by primary sources, including the extensive material available on the website of the EU institutions, for which the point of access is *www.europa.eu.int*.

Bulmer, S., and Lequesne, C. (2005) (eds.), *Member States and the European Union* (Oxford: Oxford University Press).

Cowles, M. G., Caporaso, J. A., and Risse, T. (2001) (eds.), *Transforming Europe: Europeanization and Domestic Change* (Ithaca: Cornell University Press).

Dehousse, R. (1998), *The European Court of Justice* (London: Macmillan).

Dinan, D. (2004), *Europe Recast: A History of European Union* (London: Palgrave Macmillan).

Edwards, G., and Spence, D. (1997) (eds.), *The European Commission*, 2nd edn. (London: Longman).

Hayes-Renshaw, F., and Wallace, H. (1997), *The Council of Ministers* (London: Macmillan).

Hayes-Renshaw, F., and Wallace, H. (2005), *The Council of Ministers*, 2nd edn. (London: Palgrave Macmillan), forthcoming.

Hix, S. (2005), *The Political System of the European Union*, 2nd edn. (London: Palgrave Macmillan).

Jacobs, F., Corbett, R., and Shackleton, M. (2000), *The European Parliament*, 3rd edn. (London: John Harper).

Mattli, W., and Slaughter, A.-M. (1998b), 'The ECJ, Governments, and Legal Integration in the EU', *International Organization*, 52/1: 177–210.

Maurer A., and Wessels, W. (2003) (eds.), *Fifteen into One? The European Union and its Member States* (Manchester: Manchester University Press).

Nugent, N. (2002), *The Government and Politics of the European Union*, 5th edn. (London: Palgrave Macmillan).

Page, E. (1997), *People who Run Europe* (Oxford: Clarendon Press).

Peterson, J., and Bomberg, E. (1999), *Decision-Making in the European Union* (London: Macmillan).

Peterson, J., and Shackleton, M. (2002) (eds.), *The Institutions of the European Union* 2nd edn. (Oxford: Oxford University Press).

Peterson, J., and Shackleton, M. (2005) (eds.), *The Institutions of the European Union*, 2nd edn. (Oxford: Oxford University Press), forthcoming.

Scharpf, F. W. (1999), *Governing in Europe: Effective and Democratic?* (Oxford: Oxford University Press).

Westlake, M. and Galloway, D. (2005) (eds.), *The Council of the European Union*, 3rd edn. (London: John Harper).

Part II

Policies

Chapter 4

The Single Market

A New Approach to Policy

Alasdair R. Young

Contents

Summary

The single European market programme marked a turning point in European integration. Its roots, however, stretch back well before 1985. Detailed harmonization had proved a frustrating approach to market integration, especially as external competition challenged European industry. New ideas about market regulation permeated the EU policy process and, supported by ECJ judgments and Commission entrepreneurship, facilitated legislative activism and important changes in the policy-implementing processes. Although the task of 'completing' the single market remains unfinished, it has moved to the heart of European integration and altered the pattern of state-market relations in Europe.

Introduction

The plans to complete the single market induced an explosion of academic interest in the European Union (EU). Before 1985 the theoretical debate on political integration had stalled, studies of EU policy-making were sparse, and few mainstream economists devoted themselves to the analysis of European economic integration. In the late 1980s all that changed, as competing political analyses proliferated and the economic consequences of the new legislative programme were examined. Indeed, many new theoretical approaches to the study of European integration have taken the single market as their main point of reference, just as many earlier theorists had taken agricultural policy as their stimulus. For many the single European market (SEM) programme constitutes the critical turning point between stagnation and dynamism, between the 'old' politics of European integration and the 'new' politics of European regulation.

This chapter re-examines the renewal of the single European market as a major turning point in European policy-making. In essence, it presents the argument that many of the analyses that proliferated in response to the Single European Act (SEA) and the SEM overstated their novelty and understated some of the surrounding factors that helped to induce their 'success'. Thus, accounts in the late 1980s emphasized the newness of the SEM programme, but in retrospect we can observe a significant degree of continuity with what had come before. Nonetheless, the incorporation of the SEM programme represents a very significant redefinition of the means and ends of policy. It enabled the European integration process to adapt to new constellations of ideas and interests and produced a different policy mode that has permeated many other policy areas (Majone 1994).

The SEM is also important for its impact on the European public policy model *within* the member states. Thus, market regulation at the supranational level of European governance jostles, often uneasily, with other issues on the political and economic agendas of the EU member states. There are also tensions between supranational regulation for transnational markets, engaging transnational regulators and large market operators, and encapsulated national politics, engaging those responsible for, and dependent on, the reduced domestic political space, smaller-scale entrepreneurs, local regulators, and national or regional politicians.

These repercussions have not been confined to the member states that accepted the SEA and the SEM. The formal and informal extraterritorial impact on neighbours, partners, and competitors has been powerful. The SEM has been extended formally to neighbouring countries through the European Economic Area (EEA), and the pre-accession process for central and east European states (see Chapter 16), and to many eventually by full accession. More informally, the SEM has changed the conditions under which goods and service providers from third countries may enter the world's second largest market. The economic, social, and political costs of adjustment within the single market have also generated rearguard action, sometimes focused on other EU policies that might provide compensation or displacement to external competitors.

Box 4.1 The treaty base of the single market (Treaty of Rome)

Art. 28 TEC (ex Art. 30 EEC)	Prohibition on quantitative restrictions on imports and all measures have equivalent effect
Art. 39 TEC (ex Art. 48 EEC)	Free movement of workers
Art. 43 TEC (ex Art. 52 EEC)	Right of establishment
Art. 49 TEC (ex Art. 59 EEC)	Freedom to provide services
Art. 56 TEC (ex Art. 67 EEC)	Free movement of capital
Art. 94 TEC (ex Art. 100 EEC)	Procedure for the approximation of laws that directly affect the common market

---

Background

The objective of establishing a single market started with the Treaty of Rome (see Box 4.1). It set targets for creating a customs union and the progressive approximation of legislation, as well as for establishing a 'common market', complete with free movement for goods, services, capital, and labour (the 'four freedoms'), all within a single regime of competition rules (see Chapter 5). The path was more clearly defined for the customs union than for the common market (Balassa 1975; Pelkmans 1984), reflecting the greater preoccupation of policy-makers in the 1950s with tariffs and quotas than with technical barriers to trade (TBTs) and trade in services.

In the 1960s and 1970s, however, new technologies, new products, new concerns with consumer welfare and environmental protection, and pressure from domestic firms to curb competition all contributed to the adoption of new national rules and regulations, which, whether intentionally or not, impeded trade. Thus, as tariffs among the member states were removed, other barriers were revealed, and even reinforced. Local market preferences, as well as national policy and industrial cultures, became increasingly divisive.

Harmonization and its increasing frustration

In the early 1960s the Commission began to tackle the negative impact of divergent national rules on trade. These efforts gathered pace after the complete elimination of customs duties between member states on 1 July 1968 (Dashwood 1977: 278–89). Initially the Commission tended to regard uniform or 'total' harmonization—the adoption of detailed, identical rules for all the member states—as a means of driving forward the general process of integration. After the first enlargement, however, the Commission adopted a more pragmatic approach and pursued harmonization only where it could be specifically justified. That is, it only insisted on uniform rules when an overriding interest demanded it, using 'optional' rather than 'total' harmonization.

The principal instrument of the original European Economic Community (EEC) for advancing the four freedoms was the Directive, in principle setting the essential framework of policy at the European level and leaving the 'scope and method' of its implementation to the member states. In the case of TBTs, harmonization was based on Article 94 (ex Art. 100 EEC). Other articles provided the legal foundation for the freedoms of movement for services, capital, and labour and for aligning many other national regulations (see Box 4.1).

Harmonization measures were drafted by the Commission in cooperation with sector-specific working groups, composed of experts nominated by member governments. Advice from independent specialists supplemented the Commission's resources and provided a depth and range of expertise comparable to that of the much larger national bureaucracies. The Commission also regularly invited comments on their drafts from European-level pressure groups (Dashwood 1977: 291–2). Beginning in 1973 with the 'low-voltage directive' the Commission, where possible, incorporated the work of private standard-making bodies—primarily the European Committee for Standards (CEN) and the European Electrical Standards Coordinating Committee (CENELEC)—into Community measures by 'reference to standards' (Schreiber 1991: 99).

Progress, however, was greatly impeded by the need for unanimity in the Council of Ministers. Different national approaches to regulation and the pressures on governments from domestic groups with an interest in preserving the status quo made delays and obstruction frequent (Dashwood 1977: 296). The Commission exacerbated this problem by over-emphasizing the details and paying too little attention to the genuine attachment of people to familiar ways of doing business and buying goods (Dashwood 1977: 297). As a result, only 270 directives were adopted between 1969 and 1985 (Schreiber 1991: 98).

The slow pace of European harmonization could not keep pace with the proliferation of national rules as the member states increasingly adopted national measures to protect their industries and to respond to new concerns about consumer and environmental protection in the late 1970s and early 1980s (Commission 1985b; Dashwood 1983). As a consequence, some of the earlier progress in harmonization was undone, contributing to a decline of intra-EU imports relative to total imports (Buigues and Sheehy 1994: 18), and sharply increasing the number of ECJ cases concerning the free movement of goods.

The ECJ's jurisprudence, however, began to bite at the heels of national policy-makers. In 1974 the *Dassonville* ruling established a legal basis for challenging the validity of national legislation that introduced new TBTs. The famous *Cassis de Dijon* judgment in 1979 insisted that under certain specified conditions member states should accept in their own markets products approved for sale by other member states (Alter and Meunier-Aitsahalia 1994: 540–1; Dashwood 1983: 186). Nonetheless, there was cumulative frustration in the Commission and in the business community at the slow pace of progress and the uncertainties of reliance on the ECJ, whose rulings apply only to the cases lodged. The high level of economic interdependence within the EU made these TBTs costly and visible (Cecchini, Catinat, and Jacquemin 1988; Pelkmans 1984).

At the same time there was mounting pressure for reform. In the early 1980s the governments of western Europe were facing an economic crisis. The poor competitiveness of European firms relative to those of their main trading partners in the US and, particularly, Japan contributed to large trade deficits (Pelkmans and Winters 1988: 6). Transnational companies proliferated and often squeezed the profit margins and markets of firms confined to national markets. The sharp increase in oil prices following the revolution in Iran in 1979 helped to push west European economies into recession. Inflation and unemployment both soared during the early 1980s. Business confidence was low and investment, both foreign and European, began to turn away from the Community (Pelkmans and Winters 1988: 6).

The emerging reform agenda

While the crisis was clear, the response was not (see, for example, Tugendhat 1985). Large trade deficits and high inflation constrained the ability of member governments to use expansionary economic policies to bring down unemployment. Economic interdependence further reduced the efficacy of national responses to the crisis and provided an incentive for a coordinated response to the region's economic problems.

The prospects for a collective response was enhanced by changes within the member states. These are widely described in the political integration literature as a convergence of national policy preferences during the early 1980s (Cameron 1992: 56; Moravcsik 1991: 21; 1998; Sandholtz and Zysman 1989: 111). This convergence, it was claimed, reflected widespread acceptance of neo-liberal economic ideas, which stress that markets, rather than governments, are better placed to generate economic growth. Neo-liberal ideas thus advocate that governments should interfere less in economies and concentrate on policies such as the privatization of state-owned industries and the removal of regulations, particularly those governing economic competition.

Although new government policies did certainly emerge in the early 1980s, closer examination reveals that these differed substantially between countries in terms of their origins, motivations, and intensities. Political parties advocating neo-liberal economic policies came to power in the UK, Belgium, the Netherlands, and Denmark, in part due to a rejection of the parties that had overseen the economic decline of the late 1970s (Hall 1986: 100). The rejection was less marked in Germany, where the underlying strength of its economy preserved an attachment to the established 'social market' framework. In France the 'policy learning' was explicit. Expansionary fiscal policies had led to increased inflation and unemployment, exacerbated the trade deficit, and swelled the public debt (Hall 1986: 199). By 1983 the French government had started to look for European solutions, reversing its threat of autumn 1982 to obstruct the common market (Pearce and Sutton 1985: 68). The Spanish government sought to link socialist modernization at home with transnational market disciplines abroad. Convergence is thus something of a misnomer—European market liberalization served quite different purposes for different governments and different economic actors.

New ideas about markets and competition thus started to be floated in response to the problems of the European economy. These were influenced by the wave of deregulation in the US in the late 1970s and early 1980s (Hancher and Moran 1989: 133;

Majone 1991: 81; Sandholtz and Zysman 1989: 112). Furthermore, the ECJ's 1979 *Cassis de Dijon* judgment advanced the concept of mutual recognition of national standards (see below), which provided the Commission with a lever with which to pursue greater market integration (Dashwood 1983).

From the early 1980s European Council communiqués repeatedly expressed concern about the poor state of the single market (Armstrong and Bulmer 1998: 17). In December 1982 it responded to a Commission communication that recommended the removal of TBTs, simplification of frontier formalities, the liberalization of public procurement, and closer alignment of taxes (*Bulletin of the European Communities*, 12/1982) by creating an Internal Market Council to meet regularly to consider such issues.

Throughout 1983 support for revitalizing the single market continued to grow. In April the heads of some of Europe's leading multinational corporations formed the European Round Table of Industrialists (ERT) to advocate the completion of the single market (Cowles 1994). The Union of Industrial and Employers' Confederations of Europe (UNICE) added its voice to calls for greater market integration.

The single European market programme

Meanwhile the Commission began to look for ways to attack barriers to market access, both by systematically identifying them and by exploring ways of relaxing the constraints on policy change. It suggested the 'new approach' to standards harmonization, which advanced 'mutual recognition' of equivalent national rules and restricted much of harmonization to agreeing only 'essential requirements'. It thus built on the jurisprudence of the ECJ, notably the definition in *Cassis de Dijon* of essential safety requirements (Schreiber 1991). It also built on British support for deregulation and French and German efforts to coordinate the activities of their national standards bodies (H. Wallace 1984). Towards the end of 1983 the Commission privately persuaded the British, French, and German government to accept this new approach, which was formally adopted by the Council in May 1985 (*Bulletin of the European Communities*, 5/1985).

The 'new approach' limits legislative harmonization to minimum essential requirements and explicitly leaves scope for variations in national legislation (subject to mutual recognition). Under the 'new approach' responsibility for developing detailed technical standards is delegated to CEN and CENELEC. It is paralleled in financial services by 'home country control', which sets minimum standards for national regulation of financial service providers, but then allows them to operate throughout the single market regulated by the government of the country in which they have their headquarters (home country).

In 1985, after consultations with the member governments, the new president of the Commission, Jacques Delors, decided that a drive to 'complete the single market' was perhaps the only strategic policy objective that would enjoy any sort of consensus. In his inaugural speech to the European Parliament (EP), Delors committed himself to completing the single market by 1992. The Milan European Council in June 1985 endorsed the White Paper (Commission 1985a) drawn up by Lord Cockfield, the Commissioner for the single market, containing 300 (later reduced to 282) measures that would complete the single market by 1992 (see Table 4.1).

Table 4.1 The White Paper on the single market: a taxonomy

Markets / Measures	Products	Services	Persons & labour	Capital

Market access	■ Abolition of intra-EC frontier controls
	■ Approximation of:
	  ■ technical regulations
	  ■ VAT rates and excises
	■ Unspecified implications for trade policy
		■ Mutual recognition & 'home country control', removal of licensing restrictions (in banking and insurance)
		■ Dismantling of quotas and freedom of *cabotage* (road haulage)
		■ Access to inter-regional air travel markets
		■ Multiple designation in bilaterals (air transport)
			■ Abolition of intra-EC frontier checks on persons
			■ Relaxation of residence requirements for EC persons
			■ Right of establishment for various highly educated workers
				■ Abolition of exchange controls
				■ Admission of securities listed in one member state to another
				■ Measures to facilitate industrial cooperation and migration of firms

Competitive conditions	■ Promise of special paper on state aid to industry
	■ Liberalization of public procurement
	■ Merger control
		■ Introduction of competition policy in air transport
		■ Approximation of fiscal and/or regulatory aspects in various services markets
			■ European 'vocational training card'	■ Proposals on takeovers and holdings
				■ Fiscal approximation of:
				  ■ double taxation
				  ■ security taxes
				  ■ parent-subsidiary links

Market functioning	■ Specific proposals on R&D in telecoms and IT
	■ Proposals on standards, trade marks, corporate law, etc
		■ Approximation of:
		  ■ market & firm regulation in banking
		  ■ consumer protection in insurance
		  ■ EC system of permits for road haulage
		  ■ EC standard for payment cards
			■ Approximation of:
			  ■ income tax provisions for migrants
			  ■ various training provisions
			  ■ mutual recognition of diplomas
				■ European economic interest grouping
				■ European company statute
				■ Harmonization of industrial and commercial property laws
				■ Common bankruptcy provisions

Sectoral policy	■ CAP proposals:
	  ■ abolition of frontiers
	  ■ approximation and mutual recognition in veterinary and phytosanitary policies
	■ Steel:
	  ■ call to reduce subsidies
		■ Common crisis regime in road transport
		■ Common air transport policy on access, capacity and prices
		■ Common rules on mass risks insurance
			■ Largely silent on labour-market provisions	■ Call to strengthen EMS

Source: Pelkmans and Winters (1988: 12).

During this same period, but outside the Community framework, the French and German governments in 1984 agreed the Moselle Treaty in order to mitigate the impact of border controls. In 1985 it was converted, at the insistence of the Benelux governments, into the first Schengen Agreement (see Chapter 18).

The Single European Act

Although the SEM programme laid out the course to take, there were still institutional impediments to its realization. In June 1984 the meeting of the European Council in Fontainebleau cleared the way for those institutional impediments to be addressed (Armstrong and Bulmer 1998: 18). It resolved the question of Britain's budget rebate and the outstanding issues of the Iberian enlargement, thereby clearing the way for serious consideration of revision of the treaties. At this meeting, the Commission tabled the 'new approach' and the British government tabled a memorandum that called *inter alia* for the creation of a 'genuine common market' in goods and services (Thatcher 1984). The meeting also established the Ad Hoc Committee on Institutional Reform (Dooge Committee) to consider reforms to the Community's decision-making procedures, with the Iberian enlargement in mind. Earlier that year in its Draft Treaty on European Union, the EP had sought to focus attention on institutional reform, calling *inter alia* for increased parliamentary powers and greater use of qualified majority voting (QMV) in the Council of Ministers (European Parliament 1984).

By December 1985 a remarkably quick and focused Intergovernmental Conference (IGC) had agreed the terms of institutional reform that became the SEA. In addition to its important focus on accommodating enlargement, the SEA specifically endorsed the '1992 programme' to complete the single market and altered the main decision rule for single market measures (taxation, free movement of persons, and the rights and interests of employed persons excepted) from unanimity to qualified majority voting in the Council. It also enhanced the powers of the Parliament by introducing the cooperation procedure with respect to single market measures. Thus, a strategic policy change and institutional reform were linked symbiotically and symbolically.

This linkage was crucial. First, it locked together institutional change and substantive policy goals. Secondly, the agreement to proceed with the single market was embedded in a broader set of agreements. This was connected with the accommodation of new members and budgetary redistribution, but also a number of flanking policies—such as the environment and technology policy—were included to assuage the concerns of some member governments about the liberalizing dynamic of the SEM programme (Armstrong and Bulmer 1998: 14).

Squaring the theoretical circle

Theoretical accounts of the SEM and SEA fall into two main approaches: one that emphasizes the role of supranational actors (neo-functionalism), the other that stresses the importance of the member governments (liberal intergovernmentalism).

Comparisons of the two approaches are complicated by the fact that some observers focus on the SEM, whilst others concentrate on the SEA.

Those analysts that concentrate on the single European market programme tend to stress the role of supranational actors. Cowles (1994) emphasizes the importance of transnational business interests in shaping the EU agenda in favour of the completion of the single market. Sandholtz and Zysman (1989) also give pride of place to supranational actors, although they cast the Commission in the leading role, with big business lending support. Garrett and Weingast (1993) contend that it was the ECJ's idea of mutual recognition that provided a focal point for agreement among member governments that favoured liberalization. Alter and Meunier-Aitsahalia (1994) and Pollack (2003) recognize the importance of the idea of mutual recognition, but stress the Commission's entrepreneurial exploitation of this idea as a formula for liberalization. These accounts thus are at least compatible with neo-functionalism.

Analysts that focus on the SEA, by contrast, emphasize bargaining among the member governments (intergovernmentalism). Moravcsik (1991, 1998), in particular, argues that the SEA was the product of interstate bargaining, principally between the British, French, and German governments, and that traditional tools of international statecraft, such as threats of exclusion and side payments, explain the final composition of the '1992 programme' and the SEA. Garrett (1992) argues that the member governments were willing to accept limits on their policy autonomy because they were engaged in an extended cooperative project and wanted to be able to ensure that their partners would comply with agreements. Cameron (1992) concludes that ultimately the member governments, particularly in the context of the European Council, were the crucial actors, although he concedes that supranational actors, such as the Commission, ECJ, and big business, may have influenced their preferences.

As these two theoretical approaches actually seek to explain distinct, albeit related, events, both may be broadly accurate. The Commission, transnational business interests, some member governments, and to an extent the ECJ, played the lead role in shaping the SEM programme, while bargaining among the member governments primarily determined the outcome of the SEA (Armstrong and Bulmer 1998: 19). This account is consistent with different types of actors having different impacts on different types of policy (Cowles 1994; Peterson 1995). When it comes to 'history-making' decisions, such as the SEA, the member governments are the crucial actors. When dealing with policy-setting decisions, of which the SEM is a particularly weighty example, the supranational institutions, and their allies, tend to be important.

Subsequent institutional reform

The SEA in effect set the institutional framework for the single market programme, and its broad parameters remain largely unchanged. The most significant subsequent change has been the introduction of the co-decision procedure in the Maastricht Treaty on European Union (TEU). The Treaty of Amsterdam established clearer guidelines about when member governments might adopt national rules stricter than agreed common rules. The Constitutional Treaty considered eliminating those few single market issues, such as taxation, still not subject to QMV, but met with fierce opposition from the British and Irish governments in particular. More strikingly, the institutional reforms first introduced with respect to single market measures have been subsequently extended to other areas of policy-making.

The politics of policy-making in the SEM

The SEM and SEA fundamentally changed the politics of market integration within the European Community. First, the SEM revived 'negative integration', that is, the removal of national rules that impede economic exchange. This is most obvious in the mutual recognition principle, the abolition of frontier controls and the elimination of exchange controls. Secondly, the SEA changed the institutional framework for 'positive integration'—agreeing common rules to replace national ones—by reinstating QMV and enhancing the powers of the EP. In addition, with respect to the 'new approach' and 'home country control', the SEM blurred the distinction between positive and negative integration by setting only minimum requirements. These different modes of integration have profound political implications by both affecting who the key actors are and influencing their relative power (see Table 4.2).

Negative integration

Negative integration is the elimination of national rules that impede economic exchange. It can occur as the result of political agreement among the member governments on the basis of a proposal from the Commission, as was the case with eliminating border procedures and abolishing exchange controls. In such instances,

Table 4.2 The significance of different modes of market integration

Type of integration	Mode	Description	Estimated share of intra-EU trade accounted for by affected products
Negative	mutual recognition principle	different national standards assumed to be equivalent in effect	50%
Positive	'new approach'	common objectives with reference to voluntary standards	20%
	approximation	common detailed rules	30%
	common authorization	common approval of individual products required	pharmaceuticals, GM crops and food

Source: adapted from Holmes and Young (2000), and Commission (2002b).
Note: no percentage available for 'pharmaceuticals, GM crops and food'.

negative integration, for all intents and purposes, looks much like positive integration (see below). More commonly, however, negative integration occurs as the result of a national measure being found incompatible with the treaties as the result of a judicial process. In such instances firms are usually the initiators, and the courts (ultimately the ECJ) are the decision-makers.

The principle of mutual recognition is at the heart of negative integration. It is deceptively simple. The basic idea is that all member-government regulations, whatever their differences in detail, should be deemed equivalent in effect. Consequently, products produced legally in one member state should be considered equally safe, environmentally friendly, etc. as those produced legally in any other member state. If one member government prohibits the sale of a product produced legally in another member state, the producing firm can challenge that prohibition under European law. If successful, the importing member government must accept the product, and negative integration has occurred.

Under EU law, however, member governments have the right, albeit within limits, to enforce strict national rules despite the principle of mutual recognition. Crucially, the principle applies only when the assumption holds that the national rules are equivalent in effect. This is not always the case, and Article 30 TEC (ex Art. 36 EEC) permits restrictions on trade for a number of public policy reasons, including public morality and the protection of human, animal, and plant health and safety. It is possible, therefore, that a government's more stringent regulation will be upheld. As a consequence, there are incentives for its trading partners to negotiate a common rule in order to eliminate the disruptive impact on trade of different rules (Vogel 1995; Young and Wallace 2000). This is one of the reasons why mutual recognition applies primarily to relatively simple products. It also means that strict-standard governments can play an important role in setting the agenda for positive integration. The more important their national markets, the more likely we are to see attempts to agree on a common rule.

Positive integration

Because different countries, for a wide variety of reasons, adopt different regulations and because those regulations serve public policy goals and usually only impede trade as a side effect, it is frequently not possible to simply eliminate national rules ('negative integration'). In such cases, in order to square the twin objectives of delivering public policy objectives and liberalizing trade it is necessary to replace different national rules with common European ones ('positive integration'). Given the relative importance of 'positive integration' in the EU's market integration project (see Table 4.2), it is more appropriate to describe the SEM as *re*regulatory, than *de*regulatory.

The policy cycle and institutional actors

Within the single market programme, the Commission is the formal agenda-setter as only it can propose new measures. The reality is somewhat more complicated. Member governments can request that the Commission develop proposals and, as noted above, can indirectly shape the agenda by pursuing policies that disrupt the free flow of goods or services within the single market. In addition, member governments, as part of compromises on legislation, often build in 'policy ratchets' requiring that an issue be reconsidered by some specified time in the future. Lastly, the Maastricht Treaty gave the EP the right to request that the Commission propose legislation.

As discussed earlier, the SEA introduced two important changes to the legislative process on single market measures: QMV, and the enhanced role of the EP. Although QMV is the formal decision-making procedure in the Competitiveness Council (which since June 2002 incorporates the Internal Market Council) it is used relatively infrequently. Thus, in 1989–93 only 91 decisions out of 233 taken were adopted by QMV (*Financial Times*, 13 September 1994). Somewhat perversely these votes sometimes isolated member states that had the most substantive interest in the outcome. It should be noted, however, that all decisions are taken 'in the shadow of the vote'. This means that apparently consensual decisions may mask significant compromises by isolated governments or those in small minorities.

Although the SEA increased the role of the EP by giving it the power, under the cooperation procedure, to reject or amend proposals, this power was significantly constrained. The Parliament had to vote to amend or reject a proposal by an absolute majority of its members; the Commission could choose not to integrate parliamentary amendments into its revised proposal to the Council; and the Council could overturn the Parliament's amendments or rejection by a unanimous vote. Consequently, the Parliament only very rarely rejected proposals under the cooperation procedure and only about 40 per cent of its amendments, many of which are only minor changes to the substance of the text, ended up in directives (European Parliament 1993). If some member governments favoured the amendments made by the EP, however, the EP could have a significant impact on policy, as it famously did in the 1989 Directive 89/458 setting strict new emissions limits for small cars (see Box 4.2).

The introduction of the co-decision procedure under the TEU augmented the EP's importance in single market matters, particularly strengthening its ability to reject proposals. This has led to a marked increase in the number of parliamentary amendments accepted by the Commission and Council (Hix 1999: 96). The increased influence of the Parliament formally in decision-making, and informally in proposal shaping, has had an impact on policy outcomes by enhancing the representation of

---

Box 4.2 The Small Car Emissions Directive

In 1987 the Commission advanced a proposal for standardizing limits on emissions from small cars. Member governments, reflecting the interests of their automobile manufacturers and/or the environmental concerns of their citizens, were divided over the proposals. The Danish, Dutch, and Greek governments, in particular, did not consider the proposals sufficiently stringent, but they were outvoted under QMV. Under the newly introduced cooperation procedure, however, the European Parliament also had a say. The EP also considered the proposals too weak and took a strong stand, threatening to veto the proposal if it was not made significantly more stringent. Given the fierce opposition of the Danish, Dutch, and Greek governments, there was little prospect that the Council would have been able to muster the unanimous vote necessary to overturn such a parliamentary veto. As a consequence, the Council adopted a stricter standard by QMV in June 1989.

Source: adapted from Peterson and Bomberg, 1999: 190–91.

civic interests, such as consumer and environmental groups (Peterson and Bomberg 1999; Young and Wallace 2000).

As the vast majority of the SEM legislative programme is in the form of directives, the member states have a central role in implementation. The transposition of direct-ives into national law is a necessary, but not very visible, process, since in most cases it occurs through subordinate legislation that is not much debated. Criticisms of 'Brussels bureaucracy' often relate to rules that had been transposed into national law without debate and with little attention from national parliamentarians, but then 'Brussels' is always an easy scapegoat for unpopular changes.

Although the Commission formally has a role in enforcing the single market, its staff is too small and its policy remit too broad for it to actively engage in policing all nooks and crannies of the single market. Instead, the job of ensuring compliance is decentralized and relies heavily on firms and non-governmental organizations identi-fying issues and either bringing them to the Commission's attention or addressing them directly through the courts.

The policy players

The SEM is about regulation, and, in keeping with Theodore Lowi's (1964) character-ization of regulatory politics, interest-group competition characterizes the politics of single market measures. 'Brussels' had for a long while attracted pressure groups and lobbyists from the 'cognoscenti' among the would-be influencers of Community leg-islation, but the SEM contributed to both a dramatic expansion of such activity and some changes in its form.

In part, the increase in the number of 'Eurogroups' was a simple reaction to the range and quantity of sectors and products affected by the SEM programme and the speed with which they were being addressed. Organizations (pressure groups, firms, local and regional governments, and NGOs), which had previously relied on occa-sional trips to Brussels, started to establish their own offices there or to hire lobbyists on retainer. This shift to Brussels was in part a response to the looming shadow of QMV, which meant that firms and interest groups could no longer count on 'their' member government being able to defend their interests. Building alliances with like-minded groups from other countries, other member governments, and within the Commission became crucial, and that meant having a presence in Brussels. The Commission, with limited staff and pressed for expertise, readily opened its doors to these actors.

Another change following the SEA and the launch of the SEM was the increase in the number of civic interest groups, although they found it much harder to exercise effective political muscle. The consumer and the purchaser had been the intended beneficiaries of the SEM programme and the 'minimum essential requirements' of harmonizing and liberalizing directives were often to help them or their assumed interests. However, it is easier to discern consumers as objects of policy than as part-ners in the process, although they are often sporadic participants (Young 1997; Young and Wallace 2000). In part as a consequence, in contrast to the favourable opinion of business to the SEM, wider public expectations began to wane from 1990 onwards (Franklin, Marsh, and McLaren 1994; Reif 1994), and public antipathies have emerged in response to the apparent efforts of 'Brussels' to remove differences of local taste (food standards being a particularly emotive issue). The Commission has responded by launching initiatives to make citizens aware of their rights and of the opportunities presented by the single market.

In addition to changes in the volume and types of interest groups active in Brussels, the SEM has also contributed to changes in the form of interest group participation in policy-shaping. Individual firms and direct-member associations came to rival the previously dominant conventional peak and trade associations in the consultative processes. Another change was greater reliance on consultancy (an import from the US), which started to erode the old distinctions between public policy-making and private interest representation. The Commission, member governments, and firms all found themselves relying increasingly on consultants to inject 'expertise'.

Although 'Brussels' had become much more important, firms and interest groups retained close contacts with their national governments as important players in the SEM policy process. Rather than consistently preferring national or European policy, the SEM contributed to a rise in 'forum shopping', with non-state actors pursuing their policy objectives at whichever level was considered most likely to deliver the desired result.

In this process the Commission plays a pivotal role. Its sole right of initiative ensures that, but what really matters is how the Commission has chosen to use it. Although *re*regulatory rather than *de*regulatory, the SEM did have the effect of liberalizing markets and increasing competition among firms from different member states. In such circumstances, the costs of policy change (liberalization) are concentrated on the protected firms and the benefits tend to be disbursed thinly across a wide range of actors (consumers and users), although some particularly competitive firms are likely to benefit. In such circumstances, a policy entrepreneur is required to champion change and galvanize support—a role that the Commission has grasped with gusto.

Opening up the policy space

In addition to the institutional changes introduced by the SEA, the sheer reinvigoration of European policy-making has also affected state-market relations in Europe. It has done so in two principal ways: increasing governments' autonomy from society and opening up existing policy networks. Participation in any international negotiation privileges governments with respect to societal actors (Putnam 1988; Moravcsik 1993b). In particular, governments may be able to use an international agreement or external pressure to push through desired domestic reforms that have been blocked by powerful domestic interests.

In addition, the policy networks surrounding the SEM—both because they are relatively new, and by involving actors from all the member states—tend to be more open than those in individual member states. As a result, an increasing number and variety of interests now have access to the policy process. Furthermore, if there is to be a European regulation, producers tend to want their national rules to provide the template. As a consequence, powerful business interests often compete with each other, thereby undermining the 'privileged position of business' in the European policy process.

Hence, SEM regulations are usually contested by 'advocacy alliances', tactical, often loose groupings of diverse proponents of particular policies (Young and Wallace 2000). Such 'advocacy alliances' bring together combinations of member governments, supranational European institutions, producer and civic interests. Thus, these alliances bridge the policy-shaping and policy-setting aspects of the policy cycle.

The regulatory policy mode

The SEM policy process, therefore, combines high levels of interest group engagement with Commission entrepreneurship, Council bargaining, and Parliamentary deliberation over common rules. These rules are subsequently often enforced through the courts by private actors. As such the SEM is the exemplar, not surprisingly, of the EU's regulatory policy mode (see Chapter 3).

It is, however, important to recognize that the regulatory mode actually contains two distinct dynamics: one that promotes market liberalization, the other more stringent regulation. These different dynamics apply to different types of regulation and broadly mirror patterns in other polities. With regard to economic regulations—such as controls on prices or competition—the SEM has been liberalizing. With regard to social regulations, such as consumer safety or environmental product standards, the SEM has tended to increase competition among the member states, but by producing relatively stringent common rules (Peterson 1997; Sbragia 1993; Scharpf 1999; Young and Wallace 2000).

There are two keys to these different dynamics. The first concerns policy ideas. While neo-liberalism has expounded the benefits of removing restrictions on competition (Majone 1991), post-material values and more recent ideas such as the 'precautionary principle' have supported more stringent social regulations (Weale 1992; Vogel 1989). The second key concerns how the potential for negative integration affects the bargaining power of the member governments within the Council under the shadow of QMV. With regard to economic regulations, the prospect of negative integration is pronounced, putting those member governments with restrictions in a weak position to do more than slow the pace of liberalization (Holmes and McGowan 1997; Schmidt 1998; Young and Wallace 2000).

With regard to social regulations, however, the Treaty of the European Community accepts, within limits, the right of member governments to adopt social regulations that impede trade. In addition to putting such issues on the agenda, as noted above, this puts the stricter-standard country in a stronger bargaining position; its firms are protected and its citizens are content, while foreign goods or services are excluded. The cost of no agreement, therefore, falls more heavily on its partners. Under QMV no individual government can hold out alone for stricter standards, but there is usually an 'advocacy alliance' of civic interest groups, stringent-standard producers, several member governments, the Parliament, and often the Commission in favour of more stringent standards. As a consequence, the SEM has tended to contribute to 'trading up' (Vogel 1995).

Substance and impact

Progress on the single market legislation has been impressive, with nearly 1,500 measures adopted by 2002 (Commission 2002c: 10), and the estimated economic impacts are significant (see Box 4.3). In addition, one of the most important 'outputs' of the SEM has been the change in business attitudes and business behaviour, much of it anticipating legislation (Jacquemin and Wright 1993). It is, however, important to

---

Box 4.3 The estimated impact of the single market programme

- EU GDP in 2002 was 1.8 percentage points higher due to the single market;
- about 2.5 million more jobs have been created since 1992;
- extra cumulative prosperity of €877 billion since 1992;
- EU exports to third countries increased from 7 to 11 per cent of GDP in period 1992–2002;
- inflows of FDI into the EU have more than doubled as a percentage of GDP;
- 80 per cent of EU citizens believe that the SEM has led to wider choice, and 67 per cent believe that it has led to improved quality;
- over 60 per cent of companies exporting to more than five EU member states said that the SEM has helped to boost their cross-border sales;
- electricity, natural gas, and telephone prices are now lower than in the US.

Source: Commission 2002c.

---

recognize that the benefits of the single market have been more apparent to large firms operating in multiple markets than to small and medium-sized companies (Commission 1998a) and consumers (Commission 2002c: 12).

Despite the impressive efforts, however, the single market is still not complete, and in many respects never will be, insofar as it is an on-going project requiring constant updating (Commission 2002c: 4). Indeed, there are a number of causes for concern (Commission 2004a). First, prices for the same products in different member states stopped converging before 1998, and price variation remains significantly higher in the EU than in the US. This suggests that significant obstacles to trade remain. Secondly, the net outflow of foreign investment has increased, although this may just reflect cyclical factors.

The transposition of directives into national law is less of a problem than it was, but the Commission (2004a: 16) is still not satisfied, as over 8 per cent of single market directives have not been transposed in all member states. There are four particular problem areas when it comes to completing the single market: inadequate implementation of directives; problems with the operation of the mutual recognition principle; important lasting cultural differences among the member states; and persistent gaps in the legislative programme, especially with regard to services. Each of these problems is likely to be exacerbated in an EU of twenty-five.

Although the transposition of directives into national law has eased as a problem, actual implementation is a pressing concern. In 2002 the Commission had 1,500 infringement proceedings open against member states for failing to apply directives fully (Commission 2002c: 11). France, Italy, Germany, Spain, and Greece accounted for more than half of those proceedings. The Commission (2002b: 11) considers that this does 'enormous' damage to the effective functioning of the single market.

The effective functioning of the single market is also disrupted by problems with applying the mutual recognition principle. These are most pronounced with regard to technically complex products (such as buses, lorries, construction products, and precious metals), and products that may pose a threat to safety or health (such as foods), although the principle works quite well when applied to relatively simple products (Commission 2002*b*: 2).

A contributing factor to the problems with the application of the mutual recognition principle are significant underlying cultural differences among the member states. Such differences can also complicate agreeing common new rules. Cultural differences are particularly pronounced with respect to food, as shown by the different attitudes towards biotechnology (see Chapter 13), but they also permeate other areas. In services, for example, different attitudes toward public-service obligations made the liberalization of network utilities—such as telephones, electricity, and gas—difficult. Furthermore, consumers in different markets may prefer different product characteristics or may feel more comfortable doing business with established local firms (Müller 2003). Thus, cultural differences also have a bearing on whether the removal of legal and physical barriers is sufficient to create a single market.

The most pronounced gaps in the single market's legislative programme concern services. These problems have been most pronounced in sectors dominated by public monopolies, such as energy and telecommunications markets, and in highly regulated services, such as financial services, particularly insurance (Müller 2003). Energy and telecommunications markets were finally liberalized in the 1990s. In 1999 the EU adopted the Financial Services Action Plan, a raft of forty-two measures designed to create a genuinely single market in financial services. There are, however, still a number of barriers that impede service providers from operating smoothly across borders. The Commission sees this as a particular problem in retail and business services (Commission 2002*c*: 22). The absence of coherent European company law, however, remains the most striking lacuna.

Beyond the EU level the single market programme has contributed, directly and indirectly, to changes in the institutions of regulation within the member states. This is most pronounced in network utilities and food safety, where EU directives required the establishment of at least quasi-independent national regulatory authorities to oversee competition, in the case of the former (see Chapter 5), or to provide expert, independent advice on safety, in the case of the latter (see Chapter 13). These authorities usually do not have the same degree of independence or authority as their US counterparts, and most only provide expert advice or guidance to politicians who, at least formally, take the decisions.

Policy linkages

Now that products and services move more easily between member states, attention has shifted to the processes and conditions under which they are produced and provided. Irrespective of other arguments for European policies on environmental and social issues (see Chapters 10 and 12), the preoccupation of entrepreneurs with operating on a level playing field turned attention to the relevance of such rules for costs, competitiveness, and profitability. Concerns for a level playing field also supported the case for a tough competition policy (see Chapter 5).

In addition, the single market was invoked to build support for the two big policy initiatives that followed it: economic and monetary union (EMU) (see Chapter 6); and justice and home affairs (see Chapter 18). The single market programme also has implications for the EU's external policies. It has affected the terms on which third-country goods and services enter the EU (see Chapter 15; Young 2004) and, as a consequence of the 'doctrine of implied powers', it has enhanced the EU's capacity to participate effectively in international trade negotiations (see Chapter 15; Young 2002). It has also provided a core framework for relations with the EU's 'near abroad' (see Chapter 16; Young and Wallace 2000).

The single market in an enlarged EU

Extending the single market programme to the new member states in advance of their accession has eased their adjustment to membership. Nevertheless, their member-ship is likely to complicate the single market, both by increasing the need for positive integration and by making it harder to achieve.

By increasing the diversity of membership, the new members will complicate the already delicate regulatory balance within the EU, particularly with respect to the mutual recognition principle (Holmes and Young 2000). An early indication of this was the Commission's concern with food safety standards in the new member states and the possibility that safeguard restrictions might be imposed (*Financial Times*, 23 February 2004). If the principle of mutual recognition becomes less effective, either obstacles to trade will proliferate or more common rules will have to be adopted. The larger membership, even given the revised decision rules, will significantly complic-ate agreeing such common rules. This applies particularly to new areas of policy—such as the regulation of new technologies—and areas where the single market is still incomplete. By complicating both negative and positive integration the most recent enlargement may mark the high water mark of market integration.

Conclusions: a new approach to policy

The single European market programme represents an approach to policy different both from that within the EU prior to the mid-1980s and from that found in most member states. It is an explicitly regulatory mode of policy-making. As a consequence, new relationships have been established between public and private actors at the EU level and between actors operating at the national and European levels. This has tended to open up the policy process, although business groups, especially large firms, have a 'privileged position', as they do at the national level. There is, however, more likely to be competition among such privileged actors than in member states.

The SEM has also reduced the dependence of many economic actors on national policy. The scope for national policy-makers to control economic transactions on their territories has become more limited and will remain limited as long as the trans-national legal regime of the EU holds together. That is not to say, however, that the political turf has been won by EU-level policy-makers, since the new regulatory mode involves a diffusion of policy authority rather than its concentration at the European level. Although the Commission has been heavily engaged in promoting the single market, its own net gain in authority is open to debate, not least since it has also become the butt of residual criticism about the downside effects of market liberalization. Moreover, the member governments—as participants in decision-making, the enforcers of most EU legislation, the guardians of 'home country controls', and the proponents of subsidiarity—remain key players in the regulatory process.

In addition, the member governments are in the position of defending the losers from the single market against the incursions of European regulation. Hence, the single market programme has to be seen as an important element of the legitimacy test faced by the EU since the early 1990s. It is, moreover, paradoxical that this test has been most severe in member states whose governments are strongly committed to market liberalization (the UK being a case in point).

The SEM probably would not have become such a relative 'success story' had not policy and industrial entrepreneurs been able to talk up the importance of what they were seeking to do and thus to give political sex appeal to an otherwise dreary list of separate and technical proposals. For a variety of reasons, politicians found it convenient to use the single market and the constraints from 'Brussels' as cover for changes in domestic policies and as a justification for both inaction and action at home. Commission officials were delighted to have found a theme that had such wide resonance and played it for all it was worth in developing the symbolism of European integration and its impacts on citizens as well as on firms. Sustaining political integration on the back of a programme of market liberalization has, however, proved elusive.

Further reading

On the original development of the 1992 programme, see Cockfield (1994), and Pelkmans and Winters (1988). For recent economic evaluations, see Commission (2002c, 2004a), and the Commission's biennial *Single Market Scoreboard* and website at *www.europa.eu.int/comm/ internal_market*. The introduction to the Commission's (1995) 'pre-accession strategy' summarizes the SEM and its development. For the theoretical debate, see Armstrong and Bulmer (1998), Cowles (1997), Majone (1996), Moravcsik (1991), and Sandholtz and Zysman (1989). For discussions of the political dynamics of the SEM, see Armstrong and Bulmer (1998), Scharpf (1999), and Young and Wallace (2000).

Armstrong, K., and Bulmer, S. (1998), *The Governance of the Single European Market*

(Manchester: Manchester University Press).

Cockfield, Lord (1994), *The European Union: Creating the Single Market* (London: Wiley Chancery Law).

Commission (1995), *Preparation of the Associated Countries of Central and Eastern Europe for Integration into the Internal Market of the Union, White Paper*, COM (95) 163 final.

Commission (2002c), *The Internal Market: Ten Years without Frontiers*.

Commission (2004a), *Report on the Implementation of the Internal Market Strategy (2003–6)*, COM (2004) 22 final.

Cowles, M. G. (1997), 'Organizing Industrial Coalitions: A Challenge for the Future?', in Wallace and Young (eds.), *Participation and Policy-Making in the*

European Union (Oxford: Clarendon Press), 116–40.

Majone, G. (1996), *Regulating Europe* (London: Routledge).

Moravcsik, A. (1991), 'Negotiating the Single European Act: National Interests and Conventional Statecraft in the European Community', *International Organization*, 45/1: 19–56.

Pelkmans, J., and Winters, L. A. (1988), *Europe's Domestic Market* (London: Royal Institute of International Affairs).

Sandholtz, W., and Zysman, J. (1989), '1992: Recasting the European Bargain', *World Politics*, 42/1: 95–128.

Scharpf, F. W. (1999), *Governing in Europe: Effective and Democratic?* (Oxford: Oxford University Press).

Young, A. R., and Wallace, H. (2000), *Regulatory Politics in the Enlarging European Union: Balancing Civic and Producer Interests* (Manchester: Manchester University Press).

Chapter 5
Competition Policy
Challenge and Reform

Stephen Wilks

Contents

Summary

European competition policy has steadily increased its effectiveness in controlling restrictive practices, abuse of dominant position, mergers, state aid, and the liberalization of utilities. Its success rests on the free-market approach now dominant in all European Union (EU) countries including the new member states. The central dominance of the Directorate-General for Competition (ex DGIV, now DG COMP) in the Commission has been challenged by the rapid growth and sophistication of the national competition authorities, and by increased criticism from the European courts in respect of procedure, interpretation, and economic analysis. The problems have been magnified by the scale of the workload. The Commission has responded with a bold strategy to decentralize the implementation of the competition rules through the so-called Modernization Regulation. This initiative emerges from a law-dominated epistemic community and sets in place a pan-European European Competition Network (ECN) which has the characteristics of a 'steered network', but may well reinforce the influence of European competition law and the dominance of the Commission. Competition policy is thus entering a period of potential instability as the Commission, the member states, and their competition authorities negotiate working relationships in the new world of the decentralized application of competition rules.

Introduction: competition policy and the European market

Competition policy is concerned with setting standards of conduct rather than with obtaining tangible goals, and is anchored in the principles of free-market capitalism. The character and role of competition policy have therefore been controversial across the European Union (EU) and in individual member states. Its development reflects the very varied economic systems ranging from highly liberalized markets, to those where the state has played an important role in the economy, to the post-socialist states which only started to embrace capitalism in the 1990s (Schmidt 2002). European competition policy is broad and includes antitrust, merger control, and the control of state aid (subsidies to industry). Its overall thrust has been to press on every front for the liberalization of markets.

Competition policy draws its importance from the central role that economic factors and market principles have had in the creation of the EU. The vision in 1958 was of a common market which would generate benefits for all participants through market integration. This was a liberal-economic vision, then controversial, which rested on a faith in traditional market capitalism. The vision was the natural alternative to the centrally planned economies of eastern Europe, but it was also regarded sceptically by many west European business and policy élites. It became a dominant principle only as a result of the neo-liberal revolution of the 1980s and the single market programme of 1992 (see Chapter 4). This vision was consolidated by the collapse of Soviet communism and the re-modelling of the economic systems of control in eastern Europe in alignment with the capitalist norms of the Union. Under free-market capitalism competition is the central dynamic of entrepreneurial activity and the means of energizing the economic system to deliver welfare benefits. Those aspects of economic life which hinder competition—monopoly, oligopoly, cartels, restrictive practices, market-sharing, subsidies, and state protection—also prevent it from generating and distributing wealth efficiently. Just as the European Central Bank (ECB) guarantees a sound currency and low level of inflation, so the EU competition rules guarantee a free market and economic efficiency, providing a kind of 'economic constitution' for Europe.

This emphasis placed upon the market and economic integration means that competition policy has been somewhat more important in the EU than elsewhere (with the exception of the USA, and possibly Germany). The Commission has expanded competition policy as one of its key EU competences. It has drawn on powerful treaty provisions, received support from the European Court of Justice (ECJ), and entrusted policy to DG COMP, one of the most effective Directorates-General (DGs) in the Commission, directed by a series of able commissioners. Competition policy has taken on some characteristics of a 'meta-policy', thus taking precedence over less developed policy areas (such as industrial, R&D, or environmental policy), or framing specific sectoral policies (such as media, telecoms, etc.). Indeed, competition policy has been used to discipline governments as well as companies, so that all economic actors must understand it and treat it with respect.

The salience of competition policy

Competition policy is about protecting and expanding competition as a process of rivalry between firms in order to win customers, and also as a process of creating and protecting markets. There are both political and economic rationales for competition policy. The prior political rationale comprises a commitment by governments to allow economic actors freedom to compete in the market, and to protect consumers from exploitation by powerful companies. The US is the home of competition policy, where it is still called 'antitrust', which reveals its origins in the late nineteenth century as a commitment to protect 'the little man' from the power of the big industrial 'trusts'. The more recent economic rationale is still controversial. It is based on the standard neo-classical theories of market competition, which affirm that competition creates wealth through the generation of economic efficiency, both productive efficiency (making more goods for the same cost), and allocative efficiency (giving consumers what they want). Accordingly Motta (2004: xvii) defines competition policy as 'the set of policies and laws which ensure that competition in the market place is not restricted in such a way as to reduce economic welfare'. Thus, economies where competitive pressure is intense will be more efficient than those where it is restrained, an influential argument made by Michael Porter (1990), which encouraged the Commission to reinforce competition policy as a way of making the European economy more competitive within globalized markets. This position was reinforced at the 2000 Lisbon European Council which laid out a new economic reform and competitiveness agenda, which was flagged during autumn 2004 by the incoming president of the Commission as a key priority (Commission 2004c). Competition should also be seen as a way to secure consumer welfare, although the relationship between competitiveness and consumer welfare provides a theoretical and practical tension in the operation of policy (Motta 2004: 19–30; Veljanowski 2004: 163).

The impact of EU competition policy has become far more evident on a day-to-day basis, as it increasingly affects how we do our jobs, how benefits are distributed, and how and what we consume, from football to cosmetics, the price of cars, and the proximity of supermarkets. This means that a policy area which was traditionally regarded as specialist and arcane has begun to make the headlines. This applies to the big merger cases, such as *Nestlé/Perrier* in 1993, *Boeing/McDonnell Douglas* in 1997, and *GE/Honeywell* in 2001 which also stretch beyond intra-EU cases to those with a global or extraterritorial dimension. In the *Boeing* and *GE* cases the European Commission prohibited mergers between these huge US companies due to their adverse impact on the EU market. The US was outraged and media coverage was intense. Competition issues also surface in some of the big state aid cases, such as the Commission's demand that the French electricity monopoly, EdF, be required to repay €900 million in unlawful tax breaks to the French government (*Times*, 17 October 2002). 'Big name' cases also attract great public interest, such as the Commission's findings that Microsoft abused its near monopoly and acted illegally in bundling its 'media player' software into its Windows operating system. The Commission ruled that Microsoft share details of its software design with competitors and in March 2004 Mario Monti, the Competition Commissioner, announced a fine of €497 million, the highest ever against a single company, which produced headlines such as 'Mario Monti's Broken Windows', and even 'The Full Monti' (*Financial Times*, 25 March 2004).

Such headlines dramatize the key element in assessing the impact of competition policy, and the way in which it structures the business environment for companies across Europe. EU competition policy has a 'direct effect' on companies, but until approximately a decade ago most companies treated competition policy as an after-thought, to be taken into account when drafting a major agreement, entering a joint venture, or contemplating a merger, but not at the heart of decision-making. By contrast, today, the 'competition rules' are a dominant regulatory constraint when companies formulate their corporate strategy or consider their competitive behaviour. They employ legal expertise to advise on the impact of the rules and most big firms will have an in-house 'compliance programme' to train their staff to avoid breaching the competition provisions. This shift in corporate awareness is partly due to the steady refinement and expansion of the law and the activism of the competition authorities. For corporate executives the most extreme threat is 'dawn raids' when competition officials swoop on factories, offices, and private residences across several countries to seize papers and computers in order to find evidence of secret agreements, or 'cartels' to manipulate markets. In 1996 there were only four dawn raids, but in 2003 there were twenty-one (Guersent 2003). Some arose from the successful adaptation by the Commission of a US-style leniency programme, a system of exemptions for 'whistleblowers' who provide information about a cartel in which their firms are involved. The intensification of action, in particular against 'hard core' cartels, has resulted in a huge escalation of fines. In 2001, the Commission fined fifty-six companies a total of €1,836 million, more than the cumulative total of all fines levied in the history of competition law. The first fine was imposed in 1986, and in the 1980s fines totalled only €134 million, whereas in the 1990s the cumulative total was €946 million, and in the period 2000–2003 a massive €3,080 million was levied. The biggest fines were against thirteen companies found guilty in the vitamins cartel organized by Hoffman La Roche (fined €462 million), and BASF (fined €296 million) (Arbault and Suurnakki 2002: 32–3; Guersent 2003). Policies that pack this sort of punch simply cannot be ignored.

It is worth remembering that competition policy was not always regarded with such approval and was once regarded as wasteful and destructive. For instance, in the Netherlands and Austria there was a widespread belief that 'strict competition policy would lead to cut-throat competition and decrease competitiveness' (van Waarden and Drahos 2002: 932), a belief echoed in the UK (Wilks 1999: 12). The use of cartels was widespread and not regarded as essentially illegitimate until the late 1960s. The industrial policies of many west European countries rested upon nationalization, selective intervention, indicative planning, encouragement of concentration and economies of scale, and the support of 'national champions'. Although these indus-trial policies are now largely discredited, they still attract some support among trade unions and national politicians. Thus, there remains a tension between competition policy and company support, as well as with policies to encourage regional economic development, science and technology, and small and medium-sized enterprises. In all these areas competition is being distorted by governments for alternative policy goals.

This move from planning intervention to the liberalization of markets and competition has a particular contemporary dimension *vis-à-vis* the recent enlargement of the EU in 2004. For over forty years eight of these ten new member states, with a population of 72 million, had centrally planned economies in which competition was an alien concept and capitalism was condemned. These countries have telescoped the post-war years of west European economic evolution into ten years as they have adopted the EU competition policy embodied in the *acquis communautaire*, as part of the Europe Agreements (see Chapter 16). All these countries now have competition laws, competition agencies, and a commitment to competition, out of which the Commission hopes to create a 'common competition culture'. Competition policy thus emerges as an essential component for making enlargement work and ensuring that diverse economic systems converge with the market principles that unify the EU economy.

The substance of policy

There are five components of European competition policy, each of which relies on specific legal powers:

- a prohibition on agreements between firms that limit competition (Art. 81 TEC; ex Art. 85 EEC);
- a prohibition on the abuse of a dominant position by one or more large firms (Art. 82, TEC; ex Art. 86 EEC);
- the control of mergers which create a dominant position (Regulation No. 4064/89);
- the control of aid given by a member state to a firm or category of firms (Arts. 87 and 88 TEC; ex Arts. 92 and 93 EEC); and
- the liberalization of measures by member states to favour domestic utilities, and infrastructure industries (Arts. 31 and 86 TEC; ex Arts. 37 and 85 EEC).

The sophistication and effectiveness of these components has grown over time (see Box 5.1), to create a complex agglomeration of principles and powers enshrined in practice and case law. Effective control of state aid began only in the late 1980s, control of mergers in the early 1990s, and liberalization of utilities in the late 1990s. At the heart of competition policy, however, is the prohibition on anti-competitive agreements. The first major decision taken by the Commission under Article 81 (TEU) (ex Art. 85 EEC) came in 1964, giving us forty years of development of case law, and illustrating the dynamics of competition enforcement. The Commission found that Grundig had acted illegally in granting an exclusive dealership to its French subsidiary, thus prohibiting 'parallel imports' (i.e. from other European countries). Here we see the single market imperative of integration, and the crucial role of the ECJ, which upheld the decision in *Consten and Grundig* v. *Commission* (1966), and provided

---

Box 5.1 Stages in the development of EU competition policy

	1960s	1970s	1980s	1990s	2000+
(1) Antitrust: agreements	Regulation 17; cases	develop principles	first fines	enforcement intensified	stress cartels; modernization
(2) Antitrust: abuse of dominance	dormant	first cases	develop principles; first fines	idea of collective dominance	moderate application; modernization
(3) Merger control	not in Treaty	no action[1]	Regulation in 1989	early enforcement	intensified and reform
(4) State aid	dormant	gradual development	becomes priority; first survey 1988	tighter sectoral regimes	Lisbon reinforces; steady progress
(5) Liberalized utilities	ignored[2]	ignored	more transparency; action on telecoms	becomes priority systematic challenge	continued pressure; mixed progress

[1] 'no action' means that the problem was recognized but could not be acted on without legal powers;
[2] 'ignored' means that the problem was not recognized.

---

an expansive definition of the legal term 'affecting trade' by looking at the potential effect on trade in the industry as a whole. The first three components of policy affect private sector companies, the last two, state aid and liberalization, are unique to the EU because they are targeted at the governments of the member states. The following sections review each area, concentrating on the private sector components.

Antitrust: restrictive practices

Policy on anti-competitive agreements, or restrictive practices, is specified in Article 81 which 'prohibits' all agreements and concerted practices between firms that affect trade between member states and 'have as their objective or effect the prevention, restriction or distortion of competition within the common market'. The Article also specifies exemptions from the prohibition in cases where an agreement 'contributes to improving the production or distribution of goods or to promoting technical or economic progress' (Art. 81(1) TEC, ex Art. 85(1) EEC; and Art. 81(3) TEC, ex Art. 85(3) EEC). These provisions raise extraordinary problems of interpretation. Taken literally, virtually every agreement will 'restrict or distort' competition, that is what agreements are for and every business spends much of its time and energy in foiling its competitors. On the other hand, some agreements foster competition, although interpretation will often depend on the theoretical biases of the economic analysis involved. In practice, implementation has allowed extensive discretion to the case officials in DG COMP; their interpretations of the rules have usually been confirmed in appeals to the ECJ, and only occasionally overturned.

On the basis of case law and accepted economic theory some practices are presumed to be illegal (Goyder 2003: 97). These include resale price maintenance, horizontal price fixing, export bans, and market sharing. Such practices tend to be administered through cartels among competitors in an industry so as to create or protect a collect-ive monopoly and to make excess profits. There is little doubt that cartels still prolif-erate across Europe and that the Commission has put the attack on cartels at the heart of its enforcement effort. Evidence secured by the Commission reveals astonishing illegal practices by leading companies and senior executives meeting in secret, using codes and subterfuge to outwit the authorities, which in 2001 alone prosecuted cartels in sodium gluconate, vitamins, citric acid, beer, bank charges, and (photo)copier paper. Indeed, there are serial offenders such as *Hoffman La Roche* found in breach of Article 82 (TEC) (ex Art. 86 EEC) in the famous 1979 vitamins case, and of Article 81 (TEC) (ex Art. 85 EEC) in 2002. In 2002 the Commission also concluded its first cartel case in the world of banking when it found that Austrian banking was organized by a cartel known as 'The Lombard Club', which covered all banking products, services, and advertising 'down to the smallest village' (Guersent 2003: 55). At the other end of the spectrum the majority of agreements will be perfectly legal. This applies to most distribution agreements, supply agreements (including discounts), and the many small agreements which only affect a small section of the market. Many agreements will also be exempt because they aid efficiency and 'economic progress'. In order to provide certainty the Commission has issued about a dozen 'block exemptions', which define acceptable agreements in areas such as technology, R&D, maritime transport, and insurance (Goyder 2003: 114–15). Similarly principles have evolved to define the legal-ity of agreements relating to intellectual property (where it can be pro-competitive to cooperate), and in respect of 'vertical agreements', that is, agreements between enter-prises at different stages in the supply chain, which are now generally regarded as acceptable. This is in contrast to the horizontal agreements between competitors at the same level in the supply chain which often have cartel-like qualities and are regarded with suspicion.

Antitrust: abuse of dominance

While the control of restrictive practices is regarded as a Commission success story, the same cannot be said of the second component of competition policy, controlling the abuse of dominance. This is covered by Article 82 (TEC) (ex Art. 86 EEC) which prohibits 'any abuse by one or more undertakings of a dominant position within the common market'. This prohibition is aimed at monopolies or, since full monopoly is rare, at oligopoly, where a small number of firms dominate a market. European governments are decidedly ambivalent about the control of oligopoly, the law itself has several significant flaws, and the Commission has been hesitant about exploiting this aspect of its powers. Cini and McGowan (1998: 94) go as far as to assert that 'the

Commission's monopoly policy has been largely ineffective'. This is an overstatement, but implementation is indeed impeded by the complex dynamics between the Commission and the member states.

For member states large companies have several attractive features. They enjoy economies of scale, they have financial muscle, and are representative of national industrial prowess, but most of all they can fund high technology and may operate as powerful multinationals able to compete directly with Japanese and US multinationals in global markets. These are the classic features of 'national champions', and many governments, including those of France, Germany, Italy, and the Netherlands, have been loath to see these benefits eroded by active attack from the competition authorities, particularly since Article 82 (TEC) (ex Art. 86 EEC), unlike Article 81 (TEC) (ex Art. 85 EEC), does not provide for an efficiency defence. This in part explains the hesitancy of the Commission, Article 82 (TEC) (ex Art. 86 EEC) is, however, also unsatisfactory in that it requires that the authorities first establish dominance (usually taken as at least 40 per cent of the market as indicated in the 1978 *United Brands* judgment, Whish 2003: 182); and only then can they establish 'abuse'. The law is also weak in attacking oligopolies. The Commission has attempted to establish a principle of 'collective dominance' (several companies working together in an oligopoly), but it was not until the *Italian Flat Glass* case in 1992 that it received any encouragement from the Court of First Instance (CFI), and even now the concept is not sufficiently robust (Sufrin 2000: 144). If successful in establishing illegal abuse the Commission has powers to fine, to issue a 'cease and desist' order, and in theory to enforce diversification. This last option, requiring the break up of a monopoly, is the anti-trust equivalent of a nuclear strike and has never been imposed by the Commission. In 2003 only three decisions were taken under Article 82 and they were all directed against utilities in telecoms and railways. Very few actions have been taken against the bigger European companies.

Merger control

The third component of policy is the control of mergers and acquisitions that have the potential to generate monopolies. This is the dramatic, and often controversial, face of competition policy since its main target is big firms. It attracts huge media attention and frenzied political lobbying so that big mergers present theatrical shows of Shakespearean proportions. They affect thousands of jobs, transform household name companies, make or break fortunes in financial markets and establish or destroy the reputations of captains of industry. In most EU countries, unlike the UK, 'hostile' takeovers (i.e. without the agreement of the management of the target company) are unusual and provoke acute opposition. Since 1990 DG COMP has, for example in 2003, approved (with conditions) the *Pfizer/Pharmacia* merger to create the largest pharmaceutical company in the world, and the *Pechiney/Alcan* merger (again with conditions) to create the largest aluminium company in the world. This constitutes a huge deployment of economic power and the Commission is playing on a global stage. When it blocks an international merger, as with *GE/Honeywell* in 2001, the conflict extends to the highest possible level. In this case the *GE/Honeywell* merger was the largest proposed merger in history and was approved by the US anti-trust authorities.

The Commission's rejection resulted in the merger being abandoned, but only after furious lobbying by US politicians amidst a blaze of publicity, threats of retaliation, and fresh doubts about US–Europe relations.

The Merger Regulation (Regulation 4064/89 amended by Regulation 1310/97) emerged as a result of a decade of pressure from DG COMP which persuaded the European Council finally (and rather reluctantly) to enact it in 1989. It came into effect in September 1990 and was regarded as the crowning triumph of Sir Leon Brittan's highly successful period as Competition Commissioner. It established the prestige and influence of the DG and prompted the conclusion that, by the early 1990s, the European competition regime had become globally pre-eminent (Wilks with McGowan 1996: 225). The Merger Regulation created a 'one-stop shop' which permitted the Commission to control the largest mergers above a high threshold (mergers below the threshold continue to be dealt with under national legislation). The current threshold is set at an aggregate turnover of €2,500 million (Whish 2003: 811), which catches around 300 mergers a year. Companies are in favour of the EU process which is rapid, transparent, and avoids having to seek approval from every state in which they operate. Cases can, however, be transferred. Compromises reached during the passage of the Regulation introduced Article 9, the 'German clause', so-called because it was demanded by the German authorities which wanted the opportunity to control large national mergers. It allows the Commission to give jurisdiction to a member state. On the other hand, Article 23, the 'Dutch clause', was demanded by the Dutch authorities and allows a member state to request the Commission to act on its behalf, and also (in the most recent reforms of 2003) allows the merging parties themselves to request that the Commission handle the case (Commission 2004p: 65). The Commission has pressed for greater flexibility in case handling and, in a spirit of subsidiarity, regularly transfers jurisdiction to national competition authorities (NCAs).

DG COMP rose to the merger challenge and created an effective Merger Task Force as a specialized directorate (abolished in 2004). It implements a logical two-stage process in which most mergers are cleared within one month and only the difficult cases are examined in more depth through the 'phase two' procedure. The Task Force soon earned a reputation for efficiency which put into stark relief the delays in other parts of the DG. The objective is to block or amend mergers which threaten to create a dominant position which they might then abuse. The wording of the test is of vital importance and in 2003 the Commission persuaded the Council to pass a reformed Merger Regulation which introduced an adaptation to the wording of the test (Regulation 139/2004; Commission 2004p: 59–68). This retains the dominance test which has been extensively criticized by the US and the UK (which both now use the 'substantial lessening of competition' test, Vickers 2003: 102), but it now prefaces it by attacking 'a concentration which would significantly impede effective competition'. This change may tighten European merger control, although it will continue to be based on an economic test rather than on public-interest or non-economic considerations. Throughout the 1990s the Commission gained confidence, won court cases, and became gradually more interventionist. It is still very unusual for a merger to be blocked completely (the Commission has only blocked eighteen mergers in the period 1990–2003), but it is becoming increasingly normal to accept or impose conditions before approving the merger (often divestiture of part of the merged entity). On this

Table 5.1 Merger regulation cases, 1990–2003

Year	Notifications	Phase 1 Approved	Phase 2		
			Approved No Conditions	Approved Conditions	Refused
1990	12	5	0	0	0
1991	63	50	1	3	1
1992	60	47	1	3	0
1993	58	49	1	2	0
1994	95	80	2	2	1
1995	110	93	2	3	2
1996	131	109	1	3	3
1997	172	120	1	7	1
1998	235	219	3	4	2
1999	292	255	0	8	1
2000	345	321	3	12	2
2001	335	312	5	10	5
2002	279	250	2	5	0
2003	212	223	2	6	0
Total	2,399	2,133	24	68	18

Sources: Whish (2003: 860); Commission (2004p: 61).
Note: lines do not add up horizontally due to notifications withdrawn or settled the following year.

basis the Commission built up to a crescendo of activity in 2000 when it received 345 notifications and intervened in over forty cases, 12 per cent of the total (see Table 5.1; Veljanovski 2004: 156–7).

Since 2000, merger policy has suffered some major setbacks. In 2001 the prohibition of the *GE/Honeywell* merger precipitated a torrent of criticism from the US accusing the Commission of arrogance, poor economics, outdated thinking, and incompetent analysis. The 'hammer blow' came in June 2002 when a CFI judgment overturned the Commission's prohibition of the *Airtours/First Choice* merger, the first appeal that DG COMP had lost. The shock was compounded by two further defeats in the *Schneider Electric* and *Tetra Laval* cases later in 2002. The CFI was damning. It criticized the Commission processes, its use of evidence, its reasoning, the quality of its economic analysis, and stated that the Commission had committed 'manifest errors of assessment' (Veljanovski 2004: 184). This led US critics to renew their allegation that the Commission was defending 'competitors not competition' or, in other words, protecting big European companies and not the interests of consumers (which is now the main declared objective of US antitrust policy).

In response the Commission moved to reform the merger regime. The changes are significant but not revolutionary. The new 2004 Regulation amends the merger test, makes the process more transparent, and introduces further flexibility in allocating merger cases between the Commission and member states.

One of the main changes is more informal and involves the deliberate reinforcement of economic analysis across the DG. This is symbolized by the creation of a new post of chief economist filled by Professor Lars-Hendrik Röller from Humboldt University for a three-year term. Mario Monti, Director-General of DG COMP for 2000–4 and himself an economist, noted revealingly that 'to develop an economic interpretation of EU competition rules was . . . one of my main objectives when I took office' (Monti 2003: 7). Where the balance is struck between law and economics and, indeed, what sort of economics is employed, will have a marked effect on the development of policy in mergers and across the entire policy area.

State aid

With the fourth component of policy, state aid, the style and focus of policy takes on a very different form. Here the treaty powers are less clear, the processes of implementation are less powerful, and the Commission typically enjoys less cooperation from national governments which are themselves the targets of control. In this area (as with the liberalization of utility regulation) the Commission is more than the agent of the member governments; it transcends national interests and aspires to be truly 'supranational'. Despite national hesitation the state aid regime has chalked up significant successes and has consolidated an historic move away from state subsidization of industry and, indeed, away from traditional industrial policy.

Article 87 (TEC) (ex Art. 92 EEC) affirms that aid to business, whether private or state-owned, which distorts competition is 'incompatible with the common market'. This applies most blatantly to direct state subsidies to companies. However, the concept extends to all forms of assistance, including tax breaks, preferential purchasing, loans, and even loan guarantees. Some forms of aid, and especially large subsidies, were a major tool of industrial policy as recently as the 1980s. Periodic crises in industries such as shipbuilding, coal, steel, aerospace, and the motor industry persuaded governments to grant massive rescue subsidies. These have virtually been eliminated under the tightening state aid rules, but other aspects of aid may, as Cini and McGowan (1998: 137) point out, 'be a very good thing' in areas such as R&D, small enterprise, or backward regions, where it may help create competition and guarantee social benefits. All aid must be notified to the Commission which assesses its compatibility and has developed frameworks to examine sector-specific and regional aid. A particular problem exists with the new member states, where the use of state aid is still widespread, as has been the case vis-à-vis the eastern Länder in Germany following reunification. The initial emphasis has been on transparency rather than abolition. The intention is steadily to reduce aid levels, but it is recognized that, like drug withdrawal, it is dangerous to cut the dose overnight. In respect of all state aid there was no Council regulation until 1998 when Regulations were enacted to allow exemptions and streamline monitoring. Thus, the Commission does not have fully effective implementation powers. It can take decisions prohibiting aid or demanding repayment, but it prefers to try and persuade member governments to comply. An interesting example is provided by the attack on state (Land) guarantees against default or bankruptcy which have been provided by German state governments since 1897 for German public banks. These were the biggest ever aid cases considered by the Commission and it has taken ten years of patient negotiation to eliminate them (see Box 5.2; Moser, Pesaresi, and Soukup 2002).

Box 5.2 State aid to German public banks

Issue: since 1897 the German *Länder* governments have guaranteed the debts of all German public banks (Landesbanken and Sparkassen, over 1,200 banks accounting for one third of the German market). This made bankruptcy impossible and distorted the market by giving the public banks lower borrowing costs, lower risk exposure, and by restricting market entry. Although there was no direct public spending involved this was identified as the largest regular state aid in Europe worth about €1 billion per annum to the banks.

1996   First public criticism by the Commissioner, Karel van Miert provokes strong opposition from the German Federal and *Land* governments which argue that this is part of the 'legal constitution' and provides valuable stability.

1998   At the Amsterdam European Council Germans attempt to amend the Treaty to protect public banks; Commission issues a report on the financial sector suggesting aids are incompatible with the Treaty.

1999   The European Banking Federation lodges a formal complaint against the German system, pointing out that with the euro the problem is magnified.

2001   Commission raises a formal decision declaring the guarantees to be 'incompatible' with the common market. No objection to public ownership, just to the guarantees. Mario Monti, the Commissioner, meets German leaders and agrees a compromise with a four-year transition period and some lasting concessions.

2002   German Federal and *Länder* governments agree to phase out the guarantees.

2005   Guarantees for new liabilities due to end.

2015   Guarantees for existing liabilities due to end.

Implications: this represents a major political and economic victory for the Commission. It controls state aid in the financial markets under state aid rules and provides a model which allows the Commission to address similar practices in Austria and some of the new member states.

Source: Moser, Pesaresi, and Soukup 2002.

A useful technique, developed first when Peter Sutherland was Competition Commissioner in the late 1980s, has been to 'name and shame' governments and reveal the sheer scale of state aid through periodic surveys (Commission 2001f). This was reinforced by the 2000 Lisbon European Council which pressed the Commission to reduce the level of aid, faced with the accession of countries for which aid has been 'a way of life'. This prompted the creation of a state aid register and an on-line 'scoreboard' in 2001. The Commission found itself frequently working with the grain as national governments, especially the UK, made greater efforts to reduce the use of subsidies. In 1988 state aid accounted for about 10 per cent of public expenditure or 3–5 per cent of GDP, in other words, a hugely distorting degree of cross-subsidy from the taxpayer to industry. By 2002 the figure had fallen to about 1.2 per cent of public

Table 5.2 Levels of state aid by country

Annual averages, 1997–99 (ranked by € per person employed)

Country	total, bn. €	€ per capita	€ per person employed	% GDP	% govt spending
Finland	2.0	387	914	1.74	3.21
Luxembourg	0.2	514	912	1.31	3.04
Belgium	3.1	309	830	1.41	2.76
France	17.8	304	772	1.38	2.55
Germany	26.7	326	712	1.39	2.85
Ireland	1.1	288	706	1.36	3.75
Denmark	1.7	317	622	1.08	1.90
Italy	13.6	236	607	1.28	2.56
Austria	2.2	270	550	1.16	2.15
Sweden	1.8	203	436	0.84	1.35
Spain	6.1	155	416	1.17	2.80
Netherlands	3.2	202	406	0.90	1.90
Greece	1.3	124	338	1.21	2.70
Portugal	1.5	154	326	1.56	3.50
UK	7.6	128	280	0.60	1.47
EU15	89.9	240	563	1.18	2.44

Source: Commission 2001f: 22–3.

spending and 0.6 per cent of GDP (Cini and McGowan 1998: 145; Commission 2004p: 96). This is considerable progress, although the figures are still large and state aid still proliferates. The Commission is notified of over 500 aid schemes a year and takes over 400 decisions granting approval, often after the negotiation of amendments. Table 5.2 illustrates the diverse performance across the EU. Measured by subsidy levels per capita Germany emerges as one of the worst culprits and the neo-liberal UK one of the most reluctant to award subsidies. Nonetheless, Germany, together with Italy, Finland, and Greece, have all cut subsidies dramatically since the early 1990s.

The liberalization of utilities

The fifth and final component of competition policy concerns competition in the public sector and the privatized utilities. As with state aid, the primary target is the national governments which may own nationalized industries, grant monopoly powers to state or private utilities, or operate regulatory regimes which suppress competition. The industries in question are the key utility and infrastructure sectors, such as telecoms, energy, water, post, transport, and airlines, although the issues of state control also extend to the financial sector, insurance, and the media. State ownership of these industries had become the norm from the 1950s onwards and the fact that they were often 'network' industries was often used to justify them as 'natural monopolies', on the grounds that the need for maximum efficiency through a single network (as for electricity distribution) required operation by a single company. Moreover, since these industries performed public services they were deemed to operate in the public interest, and thus potentially exempt from competition law (see Chapter 10). In many countries exemptions were incorporated into national legislation. In the 1990s this immunity was challenged by technological change, by a shift towards market solutions, and by manifest evidence that such industries were inefficient, inflexible, and far too costly (Cini and McGowan 1998: ch. 9).

The case for liberalization in these sectors, in the interests of efficiency and European competitiveness, was underlined by the single market programme of 1992 (see Chapter 4), and by the example of the UK where privatization also showed how much change could be achieved. Despite its powers under Article 86(3) (TEC) (ex Art. 90(3) EEC) to require member states to liberalize utilities, the Commission recognized how delicate and political such moves could be in areas of such vital importance to the quality of life, which often excited great public support and were typically heavily unionized and politically powerful. The Commission did not feel politically confident enough to challenge member states until the late 1980s, when it began to develop a 'new' competition policy. This is still evolving and is primarily focused on those anti-competitive practices created mainly by governments through ownership and regulation. Considerable progress towards liberalization was made, especially in telecoms, but slowed down in the late 1990s and continues to be slow and difficult. The Commission has designed complex packages of measures, including directives, restrictive practices, and merger cases in order to liberalize sectors such as electricity, gas, postal services, and air transport. The sheer scale of activity illustrates both the dedication of DG COMP in pursuing competitive markets in every setting, and the political limits to what is achievable.

Thus, European competition policy has gone through a series of cycles of development (see Box 5.1) including a legal cycle of accumulation of jurisprudence (and the creation of a cadre of career competition specialists in big international law firms), and a cycle of generational change in DG COMP which by the late 1980s had brought in a generation of bright, committed young lawyers who regarded the expansion of the competition competence with ill-concealed enthusiasm (Wilks with McGowan 1996: 247). Competition policy also needs to be assessed against the economic cycle. In boom periods merger activity increases, state aid work decreases, and on the whole the DG faces less opposition. In recession companies and governments feel more vulnerable and the interventionist voices within the Commission and its other DGs begin to prevail. There has also been a cycle of economic theory and European competition enforcement has ridden on the wave of post-Thatcher neo-liberalism. In exploiting these stages of development the single most important element lies in the nature, leadership, and competence of the responsible agencies and their staff.

Agencies and implementation: DG COMP

The development and implementation of competition policy is centred in the Commission in a Directorate-General, formerly DG IV, now DG COMP. It is a small organization which employs nearly 700 staff of whom around half are senior officials who make decisions and contribute to policy. The senior ranks are dominated by lawyers who make up nearly half the senior staff, though economists are now beginning to play a greater role. Its political head is the Commissioner, from 1999 to 2004 Mario Monti, an experienced Italian economist, and from 2004 Neelie Kroes, a Dutch businesswoman in the Barroso Commission. DG COMP is regarded as one of the most attractive postings both for the Commissioner and for the Director General, and the relationship between them is of key importance. In 2002, Philip Lowe (British) who had also been the first head of the Merger Task Force, became Director General. Until Lowe's appointment all Directors General had been German so that Lowe was preceded by Claus-Dieter Ehlermann (1990–5), and by Alexander Schaub (1995–2002), giving the DG a distinctively German feel and perhaps some influence with the traditionally powerful German competition agency, the Bundeskartellamt (BKA). The DG was reorganized in 2004 in a surprising move which abolished the Merger Task Force and distributed merger control across five sectoral directorates. The current structure of nine directorates includes two dealing with state aid, two with planning, strategy, and international links, and five organized to engage with sectors of industry.

The sectoral approach is usual amongst competition agencies and is the model used by the BKA and the Office of Fair Trading (OFT). It was argued that the reorganization would enhance staff flexibility and speed up the handling of cases by exporting the rapid response developed in the Merger Task Force to the rest of the organization where severe delays have been routine (Lowe reported in *Financial Times*, 23 February 2004). One feature of DG COMP is that many of its senior officials have spent their entire careers in its ranks. This brings benefits of continuity but at the same time carries the risk of insularity. The Commission does not practise the 'revolving door' exchange of lawyers between the private and government sectors so typical of the US (Cini and McGowan 1998).

A key question when assessing DG COMP is its level of independence. Decisions affecting competition are made by the entire college of Commissioners who are expected to reach agreement as a collective body. Nevertheless, the Competition Commissioner must expect opposition to controversial policies and decisions; member governments often press 'their' commissioner to influence policy and decisions can rest on political negotiation and compromise, and will—albeit rarely—go to a vote, especially in cases of state aid. Observers often therefore point to 'the politicized nature of European competition policy' (Cini and McGowan 1998: 214), and 'the lack of independence of the Community competition law enforcement mechanisms' (Laudati 1996: 230). Clearly DG COMP is not immune from expressions of national interest, especially in the area of state aid. The extent of its vulnerability to industrial lobbying is less clear, although it is hard to believe that powerful European companies of the stature of Fiat, Philips, or Daimler could not bring influence to bear.

On the other hand, DG COMP is relatively free from control from the Council and the Parliament for two main reasons. First, in implementing specific treaty articles it enjoys unambiguous legal authority. Secondly, in 1962 the Council delegated to the Commission extensive procedural powers to implement the relevant articles, including powers to act unilaterally (free from the member states), and the sole power to grant exemptions from the main prohibition. These delegated powers were set out in Regulation 17/1962 and have been exploited so successfully that DG COMP can be regarded as more than a mere operating agency. It has become a trustee of the competition rules. Independence is far from absolute, but can be compared with the great independent regulatory agencies of the US, such as the Federal Trade Commission (FTC) (Wilks with McGowan 1996; Wilks with Bartle 2002), and is a prized feature of competition agencies the world over. It is regarded as essential to protect the absolute values of economic competition, to avoid improper influence by business, and to avoid self-interested influence by other government departments or agencies (and, in the EU by national governments who are one of the targets of implementation).

Some have argued that this independence should be recognized more explicitly by the creation of a European Cartel Office (ECO). This was first proposed by the Germans in the 1990s as a way of avoiding any residual political bias operating through the college of Commissioners. More recently it has been advocated as part of a plan to redesign the European institutions. Commissioners and senior officials from DG COMP have mostly opposed this suggestion, pointing out that it is quite proper for competition policy to take note of the economic and political context. Indeed, there is some concern that full legal independence might involve some degree of marginalization.

The theme of independence serves to underline the claim that DG COMP is the most powerful competition authority in the world. The scale of its competence is unique, embracing not only the standard competition areas, but also state aid and the liberalization of utilities. In the US there are two powerful authorities (the FTC and the Antitrust Division of the Department of Justice), and there much of the dynamism is due to private actions in the courts which are still very unusual in the EU. The BKA and the OFT are also highly effective, but both are overshadowed by Brussels and the BKA is losing prestige, while the OFT has yet to exploit its new powers fully under the 1998 Competition Act and the 2002 Enterprise Act. With a mere 300 senior officials to police a market of 320 million consumers (soon to rise to 400 million) DG COMP was, and remains, acutely understaffed. The only plausible explanation for under-resourcing is that the member states see resources as one of the few pragmatic ways in which to restrain the ambitions of the DG.

There has been repeated criticism of DG COMP from both businesses and legal firms for its lack of accountability. It is said that the Commission is 'prosecutor, judge and jury' or, to extend the metaphor, it is 'policeman, arbitrator, prosecutor, judge, jury and prison officer'. This criticism arises essentially from the Article 81 (TEC) (ex Art. 85 EEC) restrictive practices procedure. A case is opened either following a complaint or as a result of an in-house investigation ('policeman'). The case is handled by one senior member of staff, the *rapporteur*, who investigates the abuse and often negotiates with the companies involved to change their practices ('arbitrator'). If this fails the *rapporteur* constructs a case, argues it in the office, discusses it with the Legal Service, and presses for a decision ('prosecutor'). Senior staff of the DG decide ('jury'), and settle on a penalty ('judge') which is then imposed or negotiated with the companies ('prison officer'). Not all of this is done by the same person, but much rests in the hands of the *rapporteur* and the whole process takes place within one organization, albeit with attention to natural justice and arrangements such as access to the file, information meetings, as well as the involvement of a neutral 'Hearings Officer' to see fair play. Despite efforts to improve accountability, and despite the independent sanction of the courts, there is some truth in the accountability criticism. As DG COMP has become more powerful so the problem has become more acute. The decentralization of implementation discussed below does not solve the problem where DG COMP retains control of a case.

DG COMP in context

How DG COMP operates has also to be seen in a broader EU institutional context, as well as within its network of national competition agencies. These constrain DG COMP, but can also be employed as sources of strength. No sector of industry is excluded from the competition rules although there are some exemptions, particularly in agriculture. Thus, all the sectoral DGs such as Transport and Energy need to cooperate with DG COMP. As regards competitiveness and market integration DG Internal Market and DG Industry are key partners. Historically, DG COMP and DG Industry were often at loggerheads, but today relations are less tense, and DG Industry has accepted the argument that strong competition enhances productivity and competitiveness (Commission 2004*o*, 2004*p*). The other interesting link concerns policy for consumer protection. Competition and consumer protection are combined in some national agencies (such as the OFT in the UK, and the FTC in the US), but DG COMP lost consumer protection in 1967, currently assigned to DG SANCO (health and consumer protection) (see Table 3.2). Stung by criticism from the US, DG COMP has stressed its role in serving the interests of consumers and in 2003 appointed a Consumer Liaison Officer to initiate a 'consumer dialogue'.

A constraint on DG COMP is the EU legal apparatus. Within the Commission the Legal Service has to be consulted about all legally binding acts and is therefore in constant contact with the DG. The Legal Service represents the Commission before the ECJ and the Court of First Instance (CFI), and is inherently risk-averse, which at times causes serious tension. The European courts themselves are very important. The ECJ and the CFI, created in 1986, provide the cement of European integration and are the most 'federal' of the European institutions. The ECJ was originally the venue for litigation and appeals in competition matters, and issued a series of key judgments, which not only supported the Commission, but defined market integration as a central goal of European competition policy (a goal unique to the European regime). The Court affected the development of policy in three ways. First, by establishing the supremacy of European law, it bolstered the powers of DG COMP, thus symbolizing the 'Community method' of policy-making. Secondly, like the Supreme Court in the US, it has become a policy-shaper in its own right. Its landmark decisions have developed the law through cases that have become as influential as the legislation itself, with principles and precedents that echo down the years of policy development. Thirdly, in a more subtle process, the Court has also established the influence of its distinctive legal methodology. In early cases such as *Société Technique Minière* v. *Maschinenbau Ulm* (1965) the Court dealt with the exclusive dealership issue, using a formal logic which not only carefully applied each term in the legislation, but also stressed the importance of employing economic analysis. Thus, Cini and McGowan (1998: 55) observed that 'the acceptance by national judges of the formalism of European law has been the Court's defining achievement'. This has become steadily more important as NCAs have acquired powers directly to implement the competition rules, and as national courts have therefore had to draw on the collected jurisprudence of the European Courts when reaching judgments.

The overload of complex and detailed competition cases led to the creation of the CFI as a junior court under the 1986 Single European Act. The CFI has a less formal procedure and is more specialist; it hears the majority of competition cases in small panels of five judges and in some cases (such as mergers) can operate rapidly through an 'expedited process'. The CFI has been less forgiving than the ECJ, which had been accused of being too lenient to DG COMP, especially over procedural inadequacies. In contrast the CFI has been rigorous and has reinforced the need for procedural correctness over matters such as giving a fair hearing, defining the exact case to be answered, and setting out key evidence. In more recent cases the CFI has also challenged the substantive content of decisions, challenged the reasoning and the interpretation of the evidence and emphasizing the need for more rigorous economic analysis. Thus, we are seeing a shift to a more adversarial stance in the relationship between the Commission and the Court. But the key point remains—that competition policy is being taken forward through a framework of European law within which policy developments are discussed, enacted, and resolved in a legal environment and using a legal discourse.

A third contextual factor in the Commission's ability to develop competition policy lies in its relationship with the NCAs in the member states which may include executive agencies, courts, tribunals, or government departments. In 1958 there was virtually no competition machinery in the member states (even the German BKA was not operational until late 1958), making it easier for policy to be centralized in Brussels. Over the ensuing years every member state has created its own competition agencies and appeals system. Some member states, such as the UK, Ireland, and Austria, had their own antitrust traditions embodied in laws and agencies which predated their EU membership. There is thus a pattern of long-established agencies, such as the BKA and the OFT, followed by creation or reform of established agencies in the other fifteen members up to the late 1990s. In each case the legislation and the agency roles have converged on the model of European law and DG COMP (Drahos 2001; van Waarden and Drahos 2002). The ten new members of 2004 were not given any choice. Acceptance of the competition rules and the entire weight of European jurisprudence as part of the *acquis* were conditions of accession, as was the allocation of reasonable resources to support active competition agencies and courts.

The creation of twenty-five competition regimes across the EU underlines the success of the Commission in embedding competition as a constitutive element of economic regulation, but also highlights the under-resourcing of DG COMP. In 2003, for instance, it had a budget of approximately €60 million and employed 300 'A grade' staff. In contrast, the competition agencies of the four biggest member states (Germany, France, Italy, and the UK) had a collective budget of about €120 million and employed 940 staff (all grades). In 2002 the UK alone, in the midst of a reform and expansion of its competition agencies, employed nearly as many staff and had a bigger budget than DG COMP (Global Competition Review 2003). For the smaller countries DG COMP has taken on a parental role in encouraging and training new competition agencies, a process which includes systematic exchange of staff.

Modernization of European competition policy

For over ten years DG COMP had discussed the possible decentralization of policy and the transfer of legal competence to member states. In April 1999 the team of Karel van Miert and Alexander Schaub issued a revolutionary White Paper on the *Modernization of the Rules Implementing Articles 81 and 82* (Commission 1999c). Modernization has changed the face of EU competition policy and the next section outlines the reforms, analyses their genesis, and speculates on their effects. In order to understand the revolutionary impact of modernization it is necessary to undertake a brief review of the previous system which for forty years had operated under Regulation 17/1962. It required all new agreements between firms that may affect trade between member sates to be notified to DG COMP which was required to evaluate the legality of huge numbers of submissions. The DG also had the key power of being the sole agency permitted to grant an exemption for an agreement under Article 81(3) TEC (ex Art. 85(3) EEC) in cases where an agreement could be said to contribute to efficiency and economic progress. These powers meant that Regulation 17/1962 was treasured by the DG as a precious source of authority which it was loath to give up. It feared that allowing NCAs to operate European competition policy would produce inconsistency, lax implementation, the substitution of national law, diverse economic and legal principles, delay, and the possible capture of policy by national industrial or political interests. Yet Modernization Regulation 1/2003 (Council of the European Union 2003), which came into effect in May 2004, surrendered the Commission's system of notification and its control of exemptions. As of May 2004 each NCA in the EU is free to apply Articles 81 and 82 (TEC) (ex Arts. 85-6 EEC), and each relevant national court is entitled to hear competition cases (see Box 5.3).

Part of the Commission's reason for the reforms was to free up resources to take more in-house initiatives, to use its enhanced powers of investigation much more effectively, and arguably to undertake more sectoral studies, but in particular to attack 'hard-core cartels'. The Commission's rhetoric has been fearsome, 'secret cartels between competitors are amongst the most damaging anti-competitive practices. Repeatedly denounced by Commissioner Monti as "cancers" affecting the economy, they are blatantly illegal' (Arbault and Suurnakki 2002: 15). In 1998 the Commission created a dedicated cartel unit, and added a second unit in 2002. It is attempting to increase international cooperation with the US and Canada in particular to attack cartels globally. Officials point out that cartels are not just a feature of the traditional industrial economy, but are found also in the 'new economy' of financial services, fine art auctions, and so forth. One prospect is therefore that the Commission will become an even more assertive agency, dominating the regulation of the European economy, but much depends on cooperation with the national authorities.

The Commission has established a dual strategy for mobilizing and disciplining the regiment of member state competition agencies. On the one hand, there is the legal apparatus contained in the Modernization Regulation, and on the other hand, there is the European Competition Network (ECN) which is informal and rests, at least in part, on voluntary cooperation. The Network consists of a series of (mainly virtual, electronic, and secure) links between all the formally designated NCAs and the Commission.

Box 5.3 The Modernization Regulation, 2003

- Deals with the implementation of the antitrust Arts. 81 and 82 TEC (ex Arts. 85–6 EEC), does not apply to mergers.
- Replaces Regulation 17/1962.
- Allows NCAs and national courts to apply Community law, including prohibitions, exemptions, fines, and the acceptance of commitments, but they cannot contradict or overrule Commission decisions.
- National authorities are obliged to apply Community law where the activity 'affects trade between member states'; this will marginalize national laws.
- Member states can apply stricter national laws as long as they are compatible with Arts. 81 and 82.
- Commission and NCAs should form a Network to exchange information and allocate cases. Member states designate authorities and courts to be their members of the Network.
- When the Commission initiates proceedings the national authorities have to withdraw (Art. 11(6)).
- Commission can exceptionally allow an agreement where justified by the Community 'public interest'.
- Advisory Committee will continue to meet to discuss policy and individual decisions.
- Commission acquires substantial new powers to make investigations, raid premises and homes, conduct interviews and seize material.

Source: Council Regulation 1/2003 of 16 December 2002 on the implementation of the rules of competition laid down in Arts. 81 and 82 of the Treaty [2003] OJ L1/1.

It provides the means for the mandatory exchange of information about cases and decisions, but also includes information, consultation, discussion, and debate. The Network is defined by means of a Commission Notice, a form of 'soft law' which the member states have all declared they will respect. The Notice declares that 'the Network is a forum for discussion and cooperation in the application and enforcement of EC competition policy' (Commission 2004*q*, para. 1). The ECN will undertake the crucial task of allocating cases between the NCAs and the Commission, on the following assumptions:

- the expectation that the NCA receiving the complaint or initiating the investigation will handle the case;
- that cases may be opened in parallel and closure by one NCA will not prevent another NCA taking action; and
- that where cases affect markets in more than three states the Commission will normally handle the case, and no other NCA can then act.

The Network could be described as a 'supervisory' mechanism which obliges all NCAs to inform the Commission within thirty days of a decision to open proceedings. The vital Article 11(6) of the Regulation allows the Commission to step in and open a case itself which, 'will relieve the competition authorities of the Member States of their competence'. This option to overrule the NCAs can be used in a wide range of circumstances, including when there is a disagreement between NCAs, a possible divergence from case law, if the proceedings are unduly slow, or if the Commission wishes to create new doctrine. In other words, the Commission would be able to 'cherry pick' all the interesting and important cases.

The effective operation of the Network requires trust and mutual understanding, and hence the Commission has, throughout this reform, emphasized the 'creation and maintenance of a common competition culture in Europe' (Commission 2004q: para. 1). Commission officials believe that just such a culture has developed over the past twenty years, but clearly there is work still to do to ensure that all national agencies in all countries (especially the new members) have a good understanding of the law and economics of competition and, moreover, that they are enthusiastic advocates. This makes the Network a fascinating experiment. It is a vehicle for the creation and dissemination of ideas, not just a vehicle for cooperation and exchange of information. This conjures up images of the models of network policy-making that have been identified by Majone (1996: 273) and Eising (1999) as a growing form of 'network governance' in the EU. On this basis the ECN begins to resemble the 'open method of coordination' outlined in Chapter 3. Parallels with network governance may, however, be misleading. The ECN is a consortium of public agencies, but one which is not sufficiently open to political debate. Indeed, its dynamics and influence are hard to predict. It may become a 'supervisory network', largely as the creature of DG COMP; it may become a 'coalition network' in which a small group of the more effective NCAs (such as the British OFT and the German BKA) could exert influence on their colleagues; it may become a 'protest network' through which the NCAs resist additional centralization in Brussels; and of course it might become a 'failed network', if the complexities of case allocation and the handling of many cases in parallel jurisdictions become unmanageable.

There are varying interpretations of why the Commission decided to propose this package of reforms and what its effect will be on the balance of power and the direction of policy. The two main views can be termed the 'partnership' view and the 'supranational' view. The partnership position takes the reforms at face value. They were put forward by the Commission as an exercise in decentralization through which the implementation of the competition rules would be 'shared' with the member states. Policy would operate through a partnership based on trust and cooperation. The implication was that the NCAs and their governments would be empowered as competition policy was extensively repatriated. This carried all the dangers of a centrifugal disintegration of policy, as each NCA operated differently and with varying degrees of efficiency, understanding, and national biases, including resort to their distinctive national laws. To ensure consistency across member states the Regulation therefore contains a series of formal and informal, legal and administrative safeguards. However, when the member governments approved the Regulation in the Council, they were endorsing a partnership logic.

The supranational view of the reforms looks at the legal and administrative arrangements in more detail. First it suggests that the reforms are not necessary. Secondly, it suggests that they tend to substitute EU law for national law for all significant economic transactions. Thirdly, it implies that the independence of the NCAs will be severely curtailed. And fourthly, that the modernization reforms constitute a substantial strengthening of DG COMP and increased centralization of competition policy. This thesis is now widely shared and has been articulated persuasively by Riley who writes that Regulation 1, 'for all the propaganda, does not amount to real cooperation' (2003: 664, 671–2), that 'it is the Commission who is the principal if not the sole beneficiary', and that 'the Commission has pulled off a political master-stroke'. The weight of legal comment points to the supranational view as being more plausible although the change is so substantial that it is difficult to predict the future balance of influence. The most revealing development will be the extent to which NCAs innovate and oblige DG COMP to change its policies. The message that the Commission has become even more powerful is beginning to receive wider recognition with, for instance, a *Europe Wall Street Journal* (23 January 2004) headline declaring 'EU is Set to Become a Tougher Antitrust Watchdog'—a message that the Commission is not inclined to contradict.

Competition policy as regulatory policy

Competition policy displays significant features of two of the policy models outlined in Chapter 3 (Community method, and regulatory policy), and shows virtually no similarity with the transgovernmental and distributional modes. However, recent reforms also indicate a limited move towards the policy coordination mode. It is not surprising that two of the policy modes are exemplified in competition policy. This policy area is both a leading example of the success of the Community method and provides much of the raw material that allowed Majone (1996) to develop his analysis of European regulation.

The main alignment of competition policy with the traditional Community method lies in the strong role for the Commission in designing and enforcing policy, especially over the period in which policy has been highly centralized and dominated by DG COMP. In competition policy the Commission has enjoyed exceptional freedom from the Council and the member governments. Its key partner is the courts, and so long as its actions are legally defensible the Commission has been able to act assertively and directly. In line with the Community method the Commission has pursued the goal of 'positive integration' with great determination. It has therefore sought to create a market without frontiers and has strongly attacked measures by firms (or governments) that segment markets, limit trade, or that apply different practices in different geographical areas. A key issue following modernization is whether this strong version of centralized policy will continue.

Competition policy exhibits an even closer resemblance to the regulatory mode of policy-making. This draws on the exceptionality fertile theories advanced by Majone (1996: 55, 287) about the position of the EU as a 'regulatory state', specifying behaviour in legislation and ensuring compliance through the legal system (Majone 1996: 63), where its ability to undertake regulatory policy is almost limitless. The legal process based on the treaty is enhanced by the legal apparatus of regulations and decisions supplemented by the 'soft law' of guidelines, frameworks, opinions, and notices, and has been reinforced by supportive judgments of the ECJ which have provided the foundation of Community competence. The primacy of Community law and the supremacy of the European courts mean that, as long as the Commission can win appeals in them, its decisions become binding on companies and governments across the EU—and sometimes extraterritorially. Moreover, this process is extremely inexpensive. The administrative costs of regulation are borne by the courts, the legal systems of the member states and by the clients of law firms, whilst the substantive costs of compliance and alterations of business practices are hidden and borne by firms.

The freedom of the Commission to regulate is enhanced by the weakness of the European Parliament, a feature shared in this field with national systems. Its legitimacy therefore rests on the acceptance of its market economy approach and ultimately on how far it succeeds in creating greater efficiency and ensuring some degree of equitable access to benefit from the wealth created. Majone (1996: 296, ch. 13), has argued, subtly and provocatively, that regulation does not need to be legitimized by control through the institutions of popular democracy, but can be legitimized through debate and deliberation between experts, observing due process and pursuing objective standards of efficiency. His analysis has stimulated a wider debate about 'non-majoritarian' agencies, and about the values of independence and expertise embodied in regulatory agencies. DG COMP of the Commission provides the classic example of independent European regulation (Wilks with Bartle 2002), perhaps as an extreme case of law-driven policy-making, conducted with a legal discourse through a network of legal institutions, courts, and law firms across the EU. Indeed, the recent process of modernization may perhaps best be understood as the mobilization of ideas through a legal community spreading across the member states.

Policy-making after modernization

The modernization reforms have, however, the potential to change the face of European competition policy and have created a startling new mode of policy formulation and implementation in the form of the ECN. Interpreting the impact of reform is difficult. It is quite possible that EU competition policy will roll forward in its familiar form in a process of 'path dependence' with the only major change being a coordinated implementation of familiar policy. On the other hand, modernization introduces some major areas of instability and presents possible alternative futures which are radically different from the past fifteen years of confident Commission leadership. The future shape of policy will be influenced by the politics of the new Commission and by the 'high politics' of economic policy in the stagnating economies of Germany and France. Modernization accentuates some aspects of the Community method (see Chapter 3), specifically in the legal powers which might reinforce the centralized initiating role of the Commission, and which certainly do nothing to introduce additional political or majoritarian controls. Curiously, modernization also reinforces aspects of the 'regulatory model', by further empowering the Commission as an independent regulatory agency, implementing a strengthened system of European law, and particularly downgrading the role of national competition law, which will be restricted to cases of a purely national nature. Especially interesting is the potential for the Commission to mobilize a supranational grouping of independent competition agencies in the member states and detach them from their national foundations.

The national agencies would be focused on European rules and pan-European priorities using their independence to ward off pressures from national governments and industry to create a sort of 'non-majoritarian alliance'.

This last option invites an evaluation of whether modernization and reform of merger policy can be seen as an example of the new policy mode of 'policy coordination'. The creation of independent competition agencies in all the member states since the mid-1980s means that the future implementation of policy will depend to a far greater extent on negotiation, coordination, and networking, as the coordination model both predicts and celebrates. This implies a far more volatile policy sector. As David Gerber observes, 'the courts and administrative bodies of the states will become the principal mechanisms for applying and enforcing Community law, and thus the relative power of Member States and the relative importance of their internal political landscapes will increase dramatically' reflecting 'a radical and uncharted revision of this power relationship' (Gerber 2001: 126, 128). He stresses the need for the Commission to build political support for competition policy. This suggests that the Commission may need to extend the debate about competition policy beyond a narrow legal or economic debate to assess it in terms of corporate accountability and its effects on other key policy areas such as regional development or the environment.

This chapter has stressed throughout that the power built up by agencies through effective implementation can also be deployed to take initiatives to 'make' policy in a field which reveals little by way of major political initiatives or diplomatic bargaining among member states. Much more important here have been the development and projection of ideas by (mainly legal) specialists operating in 'an epistemic community . . . a network of professionals with recognized expertise and competence in a particular policy domain and the authoritative claim to policy-relevant knowledge within that domain' (Haas 1992: 3). This fits competition policy well, where the relevant epistemic community embraces the senior officials of DG COMP, a selection of the senior people from the NCAs, prominent legal experts, the courts, the Legal Service of the Commission, and an international group of prominent academic lawyers. Latterly, the professional expertise of economists has also become more involved. Relevant 'technocrats' or policy-makers who have made their careers in competition law, embrace a commitment to competition as a benign process, and share a similar worldview. They are extremely influential in this technical world where political interests are either unclear or not articulated. Van Waarden and Drahos (2002: 931) argue that the power of this epistemic community provides the most persuasive explanation of why European competition regimes have converged. In similar terms this chapter suggests that the modernization reforms originated in the same epistemic community of experts, although it is less clear that it will be effective in implementing it.

Conclusion

This chapter argues that competition policy has a special place in the European policy matrix because it defends the essential mobilizing principle of the EU, the collective interest in economic efficiency secured through the creation of a common market.

But whilst its quasi-constitutional status makes it immune from drastic change it is not immune from criticism, and over recent years it has faced radical challenges in respect of administration, NCAs, doctrine, and competitiveness.

The challenge to administration arose from the overload suffered by DG COMP as a small centralized agency already overburdened with notifications and unable to cope with the additional workload from the ten new member states, and thus too tied to take the initiative, especially in prosecuting 'hard core cartels'. The challenge from the NCAs reflected their growth and increased competence which now offers a viable alternative to DG COMP and which in some respects offers superior analytical abilities based on more effective national laws. The challenge to doctrine is legal and economic. On the legal side, the challenge comes from the CFI which has questioned DG COMP's interpretation of legal provisions and procedural requirements to produce devastating defeats in the courts. On the economic side, criticism from economists has questioned DG COMP's treatment of vertical restraints, its doctrine of dominance, its merger test, its ability to grapple with the 'new' IT and service economy, and its inadequate commitment to consumers. Overall there has been damning criticism of its persistent lack of economic expertise. The challenge from competitiveness is linked to the relative stagnation of the EU within a globalized economy. The huge political debates in Germany, France, and across the continent pit the virtues of a neo-liberal free market against the traditional models of welfare capitalism. There is marked resistance to further liberalization and an increased inclination to favour state support for globally competitive corporations. In order to win the competitiveness argument competition policy needs to be linked to clear gains in European competitiveness and hence economic growth. Despite post-Lisbon attempts to make that link in fact the evidence is very difficult to mobilize and it is notoriously difficult to establish that micro-economic policies have identifiable macro-economic effects. The political-economic arguments for a further extension of neo-liberal competition are therefore under threat.

The response from the Commission has been bold and politically adept. As part of the post-Lisbon debate DG COMP has intensified its control of state aid, reorganized itself, increased its economic expertise, negotiated an improved merger regulation, and, most dramatically, transformed the enforcement of its core powers with the Modernization Regulation. In the interpretation offered here the epistemic community of policy-makers centred on DG COMP has managed to re-centre power in Brussels and has created a supervisory regime which has harnessed the multiple non-majoritarian agencies that make up the ECN. The key question is whether this new regime, which only came into effect in May 2004, will succeed in operating a coherent, consistent, and legally satisfactory regime which satisfies the NCAs and gives legal certainty to business. And an even bigger question, is whether it will deliver a more competitive European economy. It will be two to three years before there are adequate answers to these questions. In the meantime the concluding observation is of an exceptional level of instability in competition policy.

The period of uncertainty ushered in by the modernization reforms certainly provides the possibility that the pendulum of European policy-making may swing back from the Commission towards the national governments. Whether it does so may depend on how the NCAs in the member states choose to use their independence. Will they ally themselves with national governments and business communities which are seeking national routes to competitiveness? Or will they work within the ECN to create a novel and politically very significant supra-national network of non-majoritarian agencies across Europe?

In the coming years students of European competition policy will be observing an experiment unfolding as the relationship between Brussels and the agencies of the member states leads to new models of cooperation or conflict, and will be assessing how the new Commission rises to the challenges. It was reported that Mario Monti wished to serve a further term as Competition Commissioner. The Italian government refused to reappoint him so that the response to the challenge now lies in the hands of the new Dutch Commissioner, Neelie Kroes, and her colleagues in the Barroso Commission.

This chapter has argued that the independence, confidence, and competence of the Commission and DG COMP remains the key factor in determining the direction of policy-making. The Commission's power will be increased if economic growth recovers, if companies regard the modernized system positively, if NCAs cooperate willingly, and if neo-liberalism remains the dominant economic doctrine. Assessment of the future shape of policy will depend on how these four elements—of growth, compliance, cooperation, and economic doctrine—evolve.

Further reading

The best guide to the evolution of European competition policy is the Commission's annual report which provides a review of Commission and Court activities over the previous year, highlights strategic policy priorities, the Commission's own rationale, and, to some extent, the debates surrounding new initiatives. These latter aspects are also covered in the quarterly *Competition Policy Newsletter*, published by DG COMP. Both publications are available on the DG COMP website. More critical accounts of EU and member-state policy can be found in the *European Competition Law Review*.

A good introduction can be found in Cini and McGowan's (1998) comprehensive overview. An excellent introduction to the broader political context is provided by Amato (1997). A study emphasizing the German debates can be found in Gerber (1998), and further analysis of the Commission appears in Wilks (2005). The British House of Lords has undertaken some exceptionally useful investigations (see, for example, House of Lords 2002).

There is an excellent legal literature which is accessible to the general reader. Especially valuable are the opening and closing chapters of Goyder (2003), and the study by Drahos (2001).

Amato, G. (1997), *Antitrust and the Bounds of Power* (Oxford: Hart).

Arbault, F., and Suurnakki, S. (2002), 'Commission Adopts Eight New Decisions Imposing Fines on Hard-core Cartels', *Competition Policy Newsletter*, 2002/1: 29–43.

Cini, M., and McGowan, L. (1998), *Competition Policy in the European Union* (London: Macmillan).

Commission (1981–), *Annual Reports on Competition Policy* (Luxembourg: Office for Official Publications of the European Communities).

Drahos, M. (2001), *Convergence of Competition Laws and Policies in the European Community* (Duventer: Kluwer).

Gerber, D. (1998), *Law and Competition in Twentieth Century Europe* (Oxford: Clarendon Press).

Goyder, D. (2003), *EC Competition Law*, 4th edn. (Oxford: Oxford University Press).

House of Lords (2002), Select Committee on the European Union, *The Review of the EC Merger Regulation* (London: House of Lords), HL Paper 165.

van Waarden, F., and Drahos, M. (2002), 'Courts and (Epistemic) Communities in the Convergence of Competition Policies', *Journal of European Public Policy*, 9/6: 913–34.

Wilks, S. (2005), 'Agency Escape: Decentralisation or Dominance of the European Commission in the Modernisation of Competition Policy?', *Governance*, 18, 3, forthcoming.

Chapter 6

Economic and Monetary Union

Innovation and Challenges for the Euro

Kathleen R. McNamara

Contents

Summary

Economic and monetary union (EMU) is one of the most ambitious and successful policy projects undertaken by the European Union (EU). From the first proposals for EMU at the 1969 summit in The Hague, through to the physical introduction of the euro in 2002, European leaders have promoted EMU as a way to achieve the political goals of peace and stability through intensive economic cooperation. But while monetary integration has long been seen by key political leaders as a way to cement Europe together through the bonds of a single currency, some fundamental changes within the member states were necessary to make EMU possible. Notably, a convergence in monetary policy ideas about the value of low inflation was required, plus several decades of exchange-rate cooperation and the momentum of the Single European Act (SEA), for EMU to be enshrined in the 1992 Treaty on European Union (TEU). Today, authority for monetary policy has moved decisively to the European Central Bank (ECB), while key elements of economic union, most crucially fiscal policy, remain at the national level. If past history of currency construction is any guide, this only partially federalized system of economic governance may prove to be quite fragile. Nonetheless, the extraordinary track record of innovation and political commitment on EMU indicates that Europe's leaders may find a way to overcome the odds and meet these new challenges.

Introduction

Economic and monetary union (EMU) is one of the most innovative accomplishments of European integration. Driven in part by the political goal of cementing cooperation and solidarity among the nations of the European Union (EU), the long process of monetary integration was capped by the successful creation of the EMU and a European Central Bank in 1999 and the remarkably smooth physical introduction of the euro on 1 January 2002. Today, policy capacity in the monetary realm is truly supranational, with political authority firmly located at European level.

Yet despite these impressive accomplishments, EMU also presents some of the most vexing challenges to Europe's leaders and citizens. Many of these arise from the fact that the euro has outpaced much of the governance structure of the EU. While monetary policy-making is highly centralized, fiscal and macroeconomic policy-making remains largely national, as does political representation. The design of EMU therefore prompts a series of questions: will member governments reach agreement on how to reform the Maastricht rules regarding the Stability and Growth Pact (SGP), the agreement that currently shapes macroeconomic policy in Euroland? How can the member governments reach common positions and implement policy across a range of issues in the realm of the euro and the broader economy, both within Europe and internationally? Is the EU democratically accountable enough to sustain EMU?

Our ability to answer to these questions has been hampered in part by the seeming *sui generis* status of EMU. The euro appears unique historically because in the modern era, currencies have always been synonymous with national borders. We need to look further back for a comparison, to the nineteenth century when processes of national currency consolidation ultimately produced the 'one money, one nation' model we have today. In ways similar to the creation of the euro, multiple currencies circulating within common markets were phased out in the late nineteenth century in deference to a consolidated, national currency.

The key difference between these nineteenth century cases and the EU today is that these earlier currencies were embedded within clear projects of political integration and state formation (Helleiner 2003; McNamara 2003). Despite the remarkable development of the EU as a concrete and distinct political system, the EU has not followed the same historical path that produced today's European nation-states. The challenge for EMU, therefore, is how to be successful and sustainable despite the incomplete nature of its political integration. What is certain is that to understand how policy-making in EMU is evolving, we should extend our conceptual lenses to include theories from comparative politics as well as international relations (see Chapter 2).

The chapter begins by briefly tracing EMU's historical development with attention to the key actors and events that influenced its creation, before describing EMU's legal basis and institutional expression. I then turn to a description of the policy process of EMU, outlining the workings of the European Central Bank (ECB) and the Eurosystem, as well as discussing the related policy arenas that remain national. The comparative historical lessons we can take from other examples of currency consolidation are then explored. The conclusion outlines some of the policy challenges that face EMU today and in the future, and speculates on the tensions that arise from the 'disembedded' nature of the ECB and the euro in the broader European political system.

Historical development and motivations

The euro and the ECB, while certainly dramatic developments, have not been overnight successes; rather EMU has very deep roots in the history of European integration. Below, I summarize the underlying reasons for the move to EMU, and outline the history that brought this about.

Throughout the postwar era, west European governments have placed great value on exchange-rate stability. When the Bretton Woods global exchange-rate system began to falter in the late 1960s, European Community governments started to look for ways to create a regional exchange-rate regime to take its place. The Europeans feared that exchange-rate instability would disrupt trade in their highly open economies, as uncertainty over currency values makes it harder for buyers and sellers in different countries to calculate appropriate prices and to negotiate contracts. Despite only weak empirical evidence that currency swings dampened trade, the perception of negative trade effects long made the limiting of currency fluctuations a salient interest for the European governments. Currency fluctuations were also viewed negatively by the European governments for a second trade reason: the difficulties currency instability wrought in the administration and financing of the EC's common agricultural policy (CAP) (see Chapter 7). Finally, and perhaps most importantly, monetary integration and a single currency have also been perceived by some European élites as a way to bind together nation-states so as to ensure political stability and cooperation across the EU.

In all these motive forces, it has been national leaders and policy-making élites who have been the key actors pushing forward monetary integration, with societal interest groups providing, at best, a permissive consensus, rather than active support. Thus, the story of EMU reflects the basic assumptions of intergovernmental theory (see Chapter 2; Moravcsik 1998). However, the foundations for the major bargains along the way were forged in ways compatible with more neo-functionalist predictions of how integration proceeds. Increasing trade across the EU and the single market programme both created new incentives for actors to move forward with a single currency.

To understand EMU, we must also take account of the role played by ideas in bringing about cooperation. The structural changes occurring in the EU and in the international economy were interpreted and framed by key actors in ways that made EMU more likely. For example, political actors greatly strengthened the case for a single currency by framing it as an inevitable and necessary follow-on from the single market (Jabko 1999). This occurred despite the lack of either empirical or theoretical proof of the clear necessity of a single currency for the single market to function efficiently.

At a more foundational level, a convergence in ideas about monetary policy was a critical prior cause of the success of the European Monetary System (EMS) set up in 1979, and the subsequent adoption of the single currency (McNamara 1998). Under the early postwar policies of Keynesian macroeconomic management, governments sought the freedom to adjust their exchange rates and monetary policies at will. After the experience of inflation and low growth during the oil crisis of the early 1970s, west European governments gradually began to view stable monetary policies that targeted inflation as better than Keynesian efforts to boost employment or growth through monetary expansion. This convergence towards policies influenced by monetarist theories (rather than Keynesian theories) made exchange-rate stability achievable despite rising speculative capital flows, as policy-makers moved away from adjustments in interest rates and other policies that might destabilize currency values. Convergence in policy ideas also meant that executing a single monetary policy under the euro would be more appealing to the various national monetary authorities. Finally, the interaction of central bankers in the institutional forum of the Monetary Committee also facilitated the development of shared norms and socialized new members into the price stability culture of the EU's monetary élites (Cameron 1995; Verdun 1999). All of these various dynamics can be seen in the long run-up to today's EMU, outlined below.

As argued, EMU was no overnight success. Indeed, the first plan for monetary union was originally floated as far back as 1969 (Tsoukalis 1977). The Werner Plan, a pro-gramme for economic and monetary integration drawn up by a study group of high-ranking EC and national officials, and chaired by Pierre Werner, the Prime Minister of Luxembourg, set down a timetable for the EC to achieve a European economic and monetary union within a decade. The EMU initiative originally had been launched at the EC's 1969 summit in The Hague by Willy Brandt, the German Chancellor, in tan-dem with Georges Pompidou, the French President, beginning a long series of Franco-German efforts towards monetary integration. While the Report gave a timetable for EMU, it was vague on its exact institutional characteristics, and, although endorsed on 22 March 1971 by the EC's national political leaders, it was never implemented.

Despite the lack of progress on the ambitious plans for a single European currency, there was some more modest movement towards a collective exchange-rate regime. The so-called 'snake in the tunnel' fixed exchange-rate regime began in 1973, yet it never achieved European wide stability. Plagued by exchange-rate crises and large realignments, the snake soon collapsed and persisted through the 1970s only as a limited 'D-mark zone', consisting of Germany, the Netherlands, Belgium, Luxembourg, and, at times, Denmark.

When a new exchange-rate regime, the European Monetary System (EMS), was pro-posed in the late 1970s, it was viewed with almost universal scepticism. Its institutions looked very similar to those of the snake; moreover, it began at a time of deep pessimism regarding the ability of the EU to act collectively on any issue, much less one as complex and difficult as multilateral monetary cooperation. Yet the EMS con-founded many observers by eventually evolving into a relatively stable cooperative regime, despite the pressures of increasing international capital mobility. The EMS officially came into being in March 1979 with Germany, the Benelux countries, Denmark, France, Ireland, and Italy participating; Britain was the only then EC member not to join in the exchange-rate mechanism (ERM) that formed the heart of the EMS. The EMS suffered an initial period of adjustment and several crises, most notably during the early years of the Mitterrand presidency in France, when the new Socialist government's efforts to stimulate growth in the domestic economy caused foreign exchange traders, worried about inflation, to sell francs. Mitterrand changed the French government's macroeconomic policy course, helping to stabilize the EMS and allowing it to evolve into an extremely tight cooperative agreement.

Scholars have focused on several factors as decisive to the revival of this step towards European monetary integration. First, intra-European trade-related concerns, like those that drove the snake's creation, also played a role in the desire to construct the EMS (Frieden 1991). Secondly, on a more geopolitical level, Valéry Giscard D'Estaing, the French president, and Helmut Schmidt, the German Chancellor, sought to strengthen European institutions to compensate for what they saw as US mismanagement of the western world's affairs (Ludlow 1982). As mentioned above, a shift in ideas about the goals and instruments of monetary policy was occurring across most of Europe (Sandholtz 1993; McNamara 1998). As policy-makers' views converged around a German-influenced price stability model of policy-making, exchange-rate stability became more likely, and a necessary condition for further monetary integration was met.

The EMS consolidated its successes in stabilizing exchange rates within the EU during the 1980s, expanding to include the new member states of Spain (June 1989), and Portugal (April 1992), while the UK joined in October 1990 (see Box 6.1). By the second half of the 1980s, European leaders, led by the French in partnership with the Germans, began to consider reviving the project of monetary union that had been dormant since the Werner Report debacle of the late 1960s. The success of the single market programme (see Chapter 4) in moving towards the dismantling of barriers to trade and commerce seemed to forge a logical link with a move forward towards a single currency. The single European market project also created a sense of excitement and support for bold steps to further Europe's integration. At the June 1988 European Council in Hanover, EU heads of state and government authorized Jacques Delors, President of the European Commission, to develop a plan for economic and monetary union. The committee formed to address this goal was made up of Delors and a group of central banking officials and experts who largely shared a set of strongly held ideas about the value of price stability and monetary discipline, making the drafting of the plan relatively smooth. The group delivered its 'Delors Report' to the European leaders at the European Council in Madrid in 1989, and the report's conclusions formed the basis for the subsequent Treaty on European Union (TEU), signed in Maastricht in December 1991. A three-stage process was outlined in the Treaty, consisting of a period of convergence in policy, the creation of the ECB, and, finally, a single currency.

The starting date of the final stage of EMU remained subject to a political decision by Europe's leaders, taking into account the Maastricht 'convergence criteria', a series of economic benchmarks for membership. The convergence criteria were to be later adapted as ongoing rules for EMU in the form of the Stability and Growth Pact (see Box 6.2). The Treaty's convergence criteria were a necessary concession to those states, most importantly Germany and its Bundesbank, that feared EMU would be inflationary if the participating economies were not adequately prepared. The criteria called for member states to achieve low and convergent inflation and interest rates, a budget deficit of 3 per cent of GDP or less, public debt levels of 60 per cent or less, and a stable exchange rate. The rules of Maastricht left substantial room, however, for the heads of state and government to make their own judgment about which states should go ahead into EMU and on what timetable.

Box 6.1 A chronology of EMU

- 1969: heads of state and government agree to Werner Plan for Economic and Monetary Union.
- 10 April 1972: European exchange-rate agreement, the 'snake', set up.
- 6–7 July 1978: the European Council meeting at Bremen agrees to replace the snake with a new exchange-rate regime, the European Monetary System (EMS).
- 13 March 1979: EMS begins, the eight participating member states are required to maintain their exchange rates within a fluctuation margin of $+/-2.25\%$ ($+/-6\%$ for the lira). Creation of the European currency unit (ecu).
- 1 July 1987: The Single European Act officially takes effect.
- 24 June 1988: Council capital movements directive adopted eliminating most restrictions by 1 July 1990.
- 19 June 1989: peseta enters EMS exchange-rate mechanism (ERM).
- 26–27 June 1989: Madrid European Council receives the Delors Report and decides to convene an Intergovernmental Conference on Economic and Monetary Union.
- 1 July 1990: first phase of EMU comes into force.
- 6 October 1990: pound sterling enters ERM with a 6% fluctuation margin.
- 9–10 December 1991: Maastricht European Council reaches agreement on draft Treaty on European Union: completion of EMU and introduction of the single European currency by 1999.
- 4 April 1992: escudo enters ERM with a 6% fluctuation margin.
- 17 September 1992: the UK and Italy suspend participation in the ERM.
- 1 January 1993: single market enters into force.
- 2 August 1993: fluctuation margins of ERM currencies temporarily widened to 15%.
- 1 November 1993: Treaty on European Union comes into force.
- 1 January 1994: Stage II of EMU begins and European Monetary Institute is established.
- 9 January 1995: Austrian schilling enters the ERM.
- 15–16 December 1995: Madrid European Council names the European currency unit the euro and confirms the introduction of the single currency on 1 January 1999.
- 14 October 1996: Finnish markka enters the ERM.
- 25 November 1996: the Italian lira rejoins the ERM.
- 17 June 1997: Stability and Growth Pact (SGP) agreed.
- 1 June 1998: European Central Bank (ECB) is established, replacing the EMI.
- 1 January 1999: final stage of EMU enters into force with the irrevocable fixing of the exchange rates of the currencies of 11 member states and the conduct of a single monetary policy under the responsibility of the ECB.
- January 2001: Greece enters the third stage of EMU and adopts the euro.
- 1 January 2002: introduction of euro notes and coins and phasing out of national currencies amongst the twelve participating states.
- 22–3 March 2005: SGP rules revised.

Box 6.2 Convergence criteria (TEU) and Stability and Growth Pact (SGP)

Convergence criteria (Protocol to Art. 109j TEU; now Art. 121 TEC):

- *price stability*, measured according to the rate of inflation in the three best performing member states;
- *long-term interest rates* close to the rates in the countries with the best inflation results;
- an annual *budget deficit* which does not exceed 3 per cent of GDP;
- *total government debt* not in excess of 60 per cent of GDP, or falling steadily towards that figure;
- *stability in the exchange rate* of the national currency on exchange markets, demonstrated by participation in the exchange-rate mechanism of the European Monetary System for two years.

Stability and Growth Pact:

In June 1997 the European Council agreed the 'Amsterdam Resolution', complemented by two Regulations (1466/97 and 1467/97). These set in place the 'excessive deficit procedure' which identifies what constitutes an excessive deficit in a member state, with procedures for scrutiny, recommendations, warnings, and eventually sanctions, in the event of sustained failure to correct the deficit. Fierce debate led to modifications of the SGP by the European Council of 22–3 March 2005, which made the rules more flexible.

The run-up to EMU proved a critical test of the political commitment to the single currency. While monetary cooperation seemed to be flourishing as more countries continued to join the ERM, worked to consolidate their macroeconomic policies, and converged towards the EMU criteria, two separate exchange-rate crises threatened to derail the entire project. In September 1992, intense speculation forced the British pound sterling out of the ERM, along with the Italian lira, which only returned to the system in 1996. In August 1993, more speculative attacks led the central bank governors to widen temporarily the allowed fluctuation bands to plus or minus 15 per cent, successfully fighting off the demise of the system. The member governments held fast, and eventually, the financial markets began to reward their commitment to EMU with stabilizing currencies and lower interest rates.

The decision to begin the euro stage of EMU on 1 January 1999 was effectively made by a special European Council meeting in Brussels in May 1998. While most of the EU states had made strenuous efforts to meet the convergence criteria by the time of the launch of Stage III, not all conditions were met for all of the original eleven countries designated to adopt the euro (Austria, Belgium, Finland, France, Germany, Ireland, Italy, Luxembourg, the Netherlands, Portugal, and Spain). Despite this, the political desire to continue moving towards a common monetary authority carried the day, and the ECB opened for business, preparing for the start of EMU by the end of 1998 and the eventual replacement of national bills and coins in January 2002. Of the four states (Denmark, Greece, Sweden, and the UK) that did not initially enter the final stage of EMU, only Greece has since joined, in January 2001. The British government has so far chosen to 'optout' of membership pending an eventual referendum on the euro. Denmark and Sweden both had negative results in referenda on membership in 2000 and 2003, respectively, and are not likely to join for the foreseeable future.

Laws and institutions

The legal basis of EMU

European monetary cooperation had been a longstanding interest on the part of those leaders dissatisfied with reliance on the international monetary system. The Treaty of Rome (EEC) did not, however, specify the creation of a single European currency or monetary union as an objective. Nonetheless, it did advocate the coordination of monetary policies through the newly created Monetary Committee. Articles 105, 106, 107, and 108 EEC also stated that exchange rates were to be 'of common interest', and suggested the potential for mutual aid in the case of balance of payments difficulties. The Treaty also called for the progressive abolition of restrictions on the movement of capital 'to the extent necessary to ensure the proper functioning of the common market', but allowed national governments to 'take protective measures' to restrict capital movements if they 'lead to disturbances' in that state's markets (Arts. 67 and 73 EEC, respectively). The broader emphasis in the Treaty of Rome on the 'four freedoms' of unrestricted movement of goods, services, capital, and labour might logically be read to implicate a common monetary system as well.

Absent a European framework, the treaty which governed the monetary decisions of EU member states for the first part of the postwar period was an international one, the International Monetary Fund's Articles of Agreement governing the Bretton Woods exchange-rate system. Bretton Woods had been relatively effective at keeping exchange rates stable across the non-communist world, but as this international system began to crumble in the early 1970s, an intra-EU agreement was created to fix exchange rates among the then EU member states, namely the 'snake' or European Common Margins Agreement. Like its more successful 1980s successor, the exchange-rate mechanism of the European Monetary System, the snake did not have treaty status, but was the legal equivalent of an *ad hoc* agreement among the member states. In part, this was due to central bankers' desire to keep monetary matters firmly in their own hands, away from Brussels and the broader European framework of authority. This desire had a geographical expression: since its creation in 1964, the Committee of Central Bank Governors (CCBG) had coordinated the European exchange-rate system from meetings in Basle at the Bank for International Settlements (Andrews 2003; McNamara 2001; Russell 1977). The Swiss locale both reflected and reinforced their sense of remove from the rest of the EU policy circles.

Indeed, it was not until the 1992 TEU that laws governing EMU were enshrined in the *acquis communautaire*. At one stroke, the EU went from no treaty base for monetary integration, to detailed and extensive rules regarding the run-up to EMU, the criteria for membership, the organization, responsibility, and goals of institutions that would govern EMU, and the subsequent workings of Euroland. Yet this apparently dramatic legal change was less dramatic in substance, because in many ways the Maastricht rules simply codified existing, widely shared ideas and norms regarding the value of central bank independence and price stability in monetary policy.

The Maastricht rules apply to all EU members, with the exception of Denmark and the UK, which negotiated opt-outs. Of the three countries that joined the EU in 1995, after Maastricht was negotiated (Austria, Sweden, and Finland), only Sweden has not adopted the euro, resting on the precedent set by Denmark and the UK, albeit without a legal opt-out. The ten countries that joined in May 2004 are legally bound to join the euro, but must remain in the EMS for a period of two years in order to meet the Maastricht criteria, before their subsequent acceptance by the European Council, and adoption of the euro.

The institutions of EMU

The policy-making institutions for the monetary—as opposed to the economic—side of EMU are laid out in great detail in the TEU. The larger institutional framework for policy is the European System of Central Banks (ESCB), made up of all twenty-five of the EU's national central banks (NCBs) with the ECB at its centre. 'Eurosystem' is the term used to refer to the ECB and the national banks of the member states that have adopted the euro, numbering twelve at the time of writing. The central banks of the member states that do not participate in the euro area are members of the ESCB, but in only a limited sense, insofar as they conduct their respective national monetary policies unilaterally and do not take part in the decision-making with regard to monetary policy for the euro area.

The basic tasks of the ECB and the ESCB are the formulation and implementation of monetary policy, most prominently through: setting interest rates; the execution of exchange market operations; and holding and management of official reserves. Although the formulation of monetary policy is located solely within the ECB, subject to the priority goal of price stability, much of the execution and operation of monetary policy continues through the national central banks. The ECB is also responsible for promoting the 'smooth operation of the payment system', which refers to the workings of TARGET, the intra-European large payments clearing-house system, implying that the ECB could be a lender of last resort in the event of a crisis.

While significant policy capacity in the monetary realm has thus been transferred to the EU, it is also important to consider where the ECB does not have responsibility. In particular, two tasks traditionally vital to national central banks have not been transferred to the supranational level in Europe, namely, ultimate responsibility for stability of the European financial system, and issuing system-wide debt instruments. Uncertainty remains over how intra-EU disputes and systemic crises would be con-tained and resolved due to the limited nature of the treaty language about 'smooth operation of the payments system'. Although some have advocated it, the ECB does not yet have broader supervisory capacity over the ever more closely integrated EU financial markets. What is clear, however, is that the TEU features a 'no bail-out' clause, prohibiting the ECB from rescuing member states which find themselves in dire financial straits. The ECB is also barred from creating an EU-level financial instrument, such as a European treasury bill, to finance EU expenditures. Instead, the national central banks have individually issued their own bonds denominated in euro, and there is a highly competitive market in such bonds across the EU.

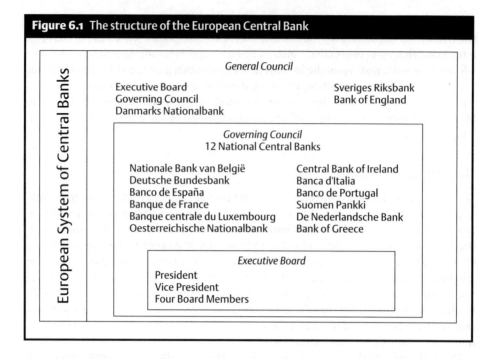

Figure 6.1 The structure of the European Central Bank

The absence of these elements of traditional national monetary capacity at the EU level may make the governance of EMU more difficult.

In terms of its internal structure, the ECB is made up of three separate, but closely linked and overlapping, decision-making bodies (see Fig. 6.1). The central body is its Executive Board, which is made up of the ECB's president, vice-president, and four other board members. These individuals are representatives of the EU as a whole rather than national representatives, and thus embody most clearly the supranational governance of EMU. Nonetheless, the job of the president of the ECB, which first went to Wim Duisenberg of the Netherlands in 1998, followed by the appointment of Jean-Claude Trichet in June 2003, has triggered some contentious political struggles between member governments wishing to ensure that this highly visible position is filled according to their national interest, and informed by the appropriate mind set. The Executive Board is responsible for the day-to-day management of monetary policy, implementing decisions made by the second body, the Governing Council, which is made up of all the central bank governors of those states participating in the euro. It also issues the necessary instructions to the national banks. Strictly speaking, the primary responsibility of this Executive Board is to carry out monetary policy, but it is also heavily involved in the formulation of policy itself in tandem with the central bank governors.

The six members of the Executive Board are appointed by common accord of the governments of the member states at the level of heads of state or government, on a recommendation from the Council and after consulting the European Parliament and the Council. The president is elected for a term of eight years, the vice-president for four years, and the remaining members for terms of between five and eight years.

As part of the rules to encourage independence from political influence and limit the temptation to curry political favour, the terms of office for the Executive Board members are non-renewable.

The third and least powerful grouping in the ECB is the General Council, comprised of the president, and vice-president of the Executive Board, and governors of all the EU national central banks, including those not participating in the euro. With the May 2004 enlargement, the central bank governors of the new EU countries became full members of the General Council. With the potential for all twenty-five EU members eventually to adopt the euro, and thus participate in the Governing Council, the ECB has recommended that the voting rights be capped at twenty-one. Under this proposal, made in 2003, there would be six permanent voting rights for the members of the Executive Board and fifteen voting rights for the governors of national central banks, exercised in rotation. All members will have the right to attend and to speak. This proposal was adopted on 21 March 2003 by the European Council, but has not been met with universal accord, and remains to be ratified by the EU member states in accordance with their respective constitutional requirements.

Policy processes and substance

The 'monetary policy' component of economic and monetary union has been transformed over the past decade by the decision to delegate centralized responsibility to an EU-level agency, the ECB. This evolution echoes processes of currency consolidation evident in earlier state formation episodes, particularly from the nineteenth century. Thus, it is useful to draw on a comparative federalism lens to understand patterns of political behaviour that have led to the achievement of the euro. Comparative federalist analysis also helps to point out that this transformation is not complete. Key policy processes within EMU still remain at the national level, complicating economic governance and creating a historically unique situation of a single currency disembedded from a broader system of economic policy-making.

Prior to the start of EMU in 1999, monetary policy-making was very much characterized by the increasingly intensive involvement of national policy-makers, the 'intensive transgovernmentalism' mode of policy (see Chapter 3). Indeed, the exchange-rate regime of the EMS evolved into a successful monetary order in no small part because key policy-makers, namely the national central bank governors, developed a strongly institutionalized network of interaction and expertise. This regime, centered on the CCBG, facilitated a convergence on policy positions towards a prioritizing of price stability, and made it easier to undertake the necessary adjustments to keep exchange rates in line. With the start of EMU in 1999, the participating national central bank governors regrouped within the ECB along with the new, supranational Executive Board and a permanent professional staff, in an explicitly supranational way.

The ECB continues to emphasize 'sound money' policies that prioritize low inflation above efforts to stimulate growth and employment. Although these substantive policy goals have been carried through from the EMS years, policy processes, in contrast, have explicitly changed. Policy is now created at the EU level within the ECB, operating within the federal system of national central banks, the ESCB. Within the ECB, the governors of the national central banks, sitting together in the Governing Council, formulate the substance of monetary policy, primarily by setting key interest rates that determine at what rate commercial banks in Euroland will be charged for borrowing money from the national central banks. These rates in turn influence the interest rates which apply to borrowers and investors throughout the eurozone. The six members of the Executive Board are responsible for implementing this policy by issuing instructions to the national central banks, preparing for meetings of the Governing Council, and managing the day-to-day business of the ECB.

On paper, it might seem that the Executive Board's role is a subordinate one of following up the directions given by the Governing Council. In practice, however, it appears that the Executive Board takes a large measure of agenda-setting power and shapes the decisions made in the Governing Council. At the twice-monthly meetings of the Governing Council, the Board presents information to the national central bank governors on the state of the Euroland economy, provides projections on future developments, and recommends a specific course of action. Given the large size of the Governing Council and the uniquely collective perspective of the Executive Board, the latter seems to have taken an increasingly lead role. This may become more pronounced as the number of central bank governors participating grows, as new members join the regime. It also appears that decisions in the Governing Council are taken by consensus rather than by vote, which means that the agenda-setting powers of the Executive Board may be more important than their minority voting position (currently totalling six versus twelve national central bank governors) might indicate.

The Executive Board members are also responsible for directing the professional and administrative staff of the ECB, who are organized into some seventeen Divisions and Directorates-General. Especially in the key policy-making divisions, such as the DGs for Economics (ECFIN), Research (JRC), and for International and European Relations, the evidence suggests that the direction provided from the Executive Board member in charge of that division is very important in shaping the staff's work and the content of policy.

Much of the substance of policy arising from these deliberations appears in keeping with the recent history of EU member governments and the TEU's statement that the 'primary objective' of the ECB is 'the maintenance of price stability' (Art. 105 TEC). The ECB must also 'support the general economic policies in the Community', but only 'without prejudice to the objective of price stability'. Price stability is not defined by the TEU in quantitative terms, but is usually agreed by observers of the ECB to mean an inflation rate of below 2 per cent.

Two strategies have been used by ECB in pursuit of this goal. The first is monetary targeting, where the amount of money flowing through the European economy is measured, and the central bank adjusts its policies to achieve a set money supply goal. The second is the use of inflation targeting, that is, the identification and publication of an inflation target that is used by the bank to guide policy. Both these strategies have their critics and adherents. When these strategies are used together, some critics claim there is a danger that the policy objectives may be too confusing for observers to determine what they are and whether they are being achieved. In addition, there has been criticism of the overriding emphasis on price stability above all things.

Observers have argued that a strict emphasis on price stability by the ECB may have a deflationary effect, slowing growth within Europe and its trading partners.

Not all of the policy processes important for the functioning of EMU are delegated to the ECB or other EU institutions, however. Significant macroeconomic policy processes remaining at the national level include regulatory oversight of the banking system, external representation and exchange-rate policy, and taxing and spending responsibilities. While the Commission plays an advocacy role in such matters, it does not have legal or political power to shape national macroeconomic policies. Discussions over such issues do occur regularly in Ecofin, the Council configuration for economic and financial ministers of the EU, but, in the absence of clear Community legal powers for the Ecofin over macroeconomic policy, the emphasis is on consensus and coordination. In addition, as regards monetary policy as such, there has been a running debate about the case for developing a special forum for only those finance ministers from countries within the euro system. After resistance from the 'outs', especially the UK, the 'Eurogroup', which is a subset of Ecofin, comprising only ministers of the euro states, was established in June 1998 in Luxembourg and now acts as a forum for coordination within the eurozone. The Eurogroup meets regularly the day before Ecofin meetings. In a compromise reached between Germany, France, and the UK, the non-euro finance ministers are allowed to attend the Eurogroup meetings, but are excluded from discussions over issues central to the euro, such as its external value vis-à-vis the dollar. At the informal Ecofin of September 2004 agreement was reached to establish new working methods for the Eurogroup. Jean-Claude Juncker, prime minister of Luxembourg, was chosen as president for a two-year period from January 2005, with Karl-Heinz Grasser, the Austrian finance minister as his deputy.

Situated more uneasily between the national and the European levels is the rule-based Stability and Growth Pact (SGP; see Box 6.2), which has proven to be one of the most politically contentious parts of EMU. The SGP, described more fully in the section on 'fiscal governance' below, continues the convergence criteria rules on national deficits and public debt, although the content and shape of fiscal policy remains a national prerogative and not all countries have remained with the targets (see the section on 'Economic governance in comparative perspective'). The SGP was adopted in the hope that macroeconomic discipline would provide a firm anchor for the single currency.

A second way of characterizing policy-making in EMU is to emphasize two distinctive and linked qualities that the ECB embodies: formal organizational independence, and the use of expertise. The ECB is distinctive in the world of central banking because its statute makes it the most politically independent central bank in the world, surpassing even historically independent entities such as the Bundesbank or the US Federal Reserve. Monetary policy is largely formulated and executed by an independent agency, whose organizational rules prohibit direct political direction. Secondly, the policy processes within the ECB are permeated by the importance of authoritative knowledge structures, the expert consensus and opinion that drive monetary policy decisions, although at the same time these can create insularity and concerns over democratic accountability.

In terms of independence, the design of the ECB embodied the view that monetary policy should be kept separate from political authority, a view which is congruent both with prevailing ideas about the organizational form of contemporary central banks, and with the prior institutional history of the monetary policy arena of the EU. The ECB's personnel and oversight procedures are designed to keep external political pressures—for example, from the national governments or from the European Commission—to a minimum so as to ensure the credible maintenance of price stability. One member of the European Commission and the President of Ecofin can participate, but not vote, in the meetings of the Governing Council. While the ECB must come before the European Parliament (EP) to present its annual report, the EP has little opportunity to influence or formal prohibition the ECB; it can only ask questions and comment. An informal tradition has developed where the President of the ECB appears quarterly in front of the EP's Economic and Monetary Affairs Committee to answer questions. The President also holds a press conference after the first Governing Council meeting of each month. These developments have been welcomed by advocates of a more open and transparent policy system, although some critics argue that minutes of the Governing Council's meetings should also be published in order to increase accountability and transparency.

Adding to its independence, the ECB's statutes cannot be changed except by treaty revision with the unanimous consent of the EU member states. This further insulates it from political interference beyond what is normal in a national setting. Internally, this autonomy is preserved as well in personnel and operational matters, as the ECB is legally separate from the rest of the EU institutional system, and thus sets its own personnel policies and other procedures.

The ECB therefore is decidedly executive in function, although within an organizational form that is expressly delegated and independent from political bodies at the executive level. This delegated organizational form is now the norm for central banks across the world, reflecting the belief that monetary policy is best kept separate from political decision-making, lest politicians be tempted to try to stimulate the economy for electoral purposes in ways that might be detrimental to the long-term health of the economy. Despite inconclusive studies on the economic value of such independence, it has become an important symbolic marker of economic prudence, and whatever its true functional effects, now has weighty symbolic properties that signal credibility and price stability policies to private actors and markets (McNamara 2002). Given the prior normative consensus in the EU on the virtues of low inflation policies, the role of the Bundesbank as a model, and the insulation of the ECB's policy precursors, it was almost inevitable that the ECB be made so very independent.

Independence has also strengthened another inherent quality of the policy process of EMU, its knowledge intensivity. More so than in many other areas of EU policy-making, EMU has its basis in a small community of technocratic experts. The knowledge structures of these policy-makers are crucial to the flow of policy-making within the ECB. The causal models they share, or disagree over, of how the economy works, and the normative judgments they make about the relative merits of various monetary policy strategies are highly consequential for outcomes in Euroland. Monetary policy is an area that is characterized more broadly by relatively little societal input, because of the relatively arcane and highly technical nature of monetary policy, the diffuse effects of interest rate changes (which create collective action problems for societal actors), and because of the institutional configuration of independence. All of these characteristics serve to reinforce the highly technocratic, knowledge-intense nature of the EMU policy process.

Economic governance in comparative perspective

While a single monetary policy is now firmly entrenched at the supranational level for the participating countries, important linked areas of economic governance remain situated at the national level, with varying degrees of *ad hoc* coordination at the EU level. The most significant of these is fiscal policy, which is presently situated uneasily between the national and the EU levels. While the SGP has set overall limits on deficits and debt, not all countries have stayed within the targets. It can be argued that the SGP is the wrong instrument to coordinate fiscal policy altogether as it provides only a very blunt and rigid instrument for policy-making. Other significant macroeconomic policy processes remaining at the national level include: regulatory oversight of the banking system; external representation of Euroland in the IMF and other fora; and exchange-rate policy. Historical examples of currency unification reveal that those that have been successful have moved such functions to the federal level. This raises the question of whether the EU can continue with a very clear collective regime for monetary policy alone, or whether it must develop a broader apparatus of economic governance and political capacity to match the euro and the ECB.

Fiscal governance

In theory, monetary unions can function without organized fiscal coordination or taxation and spending powers. However, there are reasons to view the lack of a 'federal', or EU-level fiscal institution as potentially a problem for the successful functioning of EMU. Two such factors are the 'policy mix' and automatic fiscal stabilizers. Monetary policy goals are ideally best balanced with fiscal policy to ensure the desired direction of the macroeconomy. Achieving the appropriate degree of, and balance among the goals for price stability, employment, and growth is made more likely if the policy mix between the levers of fiscal and monetary policy can be coordinated, although there are no guarantees that this will be in the case even in the most centralized and unitary economic systems. Nonetheless, separating these functions is clearly not optimal from a standpoint of coherent overall economic governance. As for the politics, a shared monetary policy is also made more palatable to those who might suffer more in a downturn, if there is a shared federal fiscal system in place. With such a system, automatic fiscal stabilizers are in place to level the playing field across regions without acrimonious debates over how to distribute resources. That is, if one region is doing well, tax revenues from that area will increase as incomes and investment earnings rise, whilst a less healthy region will be taxed less and see more transfers in the form of unemployment benefits, for example, thus automatically reducing the disparity.

History also makes a case for the need to deepen shared fiscal governance at the EU level. A comparative assessment by this author of a sample of nineteenth-century monetary unions indicates that these survived only when accompanied by fiscal union. As taxing and spending moved to the federal level along with money, political authority also become consolidated and the successful cases (nineteenth century

Germany, Switzerland, Italy, and the US) all became what we now understand as political unions or nation-states. The failed cases of the nineteenth century, the Scandinavian Monetary Union, and the Latin Monetary Union, stalled with monetary union only and soon collapsed.

The TEU did not directly address the question of fiscal governance, leaving responsibility for fiscal policy at the national level. However, within a few years, driven in part by concerns on the part of German policy-makers about the potential inflationary impact of deficit spending on the euro, the heads of state and government came to agreement at the European Council in Dublin in December 1996 on procedures for increased policy surveillance in the fiscal realm, on the specific penalties to be imposed when countries exceed the targets. The resulting SGP builds on language in the Treaty regarding 'excessive government deficits' (Art. 104, TEC). The Treaty language specifies that a government whose budget deficit exceeds 3 per cent of GDP or whose public debt exceeds 60 per cent of GDP may be required to correct its situation, and may be subject to sanctions and penalties if it fails to do so. The sanctions escalate from a requirement to put funds aside in a non-interest-bearing bank deposit, to non-reimbursable fines set as a proportion of GDP. The agreement specified that no fine will be imposed if a country is in a severe recession, defined as a drop in GDP of at least 2 per cent over a single year. If output has fallen by an amount between 0.75 per cent and 2 per cent of GDP, Ecofin may exercise discretion in applying the fines if circumstances warranted the deficits.

The SGP was not a panacea. Most obviously, by late 2004, four countries were in violation of the SGP. In 2003, France received an 'early warning' and was instructed to get its financial house in order, while Portugal, Italy, and Germany all went from initial 'early warnings' to being judged as having 'excessive deficits'. In November 2003 finance ministers rejected the Commission's recommendations to sanction these countries and voted instead to give them room to make adjustments without fines. This decision, viewed by many as effectively suspending the SGP, angered some member governments which believed that the two largest countries were being given *carte blanche* to flout the rules which their partner states were struggling to meet. The Commission decided to refer the matter to the European Court of Justice (ECJ). In August 2004 the ECJ, while condemning the EU's finance ministers for suspending the Pact's recommendations on deficits, used a technical reading of the law to uphold the rights of the national governments to ignore these recommendations and the disciplinary procedures attached to them. The European Council of 22–23 March 2005 modified the rules, widening the range of relevant factors which could be used to justify missing their targets.

Beyond the controversy about truants from the SGP, there are serious questions to be raised about its appropriateness in meeting the needs of economic governance in Europe. Although the SGP has the word 'growth' in its title, it is not likely to promote growth, but rather to be excessively restrictive at precisely the times that European states may need to stimulate their economies, as states are more likely to run up deficits in economic recessions. Many EU countries, not only those in the heart of Euroland, have been plagued by economic underperformance, making the flouting of the SGP rules less than surprising. Slow growth in Euroland has also prompted many British policy-makers, not least the Chancellor of the Exchequer and the Governor of the Bank of England, to advocate holding off on a referendum on the euro, as it might be persuasively argued that the UK is doing better outside the system.

Instead of the SGP rules, an alternative might be to pursue coordination among EU economic and finance ministers more aggressively, so that policies can be tailored to the needs of the region. In this view, greater coordination of fiscal policies is more likely within a more flexible and interactive policy setting than in that prescribed by the SGP. Even among those agreeing that fiscal policies are best directed towards rigour (because lax fiscal policies require a tighter monetary policy, which could in turn bring public pressure on the ECB and cause it to retreat to an overly lax policy stance), the SGP is seen as too blunt an instrument. Some long-time official particip-ants in the EMU project have stated privately that some form of fiscal federalism—that is, a more federal European structure with centralized redistributive policies of taxing, borrowing, and spending—is a necessity in the long run.

It was concerns such as these that prompted the second important political initiative affecting the character and organization of economic policy-making in EMU, the establishment of an informal institution, the Eurogroup, discussed above in the section on 'Policy processes and substance'.

Exchange-rate policy

While the structure of monetary policy decision-making within the ECB is relatively clear, the TEU was less clear about exchange-rate policy-making for the euro. Operational responsibility for exchange-rate values, through the conduct of foreign exchange operations, is the sole responsibility of the ECB. The TEU is less clear, how-ever, about the locus of responsibility for the formulation or creation of exchange-rate policy. The decision to enter into a formal exchange-rate agreement with non-EU countries is the responsibility of Ecofin, and any such agreement would be binding on the ECB. In the absence such an agreement, the Council, acting on a proposal from the Commission and after consultation with the ECB, may adopt (by QMV) 'general orientations' for exchange-rate policy towards non-EU currencies, but only insofar as they do not interfere with the ECB's primary goal of price stability.

As the resurrection of a formal system such as the post-war Bretton Woods interna-tional exchange-rate regime is unlikely in the foreseeable future, the vague language regarding 'general orientations' is more likely, given the informal cooperation that has characterized the international monetary system since the early 1970s. One result is an opening for increasing the Commission's institutional power. The policy discus-sion about the locus of competence for exchange-rate policy is, in any event, ongoing, despite efforts to clarify the TEU's language at the European Council meeting in Luxembourg in December 1997. The first president of the ECB, Wim Duisenberg, stated the prevailing ECB policy, however, when he noted that an exchange-rate objective is not an appropriate monetary policy strategy for the ECB, 'given that for an area as potentially as large as the eurozone, such an approach might be inconsistent with the internal goal of price stability. The external value of the euro will thus mainly be an outcome of the ECB's monetary policy'. He went on to say that formal arrange-ments with non-EU countries are unlikely, although the ESCB will have the technical capacity to 'intervene in order to counteract excessive or erratic fluctuations of the euro against the major non-EU countries' (Duisenberg 1998). In contrast, the European

Commission and some member governments, notably the French, have argued that the Treaty does leave the door open for a more activist policy on the part of Ecofin and the Commission. One likely motivation for such a stance is the desire to manage the value of the euro so as to increase the competitiveness of EU products in world markets.

The initial experience of the euro in exchange-rate markets has been marked by extreme swings in its value *vis-à-vis* the dollar. With its introduction on 1 January 1999 the euro was valued at $1.18, but by its first birthday was trading at around €1 to $1. In its second year, 2001, the euro declined to $0.87. By 2003, it had dramatically rebounded and surpassed its initial value, increasing to historic highs against the dollar by December 2004. There is disagreement on the implications, economically and politically, of these swings. The ECB has sent somewhat mixed signals at times about the desired level for the euro, and a variety of actors have criticized its Executive Board for not presenting a more coherent front. There have been some efforts at currency interventions coordinated with US officials, but it does not appear that exchange-rate management will come to prevail on the current agenda of the ECB. Fluctuations of the euro *vis-à-vis* the currencies of EU countries not participating in EMU may even be of greater ultimate concern given the high level of economic and political interaction within Europe.

Interestingly, the uncertainty regarding the legal division of responsibility for exchange-rate policy-making between Ecofin and the ECB is troublesome but not unusual when considered in the light of national policy arrangements. Historically, finance ministries have played an active role in exchange-rate management and policy-making across EU countries, but their roles have rarely been legally defined as such. The larger issue raised by the lack of assignment of the euro's exchange-rate policy authority, however, is that of the uncertain relationship of monetary policy to other economic and social policy goals in EMU (see Chapter 10). Developing the institutional capacity to integrate monetary policy into a broader set of political institutions, at both the EU and national levels, is a challenge that may remain unsolved for some time to come.

In sum, the euro is not yet 'embedded' within a well-developed institutional framework in the way that national central banks and currencies have traditionally been situated within their national policy settings. Instead, the 'monetary union' aspect of EMU leads, while the 'economic union' lags, and broader political systems of representation remain rooted at the national level. How long this will remain so is an open question: functional policy pressures may lead to spill-over into fiscal and regulatory policy areas, while democratic accountability claims and legitimacy questions may force movement towards further EU political integration. But the broader outcomes of the process of monetary integration are by no means determined.

Conclusion: looking to the future

There are several ways to categorize policy-making in EMU. Evaluating the EMU policy arena in terms of the broader conceptual framework of policy modes (see Chapter 3) allows us to see the transformation that has occurred within the monetary realm, from a policy process of a more transgovernmental nature to a supranational one. We can also delineate two linked qualities of EMU that set it apart from other policy arenas and impact the character of policy-making, namely independence and the importance of expert knowledge structures.

Against many economic and political odds, EMU has taken secure hold and the ECB is governing over the largest single market in the world. However, these accomplishments do not signal the end of the long evolution towards monetary integration, but rather the opening of a new era and a new set of challenges. This chapter has stressed one set of challenges arising from the disjuncture between a single currency firmly entrenched at the federal EU level whilst much of the political authority for economic governance remains national. The ECB does not have responsibility for providing financial stability and acting as a lender of last resort in the event of a severe financial crisis, although it may be the most logical actor to do so. Exchange-rate policy is also left indeterminate in the current legal structure. Most prominently, the SGP has proven too inflexible a mechanism to coordinate fiscal policy, and is now viewed as illegitimate in some quarters after its rules were bent to accommodate Germany and France. But there is little agreement on what should replace the SGP. Over the next few years, EU policy-makers will be forced to wrestle with the design of new institutions to coordinate fiscal policy, by revising the SGP, by strengthening the Eurogroup, or by creating an EU-level institution with the policy capacity for European-wide taxing and spending. While this sort of fiscal federalism is not likely in the near future due to the profound shift in political community and sovereignty it implies, it cannot be ruled out in the long run, particularly if the nineteenth century history of currency unions is any guide.

A broader set of challenges remains for EMU in the area of democratic accountability and legitimacy. Its central institution, the ECB, is arguably the most independent central bank in the world. While this organizational structure of delegation fits currently prevailing ideas about how central banks should be governed, it means that the ECB must be both effective at delivering positive economic outcomes and be as transparent as possible in order to gain the approval of the EU public. The ECB must also evolve in terms of its relationships with other EU institutional actors such as the EP so as to meet the expectations of democratic legitimacy within the EU political landscape. Although the recent Convention on the Future of Europe was established as a way to bring the EU project to the people and increase the perception of democratic legitimacy, the resulting Constitutional Treaty is largely silent in the area of EMU. Monetary integration has always been an élite driven, insulated process; however, the creation of the euro and the rules of the SGP have brought monetary policy-making closer to the people, and created new demands on this area of EU policy-making. Finally, the issue of whether the current EMU template will be appropriate for the ten new member states, as well as how to manage the continued absence of the UK, Sweden, and Denmark in the euro, also will challenge policy-makers over the next decade. As this chapter demonstrates, however, the history of monetary integration gives us reason to believe that EU leaders will be able to continue their innovative path towards further deepening of economic governance at the EU level despite the many challenges they face.

Further reading

The literature on EMU can be divided into works that stress the economic issues involved in its functioning, and those that focus on the political dynamics underlying monetary integration. Many of the best works straddle this divide by blending an appreciation for both the economic and the political logics at work. Thorough and clear analyses that emphasize economic factors are provided in Gros and Thygesen (1998), and De Grauwe (2002). For a comprehensive treatment of the political issues, see Dyson (1994), and Dyson and Featherstone (1999) for a detailed overview of the negotiations on the TEU. For contending theoretical perspectives on the broad political dynamics, see Moravcsik (1998), McNamara (1998), Jones (2002), and Gruber (2000). A rich literature has developed to explore more particular issues, for example, how the euro relates to political identity (Risse *et al.* 1999; Kaelberer 2004).

De Grauwe, P. (2002), *Economics of Monetary Union*, 5th edn. (Oxford: Oxford University Press).

Dyson, K. (1994), *Elusive Union: The Process of Economic and Monetary Union in Europe* (London: Longman).

Dyson, K., and Featherstone, K. (1999), *The Road to Maastricht: Negotiating Economic and Monetary Union* (Oxford: Oxford University Press).

Gros, D., and Thygesen, N. (1998), *European Monetary Integration: From the European Monetary System towards Monetary Union*, 2nd edn. (London: Longman).

Gruber, L. (2000), *Ruling the World: Power Politics and the Rise of Supranational Institutions* (Princeton: Princeton University Press).

Jones, E. (2002), *The Politics of Economic and Monetary Union: Integration and Idiosyncrasy* (Boulder: Rowman & Littlefield).

Kaelberer, M. (2004), 'The Euro and European Identity: Symbols, Power and the Politics of European Monetary Union', *Review of International Studies*, 30/2: 161–78.

McNamara, K. (1998), *The Currency of Ideas: Monetary Politics in Europe* (Ithaca: Cornell University Press).

Risse, T., Engelmann-Marten, D., Knopf, H.-J., and Roscher, K. (1999), 'To Euro or Not to Euro? The EMU and Identity Politics in the European Union', *European Journal of International Relations*, 5/2: 147–87.

Chapter 7

Agricultural Policy
Constrained Reforms

Elmar Rieger

Contents

Summary

In the 1960s the common agricultural policy (CAP) represented a striking example of the evolution of a European policy. Yet, its establishment reflected defensive, basically anti-market, national strategies of economic modernization, attaching small farmers' loyalty to rebuilt democracies, with welfare-state functions transferred to the European level and farming organizations as monopolistic intermediaries. A highly segmented system of governance developed, operating through both national and supranational mechanisms. It served to insulate agricultural policy from competing domestic political constituencies and from US demands for trade liberalization and thus helped to create a costly, cumbersome, and inefficient public policy. Rising costs forced reform in the early 1990s, with the WTO regime and US trade policies becoming major factors affecting the timing and the agenda of internal reforms. The 1999 and 2003 modifications continued a reform path which began with the reforms of Ray MacSharry, then Commissioner for Agriculture, focusing on decoupling income support from production subsidies via price policy. What had been a system centring on the administration of prices evolved into a system of direct payments to farmers. Not products, but producers are now the main focus of support. However, despite substantial changes in the institutional structure of the CAP, and notwithstanding the inclusion of agriculture in the more liberal WTO regulatory framework, the CAP remains a heavily bureaucratic system of economic regulation. This feature was strengthened, rather than weakened, by the enlargement process bringing in the large, comparatively unproductive, and manpower-heavy farming sector of the central and east European countries.

Introduction

Agricultural policy-making in the European Union (EU), despite the much acclaimed economic breakdown of the socialist countries of eastern Europe, and in defiance of global market capitalism, consists of what are basically anti-market politics. Ironically, with the accession of eight central and east European states in May 2004 the CAP enlarged its sphere of influence, extending a closed system of centralized bureaucratic governance notorious for its opacity, to countries which fought hard for democracy and free markets. Despite this, most reforms of post-communist transformation, even of political institutions, have mainly been designed from above (Blankenburg 2000).

The stated goal of the CAP is the preservation of an economic sector with supposedly distinctive institutional and social features, incompatible with the principles of industrial production and competitive markets. The outcome is a costly and conflict-ridden preservation of economic and social features, at odds both with the usual economic structure of an industrial society, and with the idea of traditional rural communities. This policy choice in the second half of the nineteenth century became entrenched in the wake of the Great Depression of the 1930s, and the autarchic policies of the second world war, and subsequent systems of economic regulation. As a result the agricultural sector of all the larger west European countries is not integrated into the overall economic and political system. Traditionally, prices were raised to a level which guaranteed even small-scale farmers a lifestyle compatible with general standards, thereby compensating for inter-sectoral disparity. However, the core elements of the CAP, that is, the regulation of markets insulated from import competition, were not invented by Brussels bureaucrats. Despite the supranational, or 'common' format of the CAP, member states' preferences are the main factors driving this policy system.

This choice gives the CAP a rationale of its own. Not only is it costly, but it also triggers unintended consequences, including major problems for international agricultural markets and heavy constraints on the ability of third-world countries to

Table 7.1 A historical perspective on agriculture in Europe

	Population active in agriculture (% total population)		Share of agriculture (% GDP)	
	1950	**2000**	**1950**	**2000**
Netherlands	17.7	3.4	12.9	2.2
Belgium	11.9	1.8	8.8	1.1
Luxembourg	24.7	2.3	9.5	0.6
France	30.9	3.4	15.0	2.2
Germany	23.0	2.5	12.3	0.9
Italy	44.4	5.3	29.5	2.4
Denmark	25.7	3.8	20.4	2.3
Ireland	40.2	10.2	31.3	2.5
UK	5.5	1.8	6.0	0.6
Portugal	53.1	14.3	26.8	2.4
Spain	51.5	7.3	35.0	3.6
Greece	48.9	13.4	33.5	6.7
Sweden	22.8	3.5	7.0	0.6
Finland	36.9	5.9	..	0.9
Austria	34.2	5.1	16.4	1.3
Estonia	..	11.3	..	1.7
Latvia	..	11.9	..	3.0
Lithuania	..	14.8	..	3.1
Poland	53.6	19.0	..	3.1
Czech Republic	39.0[1]	8.2	..	1.7
Slovakia	39.0[1]	9.0	..	1.9
Hungary	55.1	12.5	..	3.8
Slovenia	..	4.1	..	2.0
Bulgaria	74.2	9.7	..	16.0
Romania	70.0	21.8	..	11.4
Turkey	72	30.8	49.0	13.6
US	13.0	2.2	6.1	1.4

Note: [1]data for Czechoslovakia.

Sources: author's calculations based on *http://faostat.fao.org/faostat/default.jsp*; CEE country reports on the agricultural situation in candidate countries available on-line at *http://europa.eu.int/comm/agriculture/external/enlarge/publi/index_en.htm*; OEEC (1956), *Agricultural Policy in Europe and North America*.

export agricultural goods. For a long time the CAP succeeded and was indispensable for nearly all categories of farmers, often with different outcomes from those intended by its policy-makers. The variety of production systems found in Europe, and the number of farms, make it difficult to make precise evaluations about policy alternatives and their outcomes objectively in terms of economic and social adequacy, or to refuse demands for additional resources.

Between negative and positive integration

In the early years of the EU the distinctive features of the CAP were seen as laying the ground for intensified European integration. The creation of the European common market was based on the elimination of national barriers and thus constitutes a case of 'negative integration', but for agriculture this involved the coordination and fusion of six highly developed systems of state intervention (Pinder 1968). However, the CAP regime also entails positive entitlements to public assistance in the form of fixed prices and transfers. The first imposes negative restrictions on member states, whereas the latter imposes positive duties on public agencies at all levels of the European governance system. The articles in the Treaty of Rome (EEC) delineating the goals of the CAP were so vague that they needed further definition—a task the Council of Ministers quite successfully skirted. The Directorate-General for Agriculture (formerly DGVI, now DG AGRI) in the European Commission became the agency that defines the public interest in agricultural policy-making.

For farmers 'Europe' became a source of rights, not in the sense of simply having the freedom to do certain things, but by access to others' perceived entitlements; in this sense the CAP empowers farmers. Yet, unlike the social rights granted to individuals in welfare state regimes, CAP entitlements did not create zones of autonomy. However, the direct benefits of the CAP system are not immune to revision and reassessment, in that the economic positions of farmers are vulnerable to politics. With few exceptions, the European Court of Justice (ECJ) did not intervene. However, the 'radical jurisprudence' of the ECJ consisted in creating subjective rights in the field of 'negative' freedoms, but not in the field of 'positive' freedoms.

The CAP was not a political creation *ex nihilo*. National systems of agricultural support became supranational, but without direct links between the farming population of the member states and the EU. Increasingly complex forms of supranational political governance evolved around the CAP, apparently making it a positive 'story of action and success' (Lindberg and Scheingold 1970: 41). The remarkable rise of the major organization of European farmers, the Confederation of Professional Agricultural Organizations (COPA), seemed to indicate a quantum leap towards a genuinely supranational political system. Many of the general principles of European law were formed in the context of agricultural disputes (Snyder 1985; Usher 2001). Moreover, because of its size, sources, and format, the European Agricultural Guidance and Guarantee Fund (EAGGF) still dominates the Community budget, making the CAP the principal common policy of the EU, at times virtually synonymous with the general budget and expenditure (see Table 7.2).

Only with regard to agriculture did the scale of European political governance reach proportions resembling those of a federal government:

Here the community institutions have the power to legislate for the Union as a whole, without being required to refer back to the national parliaments. . . . It represents the Union's first effort to develop a common policy in major economic sphere. Such common policies are central to the successful implementation of the broader goal of economic union as well as the efficient operation of the customs union'. (Lindberg 1963: 219–20)

Table 7.2 European Union budget and expenditure on agriculture, 1965–2004[1]

	1965		1975		1985		1995		2004[2]	
	mn. €	%	mn. €	%	mn. €	%	mn. €	%	mn. €	%
General budget total	339.0	100	4,826.4	100	28,833.2	100	68,408.6	100	115,434	100
Expenditure on agriculture	28.7	8.5	4,404.4	72.2	20,413.3	70.8	37,850.1	55.3	49,305	42.7

Notes:
[1] Until 1995 general budget figures are for the EEC, ECSC, EURATOM and the European Development Fund (EDF). The EDF is financed by member states' contributions, is governed by its own financial rules, and is administered by a Steering Committee in accordance with specific procedures.
[2] Total appropriations for commitments.

Sources: Commission (2000f), *The Community Budget: The Facts in Figures*; Commission (2004r), *General Budget of the European Union for the Financial Year 2004.*

The CAP 'as a proxy for European integration' remains, 'an isolated relic' for the ambitions of the founding fathers of the European Community (Duchêne, Szczepanik, and Legg 1985: 1).

There is a widespread view that the CAP is, in the words of *The Economist* (29 September 1990), 'the single most idiotic system of economic mismanagement that the rich western countries have ever devised'. This view is not based on an analysis of the real forces shaping the agricultural policies of western Europe in the post-war era. It is simplistic to analyse the CAP in terms of 'stupidity' or 'mistakes'. More interesting is its resilience in the face of widespread hostility, even from those it was designed to help, i.e. farmers, since employment in agriculture continues to shrink and its share of the gross domestic product (GDP) of the Union stands at 1.7 per cent. Even more interesting is why the CAP was able to survive the accession in May 2004 of ten new countries with farming sectors resembling some of those in western Europe in the 1960s. With regard to agriculture, the EU had a particular—and vital—interest in ensuring that this enlargement would not increase (disruptive) diversity within the Union, and was hence actively engaged in reforms of the institutions and practices existing in the accession countries. The problem is pressing for those other countries in line for accession this decade (Bulgaria and Romania). Romania alone has more people active in agriculture than the ten new member states taken together, and Turkey has more people employed in agriculture than the EU15 (2001 figures). Looking at the history of the CAP, and the dismal situation of agriculture in nearly all central and east European countries, one is bound to ask if it is compelled to repeat its errors. The eastern enlargement of the CAP is a clear case of the politics of bureaucratic structures insofar as the solution preceded the problem. The CAP emerged once again as a constant solution apparently indifferent to the peculiar nature of the problem it was designed to resolve.

Understanding the CAP means considering it as an entity in its own right, rather than as the key to something else (be it integration theory, the dangers of supranationalism, a general theory of interest-group behaviour, rent-seeking, or joint-decision-making traps). Despite the economic revolution in rural areas, and the ups and downs of European integration, the CAP has basically remained the same. Indeed, even the growing tensions in EC–US agricultural trade relations have served to remind old and new member states alike of their attachment to this 'common' policy, despite an international environment dominated by liberal multilateralism, and thus at odds with this remnant of protectionism (Vaubel 1994: 174).

The key to understanding this policy domain is to view the CAP as an integral part of the European welfare state and its 'moral' economy. In other words, it has a *political* rationale. Unlike other welfare-state institutions, agricultural measures typically fuse production—that is, output-increasing—with income-related goals, making it hard to separate the distributive and regulatory dimensions, and in ways that defy the application of normal economic efficiency criteria. This is still true for the new regime of 'decoupled' farm aid.

The political effects can be summed up as follows:

- it facilitates the operation of an income-securing policy *vis-à-vis* a large and heterogeneous group, without requiring direct and costly contacts with individual farmers;

- it releases individual governments from having to decide on the needs of different farming groups or of individual farmers;

- it provides the farming sector with an overwhelming interest in maintaining the policy regime, since it improves the situation of all farmers, albeit larger much more than smaller ones;

- the use of comprehensive and product-specific prices has enabled governments to balance the heterogeneous needs of a highly differentiated farming sector; and

- both the member governments and national interest groups have acquired a shared purpose in sustaining a supranational policy.

Hence the CAP can be seen as a politically driven and defensive strategy to modernize European agriculture against the internal threat of an expanding industrial society and the external threat of vigorous US trade competition. This helps to explain five problems. It clarifies why decoupling income support from price policy has been so halting and is still far from complete. The more the initial legitimacy of direct income payments—compensating for cuts in the administered prices of commodity regimes—was lost, the greater the need to make the non-economic goals of agricultural policy explicit, and to avoid ends which would invite public scrutiny—something the old CAP had successfully avoided. Secondly, it clarifies why the governance of the CAP is so complex, neither pure intergovernmentalism nor real supranationalism, an addition to, and not a subtraction from, the powers of the national political systems of the member states. Thirdly, it explains why the CAP allocates resources rather perversely despite its explicit social orientation. The creation of a single agricultural support system has produced an increase in social and economic inequalities, from which large farmers, with considerable political clout, have profited disproportionately. Fourthly, it provides clues to how and why agriculture was surprisingly included in

Box 7.1 Making camel cheese safe for Europeans

When managing trade with developing countries, Brussels standards can also be a barrier to trade. Consider the case of camel milk cheese exports to the EU. Tiviski SARL, a dairy processor in Nouakchott, Mauritania, developed a technology to produce 'pâte molle' cheese from camel milk. It obtained the milk from nomad milk producers who were very poor. In return, Tiviski provided the producers with cheap access to credit and vaccinated their animals to ensure a supply of healthy milk. The camel cheese, after transport and production costs, was priced at $10 per kilogramme in the EU.

After winning a prize at a trade fair, the cheese found its way into élite stores such as Harrods in London and Fauchon in Paris. However, it proved to be difficult to find the correct tariff line for the product, and grouping it with 'other dairy, cheese' exposed it to a much higher tariff than regular cheese.

To make matters worse, the EU soon decided to abolish imports of camel cheese from Mauritania, arguing that the presence of 'foot and mouth' disease in the country could be transmitted from camels to other livestock, even though there is no real evidence that camels are capable of spreading the disease.

The EU then imposed another restriction: camel cheese could indeed be imported—but only if mechanical methods were used to obtain milk used in its production—an unworkable proposal for the low-income milk producers who were located miles away from major ports. Mauritania did not dispute this case at the WTO because of the sheer costs involved—costs that were not justified for exports of $3 million to $5 million worth of cheese per year.

Source: World Bank, *Global Economic Prospects 2004: Realizing the Development Promise of the Doha Agenda* (*www.worldbank.org/prospects/gep2004/*).

the Uruguay Round of GATT negotiations, and subsequently incorporated at least partially in the framework of the GATT and the WTO. The shift towards less trade-distorting forms of assisting farmers may be a way of reinforcing political control and economic rationality in this sector. Fifthly, it sheds light on the dismal consequences of the CAP regime for developing countries. The CAP is an inward-looking policy *par excellence*. Its task was never to improve the welfare of the world, but rather to see that European farmers were safe within it.

Defensive modernization: the CAP qua welfare state institution

Agricultural protectionism, reflected in domestic food prices, often more than double world prices, has long been the basic instrument of agricultural policy. This was not unique to the CAP; it continued the agricultural policies of the founder member states, and is still a common feature of economic modernization as developing countries switch from taxing to protecting farmers (Anderson and Hayami 1986). The CAP was not designed to increase food production, but used production-based support systems to increase the income of farmers (Milward 1981). Moreover, the oft-repeated assertion that there was a political bargain between the industrial interests of Germany, and the agricultural interests of France, should be laid to rest. The record provides no evidence for this, nor would it have made much sense economically (Willgerodt 1983: 111–14; Milward 1992: 283–4; Vaubel 1994: 174). More relevantly, all of the larger countries had sizeable farming populations which they did not want to exclude from the European Economic Community (EEC), and similarly Dutch agriculture was an integral and important part of the national export economy (Lindberg 1963: 220–5). Labour force and the economic size of the agricultural sector are a rough indicator for the equity problem at the centre of agricultural policy. In 1970, income disparity between the agricultural sector and the other sectors of the national economy was still striking. In Belgium, which had the most productive farming sector in west Europe, the income of a person employed in agriculture was equivalent to about 74 per cent of that for a person active in other sectors. The figures for the Netherlands, Italy, France, Luxembourg, and Germany are respectively 61 per cent, 51 per cent, 44 per cent, 35 per cent, and 34 per cent (GDP at factor cost per active person; see Tracy 1989: 274).

The inclusion of the CAP had two consequences. First, farmers did not block European integration, which was no small achievement, given the weight of the agricultural sector, both as a proportion of the labour force, and as a share of the economy in the late 1950s. Secondly, the CAP provided political protection *vis-à-vis* overseas agricultural exporters, notably in the US. Thus, the history and features of the CAP are more the product of how west European societies were being transformed after the second world war than of the formulations of the Treaty of Rome.

Income maintenance and the income security of farmers

The Treaty of Rome was remarkably brief on agriculture (see Box 7.2). The essence of Articles 38–46 (EEC) (now Arts. 32–38 TEC) was basically an 'agreement to agree'. The imprecision was an early indication that agriculture would be a controversial issue in European integration. The prior and highly protectionist national policies established the framework for the basic instruments of the CAP in several respects (Lindberg 1963: 223–5). First, market organizations, with fixed prices, were believed to reduce the risk and uncertainty associated with large variations in commodity prices and the volume of production. Secondly, market organizations which guarantee prices redistribute incomes from consumers and taxpayers to producers. From the Great Depression of the early 1930s onwards, income redistribution to financially stressed or low-income farmers became a major feature of farm policies (Schiller 1939; Schultz 1943). At least at the outset, the CAP was expressly designed to foster small and medium-sized family farms. Thirdly, encompassing market organizations, with fixed and guaranteed prices, provided all kinds of farmers with higher and more secure incomes. This was particularly important in the 1950s and 1960s in western Europe, with millions of smallholders remote from the normal apparatus of state bureaucracy.

> **Box 7.2** The five objectives of the CAP, Art. 33 TEC (ex Art. 39 EEC)
>
> - To increase agricultural production by promoting technical progress and by ensuring the rational development of agricultural production and optimum utilization of the factors of production, in particular labour;
> - to ensure a fair standard of living for the agricultural community, in particular by increasing the individual earnings of persons engaged in agriculture;
> - to stabilize markets;
> - to assure availability of supplies; and
> - to ensure that supplies reach consumers at reasonable prices.

In the first half of the twentieth century the parliamentary political process of mass democracy operated to bring agriculture within the mechanisms of the welfare states, rather than with a liberal market order. The initially limited role of the European Parliament (EP) meant that parties were absent as mediators of interest at the European level. Both national and transnational farm groups instead became the basic channels for mediating between farmers and the supranational political system. It was not that the agrarian interest groups defined the CAP, but that the governmental decisions to frame agricultural policy as an intrinsic element of the welfare state endowed these groups with a critical political influence.

The historical core of the CAP is the regulation of prices, aids for producing and marketing products, storage and carry-over arrangements, complemented by a common machinery for controlling imports and facilitating exports. Farmers had little autonomy in the price-fixing process or in economic competition. For a long time of utmost importance in the European context was the inability of farmers more favourably situated for production to underbid their rivals. The principal aim of the artificially created price structure was to affect directly the distribution of income, something markets do not allow. In the CAP, as in all planned economies, the prices governing farmers' decision-making did not balance supply and demand, but depended on political decisions. In order to stay in business farmers complied with decrees issued in Brussels, and not with the signals of market forces or the wishes of consumers. The matter of the demand to be satisfied by production was not dependent on the profitability of production in the market, but on the politics of the CAP. Not surprisingly, therefore, the basic economic orientation of farmers was not profit-making, in terms of income generated by markets, but rent-seeking, through exploitation of economic opportunities based on political relationships. Under these circumstances, such a strategy was not foolhardy, but a rational choice. This has changed with the 1992, 1999, and 2003 reforms, reducing price policy to a safety net and installing direct income payments as the mainstay of income support.

The CAP as a safe haven

Social policy functions for the agricultural community were not invented by the CAP, but came into being in the early 1950s in all west European countries. The need to increase agricultural production was widespread, but there was a special political need to integrate farmers into emerging welfare states and democratic politics, and a wish to keep the countryside populated. In the inter-war period major sections of the agrarian population had turned to radical right-wing parties to protest against governments that had tolerated the collapse of agricultural prices. This experience created a dramatic change in agricultural policies (Milward 2000), providing income security to farmers through guaranteed prices, but at the expense of creating tensions at the international level.

Most west European countries ran into serious trouble with the US because it too had protectionist agricultural policies, and a highly efficient and export-oriented agricultural sector on which the welfare of US farmers depended. However, in the 1950s the US tried to use the GATT, first, successfully to obtain a waiver for US programmes of agricultural subsidies, and then to force west European countries to open their agricultural markets.

The protectionist policies of Germany, Belgium, and Luxembourg were explicitly denied a legitimate position in the GATT, while France, Italy, and most other west European countries had been already targeted by the US Tariff Commission, because of the protectionist impact of their agricultural import restrictions (Dam 1970: 263). This situation made the inclusion of agriculture in the EEC a last resort for agricultural protectionism for the original six member countries. In 1962, when the common market organization for cereals was introduced as the first step in building the CAP, after serious conflicts with the US in particular, *The Economist* (15 December 1962) called the CAP a '*deus ex machina* which looks to most agricultural exporters in the GATT to be pretty diabolic', and 'a system of protection . . . about as watertight a system as could have been devised'. In particular, the system of variable levies, which changed according to changing internal prices, guaranteed that no imports would disturb the workings of the CAP.

The normal rules of the GATT do not apply to custom unions and other forms of regional economic integration, which are exempted from the most-favoured-nation principle. Notwithstanding its general commitment to eliminate non-tariff trade barriers, the GATT contained a specific exemption for agricultural import quotas and similar measures, if deemed necessary to make measures to control domestic supply work. This exemption has been a major source of disputes in international agricultural trade, particularly between the US and the EU (D. G. Johnson 1991; J. Scott 1996). The exclusion of agriculture from the GATT regime and from the rounds of tariff cuts survived until the Uruguay Round and its 'Agreement on Agriculture' of 1994.

The social and political dynamics of the CAP

Piecemeal reform became increasingly necessary because of developments triggered and shaped by the CAP itself. Initially, the international environment, changing world markets, and external political pressure, especially from the US, were of secondary importance. Insulating the farming sector from international competition had been the *raison d'être* of the CAP, for which the supranational policy format was a precondition. More important were the intra-European dynamics, with regard to both politics and policy. Member state preferences and thus intergovernmental bargains delegated to the European Commission the broad terms for running the CAP. However, the internal contradictions of the CAP soon began to dominate the agenda. The system of price support benefited larger farmers most, triggered concentration processes, and encouraged large-scale industrial production methods. Mechanical, chemical, and genetic innovations spurred the development of an agro-industrial complex which triggered a near-total rearrangement of European rural structures (see Chapter 13). Furthermore, in continental Europe the traditional way of life associated with farming and farming communities was disappearing rapidly. Finally, with the industrial appropriation of natural production processes farms became a major source of environmental problems (see Chapter 12; Goodman, Sorj, and Wilkinson 1987; Goodman and Redclift 1991). These developments were slow to impinge on the politics of the CAP. Until the MacSharry reforms of 1992 high prices were institutionally guaranteed, farmers were protected against the consequences of overproduction (i.e. falling prices), and import competition was offset by export subsidies. Raising output at all costs seemed the only way to higher and more secure incomes. It was only with the 2003 reforms that the 'greening of the CAP' became an obligatory part of support systems.

Structural measures, aimed at compensating for regional disadvantages and helping small farmers, had little impact, because the institutional and fiscal resources for this part of the CAP were dwarfed by expenditure on price support. The survival of regional production systems and of small farmers probably owes more to the in-built flexibility of family farming, than to CAP mechanisms. In particular, smaller farms survived because of two elements more important than the CAP: the rapid increase in other economic activities opened up new sources of income for agricultural households; and welfare payments, mostly child allowances and pension payments, formed a cushion (Arkleton Trust 1992). The overall effect is the persistent lag in the structural transformation of west European agriculture as a part of the larger economy. In 2000, in the EU15 three-quarters of the total volume of work on farms was performed by family members. At one end of the European spectrum, in the UK family members account for 64 per cent of total work, and at the other end, Greece reports 86 per cent.[1] However, notwithstanding the rhetoric of a 'European model of agriculture' or of Commissioner Fischler's renunciation of US-style farming, all signs point towards more, rather than less, industrialization of agricultural production. The economic modernization of the European countryside has been retarded as a result of the perverse combination of both national and supranational elements, in order to secure national interests.

In the first place, until the 2003 reform the fixed combination of price support and direct income payments to compensate for the reduction of prices produced persistent distortions. Reform was hard to achieve because what was at stake was not so much the welfare of European farmers as the fiscal balance between member states. This interest in maintaining a fiscal balance has also made it more difficult to accommodate other policy objectives—such as environmental protection and animal welfare—at the national level (Kapteyn 1996: 92–127).

A second contradiction is the interest of the Commission in improving the efficiency of CAP expenditure through direct income payments, for which it needed to supervise a transfer system also geared to achieving non-economic objectives. This required the development of a new farm audit system and dramatically increases 'red tape'. Part of the rationale for the direct income payments was that farmers must keep their land in good agricultural and environmental condition, and comply with

European standards for the environment, food safety, and animal health and welfare. Farms falling short of these requirements will face reductions in their direct payments. This system requires an enormously expanded system of surveillance to keep track of what is happening on the farm and to promote the interests of the larger community, i.e. food quality and plant and animal welfare, a more diverse farming sector, and an accessible landscape. It seems that rural development and environmental programmes are regarded as virtuous simply because they are not production aids. Function-oriented direct payments are much better suited to legitimate the stream of public money flowing to farms.

Political control of supranationalism

In the early negotiations over the regimes for common agricultural markets, the member governments took pains to retain a number of powers. Firstly, they hold the power to fix prices for individual commodities. The Commission had tried to link market organization to proposals for structural and social policy (Lindberg 1963: 238), but without success. Secondly, the main power to agree substantive legislation was retained by the Council of Ministers. Thirdly, although the responsibilities and powers of the EP increased substantially over time, its impact as regards agriculture has been limited; it was not until the bovine spongiform encephalopathy (BSE) crisis in 1996 that the EP came into the spotlight. A fourth element was the creation of the Special Committee on Agriculture (May 1960); this body of senior national civil servants prepares most meetings of the Council of Agriculture Ministers, helping to preserve the characteristic segmentation of agricultural policy-making. A fifth element is the vertical integration of national and supranational decision-making through the management committee system. The Council delegated most powers for managing the market organizations to the Commission, but required it to consult committees representing national interests. Each market organization has its own management committee, with a Commission official as chair and representatives from member governments, who vote according to qualified majority rules (Art. 148(2) EEC; now Art. 205(2) TEC). Under this procedure the Commission proposes measures to the committee for endorsement. If the measure receives a favourable opinion by a qualified majority, the Commission can put it into operation (Usher 2001: 176–8). If there is a qualified majority against, the issue goes to the Council. The same system is applied to the Guidance Section of the EAGGF.

To sum up, policy has been vertically integrated through national and Community mechanisms, limiting the autonomy of the Commission and reserving key decision-making functions for the Council. The thick web of committees ensures the prominence of national preferences in this apparently supranational process. In addition, since 1974 the European Council has circumscribed the function of the Commission as the sole initiator of Community legislation. At both the preparatory and the executive stages the national elements prevail. The Commission, in mapping out basic strategies and in sketching available alternatives, has little choice but to anticipate both the wishes and reactions of the members of the Council of Ministers. This structural feature of the process accounts for much of the content of agricultural policy, and this biases the substance of the CAP. It also helps explain why some policy actors—associations of small farmers, environmentalists, rural activists—seem to lack effective voices in this system. Policy outcomes often emerge without the underlying choices being debated, or without wider public scrutiny beyond the immediate interests involved in the regulatory or management committees. The CAP relies heavily on representational monopolies. The formal structures for channelling organized functional interests into the policy process provide legitimacy for their results, and thereby invite policy capture, since it is the results, rather than the procedures, which provide legitimacy. The classical instruments of public accountability, including judicial review, are virtually absent in the CAP. The essentially managerial and technocratic mode of policy-making creates the illusion that all problems can be resolved on the basis of technological considerations, assuming the policy goals are settled. The process makes it virtually impossible to develop truly redistributive policies, or to address normative issues which have *European* agriculture at their core, and not just the aggregate of national farming sectors.

CAP expenditure per capita varies considerably across member states, and the same is true for the new system of direct payments (see Fig. 7.1). The first and most important source of variation is farm productivity. Differences in farm size explain why per farm, the UK receives the lion's share of CAP expenditure. A second source of variation is the orientation of the national agricultural sector towards products covered by subsidy-heavy market organizations, i.e. those for arable crops, milk, olive oil, and beef and veal, which account for 66 per cent of total CAP expenditure. For example, whereas in Spain 87 per cent of agricultural production is covered by market organizations, it is only 58 per cent in the Netherlands.[2] A third source of variation is

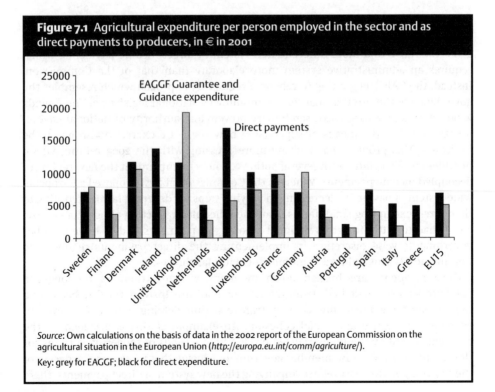

Figure 7.1 Agricultural expenditure per person employed in the sector and as direct payments to producers, in € in 2001

Source: Own calculations on the basis of data in the 2002 report of the European Commission on the agricultural situation in the European Union (*http://europa.eu.int/comm/agriculture/*).

Key: grey for EAGGF; black for direct expenditure.

the mix between expenditure on structural measures (EAGGF Guidance) and price policy/direct payments (EAGGF Guarantee). EAGGF Guidance expenditure is 7.7 per cent of total CAP expenditure, but in Portugal it is 29.4 per cent of total expenditure, and in Denmark it is almost zero.[3] The distribution of direct payments to producers also presents a strong contrast. First of all, calculating the ratio of the number of holdings to the number of beneficiaries of direct payments to producers suggests that in some countries a high number of farms seem to be outside the scope of the CAP. In Portugal 40 per cent of holdings do not receive any direct income payments. In Ireland and Denmark the ratio is greater than 1 (1.17 and 1.03), indicating several payments per farm. In the EU15, 34 per cent of farms are not covered by direct payment regimes, and 50 per cent of the total cash disbursement goes to 5 per cent of beneficiaries.[4] Secondly, intra-country distribution reveals even greater disparities. Whereas in Italy 92.6 per cent of farmers receive payments of less than €5,000 per farm and have a share of 43.2 per cent of total direct payments, in the UK 47.1 per cent of farmers receive less than €5,000 and have a share of only 3.9 per cent of total direct payments.[5] The main reason why national agricultural sectors remain worlds of their own, each of them applying different criteria for what kind of income inequality is tolerable, is the local element in the governance of the CAP.

The national dimension of the CAP

Over the years a policy process already marked by strong national influences has been brought even further back under national control. In some ways this is unavoidable given the move to a more differentiated system of direct income payments, which requires an administrative system more elaborate than that of the Commission. Instead, the CAP is beginning to rely on a regulatory approach which resembles the governance of the internal market, i.e. monitoring national legislation. The Agenda 2000 reforms increased the discretionary powers and authority of national governments, and thus the means of supervising how these are exercised also had to be increased. This problem has become more pressing with the 2003 reform, which provides member states with several options on how to implement the new regime of decoupled income payments. Whereas the Commission at first proposed a European-wide system of payments decreasing in varying steps for different farms according to their size—exempting small farms from the scheduled reduction altogether—in the end it had to settle for gross national amounts of payments and to leave member governments wide discretion in implementing the direct payments regime. The Commission is thus reduced to monitoring national choices.

Once payments are broken down by member states there is no longer a pan-European rationale in distributing CAP expenditure. Instead, the CAP becomes a mechanism for explicit inter-country transfers, thus defying notions of European economic coherence and social cohesion. An example of this is provided by the problems posed by the industrialized production methods of modernized farms for the environment. Because member governments decide themselves on the design of the environmental measures accompanying the new system of direct payments, there is no way that the Union—in the form of the Commission—will be able to allocate funds to the zones with the greatest agri-environmental problems and/or potential. The Commission has the negative power to limit what governments do in subsidizing their own farming sectors in their own way, but no positive power in forcing them to operate their policy instruments according to a European, rather than a country-specific rationale.

There have been other elements of renationalization. The Berlin European Council of March 1999, which reached a decision on Agenda 2000, invented 'national envelopes' spending on the beef and milk sectors in each member state. 'This will allow member states flexibility to compensate for regional differences in production practices and agronomic conditions which might make restructuring difficult . . .' (Commission 1999*b*). The Council now has a new tailor-made discretionary instrument at hand to buy off resistance to policy changes and to facilitate decision-making. In addition, the CAP has been increasingly redesigned to allow member governments— and those regions with some autonomy and appropriate political and financial resources—to make use of the CAP's instruments in their own way and for their own purposes. For example, both the timing and scope of decoupling direct income payments agreed in the 2003 reform depend on decisions of member governments. Together with the optional nature of some environmental programmes, designed to offset, at least partially, falling prices, the uneven pattern of implementing decoupling is likely to create new distortions in the markets for agricultural products.

The continuous strengthening of these national elements of the CAP, however, poses two major dilemmas. The first is the need to balance supranational and national elements. Because constitutionally the CAP is a common policy, the subsidiarity principle cannot be used to reorganize its basic structure. Governments want to make use of the CAP for exclusively national purposes, and at the same time they need the CAP to have enough supranational autonomy to insulate European agriculture from its international environment and from efforts to undermine its welfare function. The second dilemma is that governments are increasingly unable to pursue CAP reform because of financial repercussions. The enormous financial outlays under the CAP generated new reasons for member governments to stick to the embedded institutional arrangement whenever the centrifugal forces—fuelled mostly by the unintended effects of the CAP itself—threatened to gain ascendancy. For example, the inability of the UK government to let go of its budgetary rebate also reduces its capacity to influence reforms on the expenditure side. In addition, simply because of its scale national CAP expenditure has now become an essential element in brokering deals necessary for policy reform in areas outside agriculture.

Permutations of the CAP

Over time the CAP became the most important agent for transforming European agriculture and its original socio-structural foundations, which had given it legitimacy and rationality. Yet, increasingly it has to deal with undesired and unintended consequences. These generated demands for more corrections and a continual multiplication of policy instruments. Indeed, the power of law over economic conduct has grown weaker rather than stronger. Whatever the systems of surveillance, farmers can often use a measure quite differently from the way intended, a recurrent feature in the history of the CAP. This is the most important reason why the outcomes of revisions and amendments often contradict the intentions of the reformers.

CAP planning is premised on a view of a 'general' or European interest and notions of a basic incentive structure common to all farmers. It shares this feature with state socialism, where the diversity of interests, not properly taken into account in the planning process, spontaneously makes itself felt when individual farmers make decisions most convenient for them. CAP decisions have been made as if these objective economic laws did not apply in agriculture. Therefore, 'post-decision surprises' are a constant feature, because economic laws continue to function. Policy-makers attributed the recurrent permanent misallocation of resources to farmers' motivations and thus tried to micro-manage their behaviour, turning a blind eye to the fact that the problem lay much deeper in the political philosophy of the policy. The CAP still involves an autocratic utopia in the sense that it entails a vision of a broad transformation of the economic and social structures of European agriculture.

The Commission responded to this systemic problem not by revising the fundamentals of the CAP, but by further intensifying its regulatory mechanisms. The number of agricultural products covered by centralized market organizations steadily increased, even though other instruments were technically available, and more farmers switched to products not covered by the CAP. Existing income inequalities have been aggravated by uniform price policies and led to the introduction of so-called structural measures to offset them. The workload of the Commission became heavier, presenting ever more difficult choices. At the same time the system of agricultural decision-making was increasingly hampered by the *de facto* requirement of consensus in the Council of Ministers, although explicit vetoes of decisions have been rare (Vasey 1988: 731). Increased heterogeneity of the agricultural sector as a consequence of successive enlargements generated extra problems, and made the CAP dependent on even more complicated decisions.

The inability to control CAP expenditure or to limit its more perverse distributional effects has been a striking feature of the process. Originally the CAP was expected to be self-financing via levies on agricultural imports. Nowadays the EU budget depends on revenue contributions from the member states (see Chapter 8). Increased agricultural productivity in western Europe, induced by high guaranteed prices, and helped by export subsidies, turned the EU into a major exporter, despite the low level of world market prices. From the late 1950s to the early 1970s the degree of self-sufficiency of the then Community of six members rose from 90 to 111 per cent for wheat, and from 101 to 116 per cent for butter. As a French negotiator stated:

It is true that in the future the Common Market may no longer have such large import deficits; . . . But the Community, whose agricultural policy would by then be defined by common decisions, would . . . have to bear the consequences of that common definition; a common policy calls for common financing. (Tracy 1989: 258)

Export subsidies, along with storage, became the largest spending category of the CAP, rising from $740 million to $11.137 billion in 1993, with one-third going to cereals alone (Preeg 1995: 95), in contrast to 9 per cent of US agricultural export subsidies on cereals.

Despite early warnings by agricultural economists about the costly consequences of an output-geared system of price support, until the 1970s the CAP could be characterized

> **Box 7.3** The 2003 reform, key elements of the new CAP
>
> - *Single farm payment*: payments to farmers no longer linked to production ('decoupled');
> - *cross-compliance*: farmers who want to be eligible for the single farm payments must respect eighteen statutory requirements in the fields of environment, public, animal and plant health and animal welfare, and keep their land in good agricultural and environmental conditions;
> - strengthening of *rural development* policy as the second pillar of the CAP;
> - revision of *market support* mechanisms (e.g. intervention, storage, and export subsidies): reducing common market organization to safety nets;
> - introduction of *financial discipline* mechanism ensuring farm budget not overshot.

as a textbook case of an income-oriented policy (Rosenblatt *et al*. 1988; Tracy 1989; Anania, Carter, and McCalla 1994). The years between 1979 and the mid-1980s witnessed the onset of a more cautious price policy and the introduction of 'producer co-responsibility', with farmers bearing part of the costs of disposing of surplus production. Commission proposals for lower prices bore little fruit.

The period 1984–87 brought more serious changes: the introduction of milk quotas, and restrictive price policies for most other agricultural products. High budgetary costs started the push for a policy change; this reduced agricultural incomes and forced some small producers out of business, but the price reductions overall had little effect on production growth. In 1988 budget ceilings and stabilizers were introduced to control expenditure: by binding it to the level of the general budget of the Community through the 'agricultural guideline'; and by introducing production thresholds, which automatically trigger price cuts. This meant a further reduction in real agricultural prices.

The MacSharry reforms of 1992, piloted by Ray MacSharry, then Agriculture Commissioner, were a first step in moving the CAP away from product support to direct aid payments to farmers. This was followed by the Agenda 2000 reforms in 1999 and the 2003 reforms (see Box 7.3). Each reform package brought lower institutional prices, compensating farmers with progressively increasing direct payments. Because income support was linked to levels of production, compulsory set-aside was introduced as a supply control measure. Commodity regimes were increasingly reduced to basic safety nets, reducing costs for storage and export subsidies, the two biggest expenditure items of the old CAP. The crop sector was the first to be subject to lower intervention prices, followed by the markets for beef and veal, and finally for milk. In this way, markets could play a greater role in balancing supply and demand. Agenda 2000 presented a first attempt to institutionalize the concept of multi-functionality, bringing the mixed bag of structural measures into a single legal framework (rural development). Agriculture and rural areas were acknowledged not only as producers of agricultural commodities, but also as producers of environmental and other non-economic goods. The 2003 reform represents the biggest shift in EU support for farmers to date (see Fig. 7.2). The Agenda 2000 reforms introduced incentives to farm

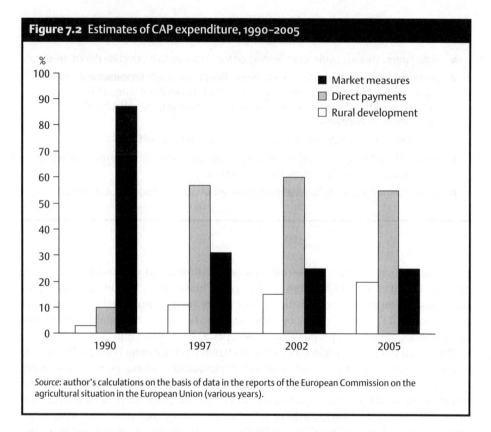

Figure 7.2 Estimates of CAP expenditure, 1990–2005

Legend: Market measures; Direct payments; Rural development

Source: author's calculations on the basis of data in the reports of the European Commission on the agricultural situation in the European Union (various years).

in an environmentally sensitive way, a shift that was substantially expanded with the 2003 reforms. Direct payments are now linked to the observance of environmental, food quality, and animal welfare standards, making payments subject to keeping farmland in good agricultural and environmental condition (cross-compliance). In addition, payments to farmers will no longer be linked to production. This 'decoupling' means that farmers obtain income payments irrespective of what—and how much—they produce, a move made possible by making price policy irrelevant for farm income. Both the scope of structural measures and the money set aside for them were expanded, a shift also symbolically marked by upgrading 'rural development' to a 'second pillar' of the CAP.

Decoupling income support from production also means that the EU has a much tighter grip on the budget, because neither market swings nor the output decisions of farmers will directly translate into increased expenditure. For this reason there is now a much greater chance to hold the so-called 'guideline' for CAP expenditures. However, the EU has still a quasi-constitutional obligation, which persists in the new Constitutional Treaty, to provide an equitable standard of living for the Community's agricultural population by way of the CAP, and if less income comes from markets, public support has to make up the difference. This limits the shifting of funds from the first (income support), to the second (rural development) pillar of the CAP, as long as expenditure on rural development does not directly translate into higher farm incomes. On the contrary, rural development measures improve cost-efficiency and raise output.

Unresolved issues: intra-sectoral inequalities and the environment

The MacSharry reforms introduced direct income payments as a compensation for the substantial cuts in prices and thus loss of income. Both the 1999 and 2003 reform packages continued this line, by linking the level of direct income support to the output of the individual farm. Three problems ensued. First, direct payments were judged by farmers solely according to whether they closed the income gap opened by falling prices. Maintaining the existing level of farm households remained a public responsibility, and farm income continued to occupy the centre of political struggles.

A second problem is the dramatically increased intra-sectoral inequality. Because of the fixation on compensating farmers for declining price support both progressivity—giving small farmers more—and degressivity—giving the largest farmers less—disappeared fast from the agenda. Instead, because 'leakage' from direct income payments is much lower compared to price support, basing payments on historic output data per farm considerably increased inter-farm inequity. An OECD study (2003) reported that the 'transfer efficiency' of price support is below 25 per cent even under the best conditions. Thus, only a quarter of every euro (or dollar) spent on market regimes improves the net income of farmers, the other three-quarters going to industries located upstream and downstream from farms. Thus, the shift to direct payments substantially improved transfer efficiency, securing higher income for farmers, but aggravated the perverse distribution of incomes in the agricultural sector. Because direct payments are based on production, they dissociate small from large farms even more, and, at the same time, help small farmers to survive, not least because the share of low-income farm households is significantly larger compared to the rest of society (OECD 2003). Direct income payments allow inefficient operators to remain farming, if they chose to subsidize their farming business with the decoupled support payment. Large farms, which are generally not the most prosperous, nevertheless benefit most both from commodity regimes and from direct payments. Clearly, neither equity-concerns nor market-failure arguments can be used to justify assisting this class of farmers. As the contrasting example of Switzerland shows, making direct payments subject to many constraints related to farm size, household income, and geographic location, can help to address intra-sector inequity to a large degree (OECD 2003: 26).

A third problem is how to link direct payments to non-economic objectives. The BSE crisis and subsequent food scares moved the issue of food safety centre stage. Increasing concerns about plant technology and animal welfare were difficult to accommodate. As for the 'greening' of the CAP, the expected environmental benefits of the reforms of 1992 and 1999 are not yet achieved to a significant extent, as the European Environment Agency's assessment of the current state of the rural environment makes clear (EEA 1999: 406–7). The environmental measures that were mostly (mis)used to channel additional money—and legitimacy—to farmers, and had a limited impact on overall environmental conditions, a situation widely replicated at the national and regional levels within member states, as the Special Report of the European Court of Auditors on 'The Greening of the CAP' pointed out (European Court of Auditors 2000, para. 51).

This short historical account provides some clues as to why the CAP proved so resistant to major changes. There are two key factors. First, the institutional apparatus of supranational policy-making, married to national and sectoral interests, brings considerable inertia into the governance of the CAP. Secondly, the distinctive 'moral economy' of the CAP has been welfare-oriented and inward-looking, making it difficult to use economic and budgetary criteria as leverage for reforms. The paradox of the past two decades consists of exploding costs, combined with a shrinking farming population, and a diminished role for agriculture in the economy. CAP expenditure per capita rose from 64.2 ecu (the shared unit of account prior to the introduction of the euro) in 1987, to 104.6 ecu in 1992 and to €120.7 in 2001. Even if expenditure fell from 0.61 per cent of GDP in 1993 to 0.43 per cent of GDP 2004, the share of agriculture in the GDP fell from 2.5 to 1.7 per cent, while CAP expenditure per farm more than doubled in the same period (Commission 2004g: 22).

The WTO and the politics of agriculture

The new politics of international trade relations have probably had more impact on CAP reform than intra-EU budgetary pressures and internal factors. The CAP had been a recurrent source of argument between the EU and its international trading partners. The Uruguay Round of the GATT provoked a struggle over whether and how agriculture would be drawn onto the agenda (Woolcock and Hodges 1996). In the final analysis the German government helped the French to hold out against extensive liberalization, while at the same time placating the US by pointing to the bigger issues at stake (Wood 1995: 228–31). The Agreement on Agriculture to include agriculture within the GATT/WTO framework, was a kind of prior international ratification by the EU of the MacSharry reforms, thus fundamentally changing the nature of bargaining in the future and paving the way for domestic reforms. These international pressures combined with internal challenges to promote more sustained efforts for reform, although not enough to revolve the fundamental tensions between the EU and the agricultural exporting countries within the Cairns Group as well as the US, or to mitigate the damage done by the CAP through EU protection to underdeveloped countries and, increasingly, central and eastern Europe (Scott 1996).

The primacy of domestic welfare

A key feature of the CAP has been 'Community preference', namely the principle that no trade agreement should result in injury to domestic producers. External relations took second place to domestic concerns in the governance of the CAP. This provided a mirror image to the US waiver of 1955 vis-à-vis the GATT, which enabled the US to use protective devices at the border to prevent domestic support arrangements from being undermined (Fennell 1997: 32).

Until the late 1980s this approach held firm, but then the context in which 'Community preference' was situated changed dramatically (Villain and Arnold 1990; Denza 1996). Politically, it became more difficult to shelter agriculture from the consequences of open markets and intensified competition. Secondly, structural and rural policies for agriculture achieved a new prominence within the EU. Thirdly, environmental concerns complicated the picture by bringing in extra demands on agriculture. Fourthly, as the population employed in agriculture shrank, it became more obvious that border protection was a very costly way of providing income maintenance to farmers. Direct income payments decoupled from production, made import protection and export subsidies dispensable (Corden 1997: 74–80). Border protection therefore became less relevant.

Thus, the real change in the agricultural policy-making arena of both the EU and the US occurred with the decision to allow domestic agricultural support systems— and not just agricultural tariffs and export subsidization—to become a topic of high priority in the Uruguay Round launched in September 1986. This opened a 'window of opportunity' for CAP reform. An extra set of players, with clearly marked preferences, was able to intervene and to feed views into the internal arguments. Nonetheless, internal disagreements, linked to the segmentation of the farming sector and the European market organizations for separate products, sharpened national profiles and raised the stakes for national politicians. Only by deliberately upgrading the external pressure, rather than pushing it aside, as in former GATT Rounds, could the EU governments convince themselves that they were better off with a reformed rather than an unreformed CAP. The long-standing fight against export subsidies, the *bête noire* of the GATT, was used by the Commission to give an extra twist of urgency to the move within the EU to direct income payments, as the means to give markets more saliency. Of course, the purpose of the WTO is not to do away with social farm policies, but to address support which has a negative impact on international trade. Therefore, CAP reform is essentially based on the switch from coupled to de-coupled payments; or in WTO speak from 'amber/blue' to 'green box' support, as a shift from trade 'distorting' to non-distorting (or minimally distorting) support (see Chapter 15).

Under pressure from the WTO both the US and the EU have undertaken significant changes to commodity policies in the past decade (US Department of Agriculture 2004). Both the EU and the US face similar pressures from tight budgets, trade policy constraints, and increasing public connection of agricultural policy with issues beyond traditional goals for supporting 'productionistic' or high-yield agriculture. Yet, despite some similarities—fewer and enlarged farms with less people employed and a declining share of the GDP—farm structures in the EU and the US remain vastly different as do policy structures, despite some convergence (see Tables 7.1 and 7.3). The 2002 Farm Act altered US policies, just as the EU has enacted reforms, but the most significant variations involve the differing reliance on tax-based income versus consumer-burdening price support, the use of surplus disposal via export subsidies and supply control, and the reliance on border measures. However, US and EU commodity policies are becoming more similar, with increased emphasis on decoupled income support and greater focus on the interactions between agriculture, the environment, and the consumer. Table 7.3 also indicates that the WTO may help to keep CAP reform on track, not least because EU officials were able to use it to bolster their own policy ideas. In the US and Japan the trend is in the opposite direction with increasing reliance on trade-distorting and consumer-burdening border measures in their farm policy mix.

Table 7.3 Basic agricultural structures in the EU15, new member states, and the US (2002)

	Utilized agricultural area (mn. ha)	No. farms (1000s)	Farm size (ha)	Employment) (1000s)	Employment (% of pop.)	Share of agriculture in GDP (%)
EU15	128	6,766	18.7	6,701	4.2	1.7
New member states	38		1.5*	3,871	13.2	3.1
USA	376	2,158	174.4	3,480	2.5	1.4

*Includes all farms, many of which are very small.

Sources: Agriculture in the EU—Statistical and Economic Information 2002, DG AGRI; Statistical Abstract of the USA (2003 edn.); United States Department of Agriculture, Economic Research Service: US–EU Food and Agriculture Comparisons, Washington, DC, 2004 (WRS-04-04).

WTO rules exempt environmental programmes from the restrictions that apply to production support, leaving both the EU and the US greater scope to use environmental programmes to support farm income, although with different policy methods. While conservation is at the heart of most US programmes, the EU's policies target rural development and provision of environmental amenities to a much greater extent. As of 2004 it is not the high politics of ministerial meetings, but the dispute settlement system of the WTO which is bearing the strain to keep order in agricultural trade, the battle over the EU banana regime being a case in point (Stevens 2000; Weiss 2003). Another arises as a result of biotechnology, where distinct regulatory approaches to consumer safety are practised on both sides of the Atlantic (see Chapter 13).

Saving the CAP: the politics of enlargement

In the years leading up to the recent enlargement many observers wondered whether the CAP could 'survive enlargement to the East' (see, for example, Josling 1998). Leszek Balcerowicz (1999: 8), the former Polish Minister of Finance, wrote in 1999 that 'without deep reforms of the CAP, it is difficult to imagine a successful outcome to enlargement . . . . A market-oriented reform of the CAP is necessary for the EU to enlarge without excessive costs'. A team of economists advising the Dutch government feared that 'the present, robust *acquis* will be undermined by a combination of lower standards of adoption, implementation, surveillance and enforcement in the CEECs, overloading an already overburdened EU system' (Pelkmans, Gros, and Núñez Ferre 2000: 9).

The most recent round of enlargement involves a dramatic change in the farm and social structures which the CAP has to address (see Table 7.4). Whereas in 2000 the population of the then twelve candidate countries[6] constituted 22 per cent of the population of the enlarged EU, their contribution to the GDP, and thereby potentially to the EU budget, was only around 5 per cent. In addition, the income difference, compared with the EU15 countries, is far greater than in earlier enlargements. This is true whether we measure at official exchange rates or at purchasing power parities, and whether compared with the EU15 average or with the lowest ranked member country in EU15. In 2002, GDP per capita in the eight CEE countries which joined the EU in 2004 stood at 23 per cent of GDP per capita in the EU15. Whereas Slovenia, the new member country with the highest GDP per capita had nearly the same level as Portugal, the poorest country in the EU15, Poland, the most populous new member state, reached 41 per cent of the Portuguese level, and Latvia, the poorest new member state, only 30 per cent.[7] Whereas the output in agriculture of the new member countries is almost 10 per cent of the output of the EU15, employment in agriculture in CEE countries is almost 58 per cent of the employment in the EU15, indicating low productivity and thus severe income problems in rural areas.[8] The level of national support has generally been much lower, and total support for farmers in the eight new member states is only 3 per cent of total support for farmers in the EU15 (see Table 7.5).

All CEE countries are plagued by taxing combinations of manpower-heavy farm sectors and high unemployment, low productivity, and a generally poor state of the infrastructure and provision of utilities in rural areas (Fernández 2002: 30). Despite collectivization a private agricultural sector persisted in the form of a large number of very small farms, with an underproductive and excessively large agricultural labour force. In most CEE countries micro-scale farming operating at subsistence levels co-exists with oversized former state and collective farms now privatized (see Table 7.4). Extending the CAP to the CEE countries will certainly deepen intra-sectoral inequities, given the failure to remove the disparity in benefits gained by large and small farmers, despite the Commission's attempts to do so in 1992, 1999, and 2003. The CEE countries have large swathes of agricultural lands, an enormous number of farms which are now subject to environmental regulations, which may constitute an insurmountable challenge to implementing the CAP efficiently. Neither the phased direct payments from the EU budget nor their own constrained national budgets provide the scope for compensating farmers for using environmentally beneficial but costly farming techniques, especially since, under the second pillar of the CAP, governments must be able to co-finance programmes for rural development. Hence EAGGF funds for rural development reserve for the ten new members only 17.5 per cent of that earmarked for EU15 countries. For the period 2004-6 Poland is expected to receive nearly the same amount as Ireland will receive for the period 2000-6, despite having thirteen times the number of farms (*Factsheet on Rural Development in the European Union* (Commission 2003)).

The reluctance to tailor new CAP instruments to the particular needs of these new member states stands in stark contrast to the 1995 enlargement, when Austria, Finland, and Sweden, being comparatively rich countries, joined the EU. In the words of the Commission, 'the design of comprehensive Rural Development Programmes for these countries was an essential ingredient to pave the way for the successful

Table 7.4 Farm structures in new member states of central and eastern Europe (2002)

Countries, running North–South		Unit	<5	5–20	20–50	50–100	>100	Total
					Farm size in ha			
Estonia	Holdings		44,060	18,577	4,239	973	1,020	68,869
	Share of total	%	64	27	6	1	2	100
	Area cultivated	ha	76,903	184,170	125,751	66,346	422,549	857,719
	Share of total	%	9	21	14	8	48	100
	Average size	ha	1.7	9.9	29.7	68.2	414.3	12.7
Latvia	Holdings		75,992	81,884	17,307	3,321	1,738	180,263
	Share of total	%	42	45	10	2	1	100
	Area cultivated	ha	209,500	821,500	507,800	224,700	465,200	2,228,700
	Share of total	%	9	37	23	10	21	100
	Average size	ha	2.8	10.0	29.3	67.7	267.7	12.4
Lithuania	Holdings		334,800	177,800	78,100	15,300	n.r	606,000
	Share of total	%	55	29	13	3	n.r	100
	Area cultivated	ha	886,500	1,110,400	593,100	310,600	n.r	2,900,600
	Share of total	%	31	38	20	11	n.r	100
	Average size	ha	2.6	6.2	7.6	20.3	n.r	4.8
Poland	Holdings		1,062,400	717,800	89,700	15,800		1,885,700
	Share of total	%	56	38	5	1		100
	Area cultivated	ha	2,633,400	6,877,500	2,489,700	3,932,300		15,932,900
	Share of total	%	16	43	16	25		100
	Average size	ha	2.5	9.6	27.8	248.9		8.4
Czech Republic	Holdings		15,756	5,530	9,433	1,830	4,036	36,585
	Share of total	%	43	15	26	5	11	100
	Area cultivated	ha	31,034	38,669	205,180	127,439	3,279,700	3,682,022
	Share of total	%	1	1	5	4	89	100
	Average size	ha	2.0	7.0	21.8	69.6	812.6	100.6
Slovakia	Holdings		63,432	1,682	1,829	486	1,779	69,208
	Share of total	%	92	3	2	1	2	100
	Area cultivated	ha	48,791	11,589	41,893	34,206	2,022,834	2,159,313
	Share of total	%	2	0	2	2	94	100
	Average size	ha	0.8	6.9	22.9	70.4	1,137.1	31,2
Hungary	Holdings		910,523	41,062	4,434	3,556	795	960,370
	Share of total	%	95	4	1	0	0	100
	Area cultivated	ha	825,776	844,057	303,075	951,692	1,726,512	4,651,112
	Share of total	%	18	18	6	21	37	100
	Average size	ha	0.9	20.6	68.4	267.6	2171.7	4.8
Slovenia	Holdings		53,383	29,587	1,729	864	864	86,427
	Share of total	%	62	34	2	1	1	100
	Area cultivated	ha	247,135	204,155	42,980	10,754	32,235	537,249
	Share of total	%	46	38	8	2	6	100
	Average size	ha	4.6	6.9	24.9	12.4	37.3	6.2

Source: Reproduced with the kind permission of Peter Weingarten, President of IAMO, Institut für Agrarenwicklong im Mittel- und Osteuropa.

Note: n.r. = not recorded; data for Poland for columns 4–5 are not differentiated in source.

Table 7.5 Producer Support Estimates for new member states in central and eastern Europe and the EU, 1997–2001

Countries running North–South	1997 Total PSE in mn. €	1997 PSE as % of total agric. product.	1998 Total PSE in mn. €	1998 PSE as % of total agric. product.	1999 Total PSE in mn. €	1999 PSE as % of total agric. product.	2000 Total PSE in mn. €	2000 PSE as % of total agric. product.	2001 Total PSE in mn. €	2001 PSE as % of total agric. product.
Estonia	27	6	91	20	24	6	31	7	44	13
Latvia	29	5	109	20	103	22	82	15	79	16
Lithuania	64	4	225	16	208	16	85	6	125	11
Poland	1,767	12	3,166	22	2,424	19	1,018	7	1,322	10
Czech Republic	221	6	878	23	796	24	578	16	534	17
Slovakia	200	11	531	31	364	25	365	23	138	11
Hungary	318	6	946	19	1,079	23	990	20	530	12
Slovenia	239	32	322	42	354	49	303	39	299	40
EU15	92,664	32	102,330	36	108,241	39	97,244	34	103,937	35

Note: The PSE (Producer Support Estimate), which shows the annual monetary transfers to farmers from policy measures has two components: policy measures that maintain domestic prices for agricultural goods at levels higher (and occasionally lower) than those at the country's border (market price support); and policy measures that provide payments to farmers, based on criteria such as the quantity of a commodity produced, the amount of inputs used, the number of animals kept, the area farmed, or the revenue or income received by farmers (budgetary payments). For more details, see Tangermann (2004).

Source: OECD (2002: 56–7), converted into euro.

integration of the agricultural sectors of these countries into the EU' (Commission 2004g: 18).

There was a near total separation of the 2003 CAP reform and enlargement. Agenda 2000, agreed at the Berlin European Council in March 1999, was designed to keep EU spending on agriculture within budgetary limits, even though it was clear that in the longer term this would have to be reviewed. As accession approached, the Commission placed great emphasis on the capacity of new member states' administrations to implement the *acquis* on schedule, never an issue in previous rounds of enlargement.

The main argument for denying the new member states direct payments was that their price levels would rise due to the extension of common market to the CEE countries, that farmers would therefore suffer no loss due to this factor and would need to pay no compensation. Commissioner Fischler even indicated that full direct payments have negative effects on production, restructuring, and income disparities

(Karlsson 2002: 58).[9] In contrast, the need to achieve full health standards for agricultural products would produce a rapid restructuring of farm structures. EU officials pronounced most of Poland's small family farms—80 per cent are tiny family plots—as inefficient, unsanitary, and perpetuating the poverty of their owners (Farnam 2001).

Agenda 2000 tried to settle both the rules and the funding for the new member states until 2006. In 2002 the Commission nonetheless used the Mid-term Review of the CAP to propose a new round of reforms, but with little support from the Council of Ministers which stated that the Commission had gone 'beyond its task' (Council of Ministers 2002). Agreement was reached in December 2002 on the terms of accession for the new members which presented the agricultural *acquis* as a *fait accompli*, although it was conceded that they would have access to some direct payments but at only 25 per cent of the levels in the EU15. Over time, however, eastern enlargement will profoundly change the shape of EU agriculture, given the prevalence of small and medium-sized farms, and given that support linked to the type of commodity and the level of production will provide powerful incentives for producers to expand output. It is hard to see how better standards of living for the agricultural community can be squared with attempts which respect market forces and keep expenditure in check, given also the limits to the Commission's exercise of discretion in reducing overproduction and/or steering farmers to new products.

The outcome on agriculture of Agenda 2000 was clearly determined, in the first place, by the national preferences of the more powerful incumbent member states (Schwaag Serger 2001). The governments—and the particular needs of the new member states—were kept at bay, despite their vehement protests. 'Never before has the conditionality been so severe' (Pelkmans, Gros, and Núñez Ferre 2000: 31). A second factor limiting reform was the way the budgetary system of the EU impacts on individual member states in terms of both contributions and receipts (see Chapter 8), given the weight of CAP expenditure. A third, and paradoxical, reason for *not* adapting the CAP to the EU25 reality is the decision-making apparatus of the EU: once this has given birth to a policy, the latter becomes very difficult to change.

Making the new members safe for the CAP

The EU relies on agencies in individual member states to implement its decisions, and the member states depend on each other to implement Community legislation. Although Article 5 EEC (now Art. 10 TEC) obliges member governments to take all the necessary measures to fulfil their obligations, the way in which they organize themselves administratively is for individual states to decide. Yet, for the European policy process to function adequately it requires a relative similarity in the quality of the administrative systems of the member states, and often involves extensive modification of national budgetary procedures. Some measure of formal convergence, though, is clearly not enough, as the example of the CAP shows, it also crucially depends on mutual confidence in each others' institutions.

The southern enlargement in the 1980s stretched the trust in the administrative capacities of the incoming member states to the limit. With eastern enlargement the problem of ensuring that sectoral administrative capacities would guarantee the application of the *acquis* was a key issue in accession negotiations. There was widespread doubt as to the quality of the administrative systems of the candidate states. This was amplified by the shift of these states towards direct income payments and sophisticated surveillance and accounting systems which set even higher demands on the administrative systems more accustomed to control and repression. In addition, democracy and administrative efficiency are not synonymous. Because 'popular sovereignty' was the rallying cry in the democratic revolutions of central and eastern Europe, the (re)organization of administration was a more difficult task than establishing democratic governments. In part, the weak links between the executives and their political and institutional environments reflect the particular features of the post-communist political systems; in part it can be explained by a lack of 'nodality', authority, and policy expertise within central government (Goetz and Margetts 1999).

Capacity-building in the new member states was not just accession-driven 'technical assistance', but was also about the more difficult task of shaping administrative cultures. This became a core preoccupation for EU policy-makers. In none of the candidate countries, not even the larger ones like Poland and Hungary, were domestic politicians a match for the bureaucratic politics transporting the CAP to them. They were faced with a powerful campaign to consolidate further the institutional identity of the CAP, and to strengthen the organizational interests attached to it. The politico-administrative status quo of the CAP is anchored, via its extension to the new member states, to a peculiar definition of reality that deters alternatives to the current institutional form of the CAP.

The more the farming sectors of the new member states resemble those of the older member states, the more secure the CAP will be. Accordingly, the enlargement process was used not to achieve a basic reform of the CAP, but to forestall future challenges by enlarging the present system.

Thus, the first principle of accession negotiations was the full acceptance by the candidates of the actual and potential rights and obligations attaching to the Union system, and thus the ability to apply the full *acquis* as it stands at the time of accession (see Chapter 16; McClintock 2004), despite its dramatically increased volume and complexity compared to previous waves of accession. This made membership conditional on the quality of the administration (SIGMA–OECD 1998), and on the still underdeveloped legal systems of central and eastern Europe. A second principle was that there would not be a general transition period. Any transitional arrangements must be: exceptional; limited in time and scope; not lead to significant distortion of competition; and accompanied by a plan to apply the *acquis*. With these principles in mind, accession terms took only limited account of the special circumstances in the acceding countries.

This is, of course, not the whole story. Eastern enlargement will strengthen the existing CAP in that rural structures in the central and east European countries are a perfect fit for the social *raison d'être* of the CAP. This does not mean, however, that *this* CAP is the best solution for the economic problems of agriculture in the new member states, although it provides their rural population with the same means of defensive modernization as earlier.

Conclusions

The CAP has passed a critical juncture with its wholesale adoption by the CEE countries. There are several reasons for arguing that its supranational features, combined with the new WTO regime, have—perversely—strengthened agricultural nationalism in the member states of the EU. Both the member governments and the Commission have exploited this contradiction to their own ends. In a sense, the political paradoxes of the CAP are the main source of its stability, since it provides the means for member governments to defend nationally defined agricultural policies, with their persistent elements of protection, welfare, and electoral concerns. After all, the most powerful organ of the EU, the Council of Ministers, is comprised of politicians with exclusively national constituents. Its reliance on forms of unanimity gives an effective guarantee of the status quo, whilst at the same time promoting compromises, which have secured continued commitment to European integration. The CAP thus helped to take agricultural policies out of divisive domestic distributional conflicts by creating a functionally segmented and politically insulated policy arena. The absence of spill-over is a core rationale of the policy. Decision-making in the EU appears to be complicated and cumbersome, but these features have made it very effective in defending national interests.

The closely aligned 2003 CAP reforms—continuing reforms started in 1992 and deepened with the Agenda 2000—and the GATT Agreement on Agriculture have in important ways pushed European governments towards new measures which can help to defuse its potentially disturbing influences on international trade relations. However, simply by its persistence the CAP constitutes a continuing source of tension on all levels of governance, internationally, supranationally, nationally, and regionally, and thus a persistent focus of problem-solving. Because of institutional complexity the solutions are always partial, and always have further consequences that in turn provide new points of tension. CAP reform is regulation through crisis, in the sense that Commissioners for Agriculture came to regard crises as the only possible occasions for reforming the system. This approach calculates political costs and concentrates on ways to manoeuvre in crisis situations, especially *vis-à-vis* the Council of Ministers, rather than on ways to rationalize the system and to eliminate the causes of repeated crisis once and for all.

For better or worse, because of agriculture the EU is more than market integration. The common interest in protecting rural sectors from the competitive forces of a capitalist market economy proved strong enough to build a centralized institutional apparatus. The peculiar policy solutions embodied in the CAP developed, once institutionalized, their own vested interests, and these interests have been relatively successful in mastering the challenge of eastern enlargement.

Notes

1 Own calculations based on data in *The Agricultural Situation in the European Union*, 2002 Report, DGAGRI.

2 Data are for 2001, the source is *The Agricultural Situation in the EU*, 2002 Report.

3 Data are for 2001 and calculated on the basis of statistics provided in the 2002 Report.

4 Own calculation based on data for 2000 on the basis of statistics in the 2001 Report.

5 Data are for 2000 and calculated on the basis of statistics provided in the 2002 Report.

6 The ten countries that joined in May 2004 plus Bulgaria and Romania which are involved in as yet uncompleted negotiations.

7 Own calculations based on data in United Nations Development Programme's Human Development Report (2004: 184).

8 Without Cyprus and Malta. Percentages are for 2000 and calculated on the basis of data in the 2002 Report. (*http://europa.eu.int/comm/agriculture*).

9 Membership provides economic security for farmers because of the bigger domestic market protected by a common tariff regime. In 2004, with twenty-five member states, the European common market was six times as large as in 1960, with six member states. In 2004 intra-European trade amounts to 65 per cent, compared to 35 per cent in 1960.

Further reading

For a detailed political history of the CAP, see Tracy (1989), and Grant (1997). Milward (1992, ch. 5) provides the best account of the prehistory. Fennell (1997) offers the most detailed, historically oriented policy analysis of the CAP. For its social consequences, see Bowler (1985). For a view of US agricultural politics and policies, see Orden, Paarlberg, and Roe (1999), and for a comparative study of the 'welfare state of farmers', see Scheingate (2001). Those interested in current developments should consult *The Agricultural Situation in the European Union*, published annually by the European Commission. For a detailed analysis of the Berlin Council and the decisions on Agenda 2000, see Schwaag Serger (2001). For more details on the financial aspects of the CAP, see also these

Reports. For a collection of articles and books dealing with the eastern enlargement of the EU and the effects on agriculture, see *www.zbw-kiel.de/dienstleist/econselect/es_eu-agrr.htm*.

Bowler, I. R. (1985), *Agriculture under the Common Agricultural Policy: A Geography* (Manchester: Manchester University Press).

Grant, W. (1997), *The Common Agricultural Policy* (New York: St Martin's Press).

Milward, A. S. (1992), *The European Rescue of the Nation-State* (London: Routledge).

Orden, D., Paarlberg, R., and Roe, T. (1999), *Policy Reform in American Agriculture: Analysis and Prognosis* (Chicaco: University of Chicago Press).

Scheingate, A. D. (2001), *The Welfare State for Farmers: Institutions and Interest Group*

Power in the United States, France, and Japan (Princeton: Princeton University Press).

Schwaag Serger, S. (2001), *Negotiating CAP Reform in the European Union: Agenda 2000* (Stockholm: Swedish Institute for Food

and Agricultural Economics), Report 2001/4.

Tracy, M. (1989), *Government and Agriculture in Western Europe* (New York: Harvester Wheatsheaf).

Chapter 8

The Budget

Who Gets What, When and How?

Brigid Laffan and Johannes Lindner

Contents

Summary

The budget is a focus for repeated negotiation among the EU member states and institutions, following firmly established rules. In 1988, after several years of bruising annual negotiations, the EU moved to multi-annual 'financial perspectives', or package deals, for which the Commission makes proposals and the 'Budgetary Authority'—the Council and the European Parliament (EP)—negotiates agreement. This has concentrated budgetary politics into periodic strategic bargains, linking national costs and benefits, reform of the common agricultural policy (CAP), regional imbalances, and enlargement. The 1992 Delors-2 package closely followed the Treaty on European Union; the 1999 Berlin package responded to the Commission's Agenda 2000 proposals, launched at the end of the 1996–7 Intergovernmental Conference (IGC). The capture of the budget by agricultural interests strengthened resistance to further increases in the overall size of the budget in the early 1980s. Mediterranean enlargement, however, brought pressure for more progressive budgetary transfers; the Delors-1 package in 1988 agreed a substantial increase in structural funds. The new Constitutional Treaty simply confirmed the current institutional set-up of budgetary decision-making and—although the camps of net contributors and net beneficiaries are more pronounced than ever—negotiations for the renewal of the financial perspective (2007–13) will probably not result in a radical change of the EU budget.

Introduction[1]

Historically budgets have been of immense importance in the evolution of the modern state and they remain fundamental to contemporary government. This chapter enters the labyrinth of European Union (EU) budgetary procedures in an attempt to unravel the characteristics of budgetary politics and policy-making. Where EU money comes from, how it is spent, and the processes by which it is distributed are the subject of intense political bargaining. Budgets matter politically, because money represents the commitment of resources to the provision of public goods. Drawing up a budget means making political choices about the allocation and distribution of scarce resources among the member states, and to regions and social groups within those states.

The politics of making and managing budgets has had considerable salience in the evolution of the EU, for a number of reasons. First, the search for an autonomous source of public finance for the original European Community (EC) was critical in building a Community that went beyond a traditional international organization. Secondly, budgetary issues have inevitably become entangled with debates about the role and competence of individual EU institutions and the balance between the European and the national levels of governance. Thirdly, budgetary flows to the member states are highly visible so that 'winners' and 'losers' can be calculated with relative ease. As a result, budgetary politics are more likely to become embroiled in national politics and national electoral competition than rule-making. Fourthly, questions about the purpose of the budget and the principles that govern the use of public finance in the Union are linked to wider questions about the nature of the EU and its evolution as a polity. As captured in the 'EU distributional mode' (see Chapter 3), changing ideas about the role of public finance in integration shape the policy agenda in areas such as economic and monetary union (EMU), regional policy, and social policy. The budget has played an important role in consolidating market integration, in facilitating agreement in many policy fields, and in the political dynamic of integration.

Analysis of budgetary politics casts light on the relationship between political and economic integration. Financial resources are an important means of applying political cement to market integration. In other words, the budget is a useful yardstick with which to measure positive integration. The size and distribution of the EU budget have implications for the operation of a vast range of policies. The process of managing, rather than just formulating, budgets, also raises questions about the management capacity of EU institutions, particularly the Commission. All EU institutions and bodies, in particular the Court of Auditors, are now paying increasing attention to the impact of fraud on the budget and searching for better ways to protect the financial interests of the EU. The poor quality of programme management in the Commission and in some member states is a recurrent theme in discussion of reform of EU financial management.

A thumbnail sketch of the budget

In the early years of the Community, the budget was a financial instrument similar to those found in traditional international organizations. The budget treaties of 1970 and 1975 led to a fundamental change in the framework of budgetary politics and policy-making. These treaties established the constitutional framework for the finances of the Union in a number of important respects (see Box 8.1).[2] The treaties created a system of 'own resources' which gave the EC an autonomous source of revenue, consisting of three elements: customs duties; agricultural levies; and a proportion of the base used for assessing VAT in the member states, up to a ceiling of 1 per cent. The 1970 agreement on own resources was subsequently altered a number of times. One basic principle was that this revenue base should apply to all member states, regardless of their size, wealth, the pattern of EC expenditure, or their ability to pay. This was to cause increasing difficulty in the years to come.[3] The budget treaties altered the institutional framework for reaching decisions on the budget. The European Parliament (EP) was granted significant budgetary powers, including the rights: to increase, to reduce, or to redistribute expenditure in areas classified as 'non-compulsory' expenditure (i.e. not agricultural spending); to adopt or reject the budget; and to give annual discharge, through a vote of approval, to the Commission for its implementation of the budget. The 'power of the purse' gave the EP leverage in its institutional battles with the Council of Ministers and allowed it to promote its autonomous policy preferences. The Council was no longer the sole budgetary authority, although it had the last word in the legislative field. The 1975 Treaty provided for the creation of the independent Court of Auditors to enhance accountability in the budgetary process and the management of expenditure.

After 1970, the emergence of the budget as a real instrument of European public policy was constrained by a basic factor which still shapes EU finances. The EU budget was, and remains, small in relation to Community gross national product (GNP), and to the level of public expenditure in the member states. In 2003, it was equivalent to no more than between 2 and 4 per cent of the combined national budgets, and its payments budget represented 1 per cent of Community gross national income (GNI). However, although the budget has little macroeconomic significance for the Union as a whole, it is very important for those member states that receive extensive transfers from the structural funds. In 2002, net receipts from the EU budget amounted to 2.39 per cent of GNI for Greece, 2.14 per cent for Portugal, 1.29 per cent for Spain, and 1.29 per cent for Ireland (see Fig. 8.2). Moreover, EU spending programmes mobilize constituencies within the member states, such as farmers and regional groups, which have a material interest in the maintenance of their receipts. The small overall size of the budget masked impressive increases in financial resources in the Delors-1 (1988–92), and Delors-2 (1993–9) budgetary agreements

---

Box 8.1 The budgetary cycle and rules

- Articles 268–280 TEC (ex Arts. 199–209 EEC) lay down the financial provisions governing the EEC Treaty, with Article 272 (TEC) (ex Art. 203a EEC) establishing the precise timetable and procedure for making the budget each year. Moreover, an interinstitutional agreement between the EP, the Council, and the Commission specifies the exchanges and interaction between the EP and the Council.

- The Commission initiates the budgetary cycle by presenting the Preliminary Draft Budget to the Council.

- The Council adopts a Draft Budget by 5 October of the year preceding its implementation. (The financial year starts in January.) The Council meets with the EP in a conciliation meeting before actually adopting the Draft Budget.

- The EP has forty-five days to complete its first reading of the Draft. It is entitled to propose modifications to compulsory expenditure, that is, expenditure needed to meet the Community's legal commitments defined as 'expenditure necessarily resulting from this Treaty and from acts adopted in accordance therewith' (Art. 272(4) TEC) (essentially agriculture guarantee spending), and amendments to non-compulsory expenditure. Its control over non-compulsory expenditure is limited to increases within a 'margin of manoeuvre', which is equal to half the 'maximum rate of increase', a percentage determined each year by the Commission on the basis of the level of economic growth, inflation, and government spending.

- The Council has fifteen days to complete its second reading of the Draft Budget. The Council has the final word on compulsory expenditure but returns the Draft to the EP, indicating its position on the EP amendments to non-compulsory expenditure. The Council meets with the EP in a conciliation meeting shortly before the second reading.

- At its second reading, the EP has the final word on non-compulsory spending within the limits of an agreed maximum rate of increase. After its second reading of fifteen days, the EP adopts or rejects the budget. If adopted, the EP President signs it into law.

- If there is no agreement on the budget by the beginning of January, the Community operates on the basis of a system of month-to-month financing, known as 'provisional twelfths', until agreement is reached between the two arms of the budgetary authority.

- The Commission then has the responsibility for implementing the budget. The Court of Auditors draws up an annual report covering the year in question, and on the basis of that report the EP decides whether or not to give a discharge to the Commission in respect of the implementation of the budget. The discharge is normally given in the second year following the year in question.

(see Fig. 8.1). The Berlin Agreement (1999–2006) did not include increases of a similar magnitude to those of Delors-1 and Delors-2.

The slenderness of EU budgetary resources highlights an important feature of the emerging European polity, namely, the significance of regulation as the main instrument of public power in the Union. The expansion of regulatory policies was an alternative to establishing extensive fiscal resources at EU level, and reflected a view which limited the role of public finance in integration. This view was not always dominant. In the 1970s the acquisition of sizeable financial resources for the budget, a form of fiscal federalism, was widely seen as essential to integration,

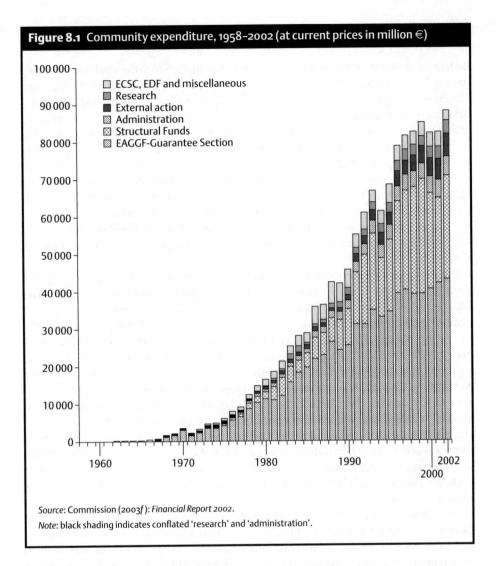

Figure 8.1 Community expenditure, 1958–2002 (at current prices in million €)

Legend:
- ☐ ECSC, EDF and miscellaneous
- ▨ Research
- ■ External action
- ▨ Administration
- ⊠ Structural Funds
- ▨ EAGGF-Guarantee Section

Source: Commission (2003f): *Financial Report 2002*.

Note: black shading indicates conflated 'research' and 'administration'.

especially to EMU. It was anticipated that a larger budget would be necessary to deal with external shocks and fiscal stabilization, which member governments could no longer deal with through management of their own currencies. In contrast, the view that there could be strong Community government, with limited financial resources, gained ground in the 1980s, as Keynesian economic policies were discredited in favour of monetarist approaches. The Keynesian economic paradigm privileged the role of budgets in macroeconomic management, whereas monetarist paradigms did not accord a central role of public finance. The capture of the EU budget by agricultural interests in the 1970s made it difficult for fiscal federalist arguments to win political ground (see Chapter 7). Since the mid-1990s, member states have subordinated their national budgets to the fiscal framework of EMU. This constraint and other pressure on national expenditure have made many member states reluctant to accept significant transfers of financial resources to the EU level.

The major players

Budgetary policy-making in the Union rests on 'history-making decisions', i.e. big package deals, an annual budgetary cycle, and thousands of management decisions within each expenditure area. 'History-making decisions', taken periodically since 1988, shape the annual budgetary cycle. The management of the budget engages many layers of government, from the Commission to central, regional, and local governmental agencies in the member states. The Commission has responsibility for establishing the draft budget each year, and for proposals intended to shape the 'grand bargains'. The Commission has traditionally been an advocate of a bigger EU budget in order to fund policy integration, but in the 1990s it was forced to pay more attention to managing EU spending. In addition, the Commission tries to play the role of honest broker in budgetary battles, charged by the member governments with drafting reports on sensitive issues, such as 'own resources' and net flows to the member states.

Different configurations of the Council play a central role in budgetary negotiations. The Budget Council, consisting of representatives from finance ministries who approve the annual budget, has well-established operating procedures and decision-making rules. The General Affairs and External Relations Council (GAERC), the Economic and Financial Affairs Council (Ecofin), and the Agricultural Council each play a key role in negotiating the big budgetary deals. The GAERC attempts to coordinate across different negotiating chapters and, not least, to contain the Agricultural Council. Ecofin tries to exert budgetary discipline and has an important role in monitoring the Maastricht budgetary criteria, whereas the Agricultural Council is locked into a clientelist relationship with farmers. Other Council configurations that develop spending programmes have to face tough negotiations about money when their programmes are reviewed and altered. However, the European Council, where heads of state or government broker the final stages of the 'history-making' bargains, still provides the most important forum for striking the big budgetary deals.

Since it was granted budgetary powers in 1975, the EP has regarded EU finances as one of its key channels of influence *vis-à-vis* the Council. The EP has tried to influence what happens at both the macro and the micro levels. As was seen in March 1999, it was an intervention by the EP, criticizing financial management, which provoked the unprecedented resignation of the whole college of commissioners. In the annual cycle of determining detailed appropriations, the EP frequently intervenes to alter the sums assigned to specific programmes and projects.

For member governments, the budget is a crucial element of EU policy. Their preferences depend on a variety of factors, notably: their net position in relation to budgetary flows; the fit between EU expenditure and their preferred policies; and the importance of the EU budget to different social groups or regions at national level. Inevitably the electoral cycle and the composition of coalition governments impinge on budgetary politics at EU level.

Budgetary politics over time

Since the first enlargement in 1973 there have been two distinct different phases of budgetary politics and policy-making in the EU. The first phase (1973–88) was characterized by intense conflict about the size and distribution of EU monies, and by institutional battles between the Council and the EP. The second phase (since 1988) has been one of relative budgetary calm as member governments succeeded in negotiating the three big budgetary bargains, known as Delors-1, Delors-2, and Agenda 2000, and the Council and the EP cooperated closely in annual budgetary decision-making. Both phases correspond to a specific set of rules and procedures, and a distinct budgetary paradigm.

Phase 1: the dominance of budgetary battles

The first enlargement disturbed the budgetary bargain established by founder member governments. In particular, between 1979 and 1984 the member govern- ments and EU institutions were locked into a protracted dispute about revenue and expenditure which contributed in no small way to a wider malaise in the early 1980s. The 1970 treaty, stemming from the summit in The Hague in December 1969, was designed to fix the rules before the UK became a member. The revenue sources suited the six founder countries, and the main spending would flow 'automatically' to support the common agricultural policy (CAP) (see Chapter 7). The package was essentially a French achievement, won in return for starting accession negotiations with the UK and the other applicants. The rules of the budgetary game were fixed to the advantage of the incumbents, above all France, making confrontation with the UK more or less inevitable (see H. Wallace 1983). Moreover, with the 1970 bud- getary treaty member states half-heartedly delegated budgetary powers to the EP introducing a complex annual procedure with a number of ill-specified rules. The mismatch between the limited desire of member states to involve the EP and the high expectations from the use of their newly acquired political powers on the part of MEPs, soon became apparent. The considerable scope for interpretation left open by the vaguely defined treaty provisions intensified this tension. In short, the UK and the EP entered a budgetary stage that was characterized by a 'de Gaulle budget'.

After accession, successive British governments struggled to get the budget issue onto the agenda and slowly managed to alter the terms of the debate to ensure that distributional issues were taken seriously. Despite being one of the 'less prosperous' member states, the UK was set to become the second largest contributor after Germany. In trying to address the problem, a key concern of British governments was the dominance of CAP expenditure (constituting 70 per cent of the EC budget) from which the UK with its small agriculture sector benefited very little. Attempts by the UK to reduce the dominance failed because other member states were unwilling to shift resources away from spending on agriculture. Moreover, there was little revenue left that would have allowed the development of other policies.

Against this background, it became clear to the British government that the UK problem was structural rather than the result of chance consequences. Hence in 1979, the new British Prime Minister, Margaret Thatcher, began to demand a rebate system, which would guarantee the UK a better balance between contributions and receipts. The Commission and the other member governments were loath to concede the British case at the outset. The Commission had always been reluctant to engage in discussion of the net financial flows to the individual member states, lest this encourage too narrow a calculation of the benefits of Community membership, and lead states to seek *juste retour*, i.e. to extract from the Community budget more or less what they put in. The key 'orthodoxy' regarding the budget at this time was that receipts flowed from EU policies and were thus automatic. This orthodoxy was challenged by the problem of UK contributions. Although Mrs Thatcher's confrontational approach was regarded as non-*communautaire*, she finally succeeded. At the Fontainebleau European Council in June 1984, the British government traded its consent to an agreement for increasing the VAT ceiling from 1 to 1.4 per cent against the establishment of a 'rebate' mechanism for dealing with excessive British contributions on a longer-term basis. The mechanism was designed to deal with the British problem and could not be generalized to other member states, even though other states became significant net contributors.

While the member governments were engaged in restructuring the budget, the EP and the Council were involved in a continuing struggle over their respective powers on budgetary matters. The EP rejected the 1980 and 1985 draft budgets, and the annual budgetary cycle was characterized by persistent struggle between the two institutions, the 'twin arms' of the budgetary authority. The EP actively exploited the broad scope for interpretation that the ill-specified treaty provisions offered. Similarly, the Council sought to limit the level of power-sharing with the EP as far as it legally could. In 1982, and again in 1986, the Council of Ministers brought an action in the European Court of Justice (ECJ) to annul the budget signed by the President of the Parliament. Repeated attempts to solve the disputes over the interpretation of the treaty provisions through joint declarations and agreements failed.

Against a Council that displayed little willingness to take the EP seriously, the Parliament was determined to use the budgetary powers which it had acquired in 1975 to enhance its position in the Community's institutional landscape and to further its policy preferences. This was done in three ways. First, the Parliament attempted to use its budgetary powers to gain some leverage in the legislative field by introducing expenditure lines in policy areas where no legal bases existed. Secondly, the Parliament used its amending power to increase expenditure in order to promote Community policies of interest to it, notably, regional policy, transport, social policy, and education. Thirdly, the Parliament used the annual budgetary cycle to expand the areas considered as non-compulsory expenditure, which meant it had a larger volume of expenditure where it could apply its margin for manoeuvre under Article 203(4) (EEC) (now Art. 272(4) TEC) (see Box 8.1). In view of these priorities, the EP tended to pay more attention to authorizing expenditure than to monitoring how it was spent, a priority reflected in the importance of the EP's budget committee, and the assignment of budgetary control to a sub-committee.

Phase 2: ordered budgetary decision-making

The year 1988 marked a turning point. After the accession of Greece, Portugal, and Spain and the adoption of the Single European Act (SEA), it became clear that the intense budgetary battles and the constant shortage of revenue could not continue. Following a proposal by the President of the Commission, Jacques Delors, the EC embarked on a far-reaching political and institutional reform in the budgetary field. On the institutional side, it introduced the multi-annual financial perspective, which balanced revenue and expenditure and constrained the ballooning CAP by dividing the budget into different headings and setting annual ceilings for spending categories. Although established by member states in the European Council, the financial perspective acquired its binding nature from the Interinstitutional Agreement between the Council, the European Parliament, and the Commission. The EP accepted the constraint on annual budgetary decision-making, because of the distributive component of the reform. The new financial perspective guaranteed a significant increase of resources and established regional spending as the second-largest part of the budget. Overall, the 1988 reform changed the rules of the game by supplanting the budget treaty with a set of superior soft-law arrangements among the budgetary actors, and it transformed the CAP-centred 'de Gaulle budget' into a redistributive and less CAP-oriented 'Delors budget'. In subsequent renewals of the financial perspective and interinstitutional agreement, the main institutional and distributive structure established in 1988 remained unchanged. The requirement for unanimity did not change. The Delors-1 package and subsequent budgetary deals required the agreement of all member states. The veto made it very difficult to tackle entrenched budgetary gains such as the British budgetary rebate or the French demands on agriculture.

Delors-1

The Mediterranean enlargements in 1981 and 1986 changed the constellation of forces on budgetary issues and heightened the salience of redistribution. Although the SEA appeared not to have overt implications for the budget, the new articles on 'economic and social cohesion' (Art. 130a EEC, now Art. 158 TEC as amended by the SEA), promoted by the Commission and the poorer member states, proved a powerful peg for the Commission to develop its strategy on redistribution. The Commission established a clear connection between the internal market process and the budget by launching two sets of proposals on budgetary reform: *The Single Act: A New Frontier for Europe* (Commission 1987*a*); and *Report on Financing of the Community Budget* (Commission 1987*b*). The proposals, known as the 'Delors Package' (later Delors-1), were negotiated at the highest political level between June 1987 and February 1988. The less prosperous states (Greece, Ireland, Portugal, and Spain) successfully linked the completion of the internal market to an increase in structural funds, designed to reinforce 'economic and social cohesion'.

The budgetary agreement reached in February 1988 was a classical EC package deal. The fact that, for the first time, all the different elements of the budget were addressed in one reform, was instrumental for the agreement. Moreover, the link to the internal market project motivated in particular Chancellor Kohl to secure an agreement, even though it meant a significant increase in German net contributions to the budget. The main elements of the agreement were:

- an increase in the financial resources available to the Community, rising to a ceiling of 1.2 per cent of GNP by 1992;

- an extension of the system of 'own resources' to include a new fourth resource based on the relative wealth of the member states as measured by GNP;

- the introduction of tighter and binding budgetary discipline to contain the growth of agricultural expenditure at not more than 74 per cent of the growth of Community GNP;

- a continuation of the complex Fontainebleau rebate system whereby the UK receives a reduction in its contribution to Community revenue equivalent to 66 per cent of the difference between its share of revenue provided and of total allocated expenditure; and

- a doubling of the financial resources available to the less prosperous areas of the Community between 1988 and 1993.

Delors-2

The pattern established by Delors-1 was replicated in the negotiations on Delors-2. The political link between the SEA and Delors-1 was followed by a similar link between the Treaty on European Union (TEU) and the Delors-2 package. The Commission launched its Delors-2 proposals in the EP in February 1992, just five days after the TEU was formally signed, with its document *From the Single Act to Maastricht and Beyond: The Means to Match our Ambitions* (Commission 1992a). It envisaged that total spending would increase by some €20 billion from 1992 to 1997, rising to a ceiling of 1.37 per cent of Community GNP. Particular increases were earmarked for structural expenditure, further strengthening the commitment to redistribution.

The debate on Delors-2 was as tortuous and controversial as the earlier debate on Delors-1. The member governments grappled with their desire to reach agreement, on the one hand, and with their determination that the terms of the agreement be as favourable as possible to their own viewpoint, on the other. At the Edinburgh European Council an agreement was reached that entailed the following main elements.

- maximum levels of revenue and expenditure were established up to 1999 (extending the financial perspective from five to seven years), with the revenue ceiling maintained at 1.2 per cent of GNP for 1993 and 1994, but set to rise to 1.27 by 1999;

- the financial flows to the poorer parts of the Community were significantly increased;

- the system of revenue-raising was slightly revised to take more account of 'contributive capacity'; and

- the UK secured the maintenance of its rebate mechanism.

Although the Commission once again played a crucial role in drafting, it was less successful than in 1988 in retaining all elements of its proposals. In particular, the Commission failed to obtain the agreement of the member governments to its proposed budgetary increases. At the same time, the cohesion countries, namely Ireland, Greece, Spain, and Portugal had reason to be very satisfied with the terms secured in Edinburgh (see Chapter 9). Against pressure from Germany, France, and the UK to limit the expenditure increase, the agreement envisaged a 41 per cent rise in spending on 'structural operations'. Furthermore, agreement was reached on financing a new instrument, the Cohesion Fund, to help the four cohesion countries to meet the convergence criteria for Economic and Monetary Union (EMU).

Agenda 2000

In the mid-1990s, the balance of forces in the Union on budgetary matters began to change radically. The sizeable expansion in the size of the budget led to the emergence of a 'net contributors' club, an austerity camp concerned about the level of their financial commitments to the EU budget. Before Delors-1 Germany and the UK had been the only major net contributors, whereas by the 1990s the majority of states were in this position. The 1988 and 1992 budgetary deals were secured in large measure by the willingness of Chancellor Kohl and the German government to bear so much of the budgetary burden. Following German unification in 1990, Germany fell from second to sixth place in the league table of per capita income, but remained the budget's main paymaster. The shock of paying for unification had a major influence on German attitudes to the EU budget; from then on the Germans took every opportunity to voice their concerns about financial burden-sharing. The Dutch government also raised equity considerations when they found themselves transformed from a net beneficiary to a significant net contributor, especially when measured in per capita terms. The 1995 enlargement added Sweden, Finland, and Austria to the growing net contributors' club, although these three new members enjoyed some mitigation of their contributions immediately following their accession.

At the Copenhagen European Council in 1993, the member governments accepted the principle of an eastward enlargement of the Union. Like all previous enlargements, this would alter the existing budgetary bargains and require considerable changes in the policy *acquis*. In addition, the accession of so many comparatively poor states would generate pressure for more redistribution and a larger budget. Moreover problems of financial management had been simmering for some time, and increasingly in the period following Maastricht, when the legitimacy of the EU was contested. The management issue exploded with dramatic effect in March 1999 when the entire Commission, presided over by Jacques Santer, was forced to resign, as a result of a report that was highly critical of its financial management.

Against these developments it is surprising that the institutional setting and the distributive character of the budget proved so robust. In contrast to the fierce budget battles of the 1970s and 1980s, discontent did not escalate or block European affairs; the tensions and conflicts were channelled towards the designated occasion for budgetary debate, namely the negotiations for the renewal of the financial perspective. Although these negotiations were intense, they nevertheless led to an agreement that was still much in line with the 'Delors budget'; thus revealing the dominance of incrementalism in post-1988 budgetary politics and the manner in which the key institutional and distributive bargains of Delors had become embedded.

The Commission followed the pattern of the Delors-1 and Delors-2 negotiations on the future financing of the Union by linking a new financial perspective to treaty changes. It launched its Agenda 2000 proposals in July 1997 (Commission 1997a) immediately following the agreement on the Treaty of Amsterdam. Yet, in contrast to its more radical proposals in 1987 and 1991, the Commission adopted a cautious strategy of incremental adjustment, rather than a bid for greatly increased resources and new sources of funding. This reflected the changing political climate following

German unification, fears about the potential costs of enlargement, and the impact of the EMU convergence criteria on national budgets. Negotiating Agenda 2000 was a real challenge and occupied EU institutions for almost two years. A key role was played by successive Council presidencies, particularly the German presidency, which in the end had to deliver an agreement at the European Council in Berlin in March 1999. The new German Chancellor, Gerhard Schröder, was determined to con- clude the negotiations, despite having a strong interest in securing a reduction of Germany's high net contributions.

The agreement, hammered out in Berlin in the early hours of the morning, fell well short of the budgetary figures proposed by the Commission. All actors, even governments from the cohesion countries, eventually signed up to the concept of 'budgetary stabilization'. Yet, at the same time, member states with a vested interest in specific expenditure programmes vetoed significant cuts or changes, for example, in the case of France and the hotly debated CAP (see Chapter 7). Therefore, the status quo was by-and-large confirmed, but, in contrast to the significant increases recorded in 1988 and 1992, the Union's budgetary resources were consolidated. The main elements of the agreement were:

- the revenue ceiling was maintained at 1.27 per cent of GNP;
- transfers to cohesion countries were marginally reduced, leaving some scope for flows to new member states in case of eastern enlargement;
- only limited changes in the size and policy structure of the CAP;
- the system of revenue-raising was again slightly revised to take more account of 'contributive capacity'; and
- the UK secured the maintenance of its rebate mechanism.

As in the case of Delors-1 and Delors-2, once an agreement was reached on a new financial perspective among the member states the Council negotiated the renewal of the interinstitutional agreement with the EP. In exchange for accepting the figures adopted by the European Council, the EP again obtained institutional concessions, which further strengthened its role in the annual procedure (i.e. changes in the classification of expenditure and extension of scope of conciliation between the EP and the Council). Since 1988, annual decision-making had changed its character. It lost its place in the interinstitutional spotlight and became the domain of budgetary experts, which cooperated closely and developed a routine of adopting annual budget in time and without major tensions. Moreover, in subsequent budgetary rounds, the net payers increasingly made their presence felt and began to question the value of regional fund expenditures.

A new style of budgetary politics?

The stability of the institutional setting and budgetary paradigm are being challenged by the accession of the ten new member states and the negotiations over a European Constitutional Treaty. In contrast to Agenda 2000 where a decision on how to reconcile the distributive interests of an enlarged Union of twenty-five member states was postponed, negotiations for a new financial perspective (2007–13) take place with the new member states at the table. Moreover, the constitutional debate brought the budgetary procedure back into the spotlight.

Negotiating the new financial perspective

The negotiations of the new financial perspective take place against the background of three developments. First, at the Lisbon European Council in 2000 the European Union set itself the strategic goal of becoming 'the most competitive economy in the world' by the end of the decade. Heads of state or government committed to take measures that would increase the competitiveness of their economies and raise investments in research and technology. The Lisbon goal was taken up by a report of an independent group of high-level experts headed by the Belgian economist, André Sapir (Sapir *et al.* 2004). Mandated by the Commission President, Romano Prodi, the group identified a number of measures that would help the EU overcome its problem of sluggish growth. The report criticized the dominance of the CAP spending and suggested refocusing the budget on European public goods, most importantly research and technology. Although fiercely criticized by some in the Commission, the report clearly established a link between the Lisbon goal and the EU budget. Secondly, most member states, in particular the large euro area members, Germany and France, have been experiencing a period of low growth rate and strong pressures on their national budgets. Their failure, in three subsequent years (2002–4), to meet the terms of the Stability and Growth Pact (SGP) which commit members of the euro area to compliance with the Maastricht criteria, further limited their willingness to accept increases of the EU budget. Thirdly, for the first time the ten new member states sit at the negotiation table with high expectations of budgetary transfers and a full veto-right. None of these states received any mitigation of their budgetary contributions at the moment of accession. The negotiations for the new financial perspective began in early 2004 with a proposal by the Commission.

The Commission's proposal

On 10 February 2004, the Commission presented its proposal for a new financial perspective for the EU budget for the years 2007 to 2013 (Commission 2004i). In his presentation of the proposal to the EP, Romano Prodi, then President of the Commission, emphasized the need to give the EU the resources to match its political priorities. Rather than fighting over details of future budget allocations, the Commission sought to engage member states in a debate over the priorities of the EU. For the first time since the inception of the financial perspective, the Commission envisaged an overhaul of the expenditure headings so as to reflect the new policies and priorities of the enlarged EU. Moreover, the Commission also proposed to increase overall expenditure (see Table 8.1).

Three zones for action were identified: (i) the Lisbon strategy; (ii) the creation of an area for freedom, security, and justice; and (iii) the strengthening of the visibility of the EU's external actions. First, as regards the Lisbon Strategy, on which most emphasis was placed, the existing headings of 'structural operations', 'pre-accession aid', and

Table 8.1 Commission proposal for the new financial perspective, 2006–2013 (€ bn.)

Appropriations for commitments (in billion €)	2006[a]	2007	2008	2009	2010	2011	2012	2013
1. Sustainable development	47.58	59.68	62.80	65.80	68.24	70.66	73.72	76.79
1a. Competitiveness for growth and employment	8.79	12.11	14.39	16.68	18.97	21.25	23.54	25.83
1b. Cohesion for growth and employment[b]	38.79	47.57	48.41	49.12	49.27	49.41	50.18	50.96
2. Preservation and management of natural resources	56.02	57.18	57.90	58.12	57.98	57.85	57.83	57.81
of which: agriculture-market related expenditure and direct payments	43.74	43.50	43.67	43.35	43.03	42.71	42.51	42.29
3. Citizenship, freedom, security, and justice	1.38	1.63	2.02	2.33	2.65	2.97	3.30	3.62
4. The EU as a global partner[c]	11.23	11.40	12.18	12.95	13.72	14.50	15.12	15.74
5. Administration[d]	3.44	3.68	3.82	3.95	4.09	4.23	4.36	4.50
Compensation	1.04							
Total appropriations for commitments	120.69	133.60	138.7	143.10	146.7	150.2	154.32	158.50
Total appropriations for payments[bc]	114.74	124.60	136.50	127.70	126.0	132.4	138.4	143.10
Appropriations for payments as a percentage of GNI (%)	1.09	1.15	1.23	1.12	1.08	1.11	1.14	1.15
Margin available (%)	0.15	0.09	0.01	0.12	0.16	0.13	0.10	0.09
Own resources ceiling as a percentage of GNI (%)	1.24	1.24	1.24	1.24	1.24	1.24	1.24	1.24

Notes:
N.B. The totals for 'appropriations' do not sum precisely.
[a] 2006 expenditure under the current financial perspective has been broken down according to the proposed new nomenclature for reference and to facilitate comparisons.
[b] Includes expenditure for the Solidarity Fund (€1 billion in 2004 at current prices) as from 2006. However, corresponding payments are calculated only as from 2007.
[c] The integration of the European Development Fund in the EU budget should take effect as of 2008. Commitments for 2006 and 2007 are included only for comparison purposes. Payments on commitments before 2008 are not taken into account in the payment figures.
[d] Includes administrative expenditure for institutions other than the Commission, pensions and European schools. Commission administrative expenditure is integrated in the first four expenditure headings.

Source: Commission (2004k), Press Release (IP/04/189), 10 February 2004.

large parts of the heading 'internal policies', were combined into a new heading of 'sustainable development' (see Table 8.1). Under this heading, considerable increases in expenditure on education, research, mobility, and trans-European networks (TENs) were planned. Secondly, the Commission planned to triple the currently very low level of expenditure allocated to freedom, security, and justice by 2013. Thirdly, as regards external actions, the Commission prioritized expenditure for neighbouring regions and EU assistance for countries and regions in crisis. Concerning agricultural expenditure, the Communication incorporated the agreement between Germany and France of 2002, which fixed ceilings for market measures and direct payments until 2013.

The Commission proposed an average spending level of 1.14 per cent of the EU's GNI over the period covered. It expected spending levels to increase in the early years due to the effects of enlargement, but anticipated that spending would fall off towards the end of the period. The GNI target was a significant increase compared to the current spending level of about 1.0 per cent of GNI. The Commission left the 'own resources' ceiling of 1.24 per cent of GNI unchanged, so as to allow a margin to cover unforeseen expenditure.[4] In summer 2004, the Commission also proposed adjustments to the 'own resources' system (Commission 2004j). It presented a proposal for a generalized correction mechanism, establishing a more transparent and equitable method to correct a budgetary burden deemed excessive in relation to any country's relative prosperity. Such a mechanism would modify and extend the 'UK rebate' to other countries.

Key cleavages and core issues

The Commission urged member states to agree on the financial perspective during the first half of 2005 under the Luxembourg presidency of the Council in order to allow sufficient time to adopt the necessary legislation for the spending programmes, although subject to input from the new Commission that took office in autumn 2004. Four key cleavages dominate negotiations on the financial perspective.

Net contributors versus net beneficiaries

In December 2003 the heads of state or government of Germany, France, the UK, the Netherlands, Austria, and Sweden issued a joint letter to the Commission President requesting that the Union's budget should not exceed the present level of spending (see Fig. 8.2). Not surprisingly, these net contributors greeted the Commission's proposal very unfavourably. By contrast, governments from beneficiary member states, such as Spain and Portugal, endorsed the Commission's proposal and stressed the importance of pursuing the objective of 'economic and social cohesion'.

Old versus new beneficiaries of regional expenditure

The Commission's proposal sought to strike a balance between spending for the new member states and the interest of current net beneficiaries of cohesion policy. Current beneficiaries want to prevent an abrupt ending of transfers to their poor regions and demand compensation should their regions lose out as a result of transfers to the new member states. This is referred to as 'statistical effect compensation'. Germany opposes this kind of compensation, whereas Italy, Spain, and Portugal insist on the need to maintain transitional support until 2014. Within Germany there are likely to be

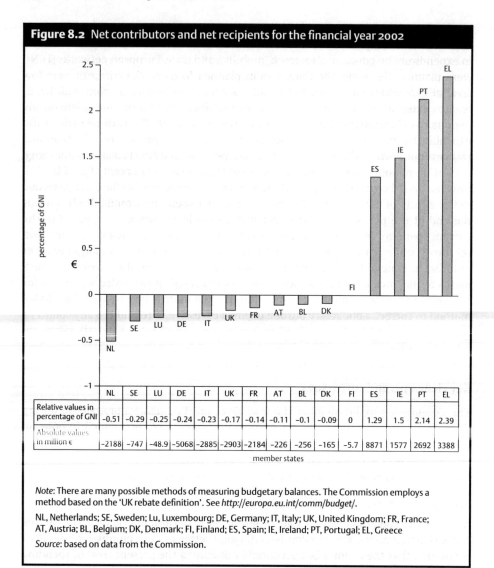

Figure 8.2 Net contributors and net recipients for the financial year 2002

	NL	SE	LU	DE	IT	UK	FR	AT	BL	DK	FI	ES	IE	PT	EL
Relative values in percentage of GNI	-0.51	-0.29	-0.25	-0.24	-0.23	-0.17	-0.14	-0.11	-0.1	-0.09	0	1.29	1.5	2.14	2.39
Absolute values in million €	-2188	-747	-48.9	-5068	-2885	-2903	-2184	-226	-256	-165	-5.7	8871	1577	2692	3388

member states

Note: There are many possible methods of measuring budgetary balances. The Commission employs a method based on the 'UK rebate definition'. See *http://europa.eu.int/comm/budget/*.

NL, Netherlands; SE, Sweden; Lu, Luxembourg; DE, Germany; IT, Italy; UK, United Kingdom; FR, France; AT, Austria; BL, Belgium; DK, Denmark; FI, Finland; ES, Spain; IE, Ireland; PT, Portugal; EL, Greece

Source: based on data from the Commission.

tensions on this issue between the Berlin government and the five new *Länder*. The new member states fear that when the net contributors insist on a zero-growth approach, these compensation payments would be financed from cuts in transfers to the east.

UK rebate versus a generalized rebate mechanism

The UK government strongly opposes any attempt to abolish the UK rebate through replacing it with a generalized mechanism, which is naturally favoured by all the other net contributors.

'Lisbon' budget versus the status quo ante

The Commission sought to transform the redistributive 'Delors budget' into a more distributive 'Lisbon budget' that would strengthen expenditure for public goods.

Yet, given the fact that agricultural expenditure is supposed to be excluded from the negotiations (under the Franco–German agreement of 2002), and that regional expenditure is dominated by strong vested interests, the proposed increases in expenditure in fields such as innovation and technology may well be rejected in order to satisfy the interest of net contributors in an austerity budget. Moreover, much of the Commission's proposal that was presented as a 'Lisbon budget' was already close to existing expenditure programmes, which were simply redefined and newly labelled.

Overall, it seems likely that the final compromise will lie somewhere between the Commission's proposal for an average spending level of 1.14 per cent GNI and the 1 per cent GNI on which net contributors insist. Thus, distributive stability would not be seriously challenged. Whether or not the institutional stability of budgetary politics will persist is, however, an open question.

The Constitutional Treaty

The budgetary procedure was raised in the Convention's constitutional debate. There was a widespread consensus among representatives at the Convention that the EU budgetary procedure needed to be simplified. Yet, the final outcome, as endorsed by the Intergovernmental Conference in June 2004, remained very close to the previous practices in budgetary decision-making. In fact, the main elements of the 'new' budgetary procedure are taken from the rules and procedures that are laid down in the Interinstitutional Agreement.

Three innovative elements have been introduced in the annual budgetary procedure: (i) the abolition of the distinction between compulsory and non-compulsory expenditure (see Box 8.1); (ii) the introduction into the Treaty of a Conciliation Committee; and (iii) granting the right of rejection to the Council. Both arms of the budgetary authority will have equal decision-making power over all components of the EU budget. Similar to the co-decision procedure in legislative politics, a Conciliation Committee will feature as the key forum for brokering a deal between the EP and the Council before their respective final readings.

These innovative features are much in line with the informal arrangements that are in place for the current procedure. First, the distinction between compulsory and non-compulsory expenditure has become less relevant over time. The Interinstitutional Agreement already gives the EP some say over compulsory expenditure through the *ad hoc* conciliation procedure. Secondly, the equivalent of a Conciliation Committee is already in place. Most of the time, the annual budget is *de facto* adopted in a conciliation meeting between the Council and the EP shortly before the second reading in Council. Thirdly, given that negotiations at the conciliation meeting cover all areas of the budget, the exclusive budgetary powers over the non-compulsory expenditure for the EP and over the compulsory expenditure for the Council have amounted to a right of rejection for both arms of the budgetary authority. The Council and EP both use their budgetary powers as bargaining chips to strike deals across the different parts of the budget. Under the new procedure, the Council will be able to prevent an agreement in the Conciliation Committee and thus trigger a new budget proposal by the Commission. The granting of this *de facto* right of rejection to the Council simply upholds the existing balance.

With regard to financial perspective, the new provisions institutionalize the current procedures for the multi-annual budget plan. From the outset, it was clear that the institutionalization of the financial perspective would probably be a minimum result of constitutional negotiations. Given the objectives of the constitutional process, namely to update and to streamline the Treaty, the contrast between the Treaty provisions and current practices was simply too pronounced in this area of the budgetary decision-making for the drafters of the Constitutional Treaty to ignore. Yet, any attempts to go beyond institutionalizing the current Interinstitutional Agreement were strongly disputed. While the Convention had settled on the introduction of qualified majority voting (QMV) for the financial perspective after 2013, heads of state or government adopted a provision that allows for the introduction of QMV only on the basis of a unanimous decision by the European Council. Similarly, the provisions concerning the revenue side do not alter the unanimity requirement for the 'own resource' ceiling.[5]

Overall, the Constitutional Treaty reforms the current budgetary procedure only to the extent that proven rules and procedures from outside the Treaty are introduced. It is clear that representatives in the Convention and, in particular, heads of state or government, did not want to alter the delicate balance between those institutional processes in which Council and member states retain some key powers and those that allow for more influential roles for the Commission and the European Parliament. If the new Constitutional Treaty is not ratified, budgetary processes are likely to conform to the decision rules and practices that have grown up around the multi-annual financial perspectives.

Managing a larger budget

The struggle for budgetary resources in the Community and the interinstitutional battles about budgetary power tended to overshadow questions of 'value for money', accountability, and the quality of the Commission's financial management. These became an increasingly important focus of budgetary politics as the financial resources of the budget grew. In the 1990s attempts were made to improve financial management, but they had proved insufficient to prevent financial mismanagement becoming an explosive political issue in 1999 when the Santer Commission was forced to resign. Time and time again the Court of Auditors drew attention to financial mismanagement in the Commission and in the member states, and two senior Commission financial control staff, Paul van Buitenen and Marta Andreasen, went public about their auditing concerns.[6]

Managing a budget that involves around 400,000 individual authorizations of expenditure and payment each year is a major challenge. The implementation of the EU budget is characterized by a fragmentation of responsibility between the Commission and public authorities in the member states: 80 per cent of the budget is managed on behalf of the Union by the member states. The Commission must rely to a large extent on the delivery and enforcement capacity of member state authorities. There is, however, a great diversity of public management and public finance cultures across the member states. At the same time, the complexity of European rules, particularly in agriculture, the customs union, and regional policy, creates loopholes, which can be exploited by those who are intent on defrauding the EU budget. The sheer number of agricultural subsidy payments and export refunds creates considerable opportunities for abuse. Reports of fraud in olive oil, beef, cigarettes, wine, and fish, running in some cases into millions of euro, undermine the credibility of the Community's policies. Press reports and investigations carried out by the European Anti-Fraud Office (OLAF), have highlighted scams involving the forging of customs documents in order to claim export refunds, avoiding anti-dumping duties, non-payment of excise duties, switching labels on foodstuffs to claim higher refunds, claiming headage payments for non-existent animals, and putting non-existent food into intervention storage. No one knows with any degree of certainty the level of fraud affecting the EU budget: estimates of between 7 and 10 per cent of the budget are often cited, but have never been convincingly proven. Investigations of fraud suggest that some member states are dilatory in following up cases of fraud against the EU budget, as this would, paradoxically, mean devoting additional national resources in order to obtain less money from the EU budget.

The 1975 agreement to create the Court of Auditors (which began work in Luxembourg in 1977) enhanced the institutional commitment to more systematic accountability. In its first report (1978) the Court raised the issue of fraud and it has continued to do so in all subsequent reports. The Court's reports have been consistently highly critical of the Commission's financial management. In the TEU, the Court of Auditors was given additional responsibilities in relation to financial management, notably the need to make a Statement of Assurance (SAD) each year to the Council and the EP to demonstrate that the financial transactions underlying the budget are legal and regular. Aware that continuing reports on fraud would undermine public confidence in European integration, the Commission, the Council, the European Council, and the ECJ began to address the issue. In 1988 the Commission established an anti-fraud unit, Unité de Coordination de la Lutte Anti-Fraude (UCLAF). A little over a decade later in 1999 this became OLAF (Office de la Lutte Anti-Fraude), an independent anti-fraud office. The ECJ became involved, underlining the legal responsibilities of the member states in combating irregularities in the use of EU funds. For example, in a 1989 case of fraud concerning maize supposedly grown in Greece, but in fact imported from Yugoslavia, it held that the member states were legally obliged under a 'loyalty clause' (Art. 5 EEC; now Art. 10 TEC) to deal with EC fraud cases in a manner similar to fraud against their national exchequers. The European Council added its authority to the fight against fraud with repeated declarations on the topic.

In January 1999, political attention was again drawn to the Commission's management of EU finances. The battleground was a classical parliamentary-executive conflict concerning accountability. It was prompted in part by allegations, in both the EP and the media, of mismanagement of the EU budget and financial irregularities. A motion of censure against the Commission was tabled in the EP, but was voted down by MEPs in January 1999 in return for a commitment from the Commission that it would cooperate with a special inquiry. A group of five 'Wise Men' (lawyers and auditors) was established by the EP with a remit to review the allegations of mismanagement and fraud in the Commissions' services. Their report, which was presented to the Commission in March 1999, highlighted problems in relation to tourism, the Mediterranean programme, educational programmes, and the European Community's Humanitarian Office (ECHO). The report (Committee of Independent Experts 1999) concluded that mismanagement in the Commission was:

... tantamount to an admission of a loss of control by the political authorities over the administration they are supposed to be running. The loss of control implies at the outset a heavy responsibility for both the commissioners individually and the Commission as a whole.

It went on to say that 'it was becoming difficult to find anyone who has even the slightest sense of responsibility' (Committee of Independent Experts 1999: 142). The political context in which the report was drafted and its tone left the Commission, after a night of drama, with little option but to resign. It had become clear that otherwise the EP would have passed a motion of censure and forced the college's resignation at the next plenary.

The Prodi Commission that took over in autumn 1999 was given a mandate to reform the Commission by the European Council. Vice President Neil Kinnock, who was given responsibility for administrative reform, proposed a White Paper on the Reform Strategy in March 2000 (Commission 2000e). Not unexpectedly following the resignation of the Santer Commission, reform of financial management and control systems was one of four priorities in the White Paper. This has involved a series of interlinked processes, notably, agreement on a new Financial Regulation (OJ L248, 16 September 2002), the establishment of an internal audit service in the Commission, the creation of an internal audit capacity in each service, a move to activity-based budgeting, decentralization of management responsibility, additional training in financial management, modernizing accounting systems, and the introduction of new information and management systems on a more systematic basis. However, the new Financial Regulation is very complex and may not facilitate financial management in the longer term. The Court of Auditors reviews the reform process each year in its Annual Report. It acknowledges that progress has been made but points to the key challenge of those parts of the budget that rely on shared management with the member states, particularly agriculture and structural measures (Court of Auditors 2003).

Conclusions

Budgetary politics in the EU is marked by both elements of continuity and factors of change. Since 1988, multi-annual bargains have become the norm, in the form of an agreed financial perspective, and are now part of the *acquis*. Although difficult and protracted negotiations have characterized all three budgetary bargains outlined in this chapter, the political process demonstrated a capacity to frame an outcome that would enjoy broad consensus. Thus the Union's annual budgetary cycle became successfully locked into a medium-term financial perspective, which in turn reduced the dangers of acrimonious arguments and interinstitutional conflicts. The influence of the Commission on the eventual outcome was, however, much stronger in relation to Delors-1 than in relation to the two subsequent packages. Having said that, the broad parameters established in the 1988 proposals—a multi-annual financial perspective, CAP reform, and an emphasis on structural spending—run through all subsequent agreements.

The capture of the EU budget in the 1960s by agricultural interests has proved relatively enduring. France, the main defender of the CAP, has been successful in preserving its interests in this policy domain. However, agricultural support in the 1990s moved decisively from market measures to compensation payments, and the funding has started to shift from consumers to taxpayers. The relative weight of agricultural support in the budget has declined from a high of 80 per cent in the 1980s to 44 per cent in 2003.

Cohesion funding assumed a central role in budgetary politics in the late 1980s with the arrival of Spain and Portugal. At about 30 per cent of total expenditure under the Berlin Agreement, structural funds remain an entrenched part of the budgetary *acquis*, and for the time being persist as a core element of the Union's finances, prompted by the continuing differentials in per capita incomes between different parts of the EU. Since 2004, the new member states also benefit from cohesion expenditure. In the negotiations for the new financial perspective, they seek to ensure that financial transfers will focus on the EU's poorest states (see Chapter 9).

The Union's budget does not conform to the principles of fiscal federalism and is unlikely to do so in the future, notwithstanding the arrival of EMU. Fiscal federalism would require far larger budgetary resources than those conceivable given the current constellation of political forces in the Union. The net contributors' club is very resistant to endowing the Union with significantly larger financial resources. There are limits to EU solidarity and to potential transfers to the east. Attempts by the Commission to refocus the EU budget towards European public goods and thus to reduce the redistributive emphasis within the existing 'EU distributional mode', are hampered by the inflexibility of the current budgetary structure. Member states defend vested distributive interests, but are very critical of spending programmes with benefits which cannot be attributed to member states.

As for the broad institutional process, four features of recent developments are worth noting. First, the Commission is under intense pressure to improve the quality of its financial management. Secondly, in spite of the rising importance of the Economic and Financial Affairs Council, within the budgetary arena both foreign ministers and heads of state or government remain at the centre of the bargaining process on the multi-annual budget deals. Having said that, within the member states, finance ministries exert considerable influence on the formation of national preferences on budgetary issues. Thirdly, in the shadow of the 'big bargains' the EP has established itself as a fully co-equal second arm of the budgetary authority and powerful guard over the implementation of the budget. Fourthly, the institutional setting established in 1988 has so far proved enduring.

Notes

1 This chapter is based on the EU budget chapter by Brigid Laffan and Michael Shackleton in the previous edition. Michael Shackleton's consent is gratefully acknowledged. The views expressed in the chapter do not necessarily reflect those of the European Central Bank.

2 For the most comprehensive and detailed treatment of the development of the EC budget and the rules that govern it, see Laffan (1997), and Lindner (2005).

3 This chapter draws heavily on the analysis of Laffan (1997), Lindner (2005), and Shackleton (1990, 1993a, 1993b).

4 The figure 1.24 per cent GNI equals 1.27 per cent GDP. The switch from GDP to GNI reflects a new national accounting methodology that the European Commission adopted in line with the 1993 System of National Accounts.

5 The Dutch government obtained an agreement on a declaration attached to the final act of the Constitutional Treaty stating that the Netherlands would support a move to qualified majority voting only once a decision on the own resource system 'has provided the Netherlands with a satisfactory solution for its excessive negative net payment position *vis-à-vis* the European Union budget'.

6 In the 2004 European elections, Paul van Buitenen was elected as one of two MEPs of his newly founded anti-fraud party 'Europa Transparant'.

Further reading

A comprehensive volume on the EU budget is Laffan (1997). Lindner (2005) presents a thorough institutionalist analysis of EU budgetary decision-making over the past three decades. For a non-academic, but detailed, account of the finances of the EU see Commission (2002e). For an analysis of the revenue side, see Begg and Grimwade (1998).

Begg, I., and N. Grimwade (1998), *Paying for Europe* (Sheffield: Sheffield Academic Press).

Commission (2002e), *European Union Public Finance* (Luxembourg: Office for Official Publications of the European Communities).

Laffan, B. (1997), *The Finances of the European Union* (London: Macmillan).

Lindner, J. (2005), *Conflict and Change in EU Budgetary Politics* (London: Routledge).

Shackleton, M. (1990), *Financing the European Community* (London: Pinter).

Chapter 9

Cohesion and the Structural Funds

Competing Pressures for Reform?

David Allen

Contents

Summary

Over the past twenty years expenditure on the structural funds grew steadily until it stabilized at around one third of the total EU budget or about 0.46 per cent of EU GDP. Since 1985 the structural funds have been specifically linked to the promotion of 'economic and social cohesion'—an objective extended to 'economic, social and *territorial* cohesion' in the Constitutional Treaty (CT). Cohesion policy in turn has been progressively associated with a growing number of broader EU objectives, such as economic growth, competitiveness, employment, sustainable development, subsidiarity, regionalism, and good governance, including the participation of civil society. This chapter argues that the structural funds have been mainly used to *compensate* member states for both the 'widening' and the 'deepening' of European integration, and that this has been *rationalized* in terms of the EU objectives mentioned above. The European Commission has also sought to *exploit* the implementation of structural fund spending in order to further the cause of multi-level governance in the EU by encouraging the participation of regional and local government, and representatives of civil society. The Commission's early success in developing a supranational policy in association with subnational government has been progressively countered by the determination of member governments to retain a 'gatekeeping' role. The 2004 enlargement of the EU presents a series of challenges to cohesion policy as it has evolved since 1985, with the member states significantly divided over whether structural fund expenditure should be expanded, maintained, or renationalized.

Introduction

Since 1985 the structural funds have been justified in terms of 'economic and social cohesion', by which was meant the removal of various disparities within the Union. The major focus has always been 'territorial', in an attempt to rectify regional and, after 1992, national disparities in per capita income. Cohesion policy has always focused on disparities in GDP per capita (Barry and Begg 2003), and has therefore privileged the macroeconomic and the territorial over the social. It can also be criticized for its failure to address significant disparities of income which can occur within a region, even when that region is itself converging with others in the EU (De Rynck and McAleavey 2001). The structural funds originally consisted of the European Regional Development Fund (ERDF), the European Social Fund (ESF), and the Guidance Section of the European Agricultural Guidance and Guarantee Fund (EAGGF). The Cohesion Fund, the Financial Instrument for Fisheries Guidance (FIFG), and the Solidarity Fund (EUSF) were added in 1992, 1993, and 2002 respectively. Under the Commission's proposals of February 2004 for 2006–13 the EAGGF and the FIFG would be separated from the other structural funds in the 'cohesion' section of the EU budget and included in the 'agricultural' section. It remains to be seen how far the Barroso Commission, which took office in November 2004, will modify these proposals.

Since 1988 the structural funds have grown to become a significant part of the EU budget (see Table 9.1), although they still represent only around 0.46 per cent of the EU's GDP. This is a figure that many feel is far too small to have a serious macro-economic effect on EU disparities, either regional or national, let alone seriously to affect EU competitiveness, growth, employment, or to achieve sustainable development. Although the ambition to promote 'harmonious development', or 'cohesion', informs a wide range of EU policies, its direct link with the structural funds is essentially a justification for expenditure that is best thought of as *compensation* for the impacts on a country or region of being part of a wider and integrated European economy. This compensation has played an important role in facilitating both the enlargement of

Table 9.1 Evolution of the structural funds for cohesion, 1975–2013

Year	mn. ecu/€	% EU budget
1975	257 ecu	4.8
1981	1,540 ecu	7.3
1987	3,311 ecu	9.1
1992	18,557 ecu	25.0
1998	33,461 ecu	37.0
2002 (includes pre-accession aid)	€34,615	35.0
2006 EU25*	€38,791	32.0
2013 EU27*	€50,960	32.0

*Excludes EAGGF—Guidance and FIFG and includes the Solidarity Fund.
Source: author's compilation from documentation.

the EU and the development of ambitious integrative packages such as the single market programme, economic and monetary union, or the Lisbon and Gothenburg agendas, designed to promote growth, competitiveness, and employment. Thus, the essence of the structural funds' operations has been determined by high-level interstate bargains—what John Peterson has called 'history-making' decisions (Peterson 1995). It is the member governments which script the cohesion 'play' (Pollack 1995: 285), even though the European Commission and a variety of regional and local actors make much of their particular roles, and their interpretation of the meaning and purpose of these plays.

This essentially intergovernmentalist explanation of the structural funds is contested by those who consider that the way in which they are implemented supports what can best be described as 'multi-level governance' (Marks 1992; Marks, Hooghe, and Blank 1996; Jeffrey 1997; Peterson and Bomberg 1999; Bache 1998; Bache and Flinders 2004). In this view the 'gatekeeping' power of the central governments in the member states is challenged by a combination of supranational (Commission), and subnational actors (local and regional authorities or representatives of civil society) (Bache 1998, 2004; Bache and Bristow 2003). In addition, some commentators see the structural funds as facilitating regionalization by giving a greater role to regional bodies in the administration of public policies (Harvie 1994; Keating 1998; Keating and Loughlin 1997).

The multi-level governance argument fundamentally draws its strength from a judgment about the way that the reforms to the structural funds, introduced by the Commission in 1988, have been implemented. A core contention of this chapter is that these reforms seem to have caught the member states by surprise. However, the 1993 and 1999 reforms, as well as the changes proposed by the Commission for the period 2007–13 (Commission 2004h), are all characterized by a significant reassertion of member-state control over the implementation process.

The arrangements for structural intervention have always privileged a philosophy of regionalism as the best means of achieving cohesion, which in turn is rationalized as a means to achieve other EU goals such as growth, competitiveness, sustainable development, and employment. Territorial cohesion is specifically mentioned for the first time only in the Constitutional Treaty (CT) and its protocol on cohesion. Article 1-3(3) of the CT refers to 'the promotion of economic, social and territorial cohesion and solidarity among member states', whereas all previous treaty references merely mention 'economic and social cohesion'. No mention is ever made in Commission literature about the compensation role that cohesion policy plays, although there are occasional references to the positive effect in terms of integration that might be gained from the visibility of structural intervention in the poorer regions of the Union. Cohesion policy is also a policy area characterized as one of 'mixed competence', with the member states supporting EU policies, while at the same time continuing to develop their own national regional policies. Here the possibility of conflict arises with EU policy on state aids, which set constraints on the public subventions that member governments are allowed to make to regions or sectors (Wishlade 1998a, 1998b; Thielemann 1998; see Chapter 5). It is significant that the most recent reforms proposed by the Commission in its Third Report on Cohesion (Commission 2004h) advocate both better coordination and EU strategic direction of national policies designed to enhance cohesion and a radical overhaul of EU state aids policies. Bachtler, Wishlade, and Yuill (2001) provide an overview of the future of regional policy in terms of a 'triangle of policies'—national regional policies, EU competition policy, and EU cohesion policy.

The biggest challenge to the structural funds and cohesion policy comes, however, from the 2004 enlargement of the Union. In the past, the structural funds were used to facilitate enlargement, and the developments leading up to May 2004 and beyond are no exception to this rule. During the 1999–2006 programming period structural funds on a significant scale have been made available (together with Phare aid) as pre- and post-accession aid to the countries which joined the EU in 2004, as well as to Romania and Bulgaria which are still negotiating accession. For the next programming period from 2007–13 the EU15 are all agreed that significant structural funds should continue to be advanced to the new members. There are, however, disagreements about whether the EU15 should continue to benefit from EU structural funding, and in that case which regions in which countries, or whether it would not be more effective to leave regional measures in these countries to national policies. Although the EU has once again proved itself incapable of significantly reducing the costs of the common agricultural policy (CAP) until 2013 at the earliest (even if the EU15 have agreed to change the way it is delivered; see Chapter 7), there remains the possibility that the EU might agree to reduce significantly the overall costs of the structural funds by limiting them to the new members (see, for example, Sapir et al. 2004). However, even if those who favour repatriating responsibility for regional development do prevail, the tradition of facilitating enlargement by providing compensation, or adjustment programmes via structural funds, is likely to be continued.

The structural funds, 1975–2004

The establishment of the European Regional Development Fund

Although the Treaty of Rome (EEC) established that the member states intended to reduce regional disparities, there was no specific provision for a regional policy or fund. It took two summits in Paris in 1972 and 1974 and recourse to Article 235 (EEC) (now Art. 308 TEC)[1] to set up the ERDF. This was rationalized by the Commission in terms of the need to deal with regional disparities, although Helen Wallace (1977) established that it could be better understood as a compensation to ease an intergovernmental deal—an exercise in 'pork barrel politics'. The deal was linked to enlargement and the need to find a means of compensating the UK for its anticipated large net contribution to the EU budget and, to a lesser extent, to the 1969 decision to move towards economic and monetary union (EMU). Deals related to enlargement and new EU objectives and competences (widening and deepening), have often been facilitated by the structural funds.

The 1975 deal established the ERDF, agreed a figure (1.3 billion ecu) for the period 1975–78, and also set out national quotas for its allocation. The fund was too small to have a significant impact on regional disparities, but once established rules had to be devised for its day-to-day management. These were devised by the Commission and were rationalized in terms of the logic of a regional policy designed to enhance cohesion.

The Commission, in particular the then Directorate-General (DG) XVI (responsible for regional policy and subsequently cohesion), hoped to influence the selection of projects submitted by the member governments, and to prevent them from simply substituting ERDF money for national expenditure. At first the Commission was constrained by the ability of the member governments to limit the total value of their project applications to the size of their agreed quotas, and by their reluctance to provide transparent financial information so that 'additionality' from this new money could be ensured. Nevertheless the implementing regulations for the ERDF, which included the creation of a Regional Policy Committee, provided the starting point for future reforms, and developed the notions of concentration, programming, additionality, and partnership (see Box 9.1). In parallel, a system for the dispersal of money from the ESF was evolving which from the very beginning sought to involve economic and social 'partners'. Thus, the ERDF was seen as promoting the economic (territorial) aspect of cohesion and the ESF as the social aspect.

Some minor reforms were introduced in 1979[2] and 1984,[3] but the Commission and most regional authorities found themselves marginalized in a policy process that rapidly became an instrument of national policy-making (Scott 1995). The primary rules governing the ERDF required unanimity in the Council, which constrained the Commission in terms of what it could plausibly propose. The European Parliament (EP), on the other hand saw an opportunity in that ERDF expenditure qualified as 'non-compulsory expenditure' in the EU budget, and was therefore subject to their endorsement and potential influence (see Chapter 8).

> **Box 9.1** The Commission's four principles for implementing the structural funds
>
> - *Concentration* of measures around priority objectives.
> - *Programming*, whereby multi-annual, multi-task, and occasionally multi-regional programmes, rather than uncoordinated individual national projects, are funded.
> - *Additionality*, making EU funds complement, rather than replace, national funding.
> - *Partnership* involving the closest possible cooperation between the Commission and the 'appropriate authorities' at 'national, regional and local level' in each member state, and at every stage in the policy process from preparation to implementation.

The Single European Act and Delors-1

It required the twin stimulus of 'widening' (Greece, Spain, and Portugal), and 'deepening' (the Single European Act (SEA), and the single market programme) to create the pressures for a 'historic' deal to develop the structural funds further. Once Greece joined the EU in 1981 it sought and gained compensation, along with France and Italy, for the presumed costs of admitting Spain and Portugal in the shape of the Integrated Mediterranean Programmes (IMPs).[4]

This compensation strategy, facilitated by structural funding, was repeated with the complex bargain that led to the apparent financial consequences of the SEA in the form of the Delors-1 package (the first multi-annual 'financial perspective'). This strategy was repeated in the early 1990s, when the Treaty on European Union (TEU) was agreed in December 1991, and then funded by the Delors-2 package (the second financial perspective) agreed in Edinburgh in December 1992 (Shackleton 1993; Laffan 1997; and Chapter 8). A similar, albeit less direct, link can be seen between the Treaty of Amsterdam (ToA), agreed in June 1997, and the Agenda 2000 proposals (Commission 1997a) launched in July 1997 and consolidated in the third financial perspective, agreed in Berlin in March 1999. This compensation saga will be extended if, by the end of 2006, the enlarged Union of twenty-five has managed to ratify the CT and to agree a fourth financial perspective. This two-stage process links distributive issues to fundamental bargains, but separates out the two phases of detailed negotiations (Majone 1994; McAleavey 1994).

The SEA for the first time linked the idea of cohesion to the reduction of regional disparities, although the structural funds (the territorial approach) were not seen as the sole solution to this problem. The SEA also referred to the use of loans from the European Investment Bank (EIB) to improve the working of the internal market (the competitive approach), and to the coordination of member states' economic policies (presumably including national regional policies). The SEA did, however, give a treaty base to the ERDF and, more significantly, to a requirement that the Commission rationalize and reform the objectives and implementation procedures of the structural funds—a power that the Commission was to exploit fully. Broad changes to the structural funds flowed from the SEA and its compensatory bargains. It is not clear from the public record how far the member states had gone in committing themselves to a particular size for the structural funds, but some observers believe that such a deal was struck (Endo 1999: 143; Ross 1995a: 40; Drake 2000: 93), and similarly so at Maastricht, Amsterdam, and Berlin.

The Delors-1 package provided for a doubling of the structural funds so that by 1992 they would account for 25 per cent of the EU budget (see Table 9.1 above). The detailed reforms of the structural funds are discussed later, but the point needs to be made here that the basic parameters of this agreement were established by high-level inter-governmental bargaining. Both the French and the UK governments demonstrated some last minute reluctance to double the structural funds, but this was overcome by the persistence of the German Presidency of the Council, the willingness of Chancellor Kohl to foot the bill, and the negotiating activism of Jacques Delors (Ross 1995a: 40–2). There is little evidence to suggest that the heads of state or government spent much time debating the advantages and disadvantages of regional policy as such as they worked to strike a deal.

The Treaty on European Union and Delors-2

The revolution in European affairs that occurred from 1989 onwards stimulated pressures for enlargement and for a further deepening of the EU. This culminated in the Treaty on European Union (TEU), agreed in Maastricht in December 1991, and the promise of a further budgetary bargain to be negotiated in 1992. In the interim, it was agreed that the special needs of the five eastern *Länder*, now included in a unified Germany, would be met by an additional allocation of 3 billion ecu for the period 1991–93. The money for the eastern *Länder* had to be an additional sum so as not to upset 'the delicate balance in the Funds' allocation of resources and their breakdown by objectives and regions' (Commission 1990b).

The Maastricht agreements were built around a complex intergovernmental bargain, much of which was negotiated at the last moment (Ross 1995a: 188–93). It is clear that further changes to the structural funds were central to the bargain. The TEU retained the cohesion objective and extended the structural funds to include a new Cohesion Fund to provide money for Greece, Spain, Portugal, and Ireland, in particular to support environmental and Trans-European Network (TEN) projects. The TEU also established a Committee of the Regions (CoR) but required only that it be consulted with regard to structural fund allocation and implementation. The CoR, like the Economic and Social Committee, has struggled to play a significant role in EU policy-making (Loughlin 1997; Jeffery 2002).

A Protocol on Economic and Social Cohesion was annexed to the TEU and it constituted an interim agreement between the member states, outlining broadly the changes to be agreed later in Edinburgh and to be incorporated into the enabling rules for the new structural funds. The Protocol recorded a 'desire for greater flexibility in the arrangements for allocations from the structural funds'. This was the start of the rot as far as the Commission was concerned, because it was a clear reference to the determination of the member states to free themselves of some of the restraints imposed by the 1988 reforms. The Protocol also indicated a willingness to devote enhanced structural funds exclusively to the poorer states, a theme often present at the start of negotiations about forthcoming financial perspectives. Since 1991 the net contributors have been looking for a way to repatriate responsibility for those elements of the structural funds that are in effect paid back to them formally through the ERDF, and subject to ERDF rules. To date, they have failed in this objective, although they are still trying (see below). In the meantime the net contributors work tirelessly to ensure that they obtain the best possible share of the allocation of ERDF payments among the member states.

The Protocol reveals more of the basic deal worked out at Maastricht in its reference to an agreement that the Cohesion Fund will go to those member states with a GNP per capita of less than 90 per cent of the Community average and which have a programme for fulfilling the economic convergence criteria for EMU. The Cohesion Fund thus represented an incentive to the poor four in the EU15 tied to the advent of EMU, rather than a regional development rationale. Both the conditions attached to the Cohesion Fund and those attached to the proposals for a general reform of the structural funds were clearly designed to enhance the power of the member governments at the expense of both the Commission and subnational actors. Nonetheless, the terms of the TEU left scope for further negotiation in what Marks (1993) refers to as 'post-treaty interpretation and institution-building', although this scope was quite significantly constrained, as can be seen in the Edinburgh agreement and the 1993 reforms.

At the 1992 Edinburgh European Council, the member governments agreed to increase the size of the structural funds from 18.6 billion ecu in 1992 to 30 billion ecu in 1999 (Shackleton 1993c) (see Table 9.1). There was also agreement about how the structural funds would be allocated between the various objectives which the Commission had established in its 1988 reforms (see Box 9.2) but only a vague understanding about the shares to be guaranteed to each member state. It was, however, evident that an agreement about how the spoils would be divided up was an essential condition for agreeing the implementing regulations (Allen 1993). At Edinburgh the European Council allocated an aggregate total of 15 billion ecu to the Cohesion Fund, and it was agreed that until 1996 Spain would receive between 52 and 58 per cent, Greece and Portugal between 16 and 20 per cent each, and Ireland between 7 and 10 per cent. The Irish Prime Minister, for instance, later claimed that he had 'firm pledges of 8 billion Irish punt' from the Edinburgh European Council (*Financial Times*, 2 July 1993), while the Spanish government said it had obtained written assurances that it would receive 6.4 billion pesetas (*Financial Times*, 5 July 1993), and the Portuguese government claimed that it was promised 3.5 billion escudos (*Financial Times*, 9 July 1993).

The exact determination of which regions would be eligible for the funds from the various objectives was left until later, although it was clear that outline promises were made in order to facilitate agreement in Edinburgh. It has been suggested, for instance, that the German government, under pressure from the *Länder*, agreed to an extension of the UK budget abatement only after it had obtained assurances that the five eastern *Länder* would be eligible for at least 13 billion ecu from Objective 1 funds. It was only after further negotiation in the Council that each member state's share was established and the enabling legislation passed in late 1993.

Between 1988 and 1999 the structural funds underwent a significant expansion. It has been argued by some that this expansion played an important role in facilitating the 'historic' decisions which underpinned the SEA and the TEU, and that much of the haggling over the details was left until later because 'the resolution of both types of decision simultaneously would be practically impossible' (McAleavey 1994). A broadly similar view can be taken of the decisions around the ToA in mid-1997, together with Agenda 2000 and the Berlin agreement of March 1999. A similar process is currently underway as the member states seek to ratify a new treaty (CT), to negotiate a new financial perspective, and to agree further reforms of cohesion policy all at the same time. Throughout the period under review both the secondary 'distributive'

Box 9.2 Structural fund objectives, 1988–2006

1988–99

- *Objective 1* was originally intended to cover regions where the GDP per capita was less than 75 per cent of the EU average. Some member states insisted that this criterion be loosened, in order to include particular additional regions, as a condition of their agreement to the overall package. The Council decides eligibility for this objective. Objective 1 draws on funds from the ERDF, ESF, and EAGGF and accounts for slightly below 70 per cent of the total funds.

- *Objective 2* covers regions affected by industrial decline, where the unemployment level is above the EU average. Eligibility for this objective is negotiated between the Commission and the Council. Objective 2 draws on funds from the ERDF and the ESF and represents around 11 per cent of the total funds.

- *Objective 3* combats long-term unemployment. In 1993 it was effectively combined with the old Objective 4, to facilitate the occupational integration of young people.

- *Objective 4*, post–1993 was to facilitate the adaptation of workers to industrial change. The two objectives draw on the ESF and together claim just under 10 per cent of the total funds.

- *Objective 5* is sub-divided between 5a, funded by the EAGGF and earmarked specifically for agricultural and forestry assistance, and 5b which draws on the ERDF, ESF, and EAGGF. Objective 5b promotes the development of rural areas mainly via diversification away from traditional agricultural activity. Objective 5 receives around 9 per cent of the total fund.

- *Objective 6* was introduced after the 1995 enlargement for developing sparsely populated Nordic areas. It draws funds from the ERDF, ESF, and EAGGF and accounts for less than 3 per cent of total funds.

2000–6

- *Objective 1* remains as above, but with a stricter application of the eligibility criterion, but also includes those areas previously eligible for Objective 6.

- *Objective 2* is for regions facing major change in the industrial, services, and fisheries sector, rural areas in serious decline and disadvantaged urban areas.

- *Objective 3* covers those regions not covered by the other objectives and is specifically aimed at encouraging the modernization of systems of education, training, and employment.

arrangements and the primary 'historic' decisions have been dependent on high-level bargaining. It was only subsequently, as the implementation process began, that other actors began to play a role.

Thus, the process of implementation does provide some scope for a challenge to the powers of the central governments of the member states, although some care needs to be taken in specifying which central powers are being challenged. Marks (1993) argues that it is necessary to 'go beyond the areas that are transparently dominated by the member states; financial decisions, major pieces of legislation and the treaties' in order to understand that 'beyond and beneath the highly visible politics of the member state bargaining lies a dimly lit process of institutional formation and here the Commission plays a vital role'. Others have argued that the implementation of the structural funds involves a mobilization of both public and private subnational actors, which is significant, because it has led to 'an enhancement of the governing capacity of the system as a whole' (Hooghe and Keating 1994). Neither of these arguments necessarily demonstrates that the central governments have lost power. It may be that they have little interest in the implementation stage once they have secured guarantees of a certain level of structural expenditure. It may be that the net contributors do have an interest in a degree of Commission oversight over the spending habits of the net recipients (Pollack 1995). It may also be the case that they are either able to control, to manipulate, or even to cooperate with, newly enfranchised subnational actors so as to consolidate, rather than weaken, their central authority. For instance, in the UK in the early 1990s the Conservative government had an interest in encouraging private subnational actors to participate in EU regional procedures, if this would disturb Labour-controlled local authorities.

Agenda 2000 and the Berlin Agreements

It was not long after the TEU and agreement on the second financial perspective that the question of enlargement arose once again. The accession of Austria, Sweden, and Finland in 1995 presented no real problems for the structural funds; it was marked only by the invention of Objective 6 (see Box 9.2). The Commission's (1996c) first assessment of cohesion policy was followed shortly by an informative report from the House of Lords' Select Committee on the European Communities (1997a). Both reports were inconclusive about the relationship between structural fund expenditure and economic cohesion, although the Lords' report attributed some significance to the political impact of the funds, in particular to the encouragement which they gave to local participation and thus a sense of 'ownership' of the EU policies. But it was hard to derive a justification for the funds in terms of their economic impact in reducing regional disparities.

The prospect of further enlargement would necessarily entail a debate about the future of the structural funds (see Chapters 8 and 16). Decisions on this were postponed while the member governments negotiated the ToA, but immediately after-wards the Commission delivered, as requested, its proposals for managing enlarge-ment. The Agenda 2000 documents (Commission 1997a; see Avery and Cameron 1998: 101–39) outlined a third financial perspective and proposed that overall spending on the structural funds, in both the EU15 and the enlarged membership, be frozen at 0.46 per cent of EU GDP (see Table 9.1). The Commission proposed a total expenditure on structural operations within this ceiling of €275 billion, at 1997 prices, between 2000 and 2006. This sum was broken down into €230 billion for the structural funds and the retained Cohesion Fund for the EU15, and €45 billion, to be ring-fenced, for both pre-accession aid for all the applicants and post-accession aid for the six candidate states that were likely to join the EU by 2006. In proposing that the structural funds should remain a high priority, but that their growth should be curtailed, the Commission was constrained by the member states which were committed to freezing the overall bud-get at a maximum of 1.27 per cent of EU GDP up to 2006, with little prospect that they could agree any significant reductions in other areas of expenditure such as agriculture.

The Commission proposed that the structural funds should be further concentrated and that their implementation should be simplified. To this end it suggested reducing the number of Objectives from seven to just three (see Box 9.2), and reducing the coverage of the structural funds from over 50 per cent of the EU population to between 35 and 40 per cent. It was also proposed that unemployment should become the major criterion for allocating structural funds in the newly created Objective 2 regions. The new rules for determining aid in Objective 2 regions and the proposed stricter application of the eligibility rules for Objective 1 would mean that many regions that had received aid between 1988 and 1999 would no longer be eligible.

The potential for sharp negotiations between member governments was high, and this is indeed what occurred between March 1998, when the Commission published its full proposals to implement Agenda 2000, and March 1999, when the European Council concluded a deal (see also Chapter 8). This established that the Commission's overall figure for structural operations expenditure between 2000 and 2006 would be reduced from €275 billion (at 1999 prices) to €258 billion. A total of €45 billion would remain ring-fenced for pre-accession aid and post-accession benefits, and the €213 billion reserved for the current EU15 would include €18 billion for the Cohesion Fund.

The character and results of this lengthy negotiation suggest a further weakening of the supranational aspects of structural funding, with the Commission forced to accept a further watering down of some of its principles, especially those of partnership and additionality. Even the effort to concentrate further the coverage of the structural funds was modified in the Berlin settlement, although the Commission did gain acceptance for the reduction of the number of objectives. The negotiations themselves were significantly affected by the German national elections, which took place in the autumn of 1998. In the intervening period between autumn 1998 and the Berlin European Council in March 1999, the Commission responded to the pressures from the member governments and announced a series of safety nets to reassure those who feared that they would lose out under the new rules. Once the Commission had conceded that special transitional arrangements would be tolerated for those regions likely to lose out, that no region would lose no more than one third of its eligible population, and that the Cohesion Fund would continue to be available for the poor four (even though three of them had apparently 'converged' enough to join the single currency), the makings of a deal were in place.

The Berlin agreement was facilitated by acceptance of the principle of providing something for everyone (see Box 9.3), which seemed to leave the member governments, especially the net recipients, in a stronger position than before. This appears to confirm the renationalization of control of structural fund expenditure, and the weakening of the Commission's four implementing principles (see Box 9.1), that has been apparent since the 1993 reforms (see following section). Formally, the 1999 reforms dealt with the immediate problem of enlargement in terms of budgetary allocations, but they had little serious impact on the problem of regional disparities. Furthermore, as Bache points out (1998: 133), the proposals addressed only the enlargement aspect of the cohesion problem. Politically, the new proposals served the function of facilitating agreement between the member governments, and the Commission may have been wise to respond to the new atmosphere by its proposals to simplify the implementation procedures, and to step back from some of its contacts with subnational actors. All of these tendencies seemed to take the policy process progressively further from the concept of multi-level governance and much closer to the modified intergovernmentalism that Bache (1999: 37–42) has described as 'extended gatekeeping'.

Box 9.3 Something for everyone! The Berlin Agreements and 'particular situations'

The Berlin European Council of March 1999 agreed structural fund spending for 2000–6, and allocated €11.142 billion for transitional support for all regions and areas which no longer meet the relevant eligibility criteria. In addition, particular situations would be funded as follows:

- €500 million for the development of the Lisbon region;

- €500 million for five more years of the Peace Programme, in recognition of the special efforts for the peace process in Northern Ireland, of which €100 million would be allocated to Ireland;

- €100 million phasing out treatment under Objective 1 for the transition in Ireland resulting from the new classification of regions, and an additional allocation of €550 million under Objective 1 as a result of the reallocation;

- €500 million for the Netherlands to take account of the particular characteristics of labour market participation;

- €150 million for Sweden for a special programme of assistance, plus €350 million for Sweden under Protocol Six of its Act of Accession;

- € 100 million to take account of the special problems of East Berlin in the transformation process;

- €96 million for Italy and €64 million for Belgium for the phasing out of allocations for Objective 2;

- €15 million for the Hainault region of Belgium for the phasing out of Objective 1;

- €300 million for a phasing out programme for the UK Highlands and Islands in view of the particular structural problems resulting from low population density, matched with a high degree of poverty;

- €450 million for Greece, €450 million for Portugal, €40 million for Ireland, and €200 million for Spain as a special financial allowance to enable these countries to maintain between 2000 and 2006 the overall average level of per capita aid reached in 1999;

- €350 million for Austria inside the Community Initiatives;

- €550 million for the Netherlands inside the Community Initiatives.

Source: Council of the European Union (1999).

Pre-accession aid

In the early years of the recent enlargement process, the Phare programme (originally Poland and Hungary Assistance for Restructuring of Economies) was used to fund individual projects and involved direct dealing between the Commission and the central governments of the candidate countries (see Chapter 16). It was much criticized for its excessive bureaucracy and for the fact that it was based on annual, rather than multiannual, programming and did little to prepare the new members for structural funding on the EU's own established model. In response to this criticism, for the 2000–6 funding period the EU introduced two new programmes which ran alongside Phare: the Instrument for Structural Policies for Pre-Accession Aid (ISPA); and the Special Accession Programme for Agricultural and Rural Development

(SAPARD). Bailey and De Propris (2004: 83) note that the idea was for Phare (€1.5bn) to prepare the new members for working with the structural funds, for ISPA (€1bn) to prepare them for the Cohesion Fund, and for SAPARD (€500mn) to prepare them for the EAGGF–Guidance Section. Nevertheless, at a time when the 1999 structural policy reforms were devolving budgetary control down to the EU15 member governments, the Commission maintained its own tight control over pre-accession structural funding—not the best way to prepare the new members for 2004. Efforts were made to build institutional capacity in the new members, in particular by the use of 'twinning' projects involving exchanges of civil servants from the EU15 with those from the candidate states. However, doubts were expressed about the likelihood of institutional *capacity* being turned into *capability* in the short time that was available before enlargement (Bailey and De Propris 2004: 90).

Implementation of the structural funds

In the early days of the structural funds the Commission was given little discretion other than over the minuscule ESF. The ERDF was distributed by a system of national quotas, which meant that the member states requested funds for projects that were already planned, or, in some cases, completed. In 1979, the Commission persuaded the Council to agree to a small non-quota section and in 1984 the quotas were relaxed into 'indicative ranges'. This gave the Commission discretion over about 11 per cent of the ERDF budget. The Commission used this new flexibility to develop its own regional priorities, and to introduce its own programmatic approach to regional assistance. In 1984 the Council agreed that 20 per cent of the ERDF would be devoted to programmes, rather than to individual projects. Although most of the programmes would be developed by the member states, some would be initiated and developed by the Commission. Steps were also taken to coordinate better the activities of the three separate funds (ESF, ERDF, and the EAGGF–Guidance Section). The IMPs and the Integrated Development Programmes (IDPs) were arguably the first to involve the structural funds as a coordinated group rather than an individual fund, although efforts had been made in this direction since the late 1970s (H. Wallace 1983).

In this early period the Commission took advantage of any opportunity to influence the activities of the funds or to shape their future. The Commission's big opportunity owed much to Delors' success in establishing the concept of cohesion in the SEA and in linking this to increased structural fund expenditure. The SEA (Art. 130d EEC now Art. 161 TEC) states that the implementation of the structural funds should be reformed on the initiative of the Commission; another Delors innovation). Once the financial perspective was agreed in 1988, the Commission duly proposed, and the Council passed, a package of regulations that amounted to a major reform. The TEU provided the opportunity for further reform in 1993, 1999, and 2006 and the Constitutional Treaty has broadly similar clauses.

In the 1988 reforms, the Commission established four principles (see Box 9.1) for the implementation of the structural funds. The Commission sought a more autonomous role for itself, in part by developing an alliance with subnational partners against the stranglehold of the national governments. The 1993 reforms suggest that this strategy had stimulated a 'backlash' as the member states took every opportunity to claw back what they conceded in 1988, in what some have described as a partial renationalization of the structural funds (Bache 1998: 127–33).

The ToA made no substantive changes, but it was agreed that the Agenda 2000 package would require yet further reform of the implementation procedures. The main guidelines for these reforms were proposed by the Commission in March 1998, formally agreed by the Council after the 1999 Berlin agreements, and became operational at the start of 2000 (Barber 1998; Bache 1998: 125–33). The Commission produced its plans for further reforms to the way that the structural funds are implemented in 2004, for agreement by the end of 2006.

Concentration

In selecting objectives for the funds (see Box 9.2), the Commission sought to impose consistent geographical and functional criteria on their management, and thereby to concentrate spending on the most needy regions and states. To a certain extent this goal has been achieved. The Cohesion Fund furthered this principle of concentration by limiting the recipients to only four member states, although from 2007 that figure will rise to eleven. There is a constant tension between the Commission's desire for more concentration (albeit with a high overall volume) for the structural funds, and the concern of all the member states to obtain and to retain as large a share of the structural funds as possible. However, if the net contributor member states could achieve a measure of repatriation of the funds, they would probably settle for a smaller total concentrated on the new members. Faced with this alternative the Commission would probably prefer to retain a high level of structural funding, even if it does have to be spread across the EU25 rather than concentrated on the new member states.

The 1993 negotiations were replete with examples of individual member states seeking to bend the agreed rules in order to preserve funds for their own favoured regions. The 1999 reforms sought to extend the principle of concentration even further by reducing the objectives to just three and by reducing the percentage of the EU's population eligible for structural aid from 51 per cent to 35–40 per cent (the Berlin European Council agreed on 42 per cent). Thus, the Commission was eventually forced to modify its proposals for further concentration with safety nets and transitional arrangements in order to facilitate an agreement that had 'something for everyone' (see Box 9.3). The Commission's proposals of February 2004 for 2007–13 would concentrate structural funding even more by mainstreaming all programmes into just three priorities (see Table 9.2).

Programming

The implementing regulations of 1988 and 1993 provided for the structural funds to be allocated to programmes rather than to individual projects. These programmes could be initiated at the national or Community level, and could be financed by one or more of the funds. In the period 1988–99, roughly 90 per cent of the funds went towards nationally initiated programmes and 9 per cent towards what became known as Community Initiatives (see Table 9.3).

Box 9.4 Structural funds, new priorities for 2007–13

Convergence: to support growth and job creation in the least developed member states and regions. This priority will receive €262.5bn (78 per cent) of the total cohesion budget and will be financed by the Cohesion Fund, the ERDF, and the ESF. It will primarily cover regions whose GDP per capita is less than 75 per cent of the EU average (i.e. the same criterion as Objective 1). This priority will include 25.6 per cent of the population of the EU25 where Objective 1 covered 22 per cent of the population of EU15.

This priority will also provide funds to the 'statistical effect' regions (those classified as Objective 1 in EU15 but not in EU25). These will cover 5.2 per cent of the EU25 population and the funding is more generous than that provided since 1999 to the Objective 1 'phase-out' regions.

Within this priority the Cohesion Fund will be available, as before, to those member states with a GNP below 90 per cent of the EU. All the new member states, except Cyprus, will be eligible along with Portugal and Greece, but there is transitional provision for Spain under the Cohesion Fund despite the fact that Spain's eligibility is lost because of the statistical effect. There will also be a special programme under this priority for the 'outermost' regions.

Competiveness and employment: replaces Objectives 2 and 3 and will have two sub-priorities and will receive €61bn (18 per cent) of the total cohesion budget.

The ERDF will be used to help *regions* to anticipate and to promote change in industrial, urban, and rural area by strengthening competiveness (50 per cent).

The ESF will be used to help *people* to anticipate and to promote change by supporting policies aimed at full employment (50 per cent).

Resources will go to those Objective 1 regions that are no longer eligible even after the statistical effect is taken into consideration (these are the new 'phasing-in' regions and cover 3.6 per cent of the EU25 population) and to all other regions not covered by the *convergence* priority. There is no guidance in the draft Regulation as to how these funds will be allocated between the member states, although there is some very general guidance as to how funds should be allocated within member states (thematic, geographic, and resource concentration).

Under this priority there will also be specific assistance to 'remote' regions such as 'islands, mountain areas and sparsely populated regions particularly in the far north of the Union'.

Territorial cooperation: to cover cross-border (land and maritime), transnational, and interregional cooperation. This priority will receive €13.5bn (4 per cent) of the total cohesion budget and is designed to further develop the INTERREG Community Initiative. All regions along the internal borders and certain regions along the external borders will qualify (where resources will be available under the New Neighbourhood Instrument).

The programmes initiated at the national level were adopted by the Commission under the 1988 rules on the basis of Community Support Frameworks (CSFs); these were separately negotiated between the Commission and each member government, on the basis of either national or regional development plans (RDPs), drawn up by the member government in partnership with its regional authorities. The 1993 reforms streamlined this process, allowing a member state to submit a Single Programming Document (SPD); these were not negotiated with the Commission, in contrast to the CSFs, and contain proposals for programmes from the outset, thus

Table 9.2 Simplifying the structural funds

2000–6		2007–13 (Commission Proposal)	
Objectives	**Financial Instruments**	**Objectives**	**Financial instruments**
Cohesion fund	Cohesion Fund		Cohesion fund
Objective 1	ERDF, ESF, EAGGF–Guidance FIFG	Convergence and competitiveness	ERDF ESF
Objective 2	ERDF, ESF	Regional competitiveness and employment	ERDF, ESF
Objective 3	ESF		
INTERREG	ERDF	European territorial cooperation	ERDF
URBAN	ERDF		
EQUAL	ESF		
LEADER+	EAGGF–Guidance		
Rural development and restructuring of fishery sector outside Objective 1	EAGGF–Guidance FIFG		
9 objectives	6 instruments	3 objectives	3 instruments

Source: Commission (2004h), *Third Report on Economic and Social Cohesion.*

shortening the process. Because of time constraints this could mean the effective exclusion (and confusion!) of 'partners', and the domination of the process by central governments. Once adopted, the programmes are monitored and assessed by monitoring committees at national, regional, and any other relevant operating level, e.g. local authorities or other agencies. The 1999 reform proposals led to a further streamlining, in response to the member governments' demand for 'simplification'; and the proposed changes from 2006 are designed to further simplify all aspects of programming from planning through operational and financial management to evaluation and accountability. Bache (1998: 127) takes this to mean reducing the role and influence of the Commission to one of framework planning and general oversight.

Initially, therefore, the Commission was successful at moving away from the uncoordinated funding of nationally selected projects towards the funding of

Table 9.3 Community initiatives, 1988–2006

Initiative	Purpose
1988–99	
Interreg	Cross-border, transnational, and inter-regional cooperation
Leader	Rural development
Regis	Support for the most remote regions
Adapt	Adaptation of the workforce to industrial change
SME	Small and medium-size firms in disadvantaged areas
Rechar	Adaptation to industrial change in coal-dependent regions
Konver	Adaptation to industrial change in defence industry-dependent regions
Resider	Adaptation to industrial change in steel-dependent regions
Retex	Adaptation to industrial change in textile-dependent regions
Urban	Urban policy
Pesca	Restructuring the fisheries sector
Employment	Integration into working life of women, young people, and the disadvantaged
2000–6	
Interreg	Cross-border, transnational, and inter-regional cooperation
Leader	Rural development
Equal	Transnational cooperation to combat all forms of discrimination and inequalities in the labour market

programmes, designed in consultation with the member governments and using Commission-determined criteria. However, over time it has been forced to concede more and more of the programming to the member governments. As we shall see, the designation of objectives, of the areas that they will cover, and of the programming criteria are increasingly influenced by the bargains struck internally by the member states. The Commission was able to push its programming principle furthest in the one area where it has had considerable autonomy: Community Initiatives (see Table 9.3), but these were reduced to just three (then four) in 1999, and are scheduled to be totally subsumed to the mainstream programmes from 2007 onwards. As Hooghe and Keating (1994) pointed out, the Commission's exercise of autonomy with regard to Community Initiatives caused considerable friction with the national authorities—friction that has often been exacerbated by coordination failures within the Commission itself, resulting in conflicts and contradictions between Commission-initiated programmes and national programmes. In the 1993 reforms a new Council Committee on Community Initiatives was established to tighten member governments' control. For the period 1993–9 the Commission optimistically proposed that the percentage of the structural funds devoted to Community Initiatives be expanded from 9 per cent to 15 per cent. The member governments responded by retaining the 9 per cent limit, in 2000–6 they reduced this to just 5 per cent and from 2007 they will disappear altogether as a separate item in the cohesion budget.

Additionality

The Commission has repeatedly tried to insist on additionality as a principle for structural fund expenditure. It was successful in the 1988 reforms in making this more respected by the member states, and in constraining them from reducing national expenditure, as they had tended to do in the past. Bache (1998: 77–9 and 105–12, 2004: 174–8) documents the battles that the Commission has had over this issue, in particular with the UK, but also with the other member states. On this issue the Commission was actively supported by many local and regional authorities, a development which provided Marks (1993) with the evidence that he needed to confirm his view that subnational authorities and the Commission had become significant participants and partners in the EU policy process. However, this overall conclusion was challenged by Pollack (1995), and the actual outcome of the UK dispute is questioned by Bache (1999). Nevertheless the Commission has pushed the member governments to 'account openly and transparently for the structural funding they receive and for the continuing implementation of national expenditure' (Scott 1995). Member governments are now required to demonstrate additionality, and the Commission has successfully threatened to withhold funds from recalcitrant states if they do not comply. Nevertheless, it still has enormous problems in seeking to monitor effectively the devious financial practices of member governments. In the 1999 reforms these problems were acknowledged; as part of its 'simplification' drive the Commission came up with the notion of 'negotiated additionality'. It was, however, still complaining in The Third Report on Cohesion (Commission 2004h) that additionality was proving difficult to verify, especially in Objective 2 and 3 regions. The Commission's answer is to pass the responsibility for ensuring additionality back to the member states.

The Cohesion Fund, on the other hand, appears to strike at the very principle of additionality. This is partly because until 2004 cohesion money was primarily viewed as aid to promote convergence for the purposes of EMU. It was thus specifically designed to assist governments from the poorer member states of the EU15 to receive structural assistance without increasing the burden on overall government expenditure. It became harder to retain this rationale when three of the four beneficiaries of the Cohesion Fund joined the single currency. However, the 1999 agreement retained the Cohesion Fund until 2006, with a view to helping those eligible to 'maintain' the convergence that they have managed to date, and the proposed allocations for 2007 onwards increase the share of the total structural funds taken up by the Cohesion Fund.

Partnership

A great deal of excitement has been generated by the Commission's advocacy of the principle of partnership in the management of the structural funds (Bache 1998: 93–104, 1999; Bache and Flinders 2004: 166–74). The 1988 reforms called for the close involvement of regional and local bodies with the Commission and the national authorities in the planning, decision-making, and implementation of the structural funds. It is this which is the basis for the interest in subnational actors (Hooghe 1996), and the notion of multi-level governance (Marks 1993; Bache and Flinders 2004) in this area of policy. The intent was clear: it was not just to improve the efficiency of regional policy, but to give it features specifically designed to penetrate national policy processes (Hooghe 1996). In this sense one core goal was a policy made for the regions and by the regions; in other words, a policy that encouraged not just regionalization, but regionalism. Such an objective was almost certain to encounter resistance from central governments, especially in the more highly centralized member states such as the UK in the 1980s and early 1990s, and especially at a time when they were facing demands for devolution.

The 1988 partnership proposals included some interesting innovations, which were seized upon by a host of academics searching for a convincing alternative to the inter-governmentalism that had begun to dominate studies of the EU policy process. An advisory Consultative Council of Regional and Local Authorities was established, the forerunner of the CoR (Committee of the Regions). Regional and local authorities became much more active, both individually and collectively, in lobbying in Brussels and in national capitals (McAleavey 1994; Mazey and Richardson 1993b; Hooghe 1996). While some authors have argued that the partnership principle has enhanced regional and local governmental involvement in the policy process (Landábru 1994; Laffan 1996; Nanetti 1996), others contend that, despite a great deal of mobilization, much of the activity has been symbolic or has been countered by the gatekeeping activities of central governments (Sutcliffe 2000; Bache and Bristow 2003; Gualina 2003; Hughes, Sasse, and Gordon 2004; Bailey and De Propris 2004). On this latter view, very little real power has been wrested from national central governments, and very little additional power has flowed to the regions in those member states such as Germany or Spain with an already decentralized federal structure (Hooghe and Keating 1994; Anderson 1995; Bache 1999). McAleavey's (1994) study covers the extensive activity of the lobby which promoted Objective 2 and sought to preserve it in the 1994–9 period. He concluded that the impact of the lobbying had been minimal, and that it was not possible to detect subnational influence on the intergovernmental bargaining in Edinburgh.

Perhaps not surprisingly, the extent of influence of the many regional offices based in Brussels has been questioned by central government officials, in contrast to the claims from regional and local authorities to the political credit for any EU funds that have come their way. Subnational actors involved in structural fund partnerships have been the subject of a great deal of academic scrutiny (Bache 1998: 93–104; A. Smith 1998), and it is hard to draw firm conclusions across the great variety of EU member states. It appears that the effectiveness of subnational access is determined more by the nature of the constitutional arrangements in a particular member state than by the Commission's partnership arrangements. In some cases central governments have been able to strengthen their powers by using Commission procedures to play one set of subnational actors off against another, or by joining forces with subnational actors to do battle with the Commission. Examples of the latter case support the liberal intergovernmentalist approach of Moravcsik (1998), in so far as they show subnational actors as important in national preference formation, rather than as independent actors at the EU level.

The Commission has been criticized for its choice of partners; in some programmes, the Commission prefers regional authorities, in others local authorities, and in yet others partners from the private sector. In recent years cities have strengthened their claims for attention especially as the overall affluence of many of Europe's major cities disguises pockets of extreme poverty, and thus the need for programmes designed to enhance social as opposed to territorial cohesion. There is also a tension between the Commission's desire for partnership and its desire for consistent, coherent, and well-coordinated programmes. If the partnership principle really did lead to significant subnational participation in the design and management of the structural funds, then the enormous variety across the EU, in terms both of organization and influence, would lead to different regions funding many different solutions to similar problems (A. Smith 1998; Bache 1998). We can indeed observe a great deal of regional mobilization; in the Flanders region of Belgium and in the German *Länder* there is extensive involvement in the preparation, financing, monitoring, and assessment of programmes, although Anderson (1995) doubts whether the *Länder* have increased their powers *vis-à-vis* the federal government. This was clearly not the case in the UK before 1997 (Bache, George, and Rhodes 1996; see also Bulmer and Burch 2002), or in countries such as Greece, Ireland, and Portugal or a number of the new members, which have no elected regional tiers. In these cases the powers of the central government have probably increased, drawing on their ability to influence significantly who participates in the implementation of the structural funds. Devolution in the UK and the recasting of the eligible areas in Ireland may change the patterns of influence (Bulmer and Burch 2002).

It is, however, quite hard to demonstrate that the Commission's advocacy of the partnership principle in itself has significantly challenged the autonomy of the central governments. Where that autonomy is under challenge for different reasons, the management of the structural funds provides an opportunity structure for political positioning, as may well be the case as regards the participation of the UK Highlands and Islands in Objective 1 funding after 1999. Some EU countries have experimented a good deal with regionalization in recent years, but this should not necessarily be equated with regionalism as such. As Tsoukalis (1997: 208) concludes, 'European integration may indeed strengthen in the long term the centrifugal tendencies inside some member states. But this will have little to do with the principle of partnership or other such ideas which have often been blown completely out of proportion in the literature'.

The structural funds post-enlargement, 2004–13

The impact of enlargement

The 2004 enlargement was certainly partially facilitated by the use of EU funding, based on the model of the structural funds, to provide pre- (and post-) accession aid. The new member states clearly expect to be significant beneficiaries of structural funding under the 2007–13 financial perspective. The Prodi Commission proposed to spend a total of €335bn under the fourth financial perspective to run from 2007–13. This figure has to be agreed with the member states by the end of 2005 and it may be that the new Barroso Commission will modify the proposal itself. There is a fundamental disagreement among the old member states about how this enlargement should bear on the structural funds overall. In particular there is a significant dispute between those member countries (mainly net contributors), which would restrict future structural operations to the new members, and those which want to see the structural funds continue to provide 'something for everyone'. As Barry and Begg (2003: 790) point out, however, the budgetary arithmetic is such, given an agreed limit of 4 per cent of GDP on what any new member can receive, that the EU25 are effectively left with a choice between maintaining the present system of structural funding (albeit reformed), as the Commission advocates, or halving the anticipated costs by confining funding to the new member states. These latter have a combined GDP of just 4 per cent of the EU total, and 4 per cent of this amounts to just 0.16 per cent of EU GDP, compared with the 0.46 per cent that is currently spent on the structural funds—a percentage that the Commission proposes to maintain.

The context for planning the next financial perspective, and thus the funds available for structural operations, have been significantly altered by the 2004 enlargement and the planned admission of Bulgaria and Romania in 2007. Enlargement to EU25 has increased the population of the EU by 20 per cent, but the GDP by only 4–5 per cent, with the result that the EU's average per capita income has fallen by 10 per cent. By the time that the EU has twenty-seven members more than one third of the EU population will live in member states with a per capita income of less than 90 per cent of the EU average (the criteria for Cohesion Fund assistance) compared to just one sixth in the EU15. In the EU27 the poorest 10 per cent of the population will earn just 31 per cent of the EU27 average, compared to the 61 per cent of the EU15 average income earned by the poorest 10 per cent in the EU15.

Nearly all the regions of the new member states will qualify for EU structural funding under the present Objective 1 criterion (GDP per capita of less than 75 per cent of the EU average). At present around 70 per cent of the structural funds are allocated to this objective and under the Commission's proposals of February 2004 (Commission 2004i), which retain the same criterion, this figure will be raised to 78 per cent. The reduction in the average per capita income in the EU25 means that most of the regions in the EU15 which qualify for funding under Objective 1 will do so no longer because their relative prosperity—albeit not their absolute prosperity—has changed; they are the victims of the so-called 'statistical effect'.

As a result of the 2004 enlargement an increased number of the EU15 states will become net contributors to the EU budget (see Chapter 8). Most of the new members should stand to become net recipients,[5] if the budgetary structure remains fundamentally unchanged, as the Commission has in effect suggested with its proposals for the fourth financial perspective (Commission 2004i). However, a significant group of net contributor countries in the old member states have already indicated that they wish to cap the size of the EU budget at a lower level, perhaps with new priorities. Hence the pressure will be on the structural funds, especially if the agreement driven by the French and German governments is retained, which renders agricultural expenditure 'untouchable' until after 2013. A proposal to respond to enlargement by restricting structural funding to the new members could find favour with a formidable combination of new members and net contributors. However, decisions on the financial perspective, including the structural funds, have to be taken by unanimity, and hence yet another compromise will have to be found.

Enlargement has increased the problem of achieving the goal of cohesion, because of the widened range of diversity within the EU25. It is, however, by no means clear that the structural funds, which will represent 0.46 per cent of EU GDP at the most, are the best means to attain economic convergence. Opinions are heavily divided about the effectiveness of the structural funds as an instrument for reducing divergence, with some commentators preferring to rely on the workings of the market, supported by a competition policy, while others are convinced that diversity within and between regions is best rectified by national rather than EU measures. The new member states do not, however, have well-developed national regional policies to fall back on, should the EU fundamentally change its approach. This may not, however, be so relevant for the smaller new members, many of which are smaller than regions in larger countries under the current EU definitions. In addition, there is the question of the capacity and the capability of the new member states to implement structural spending programmes, either under the present regime (in which subnational partnerships with the Commission are encouraged), or under a reformed system, that might place more weight on the roles of central governments.

Continuing pre-accession aid, 2004–6

On their accession the ten new member states immediately became involved in negotiations with the other member states and the Commission over the fourth financial perspective and the detailed arrangements for the dispersal of the structural funds in the next programming period. It is interesting to note that the portfolio for regional policy has gone to Danuta Hübner, the Commissioner from Poland, and that the overall budget portfolio has gone to Dalia Grybauskaite, the Commissioner from Lithuania. The successor arrangements will cover the period 2007–13, and meanwhile an adjustment of Agenda 2000 provides just under €25bn for structural aid, as well as continuing pre-accession aid, for the new members until the end of 2006 (see Table 9.4).

Despite the fact that the new members received considerable amounts of pre-accession aid as well as assistance from the Phare programmes, doubts have been expressed about their capacity to manage structural programmes, and in particular about the existence of capacity below the national governmental level. This has been a repeated concern of the Commission in its regular reports over the pre-accession period. Bailey and De Propris (2004) argue that the new members are ill-equipped to participate in the multi-level governance partnership schemes, partly because the local and regional institutions are weak, and partly because of the conscious and effective 'gatekeeping' of the new member state central governments (Baun 2002). Nonetheless, the new member governments have been engaged in reform initiatives to improve the quality of regional and local government over the past decade, generally using templates from the old member states, and seeking to make these compatible with EU funding criteria and practices. For example, both Poland and Hungary have undertaken extensive reforms with a clear view to EU funding (see Keating and Hughes 2003; Hughes, Sasse, and Gordon 2004). We know from the

Table 9.4 EU aid to new members, 2004–6

Objective	1	2	3	INTERREG	Equal	Cohesion Fund	Total
Czech Republic	1,454.27	71.3	58.79	68.68	32.1	938.05	2,621.19
Cyprus	0	28.02	21.95	4.30	1.81	53.94	113.44
Estonia	371.36	0	0	10.60	4.07	309.03	695.06
Hungary	1,995.72	0	0	68.68	30.29	1,112.67	3,207.36
Latvia	625.57	0	0	15.26	8.03	515.43	1,164.29
Lithuania	895.17	0	0	22.49	11.87	608.17	1,537.70
Malta	63.19	0	0	2.37	1.24	21.94	88.74
Poland	8,275.81	0	0	221.36	133.93	4178.60	1,2809.70
Slovakia	1,041.04	37.17	44.94	41.47	22.27	570.50	1,757.39
Slovenia	2,37.51	0	0	23.65	6.44	188.71	456.31
Total	14,959.64	136.49	125.68	478.86	252.05	8,495.04	24,451.18

Source: Euro News April 2004 (Newsletter of the UK Network of European Information Centres).

diverse experiences of the EU15 that an important distinction must be made between indicators of *activity* or *participation* and the capability that depends on effective *governance*. There is some evidence that the Commission is losing out to the newly acquired 'gatekeeping' skills of the central governments. Critics from the new member states also argue that the Commission has been heavy-handed and some-times inept in its efforts to impose reforms (Hughes, Sasse, and Gordon 2004). Many, however, still doubt their capacity to participate effectively in the national regional development planning process which forms a part of the Commission's proposals for the period 2007–13. Doubts in addition about the 'absorptive capacity' of the new members have already led to an EU decision that, at least until 2013, a cap of 4 per cent of GDP will be set on the total amount of structural aid that any member state can receive. Moreover there is the possibility that they will increase regional and national disparities among the new members, as the richer ones with higher GDPs may be more successful in exploiting this assistance.

The fourth financial perspective

In February 2004 the Commission (2004i) published its proposals for the fourth financial perspective (2007–13), which shapes the budgetary context for the decisions to be made during 2005. The incoming Barroso Commission will have a chance to develop its own approach: first, when presenting a fully-fledged proposal in spring 2005, and then in the subsequent negotiations with the member states, which are due to end in 2005, but which may well spill over into 2006. At the time of writing (December 2004), it is still too early to tell how far the new Commission will adapt the proposals from its predecessor. Whatever is decided will effectively be the second instalment of the 'bill for enlargement' (Agenda 2000 being the first instalment).

The fourth financial perspective has to assume an EU membership of at least twenty-seven (twenty-eight if Croatia joins the EU before 2013) during the programming period. Structural and cohesion funding represent the only significant area of expenditure where there is a potential margin for manoeuvre, if the level of agriculture spending remains locked to what was agreed in 2002 (see Chapter 7). There are already indications that some of the old member states, in particular the net contributors, want to challenge the inherited framework for EU spending. Moreover, various proposals have been made (Kok 2004; Sapir *et al.* 2004) for shifting spending to other kinds of policy goals, especially those associated with the Lisbon Agenda.

Specifically as regards regional policy a real choice will have to be made between the Commission's proposal of February 2004 that around €336 billion be allocated to the structural funds over the period, and the counter proposal from the UK (HMSO 2003) that would lead to approximately half that figure being allocated at the European level. Four arguments weigh in the balance here. First, there is the overall question of fiscal policy stance, given EMU and the Maastricht criteria on public spending (see Chapter 6). Secondly, there is the debate about whether or not EU spending on regional policy and cohesion has actually contributed to economic convergence and the reduction of disparities within or between regions. Thirdly, there is the issue of the polarized and highly politicized tensions among: net contributors; existing beneficiaries of the structural and cohesion funds in the old member states; and claimants from the new member states. Fourthly, there are the pressures for funding on other EU policy goals. Past experience suggests that a compromise is the most likely outcome, bearing in mind that negotiations over the financial perspective and the future structural funds will coincide with referenda on the CT in a number of member states—a significant complicating factor.

The Commission's proposals have rearranged the categories of expenditure for the EU budget (see Chapter 8, Table 8.1). Now the two main budget lines are: sustainable growth, subdivided into competitiveness and cohesion; and natural resources, subdivided into agricultural payments and other natural resources. This makes precise comparison with the past difficult. Broadly speaking, most of what was 'structural operations' now appears under the cohesion heading of 'sustainable growth'.

The Commission proposed that the budget as a whole should grow by around 30 per cent over the period, with cohesion spending tracking this growth. This represents a significant increase in the funds available for cohesion over the period 2007–13 of €336bn, compared with €257bn for the period 2000–6. Total planned cohesion spending (minus EAGGF, Guidance, and FIFG spending, which has been relocated to the agriculture heading) amounts to around 0.4 per cent of EU GDP. Under the proposed capping rule a maximum of between 0.16 and 0.20 per cent of EU GDP can be spent in the new member states. Thus, at least half the proposed cohesion expenditure over the period would be spent in the old member states that constitute the EU15. Finally, the Commission wants to simplify the spending instruments by identifying one instrument per policy area and one fund per programme. This is in line with the Commission's proposals for reforming the cohesion programmes and would lead, for instance, to all the pre- and post-accession programmes (Phare, SAPARD, and ISPA) being grouped together.

The further reform of cohesion policy, 2007–13

In February 2004, building on the work that followed the second cohesion report (Commission 2001g), the Commission published its third report on economic and social cohesion (Commission 2004h), in which it presented it proposals for future structural funding, with an unsurprisingly positive assessment of the impact of the current programmes. The Commission proposed that the six priorities or objectives of the period 1999–2006 be reduced to three, and that they should be funded only by the ERDF, the ESF, and the Cohesion Fund (see Box 9.4). It also suggested changes to both the implementation and evaluation procedures.

The Sapir Report (Sapir et al. 2004) noted the compensation function of the structural funds, but could find no hard evidence to support either the argument that the funds had made a significant difference to the performance of lagging regions, or the argument that they had not. Sapir went on to state that a national approach (as with the Cohesion Fund whose success especially in Ireland and Spain is universally acknowledged) was preferable to a regional one (ERDF) for determining eligibility for structural funding. They recommended that in future cohesion resources would be best spent on building institutional and physical capacity together with developing human capital. However, these recommendations provoked some irritation on the part of Michel Barnier, the then Commissioner responsible for regional policy, and thus were not subsequently endorsed in the February 2004 report (Barry and Begg 2003: 791). Nonetheless, the Kok Report (2004) echoes a good deal of the arguments presented by Sapir when first published in an on-line version by the Commission in 2003.

The new reforms would bring all the previous Community Initiatives (INTERREG, EQUAL, LEADER, and URBAN) into the three mainstream programmes and the Commission is particularly keen to involve city authorities in the planning and implementation of programmes to a greater extent than before.

Programming, partnership, additionality (although this will prove difficult with cross-border programmes between member and non-member states), and concentration remain the key principles of implementation. There are proposals to make programming more strategic and to simplify implementation, while enhancing transparency and financial accountability. This is to be achieved by the reduction of both funds and priorities to three, and by a new planning framework involving: (1) an EU cohesion strategy adopted by the Council; (2) a national development strategy devised by each member state; (3) national regional operational programmes; and (4) annual reporting to the Council. Financial control is to be made more 'proportionate' and devolved downwards as much as possible to deal with the charge of excessive bureaucracy by the Commission. The Commission's plans, which split the funds between the 'new' and 'old' members, do little to further concentrate resources, although limiting structural funds to the new members would have a significant concentration impact. There is an increased emphasis on partnership with proposals for further decentralization to 'partnerships on the ground' underpinned by 'tripartite' contracts between the member states, the regions, and local authorities. The aim is clearly that of enhanced multi-level governance, but the actual impact will be dependent on the extent of central government 'gatekeeping' in each member state. Much the same caution needs to be expressed about the Commission's plans to further involve the social partners and civil society. Under these arrangements cohesion policy will be given a higher profile in the Council, and the tendency to devolve responsibility down to the member states will continue, albeit with enhanced accountability.

The Commission plans were presented to the Cohesion Forum, which met in May 2004, and were then turned into draft regulations for the Council and Parliament to consider during 2005 and 2006, depending on how long it takes the member states to reach agreement on the fourth financial perspective. The Commission would prefer this to be sooner rather than later in order to prepare programmes during 2006 for introduction in 2007. However, if previous rounds are any guide the major financial decision will be postponed until the last possible moment. In 2005–6 this decision is also likely to become entangled with the debate on the ratification of the CT as one or two of the key players in the battle over the financial perspective will be at their most sensitive to domestic public opinion as they try to reach an agreement.

Conclusions

The CT, with its Cohesion Protocol, makes clear that the EU intends to continue pursuing the objective of economic, social, and territorial cohesion. The structural funds are most clearly directed at the territorial aspect. The logic assumes that economic convergence among countries and among regions will deliver cohesion, which in turn will deliver growth, competitiveness, employment, and sustainable development, and thus the Lisbon and Gothenburg objectives.

What remains in doubt are the overall size and beneficiaries of the structural funds in an enlarged Union. Decisions about these two factors will be reflected in whatever agreement is reached about the fourth financial perspective. The amount of money allocated to the structural funds for 2007–13 will indicate the degree of compensation for enlargement that the member states agree to pay each other in an intergovernmental package. It has already been agreed that the new member states will receive structural funding, but limited to a maximum of 4 per cent of EU GDP. What is not yet agreed is the extent to which, if at all, the 'old' member states of the EU15 will continue to receive structural assistance.

This compensation bargain will determine the extent to which the Commission's plans for the reform of the structural funds will be taken forward. Irrespective of the level of funding, it is likely that the process of renationalizing the means of delivery, financial management, and evaluation of structural funding will continue. This would increase the emphasis on the role of national regional policies, which already account for over 75 per cent of regional spending in the EU. There is some evidence to suggest that national regional policy has to a minor extent been Europeanized over the years. Involvement in EU cohesion policy has influenced the way the member states define their regions, and has also led to a greater awareness within the member states of the need to attend to regional divergence. EU programmes may have enhanced the visibility of the EU in those regions and localities that have benefited from structural funding, but there is little evidence to suggest that this has enhanced the popularity of the EU in public opinion as a whole. Opinions remain divided about the precise extent of the impact of EU structural funding on regional and national convergence, because of the difficulty of separating this from the impacts of other factors, such as national regional programmes, other national macroeconomic policies, and globalization. Although the structural funds to date have accounted for a significant percentage of the EU budget, the absolute sums remain small at below 0.46 per cent of EU GDP.

This chapter takes issue with the argument that the manner in which the structural funds have been implemented has had a significant impact on the development of multi-level governance. Despite the initial thrust of the 'partnership' provisions of the 1988 reforms, the national governments of both the 'old' and the 'new' member states have either retained, or learned, 'gatekeeping' skills. These enable public and private, regional and local interests to *participate*, but little else. The implementation of the structural funds has encouraged multi-level participation, but this should not be confused with multi-level governance. It is hard to demonstrate that regional and local actors are any more effective individually in relation to the structural funds and EU governance than they are collectively within the Committee of the Regions or the Economic and Social Committee, although these are clearly weak bodies (Jeffery 2002). In general, the degree of subnational participation in the EU governance of the structural funds remains primarily a product of the nature of the constitutional arrangements within particular member states. Where changes in these arrangements have occurred, as in the UK since 1997, then these changes have not been as a direct result of participation in EU structural fund governance. In the UK, devolution owes nothing either to the EU, or to the structural funds, although it may well be that authorities in Scotland and Wales will express a preference for EU rather than UK regional funding.

Finally, it should be noted that the recent preference amongst the member states for the open method of coordination (OMC) rather than the 'Community method' has spread to notions of cohesion and regional intervention. Some member states see the pursuit of best practice and benchmarking in national regional policies as an attractive alternative to EU-level regional policy. The Commission has already made concessions to this tendency in its proposals for the coordination and standardization of national regional programmes as part of its structural fund implementation reforms. If member states which are net contributors get their way with the next financial perspective, such that structural interventions are partially or totally 'renationalized', then overseeing the coordination of national regional policies may be all that is left of this particular aspect of EU cohesion policy after 2013.

Notes

1 Article 235 of the Treaty of Rome (EEC) reads 'if action by the Community should prove necessary to attain, in the course of the operation of the common market, one of the objectives of the Community and this Treaty has not provided the necessary powers, the Council shall, acting unanimously on a proposal from the Commission and after consulting the assembly, take the appropriate measures'.

2 A small non-quota section, under the exclusive control of the Commission, was built into the ERDF allocation process—a predecessor of the Community Initiatives that were introduced in 1988.

3 Instead of rigid national quotas a system based on 'indicative ranges' was introduced, giving the Commission a bit more flexibility (around 12 per cent of the ERDF was now effectively at the discretion of the Commission). In 1984 the Commission also made some progress towards replacing the funding of individual projects with the establishment of more wide-ranging 'programmes'. These were designed to give the Commission a greater input into regional expenditure plans.

4 The Integrated Mediterranean Programmes were first established in 1985 and involved the transfer of 6.6 billion ecu over seven years to parts of France and Italy and all of Greece. The Commission advanced its own procedural agenda by only funding integrated programmes rather than individual projects selected by the recipient states.

5 The new members did not, however, have any traditional alleviation of their EU budget contributions at the moment of accession. Their actual net receipts will depend a great deal on how spending programmes are implemented by both the Commission and their own national administrations.

Further Reading

For an overview of the development of EU regional policy and the theoretical debate see Hooghe and Keating (1994), Bache (1998), and more recently Tarschys (2003). For a good review of the literature on 'territorial politics', see the review article by Christiansen (1999). Peterson and Bomberg (1999) provide a useful overview of cohesion policy and the debate about the significance of subnational actors, while Hooghe (1996) provides a thorough account of research on the subject. Marks (1992) remains a clear statement of the 'multi-level governance' concept applied to EU structural policy and Pollack (1995) stands out as a detailed rebuttal of this view. More recent studies include Bailey and De Propris (2002), Gualini (2003), and Bache (2004). There have been several studies of the new members and cohesion policy; Bailey and De Propris (2004), and Hughes, Sasse, and Gordon (2004) are particularly useful. Scott (1995) remains essential on the regional development debate, and Barry and Begg (2003) provide a useful introduction to the special issue of the *Journal of Common Market Studies* that they edited on 'EMU and Cohesion'.

Bache, I. (1998), *The Politics of European Union Regional Policy: Multi-Level Governance or Flexible Gatekeeping?* (Sheffield: Sheffield Academic Press).

Bache, I. (2004), 'Multi-Level Governance and EU Regional Policy', in Bache and Flinders (eds.), *Multi-Level Governance* (Oxford: Oxford University Press), 165–78.

Bailey, D., and De Propris, L. (2002), 'The 1988 Reform of the Structural Funds: Entitlement or Empowerment?', *Journal of European Public Policy*, 9/3: 408–28.

Bailey, D., and De Propris, L. (2004), 'A Bridge too Phare? EU Pre-Accession Aid and Capacity Building in the Candidate Countries', *Journal of Common Market Studies*, 42/1: 77–98.

Barry, F., and Begg, I. (2003), 'EMU and Cohesion: Introduction', *Journal of Common Market Studies*, special issue, *EMU and Cohesion*, 41/5: 781–96.

Christiansen, T. (1999), 'Territorial Politics in the European Union', *Journal of European Public Policy*, 6/2: 349–57.

Gualina, E. (2003), 'Challenges to Multi-level Governance: Contradictions and Conflicts in the Europeanization of Italian Regional Policy', *Journal of European Public Policy*, 10/4: 618–36.

Hooghe, L. (1996) (ed.), *Cohesion Policy and European Integration: Building Multi-level Governance* (Oxford: Oxford University Press).

Hooghe, L., and Keating, M. (1994), 'The Politics of European Union Regional Policy', *Journal of European Public Policy*, 1/3: 367–93.

Hughes, J., Sasse, G., and Gordon, C. (2004), 'Conditionality and Compliance in the EU's Eastward Enlargement: Regional Policy and the reform of Sub-national Government', *Journal of Common Market Studies*, 42/3: 523–51.

Marks, G. (1992), 'Structural Policy in the European Community', in Sbragia (ed.), *Euro-Politics: Institutions and Policy-making in the 'New' European Community* (Washington: Brookings Institution), 191–224.

Peterson, J., and Bomberg, E. (1999), *Decision-making in the European Union* (London: Macmillan).

Pollack, M. (1995), 'Regional Actors in an Intergovernmental Play: The Making and Implementation of EC Structural Policy', in Rhodes and Mazey (eds.), *The State of the European Union, iii, Building a European Polity?* (Boulder: Lynne Rienner), 361–90.

Scott, J. (1995), *Development Dilemmas in the European Community* (Buckingham: Open University Press).

Tarschys, D. (2003), *Reinventing Cohesion: The Future of European Structural Policy* (Stockholm: Swedish Institute for European Policy Studies).

Chapter 10

Social Policy

Left to the Judges and the Markets?

Stephan Leibfried

Contents

Summary

Despite the widespread assumption that European Union (EU) involvement in social policy has been minimal, the dynamics of market integration have led to a substantial spill-over onto the EU level. Resistance by national governments to a loss of autonomy, and conflicts of interests between rich and poor regions, or between employer and employee interests, present formidable obstacles to EU policies. However, in the 1980s, and especially in the 1990s, the EU accumulated substantial regulatory mandates in social policy, more recently reaching out further to anti-discrimination politics. Nevertheless, member governments have lost more control over national welfare policies, in the face of the pressures of integrated markets, than the EU has gained *de facto* in transferred authority, although this development appears to have come to a halt. The multi-tiered pattern which has emerged is largely law-driven and court-driven, marked by policy immobilism at the centre and by 'negative' market integration, which imposes significant constraints on national social policies. Eastern enlargement and the attendant increase in heterogeneity may mark the highpoint of *traditional* twentieth century European social policy, and point to *new* regulatory horizons for the twenty-first.

Introduction[1]

Accounts of European social policy still present a minimalist interpretation of European Union (EU) involvement (see Collins 1975; Falkner 1998). The sovereign nation-state, so the argument goes, leaves little social policy role for the EU. It is regarded as focused on 'market-building', leaving an exclusive, citizen-focused, national welfare state, its sovereignty formally untouched, though perhaps endangered indirectly by growing economic interdependence. 'Welfare states are national states' (de Swaan 1992: 33; Offe 2000, 2003), and on the face of it, the European welfare state does indeed look national. There is no European welfare law granting individual entitlements *vis-à-vis* Brussels; there are no direct taxes or contributions, and no funding of a 'social budget' to back such entitlements; and there is no Brussels welfare bureaucracy to speak of. 'Territorial sovereignty' in social policy, so conventional wisdom holds, is alive and well. Today, however, an alternative view is more plausible. The process of European integration has eroded both the sovereignty (the legal authority), and autonomy (*de facto* regulatory capacity) of member states in social policy. What began as a parallel universe turned into a single arena of conflict (Becker 2004a). National welfare states remain the primary institutions of European social policy, but they do so in the context of an increasingly constraining multi-tiered polity (Pierson and Leibfried 1995).

While there have been extensive barriers to any true federalization of European social policy (on the varieties of federalizing welfare, see Obinger, Leibfried, and Castles 2005), the economic and institutional dynamics of creating a single market have made it increasingly difficult to exclude social issues from the EU's agenda. The emergence of a multi-tiered structure (Pierson 1995b), however, is less the result of the welfare-state-building ambitions of Eurocrats than of spill-over from the single market initiative where 'spill-over' refers to the process whereby the completion of the internal market invades the domain of social policy (Haas [1958] 2004; Lindberg and Scheingold 1970; Falkner 1998). In the 1980s the single market initiative was based on a deregulatory agenda, and it was assumed that initiatives to ensure the free movement of goods, persons, services, and capital could be insulated from social policy issues, which would remain the province of member states. This dubious assumption runs directly contrary to the central tenets of political economy, which stress that economic action is embedded within dense networks of social and political institutions (Hall 1986, 1999; North 1990). There is significant evidence that the neat separation between 'market issues', belonging to the supranational sphere, and 'social issues', belonging to the national spheres, is unsustainable. Irrespective of the results of 'high politics' struggles over social charters and treaty revisions the movement towards market integration carries with it a gradual erosion of the autonomy of national welfare states *and* their sovereignty, increasingly situating national regimes in a complex, multi-tiered web of public policy.

This transformation occurs through three processes (see Table 10.1). 'Positive', or activist, reform results from social policy initiatives taken at the 'centre' by the Commission and the Council, increasingly pushed by the European Parliament (EP), along with the European Court of Justice's (ECJ) often expansive interpretations of what those initiatives mean; in the 1990s the treaty mandate was strengthened, providing a 'Euro-corporatist' anchor, which drew European trade unions and employer

Table 10.1 National welfare states transformed through European integration: processes, key actors, and examples

Processes	Key actors	Examples
Direct pressures of integration –> '*positive*' initiatives to develop uniform social standards at EU level	Commission, expert committees, ECJ, and since 1992 institutionally entrusted corporate actors (UNICE, CEEP, ETUC) (background actors: EP, ESC; diverse lobbies)	■ *Old politics*: national and gender equality; health and safety; Social Protocol 'corporatism' since 1992, generalized 1997, with expansion of competences and of QMV; 1989 EC Social Charter, 'incorporated' in ToA; extending notion of European citizenship ■ *New politics*: expanding anti-discrimination law beyond nationality and gender to 'any ground such as *race*, colour, *ethnic* or social *origin*, genetic features, language, *religion or belief*, political or any other opinion, membership of a national minority, property, birth, *disability, age or sexual orientation*' (Art. 81 CT; items in italics already in Art. 13 TEC)
Direct pressures of integration –> '*negative*' policy reform via market compatibility requirements	ECJ, Commission; Council (national governments), national legal institutions	Labour mobility, since late 1980s freedom to provide and consume services, combined with impact of the European Treaty's 'competition regime'
Indirect pressures of integration –> adaptation of national welfare states	market actors (employers, unions; sensitive sectors: private insurance, provider groups), Council, individual national governments in fields outside social policy	Further 'social dumping' accented by eastern enlargement, EMU and Maastricht criteria; harmonization of tax systems; single market for private insurance; dispensing with the public utilities state since the 1980s, which was the traditional outer mantle of the welfare state; affecting the education profile of the welfare state professions through standardized European educational standards

organizations towards the activist 'centre'. In the last decade a softer version of integration[2] has expanded via the 'open method of coordination' (OMC; see Chapter 11), which can either amplify positive integration—as in the modernization of social protection systems—or step in where Europe would otherwise have little legal effect. '*Negative*' reform occurs through the ECJ's imposition of market compatibility requirements—via the four freedoms (Barnard 2004)—that restrict, but also redefine the social policies of member states. Both positive and negative initiatives create direct pressures on national welfare states through new instruments of European social policy. Finally, the process of European integration creates an escalating range of indirect pressures that do not legally require, but nonetheless encourage, adaptations—convergence—of national welfare states. These 'ecological' pressures strongly affect national welfare states, but they are not systematically connected to the development of social policy instruments at the European level.

In the first section the initially modest direct efforts to develop an activist European social policy are reviewed. The formidable obstacles for such policy are highlighted: institutions that make reform difficult; limited fiscal resources; jealous member-state protection of 'state-building' resources; and an unfavourable distribution of power among interest groups. However, the 1990s also reveal a growing 'activity' potential and profile. In the second section the development of 'market compatibility require-ments' is evaluated—legal challenges to those aspects of national welfare states that conflict with the single market's call for unhindered labour mobility and open com-petition for welfare provision. In the third section the *de facto*, rather than *de jure*, pres-sures on national regimes are taken up. These result from factors such as competitive demands for adaptations of national economies and their institutional environments to a single market and, since January 1999, a single currency area for the now twelve member states. In the final section these arguments are pulled together to highlight some of the distinctive features of this emerging multi-tiered system of social policy.

'Positive' initiatives from the centre go hand in hand with major and visible social conflicts, and have been attempted since the foundation of the European Economic Community (EEC), since 1997 the European Community (EC). The 1957 Treaty of Rome, for instance, met stiff resistance in the French National Assembly in part because of con-cern that weak social clauses endangered the well-developed French welfare state, mak-ing French industry less competitive (Marjolin 1989). 'Negative' integration efforts were historically less visible, but are just as old. The coordination of rules governing labour mobility was enshrined in one of the earliest EC legislative acts of 1958, although sim-ilar action on services dates only from the mid-1980s, reaching a high plateau at the end of the 1990s. Naturally, 'indirect pressures' (see Table 10.1), are more recent, since such pressures could only build up as integration increased and intensified.

In general, under the hegemony of centre-right parties the economic integration perspective was locked firmly in at the EC level from 1957 onwards, whilst the social democrats in their two phases of hegemony in the 1970s and late 1990s, were unable—and often unwilling—to lock in a social integration perspective in a similarly effective manner (Manow, Schäfer, and Zorn 2004); they invented OMC instead.

The limited success of activist social policy

Discussions of social policy generally focus on such prominent actors as the Council, the Commission (often in tandem with the Directorate-General for Employment, Industrial Relations and Social Affairs), and progressively more, the EP (with its Committee on Employment and Social Affairs), and the representatives of business and labour interests with their recently matured 'corporatist policy community' (Falkner 1998). The Commission, in particular, has been a central actor in direct attempts to construct a significant 'social dimension' for its 'European social model'

(Commission 1994*b*, 2000*d*, 2003*c*)—areas of social policy mandating where uniform or at least minimum standards are set at the European level. These attempts have occurred in fits and starts during the past few decades, with high aspirations and modest results, marked by a plenitude of 'cheap talk', produced in the confident knowledge that the requirements of unanimous votes in the Council meant that ambitious blueprints would remain unexecuted (Streeck and Schmitter 1991; Vogel-Polsky and Vogel 1991; Lange 1992). Here only the broadest outlines are reported, the main argument being that the analytical focus on the efforts of Euro-federalists to foist an activist 'social dimension' on a reluctant Council—a perspective still informing many recent analyses—has been somewhat misleading. European integration has indeed altered European social policy-making, but largely through quite different mechanisms operating outside the welfare dimension proper.

The obstacles to an activist role for Brussels in social policy development are formidable (Pierson and Leibfried 1995), and are increasing. These include both institutional constraints and the balance of power among relevant social interests. EU institutions make it much easier to block reforms than to enact them. Generally, only narrow, market-related openings for social legislation have been available (see Table 10.2). Even on this limited terrain reform requires a *super*-majority, i.e. a *qualified* majority. The member governments themselves, which act as gatekeepers for initiatives requiring Council approval, jealously protect social policy prerogatives. Since the second world war, economic and geopolitical changes have gradually diminished the scope of national sovereignty in a variety of domains. The welfare state remains one of the few key realms of policy mandates where national governments still appear to reign supreme. Given the popularity and the electoral significance of most social programmes, national executives have usually resisted losses of social policy authority.

A further barrier is the relative weakness—and the entrenched Euro-scepticism—of the 'social democratic' forces most interested in a strong social dimension (Manow, Schäfer, and Zorn 2004). In most of Europe, unions and social democratic parties had become weaker since the 1980s, especially among the founding members of the EU. Though social democracy—then bent less on traditional social than on 'new' employment policy—had grown again among EU member states in the second half of the 1990s, union power had not. At the European level, organizational difficulties and profound conflicts of interest between high-wage and low-wage areas of the EU limit labour's influence, sometimes leading to new regional inter-class alliances. At the same time, business power has grown considerably, in part because of the increasing capital mobility fostered by European integration and OECD-wide capital markets. This balance of power among social interests has further hindered efforts to deal with institutional blockages, limited fiscal resources, and the tremendous difficulties of harmonizing already widely divergent and deeply institutionalized national social policies.[3]

In this context, substantive policy applications have been rare (see Falkner 2003*b*; Falkner *et al.* 2005). Expansive visions of EU social policy have had far lower priority than initiatives for an integrated market. Knowing that—at least until the Social Protocol became effective in 1993—UK opposition rendered serious initiatives impossible (Kleinman and Piachaud 1992*b*), member governments, European officials, and interest groups have made rhetorical commitments to the construction of a social dimension (Lange 1992; Ross 1995*a*, 1995*b*; Streeck 1995). The last two decades of the twentieth century witnessed noisy public fights over a series of initiatives to increase the social policy mandates of the EU which in most cases far exceeded the true implications of the proposals made. These initiatives were invariably defeated outright or dramatically scaled down. The struggle over the Social Charter in the 1980s was typical (Falkner 1998), though in the meantime the 1989 Community Charter of the Fundamental Social Rights of Workers and the 1961 European Social Charter of the Council of Europe have both been silently incorporated by simple reference in the preamble to the 1997 Treaty of Amsterdam (ToA) under Article 136(1) (TEC), and carried forward in the Treaty of Nice (ToN) signed in February 2001. All these rights now reappear directly in the Charter of Fundamental Rights of the EU, proclaimed in Nice on 7 December 2000 by the European Council (though not part of the ToN), now transposed into the Charter of Fundamental Rights of the Union (Part II of the 2004 Constitutional Treaty, CT), with its social policy Title IV 'Solidarity' (Arts. II 87–98 CT) (see Becker 2004a; Treib 2004; Falke 2000, Table 4).

At the end of the 1980s attempts to establish an ambitious programme for European-level legislation were still rebuffed by the UK, which eventually refused to agree to even the watered-down version of the EU Social Charter signed by the other member governments in 1989. The exercise allowed various actors to adopt politically useful public postures, but seemed to give only modest momentum to actual policy initiatives.

Until the early 1990s legislative reform was limited to a few areas where the Treaty of Rome, or the single market project, allowed more significant latitude. A notable example concerns the gender-equality provisions of Article 119 of the Treaty of Rome (EEC) (now Art. 141 TEC). Until 1986 this was the only major (then implicit) social policy mandate in reach of the then EC. This provision, offered as a face-saving concession to France, lay dormant for almost two decades. In the 1970s, however, the Council unanimously agreed to a number of directives which gave the 'equal treatment' provision some content. Over the past twenty years, the ECJ has played a crucial activist role, turning Article 119 (EEC) and the directives into an extensive set of requirements and prohibitions related to the treatment of female (and occasionally male) workers (Falkner 1994; Ostner and Lewis 1995; Hoskyns 1996; Bieback 1997; Mazey 1998). These rulings have required extensive national reforms—although not always to the benefit of women.

For example, ECJ decisions have had a dramatic impact on private and, indirectly, on public pension schemes. The Court's insistence on equal retirement ages in occupational pension schemes forced the UK to level ages up or down. By choosing to raise the retirement age for women the government saved billions of pounds, whilst avoiding much of the blame for the cuts. In 1990, when the ECJ made a similar ruling for occupational pensions in *Barber*, fear that this ruling might be applied retroactively to private pensions (at a cost estimated at up to £40 billion in the UK and DM 35 [€17.5] billion in Germany) fuelled 'what is probably the most intense lobbying campaign yet seen in Brussels' (Mazey and Richardson 1993: 15). While this pressure led the negotiators of the 1992 Maastricht Treaty on European Union (TEU) explicitly to limit retroactivity, the impact of the Court's rulings was still dramatic.[4] Thus, the EU has come to play a considerable role in gender issues, although the market-oriented nature of the Union and its restricted focus on the paid-labour market had circumscribed such interventions for some time. Treaty changes and ECJ activity also indicate that such discrimination issues are continuously expanding, be it 'in intensity' by including other policy areas (through mainstreaming; see Pollack and Hafner-Burton 2000), or 'in extensity', by moving outward from European hard-core nationality and gender, to age, ethnicity, religion, sexual preferences, etc. The latter is, after all, primary EC law, directly applicable by the ECJ, without a strong need for directives, and the Court can rely on a longstanding and extensive series of precedents. If fused with sufficient sanctions, for example in tort law, it may well be that the future of the regulatory EU welfare approach lies in anti-discrimination (for a US parallel, see Nivola 1998; Kagan 2001).

A second example is the extension of regulations governing health and safety in the workplace (see Eichener 1993, 1997, 2000). The Single European Act (SEA) of 1986 allowed qualified majority voting (QMV) in this area for fear that national regulations could be used as non-tariff barriers to trade. Surprisingly, policy-making has produced neither stalemate nor lowest-common-denominator regulations. Instead, extensive regulations have generally produced a high level of standards. Furthermore, European regulators moved beyond the regulation of products to the regulation of production processes, where the concerns about barriers to trade would seem inapplicable. As Eichener has documented, the Commission's role as 'process manager' appears to have been critical in this low-profile environment. Much crucial decision-making took place in committees composed of policy experts (Joerges and Neyer 1997a; Joerges 2003). Some of these experts were linked to business and labour groups, but business interests did not have the option of simply refusing to participate, since regulatory action was likely to proceed without them. Representatives in these committees were often interested in innovation, having gravitated towards Brussels, because in regulatory issues it seemed to be 'where the action is'. In this technocratic context, 'best practices' from many member states were pieced together to form a relatively interventionist structure of social regulation. The Commission played a central part by linking together the work of different committees, incorporating concerns of other actors such as the EP, and founding a specialized 'expertocratic' institution, the European Agency for Safety and Health at Work, active since 1996 in Bilbao, and by actively promoting innovative proposals.

This development provided one indication that the institutional restrictions on social policy initiatives had loosened somewhat since the mid-1980s. The introduction of QMV in some domains has made social policy the focus of sharp conflict. There have been significant struggles to determine the range of issues that can be decided by QMV, either under Article 100a (EEC) (now Art. 95 TEC) (covering harmonization of legislation as to avoid distortions of competition), or under the SEA's exception for proposals governing the health and safety of workers: 'the treaty-base game' (Rhodes 1995). Members of the Commission, the EP, and the European Trade Union Confederation (ETUC) have pushed with some success for expansive readings of these clauses. UNICE, the main employers' organization, has strongly opposed such a move (Lange 1992; see also, Falkner 1998). While many proposals connected to the Social Charter and the 1989 Action Programme had been watered down or stalled until the early 1990s, even then the combined impact of what was passed was far from trivial (Addison and Siebert 1993). Early signs of growing room for social policy initiatives were the enactment of the Atypical Work (health and safety) Directive in 1991, and the Maternity Directive in 1992, both passed under the 'health and safety' provisions allowing QMV—and both opposed by the UK, and the latter also by Italy.[5] This legislation required more generous policies in several EU countries. At the same time, it introduced a policy 'ratchet', prohibiting other countries from cutting back their existing regimes. But the 1992 TEU and its Social Protocol achieved a procedural breakthrough and an expansion of mandates which led to a series of additional directives (see Table 10.2).

Table 10.2 Assignment of explicit[a] social policy mandates to the EU up to the ToN, with preview of the Constitutional Treaty

Field of mandate	European Economic Community EEC 1957 (1958)	Single European Act (SEA) EEC 1986 (1987)	Maastricht Treaty on European Union TEU 1992 (1993)	Social Protocol SP 1992 (1993)	ToA ToA 1997 (1999)	ToN ToN 2000 (2003)	Rome (II) Constitutional Treaty CT 2004
1 Discrimination on grounds of nationality	Unan 7	No ref	QMV 6	No ref	QMV 12	QMV 12	QMV III-123
2 Other anti-discrimination measures, harmonization excluded	No ref	No ref	No ref	No ref	QMV 13 (2)	QMV 13 (2)	QMV III-124 (2)
3 Free labour movement	Unan 48–50	QMV 48–50	QMV 48–50	No impact	QMV 39–40	QMV 39–40	QMV III-133–134
4 Gender equality in pay[b]	(Unan) 119	(Unan) 119	(Unan) 119	(Unan) 6	QMV 141	QMV 141	QMV III-214
5 Gender equality for labour force[b]	No ref	No ref	No ref	QMV 2 (1) v	QMV 137 (1) v	QMV 137 (1) i	QMV III-210 (1)(i)
6 Working environment	No ref	QMV 118°	QMV 118a	QMV 2 (1) i	QMV 137 (1) i	QMV 137 (1) a	QMV III-210 (1)(a)
7 Working conditions (outside former Art. 118a, line 6)	No ref	No ref	No ref	QMV 2 (1) ii	QMV 137 (1) ii	QMV 137 (1) b	QMV III-210 (1)(b)
8 Worker information and consultation	No ref	No ref	No ref	QMV 2 (1) iii	QMV 137 (1) iii	QMV 137 (1) e	QMV III-210 (1)(e)

#								
9	Integration of persons excluded from labour market[c]	No ref	No ref	No ref	QMV 2(1)iv	QMV 137(1)iv	QMV 137(1)h	QMV III-210(1)(h)
10	Combating of social exclusion	No ref	No ref	No ref	No ref	No ref	QMV 137(1)j	QMV III-210(1)(j)
11	Modernisation of social protection systems	No ref	No ref	No ref	No ref	No ref	QMV 137(1)k	QMV III-210(1)(k)
12	Public health	No ref	No ref	QMV 129	No ref	QMV 152	QMV 152	QMV III-278
13	Social security coordination	Unan 51	Unan 51	Unan 51	n.a.	Unan 42	Unan 42	QMV III-136 (but see III-136(2))
14	Harmonization of other anti-discrimination measures (see line 2)[d]	No ref	No ref	No ref	No ref	Unan 13(1)	Unan 13(1)	Unan III-124(1)`
15	Social security and protection of workers	No ref	No ref	No ref	Unan 2(3)i	Unan 137(3)i	Unan 137(1)c	Unan III-210(1)c
16	Protection of workers (employment contract termination)	No ref	No ref	No ref	Unan 2(3)ii	Unan 137(3)ii	Unan 137(1)d	Unan III-210(1)d
17	Collective interest representation, codetermination	No ref	No ref	No ref	Unan 2(3)iii	Unan 137(3)iii	Unan 137(1)f	Unan III-210(1)f
18	Employment of third-country nationals	No ref	No ref	No ref	Unan 2(3)iv	Unan 137(3)iv	Unan 137(1)g	Unan III-210(1)g
19	Funding for employment policy[c]	No ref	No ref	No ref	Unan 2(3)v	Unan 137(3)v	No ref	No ref

Table 10.2 (Continued)

Field of mandate	European Economic Community EEC 1957 (1958)	Single European Act (SEA) EEC 1986 (1987)	Maastricht Treaty on European Union TEU 1992 (1993)	Social Protocol SP 1992 (1993)	ToA ToA 1997 (1999)	ToN ToN 2000 (2003)	Rome (II) Constitutional Treaty CT 2004
20 Pay	No ref	No ref^e	No ref in 100a (2)^e	Excl in 2 (6)	Excl 137 (6)	Excl 137 (5)	Excl III 210 (6)
21 Right of association	No ref	No ref^e	No ref in 100a (2)^e	Excl in 2 (6)	Excl 137 (6)	Excl 137 (5)	Excl III-210 (6)
22 Right to strike and to impose lock-outs	No ref	No ref^e	No ref in 100a (2)^e	Excl in 2 (6)	Excl 137 (6)	Excl 137 (5)	Excl III-210 (6)
23 Mandates for the Open Method of Coordination^g (OMC)	Employment				(128) 140^f	(128) 140^f	III-213 a
	Labour market and working conditions					140	III-213 b
	Professional education and training					140	III-213 c
	Social security					140	III-213 d
	Prevention of occupational accidents and diseases					140	III-213 e
	Protection of health at work					140	III-213 f
	Law of coalitions and collective agreements between employers and employees					140	III-213 g

Notes: Years for treaties refer to the signing and (in parentheses) the ratification of the treaty. Numbers listed in the table refer to articles in each treaty.

Unan = unanimity required;
QMV = qualified majority voting;
No ref = no reference to mandate;
n.a. = not applicable;
Excl = mandate explicitly excluded.
Heavier shading denotes weaker mandate. Heaviest shading shows explicit denial of mandates, anchored in the treaties only since 1992 in these areas.

[a] As a rule the table refers to *explicit* powers mentioned in the treaties, in contrast to *unspecified general* powers, as under Arts. 100 and 235 EEC (now Arts. 95 and 308 TEC), or to *non-enabling* norms (on an exception see note b and note d, para. 2).

[b] Between the original Treaty of Rome and the 1992 Social Protocol, the ECJ had interpreted gender equality ever more widely. Art. 119 EEC (now Art. 141 TEC) contained no express enabling clause; respective Directives were based on Art. 100 or 235 EEC which required unanimous decisions. In the end Art. 141(3) TEC in 1997 brought the first special mandate and QMV.

[c] From 1992 to 1997 this QMV-mandate excluded the one for *funding*, where *unanimity* was required according to Art. 2(3) of the Social Protocol and then Art. 137(3) TEC, thus maintaining anti-poverty spending programmes as highly veto prone.

[d] On top of the original *two* anti-discrimination articles—gender (equality in pay only; Art. 119 EEC, see table lines 4, 5 [and note b], and since ToA generally prohibiting any discrimination based on 'sex' see lines 2 and 14) and nationality (Art. 12 TEC; ex Art. 6 EEC; QMV; see line 1)—dating already to 1957, Art. 13 TEC in 1997 silently added *seven new* anti-discrimination categories: racial or ethnic origin, religion or belief, disability, and age or sexual orientation. These *nine* categories are picked up in lines 1, 2, and 14 of the table. Art. 21 of the European Charter of Fundamental Rights—identical with the Art. II-81 CT—includes the above and adds *nine* novel categories: colour, social origin, genetic features, language, political or any other opinion, membership of a national minority, property, birth, and disability. Altogether these *eighteen* categories of anti-discrimination serve as *examples* only ('on any ground such as') when the 2004 CT becomes law. But Art. II-81 CT does *not* give the EU a special regulatory mandate (and see Arts. II-111–114). However, as the case of gender equality has shown, these nine categories of EU primary law to be, together with the open-ended thematic mandate, might unfold an unforeseeable dynamics—especially with an ECJ that can rely on long and developed chains of anti-discrimination precedents in nationality and gender (and see *seven* new categories to be explored), with gender equality starting out from just that unmandated situation in 1957 (see note b).

[e] From 1986 to 1997, first Art. 100a EEC introduced by the SEA, and then Art. 100a (2) amended by the TEU (now Art. 95 TEC) exempted provisions on taxes, free movement of persons, and on the rights and interests of employees from QMV, but did not preclude action by unanimity, whereas Art. 2(6) of the Social Protocol and the later Art. 137(6) TEC amended by ToA specifically withholds mandates on pay, etc. as such.

[f] Art. 128 (2) TEC in the new ToA 'Employment Chapter' (Arts. 125–30 TEC) already spoke of 'guidelines' and Art. 140 TEC provided a loose mandate only, with the situation in public health being similarly opaque (see Art. 152 (2) versus (4) TEC). The full materialization of the 'open method of coordination' (OMC) took much longer, and evolved in the main extra-constitutionally, until picked up in 2004 by Art. III-213 CT, where OMC instruments of the Commission are specified in the second paragraph. Already in the 2001 ToN the OMC subject areas are listed as *examples*, allowing an extension of OMC to many other like fields.

[g] The term 'open method of coordination' is not mentioned in any of the treaties.

Source: Falkner (1998: 82), supplemented by the author, with special thanks to Josef Falke, Centre for European Law and Politics (ZERP) and Research Centre Transformations of the State (TranState), both University of Bremen, for his continuous help in updating and legal advice.

The watershed and high point in the development of social policy mandates dates to the mid-1990s. The 1997 ToA reveals a fully developed 'Social Chapter', a 'one track' Social Europe as a first hard 'constitutional' endpoint of a soft 1989 Social Charter, all of this affirmed in the ToN. The two 'original' mandates (health and safety in the 'working environment'—Art. 118a EEC (now Art. 137(1) TEC); and gender equality 'in pay'—Art. 119 (EEC) (now Art. 141 TEC), were kept, but health and safety was broadened to all 'working conditions' and gender equality was extended to all 'labour force' issues (partly following EC practice and the ECJ); all were placed under QMV, an innovation for gender equality. Two additional QMV mandates were introduced in the ToA: worker information and consultation; and integration of persons excluded from the labour market (but not the attendant finances). Unanimous decision-making was explicitly extended to five new topics: social security and worker protection; protection of workers when employment contract is terminated; collective interest representation; employment of third-country nationals; and financing measures to integrate the excluded. Moreover, to tame the scope of treaty clauses with wide powers, three topics were explicitly declared off-limits: pay; the right of association; and the right to strike, and to impose lock-outs. In all these revisions the ToA consolidated and universalized a state of the Union that dated to the 1992 Social Protocol for all EU members except the UK which had opted out of its provisions.[6] In 1997 the new British government reversed its predecessor's opt-out, and did so without exception. Amsterdam thus extended Maastricht progress to the UK. Agreement was also reached to universalize the new 1992 Euro-corporatist legislative powers of the 'social partners', i.e. the unions and the employers, in what became Articles 138-9 (TEC) (ex Arts. 118a and 118b EEC).

But the ToA also has some original social policy aspects: based on a Swedish initiative, it also included a new Title VIII on employment (Arts. 125–30 TEC, replacing Arts. 109 n–s TEC in TEU) (Johansson 1999; Tidow 2003). Although stressing the importance of activist policy, the provisions call for largely symbolic actions—the exchange of goals, procedures, guidelines, and reports. In striking contrast to economic and monetary union (EMU), it does not provide additional fiscal or legal instruments for effective 'positive integration' beyond the small European Social Fund (J. A. Anderson 1995; Kaluza 1998). The employment mandate assigned to the EU level therefore is less about EU employment policy than about coordinating national employment initiatives via the OMC. Since then OMC has been extended to other fields such as pensions (Eichenhofer 2004a; Schmähl 2003; Sommer 2003; EDS 2004), social inclusion, health (Eureport social 2004, 12/9–10), and migration and is currently being 'streamlined' beyond recognition (Commission 2003b; Casey 2003; Eureport social 2003, 11/6).

In principle, the revised 'Social Chapter' (Arts. 136–45 TEC) facilitates efforts to expand EU social policy, in line with the 1992 Social Protocol. First, a country's capacity to obstruct legislation has diminished. By 1992, the four cohesion states—Greece, Ireland, Portugal, and Spain—no longer commanded enough votes to block reform under the Social Protocol's rules on QMV. This minority status became more pronounced after the 'northern expansion' to an EU15 in 1995—and is now even more marked in the EU25. While blocking initiatives through a minority procedurally now requires more countries than ever before, cohesion, in essence, has lessened, giving rise to few social policy initiatives to be blocked in the first place. The obstruction that had met the 1989 Social Action Programme (Falkner 1998) had been made impossible.

In 1994 a long-delayed European Works Councils Directive was approved under these procedures (Rhodes 1995; Falkner 1998), even though in this case the new Euro-corporatist legislative procedure still remained stalled. In 1996 the Parental Leave, and in 1997 the Atypical Work (working conditions and distortion of competition) directives followed suit (Falkner 1998), and in 1999 Fixed-term Contracts. These became the prime successes for a functioning Euro-corporatism endowed with legislative powers. The social partners seemed ready to negotiate, now 'in the shadow of the [Council] vote', and based on their own learning experience. But no other major directives followed in the new century. Instead, the social partners side-stepped this shadow with a Framework Agreement on Teleworking (16 July 2002).[7] In this agreement, for the first time, the social partners committed their own members to direct implementation, and sought no ratification through the Council of Ministers; this was seen as having greater political promise—but also the risk of having little effect.

Yet, while most aspects of the Social Charter have moved forward, further initiatives are likely to be modest and 'consolidating' in nature, as indicated by the 1998 Social Action Programme. Throughout the early 1990s the Commission was involved in intensive soul-searching concerning its proper social policy role (Ross 1995b), and this continued all the way through to the eastern enlargement. Efforts to combat stubbornly high levels of European unemployment then moved centre stage (Commission 1994b, 2003a, 2003c), as reflected in the ToA in 1997, and since the ToN in 2003 combined with efforts to 'modernize social protection systems' (Art. 137(1)(k) TEC) in times of budget austerity, and to combat 'social exclusion' (Art. 137(1)(j) TEC)—these two new QMV mandates were the only original contributions to social policy brought about by the ToN. The Commission seems to have accepted at least part of the British case for the need to promote 'flexibility'. The White Paper, *Growth, Competitiveness, Employment* had revealed a change in emphasis towards reducing labour costs, calling for tax reforms to generate 'a substantial reduction of non-wage labour costs, particularly for the least-skilled workers' (Commission 1993c: 116ff). This trend has since intensified, with the 'slimming down' of national welfare states now a regular and prominent topic on the agenda of Ecofin, the European Council, and the Commission[8]—and with the Ministers' Employment and Social Policy Council and the corresponding DGs in the Commission mostly put on the defensive. The member governments seem unlikely to allow the Commission to take the lead on such issues, suggesting that the immediate prospect is for consolidation, with the completion of some current agenda items, but few new initiatives.

Somewhat less noted by member governments has been the silent anti-discrimination revolution in the treaties. While the TEU (1992) was basically characterized by the old politics of prohibiting labour discrimination by nationality and gender, the 1997 Article 13 (TEC), introduced via the ToA, added 'racial and other origins, religion or belief, disability, age or sexual orientation'—unchanged in the ToN (2001)—and Article II-81 (CT) (2004) would amplify this by 'any' further 'ground such as' 'colour, social origin, genetic features, language, political or any other opinion, membership of a national minority, property, and birth'. In a more heterogeneous and veto-prone Europe this could become the regulatory route leading into the EU's social policy of the twenty-first century. An 'Article 13 Package' of two Directives (Anti-Racism, Employment), and one Action Programme was packed in 2000 to make legislation effective (Directives 2000/43, 29 June 2000, and 2000/78, 27 November 2000; see Eichenhofer 2004b).

In the US, the New Deal was contained and strangled by an ever-expanding body of anti-discrimination 'regulatory' politics in the two decades following the civil rights reforms of the 1960s (Kochan *et al.* 2001; Nivola 1998). Similarly, traditional European labour-oriented social policy might well be displaced by this new and expanding domain. For the same reasons that anti-discrimination became an easy fit in the US— burdening third parties only, making political promises of well-being whilst by-passing the burden on public budgets, and relying mainly on legal strategies—it may also develop into a European panacea for a state that guarantees security (Franzius 2003), as foreshadowed in the European post-Nice struggles over 'unisex' private insurance tariffs.[9] Anti-discrimination may also offer a way out of an increasingly heterogeneous EU. This structural transformation would overcome the mono-focal EU orientation on employment and move it toward the 'citizenship-consumer' frontier. In doing so, it would by-pass, and accommodate Bismarck-oriented and Beveridge-type traditions plus those of US consumer welfare (Rieger and Leibfried 2003). Europe is not likely to rely on high-yield torts approaches Western-style as does the US (Nivola 1998), since sanctions are a matter of member-state legislation. A slow process of legal converg-ence and harmonization can be foreseen, where countries with experience in anti-discrimination, such as the UK and the Netherlands, may take the lead (House of Lords 2000).

The dismissals of claims that a significant EU role now exists in social policy are largely based on an examination of 'high politics'—the widely publicized struggles over positive, centre-imposed social policies through devices such as the Social Charter in the 1980s and the Social Protocol in the early 1990s. Developments such as the Maternity Directive, the directives under the Social Protocol (1992), and the 'con-stitutionalized' Social Chapter (1997) suggest that the room for European initiatives was still growing in the 1990s. EU legislative activity is now at least as extensive as, for example, federal social policy activity in the USA on the eve of the New Deal (Robertson 1989; Pierson 1995a; Obinger, Leibfried, and Castles 2005)—and it moves in great strides to match the US anti-discrimination era dating from the 1960s to the 1980s. Yet, if member states have lost considerable control over social policy in the EU, this is primarily because of processes other than the efforts of EU officials to develop social policy legislation for a new European universe.

European integration and *de jure* market compatibility requirements

Lost amidst the noisy fights over the Social Charter and the Social Protocol has been the quiet accumulation of EU constraints on social policy connected with market integ-ration. The last four decades have witnessed a gradual, if incremental, expansion of EU-generated regulations and, especially, court decisions that have seriously eroded the sovereignties of the national welfare-state and have overlaid European welfare states with a new mobility-friendly and competition-friendly regime. Until recently (Falkner 1998; Falkner *et al.* 2005) political scientists paid scant attention to this area of 'low politics', entranced by the world of 'high politics' and 'high conflicts' in treaty bargaining. The topic was left to a small set of European labour law, welfare, and social security lawyers and national government officials who monitored another centre of policy-making: the courts.[10]

Since the 1960s the ECJ has delivered about 900 decisions (*output*) on social policy topics, with free movement and workers and their (plus third-country migrants') social security amounting to around 600 decisions and circa 300 decisions on other 'social policy' matters (within the scope of Arts. 117–22 EEC, now Arts. 136–45 TEC) (see Table 10.3). In addition, the Commission also brought to court violations of the treaties by member governments concerning social policy.

The social policy caseload for 1992–2003 (*input*, see Chapter 3, Table 3.4*b*), was second only to agriculture, and on a par with environmental and consumer issues, with the number of cases decreasing after 1999, which puts social policy in second place for demand of ECJ decisions—staying firmly in the ECJ's 'major league'. These statistics do not include cases based on the freedom of services, and those of all other categories that may occasionally impinge heavily on national welfare states.

They do not include law suits initiated by the staff of the EU for whom the ECJ serves as a labour and social security court (Tables 3.4*a*, 3.4*b*). This huge demand on ECJ resources, among others, had led to the founding of the Court of First Instance (CFI) in 1989 (Emmert 1996), with the ECJ now serving only as a court of appeal—and may result in a completely separate ECJ jurisdiction (*Eureport social* 2003, 11/12: 8). But the social status of these civil servants does not serve as a welfare model for EU citizens—as it had in some member states, such as Germany and France—so these cases do not affect national social policy. Nor do the statistics include the almost 100 decisions of the CFI on social policy issues (Chapter 3, Table 3.5), which mostly address conflicts over distributive criteria in the European Social Fund (ESF). Stepping back further, it is worth noting that social policy cases were already on par with competition cases from 1971 to 1991 (Table 3.5*a*), slowly overtaking them to about double the caseload by 2003—almost paralleling the development of the caseload on the free movement of goods.

The approximately 900 social policy cases (*output*) have a distinct pattern of origin (see Table 10.4). Even after several enlargements, cases emerged mostly from the original EC6—with Germany, Belgium, and the Netherlands leading the pack—and, from the newcomers, mostly and interestingly from the UK which became quite active in the European legal system, with a focus on workers' protection and equal treatment. Remarkably, the smaller states, such as Belgium, and the Netherlands, have given rise to a disproportionate share of the social caseload, especially for social security of migrant workers, while France and Italy have consistently produced few, with Germany especially active only for cases on the free movement of persons (Stone Sweet and Brunell 1997). However, small countries with very few cases, like Luxembourg, may nevertheless initiate big consequences as the 1998 *Kohll* and *Decker* decisions show. Since plaintiffs usually may not appeal to the ECJ directly, the national legal profession plays a critical 'intermediary' role in feeding cases to the ECJ. Indeed, the activist stance of the legal profession seems crucial. In Germany, for instance, lower welfare and labour courts often try to outmanoeuvre their national courts, employing the ECJ to overturn firm national precedents 'from above'.

The EU's social dimension is usually discussed as a corrective or counter to market-building, but instead appears to have proceeded largely as part of the market-building

Table 10.3 Distribution of ECJ judgments on social policy by functional subcategories, 1954–2003

Period	Sum Total ECJ judgments	Freedom of movement for workers		Social security of EU migrant workers[1]		Social security of third-country migrant workers[2]		Workers' protection and equal treatment		Social policy (all)	
All treaty articles		Arts. 39–41 TEC (ex Arts. 48–50 EEC)		Art. 42 TEC (ex Art. 51 EEC)		Arts. 300 and 310 TEC (ex Arts. 228 and 238 EEC)		Arts. 136–45 TEC (ex Arts. 117–22 EEC)			
	cases	cases		cases		cases		cases		cases	
	No. (= 100%)	%	No.	%	No.	%	No.	%	No.	%	No.
1954–60	50										
1961–65	52			15.4	8					15.4	8
1966–70	45	2.2	1	44.4	20					46.6	21
1971–75	249	4.4	11	15.7	39			0.4	1	20.5	51
1976–80	462	2.4	11	14.7	68			0.6	3	17.7	82
1981–85	657	2.4	16	6.7	44			3.2	21	12.3	81
1986–90	855	3.4	29	6.7	57	0.2	2	4.6	39	14.9	127
1991–95	929	4.4	41	7.6	71	0.6	6	6.7	62	19.3	180
1996–00	1,084	4.2	45	5.1	55	1.6	17	8.9	96	19.8	213
2001–03	751	3.6	27	3.9	29	0.7	5	6.7	50	14.9	111

1996	182	5.5	10	4.9	9	1.1	2	7.7	14	19.2	35
1997	225	3.1	7	6.7	15	2.7	6	8.0	18	20.5	46
1998	233	4.3	10	5.2	12	1.3	3	8.6	20	19.4	45
1999	208	3.8	8	3.4	7	1.0	2	8.7	18	16.9	35
2000	236	4.2	10	5.1	12	1.7	4	11.0	26	22.0	52
2001	224	3.1	7	5.8	13	0.4	1	7.6	17	16.9	38
2002	251	2.4	6	4.4	11	0.4	1	4.8	12	12.0	30
2003	276	5.1	14	1.8	5	1.1	3	7.6	21	15.6	43
1954–2003	5,239	3.5	181	7.5	391	0.6	30	5.2	272	16.8	874

Source: Data on the distribution of ECJ decisions were obtained by Andreas Obermaier from the analytical indices of the *Reports of Cases before the Court of Justice and Court of First Instance* (Luxembourg: ECJ), and verified by inspecting the individual cases (available on-line at *http://curia.eu.int*). Decisions concerning the staff of the European Communities and appeals were not included.

Notes:
[1] This column reports the decisions based on Regulations 3/58, 1408/71, 574/72 (and amendments). These regulations are based on Art. 51 EEC (now Art. 42 TEC).
[2] This column reports the decisions based on Association and Cooperation Agreements with third countries (like Turkey, Algeria, Morocco, Slovakia), insofar as they address social security concerns of third-country migrant workers.

Table 10.4 ECJ rulings on social policy by functional subcategories and EU member states, 1954–2003

Countries	AU	BE	DK	FI	FR	DE	GR	IE	IT	LX	NL	PT	ES	SW	UK	All
Freedom of movement for workers																
1 Referral by European Commission	5	12			6	2	5		11	6	1		5			48
2 Preliminary rulings	5	17			16	32	2	1	15	5	18	1	2		18	132
3 All	5	29			22	34	7	1	26	11	19	1	7	—	18	180
Social security of EU migrant workers																
4 Referral by European Commission		5			5	1	1			1	2					16
5 Preliminary rulings	6	121	1	2	40	93	2		9	5	67		7	2	20	375
6 All	8	126	1	2	45	94	3		9	6	69		7	2	21	391
Social security of third-country migrant workers																
7 Preliminary rulings	2	4			1	18					5					30
Workers' protection and equal treatment																
8 Referral under Article 230 (ex 173)																2
9 Referral by European Commission	4	6	1	1	8	4	3	2	15	6	1	1			4	56
10 Preliminary rulings	6	15	18	2	9	54	1	5	12	6	30		7	4	52	215
11 All	10	21	19	3	17	58	4	7	27	6	31	1	7	4	**56**	273

Social policy—all

12 Referral under Article 230 (ex 173)																2
13 Referral by European Commission	4	23	1	1	19	7	9	2	26	13	4	1	5	0	5	120
14 Preliminary rulings	19	157	19	4	66	197	5	6	36	10	120	1	16	6	90	752
15 All cases	23	180	20	5	85	204	14	8	62	23	124	2	21	6	95	874
16 Union member since	1994	1957	1972	1994	1957	1957	1980	1972	1957	1957	1957	1985	1985	1994	1972	—
17 Years: 2003 minus (line 16 or 1961)	10	43	22	10	43	43	24	32	43	43	43	19	19	10	22	426
18 Cases/year membership (115/117)	2,3	**4,2**	0,9	0,5	2	**4,7**	0,6	2,5	1,4	0,5	2,9	0,1	1,1	0,6	**4,3**	2,1

Source: See Table 10.3. Higher than average values per country are in bold.

process, and was sucked into a free mobility and competition-enhancing process. It is this which has spurred the demand for court decisions, and thus expanded European law in several areas of importance to systems of national social provisions. Only insofar as social dimension would follow straight from European citizenship (Bieback 2003), or from legitimate residency (Eichenhofer 2003a), would we discern an approach external to market-building. There are some signs that such an extra layer is evolving out of Union citizenship (Art. 17 TEC, ex Art. 8 EEC), as the heated exchanges over the *Grzelczyk* decision of 2001 indicate (Hailbronner 2004; Sieveking 2004). In its interpretation of EC law the Court increasingly takes direct recourse to treaty citizenship in undoing, revising, or adjusting secondary EC law.

Freedom of movement for workers

The nexus between the market and social policy was at least partially acknowledged at the outset, when social policy in the EU was addressed largely in relation to reducing restrictions on labour mobility. Articles 48–51 EEC (now Arts. 39–42 TEC) deal with the freedom of movement for workers, with Article 51 EEC (now Art. 42 TEC), providing for the direct social policy effects: 'The Council shall, acting unanimously on a proposal from the Commission, adopt such measures in the field of social security as are necessary to provide freedom of movement for workers . . . ' (see also Commission 2002d).

The fact that a labour mobility regime of 'coordination' tends to restrict welfare-state sovereignty was on the minds of treaty-makers in 1957, when Italy, as a labour exporter, and France, with early equal pay legislation, pushed for EU mandates (Romero 1993). At the time such impacts were neither particularly visible nor contentious. An entrenched intergovernmental consensus already existed on which the treaties could build, including: bilateral and multi-lateral social security treaties, the Treaty of Paris establishing in 1951 the European Coal and Steel Community, a social security treaty for miners and steelworkers, and the standards set by the International Labour Organization (ILO) in Geneva (Schulte 1994, 2004). These embedded international legal norms and the concomitant obligations for member states,[11] gradually became more deeply institutionalized—mostly in the quiet of the Court's chambers. It was not until the end of the 1980s that member states began to wake up to the full importance of 'coordination', and to struggle with or against it (Conant 2002).

One of the points of tension between national welfare states and the developing common market has arisen over regulations governing the mobility of labour across the jurisdictional boundaries of member states. Compared with the US, intra-European migration is small, and member states are quite different in their active migration profiles.[12] Prior to the 2004 enlargement there were still only about five million workers in the EU, including their dependants, who exercised this freedom, far outnumbered by third-country migration into the EU (Angenendt 1997). Today, third-country nationals still far outnumber intra-EU migrants, but eastern enlargement is likely to bring the proportions closer to parity in the coming decade. But these numbers provided more than the 'critical mass' necessary to generate continuous and increasing litigation at the ECJ level. In legal terms, the adaptation of social policy to a developed context of European 'interstate commerce' does not require a quantum leap in intra-EU migration. Individuals as litigants and national courts which refer cases to the ECJ are, together with the ECJ, the central actors in shaping this multi-tiered EU policy domain. They have instigated a large corpus of national and, especially, supranational, adjudication since 1959. Third-country migrants have also prompted important cases, and concerns about irregular labour migration has been one of the driving forces behind the third pillar and the innovations of the ToN (see Chapter 18).

Over a period of fifty years a complex patchwork of regulations and court decisions has partially suspended the principle of member-state sovereignty over social policy in the interest of European labour-market mobility (Jorens and Schulte 1998; Barwig and Schulte 1999; Slaughter, Stone Sweet, and Weiler 1997; Eichenhofer 2003a; Schulte 2004). It now spreads to the freedom of service users and providers. The net effect is to limit national capacities to contain transfers 'by territory' (Maydell 1991: 231), and to shape welfare state reform trajectories, as we can see from just two examples. First, attempts to create a minimum pension benefit in Germany during the 1980s foundered in part because of concerns that the benefit would be 'exportable' to non-German EC citizens who had worked for some time in Germany (Zuleeg 1993). Secondly, in 1994 German long-term care insurance was strategically targeted to include benefits 'in kind', that is, straight monetary transfers treated as 'in-kind' surrogates, so as to prevent a Europeanization of benefits, and thus to preserve territorialization. But in 1998 in *Molenaar* the ECJ did not find this strategy convincing (Sieveking 1998; see also, Bahle 2003; Bahle and Pfennig 2001).

To summarize some of the key implications of this section:

- A member state may no longer limit most social benefits to its citizens. As regards 'non-nationals' from within the EU, the state in which they legally reside no longer has any power to determine whether non-nationals are entitled to benefits or not. Benefits must be granted to all—or withheld from all. This development is remarkable, since 'citizen-making' through social benefits—demarcating the 'outsider'— was a watershed in the history of state-building on the continent, especially in France and Germany. This restriction tends to encourage attempts to develop what are innocent-looking, but devious, mechanisms at the national level.

- A member state may no longer insist that its rights and benefits only apply to, and can only be provided within, its territory, and today states can exercise their power to determine the territory of benefit consumption only to a limited extent—basically when providing in-kind or universal means-tested benefits, and in unemployment insurance (see Husmann 1998), though the latter is about to change in the reform of coordination legislation (Regulation EC 883/04; *Eureport social* 2004, 11/12).

- A member state is no longer entirely free to prevent other social policy regimes from directly competing on its own territory. In Germany, for instance, there are many 'posted' construction workers from other EU countries, who work for extended periods at their national wage level, while covered by many of their home country's social regulations. Thus, the state has lost some of its exclusive power to determine how the people living within its borders are protected, though there have been successful attempts in the 1990s to contain these losses through obligatory minimum wages and holidays (see Eichhorst 1998, 2000; Streeck 1998; Menz 2003; *Eureport social* 2004, 12/3).[13]

■ Member states do not have an exclusive right to administer claims to welfare benefits from migrants. Instead, the authorities of other states may also have a decisive say in adjudicating benefit status in individual cases—as controversial cases like *Paletta* of 1992 revealed repeatedly in Germany and other countries.

If complete national *de jure* authority in these respects is what sovereignty in social policy is all about, then it has ceased to exist in the EU. This has been a complex process, in which supranational efforts to broaden access and national efforts to maintain control go hand in hand, are calibrated from one conflict to another, and case by case, are thus moving piecemeal into a new, albeit unknown, system.

This transformation has not occurred without resistance from the member governments. Individually, the latter have baulked at implementing particular facets of coordination, although they have often been effectively taken to task for this by the ECJ. Collectively, they sought to roll back some aspects of coordination in the early 1990s, unanimously agreeing to revisions that would allow them to restrict portability in a somewhat broader range of cases following proper 'notification' (Schuler 2002; applied by the ECJ *inter alia* in *Skalka* in 1992; *Eureport social* 2004, 12/7–8). The impact of this shift has been modest and efforts to contain it persist, though it has partially offset some of the loss of sovereignty.

Coordination, however, can be perceived as the lever for an incremental, rights-based 'homogenization' of social policy. Neither 'supranationalization' nor 'harmonization' seems an appropriate label for this dynamic, since each implies more policy control at the centre than currently exists. The process is more like a market-place of 'coordination', with the ECJ acting as market police, a light and visible, but far-reaching, hand, reshaping the boundaries of national autonomy. It structures the interfaces of twenty-five national social policy systems, integrating their legal benefit-language and making them comparable, with potentially far-reaching consequences for the visibility and the range of policy options available to national welfare states.

Freedom of services and the European competition regime

In line with the EU's agenda on market integration, Articles 59–66 (EEC) (now Arts. 49–55 TEC, with old Arts. 62 and 63 repealed), also from the outset provided a mandate to regulate and ensure the freedom to provide services. This mandate does not appear to allow much room for social policy. In contrast to coordination, the EEC Treaty's signatories at the time saw *no* real connection between the freedom of services and their sovereign welfare state-building—they only had the markets for financial services (banks and private insurers) in mind. But developments since the mid-1980s forced by the SEA (1986), have shown that this constitutional principle and its implementation entail far-reaching consequences for national social policy regimes. It guarantees both the freedom of movement to consumers 'of social policy' to shop where they want, and the right of service providers to deliver their services 'across the border' in another welfare state. Through the freedom of services, especially combined with the EU competition regime for private actors, the demarcation line between welfare state and market has been redrawn across all member states (see, for example, Becker 2003, 2004b; Ebsen 2002; on the German example of policy modernization, Kingreen 2004). This spillover has become a major terrain for European conflicts over social policy—especially health—reform, as several ECJ decisions since 1998 clearly revealed. In the rest of this section, we briefly indicate how creating a free market for labour and services has directly intruded on the sovereignty of national welfare states.

The treaties, and also secondary European law, focus on 'economic activity', and entrepreneurial freedoms. Are welfare state measures 'economic activity', are its institutions 'enterprises'? If so, the freedom of (financial or social) 'services' (Arts. 59–66 EEC; now Arts. 49–55 TEC) would apply,[14] as would the general European competition regime (see Chapter 5).Wherever the welfare state is involved in 'economic activity' both normative domains usually become relevant at the same time. European integration does acknowledge non-economic, true, i.e. redistributive, welfare state activity— but when in doubt 'economic' and not 'welfare state' activity is presumed. There is, as ECJ cases show, no general 'exemption' for welfare state activity from the market freedoms established by the treaties (Becker 1998). Instead, drawing—and continuously redrawing—this fine line between 'economic' and 'solidaristic' action is what much of the legal conflict is about (see *Sodemare* in 1997). Only at the end of a long process will we know the real contours of the interface between European law and national welfare states (Graser 2004).

Schulz-Weidner (1997: 449) has posed the general dilemma well:

There is a permanent tension between the European economic constitution on the one hand, and the sovereignty of its member states to shape their welfare states on the other. The European economic constitution and its competition regime have moved out of the national sphere and have become a mostly European mandate . . . As soon as social security institutions are active 'economically'—and the ECJ interprets this quite liberally—they lose their national privileges, and have to conform to the European competition regime and the basic freedoms. Otherwise these institutions would forfeit their (national) 'social security monopoly'.[15]

It is now clear that these stark 'alternatives'—'economic v. solidaristic', and (if economic) the freedom to provide services and application of the European 'competition regime'—affect national welfare states directly and deeply. How this constellation shapes the contours of welfare states is opaque and continuously contested. To clarify Schulz-Weidner's point some examples may be helpful. A number of reforms to national pension systems are under discussion in member states, such as changing over to a 'capital stock' principle, or staying with the 'pay-as-you-go' system, but weeding out 'foreign' elements, such as maternity pension credits, survivor insurance, and the costless co-insurance of non-working family members. Many of these shift social insurance away from 'redistribution' and 'solidarity'. Beyond some, as yet unidentified, threshold such programmes would become just another economic enterprise that must compete with private (pension) insurance and other competitors on a level playing field. Then a provider monopoly for public insurance would become unsustainable.

The principles concerning the free movement of workers have been continuously worked out in hundreds of ECJ decisions spanning almost four decades. However, the influence of the 'economic action' doctrine, of the freedom to provide services, and of the competition regime on national welfare states emerged only slowly after the passage of the SEA in 1986, and have been confronted more systematically only since the late 1990s. Furthermore, the related influence of the freedom of establishment provisions (Arts. 52–8 EEC, now Arts. 43–8 TEC) has been felt only quite recently, although there are a few leading cases. There are significant prospects for a substantial remoulding of national social policies through this 'market filter', which absorbs some 7 per cent of the EU15 labour force, and is actually a growing sector in an ageing continent, and has been exposed to some turmoil in recent ECJ history. Some consequences of these 'regime changes' are detailed by Schulte (1999):

> The struggle is about delimiting a sphere for the welfare state which is intervention-free, be it from the EU or through the market. . . . member states remain competent to make insurance obligatory, to implement solidarity and to install a redistributive financing system. But wherever there are market traces, national hindrances of any sort are prohibited. It does not matter whether a consumer is buying his own health care (and then is reimbursed), or whether a health care scheme does this for him or her (through 'in kind' provision or 'national health care'). . . . As the health care deliverer steps in for the individual it will also have to respect *Kohll* and *Decker*: in-kind providers from other member states have a right to a level playing field *vis-à-vis* local providers, so alternatively refund systems will have to be offered for demand and supply from 'out-of-state'. National health systems are affected as well, if they have market or 'quasi-market' elements, as does the UK; the 'vouchers' in use there should be extended to the EC. Why should consumer demand in an influenza epidemic, as in 1998, stop at the UK border? Why should hospital beds in France or Benelux—just beyond the Tunnel—not be just as much on offer as (scarce) UK beds?

Kohll, and *Decker*, both of 28 April 1998, are the key ECJ cases testing the 'freedom to provide services' (Maydell 1999; Kötter 1998).[16] In particular, *Kohll* from 1998 helps illustrate the continuing struggle over where to draw the line between the market and welfare-state privileges. The intensity of the turf fight appears in the spontaneous reactions of one of the member governments concerned. The German government feared an 'Americanization' of the health sector and financial instability for the welfare state in general. But, some sick funds saw new opportunities to cut costs, and the popular press was drawn to horizons for 'treatment under palm trees' (Becker 1998; Kötter 1998). Both cases focused on whether a member of a sickness insurance fund could make use of 'service providers' in other member states. This issue concerns some 90 per cent or more of the population (the insured) in most countries, together with provider groups.

Both cases are from Luxembourg, a small country with a natural bent for cross-border markets. *Kohll* deals with remunerative orthodontist work carried out in Germany, outside a hospital infrastructure, by doctors in private practice. *Decker* deals with the purchase of a pair of spectacles with corrective lenses on a Luxembourg prescription from a Belgian optician. In both cases the sick fund refused to reimburse. In *Kohll*, this was because it saw no basis for defining it as a case of 'emergency treatment received in the event of illness or accident abroad'; and, since the fund had rejected Kohll's request with reason, the required 'prior authorization of the competent social security institution' was out of order. Decker had not requested prior authorization, but had only submitted the bill.

These cases caught the attention of many member governments, since national interests are highly affected by prying open 'closed shop' health delivery systems. The Court found such authorizations, or administrative 'necessity testing', not in compliance with EC law. In *Kohll* the Court applied the 'freedom of services':

> Article 59 of the EEC Treaty precludes the application of any national rules which have the effect of making the provision of services between Member States more difficult than the provision of services purely within one Member State.

Moreover, the Court saw no 'objective' justification for such a rule, since it did not see any 'risk of seriously undermining the financial balance of the social security system', which could be an 'overriding reason in the general interest':

It should be noted . . . that under Articles 56 and 66 of the EC Treaty Member States may limit freedom to provide services on grounds of public health. However, that does not permit them to exclude the public health sector as a sector of economic activity and from the point of view of freedom to provide services, from the application of the fundamental principles of freedom of movement . . .

The conditions for practising as a doctor or dentist have been dealt with in several coordination and harmonization directives. It follows that medical professionals practising in one member state should enjoy the same guarantees accorded to medical professionals operating on their own national territory, for the purpose of freedom of services. Nor could the Court find that these rules 'were necessary to provide a balanced medical and hospital service accessible to all'. In *Decker*—as for all pharmaceuticals—the focus was on the free movement of goods (Art. 30 EEC, now Art. 28 TEC) rather than on services. Protection of public health (Art. 36 EEC, now Art. 30 TEC) was again seen as unaffected, especially since a national ophthalmologist had prescribed the spectacles.

This opening of one major social insurance system to the European market is probably just the beginning, as other cases are pending which test the limits of welfare state 'closed shops'. Since 2002 the important strategic issue of normal access to hospital treatment in other member states was subject to several ECJ decisions, starting in 2001 with *Vanbraekel*. Here the ECJ showed more respect for how member states organized their welfare states, requiring permits for out-of-state treatment, but respecting only 'medical necessity' and stipulating a right to a permit. In the medium term such 'deregulation' may provoke 're-regulation' in order to provide particular social goods.

The balance between a market and institutionally autonomous national welfare states, two principles embedded in the EU treaties, is not static but has become dynamic, with national reforms heading for privatization *cum* deregulation and the diverse Brussels 'single market regimes' both feeding into each other in a race towards 'marketization' (Bieback 2003). Brussels finds a wide open terrain here, with a large potential for restructuring welfare-state delivery regimes. The Commission's *White Paper on Services of General Interest* (Commission 2004n; *Eureport social* 2003, 11/6), and the struggle over the Services Directive (Commission 2004m; *Eureport social* 2004, 12/4–5; 2003, 11/4–5), with a sectoral Social Services Directive still in preparation (*Eureport social* 2004, 12/11), indicate a much more prominent role for the Commission here than in the coordination arena. The restructuring problem is likely to be particularly severe for Sweden and Finland, the two Nordic countries which joined the EU in 1995, since they have built up the most encompassing welfare states, and have also systematically pursued a policy of marginalizing competitive pressures in welfare state activity. In the early 1990s, Kåre P. Hagen (1992: 289), seeing the welfare state *per se* as endangered, argued that:

Political ambitions of providing high- and equal-quality health care to all segments of the population, have required the extensive use of public monopolies that may militate against enterprise freedoms guaranteed by Community legislation. . . . In general, any kind of state welfare policy which is deliberately designed to prevent private purchasing power from being reproduced in the consumption of welfare goods supplied by the market, will run counter to the freedoms of the common market (see also Hagen 1998).

This position is somewhat overdrawn, but we can now can add three further general points to our list of restrictions on member-state autonomy:

- The Treaty constellation— 'economic' v. 'solidaristic' action, freedom to provide services, and competition regime—now frames the welfare state. It seems to prioritize two polarized trajectories: it sets contours for protecting core welfare state components (redistribution, pay-as-you-go, etc.); but, when redistribution recedes, it moves the welfare state (in whole or in part) over the borderline into the sphere of 'economic action', thus slowly submerging its activity in a single European 'social security' *market*.

- Consumer and provider rights in 'services' have come to the fore since the mid-1990s, also in relation to questioning welfare state 'closed shops'. Member governments can no longer exclusively decide who provides social services or benefits. They can no longer exclusively organize social-service occupations, since the mutual recognition of degrees and licences from other member states intervenes. And they have a radically limited capacity to protect their national service organizations from the competitive inroads of service organizations in other member states.

- The health area is a first, *and crucial*, Europe-wide testing ground for the turf battle between national welfare states and the EU plus the market, as represented by private insurance, producers, etc. (see Mossialos *et al.* 2002; Mossialos and McKee 2002; Commission 2004n especially section 4.4).[17] Compared with pensions, health insurance has more 'market traces' in most national systems, is more fragmented by provider groups already operating in markets (medical instruments, pharmaceuticals), or quasi-markets (doctors in sick fund private practice), and has been traditionally exposed to substantial private provision in most countries. In recent decades, national reforms have pointed increasingly to 'market cures'.[18] As health is a general concern for Europeans, the idea of a European Health Insurance Card (Commission 2004l) should be well received, and is seen by some as the social policy equivalent of the euro. The card is scheduled to be fully introduced by 2006 (*EDS* 2004: 17ff), and should also function as a single market-maker (*Eureport social* 2003, 11/11; 11/3).

To summarize, even if we focus exclusively on issues of freedom of movement for workers and freedom to provide services, one can see a wide range of market compatibility requirements, through which either EU regulations or ECJ decisions impinge on the design and the reform of national social policies. Examples of other welfare state effects of single market measures could easily be multiplied—for example, restrictions related to subsidies (Schulz-Weidner 2004) for economic activities in regional policy. In Italy, for instance, the government used abatements of social insurance taxes as a strategy to attract investment to the Mezzogiorno. While the Commission agreed to permit this until the end of 1993, it then initiated ECJ proceedings against the continuation of the practice on the grounds of 'unfair competition' (*Eureport* 1994, 2/5). In 1993 and 1994 Belgium continued a Maribel scheme in which it also lowered contributions for companies especially exposed to European market competition. The Commission deemed this state aid to be in violation of Article 87(1) TEC (ex Art. 92 EEC), and intervened. Belgium took recourse to the ECJ in *Maribel*, and in 1999 the Court held that the legality of *Maribel* was to be assessed solely in relation to its effects, and not to the intention of the state to generalize them to the whole economy; since in effect such aid put other companies in the European market at a disadvantage it was declared illegal. Due to the European Economic Area non-EU member Norway faced precisely these barriers in 1998 (*Eureport social* 1998, 6/8). Similarly, improvements in Germany's social insurance for farmers require Brussels' approval, since such changes in a non-universal insurance could constitute sectoral subsidies if part of a package deal with the lowering of prices for agricultural commodities. The broader point is clear: a whole range of social policy designs that would be available to sovereign welfare states—and belong to the traditional policy 'toolkit'—are prohibited, or made more costly, to member states within the EC's multi-tiered polity.

European integration and *de facto* pressures on national welfare states

The EU now intervenes directly in the social policies of member states in two ways: by enacting significant social policy initiatives of its own; and by striking down those features of national systems deemed incompatible with the development of the single market. In addition, the process of European integration also has a less direct, albeit significant, effect on national social policies, as both the economic policies of the EU, and the responses of social actors to those policies, put pressure on national welfare states. These effects are difficult to measure because they are indirect, but they nonetheless add to the general picture of increasing supranational influence over the design of national social policy.

The most frequently cited source of pressure on welfare states within the EU is the likelihood that heightened integration may lead to 'social dumping', a debate still going strong, though it has been partly submerged in the 'globalization' discussion (Rieger and Leibfried 2003). The term refers to the prospect that firms operating where 'social wages' are low may undercut the prices of competitors, forcing higher-cost firms either to go out of business or to relocate to low social wage areas, or to pressure their governments to reduce social wage costs (Vaughan-Whitehead 2003). In extreme scenarios, now 'in vogue' with eastern enlargement in countries bordering on the eastern enlargement, such as Germany, Austria, and Italy, these actions could fuel a downward spiral in social provision, eventually producing very rudimentary, 'lowest common denominator', national welfare states. Supporters of social policy in the EU countries with well-developed welfare states—for example, labour confederations such as the German Deutscher Gewerkschaftsbund—have particularly stressed this concern.

There is some evidence that these kinds of pressures have restricted social expenditure in the US, where labour (and capital) mobility is far greater than is currently the case in the EU (P. E. Peterson and Rom 1990; see also, Boltho 1989). Despite widespread attention to this issue, however, the evidence that European integration will fuel a process of social dumping remains limited (Majone 2005). As a number of observers have noted, the 'social wage' is only one factor in investment decisions, and firms will not invest in low social wage countries unless worker productivity (relative to wages) justifies such investments (Hauser 1996). Even in eastern enlargement—today's focus for the social dumping debate—a huge wage disparity only leads to a relatively small disparity in productivity (about one sixth) to the advantage of the east (Vaughan-Whitehead 2003; for a social policy overview, see Tomka 2004; Guillén and Palier 2004). Furthermore, price and quality competition should be distinguished. Neo-classical trade theory suggests that high social wage countries should be able to continue their policies as long as overall conditions allow profitable investment. One sign of the ambiguous consequences of integration is the fact that northern Europe's concerns about 'sunbelt effects' are mirrored by south, and now east, Europe's concerns about 'agglomeration effects' in which investment would flow towards the superior infrastructures and high-skilled workforces of Europe's most developed regions.

Social dumping may generate greater fears than current evidence warrants. The opposite could be the case for some of the other ways that economic integration creates pressures on national social policy systems. The single market is encouraging a gradual movement towards a narrowed band of value-added tax rates. In theory, governments whose VAT revenues have been lowered will be free to increase other taxes, but this may not be easy. Because it is politically easier to sustain indirect taxes, the new rules may create growing constraints on member-state budgets, with clear implications for national social policies (Wilensky 1976; Hibbs and Madsen 1981). This is likely to be a problem for Denmark, which relies heavily on indirect, rather than payroll, taxes, to finance its generous welfare state (J. H. Petersen 1991, 1993, 2000; Hagen, Norrman, and Sørensen 1998). Thus, countries such as Denmark and Sweden are resisting 'upper limits' for value-added taxes, to ensure that they can finance their welfare states.

The move towards EMU (Martin and Ross 2004), with its tough requirements for budgetary discipline, may also encourage downward adjustments in welfare provision (see Chapter 6). For example, to participate in the final stage of monetary union, Italy had to reduce its budget deficit from 10 to about 3 per cent of GDP by the end of the 1990s (Gohr 2001; Ferrera and Gualmini 2000, 2004; della Sala 2004). This served mainly to legitimate efforts by successive governments to pursue major cuts in old-age pensions and other social benefits in 1994 and 1995 (Brunetta and Trenti 1995). EMU seems to have triggered a systematic rebuilding and retrenchment of the Italian welfare state. While most other countries face less radical adjustments—at least in the short run—the convergence criteria presented formidable problems for almost all of them (Krupp 1995), and have increased the level of the reform pressures obtaining in any case (Martin and Ross 2004: 316–21). Here again, the significance of the EU's indirect effects is hard to ascertain. Governments would have faced such pressure for austerity in any event (see Pierson 1998, 2001). The convergence criteria do not, of course require budget reductions—tax increases are also possible—but they do strengthen the hand of those seeking such cuts. We should also note, however, that a backlash against the Maastricht criteria has built up since 2002, and this can be read under the heading 'national welfare states strike back'.

EMU would not only put pressure on national social programmes, but could also prod the EU into a more active role in combating unemployment, a stance the Union has symbolically enshrined in the 1997 ToA (see Chapter 11). Analysis of the prospects for monetary integration in Europe was historically coupled with discussion on the need for accompanying social policies to address the probable emergence of regional imbalances (Ross 1995b). EMU would strip national governments of significant macro-economic policy levers, and a EU-wide macroeconomic stance would create signific-ant regional unemployment problems. More flexible exchange rates allow local adaptations to local economic conditions. Once these instruments are dismantled, combating pockets of regional unemployment at the national level will be more difficult (Eichengreen 1992).

A further indirect pressure on national welfare states stems from the dismantling of the 'public service' or 'public infrastructure state' with its different national labels. Trains, postal services, air transport, electricity, gas, and water, together with local services—from waste disposal to public baths and hospitals—were public enterprises, financed by tariffs that assured equal service across the country, and in urban and rural areas, often resorting to cross subsidies between rich and poor services to achieve this equality. Starting with telecommunications in the mid-1980s, branch after branch of these public structures has crumbled and been privatized (Schneider and Tenbrücken 2004; Schneider, Fink, and Tenbrücken 2005). Direct supranational prodding via EU regulation based on competition law (Eureport social 2004, 12/7–8; S. K. Schmidt 2004a, 2004b), and privatization and deregulation in the UK and US, were exacerbated by domestic attempts to cut state spending and level out the playing field for different kinds of enterprises, and resulted in radically increased competitive pres-sure in newly internationalized markets (see Chapter 5). The reconfigured public-service state often consists of private, multinational companies formed in branches of public service that had been national or regional. We have seen a separation of the two—a 'transnationalization' of the public-service state and, comparatively speaking, a national lock-in of welfare state change (Leibfried and Zürn 2005)—and thus the loss of one of the welfare state's protective outer skins (Leibfried 2001). And, the principles established in the privatization of the public service state are now applied—to a smaller or larger extent—to the welfare state proper (Haverkate and Huster 1998; Schwarze 2001; Pielow 2001, 2002; Commission 2004n; Eureport social 2004, 12/6, 12/3, 12/1–2; ECJ Altmark Trans, 2002; Schulz-Weidner 2004).

A final indirect pressure on national welfare states stems from the rapidly evolving European single private insurance market. As of July 1994 national private insurance has been drawn into the common market of the EU, with the Commission most active in establishing a single occupational pensions market (Eureport social 2004, 12/1–2; 2003, 11/9–10, 11/3), among others with a Pension Fund Directive (Eureport social 2003, 11/4–5), also supported by the ECJ (Eureport social 2004 12/11; Schulz-Weidner 2003; Skandia 2003; Danner 2002). The furious pace of cross-border mergers and acquisitions is creating a heavily concentrated, or interlocked, insurance sector operating at the European level, though mostly in still very balkanized national markets (due to the 'salesman dependency' and 'label recognition'). Integrated European insurance mar-kets allow for a greater differentiation of policy holders by risk groups (Stone 1989), and thus for cheaper policies with lower operational costs—unless certain risks, such as 'genetic features' (Art. II-81 CT), and 'sex', were disallowed—in 2004 there was an unsuccessful attempt to do this with mandating unisex tariffs. Furthermore, such an integrated private sector would confront 25 national, internally segmented, public insurance domains, themselves often caught up in spirals of deregulation and thus already exposed to challenges from these private markets (Hagen 1998). Insurance providers with the option of relocating to more lenient member states will gain a growing influence over national social regulation. At the same time, the clash between particular national regulatory styles and the different traditions of competing insurers from other member states is likely to be intense.

The results of 'public/private' interplay in the context of a radically altered private sector are difficult to anticipate. There is, however, considerable evidence from studies of national welfare states that the reform of private-sector markets can have dramatic effects on the provision of public services (Rein and Rainwater 1986). Public and private insurance compete mainly in areas such as occupational pensions (Pedersen 2004; Pochet 2003), life insurance, and supplemental health insurance. Permanent turf battles between public and private seem likely concerning where 'basic' (public) coverage should end and 'additional' (private) insurance may begin. Private (or competing 'out-of-state' public) actors in this turf battle may arm themselves with the 'economic action' approach. Since the periphery of 'private insurance' is likely to be considered 'economic' action, freedom to provide services and the European competition regime reign freely. This may be seen as part of a broader process in which movement towards the single market challenges existing demarcations between the public and private spheres. The welfare state, which has traditionally been a key area for establishing these demarcation lines, is bound to be affected by such gradual and often indirect redrawing of boundaries (Hagen 1998), frequently taking place in fields beyond the welfare state.

It is difficult to evaluate the consequences of these indirect pressures for national welfare states. Many of the potential problem areas lie in the future, and some of the others, such as social dumping, are difficult to measure. One has to weigh the pressures for reform against the welfare state's considerable sources of resilience (Pierson 1996a, 1998, 2001). Yet, the picture that emerges is of national governments with diminished control over many of the policies that have traditionally supported national welfare states—the currency, macroeconomic policies, public finance, tax policies, and also industrial-relations systems. Again, these developments challenge the dominant view that European integration is a 'market-building' process that advances relentlessly, whilst leaving the development of social policy a purely national affair.

Social policy in Europe's emerging multi-tiered system

Scholarly attention has focused largely on the Commission's efforts to establish a 'social dimension' of EU-wide policies or at least minimum standards. To date these efforts have modified member-state social policies in relatively few areas—most systematically, though, in labour law (see, for example, Weiler 1991, 1999; Burley and Mattli 1993; Stone Sweet and Caporaso 1998), but the expansion of EU mandates, buttressed by the extended use of QMV, indicates that an 'activist' threshold may have been crossed in the 1990s. Important, though much less visible, have been the social policy effects of the single market's development itself. These have occurred either directly, as the Commission, national courts, and the ECJ have sought to reconcile member-state policy autonomy with the effort to create a unified economic space, or indirectly, through pressures on the support structures of national welfare states.

We are living through a period of rapid change in the relations between nation-states and an increasingly global market system (Leibfried and Zürn 2005). '[T]he central question to pose is: has sovereignty remained intact while the autonomy of the state has diminished or has the modern state faced a loss of sovereignty?' (Held 1991: 213). In the EU, both member-state sovereignty and autonomy have diminished in tandem (Leibfried 1994; Pierson 1996b). The process has been subtle and incremental, but developments within the Union as a whole increasingly constrain national welfare states. Member governments now find their revenue bases under assault, their welfare-reform options circumscribed, many of their delivery regimes under threat of new competition, and their administrators obliged to share control over policy enforcement.

What is emerging is a unique multi-tiered system of social policy, with three distinctive characteristics: a propensity towards 'joint-decision traps' and policy immobilism; a prominent role for courts in policy development; and an unusually tight coupling to market-making processes.

First, European-level policy-makers are tightly hemmed in by the scepticism of the Council, the density of existing national-level social policy commitments, and the limited fiscal and administrative capacities of the EU. Compared with any other 'multi-tiered' system the EU's social policy-making apparatus is extremely bottom-heavy (Kleinman and Piachaud 1992a; Pierson and Leibfried 1995; Kleinman 2001). The relatively weak 'centre' has limited capacity to formulate positive social policy. As a result, social policy evolution is more likely to be the result of mutual adjustment and incremental accommodation than of central guidance. The centre generates a variety of pressures and constraints on social policy development, but much less by way of clear mandates for positive action.

Yet there has also been a considerable weakening of the member states' positions (Pierson 1995b). With the gravitation of authority, even of a largely negative kind, to the European level, the capacity of member governments to design their welfare states as they choose is also diminishing. Significant losses of autonomy and sovereignty occurred without member governments paying a great deal of attention. In some cases—such as Italy's role in pushing for enhanced labour mobility in the Treaty of Rome—member governments actively pursued sovereignty-eroding initiatives. While member governments currently resist some of the single market's implications for their own power, their capacity to do so is limited by their fear of jeopardizing the hard-won benefits of European integration. Their resistance is further limited by an institutional ratchet effect. Once a member of the EU a country is bound by all ECJ rulings, and can pursue reforms only through the slow and difficult procedures available under EU rules. The combination of diminished member-state authority and continued weakness at the EU level is likely to restrict the room for innovative policy. As Fritz Scharpf observes, 'the policy-making capacities of the union have not been strengthened nearly as much as capabilities at the level of member states have declined' (1994a: 219, 1994b; Offe 2003).

Member governments still 'choose', but they do so from an increasingly restricted menu. At a time when control over social policy often means responsibility for announcing unpopular cut-backs, member governments are sometimes happy to accept arrangements that constrain their own options. Given the unpopularity of retrenchment, governments may find that the growing ability to blame the EU allows changes which they would otherwise be afraid to contemplate. The movement towards a multi-tiered political system opens up major new avenues for the politics of 'blame avoidance' (Weaver 1986). It has been suggested that this dynamic may strengthen national executives at the expense of domestic opponents (Milward 1992; Moravcsik 1994, 1998; Wolf 1997). Yet in the process of escaping from domestic constraints, national executives have created new ones that profoundly limit their options. Decision-making bodies at both the national and supranational levels face serious restrictions on their capacity for social policy intervention, since they have partly 'locked themselves in' through previous steps towards integration.

The second distinctive characteristic of social policy-making in the EU is that the constraints and requirements which develop from the centre are normally law-driven or court-driven.[19] It is as much a series of ECJ rulings as the process of Commission and Council initiative that has been the source of new social policy. While the Council and Commission are prone to stasis, the ECJ's institutional design fosters activism—a situation emphasized in the 2004 Constitutional Treaty. Faced with litigation, the ECJ cannot avoid making what are essentially policy decisions as a matter of routine. The Court also relies on simple majority votes, taken in secret, sheltering it from the political immobility often a feature of the EU. Only a unanimous vote of the Council can generally undo ECJ decisions when they relate to primary European law. The structure of EU institutions places the ECJ centre stage. Attempts at corporatist policy-making have generated much of the drama surrounding Europe's social dimension, but until recently (Falkner 1998) businesses and unions have had little direct involvement in the decisions that have actually created legally binding requirements for the social policies of member states. But this seems to be changing.

Legal strategies have had the advantage of leaving taxing, spending, and administrative powers at the national level—even more so, the more they are regulatory in nature. One should emphasize, however, that such a court-led process of social policy development has its own logic. Decisions are likely to reflect demands for doctrinal coherence as much as, or more than, substantive debates as to the desirability of various social policy outcomes. The capacity of reforms built around a judicial logic to achieve substantive goals may be limited. Furthermore, courts may have less need to consider political constraints in prescribing solutions. One danger is that Court initiatives may exceed the tolerance of important political actors within the system. After all, centralized policy-making was made difficult in the EU precisely because ECJ activism may generate resentment. This is, of course, one aspect of the current disquiet over the 'democratic deficit'.

Finally, Europe's emerging multi-tiered system of social policy is uniquely connected to a process of market-building. Of course, social policies in mixed economies intersect in a variety of complex ways with market systems. In the past, however, social policy had generally been seen as part of what Karl Polanyi (1994 [1944]) describes as a spontaneous 'protective reaction' against the expansion of market relations. Social policies that have developed in response to the shortcomings of market arrangements, have become an outcome of politics *against* markets.

At the EU level, however, interventions in the traditional spheres of social policy have generally not taken this Polanyian form. Even in areas such as gender issues where the EU has been activist, policies have been directly connected to labour-market participation, while broad issues of family policy and windows of opportunity to synthesize social inclusion and educational policy, provided EU-wide by the OECD PISA study (Allmendinger and Leibfried 2003), have been ignored, although they were thoroughly explored in an Observatory on National Family Policies after 1989. Instead, as the centrality of decisions regarding labour mobility and free service markets reveals, EU social policy interventions have developed as *part of* the process of market-building itself. Never before has the construction of markets shaped the development of social policy initiatives so visibly and intensively.

The overall scope of EU interventions has indeed been extensive. These interventions reveal that national welfare-state regimes are now part of a larger, multi-tiered system of social policy. Member governments profoundly influence this structure, but they no longer fully control it. While the governance of social policy occurs at multiple levels, however, the EU's peculiar arrangement is also different in many respects from traditional federal states, distinguished by a weak policy-making centre, court-driven regulation, and strong links with market-making processes. The EU's unique political arrangement is producing a pattern of policy-making quite different from that of any national welfare state (see Streeck 1995, 1998, 2000). Nevertheless, especially in this unique multi-tiered arrangement we should heed Harold Laski's 1939 federalist warning—and also not become trapped in its inherited economic mantle and not be consumed by the costs of *non*-social Europe:

> Federalism . . . is insufficiently positive in character, it does not provide for sufficient rapidity of action: it inhibits the emergence of necessary standards of uniformity; it relies upon compacts and compromises which take insufficient account of the urgent category of time; . . . its psychological results, especially in an age of crisis, are depressing to a democracy that needs the drama of positive achievement to retain its faith. (cited in Barnard 2000: 68)

Notes

1 This chapter is based on, but substantially revises and updates, Leibfried and Pierson (2000). I am indebted to Andreas Obermaier, Eberhard Eichenhofer, Josef Falke, Hanna Piotter, Bernd Schulte, and Dieter Wolf for their help.

2 As Arts. III–107, para. 2, and –179(2), para. 2 of the Constitutional Treaty of 2004 show, soft law could rapidly turn into something more binding, where the Commission is empowered to become active, especially by way of initiatives, designed to set guidelines and indicators, facilitate the exchange of national experiences, and distil the elements necessary for a regular oversight and evaluation.

3 Recommendations 92/441 (Common Criteria Concerning Sufficient Resources and Social Assistance in Social Protection Systems, 24 June 1992), and 92/442 (Objectives and Policies of Social Security Systems, 27 July 1992) reflect these difficulties and point to social policy 'convergence' (Maydell 1999). In contrast, in the 1970s 'harmonization' was still the major focus (see Fuchs 2003).

4 The retroactivity of the *Barber* case was weakened by a unanimous amendment to the treaties in the TEU, which

established a less costly—but not the least costly—version of retroactivity. Thus restrained, the ECJ upheld the TEU solution of 1993 in *Ten Oever*. Estimated costs of full retroactivity for Germany are from Berenz (1994); for the UK see Mazey and Richardson (1993: 15); see also, Pollack (2003).

5 Two further directives were passed: the Young Workers Directive; and the Working Time Directive. Italy, Greece, and Spain opposed the former and the UK the latter (on the latter, see Pollack 2003). Three further framework agreements should be mentioned here: Parental Leave (1996), Part-time Work (1997), and Fixed-term Contracts/Temporary Work (1997). More recently, Teleworking (2002). On the trajectory of directives, see Falkner *et al.* (2005).

6 The UK opt-out from both decision-making and policies *de facto* cautioned the eleven, later fourteen, in their use of the Social Protocol as they feared distortions of competition and instinctively preferred to maximize unanimity. Many UK-based firms voluntarily implemented the 1995 European Works Council Directive in order to preserve intra-firm uniformity, and to ward off possible consumer conflicts (Falkner 1998: 197). The ECJ never ruled on the legality of the Protocol. Once the UK had opted in, it became bound by the new *acquis* of decisions taken between 1993 and 1997.

7 See *http://europa.eu.int/comm/employment_social/news/2002/*.

8 Respectively, *Eureport social* 2004, 12/1–2; 2003, 11/6; *Eureport social* 2004, 12/3; Commission 2003a, 2003c; *Eureport social* 2003, 11/11; 11/9–10. The orientation might even be labelled tending to the 'market radical', turning every European citizen into an entrepreneur and away from standard employee social protection.

9 *Eureport social* 2004, 12/9–10; *EDS* 2004; *Eureport social* 2004, 12/6; 2004, 12/3;

Eureport social 2003, 11/12; 2003, 11/7–8; House of Lords 2004a.

10 See Weiler (1991, 1999); Burley and Mattli (1993); Stone Sweet and Caporaso (1998). On the general myopia about courts, see Shapiro and Stone (1994). On the state of welfare law, see Schulte (2004), and Eichenhofer (2003a, 2003b). For labour law, see Barnard (2000), Bercusson (2000), O'Leary (2002). And for a general background on ECJ development, see Chalmers (2004).

11 The first regulations were EEC 3/58 and 4/58; later EEC 1408/71 and 574/72. These were extended to third-country nationals in Regulation EC 859/03. As of 29 April 2004, all coordination regulation is being modernized under Regulation EC 883/04.

12 An EU study reported that in 1995 about 155,000 Germans worked in another EU country, 177,000 French, and 197,000 British, and 625,000 Italians; of the 3.5 million foreign workers in Germany less than a third were EU citizens, notably 365,400 Italians and 233,000 Greeks (*Eureport social* 1998, 6/3).

13 The 1996 Directive on the Posting of Workers was advocated by the governments of Austria, France, and Germany, and resisted by the UK and Portugal, both 'donor nations'. The continuing controversy is over the competition of several social policy regimes on one territory, when workers migrate to benefit from wage differentials, whilst taking with them some of the social and wage policy 'frames' of their country of origin, as when the centre of unified Berlin was rebuilt after 1990.

14 Much welfare state activity falls under 'services' in the terms of the treaty, not only 'social services'. Private insurance is a matter of financial services. So is the (monetary) 'transfer state', when considered as 'economic' activity rather than 'true welfare state activity', as, for example, when public pensions

are shorn of all their redistributive elements in welfare state reform.

15 Where 'monopoly' means supply by particular public institutions, i.e. a provider monopoly (see Giesen 1995, 2001, 2004). Giesen's focus is accident insurance, where the monopoly is most controversial and where several member states already allow for private competitive provision.

16 In a 1991 judgment, *Höfner & Elser v. Macotron*, the ECJ declared the monopoly in employment services of German unemployment insurance illegal as regards senior white-collar employees.

17 Some producers are more likely to take the European route than others, especially private international service organizations involved in hospitals, markets for medical drugs, and the provision of medical equipment (Bieback 1993: 171). These producers are likely to become strong actors at the EU level, *vis-à-vis* the Commission or in the Courts.

18 Directive 89/105 set minimum standards for all national systems of drug price control and price-fixing. The Commission has developed proposals for a single drug market, which would strongly, though indirectly, harmonize parts of national-health insurance systems, for example by undoing price controls and introducing significant co-payments (Kotzian 2002, 2003). In 1994 the European Medicines Agency (EMEA) in London started surveillance and licensing work

(*Eureport* 1994, 2/2; EMEA Yearly Reports). Commission competition policy also provides instruments for influencing drug pricing, with wide potential impact on health policies. Since equivalent pharmaceuticals are much cheaper in most southern European countries, among others German sickness funds have been quite interested in 'importing' such drugs (Schwarze 1998)—and the euro will give another boost to these trends. This ongoing conflict reveals 'the close links between drug prices and health care policy' (Woolcock 1996: 314), and an unresolvable conflict which Michael Noonan, the Irish Secretary of Health, described thus in 1996: '. . . Member States cannot give ground on their prerogative to set health policy within their own jurisdiction. Nor is it acceptable that one country can or should impose its choice of health policy on its neighbours by the action of parallel trade' (cited in Schwarze 1998: 63). One possible resolution, Europe-wide standardization according to Arts. 94 and 95 TEC which would replace diverse national health policies, has met with strong resistance from the pharmaceutical industry.

19 Gerda Falkner pointed us to a budget-driven factor which shapes national thinking on some social problems and policies, insofar as national agencies tailor their projects to specific EU programmes as a way of obtaining complementary funding.

Further reading

For the main contours of the subject, see Leibfried and Pierson (1995*b*); the first and last chapters provide a guide to theoretical explanations, and the second chapter details the core contours of social policy. For more recent analyses, see Hine and Kassim (1998), Kaelble and Schmid (2004), and Offe (2000). For a UK 'social policy' view, see Kleinman (2001). For a broad 'continental' political science view, see Scharpf (1999: ch. 4). On enlargement, see Schmähl (2004). For an overview of the legal dimension, see Eichenhofer (2003a), Schulte (2004), and Fuchs (2002). For a comprehensive constitutional perspective with a health focus, see Kingreen (2003). On health law, see Mossialos and McKee (2002), and on health policy, see Mossialos *et al.* (2002). On the withering away of the services—public utilities—mantle of the welfare state due to EC competition law, see Leibfried (2001). Recent ECJ cases may be consulted on the web under *www.curia.eu.int/*. For a comprehensive analysis of the new corporatist perspectives, see Falkner (1998). Both the *Journal of European Social Policy* (1991–), and the *Journal of European Public Policy* (1994–) contain useful articles. Since 1993 regular policy news is reported monthly in German bulletin, *Eureport social*, until (Feb. 1995) entitled *Eureport*, published by the European representation of the German social insurance (*dsv@esip.org*) in Brussels, which is a member of the network European Social Insurance Partners (ESIP; *www.esip.org*).

Eichenhofer, E. (2003a), *Sozialrecht der Europäischen Union* (Berlin: Erich Schmidt).

Falkner, G. (1998), *EU Social Policy in the 1990s: Towards a Corporatist Policy Community* (London: Routledge).

Fuchs, M. (2002) (ed.), *Nomos Kommentar zum europäischen Sozialrecht* (Baden-Baden: Nomos).

Hine, D., and Kassim, H. (1998) (eds.), *Beyond the Market: The EU and National Social Policy* (London: Routledge).

Kaelble, H., and Schmid, G. (2004) (eds.), *Das europäische Sozialmodell: auf dem Weg zum transnationalen Sozialstaat* (Berlin: Sigma).

Kingreen, T. (2003), *Das Sozialstaatsprinzip im europäische Verfassungsverbund.*

Gemeinschaftsrechtliche Einflüsse auf das deutsche Recht der gesetzlichen Krankenversicherung (Tübingen: Mohr Siebeck).

Kleinman, M. (2001), *A European Welfare State? European Union Social Policy in Context* (London: Palgrave Macmillan).

Leibfried, S. (2001), 'Über die Hinfälligkeit des Staates der Daseinsvorsorge. Thesen zur Zerstörung des äußeren Verteidigungsringes des Sozialstaats', in Schader-Stiftung, *Die Zukunft der Daseinsvorsorge: öffentliche Unternehmen im Wettbewerb* (Darmstadt: Schader-Stiftung), 158–66.

Leibfried, S., and Pierson, P. (1995b) (eds.), *European Social Policy: Between Fragmentation and Integration* (Washington: Brookings Institution).

Mossialos, E., Dixon, A., Figueras, J., and Kutzin, J. (2002) (eds.), *Funding Health Care: Options for Europe* (Buckingham: Open University Press).

Mossialos, E., and McKee, M. (2002), *EU Law and the Social Character of Health Care* (Brussels: P.I.E-Peter Lang).

Offe, C. (2000), 'The Democratic Welfare State in an Integrating Europe', in Greven and Pauly (eds.), *Democracy Beyond the State? The European Dilemma and the Emerging Global Order* (Boston: Rowman & Littlefield), 63–89.

O'Leary, S. (2002), *Employment Law in the European Court of Justice: Judicial Structures, Policies and Processes* (Oxford: Hart).

Scharpf, F. W. (1999), *Governing in Europe: Effective and Democratic?* (Oxford: Oxford University Press), 121–55.

Schmähl, W. (2004), 'EU Enlargement and Social Security: Some Dimensions of a Complex Topic', *Intereconomics: Review of European Economic Policy*, 9/1: 21–8.

Schulte, B. (2004), 'Supranationales Recht', in von Maydell and Ruland (eds.), *Sozialrechtshandbuch (SRH)*, 3rd edn. (Baden-Baden: Nomos), 1611–76.

Chapter 11

Employment Policy

Between Efficacy and Experimentation

Martin Rhodes[1]

Contents

Summary

Attempts to put in place an employment policy for the European Union (EU) have been bedevilled from the outset by one of the EU's most complex regulatory conundrums: how to create a system of regulation that accommodates the diversity of historical, legal, and institutional traditions of the member states *and* resolves continuing conflict, over both the desirability of new forms of labour-market regulation, and the assignment to the EU of policy powers in this domain. Nevertheless, the past several decades have witnessed the creation of a regulatory system based on three pillars, each with a different mode of policy-making and governance: (1) EU legislation promotes employment rights, produced by a version of the 'Community method'; (2) 'law via collective agreement' is a negotiated alternative to pillar one, and involves agreement among the social partners prior to legislation; and (3) a more recent and more radical shift from hard law to soft law embraces an expansion from employment protection to employment *promotion*, through the European Employment Strategy (EES). All three modes have been character-ized by: a continuing contestation of the form, substance, and level of regulation; the centrality, especially since the 1980s, of the Commission, acting as a policy and norm entrepreneur and as mediator between the member states; the weaknesses of the institutional architecture underpinning this policy arena; political power games, involving the member states and the supranational institutions, that have driven the locus of policy-making over time from one governance mode to the next; and a series of trade-offs over time between efficacy and experimentation in policy formulation and execution.

Introduction

Employment policy has always appeared to be marginalized in European policy-making, and was written only lightly into the original treaties. Its peripheral role has often been associated more with a general failure to create a 'social dimension' of 'positive' integration to accompany the 'negative integration' of the EU's more central market-making mission. Chapter 10 in this volume argues that interpretations minimizing the importance of the EU involvement in social policy are profoundly mistaken in that European social integration has eroded both the sovereignty and the autonomy of national welfare states. The history of European employment policy development has run parallel to, and frequently overlapped with, that of social policy. Employment policy—in its multiple forms—has contributed to a reordering of relations between national and supranational power and influence. National employment policy is understood here as the laws and conventions that establish the rights and entitlements of workers and structure the work relationship, as well as measures to protect and promote employment more generally. A complete understanding of this evolution is impossible without taking the European dimension closely into account.

Nevertheless, employment has been and remains one of the most contested areas of policy-making in the EU and the structural obstacles to a 'European' policy, rather than a weak European coordination of national policies, are considerable. Employment policy may have moved closer to the centre of EU policy preoccupations, after several decades of policy initiatives, institutional and treaty innovations, experimentation with negotiated and 'new' modes of governance, and the creation of new fora for policy interaction. However, it remains a 'Cinderella' of the European integration project. In the absence of firm treaty foundations, the development of employment policy has relied critically throughout the entire period on the capacity of the Commission to engage in entrepreneurial agenda-setting and coalition-building around its legislative agenda, to solicit the support (which has been frequently provided) of the European Court of Justice (ECJ), and to forge coalitions—both with member states, behind social action programmes and treaty innovations, and with the national and European associations of capital and labour in support of new methods of policy-making. More recently, a more experimental technique has become evident, namely the creation of new 'policy spaces' for actors to fill and to develop across the multiple levels of the EU, providing a weak and insubstantial proxy for more traditional forms of institutionalization.

To employ the categories of EU policy-making set out in Chapter 3 of this volume, employment policy reveals a series of policy modes, ranging from the use of the Community method of legislating (albeit somewhat hesitantly due to the fragility of its treaty bases), through a peculiar and unique hybrid of the Community method and the regulatory approach in the post-Maastricht method of 'making law via collective agreement', to the softer modes of intervention characteristic of policy coordination and benchmarking in the EES. This transition is explained in our analysis of the three modes of policy-making currently extant in this sector. This analysis of EU policy is necessarily mainly rooted in the experience of western European countries, the old members of the EU. The contemporary EU25 brings into the frame a group of central and east, as well as south, European countries with other features.

Why has there been so much instability and continuous renovations to the architecture of European employment policy? There are several reasons: the changing nature of the employment 'problem'; the diversity of European labour-market organization and industrial relations; and the 'essentially contested' nature of employment regulation. First, the focus of employment policy-making has shifted quite radically over time, as the full employment in western Europe of the 1950s and 1960s gave way to a period of rising unemployment and declining employment rates in the crisis following the twin oil shocks of the 1970s. From then on, the link between GDP and job growth was broken. Successive economic upturns failed to return employment rates to pre-recession levels, revealing problems of industrial adjust-ment, mismatches between the supply and demand for skills, and a more general failure of west European welfare states to respond to the challenges of post-industrial economic development. By the 1990s, many west European countries were forced to cope with a crisis of 'welfare without work' and increasingly constrained policy choices. While still dealing with the legacy of the 1970s and 1980s in the form of long-term structural unemployment, they were also faced with a 'service sector trilemma' (Iversen and Wren 1998), in which the goals of employment growth, wage equality, and budgetary constraint come increasingly into conflict.

As some countries have discovered (the UK and Ireland), if service-sector employ-ment is to be generated in the private sector, then adjustments to wage and non-wage costs for the less skilled and greater wage inequality (unless compensated for by tax credits or in-work benefits) may have to be tolerated. Creating such employment through the public sector (the traditional Scandinavian solution) entails increased budgetary pressure at a time when deficits and higher taxes are definitely out of fashion. The alternative to doing neither would appear to be continuing, if not rising, unemployment—the unpalatable choice made *de facto* by those continental countries (France, Germany, and Italy) which have retained their high levels of labour-market regulation and employment protection, but have also lost their capacity for state-promoted job-creation (Ferrera, Hemerijck, and Rhodes 2001). But if European policy-makers have therefore had to shift their attention accordingly from employment protection to employment promotion, the diversity of European labour-market regulation and industrial relations complicates and frustrates attempts to tackle both of those goals with European rather than nation-specific policies.

National labour-market regimes are embedded in diverse social, political, and economic systems, or 'varieties of capitalism' (Hall and Soskice 2000), which render impossible both the harmonization of social protection and uniform approaches to job-creation. If 'welfare states are national states' (see Chapter 10), then employment regimes are coupled closely with them, and their social security, pensions, and unem-ployment benefit systems. Employment regime 'policy spaces' are densely occupied by national behavioural norms, long-standing entitlements backed by vested interest and client groups, and diverse forms of labour-market organization. Their industrial relations rules—derived from law or collective agreement, or complex combinations of the two—differ considerably. Broadly speaking, European industrial relations systems break down into: those in which the state plays a central role through both the constitutional provision of workers' rights and comprehensive labour-market legislation (Belgium, France, Germany, the Netherlands, Luxembourg, Italy, and Greece); those where the state has traditionally abstained from regulating industrial relations extensively by codes and legislation (the UK and Ireland); and those where a functional equivalent to legal and legislative frameworks is provided by corporatist-type agreements between employers and unions (Denmark and Sweden). However, systems of labour-market regulation map imperfectly on to this configuration. If employers in Germany, the Netherlands, Belgium, and the Nordic countries are heavily constrained by hiring, dismissals, and contract regulations, but enjoy more within-firm flexibility (due to high levels of skills and consensual workplace rule-setting), those in the UK and Ireland enjoy higher levels of internal and external flexibility (though a less-skilled workforce can constrain adjustment capacities), while their southern counterparts (Italy, Greece, Portugal, and Spain) have typically enjoyed neither, due to tightly constraining, state-legislated labour regulations and adversarial industrial relations. Flexibility has been delivered instead through the evasion of regulations and the emergence of dual labour-markets, dividing those on full-time contracts, and who are protected by law or collective bargaining, from a growing number of less protected fixed-term and part-time workers. Enlargement to the east complicates the mix still further by adding a fourth model, one in which state intervention, akin to that of the southern countries, is combined with the weak levels of unionization and firm-level representation of the Anglo-Irish group.

The third reason for instability and volatility in this domain of policy-making is that the issue of employment inevitably touches on core ideological differences concerning the appropriate degrees of economic regulation and the levels at which it is applied. Thus the process of EU employment policy development has been riven by a two-way conflict, or double cleavage, from the early days of the European project, and in particular from the 1970s on: between the supporters and opponents of an EU social dimension which would elevate distributive policies and politics to the European level (i.e. between 'federalists' and 'subsidiarists'); and between competing conceptions of how labour markets and social systems should be organized (crudely put, between socialists/social democrats and market liberals) (Rhodes 1992). Actors (politicians, trade unionists, and public officials, both national and European) can be found in various locations across the 2 x 2 space of political contestation and policy debates produced by this twin dichotomy.

Note that 'subsidiarists' are not always market liberals and centralizers are not always hyper-protectionists or even social democrats. However, this characterization is a useful first step in understanding the nature of the coalitions that have mobilized behind or against EU employment policy over the past several decades. It helps us to appreciate the continuing institutional weaknesses of Europe's employment policy-making architecture, and to assess the extent to which both 'old modes' and 'new modes' of governance in this policy arena have succeeded or failed. These difficulties confront both the traditional and the more innovative (albeit now ageing) channels of policy-making in employment policy, respectively the Community method and what we term below the 'negotiated' method of law-making. The great strength of the EES—albeit also a critical source of weaknesses—has been its explicit and quite novel attempt to bridge these twin dichotomies, so as to overcome the 'sovereignty' disputes endemic to EU employment policy, to dilute opposition to a further development of the 'social dimension', and to accommodate the diversity of the employment and welfare systems discussed above. Its success in doing so is assessed below. Its fate as the most ambitious, but also the most weakly institutionalized, mode of EU employment policy-making will depend on whether greater effectiveness can be achieved. This would also depend on forging links with the other, more traditional, modes of governance in this arena.

The three pillars of policy

Three institutional pillars of European employment policy have been constructed since the 1960s. The first is the legislated 'rights' pillar, based on the standard Community method, and used in fits and starts for employment issues from the 1960s onwards. Policy-making in this pillar has been conducted via decision-making rules based on both unanimity and (after the Single European Act, SEA) qualified majority voting (QMV) in the Council and implemented via directives, in which scope for variation in implementation has been restricted. The second pillar of 'law via collective agreement' has its roots in the sporadic instances of social dialogue promoted by the Commission between European-level employer and trade union confederations in the 1980s. This was backed by Article 118b (EEC) (now Art. 138 TEC), and formally institutionalized in the social policy agreement (Art. 4; now Art. 139 TEC) of the Maastricht Treaty on European Union (TEU). This allowed the social partners to request a Council decision on an employment policy agreement, or alternatively the implementation of directives via collective bargaining and 'national practice'. The third pillar is the more recent, more experimental, and more ambitious European Employment Strategy (EES)—a radically 'new' mode of governance (or 'open method of coordination'), dependent for implementation on persuasion and 'soft' compliance via benchmarking and peer review. The construction of each of these pillars has been limited by the need to account for the member state diversity mentioned above, by the rapidly evolving nature of labour markets, employment challenges, and business organization over recent decades, and by the two-way conflict over appropriate forms and levels of regulation and over the assumption and extension of supranational jurisdiction.

Each pillar links a particular form of policy-making with a specific mode of governance. In order to clarify those linkages and their implications for policy outcomes, we adopt the typology developed by Treib, Bühr, and Falkner (2004) (see Fig. 11.1). The first pillar employs binding legal instruments (directives) with a rigid form of implementation via labour law, backed by the courts (national and European). This constitutes the most coercive form of governance. However, the treaty requirements insist that employment legislation respect variations in industrial relations and labour law systems. Employment directives therefore typically avoid harmonizing objectives and aspire instead to 'partial harmonization' or 'diversity built on common standards'

Figure 11.1 Policy instruments and modes of governance

		Legal instrument	
		binding	non-binding
Implementation	rigid	I Coercion (pillar 1)	III Targeting (pillar 2)
	flexible	II Framework Regulation (pillar 2)	IV Voluntarism (pillar 3)

Source: Treib, Bühr, and Falkner (2004).

(Kenner 2003: 30–1). Thus, except in those cases, such as equal opportunities and equal pay, where there has been a stronger treaty base for legislation, and in particular for ECJ case law, the real extent of coercion has been limited by the problems of implementing EU labour law across very different national systems. The second pillar of 'law via collective agreement' produces binding but flexible instruments (e.g. framework legislation that offers a menu of alternatives for member states to choose), as well as non-binding but rigid instruments (e.g. targeted recommendations that contain explicit rules of conduct for workers and employers). This approach relies heavily on negotiation—at both the European and national levels—between social actors. This is a flexible form of governance, but one still potentially conducive to effective implementation. Nonetheless, the impact of directives produced in this pillar has been weak, owing to political opposition to upward harmonization and the institutional fragility of this experimental form of law-making. The third pillar comprises the EES through the open method of coordination, using non-binding and flexible instruments. This is a 'voluntarist' form of governance with still weaker implementation capacities than the second pillar, and uncertain links between policy inputs and outputs. Open-ended experimentation, in both the form and substance of policy-making, takes priority over the search for efficacy as such.

Over time, there has been a shift of focus from the first, to the second, and then to the third pillars, involving (to use the terminology of Chapter 3) a diversification of policy modes away from the distinctive Community method, through the EU regulatory model, to policy coordination and benchmarking in a context of multi-party, multilevel interaction. This is largely due, I argue, to the efforts of the Commission and pro-integration élites to work around vetoes and to neutralize the operation of the 'double cleavage'. However, 'new' and experimental modes of governance and policy instruments have not decisively replaced the old: policy-making continues to be conducted differently in each of the three pillars. Moreover, it is important to note that 'soft law', in various forms, has a long history in European employment policy-making. It has promoted, consolidated, and sometimes supplanted more coercive 'hard law' initiatives, and is far from being restricted to the more recent phase of the EES.

Employment policy-making before Amsterdam

Pillar one: between the 'Community method' and the EU regulatory model

In the first pillar of employment policy, that concerned with the production of directives, the distinctive Community method defined in Chapter 3—with a strong Commission involved in policy design, policy-brokering, and policy execution, and a fully-empowered Council engaged in strategic bargaining and package deals—has been an aspiration rather than a reality. Much of the frenetic political activity in this arena since the 1960s has been linked to this ambition, and each of the major treaty revisions has witnessed a struggle over providing a more solid legal base for European employment intervention. However, the history of EU employment legislation has been a tortured one, with the Commission acting as tireless promoter of new regulatory objectives and rules, often in the face of intense political opposition, the Council forging agreement on minimum standards, to be implemented differentially in individual countries, and the ECJ providing backing for those standards, but refraining from over-zealous judgments where the treaty basis was unclear. These are all characteristics of the EU regulatory model, and use of the Community method as such has been restricted to those few areas where there has been a sound treaty basis for legislation (some aspects of health and safety, for example, and gender equality at work), or where the original legal base for employment directives has, in certain limited cases, been replaced by a stronger treaty alternative.

Certainly, the main obstacles to an EU-wide regime of employment regulation have been structural—the contrasts between national employment and industrial relations systems, the close links between employment protection and national welfare systems, and the constantly moving target of employment policy over recent decades, as the economic and business environment has evolved. However, even this constrained approached has been made more difficult by member states' jealousy of their jurisdiction over social and employment policy, which has limited efforts to strengthen the legal foundations for European intervention. The Treaty of Rome (EEC) made only highly ambiguous provision for EU social or employment policy. Articles 117–122 (EEC) (social provisions) conferred few real powers upon the EU institutions. Under Article 117 (EEC) working conditions and standards were intended to flow from the functioning of the common market, as well as from law, regulation, or administrative action, thus providing the basis for the ensuing conflict between pro-integration forces which relied on the first, and their opponents which invoked the second. Article 118 (EEC) simply required the Commission to promote cooperation between the member states through studies, opinions, and consultations. Given the market-oriented nature of the Treaty of Rome, social and employment policies were to be used for correcting obvious market failures, not for creating a supranational welfare state. But there was early intergovernmental conflict over when European regulation could be used to defend national systems from regulatory competition. The French believed that some form of social security harmonization would protect their high social charges from creating competitive disadvantage, and that gender equality provisions in the French constitution should be transferred to the Treaty, while the

Germans were opposed to any legal competence for the supranational authorities in this area (Rhodes 1999). The only substantial concession made to the French position was Article 119 (EEC) on the principle of equal pay. As a result, many of the employment policy advances from the 1960s onwards were based on alternative articles. In the early 1970s, for example, the Council of Ministers made use of Articles 100 and 235 (EEC). These empowered the Council to issue directives and regulations for the approximation of national regulatory systems, including laws, insofar as they directly affected the establishment and functioning of the common market, and led to directives on dismissals (in 1974) and workers' rights in the event of mergers (1975).

Subsequent treaty revisions sought to strengthen the basis for employment policy, but only meagre steps were made, and each time only after major clashes and compromises between member states. In the SEA, Community competences were bolstered, but only for health and safety issues where regulation could be justified as preventing potential market distortions. Article 118a (EEC) thus granted the Commission the power of proposition in health and safety legislation after consultation with the Economic and Social Committee, gave the EP a second reading of proposals through the then new cooperation procedure, and allowed the Council to act under QMV. Yet such directives were constrained by the proviso that small and medium-sized firms should be protected from excessive regulatory burdens. Elsewhere in the SEA, although Article 100a (EEC) introduced QMV for measures essential for the construction of the single market, British and German opposition ensured that those relating to the free movement of persons and rights and interests of workers were explicitly excluded (Rhodes 1992; Majone 1993).

By the time of the TEU, there was a broader coalition of member states in favour of European regulation of employment and other social issues to provide safeguards against a regulatory 'race-to-the-bottom', as the single market deepened and the prospect of eventual currency union became closer. Yet ferocious opposition from the British government placed a major constraint on any new supranational transfer of powers, and the reinforced subsidiarity principle in treaty terms as a means of forestalling federalism also limited the effect of new provisions (van Kersbergen and Verbeek 2004). The ambition, especially of the northern member states (apart from the UK), was to resolve procedural disputes by bringing most areas of labour-market policy under QMV, and to extend Community competence to contractual rights and workers' representation and consultation. In the final agreement adopted as the Social Protocol by eleven member states (the UK opted out), only health and safety, work conditions, and equality at work fell under QMV. In the revised Articles 117–18 (TEC) (Arts. 1–2 of the Social Agreement), there were bolstered references to the need to respect member state differences and to avoid new regulatory burdens on small and medium-sized firms.

Only with the Treaty of Amsterdam (ToA) in 1997—when the UK also revoked its opt-out under a new Labour government—was QMV extended to worker information and consultation and the integration of persons excluded from the labour market. But most areas of employment policy remained under unanimity voting, while pay, the right of association, and the right to strike and to impose lock-outs were excluded from Community competence altogether (Art. 137(6) TEC).

Given these constraints, the Commission sought to exploit the fragile treaty bases to the maximum, sometimes backed up by the ECJ in its case law, and sometimes by making what lawyers call 'soft law' initiatives. Thus, it put forward recommendations and codes of practice so as to strengthen the application of existing laws, and 'solemn declarations', such as the 1989 Social Charter, or 'social action programmes', to push forward the processes of coalition-building and to set the agenda for further measures. Thus, in the mid-1970s, the Commission's Social Action Programme, adopted by a Council Resolution, provided the soft-law basis for negotiation and coalition-building around a new series of subsequent employment policy directives (see Kenner 2003: ch. 2). During the period of acute intergovernmental conflict over social policy between the SEA and Maastricht, the Commission proposed a series of employment initiatives by playing the 'treaty-base game', in which it stretched as far as possible the interpretation of 'health and safety' to include workplace directives, using QMV for the treaty base in order to minimize member-state opposition (Rhodes 1995). Even the 1989 Social Charter emerged from a process of conflict and eventual compromise as a vague and non-binding document setting out the basic social rights of workers in the EU. Efforts to introduce 'harder' instruments, such as a framework directive on basic rights and a binding European workers' statute, were defeated. Nonetheless, an important social action programme of legislative proposals emerged in the early 1990s and provided an important impetus for mobilizing the social policy advances eventually achieved at Maastricht and Amsterdam (Rhodes 1991).

This did not, however, add up to a more solid legal base. The 1974 Social Action Programme and the 'treaty-base game' of the 1980s and 1990s revealed a considerable difference in the nature and quality of regulation in those areas with solid legal foundations, from those based on 'creative regulation' and justified as 'health and safety', which usually translated into poor law with limited effects. The Social Action Programme, developed at the time of the first oil shock, allowed for a series of innovations in employment protection. The Council went along with the occasional use of Article 100 (EEC) (now Art. 94 TEC) for single market measures and Article 235 (EEC) (now Art. 308 TEC), providing for law-making not covered specifically in the Treaty. Measures were agreed to improve labour mobility and to create a level-playing field for competition, including Directive 75/129 on procedural rights under collective redundancies, Directive 77/187 on rights of employees under changes of ownership of undertakings, and Directive 80/987 guaranteeing state compensation to employees of insolvent companies. These were deemed appropriate in a period of extensive industrial restructuring and could be subject to different forms of implementation in line with national practices. A further half dozen directives on equal pay and equal treatment were based on the more solid Article 119 (EEC) (now Art. 141 TEC), which has a legal base of unanimity, in the mid-1980s. These were spurred on by the role of the ECJ, which had linked direct effect with the principle that community law had supremacy over national law. Jurisprudence on equal pay and equal treatment helped ensure the implementation of directives. Furthermore, the first framework directive (80/1107) on health and safety at work, produced a series of 'daughter directives' on specific hazards, plus further soft law in the form of a Council Recommendation on a forty-hour week and four weeks annual paid holiday (a forerunner of the later working time directive). A second framework directive (89/391) laid down general objectives and obligations on employers and workers, while leaving scope for varied application at the national level, and ultimately producing fourteen daughter directives and a series of action programmes.

The legislation of the late 1980s and early 1990s based on creative regulation was much less successful. The effort to define workers' rights as a health and safety issue, thus subject to QMV so as to avoid the British veto (during the Thatcher, then Major, Conservative governments), severely weakened the impact of the directives. Thus, the Pregnancy and Maternity Directive (92/85) has ensured health protection, but has been less effective with regard to employment discrimination. The Working Time Directive (93/104) was innovative in allowing some elements to be implemented through collective agreements (a practice which widened under negotiated pillar two), but it excluded a number of sectors, and allowed important derogations for member states, such as the UK opt-out for individual workers. The Young Workers Directive (94/33) created rights for workers under the age of eighteen, and banned work under the age of fifteen, but contained many derogations, such as the UK's special entitlement to delay implementation (Kenner 2003).

Pillar two: the social dialogue and law via collective agreement

One of the key innovations of the Maastricht TEU as regards social policy was its creation of an alternative mode of law-making involving the European social partners, in an 'inter-professional social dialogue' at the European level. There were several motives for this. The first was that it gave formal status and potentially considerable influence to employers and trade unions at the European level through a process of dialogue that had been promoted by the European Commission and lobbied for by Europe's most powerful labour movements. The German unions in particular, following their disappointment with the anodyne final form of the 1989 Social Charter, committed themselves to a reorganization and reinvigoration of the rather weak European Trade Union Confederation (ETUC). The second was the hope that, given continuing British opposition to any advances in European social and employment policy, this new approach to law-making would provide an alternative means for mobilizing support for such initiatives. Thirdly, this shift to directives produced at EU level, but implemented in the member states via negotiation, would better accommodate the diversity of European industrial relations, given the range between collective agreements and legal codes as systems for underpinning labour-market relations and policy development.

By 1991, employers had accepted, at least in principle, the procedural importance of rule-setting at the EC level through the social dialogue. In the past, employers had tried to keep the social dialogue in check, and the Union of Industrial and Employers' Confederations (UNICE), the peak European association, had consistently opposed both EU-level collective bargaining and any legislative enhancement of workers' participation rights in transnational companies. But Article 118b (SEA) obliged the Commission to promote dialogue between management and labour, and in October 1991 UNICE and ETUC were able to agree to a joint proposal for a new form of bargaining over employment legislation. In the meantime, the Commission had promoted discussions between UNICE, CEEP (European Centre of Enterprises with Public Participation and of Enterprises of General Economic Interest), and the ETUC through joint union-employer working parties on the economy, employment, social dialogue, and new technologies. Thus, the Commission succeeded in creating new 'policy spaces' and extending European responsibilities into new domains as the basis for future institutional development. After 1989 this process became more focused, prioritizing education and training, and producing four joint opinions on: the promotion of labour mobility; education; vocational guidance; and management-labour partnerships. These provided the groundwork for two key agreements: the September 1990 framework agreement, signed by CEEP and the ETUC, on improving vocational training and health and safety via social dialogue; and, most importantly, a joint submission to the Intergovernmental Conferences, which in 1991 negotiated the TEU, proposing a new role for the social partners in making and implementing EC policy (Rhodes 1995; Falkner 1998).

To the surprise of its proponents, this submission was inserted almost *verbatim* into the Social Protocol of the TEU (later integrated into the ToA), creating a complex set of procedures for the pursuit of law via collective agreement. First, all directives, whether adopted by QMV or by unanimity, can be entrusted to 'management and labour' at their joint request for implementation via collective agreement. Secondly, the Commission is obliged, before submitting proposals, to consult management and labour on the possible consequences of Community action. The social partners may in response forward an opinion or, if appropriate, a recommendation. Thirdly, and most importantly for the discussion here, the social partners can opt for the contractual option and negotiate directly the content of Commission proposals, proceeding, if they are able, to a collective agreement. With even more flexibility, any such agreements can then be implemented by a further negotiation in the member states in accordance with their own procedures and practices, or via a Council decision on a proposal from the Commission.

The negotiation procedure was first used in 1993 when the Commission presented a modified version of a legislative proposal on the creation of European works councils that had failed the normal legislative route in various forms in preceding years. However, this tactic failed when the British employers in effect vetoed any agreement on the part of UNICE, and the Commission was forced to return to the standard method of submitting proposals for legislation to the Council. It finally steered through a directive on the establishment of European works councils under the Social Protocol (i.e. the standard legislative process, but excluding the UK), under which management must institute fora for informing and consulting employees in all companies with more than one thousand employees and more than 150 in at least two member states. Several other proposals have been successfully translated into social framework agreements in subsequent years: Directive 96/34 on parental leave; Directive 97/81 on part-time work; and Directive 99/70 on fixed-term work. Like the proposal on European works councils, all three were redirected by the Commission to the social agreement channel after failure to achieve success via the standard legislative route.

Although apparently a triumph for those seeking a European level of employment regulation, the limited use of the new social policy agreement procedures prior to Amsterdam has been described as 'a derisory outcome' for those who had worked to break the impasse in social and employment policy-making at Maastricht (Kenner 2003: 291). The legislation does provide real regulatory added value, in that its minimal standards and flexibility limited its impact to the least well regulated countries. While the directive on parental leave has been criticized as a 'lowest common denominator' agreement, the directive on part-time work has been characterized as weak, consisting of a series of non-obligatory provisions that are unlikely to achieve the objective of removing discrimination against this category of workers, and the directive on fixed-term work has been called a 'missed opportunity' to regulate one of the most insecure forms of agency work, and in most member states little or no change was required to existing national laws (Kenner 2003: 290).

The gradual shift towards negotiated and 'non-coercive' framework agreements of this kind had facilitated political agreement in a period of intransigent opposition to European employment policy initiatives; this came especially from European employers and the British government, but also from other member states committed to enhanced subsidiarity. However, the compromises required to achieve this meant a major loss in policy effectiveness. At most, the negotiated framework legislation put a minimum floor of rights under existing systems of regulation. The relative weaknesses in the organization and representation of the social partners at the European level also militated against a major leap forward. Most important, however, was the shift in focus of European policy-making soon after Maastricht away from employment *protection* towards new objectives of *employment* promotion.

Employment policy post-Amsterdam

Pillar three: the EES and the OMC

The European Employment Strategy (EES) marks a radical departure from the policy developments of the past, in at least two ways. First, it moves beyond the traditional preoccupation with employment protection to the issue of creating new employment. This implied the involvement of 'Europe' in areas of national sovereignty that had previously been jealously guarded from intervention. The second innovation was the elaboration of a strategy and instruments that would simultaneously target the issue of job-creation—in terms of both quantity and quality—while also allaying fears in the member states of unwarranted intrusion into their domestic social, employment, and broader economic policies. In part the EES was a policy response from a pro-integration coalition, spanning the Commission, the Parliament, and member states, to the failures and blockages afflicting policy development over the years in the other two pillars. It was also a political response to economic and monetary union (EMU) which prevented individual countries from using expansionist monetary and fiscal policies to stimulate economic and employment growth (see Chapter 6). What emerged was a broad, multi-faceted job-creation strategy, based on non-binding, soft-law instruments of peer review, benchmarking, and persuasion. The EES also represents an ambitious attempt to overcome the enduring double cleavage between 'federalists' and 'subsidiarists' on the one hand, and between socialists/social democrats and market liberals on the other, by means of a new, experimental method of policy-making. This aim of accommodating and defusing ideological divisions and

Table 11.1 The European employment strategy (EES) and the open method of coordination (OMC)

	EES	OMC
Source of legitimacy	Legal	Political
Legal or political	Treaty of Amsterdam: Employment Title	Lisbon Summit (2000) Part 3 Draft Constitutional Treaty
Policy area	employment	social inclusion, pensions, education, research, and innovation
Policy aim	unidimensional	multi-dimensional
Instrumental differences	stronger	weaker

sovereignty dispute, is the major strength of the EES, but also a critical source of its weakness. Tables 11.1 summarizes developments.

Origins and institutional development

How did the notion of a common European employment policy arrive on the agenda in the period leading up to Amsterdam? In essence, the Commission, by operating in full entrepreneurial mode, managed to fashion a coalition of social-democratic governments around the relaunching of employment policy as an active policy domain (Arnold 2002). It had to negotiate around the traditional vetoes to boosting supranational competences in this arena. Many countries, for example, Sweden and the Netherlands, were sympathetic to the new emphasis on employment issues, but were keen advocates of subsidiarity and opposed to an unbridled transfer of power to Brussels. The spill-over from EMU was political rather than functional, and flowed from the need of social democratic governments to legitimize their almost unanimous support for EMU with their electorates and other domestic constituencies, primarily the labour movement (Notermans 2001; van Riel and van Meer 2002).

The EES began to take form after the Essen European Council (1994), following the spur to change in EU policy orientations given by the Delors Commission's White Paper, *Growth, Competitiveness and Employment* in 1993 (Commission 1993c). Highlighting Europe's poor performance in an era of accelerating economic and technological change, the Commission advanced a series of guidelines for reform. In an attempt to blend the political priorities of European social democrats, christian democrats, and liberals, the tactical aim was to strike a balance between solidarity and competitiveness. But due to counter-pressures from several member states, there was little real progress at the time (Goetschy 2003; Mosher and Trubek 2003). A stronger interpretation of the Delors vision developed through negotiations and bargaining between the member states, notably in sessions of the European Council, in Madrid in December 1995 and in Dublin in 1996, with the Commission spurring progress along, by striking alliances with key European coalitions (most importantly the Group of European Socialists) and organizing peer-pressure on the most reluctant states, principally Germany.

An agreement was reached on the form of the employment strategy at the 1997 European Council in Amsterdam. The aim and mode of functioning of the EES is set out in the Title VIII (later XI) of the ToA (Arts. 125–30) on employment. The main objective was the achievement of a high level of employment, through the promotion of a 'skilled, trained and adaptable workforce and labour markets responsive to economic change'. Under Article 126 (TEC), the Community should contribute to that end 'by encouraging cooperation between member states and by supporting, and if necessary complementing, their action'. The guidelines are not binding—an essential feature for the compromise that eventually brought all members states on board; but by its inclusion in the ToA, the EES became part of the processes in which member states are obliged to participate. The process of policy deliberation envisaged was put into effect at the Luxembourg European Council in November 1997, since when it has been repeated on a yearly basis. The first set of (nineteen) European Employment Guidelines (EEGs) was adopted, based on four strands: employability, entrepreneurship, adaptability, and equal opportunities, each containing between three and seven guidelines.[2] The 2000 Lisbon European Council confirmed its support for the EES method, and also began its extension as a method of policy-making to other areas. It committed the member states to striving for 'full employment', coupled with new quantitative objectives: a 70 per cent overall employment rate and a 60 per cent female employment rate by 2010 (targets that had been lobbied for by the Commission, gathering allies where possible, but without result since the 1993 Delors White Paper). At Lisbon, and in the European Councils that followed at Nice and Stockholm, successive Council presidencies, held by social democratic governments, acted closely in alliance with the Commission and the EP to sustain their coalition, to propel the EES forward, and to extend the coverage of OMC (van Riel and van Meer 2002). Nevertheless, and regardless of the attempt to appease those who opposed new EU powers over employment policy, the EES was to remain contested terrain, both ideologically and in power games between the Council and the Commission.

The EES as a 'new mode of governance'

When first launched, the EES had a relatively low profile as a complement to the process of building EMU. It is only since the elevating of the term 'open method of coordination' (OMC) at the Lisbon European Council in 2000, and its extension beyond the EES to other areas of policy-making, such as social exclusion, that the EES has become a topic of intense interest and debate. It exemplifies a 'new mode of governance', which differs along numerous dimensions both from the traditional Community method and from the older hard-law and soft-law procedures that preceded it. The growing literature on the subject has identified as its key characteristics: the heterarchical (i.e. non-hierarchical) participation of actors; a 'new' problem-solving logic based on deliberation and 'policy learning'; the use of benchmarking and reference to 'best practice'; and both vertical and horizontal policy integration across the EU's multi-level polity (Scott and Trubeck 2002; Cohen and Sabel 2003; Borrás and

Jacobsson 2004). Undoubtedly, these features can all be found in the EES. They are argued to be in part a response to the functional requirements of an expanding (and deepening) EU, given its coordination problems, stalemates due to blocked or delayed transfers of policy powers, and the increasing functional interdependence of policy areas (Borrás and Jacobsson 2004).

Ultimately, the EES is a political strategy and the success of these new 'voluntary' methods is linked to hard political realities. In terms of policy aims, the EES is closely linked politically to the Maastricht process and EMU. The EES was used to gain support for EMU and owes its existence—and institutionalization—to that strategy and the political coalition behind it. While that linkage helps make the EES stronger than other areas using OMC (social exclusion, pensions, etc.), helped by the available range of policy instruments (relatively 'hard' forms of 'soft law', tough 'peer review', and so forth), it is much weaker than the Maastricht Social Protocol, and some would argue than the EMU's Stability and Growth Pact (SGP) in one critical respect, namely the incentive structure—or 'shadow of hierarchy' (Héritier 2003)—to compel member-state compliance. Both 'competition incentives' (exposure to market sanctions, whether for the individual country or for the EU as a whole), and 'cooperation incentives' (peer pressure on poor performers triggered by the adverse impact on the rest of the 'club') operate very differently in the two cases (Morelli, Padoan, and Rodano 2002). In principle, at least, the rules for conformity in economic policy behaviour (regardless of recent infringements of the SGP by large member states), are easier to establish and to police than are targets for social policy and job-creation.

The core issue at stake here is the extent to which 'new modes of governance' such as OMC, based on guidelines, benchmarks, and notions of best practice, translate into the real world of policy influence and impact. As Héritier (2003: 118–19) has argued, there is a trade-off between *political capacity* (the costs involved in reaching agreement) and *policy effectiveness*, but even political capacity can be reduced, once an initial focus on general principles turns to efforts to agree more specific goals and indicators. It is certainly true that the EES has been a far from conflict-free zone. Its effectiveness is indeed difficult to determine, unless 'effectiveness' is redefined to include changes in policy outlook, the creation of new alliances, altered ways of thinking, and shifts in the equilibrium of domestic policy-making (Mosher and Trubek 2003).

Actors and the EES policy process

In formal terms, the roles of the actors and relations between them can be set out in terms of the EES cycle of 'policy coordination'. This cycle was reformed substantially at the Brussels European Council in June 2003, not only to 'mainstream' the EES within the Lisbon Strategy, but also in response to complaints from the member states over the excessive complexity and high level of detail in EES guidelines, the considerable overlap between the EES and other processes, and the duplication of work for national officials (see Jacobsson 2004a). The pre- and post-reform policy cycles are illustrated in Table 11.2.

From 1997 to 2002, the policy cycle was repeated on a yearly basis. It began with agenda-setting. In practice, the rotating presidency of the Council has considerable influence in the agenda-setting process, as does the Commission, which provides the 'support team' as well as analytical and preparatory documents. Policy objectives

Table 11.2 Key characteristics of the EES

Features/Process	European Employment Strategy (EES), 1997–2002	After adaptations, 2003
Started	1997	2003
Cycle	Annual	Tri-annual; synchronized with Broad Economic Policy Guidelines (BEPG)
Policy objectives	+/− twenty guidelines organized around four strands	Ten 'result-oriented' priorities around three overarching aims
Number of cycles undergone	Five	One
Key participants, those who make the actual decisions	Ministers of employment and social affairs (in Council formation) in close collaboration with the European Commission	Ministers of employment and social affairs (in Council formation) in collaboration with the European Commission
Final veto point, through QMV	Ministers of social affairs and employment (in Council formation)	Ministers of social affairs and employment (in Council formation)
Mandatory consultative participants	European and national social partners, European Parliament, ECOSOC, Committee of Regions (CoR)	European and national social partners, European Parliament, ECOSOC, CoR
Legal basis of process	Employment Chapter of ToA, 1997	Employment Chapter of ToA, 1997
Technical indicators and targets	99 indicators in 2002, 35 key indicators, and 64 context indicators; 70% overall employment rate (2000) to be reached 2010; 60% female employment rate (2000) to be reached 2010; 50% older workers employment rate (2001) to be reached 2010	64 indicators in 2003: 39 key indicators and 25 context indicators
Peer review (or in-built incentive structures for 'learning')	Annual peer review of the National Actions Plans (NAPs) ('Cambridge process'); peer review programme on active labour market policies (from 1999 onwards)	Annual peer review of the NAP ('Cambridge process'); peer review programme on active labour market policies (from 1999 onwards); political aim to focus the 'Cambridge process' on one objective only to render it more effective

were decided in phase two. Until 2002 these objectives were set out in terms of twenty or so guidelines, organized around the four strands of employability, entrepreneurship, adaptability, and equal opportunities. Since 2003 they have been presented in the form of ten 'results-oriented' priorities structured around three objectives: full employment; quality and productivity at work; and social cohesion and inclusion (see Table 11.3). The Commission draws up the guidelines, which are then endorsed by the Council on a legal base of QMV. In the third phase, member governments prepare national action plans (NAPs), in which they set out the measures they will take to 'comply' with these objectives. The Commission prepares the draft of the joint employment report, assessing the overall change in the employment situation in the EU and the implementation of the employment guidelines. This is then modified, if deemed appropriate, and endorsed by the Employment, Social Affairs, Health and Consumer Affairs Council (EPSCO). Finally, it is approved by the European Council. In parallel, the Commission makes individual recommendations, which are also endorsed by the Council, to each member state. The recommendation tool, as defined in the ToA,[3] is a key element that distinguishes the EES from other areas covered by OMC. The Commission was given the right to make recommendations, subject to the approval of EPSCO. They were used for the first time in 1999, and have since then been deployed on a yearly basis as a means of placing pressure on the member governments to meet the guideline objectives. In the fourth stage of the cycle, member governments prepare their NAPs in response to the recommendations. These are then 'peer reviewed' in the so-called 'Cambridge process'—a closed two-day meeting of the Employment Committee (EMCO), which is comprised of two delegates from each member state and two members from the Commission, and which monitors employment and employment policies in the member states.[4] The peer review is followed by bilateral meetings on the NAPs between representatives of governments and the Commission. From 2003, it was decided that the peer review session should focus more closely on the implementation of the employment recommendations (King 2003).

In principle, this process is given an important infusion of democracy and legitimacy by the involvement of political and interest group representatives. According to the ToA, the EP has to be consulted on the EES, although in practice its role was somewhat marginal during the first five years. This was due, among other reasons, to the lack of time allowed by the process for the preparation of positions or opinions (European Parliament 2002; King 2003). However, the timetable of the EES as modified from 2003 creates additional time for the EP to prepare its opinion for the annual June European Council, where the EES is discussed (Commission 2002f), and this may provide an opportunity for closer involvement. The social partners have a treaty-based mandate for participating in the EES, although it is rather vague. According to Article 130 (TEC), in fulfilling its mandate EMCO 'shall consult management and labour', which in practice means employer and union organizations at the European level. The main treaty reference to *national* level social partner involvement is in Article 126(2), which states that 'Member States, *having regard to national practices related to the responsibilities of management and labour*, shall regard promoting employment as a matter of common concern' (our emphasis). While there is no formal requirement for the involvement of the social partners in drawing up the NAPs, in practice they are consulted, though their degree of involvement and satisfaction with their role vary greatly from one country to the next.

Table 11.3 The 2003 revision of the EES four-strand structure

Guidelines 1997–2002	Result-oriented priorities since 2003
Activation and the prevention of long-term unemployment, especially addressing young unemployed (employability strand)	Active and preventive measures for the unemployed and the inactive
Reviewing benefit, tax, and training systems to reduce poverty traps and to make it more attractive and easier for the unemployed to access training and employment (employability strand)	Making work pay
1. Making it easier to start up and run businesses, with a particular focus on promoting small and medium-sized enterprises (SMEs). Activities include the encouragement of greater entrepreneurial awareness across society and in educational curricula, the provision of clear and stable rules for the development of, and access to, risk capital markets, and the reduction and simplification of administrative and tax burdens on SMEs. 2. Creating new opportunities for employment in the knowledge-based society and in services, where there is a considerable potential for job creation. There should not only be a focus on the quantity, but also on the quality of the jobs created. 3. Enhancing regional and local action for employment by identifying and encouraging the potential of job creation at local and regional levels. 4. Reforming taxation to favour employment and training. (4 guidelines under the entrepreneurship strand)	Fostering entrepreneurship to create more and better jobs
	Transforming undeclared work into regular employment
Developing a comprehensive policy for active ageing (employability strand)	Promoting active ageing
	Immigration
1. Modernizing the organization of work to achieve an appropriate balance between flexibility and security, and to contribute to improving the quality of work. Flexible	Promoting adaptability in the labour market

work arrangements are to be developed further. Atypical work contracts are also to be incorporated further into the national law, to provide atypical workers with more security and higher occupational status. 2. Supporting adaptability and innovation in enterprises as a component of lifelong learning. All workers should be provided with the possibility to achieve information society literacy by 2003. (Both guidelines from the adaptability strand)	
Skill-development for a perpetually changing labour market in the context of life-long learning. This guideline targets the improvement of the quality of education and training systems, for optimal adaptation to the labour market. Special reference is made to e-learning. Particular attention is to be paid to youth in disadvantaged groups and to adult illiteracy (employability strand).	Investment in human capital and strategies for lifelong learning
1. Gender mainstreaming approach calling for integrating gender issues transversally into the EES. 2. Tackling gender gaps in unemployment rates, ensuring a balanced representation of men and women in all sectors and occupations, and taking measures to achieve gender pay equality in both the public and private sectors. 3. Reconciling work and family life through the design and the implementation of family-friendly policies, including affordable, and high-quality care services for children and other dependants, as well as parental and other leave schemes. (3 guidelines under the gender equality strand)	Gender equality
Combating discrimination of access to and on the labour market. This guideline calls for the establishment of a coherent set of policies to promote the social inclusion of disadvantaged groups through employment (employability strand).	Supporting integration and combating discrimination in the labour market for people at a disadvantage
	Addressing regional disparities

Note: The new result-oriented priorities do not include under-employability: setting out active policies to develop job-matching and to combat emerging bottlenecks in the new European labour markets.

Efficacy versus experimentation

As we have seen, employment policy in the past has been characterized by conflict over the transfer of policy powers to the supranational authorities and the appropriate degree of EU-wide regulation. With the EES it was hoped that a political consensus on employment policy could be more easily achieved given the soft-law character of its policy instruments and its explicit acceptance of diversity among member states in the implementation of EES objectives. Much of the literature on the EES has focused on these deliberative, positive-sum, consensus-seeking qualities, as if the efforts on the part of certain European élites to escape from decades of political conflict in this arena had indeed been achieved. A closer analysis of the EES in operation reveals, however, several key features reminiscent of experience in the first two employment pillars: a struggle between the 'competence-maximizing' aspirations of the Commission and concern from the member states to contain them; sovereignty disputes over the extent to which European policy would penetrate still jealously-guarded national policy domains; and tension between the 'heterarchical' or 'network governance' pretensions of the EES and its tendency in practice to replicate more traditional top-down policy hierarchies.

All three conflicts have characterized the functioning of EMCO, which lies at the core of the process. This has been characterized as a kind of 'deliberative institution' located between the Commission and the member states, although it has continued to be driven by intergovernmental, interest-driven bargaining rather than results-oriented open deliberation. It has become increasingly politicized as member governments have sought to use it as a forum for shaping the policy agenda. Thus, in an early 'sovereignty dispute' in the late 1990s, many member governments reacted with hostility to the overt early use of the recommendation tool. They were especially dismayed at the quasi-secretive manner in which the Commission had engineered the process, and then extensively publicized its recommendations so as to exert peer pressure. After intense debate, the Commission and EMCO jointly agreed that they should refrain from being polemical, should be open to amendments, and, rather than classify member states according to their performance, they should treat them on an equal footing. Member governments have since become closely involved in the elaboration of recommendations, and Commission proposals are discussed horizontally among governments, rather than being imposed top-down (Barbier and Samba Sylla 2004). But this often amounts less to deliberation than to old-fashioned bargaining. Discussions in EMCO, report Jacobsson and Vifell (2003: 16), have increasingly taken the form of negotiations based on national positions rather than open-ended exchanges of opinion or reflections on best practice.[5]

A second 'sovereignty dispute' took place over a period of eighteen months in 2002–3 preceding the transformation of the EES guidelines, in line with pressure from member governments. Jobelius (2003) illustrates how preferences were mobilized on both sides and with what effect. While the Commission sought to promote further integration via new channels of influence over national policies, the latter actively resisted. The conflict was resolved only when the Commission abandoned its proposed new quantitative targets in all areas except for education and measures to 'activate' the unemployed. A Commission injunction on member states to ensure that adequate financial resources were deployed behind the employment policy guidelines was also replaced by a call for more 'transparent and cost-effective' finance (Watt 2004: 131). The OMC and soft law supposedly provide the Commission with a proactive role in taking a broad rather than piecemeal approach to policy, allowing it to expand cooperation to new areas formerly under national competence, thus effectively by-passing the subsidiarity principle (Jacobsson 2004b). But the Council has fiercely resisted this *de facto* extension of Commission influence, and has arguably been the winner in the OMC power stakes (King 2003; Borrás and Jacobsson 2004).

A further strengthening of member states' power *vis-à-vis* the Council is evident in other aspects of the EES reform. Although it has been claimed that the EES has survived the 'litmus test of governmental shifts', the 2003 reform occurred at a time when right-wing governments dominated the European political landscape. The earlier social democratic coalition had fragmented. This had an inevitable impact on employment priorities. Liberal market concerns were evident in the shift from the four-strand approach to the three 'core objective' structure. They were also reflected in an increasingly tortured discourse to depict EES aims, given the difficulty of reconciling the priorities of social democratic solidarity with those of liberal market flexibility. Thus the Commission's 2003 statement on *The Future of the European Employment Strategy* (Commission 2003d) argued that labour-market flexibility should be encouraged, especially in the form of different contractual arrangements, 'while at the same time steps should be taken to prevent a segmentation of the labour market between different types of workers' (Raveaud 2005), two contradictory aims.

A good deal of prominence has been given to the involvement and participation in the EES of the social partners and other interest groups. Grand claims have been made for the development of a new form of 'networked governance'. The reality is rather more prosaic. The participation of the social partners, the ETUC on the union side, and UNICE, the CEEP, and the UEAPME (European Association of Craft, Small and Medium-sized Enterprises) on the employers' side, has been patchy to date, and the participation of labour and management in the EES has been widely recognized as one of its weakest parts (Smismans 2003; De La Porte and Pochet 2004). The EES policy cycle is not a heterarchical and deliberative process with open access to a wide range of groups. It is actually rather closed, élitist, and arguably much less democratic and accountable than standard community methods (Syrpis 2002). In particular, parliamentary influence (whether national or European) is extremely limited, and there is no judicial review. The Council and the Commission are in practice the key decision-makers.

What does this imply for the linkages between EU-level impulses and the transformation of national employment policies? One view suggests that the linkages between supranational and national policy arenas in the EES are creating a new form of rationality in policy-making, in which efficiency and performance are backed by a new system of 'surveillance' (Haahr 2004). The truth, as usual, is less dramatic. For if the EES fails to break new ground in terms of experimental governance, its effectiveness as a means of shaping policy reform leaves a great deal to be desired. The adaptation of the employment strategy to the national level is essentially decided on by governmental actors—more closely resembling traditional top-down, technocratic government than multi-level governance (De La Porte and Pochet 2004). Despite some improvements in social partner participation within the member states in recent years, the national adaptation and implementation of the EES depend to a great extent on existing institutional dynamics, the agendas of the social partners (not always or in all countries conducive to accepting and implementing EU recommendations), and national political circumstances. In addition, there is the problematic issue of how broad policy initiatives apply to the complex, interdependent policy systems of national welfare states.

The most authoritative recent empirical investigations of the EES in practice are to be found in Jacobsson and Schmid (2002) and Jacobsson and Vifell (2003). They conclude that NAP procedures have been insufficiently integrated into national decision-making structures and budget allocations. Not so much a deliberative process of policy learning or best-practice diffusion, the EES can be more accurately described as a rational, two-level game between the Commission and the Council, in which governments do their utmost to retain control of domestic policy processes. They observe few examples of an upward transfer of learning from promising local solutions to the national or European levels, or of its subsequent cross-national diffusion. Far from being a force for decentralization, or the modification of national programmes and EU guidelines in the light of negative or positive experiences, for some observers (e.g. Syrpis 2002; Smismans 2004) the EES process actually *centralizes* the key locus of employment policy initiatives. In its most cynical manifestation, this amounts to a 'double standards game' in which governments endorse European guidelines, but fail to take responsibility for their implementation at home. A more optimistic appraisal, among the best surveys to date, can be found in Zeitlin and Pochet with Magnusson (2005).

One of the most thorough investigations to date, the Cologne-based Govecor project, concludes in its 2003 Interim Report that, at its best, the EES has encouraged better coordination among ministries, as well as between administrations and interest groups, in a limited number of member states (Govecor 2003; Zeitlin and Pochet with Magnusson 2005). But even that conclusion is qualified by evidence that such influence is limited to a small group of actors, leading to little by way of institutional innovation, and figuring hardly at all in public discourse or inter-party competition. Moreover, as we have demonstrated above, after five years of the EES, there is little of a political support base for a hardening or upgrading of the rules for employment policy coordination. This was evident not just in the second round of the 'sovereignty struggle' in 2003 over attaching new quantitative targets for the EES, but also, in the same year, in divisions within the Economic Policy Working Group of the Convention on the Future of Europe over issues of economic government, and in the more general opposition to constitutionalizing the OMC.

Conclusions: assessing European employment policy

This chapter began by noting that employment policy poses some of the most difficult regulatory problems in the EU because it has been 'essentially contested', with regard to both the assumption of Community competences and the nature of the regulation it attempted. The analysis above has shown how, over time, the efforts of an EU employment advocacy coalition—spanning the Commission, the European labour movement, and certain supportive member states—have kept the issue alive, and dealt with opposition and blockages by shifting the political parameters of the regulatory system. First, a creative interpretation of the treaty base for employment legislation was used; then legislative proposals were shifted to a second, alternative method of making law via collective agreement; and, finally, in the radically changed circumstances of the mid-to-late 1990s, with EMU and an eastward enlargement on the horizon, the emphasis moved to the wholly soft-law-based EES.

This shift has added to, rather than subtracted from, the regulatory options available for employment policy. Each pillar remains in place, holding out the possibility of a complementary or integrated use of policy instruments, so that efficacy is not necessarily sacrificed as the scope for experimentation widens. But what does an assessment of recent developments in each pillar reveal about the locus of innovation? The first pillar of traditional EU legislative policy-making remains surprisingly active. Significant advances in recent years include: the adoption of a framework equal treatment directive in 2000 (to combat employment discrimination on the grounds of religion or belief, disability, age, or sexual orientation; see Chapter 10); the adoption in 2001 of a regulation governing the creation of a European Company Statute and an accompanying directive on worker involvement; the adoption in 2002 of a highly controversial directive on national information and consultation rules (under which firms over a certain size must put in place mechanisms for informing and consulting employees, with a major potential impact on the Anglo-Irish countries); continuing discussion in the Council on a draft directive on working conditions for temporary (agency) workers, first proposed by the Commission in 2002; Commission proposals to amend and strengthen the Working Time Directive (2003); and political agreement in the Council on a draft directive implementing equal treatment between men and women outside the work place (2004).

However, pillar two—the more experimental social dialogue track—has visibly weakened over time, as the flow of draft directives transferred from the first legislative pillar has dried up and the focus has shifted to 'new generation' framework agreements. These latter include agreements on 'teleworking' (2002), and 'work-related stress' (2004), that are well-intentioned but (very much in line with UNICE preferences) do not have the force of a directive, and are fully open to interpretation by employers and employees in member state. The 'mainstreaming' of the social dialogue—for example, within the EES, where its role has been rather weak—has dispersed rather than reinforced its impact. As for the EES, the third pillar, the most significant recent innovation has been a shift in priorities which followed the creation of a European Employment Taskforce (EET) in March 2003 on a mandate from the European Council. Its first Report, *Jobs, Jobs, Jobs: Creating More Employment in Europe* (EET 2003), refocused EES objectives on the adaptability of workers and enterprises, attracting more people into the labour market, and investment in human capital. Rather than deliberation or 'iterative learning' through the EES peer-review process, it was the latter which provided the basis for the EU's recommendations on national employment policies in 2004.

Against this background, there are two key challenges to EU employment policy. The first, enlargement, poses a critical challenge, for the accession of the new member states has further extended the variety of social conditions, labour law standards, and social dialogue traditions in the EU. Their jobless growth casts a shadow over the EU's already poor employment prospects (Falkner 2003a, 2003b; Ingham and Ingham 2003).

The second concerns the EES and how to gain real value-added from the considerable investment that has been made in terms of political commitment and expectations over recent years. As has been observed by Jacobsson and Vifell (2003), the EES has had three aims: cooperation among actors; coordination of national employment policies; and convergence in outcomes. However, there is no clear institutional commitment to any of these goals across the EU member states, or to developing the means for achieving them. Once again, the eastward enlargement complicates the task of delivering results, as opposed to multiplying policy processes and procedures.

One solution to the trade-off between efficacy and experimentation (in evident favour of the former) in the social dialogue and the four strands of EES would be to strengthen the links with the still vigorous first pillar, either by using instruments of soft law (e.g. peer review, and benchmarks) to facilitate the implementation of hard law, or by using hard law to ensure the implementation of soft-law directives. As revealed by the analysis of the first pillar, there is a long history of using soft-law methods to lay the groundwork for hard-law intervention, and to strengthen instruments of hard law once they are in place. This evolution suggests that the Community method, European social agreements, and the coordination mechanisms of the EES could be deployed together in pushing forward the employment policy agenda. Indeed, there have been numerous proposals (e.g. Scharpf 2002) for giving the OMC real bite by linking its provisions to framework directives, so as to harness the flexibility of this new mode of governance, and its associated utility in an age of subsidiarity, to the ultimate sanction of law and the courts. Detailed analysis of the use of binding legislative policy tools (regulations, directives, and decisions) in the employment policy area reveals that there has been no clear substitution of non-binding instruments for the Community method in the period since 1997 (Arnold, Hosli, and Pennings 2004). This suggests that the panoply of policy instruments and modes of governance remains wide, and that, at least in theory, there is scope for such regulatory, 'cross-pillar' innovation. If that occurred, it might help rescue the EES from ultimate irrelevance and back its promise to provide a more effective and more legitimate form of policy-making (Eberlein and Kerwer 2004: 135).

Notes

1 This chapter has been written with the assistance and input of Caroline De La Porte.

2 These are usually referred to as the 'four pillars' of the EES, but the term 'pillar' has been avoided so as to avoid confusion with its use in this chapter to characterize European employment policy more generally.

3 Article 128, para. 4, sets out the process as follows: 'The Council, on the basis of the reports referred to in paragraph 3 and having received the views of the Employment Committee, shall each year carry out an examination of the implementation of the employment policies of the Member States in the light of the guidelines for employment. The Council, acting by a qualified majority on a recommendation from the Commission, may, if it considers it appropriate in the light of that examination, make recommendations to Member States'.

4 Before the meeting, each member state's NAP is read by one other member state and by the Commission, which is followed by a fifty-minute examination of each NAP that includes a short presentation by the member state, questions and comments from the examining member state, and a response from the Commission. The other member states (including observers from the new member states since 2000) then have the opportunity to ask questions.

5 If there *is* a locus of deliberative policy-making in the EES, it lies in the specific—albeit voluntary—'peer review programme' established in 1999 to identify, evaluate, and disseminate 'good practice' in active labour market policies in which country representatives discuss cases of policy success that they might like to emulate. Nevertheless, the obstacles to policy influence via learning and deliberation are not just procedural and institutional, but are also due to the structural and practical differences between systems.

Further reading

Employment policy is very much a moving target, and a full understanding of the issues discussed in this chapter requires excursions into the related literatures of law and political economy. For a legal perspective, see the authoritative contribution by Kenner (2003), and the analyses in Shaw (2000) and Sciarra (2001). Falkner, Treib, Hartlapp, and Leiber (2005) provide the best analysis of EU employment regulation from a political science perspective. For the development of EU and national employment policy, ECJ judgments, and industrial relations issues, including the European social dialogue, the European industrial relations observatory on-line (*www.eiro.eurofound.eu.int/ index.html*) provides an indispensable resource. For an in-depth analysis of the first five years of the EES, see Foden and Magnusson (2003). One of the best recent analyses of European employment policies in comparative context is Zeitlin and Trubek (2003). Zeitlin and Pochet with Magnusson (2005) provide an in-depth treatment of the EES and OMC, while Borrás and Greve (2004) give a more general analysis of the OMC extending to other policy areas. The Cologne-based Govecor (Economic Governance through Self-Coordination) project (*www.govecor.org/home/welcome.asp*) has focused on the combined impact of the legal provisions for the coordination of employment policy as set out by the ToA and the Stability and Growth Pact and provides a wealth of reports on this subject.

Borrás, S., and Greve, B. (2004) (eds.), 'The Open Method of Coordination in the European Union', special issue, *Journal of European Public Policy*, 11/2: 185–208.

Falkner, G., Treib, O., Hartlapp, M., and Leiber, S. (2005), *Complying with Europe? Theory and Practice of Minimum Harmonisation and Soft Law in the Multilevel System* (Cambridge: Cambridge University Press).

Foden, D., and Magnusson, L. (2003) (eds.), *Five Years' Experience of the Luxembourg Employment Strategy* (Brussels: European Trade Union Institute).

Kenner, J. (2003), *EU Employment Law: From Rome to Amsterdam and Beyond* (Oxford: Hart).

Sciarra, S. (2001) (ed.), *Labour Law in the Courts: National Judges and the European Court of Justice* (Oxford: Hart).

Shaw, J. (2000) (ed.), *Social Law and Policy in an Evolving European Union* (Oxford: Hart).

Zeitlin, J., and Pochet, P. with L. Magnusson (2005) (eds.), *The Open Method of Coordination in Action: The European* *Employment and Social Inclusion Strategies* (Brussels: P.I.E.-Peter Lang).

Zeitlin, J., and Trubek, D. (2003) (eds.), *Governing Work and Welfare in the New Economy: European and American Experiments* (Oxford: Oxford University Press).

Chapter 12

Environmental Policy

Contending Dynamics of Policy Change

Andrea Lenschow

Contents

Summary

EU environmental policy appears under siege. The accession of ten new members to the Union, economic pressures, and doubts as to the effectiveness of the existing environmental *acquis* seem to suggest that policy-making in this field will slow down or even regress in the coming years. But, looking at the historical evolution of environmental policy as well as the actor dynamics that have characterized policy-making this chapter warns against jumping to conclusions. In the past, we have witnessed the 'constitutionalization' of environmental policy, a fluid constellation of 'leaders and laggards', and trends to supersede supranational versus intergovernmental conflict lines—opening ways to substantial and procedural innovation. This chapter identifies some areas of recent change which may be reinforced, rather than blocked, by eastern enlargement.

Introduction

Formally speaking, environmental policy is one of the younger policies of the EU, gaining treaty recognition in 1986 with the adoption of the Single European Act (SEA). In reality, however, we can look back at half a century of environmental policy-making in the EU during which time policy moved from the margins of the single market project to become a central goal of the EU. This process has been accompanied by several interesting dynamics that will guide students of the EU towards a differentiated perspective on EU policy-making.

The historical section highlights the close relationship between the European treaty law and the evolution of a specific policy sector. This relationship is not, as one might expect, one-sided with only the formal rules set out in the treaties constraining substantive policy, but also involves formal and informal processes of policy-making which feed back to treaty adaptation. The second section develops an understanding of the role of policy-making actors and the dynamics between them during the various policy phases from agenda-setting to implementation. We note that binary perspectives, juxtaposing supranational against intergovernmental influence or—within the Council—the rich, northern environmental proponents against the poorer, southern states, do not do justice to the far more varied dynamics in space and time. Finally, the chapter addresses recent changes in regulatory policy-making in the EU. Environmental policy, which has long been a prototype of the regulatory mode, is undergoing interesting reforms. These relate to concerns about the lack of efficiency and effectiveness of old-style regulation, captured also in the general 'new governance' debate. In addition, the recent enlargements have raised the issue of redistribution in this field. Is environmental policy at a crossroads leading to new forms and directions? This chapter ends with preliminary answers to this question.

History

In the late 1950s and early 1960s the members of the then European Community (EC) had already passed important environmental legislation on safety standards related to radiation or the control of dangerous chemicals.[1] These pieces of legislation were linked to the development and modernization of the industrial sector in Europe. The explicit notion of environmental policy, however, developed only in the 1970s. In the economically 'golden' early 1970s there was growing concern about environmentally harmful effects of economic development and growth. In the light of transboundary effects of air and water pollution the heads of state and government of EC member states decided during the Paris summit in 1972 to push forward the development of a common environment policy. The Commission responded to these signals by publishing a first European Environmental Action Programme (EAP) in 1973, which defined general principles of environmental policy such as 'prevention', 'action at source', and 'the polluter pays'. These were not only very progressive at the time, but remain core principles of EU environmental policy-making today.

In parallel, the Commission began to develop and to propose 'green' policies. But, despite all the environmental rhetoric, it proved difficult to pass tough, mandatory standards in the Council. The first directive on car emissions from 1970, for instance, provided only for 'optional harmonization' (Haigh 2004: 6.8), in the sense that no country was obliged to meet the defined limit values. However, now no country could refuse to approve (and import) any car meeting these values, triggering some regulatory competition between the member states.[2] Once recession hit western Europe in the second half of the 1970s, agreements were even harder to reach. To stand a chance of success, the Commission couched most proposals as economic measures intended to improve European or international competitiveness. Secure market access within the Community was, for instance, the basis for several 'follow-up' directives on car emissions in the 1970s.[3] In an international context, tough environmental requirements for the US chemicals sector that had the potential to close this market to European exporters set the stage for several amendments to the early 1967 directive on the labelling and packaging of dangerous chemicals. Environmental protection was only a secondary motivation to the decision-makers.

The issue-linkage between environmental and market objectives had become an important strategic option for the Commission in responding to the prevailing value and interest structure in the Council (Weale *et al.* 2000). This, however, was also due to the legal framework of the Community. In the absence of any explicit reference to environmental policy in the Treaty of Rome, Article 100 (EEC) (now Art. 94 TEC) on the single market provided an opportunity for Commission proposals under the condition that environmental policy was 'packaged' as market regulation to remove non-trade barriers between the member states. Alternatively, the 'catch all' Article 235 (EEC) (now Art. 308 TEC), allowing action in all areas in line with the general mission of the Community, such as the establishment of harmonious living conditions, served as a basis for proposing environmental policy measures. Generally, this latter basis encountered more sceptical reactions in the Council than the former basis of market association, and often resulted in lengthy negotiations. The adoption of the 1979 directive (79/409/EEC) on the protection of birds and their habitat, for instance, which was based on Article 235, took eight years of preparation and negotiation.

In the light of these complications, the informal status of EC environmental policy was ended with the SEA. The new Article 100a EEC (now Art. 95 TEC) explicitly acknowledged the Community's competence to regulate environmental matters in areas that affect the creation of the internal market. Article 130 r–t (EEC) (now Arts. 174–6 TEC) established the basis for explicit European environmental policy, in effective by-passing recourse to Article 235. The decision-making procedure to be applied in adopting environmental legislation, however, varied between the legal bases. Qualified majority voting (QMV) and the new cooperation procedure with the European Parliament (EP) applied to single market-related measures, whereas unanimity in the Council and mere consultation with the EP were required for environmental policy not linked to the internal market.

The more formal status contributed to a rapid expansion of the environmental *acquis* and at the turn of the century about 300 environmental directives and regulations were in place. The uneven decision-making arrangements, however, invited policy-makers to continue forum shopping in order to push environmental proposals through the easier route provided for market-building measures. As regards disputes between Commission and Council the best known example, insofar as it led to a major controversy, is the Council Directive 89/428/EEC on procedures for harmonizing the programmes for the reduction and eventual elimination of pollution caused by waste from the titanium dioxide industry. The Council had adopted the directive unanimously, after consulting the Parliament, on the basis of Article 130s (EEC) (now Art. 175 TEC), although the Commission had based its proposal on Article 100a EEC (now Art. 95 TEC). The Commission asked the European Court of Justice (ECJ) to annul the directive, arguing that the directive's principal objective was to improve the market conditions for the titanium dioxide industry and not, as argued by the Council, the protection of the environment. The Court ruled in favour of the Commission (Case 300/89, *Commission v. Council* [1991] ECR I-2867), although it argued that Articles 100a and 130s were equally applicable. In such cases, it argued, Article 100a was to be used as it provided for stronger involvement of the Parliament which had become a general treaty objective after 1987 (Koppen 1993). This ruling further supported the Commission in its inclination to base environmental proposals on the single market article.

In short, incidental policy-making had been the pattern in the early 'unofficial' years of EU environmental policy; active initiative combined with the use of treaty games—with the Commission 'picking' the legal basis for its proposals according to procedure rather than substance—shaped the period following the adoption of the SEA. And yet, environmental policy was taking shape (see Fig. 12.1). Despite their

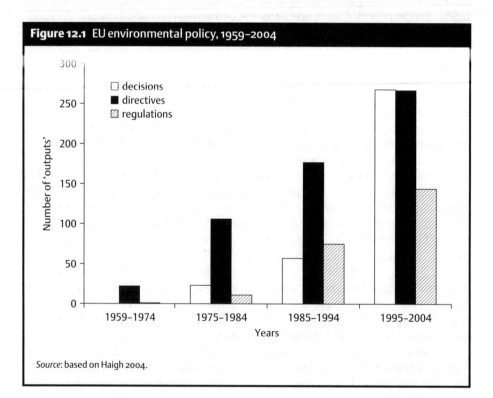

Figure 12.1 EU environmental policy, 1959–2004

Source: based on Haigh 2004.

non-binding status, EAPs (covering five-year periods) became an important vehicle for the Commission to announce and substantiate policy initiatives for subsequent years. Bodies of law developed as regards water, air, and waste, chemicals, nature, and noise policy. In addition, more general and procedural measures were adopted, ranging from impact assessments to information rights. More recently, the Commission has moved from the medium-specific to a theme-oriented approach, focusing on climate change, biodiversity, the link between environment and health, and the like.

While the autonomous role and strategic finesse of the Commission in placing environmental policy on the agenda were important factors in explaining the expansion of the *acquis*, the interests of member governments were a constant point of reference for the Commission. It was responsive to their demands for Community legislation, while trying to anticipate potential conflicts in the Council and to temper its own proposals accordingly. In this context, those states which were leaders in developing national environmental regulation provided regular input for Commission initiatives, because they wished to limit transboundary effects of environmental pollution as well as to limit the potentially negative effects of progressive national standards on the competitiveness of their industries. Furthermore, in terms of procedural rules, member governments liked to be on the initiating side in order keep down the costs of any subsequent adaptation. These dynamics will be illustrated below. It must be noted, however, that to date the conflicts of interest that emerged between leaders and laggards have not prevented the considerable expansion of environmental policy. Both the inter-institutional and intra-institutional dynamics are set out below.

The treaty revisions adopted in the Maastricht Treaty of European Union (TEU) (1992), and the Treaty of Amsterdam (ToA) (1997) contributed to the expansion by further easing decision-making. As a result of making QMV and the co-decision procedure the rule for most environmental policies, the pattern of environmental policy objectives which matched pragmatically with legal and procedural opportunity structures in the treaties largely disappeared—a sign of the political consolidation of the policy field. Policy principles and concepts that had been introduced informally in the EAPs and in individual directives, were upgraded to treaty rank in 1987 and gained further visibility when inserted into Part One of the TEC on the general principles of the Union (see Box 12.1). The EU is committed to 'a high level of protection and improvement of the quality of the environment' (Art. 2 TEC), and to the integration of environmental protection requirements into 'the definition and implementation of the Community policies and activities . . . , in particular with a view to promoting sustainable development' (Art. 6 TEC; ex Art. 3c EEC). Title XIX of the Treaty lists the objectives and principles of environmental policy (Art. 174 TEC; ex Art. 130 EEC), and specifies the decision-making procedures (Art. 175 TEC; ex Art. 130s EEC). Responding to pressure from member states with an interest in high environmental standards, especially voiced from the new entrants, Sweden, Finland, and Austria, Article 176 (TEC) (ex Art. 130t EEC) permits member states to maintain or to introduce more stringent protective measures, as long as these are 'compatible with [the] treaty' and notified to the Commission, whereby the issue of compatibility relates essentially to the provisions on the free movement of goods.[4]

The treaty revision agreed in Nice in December 2000 failed to round off previous reforms and raised doubts about the true environmental profile of the EU. QMV was not extended to the few remaining areas—most importantly (environmental) taxation issues—and the threshold for reaching a qualified majority was slightly

Box 12.1 Key treaty changes and policy decisions affecting environmental policy-making

Treaty base	Key policy decisions
Until 1986 no explicit treaty basis for environmental policy exists	■ 1967: 1st Directive on classification, packaging, and labelling of dangerous substances (67/548)
→ Article 100 (EEC) on the single market and the catch-all Article 235 (EEC) provide legal foundation for first environmental legislation	■ 1970: Directive establishing a framework for measures to combat air pollution from motor vehicles (70/220)
	■ 1973: Launch of first European Environmental Action Programme
1973: UK, Ireland, and Denmark join EC	■ 1979: Birds Directive on the protection of birds and their habitats (79/409)
1981/1986: Greece, followed by Spain and Portugal, join the EC	■ 1980: Directive setting minimum standards for drinking water (80/778)
	■ 1985: Directive requiring environmental impact assessments, especially for large development projects (85/337)
1987: Single European Act (SEA) in force	■ 1988: Directive to limit emissions from large combustion plants (88/609)
→ New environmental policy title introduced, with unanimous voting in the Council	■ 1989: Directive about the harmonization of programmes to reduce waste from the titanium dioxide industry (89/428)
→ Article 100a (EEC) on the single market cites environmental regulation explicitly; this article allowed for QMV	■ 1990: Directive on public access to environmental information (90/313)
	■ 1991: Directive on controlling the pollution through urban waste water (91/271)
	■ 1992: Habitats Directive on the conservation of natural habitats and wild flora and fauna (92/43)

1993: Treaty on European Union (TEU) → QMV is extended to most, though not all, areas of environmental policy → Co-decision-making with the EP is introduced for measures linked to the internal market → Concept of sustainable growth respecting the environment (Art. 2 TEC), the precautionary principle and the principle to integrate environmental objectives in all non-environmental policies (Art. 130r TEC) **1995: Austria, Finland, Sweden join EU**	■ 1994: Establishment of the European Environment Agency ■ 1994: Directive on limiting the volume and increasing the recovery of packaging waste (94/62) ■ 1994: Regulation implementing the Montreal Protocol of the Vienna Convention on the protection of the ozone layer (3093/94) ■ 1996: Directive on integrated (cross-media) pollution prevention and control (96/61) ■ 1996: Framework Directive on air quality, consolidating earlier typically substance-specific directives on air pollution (96/62)
1999: Treaty of Amsterdam (ToA) → Concept of sustainable development (Art. 2 TEC and Preamble); strengthened commitment to integration principle → Co-decision-making (Art. 175 TEC) for measures adopted under Art. 174 TEC (ex Art. 130r TEC)	■ 2000: Framework Directive on water, consolidating earlier directive dealing with water pollution (2000/60) ■ 2001: Launch of 6th European Environmental Action Programme ■ 2002: Ratification of Kyoto Protocol on Climate Change
2003: Treaty of Nice (ToN) → Raises the threshold for reaching qualified majority **2004: Ten new members join the EU** **2004: Constitutional Treaty (CT)[a]**	■ 2003: Directive establishing a scheme for greenhouse gas emission allowance trading within the Community (amending a 1996 Council directive) (2003/87) ■ 2003: Directive restructuring the Community framework for the taxation of energy products and electricity (2003/96) ■ 2004: Directive to establish a framework of environmental liability based on the polluter-pays principle (2004/35)

a Awaiting ratification

raised. Under this rule, it may be easier to block the enactment of more active environmental policy, a factor that is particularly significant in the enlarged EU (Jordan and Fairbrass 2002). The Constitutional Treaty (CT) introduces a double major-ity rule of 55 per cent of the member states and 65 per cent of the population which lowers this threshold again somewhat. Devuyst (2004: 1) argues that this is 'unlikely to foster a dynamic decision-making process in an expanded EU of twenty-five Member States'. Given the already high investments that were required from the new mem-bers in order to meet the terms of the *acquis communautaire* as a condition of EU acces-sion it seems improbable that they will be supportive of still further tightening of environmental standards in the short to medium term.

Key players

This section introduces the main actors in EU environmental policy-making, putting specific emphasis on the intra- and inter-institutional relations that are characteristic of this policy field.

The Commission

The Commission is present throughout the entire policy cycle. Its primary powers lie in the policy formulation phase based on its power of initiative. During decision-making the Commission performs as an intervening and mediating actor; although its right to withdraw a proposal at the legislative stage confers some veto power on the Commission, operative primarily in the sense of an implied power. Furthermore, in its role as the 'guardian of the Treaty' the Commission is responsible for ensuring the implementation of EU law, for which it depends on the cooperation of the national or regional governments and administrations, which are responsible for legal and pract-ical implementation. Finally, the Commission is involved in facilitating the execu-tion of certain tasks laid down in EU legislation. Here the Commission relies on committees of mostly national officials that have been created for specific aspects of environmental policy following the comitology procedures (Weale *et al.* 2000: 90).

The sectoral organization of the Commission into Directorates-General (DGs) and its limited staff resources have a strong impact on its capacities to perform these mul-tiple functions. During the early stages of policy formulation DG ENV carries the main responsibility; it also depends on the support of other DGs and on wide support in the college of Commissioners before any policy proposal can be passed to the Council and the Parliament for consideration. Given the horizontal nature of environmental pol-icy, affecting economic sectors ranging from agriculture to transportation, the path towards approval within the Commission can be a rocky one. The often conflictual relationship between DGs poses problems for coordinated and coherent policy formulation. Generally, DG Environment may find it opportune to emphasize the pos-itive economic and developmental effects of any given environmental proposal and to de-emphasize any potential burden for industry or national budgets. Therefore, the issue-linkage between environment and the economy is (or has been) due not only to particular legal structures or member state interests, but also to the decision-making structure inside the Commission.[5]

In the past, policy formulation was considered the main responsibility of the Commission. Here the Commission has opportunities to advance its role as a supranational actor and to develop proposals that go beyond the status quo in the member states in the sense that it has often sought to be more the promoter of tougher environmental rules, thus seeking to conflate 'Europeanness' and 'greenness'. This role seems to put the Commission in almost natural opposition to the member states and the Council, whereas the EP—speaking for the European electorate—appears as a 'natural ally'. Particularly during the early ambitious efforts of the Commission this was often an accurate description of the inter-institutional relations shaping environmental policy-making. But even then, reality has been more complex. Not only did the Commission react regularly to national demands for European policy,[6] but with limited staff of about 500 A grade officials, it has been dependent on national expertise and regularly sought the opinion of the national ministries to ensure the feasibility of its proposals and to anticipate the conflicts that might otherwise hamper decision-making.

Arguably, this attentiveness to the member states' points of view increased during the last decade due to a re-ordering of the Commission's priorities. As will be discussed below, deficient implementation, in the environmental field as elsewhere, has come to undermine the legitimacy of the Commission. In response, the Commission had already tried to improve its relations with the 'real' implementers, namely the relevant agencies in the member states, during the policy design stage. Beginning with the fifth environmental action programmes, the Commission speaks of the member states as partners; formal and informal dialogue networks aim to put this cooperative approach into practice (Commission 1993*a*: 113–16).

The Council of Ministers

The Council of Ministers, like the Commission, is characterized by segmentation. There is little coordination between the Environment Council and the various other Councils. Both the Secretariat General of the Council and the pyramid of Council committees, follow by and large a sector-specific approach. This 'insularity' allows the environment ministers some escape from domestic constraints. At some distance from influential colleagues in charge of the economy, finance, or agriculture, environment ministers may seek the opportunity to give support to an agenda that would stand little or no chance domestically, although this depends also on how tightly national positions are coordinated across ministries. Back home, controversial decisions may then be blamed on 'Brussels' or a too powerful alliance of environmental leader states. Enhanced transparency of Council negotiations, as well as the stronger accountability of governments as regards their previously agreed mandates, may reduce this informal leeway of national policy-makers in Brussels. To what extent increased democratic control really undermines the 'problem-solving mode' that sometimes develops between policy specialists in the Council and instead favours strict bargaining between states is debatable (Jachtenfuchs 2000).

At first sight a single cleavage, separating leaders from environmental laggards, runs through the Council of Ministers. Simply put, the leaders appear to be countries like Germany, the Netherlands, Sweden, and Denmark, i.e. the richer, northern states—whereas the laggards are the poorer, southern states like Greece, Spain, Portugal, and the new member states, which have other investment priorities and do not face an electorate pushing for tougher environmental standards. But also the UK, given its insular location (protecting it from some transboundary effects), and the legacy of its heavy industry sector, was long considered the 'dirty man' of Europe, although this has changed in the past decade (Jordan 2002b). The existence of this north-south, rich-poor cleavage was visible in previous rounds of enlargement. The southern enlargements in 1981 and 1986 were accompanied by a substantial increase and refocusing of the Communities' financial support schemes for environmental investments. In 1993 the Cohesion Fund, which spends about 50 per cent of its monies on environmental projects, was launched. The 'northern' countries which joined in 1995, in turn, negotiated a treaty revision that allows them to exceed EU environmental standards under certain conditions. Only the new, mostly central European, member states have had to adopt the entire environmental *acquis* with very few derogations and without comparable side-payments. It is to be expected that these countries will now attempt to limit the environmental 'burden of accession' from the inside; hence, the effect of their membership will be felt in future policy negotiations.

Box 12.2 Car emissions (phase 1)

■ The early directive on car emissions was characterized by largely optional standards. This changed in the 1980s due to the initiative of Germany, where the impact of acid rain began to be felt as large forests showed signs of great distress. The German public had reacted to these (and other) signs of environmental damage by giving increasing support to the new Green Party, forcing the large Social Democratic and Christian Democratic parties to develop an environmental policy agenda.

■ In targeting car emissions a second, non-environmental factor was critical. In the US (California), legislation had been passed requiring cars to be fitted with the three-way catalytic converter. Especially those German producers exporting to the American market needed to adopt this new technology and had an interest to not be the only ones in Europe making this investment. Germany was supported by the Netherlands and Denmark, but opposed by France, Italy, and the UK. France and Italy feared disproportional cost increases for their smaller cars; they and the UK favoured the development of the lean-burn engine to control pollution. As Germany threatened unilateral action, the Commission put forward a proposal in 1984 which set emission standards at a limit that could be met only by cars fitted with this new technology. In 1985 a compromise seemed in sight, effectively requiring the three-way catalytic converter only for large cars whereas the new limit values for medium-sized and small cars would be achievable by alternative means. Formal agreement with the directive was blocked by Denmark and Greece. Greece had no car industry which could face rising production costs and in Athens people and antiquities suffered from traffic-induced air pollution. Greece therefore made its agreement to the compromise contingent on greater EC support for environmental protection projects in Athens.

■ The Single European Act introduced QMV in matters related to the single market (such as cars). The opponents to the compromise were overruled and Directive 88/76 was adopted. It was the first time QMV was used in the field of environmental policy (Holzinger 1994; Haigh 2004).

Box 12.3 Access to information

The role of leaders and laggards are played by, at first sight, surprising actors in the case of Directive (90/313) ensuring free public access to environmental information from those public authorities which carry out tasks in the field of environmental protection. Here the UK joined after some hesitation the group of front-runners (Denmark, France, the Netherlands, and Luxembourg), whereas Germany together with Spain appeared on the opposing side. Referring to plans specified in the fourth EAP, the initiative for a European environmental information directive came from the environment committee of the European Parliament.

The Commission reacted positively, preparing a proposal in 1987. The initiative was politically sensitive, however, as it potentially affected information that used to fall under rules of data protection. Germany used to handle data access traditionally very restrictively; data protection from potential abuse had priority over offering information in the name of public service. The opposite was true in the UK especially since a new public service philosophy had been adopted under the conservative government. Yet, the Department of the Environment (DoE) first did not see the 'value added' of the directive; the House of Lords favoured an approach going beyond the legislative proposal (combining active provision of information in the form of open registers with the passive access right).

In 1989 under the French presidency the DoE changed its mind and supported a revised Commission proposal. Germany remained resistant until last, but in 1990 the directive could be adopted in the Council. Notably, the cleavage line that put Germany on the opposing end had less to do with environmental progressiveness than with national administrative and legal traditions. On this dimension there had been recent reforms in the UK contributing to a more favourable view (Héritier, Knill, and Mingers 1996). Directive 2003/4 later revised the rules.

The cleavage structure in the Council has, however, never been quite so two-dimensional as suggested above. Three reasons account for greater complexity. In the first place, member states face different environmental problems. Highly industrialized countries are likely to be more concerned with air quality, waste treatment, and noise, than countries with a larger rural sector and dependence on tourism which place greater value on the quality of soil, nature protection, and sufficient quantities of water. Secondly, countries differ in their regulatory philosophies and styles (Richardson 1982; Vogel 1986). Hence, their governments argue not only about the level of standards, but also about the kind of policy instruments to be employed, the amount of administrative or regional flexibility desirable, and the degree of scientific uncertainty acceptable before imposing EU measures. Thirdly, member governments alter their positions over time, if either the economic and environmental conditions change or a new government with different policy priorities comes to power. The two examples in Box 12.2 and Box 12.3 illustrate the impact of these factors on the decision-making dynamics in the Council.

The European Parliament

As indicated, the EP has gained decision-making power over the years. Under the most recent treaty arrangements the co-decision procedure applies to most aspects of environmental policy—making the EP the equal partner of the Council. But even earlier the EP had left its mark.

Traditionally, the EP has been the 'greenest' of the three main policy-making bodies. Even prior to its direct election it had pushed the Commission to propose environmental policy. In the case of the Birds Directive, for instance, the EP had been petitioned by several animal rights groups concerned with the hunting of migratory birds, and in 1971 requested the Commission to take up this issue. The Commission responded in the first EAP and, after consulting numerous experts, presented a draft directive in 1976 (Haigh 2004: 9.2). More recently, in the 1990s, the EP brought the issue of implementation in environmental policy to the fore and pushed the Commission to engage more systematically with societal and administrative actors on the ground (European Parliament 1996b; Collins and Earnshaw 1992). Generally, the EP works to enhance control both in Brussels and on the ground. Finally, under certain conditions the EP effectively pursues its interest during decision-making, as, for example in the case of car emissions (see Box 12.4).

The effects of co-decision on the nature of environmental policy decisions are hard to generalize. While a 'green' EP may push the passage of stringent rules, some argue that conciliatory behaviour may replace previous vigorous advocacy (Holzinger 1994: 114–16). Under the early consultation procedure advocacy was the only possible route towards success; under the cooperation procedure the EP could constrain decision-making in the Council by pushing it to a critical limit (Tsebelis 1994). Co-decision provides potential true veto power and hence visible responsibility for the outcome, thus making the EP

Box 12.4 Car emissions (phase 2)

- Directive 88/76 stipulated that the Council decide on more restrictive emission norms for small cars applicable after 10/1992 (new models) or 10/1993 (new cars). After consulting intensively with national experts, the car industry, as well as environmental groups, in early 1988 the Commission tabled a proposal which extended the norms already agreed for medium-sized cars to small vehicles. Although further limiting car emissions, the proposed standards would not make the three-way catalytic converter obligatory for small cars, as had been demanded by Germany, Denmark, Greece, and the Netherlands, as well as the European Environment Bureau. Nevertheless, the Council supported the Commission proposal in its common position. In this the Council disregarded the position of the EP, which in its first reading had asked to adopt the stricter standards advocated by the environmental 'leader' states. As the Single European Act had not only introduced QMV but also the cooperation procedure, the Parliament had the right to a second reading, reacting to the Council's common position. In its second reading the EP reaffirmed its initial position and the Commission now followed the EP in presenting a revised proposal. According to the cooperation procedure the Council now needed a unanimous vote in order to overrule the Commission and the EP. Given the continuous opposition of Denmark, Greece, and the Netherlands this was not forthcoming and the Council agreed with a qualified majority to adopt the revised Directive 89/458 which made the three-way catalytic converter mandatory for large and small cars—though not (yet) for medium-sized cars.

- While the effective use of the EP's (new) powers cannot be denied, its success depended on the member states' preferring largely unwanted standards over no agreement at all. Both the importance of a common car market and a rising environmental awareness throughout Europe had softened the previous categorical opposition of particularly Italy and France towards the new engine technology and made the decision possible in 1989 (Holzinger 1994).

more accountable for decisional failure, which may make it adopt a more cautious approach, as long as reaching some solution is its objective.

However, not everything depends on strategy, since policy style may also be related to personalities. The policy driver inside the EP has been its Committee on the Environment, Public Health and Consumer Protection. A pro-active and often uncompromising attitude characterized the operations of this committee in the 1980s and 1990s under the chairmanship of Ken Collins (1979–99),[7] a Scottish Labour MEP (Sbragia 2000: 301–2). His successors, Carolyn Jackson (1999–2004), and Karl Heinz Florenz, who became chairman in 2004, are both members of the European Peoples' Party and politically less prone to radical environmental views. But, as long-time active members of the committee, they have contributed to continuity and expertise in its work, ensuring its influence despite some moderation in style.

Although decision-making procedures within the Parliament place committees in a core position, the overall political composition of the EP must not be underestimated. This influences plenary majorities, as well as committee opinions, because the membership of all committees broadly reflects the overall party strengths. Compared to most national parliaments the green faction is quite large;[8] during the fifth term (1999–2004) 7.7 per cent of the seats went to the Group of the Greens/European Free Alliance. This proportion dropped to 5.9 per cent at the 2004 elections, however, with the arrival of the ten new member states with different political preferences (only Latvia elected a green party MEP). Consequently, the effects of enlargement on environmental policy will be felt not only in more difficult negotiation processes within the Council, but also in less environment-friendly attitudes inside the Parliament.

The European Court of Justice

In the past the ECJ through its case law has contributed to the development of EU environmental policy, and continues to do so today. Until the SEA the ECJ used its opportunities to develop legal norms to confirm the legitimacy of environmental measures in the absence of an explicit reference in the EEC Treaty.[9] Subsequently, the Court was instrumental in emancipating the environmental agenda from the single market agenda. In the Danish bottle case it ruled that the principle of free movement of goods can be overridden if this serves to achieve common environmental objectives (C-302/86 *Commission v. Denmark* [1988] ECR 4607). In the titanium dioxide case (C-300/89 *Commission v. Council* [1991] ECR I-02867), the Court eased the way towards delineating the decision-making procedures in the environmental field and supported further empowerment of the Parliament.

The main responsibilities of the Court in the present legally consolidated phase of environmental policy relate to implementation and enforcement. First, in infringement proceedings usually initiated by the Commission against member states (Art. 226 TEC; ex Art. 169 EEC; Art. 141 EEC (litigation)), the Court ensures compliance with EU law. Under the Art. 228 TEC (ex Art. 171 EEC) procedure it may impose pecuniary sanctions in cases of prolonged non-compliance or poor compliance. Although the number of cases brought under this procedure has been rising quickly, so far there have been only two cases where the Court ordered fines against member states. In 2000 the Court imposed a fine of €20,000 for each day following the ruling against Greece (C-387/97) until it ended the uncontrolled tipping of waste at a site in Crete that violated Directives 75/442/EEC and 78/319/EEC on waste, and toxic and dangerous waste, respectively. In a second ruling from November 2003 (C-278/01) the Court ordered Spain to pay an annual fine of €624,150 for each per cent of inland bathing waters that did not comply with the limit values set in Council Directive 76/160/EEC of 8 December 1975 concerning the quality of bathing water.

Under Article 234 TEC, if an individual argues before a national court that a national law or policy conflicts with EU law, the national court may seek guidance from the ECJ by making a preliminary ruling reference. This procedure operates analogously to an enforcement mechanism, as individuals or groups are able to bring legal action against national authorities that have failed to transpose or comply with EU law. The implementation of the Directive on the conservation of wild birds (79/409/EEC), which was adopted in 1979 to limit the annual hunting of migratory birds, benefited from a bottom-up judicial dynamic of this kind. Due to the weak legal basis for environmental rule-making at the time and the controversial nature of this issue (see above), the Commission had manoeuvred carefully in the proposal phase and the final directive included very general requirements and made derogations for numerous special cases. Ambiguities led to uncertainty among national authorities about the appropriate implementation measures but also to a tendency to resist implementation altogether. Environmental and animal associations, who could not initiate legal proceedings at the Community level directly,[10] sought administrative or legal recourse on the national level against those authorities that failed to comply with the directive. On several such occasions, the national courts requested a preliminary ruling from the ECJ, which used these opportunities—as well as infringement cases brought by the Commission—to give far-reaching readings to the directives, extending the level of protection afforded to birds as well as their habitat (Cichowski 2001).

Environmental interest groups

Seven environmental NGOs are the core organizations representing environmental interests at the European level: the European Environmental Bureau (EBB), Friends of the Earth (FoE), Greenpeace International, the World-Wide Fund for Nature (WWF), the Climate Network Europe (CNE), the European Federation for Transport and Environment (T&E), and BirdLife International. Among this 'gang of seven' the EEB has the longest history in Brussels. It was set up in 1974 with the help of the European Commission which had an interest in garnering societal support for its—after all, legally questionable—activities in the environmental field. Today the EEB is a federation of 132 organizations from twenty-four European countries. The other environmental groups established their Brussels offices from the late 1980s to the early 1990s.

Their number of staff is small and their financial resources modest. In order to compensate for the limited resources all groups focus their activities on a defined range of topics which is coordinated among them (Webster 1998). All, except Greenpeace, also receive some Commission funding for regular operations; from 2002 to 2006 a total of €32 million is being made available to support environmental NGOs registered in the member states, old and new, and other candidate countries, as well as a number of Balkan countries (Decision 466/2002/EC). In recent years, however, the funding policy of the Commission for NGOs has come under critical scrutiny (Eising 2003: 203–4).

The Brussels-based staffs concentrate activities on the policy formulation phase. Here they act both as a pressure group, mobilizing the general public or member states on their behalf, and as 'think tanks', offering expertise and detailed information from the ground. The Commission regularly employs interest group representatives on temporary contracts in order to internalize this expertise. During the decision-making phase, NGOs use public campaigns, and direct contacts with member governments and MEPs to ensure the desired majorities. At this stage the national members of the Brussels-based groups assume an important role. Finally, national NGOs are crucial during the implementation and enforcement phases of policy-making (see the example of the Birds Directive above). In addition to national legal action, environmental groups use the complaints procedure[11] to inform the Commission of any gap in implementation that is detected in the member states. In 2002, the Commission received 555 new complaints alleging breaches of EU environmental law (Commission 2003e: 33).

Regulatory policy-making at the crossroads

The regulatory policy mode under siege?

Years of EU environmental activism had not significantly improved the state of the environment (EEA 1999). Some critics condemned the cost of environmental regulation, and the EU's tendency toward *ad hoc* and 'wild' regulatory expansion. Others deplored the apparent lack of coordination between environmental and other EU policy areas, such as transport, energy, agriculture, or the single market, and wished to see better integration of environmental objectives into general policy-making in the EU. Arguably, EU environmental policy suffers from an implementation deficit exceeding that of other policy areas such as the single market, industry, and consumer affairs (see Fig. 12.2).

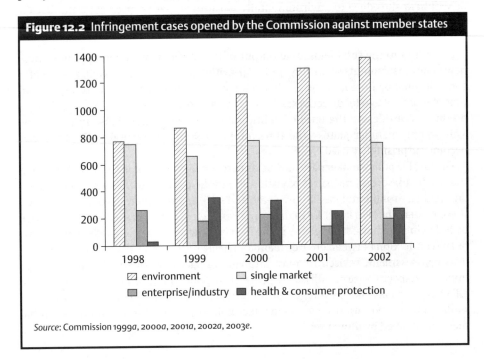

Figure 12.2 Infringement cases opened by the Commission against member states

Source: Commission 1999a, 2000a, 2001a, 2002a, 2003e.

Reflecting the high imperative to reform, the overall legitimacy of environmental policy was questioned both by eternal sceptics, who perceived such policy as a burden on the economy, and by the advocates of further 'greening' of the EU.

EU policy-makers responded to these challenges in several ways. First, the Commission has made several proposals to improve implementation and enforcement. Most significantly, the environmental network for the implementation and enforcement of environmental law (IMPEL), made up of Commission officials and representatives of relevant national (or local) authorities has become an important forum for considering the feasibility of EU proposals early in the game, as well as for improving the capacity and willingness of local implementers through the exchange of experiences. The Commission has also made extra efforts to develop implementation guidelines. In the light of continuing problems, especially with regard to compliance with the principle of environmental policy integration and in meeting the climate change target, Environment Commissioner, Margot Wallström reflected in an interview with the *European Voice* in November 1999 that 'In the long run I would prefer to be more of a consultant or advisor to member states, but until then I will have to be more of a policewoman' (*European Voice*, 11 November 1999, 2). Figure 12.2 indicates that the use of infringement proceedings by the Commission in the environmental field was stepped up.[12]

Secondly, the Commission has started reforms in the choice of proposed policy instruments. In addition to efforts to generate simpler and more comprehensible legislation,[13] it experiments with a more context-oriented and flexible approach. This represents a change in regulatory philosophy, away from the 'German' legal, interventionist style towards a 'British' 'hands-off' approach and procedural regulation. Generally speaking, information-based instruments aim at raising awareness and triggering learning effects; economic instruments attach a price (in the form of fees, taxes, or withheld subsidies) to environmentally harmful activities or create a market for permits or allowances. Box 12.5 summarizes the most important 'new' instruments adopted on the EU level.

Compared to the total legislative output of the EU in environmental policy, these new policy instruments seem very limited (Héritier 2002; Holzinger, Knill, and Schäfer 2003). It must be noted, however, that the scope of these instruments is larger than that of many 'old-style' directives, which set very specific standards for operations or products. Considering the level of political contestation—related also to new cleavages among member states—the repertoire of EU environmental policy tools has become surprisingly varied.

Thirdly, EU policy-makers are aiming at better policy integration in two senses. On the one hand, several measures pay attention to the combined effects of pollution on different environmental media (air, water, and soil), and the interdependency between these media. The two latest EAPs, from 1993 and 2002, have pursued this perspective by following thematic strategies, e.g. the focus is now on climate change, biodiversity, or the connection between environment and health. The directives on environmental impact assessment, revised in 1997, strategic impact assessment that extends the impact perspective from individual projects to policy programmes, which became effective in 2004, and on integrated pollution prevention and control, adopted in 1996, facilitate pollution control (and technologies permitting) beyond the initial medium affected by discharge.

Box 12.5 'New' environmental policy instruments in the EU

- The Council Directive 90/313/EEC on the freedom of access to information on the environment is a tool to raise the environmental performance of public authorities (and industrial actors under their control) by introducing stronger public scrutiny. Directive 2003/4/EC updates and amends the earlier directive.

- The Eco-management and audit scheme (EMAS) (Regulation 761/2001) allows a firm to be registered as an 'EMAS business', if it adopts an officially verified environmental management system. This voluntary scheme aims at inducing firms to take account of environmental effects early in the production process; in addition industry may use the EMAS logo in public relation campaigns.

- Following Regulation 1980/2000 manufacturers, service providers, traders, and retailers may apply for the award of the EU eco-label to their products. The label may be used as a 'sales-pitch' while informing the consumers about environmental qualities of the product.

- After unsuccessful attempts to adopt a European carbon/energy tax, in 2003, after six years of negotiation, a much toned down Framework Directive on Energy Taxation (2003/96) was passed, which aims at harmonizing and gradually increasing the minimum rates of duty applicable to a range of energy products.

- The Directive 2003/87/EC of the European Parliament and the Council of 13 October 2003 establishing a scheme for greenhouse gas emission allowance trading within the Community (amending Council Directive 96/61/EC) comes into force in 2005. It aims to meet the Kyoto target of 8 per cent emission reduction, calculated from emission in 1990 as the base-level and taking 2008 to 2012 as target years. In each member state a set number of allowances for emitting greenhouse gases are allocated and then traded by the relevant operators. Depending on the price for emission allowances, they may find it advantageous to invest in emission reduction.

- On 21 April 2004 Directive 2004/35/EC of the European Union and the Council on environmental liability with regard to the prevention and remedying of environmental damages was passed after years of debate (Tsekouras 2000).

Policy integration in a second sense applies to policy coordination. In June 1988 the Cardiff European Council represented something of a breakthrough for the policy integration principle. Most configurations of the Council, ranging from agriculture to Ecofin, have to develop an environmental integration strategy, and member governments are supposed to exchange 'best practice' models (Lenschow 2003). Some first improvements can be detected, for instance in the reform of the CAP in 2003 (see Chapter 7). But, the commitment of the EU's political leadership to environmental integration remains volatile, especially during difficult economic times. Ultimately, the economic preoccupations of the EU may trump its environmental agenda and the historical policy-making mode of opportunistic 'niche seeking' may turn out to be far from obsolete for policy-makers dedicated to environmental objectives.

In 1992 the Edinburgh European Council called for priority to be given to simplifying and improving the regulatory environment in the EU. In 2001, the Commission acknowledged that 'nine years on, it has to be said that the results still fall short of the objectives . . . most of the work still remains to be done' (Commission 2001b: 2). In 2004 it announced 'a *further renewed approach* . . . that focuses on integration, implementation and information' (Commission 2004b: 20; emphasis added). And yet, the reforms of recent years have moved EU environmental policy-making just beyond the crossroads, slowly altering the previous 'top-down' and non-integrated patterns. But in light of the eastern enlargement the quest for renewal may pose yet another challenge.

Is there a distributive agenda?

During the southern enlargements, the EU member states realized that the socio-economic characteristics of the new (and some old) member states could bring EU environmental policy-making to a halt and adopted several special programmes (ENVIREG, MEDSPA, LIFE,[14] and most importantly, the Cohesion Fund) to facilitate southern 'greening'. About half of the Cohesion Fund monies, which amount to €18 billion for the seven-year period 2000–5, are dedicated to environmental projects in Spain, Portugal, Greece, and Ireland. The Financial Instrument for the Environment (LIFE), is endowed with €640 million for the period 2000–4 (or less than 0.2 per cent of the Community's annual budget); it aims specifically at nature protection, innovative techniques of environmental policy, and the build-up of capacities in non-candidate third countries bordering on the Union. In addition, the structural funds (see Chapter 9), which amount to about one-third of the EU budget, are the main EU source of direct environmental funding in disadvantaged or rural regions; non-environmental projects supported through these funds also need to show compliance with EU environmental law and hence to contribute to its proper implementation.

With the accession of ten new member states in 2004 the EU's budgetary provisions were not sufficient to meet their funding needs (see Chapter 8). Agenda 2000, the EU's financial perspective for the period 2000–6, assumed that only 4 per cent of the investment needs of the new member states, which are estimated at around €100 billion in the environmental field (*Süddeutsche Zeitung*, 23 March 2004, 7; Commission 2001c), could be covered by Community funds. Drinking water, waste water, waste management, and air quality, in particular, are areas requiring urgent action in these countries as their temporary derogations will expire.[15] Economic and monetary union (EMU), and the associated Maastricht criteria, pose additional constraints on the investment capacity of the new member states. Although not yet full participants in EMU, they all hope to join eventually, with the result that local and regional authorities and industry can hardly afford to make investments in environmental infrastructure. Not surprisingly, the widely held environment-friendly views after 1989 have changed (recall the EP election results), and the environmental *acquis* is perceived as a 'structural imperative' and a burden from accession (Slocock 1996).

Several scenarios follow from this. First, the practical implementation of the environmental *acquis* will be deficient in many instances. Secondly, the new member states will step on the brake when new, and potentially costly, EU measures are discussed. Thirdly, on a more positive note, with respect to the new procedural instruments discussed above, the new member governments may show more favourable attitudes as they proceed with the ongoing process of administrative modernization (Jehlička 2002). Here the 'renewal' of EU policy may be pushed rather than hampered.

The EU as an international actor

So far EU environmental policy has been presented as being largely internally motivated, either to facilitate the internal market or to deal with European transboundary effects. According to one Commission official, however, over one-third of current EU environmental measures can be traced back to international agreements related to water, the atmosphere, waste, wildlife, etc. (Baker 2003: 25, citing Commission official Nick Hanley). Hence the EU has stepped up efforts to gain formal recognition as an international actor in environmental policy (see, e.g., Sbragia and Damro 1999). As international conventions are usually formal agreements between sovereign states, and as the EU obviously is not a state, this process involved the establishment of new procedures and routines, both internationally and within the EU, challenging traditional multi-lateral practices.

The question of whether to accept the Community as a party to a convention at the international level had to be answered and is controversial both internally and externally. Non-EU states are not always ready to accept the EU as a signatory, unless it is made sufficiently clear how the agreed obligations will be implemented internally. The Convention on International Trade in Endangered Species (CITES) from 1973 still prohibits the Community from acceding, the Vienna Convention on the Ozone Layer (1985), and the subsequent Montreal Protocol (1987) included—after heated arguments— both the Community and the member states. This form of a 'mixed agreement' has also been chosen for the Climate Change Convention (1994). But also within the EU, the form of representation is controversial, since it has to be clarified whether the EU has the legal competence to deal with the problem under consideration. Prior to the SEA and the establishment of a legal base for European environmental policy this was highly contested. But even now the exact policy competences are never quite clear, and hence the practice of mixed—member state and EU—representation. A second and related issue is who should speak on behalf of the EU—the Commission or the presidency of the Council of Ministers? Despite these persisting ambiguities, EU member governments have become increasingly willing to coordinate their positions and act collectively, while international partners have come to expect 'the Union' in some formation at the negotiation table.

During this process of institutionalization, the EU has evolved from a 'Vienna laggard to a Kyoto leader' in global environmental negotiations (Sbragia and Damro 1999: 53). By the time of negotiating the Kyoto Protocol, the EU's member states had not only got used to complex representation structures—in this instance most of the negotiating was done by the Council presidency—but, more importantly, they had become quite used to accepting national restrictions due to European—and now global—rules and even to agree on differential treatments among themselves.[16] In the case of Kyoto the intra-EU burden-sharing agreement allocated different commitments to the reduction of greenhouse gases to the member states; this strengthened the EU's negotiation position as it was able to commit itself to the toughest (collective) target of an 8 per cent reduction.[17] This commitment (together with the burden-sharing agreement), will become binding when the Protocol comes into force, which has become increasingly likely now that the Russian Federation has signalled its willingness to ratify. Credible EU leadership in international environmental policy in the future will much depend on its capacity to meet its Kyoto commitments.

Conclusions

What—in a nutshell—are the key features of EU environmental policy-making? Empirically, it is a story of policy expansion, deepening, and institutionalization, which has been traced back to pragmatic and adaptive policy-makers in the Commission, a competitive dynamic between the member states, and the facilitating roles of the Court, the EP, and societal interests. Processes of gradual institutionaliza-tion moved environmental policy principles from the status of programmatic state-ments into a formal *acquis* and finally into prominent treaty provisions. This prevents a rolling back, even at times of little political enthusiasm for new initiatives and ris-ing criticism about high degrees of interventionism, excessive costs, and poor records of implementation. Not contraction but adaptation appears the pattern of change, with the critics from yesterday becoming the reformers of tomorrow.

Will this dynamism continue even after the latest enlargement? The enormous financial burden implied in adopting the environmental *acquis*, on the one hand, and little societal interest in pushing a 'green' regulatory agenda, on the other, may sug-gest that environmental policy-making will be blocked for some time to come. The economic and financial consequences of regulatory policies are likely to dominate the negotiation processes. But, the progression of EU environmental policy so far has pointed to the multiple dimensions of environmental policy and fluid constellations of actors. To the extent that new procedural rules or economic instruments fit the administrative and economic reform agenda in the new member states these may well push the new governance agenda while blocking the 'old' one.

Notes

1 On radiation see Council Directive 59/221 laying down the basic standards for the protection of the health of workers and the general public against the dangers arising from ionising radiations (no longer in force), and Council Directive 66/45/Euratom of 27 October 1966 amending the Directives stipulating the basic standards for the protection of the health of workers and the general public against the dangers arising from ionising radiations (no longer in force). On chemicals see Council Directive 67/548/EEC of 27 June 1967 on the approximation of laws, regulations and administrative provisions relating to the classification, packaging and labelling of dangerous substances.

2 The concept of regulatory competition is important for understanding policy-making in the EU. In the literature we find two distinct meanings of this concept (Knill 2003: 124–35): the

existence of the internal market forces member states to keep in mind the cross-boundary market effects of domestic (environmental) legislation in order to ensure the European competitiveness of their producers; EU legislation may intervene in this dynamic by establishing either minimum or uniform standards; and member governments often have an interest in pushing their domestic regulatory approaches and standards up to the European level; if successful, a member state profits from the levelled playing field at minimum adaptation costs.

3 Council Directive 72/306 on measures to be taken against the emission of pollutants from diesel engines for use in vehicles; Council Directive 74/290/EEC adapting to technical progress Council Directive 70/220/EEC on the approximation of the laws of the member states relating to measures to be taken against air pollution by gases from positive ignition engines of motor vehicles; Commission Directive 77/102/EEC adapting to technical progress Council Directive 70/220/EEC of 20 March 1970 on the approximation of the laws of the Member States relating to measures to be taken against air pollution by gases from positive ignition engines of motor vehicles; Commission Directive 78/665/EEC adapting to technical progress Directive 70/220/EEC on the approximation of the laws of the member states relating to measures to be taken against pollution of the air by gases from positive ignition engines installed in motor vehicles.

4 Among the principles listed in Article 174 EEC (ex Art. 130r EEC) of the Treaty of Amsterdam (which remain unchanged in the Treaty of Nice) are the commitment for a high level of protection, the precautionary principle, the preventive action principle, and that environmental damage should as a priority be rectified at source, as well as that the polluter should pay. There are a number of contextual issues to be taken into account: (a) available scientific and technical data; (b) regional differences in terms of environmental conditions; (c) the potential benefits and costs of action or lack of action and the economic and social development of the Community as a whole and the balanced development of its regions. While the co-decision procedure and QMV apply to most environmental policy-making, the Council acts unanimously on provisions primarily of a fiscal nature and measures affecting town and country planning, the management of water resources, land use (with the exception of waste management), and a member state's choice between energy sources or the structure of its energy supply (Art. 175 TEC; ex Art. 130s EEC). Finally, temporary derogations or financial support from the Cohesion Fund may assist member states to deal with costs that are deemed disproportionate for the public authorities.

5 This is generally also true at the member-state level, where inter-ministerial relations and the level of ministerial autonomy from the head of government or the cabinet affect the final decisions.

6 See n. 2 above.

7 Ken Collins was chairman from 1979 until 1984 and 1989 until 1999, and vice chairman from 1984 until 1989.

8 Proportional voting for EP elections is responsible for the UK currently having five green MEPs, whereas domestically first-past-the-post voting works against the representation of smaller, non-regional parties.

9 See the cases on detergents and sulphur content in liquid fuel (91/79 and 92/79 *Commission v. Italy*, ECR 1980: 1099, 1115).

10 Direct litigation proceedings give private actors and environmental

groups only restricted *locus standi* before the court, namely when they can show direct and individual concern (Nollkaemper 2002).

11 See standard form for complaints to the Commission [1995] OJ C119/5.

12 The data would lead the reader into thinking that the implementation performance in the member states is steadily worsening. But the data merely reflect the Commission's activities in pursuing potential infringements in the member states (Börzel 2001).

13 The Water Framework Directive of 2000, for instance, consolidates previous regulatory output by replacing seven of the 'first wave' water directives. By requiring all member states to cooperate in the management of river basins, the EU brought the hitherto neglected cross-boundary and cross-media effects of water pollution into focus (Grant *et al.* 2000: 167–75). In 2004, waste and air quality legislation were to be screened for potential simplication and consolidation (Commission 2004b: 27).

14 ENVIREG was a Community initiative under the structural funds (initiated in 1990) to encourage regions to utilize resources for economic development more efficiently within the context of environmental protection. The Mediterranean Special Programme of Action (MEDSPA) was a 1991 initiative (Regulation 563/91) on the protection and improvement of the environment in the Mediterranean region, within and outside the Community.

15 The new member states have received between three (Czech Republic) and ten (Poland) transitional arrangements; the transition periods vary between countries and environmental sectors (the longest periods apply to industrial pollution). Complete data can be accessed at the Commission website: *http://europa.eu.int/comm/enlargement/ negotiations/*.

16 Besides the explicit financial support for less prosperous states, regulatory derogations and differential emission limits also imply redistributive effects.

17 Compared to 7 per cent for the US (albeit still hypothetical in the absence of a US signature), and 6 per cent for Japan.

Further reading

The recently updated manual of EU environmental policy (Haigh 2004) provides a brief overview of all EU environmental legislation and their political development; it pays particular attention to the British role in decision-making as well as implementation. Weale *et al.* (2000) provides a good overview of EU environmental governance, including several case studies. Jordan (ed.) (2002a) puts together core articles on this topic from the past ten years and a new edition is currently under preparation. Wurzel (2002), Jordan (2002b), Knill (2002), and Liefferink with Jordan (2004) look at the interplay between (selected) member states and EU policy-making—a topic only alluded to in this chapter. On new policy instruments in the EU and in the member states, see Jordan, Wurzel, and Zito (2003) and for implementation, Knill and Lenschow (2000).

Jordan, A. (2002a) (ed.), *Environmental Policy in the European Union: Actors, Institutions and Processes* (London: Earthscan).

Jordan, A. (2002b), *The Europeanization of British Environmental Policy: A Departmental Perspective* (Basingstoke: Palgrave Macmillan).

Jordan, A., Wurzel, R., and Zito, A. (2003), *'New' Instruments of Environmental Governance: National Experiences and Prospects* (London: Frank Cass).

Haigh, N. (2004) (ed.), *Manual of Environmental Policy: The EU and Britain*, Institute of European Environmental Policy (IEEP) (Leeds: Maney Publishing).

Knill, C. (2002), *The Europeanisation of National Administrations: Patterns of Institutional Change and Persistence* (Cambridge: Cambridge University Press).

Knill, C., and Lenschow, A. (2000) (eds.), *Implementing EU Environmental Policy: New Directions and Old Problems* (Manchester: Manchester University Press).

Liefferink, D., and Jordan, A. (2004) (eds.), *Environmental Policy in Europe: The Europeanisation of National Environmental Policy* (London: Routledge).

Weale, A., Pridham, G., Cini, M., Konstadakopolos, D., Porter, M., and Flynn, B. (2000), *Environmental Governance in Europe* (Oxford: Oxford University Press).

Wurzel, R. (2002), *Environmental Policy-making in Britain, Germany and the European Union* (Manchester: Manchester University Press).

Chapter 13

Biotechnology Policy

Between National Fears and Global Disciplines

Mark A. Pollack and Gregory C. Shaffer

Contents

Summary

Over the past two decades the institutions of the European Union (EU) have emerged as the primary regulators of genetically modified (GM) foods and crops, one of the most controversial and complex policy issues facing the Union today. Agricultural biotechnology presents three special challenges to the EU. It is multi-sectoral (cutting across multiple 'issue areas'); multi-level (cutting across national, supranational, and global levels of governance); and inherently concerned with *risk regulation* (which raises both scientific and ethical challenges to the EU and its institutions). The Union adopted its first binding regulations on GM foods and crops in 1990. The implementation of these regulations proved controversial, provoking a revolt among member governments that responded with a *de facto* moratorium on the approval of new GM varieties. Faced with widespread governmental and public calls for a stricter and more comprehensive approach, since 2000 the Union has engaged in a root-and-branch reform of EU policies, setting out detailed rules on labelling for GM foods and the traceability of GM crops 'from farm to fork'. EU regulations have not developed in isolation, however. Instead, EU policies have been shaped by international pressures from the United States (US) and the World Trade Organization (WTO), while the EU has sought to export its domestic regulatory principles internationally.

Introduction[1]

Few issues of European law and policy excite as much attention and concern as the creation and marketing of genetically modified organisms (GMOs). Lauded by many scientists, policy élites, and members of the biotech industry as a scientific and economic step forward, genetically modified (GM) foods and crops have also been rejected as unsafe or undesirable by many environmentalists and consumer advocates, and by the greater part of the European public. Into this controversy have stepped the institutions of the EU, which increasingly play the leading role in establishing the regulatory framework for the growing and marketing of GM foods and crops in the Union's twenty-five member states.

In this chapter, we examine EU policy and policy-making in the area of biotechnology, with a specific focus on agricultural biotechnology—namely, the development and marketing of GM crops and foods. More specifically, the chapter summarizes both the *content* of the EU's rapidly evolving regulations, and the *process* whereby these regulations have been promulgated, implemented, and comprehensively reformed in the space of little more than a decade. EU policy in this area is predominantly regulatory in character, setting the increasingly detailed regulatory framework within which GM foods and crops may be developed, introduced into the environment, and work their way into the food supply.

This chapter examines the challenges posed by biotechnology as a multi-sectoral and multi-level area of policy-making, involving the regulation of risk. It then provides a historical background to EU biotech policy, followed by a section on the problems of implementing the Union's early regulations. The chapter next examines recent EU reforms of GM regulatory policy and the relationship between EU regulations and international trade and environmental rules. The concluding section assesses EU biotech policy in relation to the typology of modes of governance discussed in Chapter 3, and in particular the 'regulatory mode'. The chapter does not deal with the similarly interesting issues that arise in other areas of biotech policy, such as developing patenting rules for new and controversial inventions.

Regulating GMOs: three challenges

GMOs pose three fundamental challenges to the Union's regulatory capacity. Biotechnology is an issue that is inherently *multi-sectoral*, requiring horizontal coordination across a range of issue areas; inherently *multi-level*, requiring vertical coordination across the national, supranational, and international arenas; and inherently concerned with *risk regulation*, requiring difficult, highly contested decisions about the role of science and politics in the assessment and management of risk to modern European societies.

A multi-sectoral challenge

The regulation of biotechnology is a complex and multi-sectoral policy, involving actors and perspectives from many distinct issue areas. For example, within the Commission biotech policy raises important questions for the DGs with responsibility for the internal market, industrial policy, research and technological development, environmental protection, food safety and consumer protection, agriculture, and international trade. Each of these issue areas, moreover, raises the following distinct matters regarding the regulation of GMOs:

The *internal market* has as its primary goal the free movement of goods, services, labour and capital, and hence specifically the free movement of GM seeds, crops, and food within the Union. Indeed, the need to complete the internal market was claimed by the Commission as the primary legal basis of much EU legislation in this area.

Biotechnology has consistently been an important question for the Union's *industrial policy*, as the Commission and others have sought to secure a regulatory environment conducive to the development of a European biotech industry able to compete with that of the US.

Biotechnology appeared at an early stage on the agenda of the Union's *research and technological development policy*, as a priority area for collaborative cross-national scientific research.

The promotion of biotechnology, however, must contend with the potential *environmental* effects of its use, particularly with regard to the release of living GMOs (i.e. seeds and crops) into the environment. Largely for this reason, the Commission's Directorate-General for the Environment has played a leading role in the formulation of EU biotech policy, which has been negotiated and adopted predominantly by the Council of Environment Ministers, together with the European Parliament (EP).

Finally, marketing GM foods raises questions of *food safety and consumer protection*, insofar as EU consumers worry about the safety of GM foods or simply insist on the right to know whether the foods they buy are genetically modified or contain a genetically modified ingredient. Consumer concerns about food safety have played a key role in the controversies regarding the regulation and marketing of GM foods. By the same token, EU regulations on traceability and labelling of GM animal feed, food, and crops have significant implications for the Union's common agricultural policy (CAP; see Chapter 7).

The EU's regulation of GM foods does not take place in a vacuum, but has repercussions for the Union's international trade relations. Even when adopted for entirely domestic reasons, EU regulation can have an impact on the flow of GM foods and crops from third countries such as the US, and hence must be addressed by DG Trade. Indeed, the need to justify EU policies within the legal framework of the WTO has led to substantial reforms of EU biotech policy over the past decade, although it is controversial whether these changes constitute a 'watering down' or a 'trading up' of EU regulations (Young 2003).

As a multi-sectoral issue, the regulation of GMOs raises the challenge of coordinating policy-making horizontally among a large number of actors with diverse perspectives on the aims and the context of EU regulation. Not surprisingly, it has proven difficult for the European Commission and the other institutions of the Union to coordinate policy-making across so many issue areas. The Commission has established, and repeatedly reformed, multi-sectoral working groups to coordinate policy across all DGs with an interest in the issue. The multi-sectoral nature of GMOs has also rallied a range of individuals and interest groups in organized opposition to GMOs from a variety of perspectives (environmental, food safety, and anti-globalization). From this hybrid mix of politics, GMO policy-making has emerged as a volatile issue.

A multi-level process: three arenas

The regulation of biotechnology has also been marked by a multi-level process which involves overlapping and sometimes conflicting regulations promulgated at the national, supranational/EU, and international levels. EU policy-makers, therefore, face not only the challenge of horizontal coordination across issue areas, but also the vertical coordination of EU policies with a diverse and politically sensitive set of national policies, and a growing body of international trade and environmental law governing the release and marketing of GMOs. EU policy has faced sharp political and legal challenges from below (in the form of national revolts against the licensing of individual GM foods and crops), and from above (in the form of challenges from other countries within the WTO).

Prior to the adoption of the first EU regulations in 1990, biotech R&D in Europe was regulated entirely at the national level. These national regulations varied across the member states, with countries such as Denmark and Germany imposing tight restrictions on genetic engineering research, with others, such as the UK and France, being more permissive, and relying mainly on self-regulation, and a large third group which had not yet adopted any regulations (Cantley 1995).

The European Commission came forward during the latter half of the 1980s with its first proposals for the regulation of GMOs. On the basis of these proposals, in 1990 the Council of Ministers adopted the first binding EU directives on the contained use and deliberate release of GMOs. However, those directives featured substantial roles for the EU's member governments, which would play an important part in the initial approval of GM foods and crops, and retain the ability to impose national-level safeguards against GMOs authorized at the EU level.

Biotech regulation has become an increasingly important matter for the global trade, environment, and food safety regimes. National and EU regulation of biotechnology, while aiming primarily at environmental protection, consumer protection, or food safety, also has important implications for international trade, since these regulations can serve as non-tariff barriers impeding the free movement of GM foods and crops across national borders. The question of biotech regulation as non-tariff barriers became an important political and legal issue from the late-1990s when US farmers rapidly adopted GM foods and crops only to find themselves unable to export them to the EU, where new varieties were slow to meet with regulatory approval, and where even approved varieties encountered national barriers and strict EU labelling requirements. In the US, the EU's stringent regulations, and the *de facto* moratorium on new approvals after 1998, smacked of protectionism and irrationality. The US placed increasing pressure on the Commission to end the moratorium and to resume approval of new GM varieties, culminating in the US filing a WTO legal dispute against the EU in May 2003. Within Europe, however, US pressure prompted a backlash from environmental, consumer, and agricultural groups, and from some member governments, further politicizing an already sensitive issue. Caught between these conflicting national and international pressures, the European Commission sought, albeit with limited success, to reconcile the political demands of European citizens and national governments, on the one hand, with the legal obligations and political pressures from the international arena, on the other.

Risk regulation and legitimacy

Finally, the regulation of biotechnology intersects with two broader, vitally important, and interrelated questions for the Union, namely the regulation of risk and the legitimacy of EU governance. In particular, risk regulation raises fundamental normative questions about the roles of science and politics in the management of risk, calling into question the legitimacy of EU decision-making in a context in which democratic control of EU institutions is widely considered to be inadequate (Scharpf 1999; Greven 2000).

In modern societies, governmental actors are frequently called upon to adopt regulations regarding the acceptable degree of risk posed to society by products or by industrial processes. Risk, in this context, refers to 'the combination of the likelihood (*probability*), and the harm (*adverse outcome*, e.g. mortality, morbidity, ecological damage, or impaired quality of life), resulting from exposure to an activity (*hazard*)' (Wiener and Rogers 2002: 320, emphasis in original). In principle, therefore, regulators faced with a novel product or process—such as the genetic modification of foods and crops—need to ascertain the potential harm caused by such activities, as well as the probability of such harm, before deciding on the legality or illegality of a product or process.

In practice, risk regulation frequently requires regulators to act in the face of *uncertainty* regarding the nature and extent of the risks posed by new products and processes, raising the fundamental political question of how governments should regulate risk in the face of such uncertainty. Frequently, regulators take *precautionary* measures, regulating or even banning products or activities, in the absence of complete information about the risks posed. All government regulators engage in some form of precautionary regulation. In the US, for example, federal government regulators began in the 1970s with relatively blunt approaches, such as banning potentially harmful or carcinogenic products, and have gradually moved towards more discriminating approaches, such as the conduct of scientific risk assessments to assess the likelihood of risk and cost-benefit analysis to weigh potential gains to society from alternative types of regulation (Majone 2003).

By contrast, risk regulation in Europe took place largely at the national level until the 1980s, when EU institutions began to play an increasing role in harmonizing risk regulation across the member states. The EU's approach to risk regulation has evolved quite differently from that of the US (Vogel 2001). Whereas the former began with highly precautionary legislation in areas such as the environment, consumer protection, and worker health and safety, only to adopt scientific risk assessment and cost-benefit analysis more recently, regulators in the EU have become more precautionary and more risk-averse over time. Vogel argues that US and EU risk regulation resemble 'ships passing in the night', with the EU becoming more precautionary, and the US less precautionary over time. Vogel and others argue that a key cause has been a series of European regulatory failures and crises over the past decades, including the BSE or 'mad cow' crisis, which have weakened public trust in EU regulators and scientific risk assessments, increased support for highly precautionary regulations, and called into question the *legitimacy* of EU regulations and EU institutions in European public opinion. Responding to this crisis of legitimacy, EU institutions have moved aggressively to overhaul EU risk regulation across a range of areas (see, e.g., Bodansky 1991; Commission 2000c; Wiener and Rogers 2002; and Majone 2002).

Other scholars dispute Vogel's characterization, noting that the purported 'flip-flop' in US and EU approaches draws disproportionately from a few controversial issue areas, such as the use of growth hormones in beef cattle, and the regulation of GMOs. In a wide-ranging survey of US and European risk regulation, Wiener and Rogers (2002) find a more complex set of outcomes, in which the US is more precautionary in some areas (e.g. nuclear energy, particulate air pollution), and the EU in others (GMOs, hormone-treated beef). For this reason, we will not generalize from our study of GMO regulation to the question of comparative precaution in general. Yet, we do emphasize the challenges posed to the EU's regulatory capacity and legitimacy by questions of risk regulation (see, e.g., Neyer 2000; Vos 2000; Joerges 2001b; Vogel 2001; Chalmers 2003; and Majone 2003).

Historical origins of EU biotech policy

The 1957 Treaty of Rome (EEC) made no explicit mention of a policy for biotechnology, or even for the closely related areas of environmental protection and food safety, which remained primarily national responsibilities within each of the member states. However, over the past three decades the Union developed *de facto* policies on biotechnology, as the EU's policies on R&D, agriculture, food safety, and the internal market have 'spilled over' into the regulation of the content and labelling of GM foods and crops.

Genetic engineering is a technology used to isolate genes from one organism, manipulate them in the laboratory, and inject them into another organism. This technology, also known as recombinant DNA (rDNA) research, first emerged as a concern for national and international regulators in the 1970s, as biological scientists began making crucial advances in rDNA research.[2] The debate over the regulation of such research is often dated to the international meeting of scientists at Asilomar, California, in 1975, which highlighted the promise of biotechnology, but also called on the scientific community to exercise caution and restraint in the creation of genetically engineered organisms that might prove hazardous. During this period, from the 1970s through the mid-1980s, the development and marketing of GM foods and crops was a distant goal, and regulators in Europe and elsewhere focused primarily on issues relating to laboratory research and the development of a competitive biotech industry. In 1978, the Commission DG for Science, Research and Development (then DG XII) proposed a Community R&D programme in molecular biology, together with a draft directive requiring notification and prior authorization by national authorities for all biotech research. This latter proposal was withdrawn by the Commission in 1980, in favour of a non-binding 1982 Council Resolution calling for notification of rDNA research to national authorities. Commission concerns about the competitiveness of the EU's biotech industry remained, however, and in 1983 it incorporated biotechnology into its multi-annual Framework Programme for research and technological development.

By the mid-1980s, with the rapid development of genetic engineering and the early efforts to regulate biotechnology among the member governments, the Commission began to explore the development of a Community framework for biotech regulation more actively. The Commission created inter-departmental coordinating bodies, notably the Biotechnology Steering Committee (1984), and the Biotechnology Regulation Inter-service Committee (1985), to determine a new regulatory approach (Patterson 2000: 324–32). Within these groupings, the centre of gravity gradually shifted away from DG XII, and towards other DGs, particularly Environment (DG XI), which became involved in the late 1980s, as biotechnology moved increasingly out of the laboratory and toward releases into the environment and the marketing of GM foods and crops. With DG ENV taking the lead, in 1986, the Commission released another Communication, 'A Community Framework for the Regulation of Biotechnology', which laid out the Commission's rationale for a European regulatory regime and its plans for specific EC regulations (see Box 13.1). 'The internal market arguments for Community-wide regulation of biotechnology are clear', it argued. 'Micro-organisms are no respecters of national frontiers, and nothing short of Community-wide regulation can offer the necessary consumer and environmental protection' (Commission 1986).

The 'Deliberate Release' Directive 90/220

The Commission came forward in May 1988 with its proposal for two new directives, which ultimately became Directive 90/219 on the Contained Use of Genetically Modified Micro-organisms, and Directive 90/220 on the Deliberate Release into the Environment of Genetically Modified Organisms. The first relates primarily to the safety procedures for laboratory research involving genetic modification, whereas the second concerned the release of GMOs from the laboratory into the environment, as well as the marketing of GM foods and crops. We concentrate on Directive 90/220, which emerged during the 1990s as the primary, and most controversial, EU regulation governing the approval and marketing of GM foods and crops.

The Commission's (1988) proposal for a 'Deliberate Release Directive' began by noting the extraordinary diversity of existing national regulations across the member states, including: (a) a ban on deliberate release (subject to exceptions) in Denmark and Germany; (b) a case-by-case approach to the release of individual GMOs in a number of member states (UK, France, Belgium, Netherlands, and Luxembourg); and (c) an absence of legislation in other member states (Ireland, Greece, Italy, Spain, and Portugal). These differences, the Commission argued, could distort competition among member states in the biotech sector, and impede the development of a competitive European biotech industry. Accordingly, the Commission proposed a draft directive to be adopted under Article 100a (EEC) (now Art. 95 TEC), and hence using

Box 13.1 Key events in EU biotech regulation

1975	Asilomar conference on biohazards posed by GMOs
1978	Commission proposes Directive requiring prior notification and authorization of GM research (withdrawn 1980)
1983	Biotechnology included in EU Framework R&D Programme
1984	Commission forms Biotech Steering Committee
1986 (Nov.)	Commission report, *A Community Framework for the Regulation of Biotechnology*
1988	Commission proposes twin directives on Contained Use and Deliberate Release of GMOs
1990	Council adopts Directives 90/219 and 90/220
1996 (March)	Start of BSE Crisis, questioning of EU food safety regulation
1997 (Jan.)	Council adopts Novel Foods Regulation
1997 (Jan.)	Commission approves sale of GM maize; three member states invoke safeguard clause
1998 (Oct.)	Start of *de facto* moratorium on approval of new GM varieties
1999 (June)	Declaration of moratorium on GM approvals by five member states
2000 (Jan.)	White Paper on Food Safety
2000 (Jan.)	White Paper on the Precautionary Principle
2000 (Jan.)	Cartagena Protocol on Biosafety Adopted
2001 (March)	Council and EP adopt Directive 2001/18, replacing 90/220, on deliberate release of GMOs
2002 (Jan.)	Establishment of European Food Safety Authority
2003 (May)	US launches WTO complaint over EU regulation of GMOs
2003 (Sept.)	Council and EP adopt Regulation 1830/2003 on Traceability and Labelling of GMOs
2003 (Sept.)	Council and EP adopt Regulation 1829/2003 on Genetically Modified Food and Feed
2004 (Apr.)	Entry into force of Regulations 1829/2003 and 1830/2003
2004 (May)	Commission ends moratorium with approval of Bt-11 maize

the cooperation legislative procedure involving the European Parliament (EP). By contrast with the regulatory approach of the US, which regulated GMOs according to the characteristics of the final *product* rather than genetic modification as a *process*, the Commission's proposal followed the approaches of countries such as Germany and Denmark in adopting a process-based approach, creating special and distinct regulations for the approval and marketing of GMOs.

The Commission's proposal emphasized the scientific uncertainty associated with genetic engineering, and proposed a scheme that would provide for case-by-case assessment and authorization of the release of new GM varieties into the environment. Significantly, the Commission proposed a procedure that, at least in the first instance, involved regulatory assessment and approval by a national regulatory authority, followed by the sharing of information among the member states, with EU institutions intervening to regulate directly only if member governments disagreed on the safety of a given GM variety.

More specifically, the Commission's proposal would require any individual wishing to release GMOs into the environment (e.g. for farming or marketing) to notify and to provide a detailed risk assessment to the competent regulatory authority of the EU member government where the release was proposed. That member government would then be made responsible for evaluating the application in line with the criteria laid down in the Directive. If the member government rejected the proposal, the procedure would end, but if the proposal was accepted, the dossier would be forwarded to the Commission and to the other member governments, which would have a limited period to object to the authorization. If no objections were raised, the product would be authorized for release and/or placement on the market throughout the EU. By contrast, if one or more member government or the Commission objected, the latter would undertake its own assessment and formulate a Decision to approve or to deny the application. The Commission's draft Decision would be circulated to an advisory committee of member-state representatives, whose opinion the Commission would take into 'utmost account'; the final decision, however, would remain with the Commission. In a final acknowledgement of member-state prerogatives, the Commission proposed a 'safeguard procedure', whereby a member government could, if it had evidence of a serious risk to people or the environment from a previously approved GMO, 'provisionally restrict or prohibit the use or sale of that product on its territory'. Here again, the member government in question would have to inform the Commission of its actions and give reasons for its decision, and the Commission would retain the power to approve or reject the measures in question.

In its first (1989) and second (1990) readings, the EP criticized the Commission proposal as too lax on a number of points, and proposed a number of amendments that would have substantially tightened regulatory restrictions on the approval of new GMOs. By contrast, the US government criticized both the Commission proposal and the EP's proposed amendments as unnecessarily strict and arbitrary, particularly insofar as they proposed to regulate all GMOs regardless of the characteristics of any resulting products (Cantley 1995: 559).

The Council followed the broad lines of the original Commission proposal, thus rebuffing the core US objections, whilst at the same time rejecting the Parliament's most far-reaching amendments. The Council's final text of Directive 90/220 therefore laid out a complicated, multi-level approval process for the release and marketing of GM foods and crops. Under the Directive, as under the original Commission proposal, a manufacturer or importer seeking to market a GMO or release it into the environment first had to submit an application to the competent national authority of a member state, including an extensive scientific risk assessment. The member state to which the application was submitted then examined the dossier, and either accepted or rejected the application. In the case of a favourable opinion, the dossier was then forwarded to the European Commission and to the other member governments, each of which had a right to raise objections. If no objections were raised, then the member state carrying out the original evaluation formally approved the product, which could be marketed throughout the EU.

If one or more member states raised an objection, however, a decision was taken at the EU level. The Commission, acting on the basis of an opinion from its scientific committees, adopted a draft decision, as in the original Commission proposal. However, whereas the original Commission text provided for the Commission to be aided only by an 'advisory committee' of member-state representatives, the final text featured a more constraining 'regulatory committee'. Under the regulatory committee procedure, the Commission's draft decision was forwarded to a committee of member-state representatives, who could approve the decision by a qualified majority vote (QMV). If the regulatory committee did not approve the decision, it would be sent to the Council of Ministers, which could approve the Commission decision by QMV or reject it by a unanimous vote. If the Council failed to act within three months, the Directive provided that 'the proposed measures shall be adopted by the Commission' (Art. 21, Directive 90/220). Finally, and significantly in the light of later developments, the Council retained a slightly modified version of the Commission's safeguard clause, whereby a member state could, on the basis of new evidence about risks to human health or the environment, 'provisionally restrict or prohibit the use and/or sale of that product on its territory'. The member state in question would be required to inform the Commission, which would approve or reject the member-state measures subject to the regulatory committee procedures just described.

The Novel Foods Regulation

In 1997, the Directive 90/220 was supplemented by Regulation 258/97, the so-called Novel Foods Regulation. This regulation defined 'novel foods' as all foods and food ingredients that had 'not hitherto been used for human consumption to a significant degree within the Community', which included foods that were genetically modified and foods produced from, but not containing, GMOs (for example, oils processed from GM crops, but no longer containing any traces of GM material).

The regulation also created an authorization procedure for such novel foods, similar to that of Directive 90/220. Any individual seeking to market a novel food would be required to submit an application in the member state in which the food would first be placed on the market. That state would conduct a thorough assessment and take a decision, which could be contested by any member state. Such contestation would trigger a centralized EU regulatory procedure in which the Commission would again take the leading role, overseen by the Standing Committee on Foodstuffs, consisting of representatives of the member states. The regulation also imposed requirements on novel foods that were authorized for marketing, including the labelling of foods containing GMOs or derived from GMOs, provided that the latter were deemed 'no longer equivalent' to their conventional counterparts.

Significantly, however, the regulation created a simplified procedure for foods derived from, but no longer containing, GMOs, provided these remained 'substantially equivalent' to existing foods in terms of 'their composition, nutritional value, metabolism, intended use and the level of undesirable substances contained therein' (Art. 3, Regulation 258/97). In practice, this provision would prove important in the coming years, as member states would approve a number of products derived from GMOs as being 'substantially equivalent' to their conventional counterparts.

Finally, and significantly in terms of later developments, the regulation (like the earlier Directive 90/220) contained a safeguard clause allowing member states, 'as a result of new information or a reassessment of existing information' to 'temporarily restrict or suspend the trade in and use of the food or food ingredient in question in its territory' (Art. 12, Regulation 258/97). This safeguard clause would later be invoked to contest the 'substantial equivalence' of approved products, raising questions about the adequacy of the existing regulatory structure.

The problem of implementation: member-state revolt and international reaction

To understand successive attempts to regulate agricultural biotechnology in the EU, and the subsequent difficulties of implementation, we need to place these in the context of other developments in the mid-1990s, including the BSE food-safety scandal that struck in 1996. In March 1996, the British government revealed a possible connection between the human illness, Creutzfeldt-Jacob's disease, and bovine spongiform encephalopathy (BSE), spread by the consumption of contaminated feed, and known as 'mad cow disease'. BSE infected some 150,000 cattle in the UK, triggering a wide-scale slaughter of cattle, a Community ban on the export of British beef, a plummet in beef sales throughout Europe, and a loss of consumer confidence in regulatory officials. While the ban on British beef was eventually rescinded, the BSE scandal raised the question of risk regulation 'to the level of high politics, and indeed of constitutional significance' (Chalmers 2003: 534–8), generating extraordinary public awareness of food safety issues and widespread public distrust of regulators and scientific assessments.

It was in this political context that GM crops were first commercially introduced in the US and Europe. In April 1996, within a month of the ban on British beef, the Commission approved the sale of GM soya products over the objections of many member states. In November 1996, GM soya was imported from the US to the EU, spurring widespread protest by Greenpeace and other groups. Media coverage and public debate about GM foods, therefore, began just as the BSE food crisis struck.

Two other critical events occurred in late 1996. In December, a Scottish scientist announced to the world the first successful reproduction of a cloned mammal, a sheep named 'Dolly'. The announcement spurred ethical challenges to biotechnological research. Also in December, the US and Canada lodged complaints with the WTO challenging the EU's ban on hormone-treated beef, on the grounds that it constituted a disguised barrier to trade and was not justified on the basis of a scientific risk assessment. The WTO subsequently ruled against the EU, and, when the EU failed to comply with the ruling, authorized the US and Canada to retaliate by withdrawing trade concessions in an amount equivalent to their trading losses, which they did, imposing trade sanctions worth US$116.8 million and CND$1.3 million per year. Targeted products included traditional French foods such as *foie gras*, Roquefort cheese, and Dijon mustard. The WTO case further rallied a federation of smaller French farm producers and a fervent opponent of GMOs, the Confédération Paysanne, led by José Bové, who became a symbol for anti-globalization and anti-WTO movements worldwide, and a French national hero.

The close succession of these events illustrates how the popular understanding of GM products in Europe became associated with consumer anxieties related to food safety crises, distrust of regulators and scientific assessments, disquiet over corporate control of agricultural production, ethical unease over GM techniques, environmental concerns, and anger over the use by the US of international trade rules to attempt to force 'unnatural' foods on Europeans. A widespread cross-sectoral movement organized to oppose GMOs in Europe, bringing together environmentalists, consumers, and small farmers. The movement operated at multiple levels, working the media and local and national political processes, coordinating transnationally, and lobbying the Commission and EP (Ansell, Rahsaan, and Sicurelli 2005). The British media dubbed GM products 'Frankenstein' foods, playing on fears that scientists and public agencies could not control the release of GM products. Negative European attitudes toward GM crops and foods rose rapidly. In early 1996, 46 per cent of the French were against GMOs, a figure that rose to 65 per cent in 1999, and 75 per cent in 2002. Similarly, over 80 per cent of Germans expressed negative opinions about GMOs by late 1998 (Gaskell, Allum, and Stares 2003).

In the midst of the fray, the Commission approved the sale of another GM food crop (Bt-maize) in January 1997, over the objection or abstention of all but one of the fifteen member governments. The Commission was able to do so because of the approval procedure in Directive 90/220 (Commission 1996b). A member state (in this case France) could approve a GM variety and forward its decision to the Commission and the other member states so that the variety could be marketed throughout the EU. Since some member states objected to this approval, the Commission reviewed the dossier, and approved it. The Commission then submitted a draft authorization to the regulatory committee consisting of representatives from each of the member states. Eight representatives abstained or voted against the approval, so that the Commission forwarded its proposal to the Council. The Council could amend the Commission's proposal only by a unanimous vote, and France announced that it supported the Commission's authorization (Bradley 1998: 212). As a result, even though fourteen member states refused to support the Commission, the approval went forward.

Member governments did not simply accept the Commission's decision. They undermined its implementation, invoking the safeguard clause of Directive 90/220 which permitted a member state to prohibit an approved GM variety in its territory if it had 'justifiable reasons to consider that [the] product . . . constitutes a risk to human health or the environment'. Austria was the first to act, promptly prohibiting the cultivation and marketing of the GM maize variety in February 1997. Luxembourg followed suit in March. In April, the EP, which held no power to block the approvals, nonetheless passed a resolution condemning the 'lack of responsibility of the Commission in unilaterally taking decisions . . . in spite of the negative positions of most member states and the European Parliament'.

Member-state deployment of safeguard bans grew, undermining the central purpose of Directive 90/220 to create a single market for GM crops under a harmonized regulatory system. By January 2004, Austria, France, Greece, Germany, Luxembourg, and the UK had respectively invoked nine safeguard bans (Commission 2004ƒ). Italy invoked an analogous safeguard procedure under Article 12 of the Novel Foods Regulation (Regulation 258/97) to ban the sale of food products containing ingredients from four varieties of GM maize. The Commission forwarded to the regulatory committee a proposal to initiate a legal challenge against these member state bans, but proceeded no further when the committee refused to support it. The Commission decided to bide its time while it proposed new legislation.

Opponents of GMOs worked not only the political process, but also took their battle to the market-place. Under pressure from potential consumer boycotts of their foods, many large European retailers refused to stock GM foods. Large UK supermarket chains, such as Sainsbury, and food processors, such as Haldane Foods, pledged that their company-labelled foods would be GM-free. Thus, although GM soya and maize varieties had been legally authorized for marketing throughout the EU and validated by risk assessments conducted by EU scientific committees, they were subject to bans by member states and were barely commercialized (Vogel 2001: 11).

Responding to the popular backlash against GMOs, in June a group of member states pronounced the need to impose a moratorium on approvals of GM products. Since the earlier date of October 1998 (when two GM varieties of carnations were approved), no GM varieties had been authorized for sale in the EU market, the only exception being for foods derived from GM varieties deemed 'equivalent' to traditional foods under the Novel Foods Regulation. For all these reasons, any account of EU policy-making in the sphere of biotechnology must address not only the *legislative* politics of adopting EU regulations and directives, but also the subsequent and equally acrimonious politics of *implementation*.

The Commission was in a particularly delicate situation at the time. In February 1997, the EP adopted a report that criticized the Commission for its handling of the BSE issue and threatened censure. Parliament's concern over the Commission's handling of EU finances eventually led to a highly critical report from five independent experts in January 1999 that triggered the resignation of the Santer Commission (see Chapter 8). Under the circumstances, the Commission did not wish to further provoke the member governments and the EP by using its powers under existing regulatory procedures to approve GM crops over their objections.

The Commission, nonetheless, was caught in a vice, as it faced determined opposition to the moratorium from the US, where regulatory policy tends to treat GM crops and foods as 'substantially equivalent' to non-GM varieties, and, in consequence, relies largely on industry self-regulation. Unlike Europeans' reactions to GM products, most US consumers have not contested the marketing of GM foods. As a result, the vast majority of GM research, development, and production occur in the US, where around two-thirds of all GM crops are grown. By the end of 2003, around 81 per cent of soya beans, 73 per cent of cotton, and 40 per cent of corn grown in the US were GM varieties, and these figures were rising annually. US exports of soya to the EU were valued at $1.5 billion in 1998, but these sales have since dropped, leading to cries of protectionism from US farmers. In the light of the growth and prospects of agricultural biotechnology for US farmers and industry, their trade associations pressured US authorities to challenge EU trade restrictions bilaterally and under WTO rules. GMO regulation in the Union faced not only the challenge of multi-sectoral coordination, but also a multi-level one.

Reform of EU policy since January 2000

Facing pressure on multiple fronts, the Commission looked for a way to resume approvals of GM varieties, to free up commerce in the internal market, to assuage member states and their constituents that adequate controls were in place, and to restrict the opt-out rights of member governments under 'safeguard' provisions. In particular, the Commission hoped that the moratorium on GM approvals could be addressed through new legislation that would replace or complement Directive 90/220 and the Novel Foods Regulation.

In January 2000 the Commission (2000*b*) issued a preliminary policy initiative in the form of a White Paper, in which it proposed that the EU overhaul its food safety system and establish a new centralized EU agency, the European Food Safety Authority (EFSA).[3] The White Paper's general approach to risk regulation in the food sector divided 'risk assessment' from 'risk management'. Specialized scientific committees within the new agency would conduct risk assessments, and provide food safety information to consumers and operate a rapid alert system in conjunction with member-state authorities to respond to food safety emergencies. Risk *management*, in contrast, would remain under the control of the EU's political bodies. In an annexed 'action plan', the Commission listed over eighty proposed food safety-related measures to adopt, including amendments to Directive 90/220 and the Novel Foods Regulation.

The following month, the Commission (2000*c*) issued a Communication on the precautionary principle, indicative of a more risk-averse approach in an increasingly politicized domain that challenged the legitimacy of EU law. The Commission declared that the 'precautionary principle' would be applied whenever decision-makers identify 'potentially negative effects resulting from a phenomenon, product or process' and 'a scientific evaluation of the risk . . . makes it impossible to determine with sufficient certainty the risk in question [on account] of the insufficiency of the data, their inconclusiveness or imprecise nature'. It stressed that 'judging what is an "acceptable" level of risk for society is an eminently *political* responsibility' (Commission's emphasis). The Commission promised further guidance regarding the application of the principle, which it acknowledged, was 'giving rise to much debate and to mixed and sometimes contradictory views'. The Commission stated that where regulatory decisions were adopted in accordance with the principle, the resulting measures should be proportionate, non-discriminatory, consistent, based on cost-benefit analyses where feasible, and subject to review and ongoing risk assessment. A resolution on the precautionary principle adopted at the Nice European Council in December 2000, granted policy-makers further flexibility. It maintained that risk assessments might not always be possible on account of insufficient data, and that cost-benefit analyses should consider the 'public acceptability' of risk management decisions. This version of the precautionary principle, already too permissive in the views of US policy-makers, had just become more so.

In 1998 the Commission proposed a new directive to replace Directive 90/220, which was eventually enacted in 2001. In the wake of the BSE crisis, the Commission had already reorganized its internal handling of food safety matters within a recast (and renamed) Directorate-General for Health and Consumer Protection (using the

French acronym, SANCO) in 1997 (Skogstad 2003: 6). Once more, the Commission was divided between those who desired less-restrictive authorization and labelling requirements (DG Industry, DG Research, and DG Trade), and those who sought stricter controls (such as DG Environment and DG SANCO) (Stewart and Johanson 1999: 273). The leading players were DG ENV and DG SANCO, both of which favoured a precautionary approach to risk regulation. Overall, the Commission was eager to establish a system that would meet member-state demands for environmental and consumer protection, and in so doing, to bring an end to the *de facto* moratorium and to fend off a potential legal challenge from the US.

Both the EP and Council pressed the Commission for further regulatory controls. The majority of MEPs insisted on tighter labelling requirements and lower thresholds for traces of GMOs in products sold in the EU. The member governments varied in their views, with some determined that no GM crops would be grown in their territories (such as Austria and Luxembourg), and others torn between the demands of GM opponents and those of the biotech sector (such as Germany and the UK).

The resulting legislation, Directive 2001/18, was adopted in March 2001 by co-decision between the Council and European Parliament. The Directive's twin objectives were to protect the environment and human health when GMOs are released into the environment and placed on the market 'as or in products', in both cases to be applied '[i]n accordance with the precautionary principle'. The need to assuage those member governments that desired stringent regulation led to a ratcheting up of EU regulatory requirements (Young 2003). The directive tightened requirements on commercial applicants and member governments, requiring more extensive environmental risk assessment, further information concerning the conditions of the release, and monitoring and remedial plans. Although touted by the EP's rapporteur David Bowe as 'the toughest laws on GMOs in the whole world', the adoption of Directive 2001/18 did not satisfy a core of member governments (in particular, Austria, Denmark, France, Greece, Italy, and Luxembourg), which insisted on continuing the moratorium, and on the need to impose national safeguard bans in the absence of still more stringent EU regulations.

Faced with this continuing resistance, in 2001 the Commission proposed two additional legislative instruments, on the labelling and traceability of GM foods and their use in food and feed. Adopted after drawn-out bargaining between the Commission, Council, and EP, both measures took the form of regulations, and not directives, placing authority predominantly in the hands of Community institutions. Regulation 1829/2003, on the authorization of GMOs in food and feed, replaced the provisions of Directive 2001/18 governing the authorization for marketing GMOs as, or in, products, and the labelling provisions of the Novel Foods Regulation. Regulation 1830/2003, in turn, created new rules on the traceability of GM products throughout the production and distribution process. Both regulations became effective in April 2004 (see Box 13.2).

Regulation 1829/2003 established a more centralized procedure for authorizing the release and marketing of new GM varieties. In this way, the Commission hoped to manage divergent challenges from member governments and the US. The procedural scheme at the EU level became more centralized in two primary respects. First, although the application process still begins when an operator submits an application dossier to the competent authority of a member government, that member government authority now immediately provides the dossier to the EFSA, a centralized EU agency, which in turn issues the risk assessment, working in conjunction with the competent national authority and a Community reference laboratory. The remainder of the new

---

Box 13.2 EU legislation governing GMOs and GM products, May 2004

Step-by-step activities in the production process	Applicable EU legislation
GMO research in laboratories	Contained Use Directive 90/219
GMO experimental releases (trials)	Directive 2001/18
GMO environmental releases for crops	Regulation 1829/2003 and Directive 98/95/EC (common seed catalogue)
Authorization for marketing of GM seeds (for environmental releases of crops)	Regulation 1829/2003 and Directive 98/95/EC (common seed catalogue)
Authorization for marketing of GM food and feed	Regulation 1829/2003
Labelling of GM seed, food, and feed	Regulation 1829/2003
Traceability and labelling of GM products	Regulation 1830/2003

Box 13.3 Authorization for GM products (food and feed) under Regulation 1829/2003

Operator	An operator submits an application to the competent authority from one of the member states
Member state	The member state provides the file to the new European Food Safety Authority (EFSA)
EFSA	The EFSA provides a copy to the other member states and the Commission, and makes a summary of the file publicly available
EFSA	Within six months, the EFSA submits its opinion, based on risk assessments, to the Commission, the member states, and the applicant, and, after the deletion of any confidential information, makes it publicly available
Commission	The Commission is then to issue a draft decision, which may vary from EFSA's opinion, to the regulatory committee consisting of member state representatives
Regulatory Committee Council Commission	The regulatory committee is to deliver its opinion on the Commission's draft decision by a qualified majority. If the committee delivers no opinion or a negative opinion, the Commission must submit its proposal to the Council. If the Council does not adopt (or indicate its opposition to) the Commission's proposal by a qualified majority vote, then the proposed decision 'shall be adopted by the Commission'.

---

authorization procedure is largely similar to that provided under Directives 90/220 and 2001/18 (see Box 13.3). Any authorization of a GM variety, however, is now limited to a term of ten years, although authorizations are subject to renewal.

Secondly, the regulation restricts the grounds on which member states may ban GMOs unilaterally as a 'safeguard measure'. A member state may adopt 'interim protective measures . . . where it is evident that products authorized . . . are likely to constitute a serious risk to human health, animal health or the environment', provided it first informs the Commission of the 'emergency' situation and the Commission does not act. The Commission's original proposal had provided for no such safeguard powers, but the EP and the Council succeeded in including this clause (Scott 2003: 224).

Regulation 1829/2003 also broadened the scope of product coverage in two ways. First, GM animal feed is covered by these regulations for the first time, in addition to GM food for human consumption. Secondly, the new regulation also covers food and feed that do not contain, or consist of, GMOs, but nonetheless are 'derived', in whole or in part, from GMOs, or contain ingredients 'derived in whole or in part from GMOs'. The former 'simplified procedure' has thus been eliminated.

One of the most controversial elements of the new regulation was the establishment of a set of thresholds for permitted traces of GM ingredients, provided their presence is 'adventitious'. Recognizing that it is practically impossible to ensure that any shipment is entirely free of GM material because of the way crops are threshed, stored, and transported, the Commission initially proposed a threshold of 1 per cent GM material, below which any crop would not have to be labelled as containing GM foods. However, environmental and consumer groups, the EP, and several member governments called for lower thresholds. European biotech companies and the US government, by contrast, criticized it as unrealistic, costly, and scientifically unjustified. These divisions were mirrored in the Council, where the UK favoured the Commission's proposed 1 per cent threshold, while Austria at the other extreme favoured thresholds as low as 0.1 per cent. The final wording, in a compromise, established two distinct thresholds. First, food products will not violate labelling requirements if they contain material from EU-approved GMOs 'in a proportion no higher than 0.9 per cent of the food ingredients considered individually . . . provided that this presence is adventitious or technically unavoidable'. Secondly, the regulation establishes a second and stricter threshold of 0.5 per cent for GMOs not yet approved for environmental release in the EU, and establishes a three-year window after which no residues of non-approved GMOs will be allowed in food or feed products.

Regulation 1830/2003, finally, included a more centralized framework for tracing GM products, as Directive 2001/18 had left this responsibility to the member states. The regulation required the Commission to establish a system of unique identifiers for each GMO in order 'to trace GMOs and products produced from GMOs at all stages of their placing on the market through the production and distribution chain'. More specifically, producers must collect and retain data on the GM content of foods and crops one step upstream and one step downstream in the distribution chain, for five years. These strict traceability requirements have been bitterly criticized by many US producers, as well as by some European producers. The Commission has justified these requirements as vital to the EU labelling system and for any future recalls of GM foods or crops.

In 2003 the Commission and biotech companies tried to step up enforcement against non-compliance by member governments with some EU regulatory requirements. In April the Commission issued a 'letter of formal notice' to twelve member states that had failed to implement Directive 2001/18. It initiated a lawsuit against eleven of them in July pursuant to Article 226 (TEC) (ex Art. 169 EEC). When Austria proposed to make the region of Upper Austria a GM-free zone in March 2003, the Commission (following an opinion from EFSA) ruled that Austria's general ban would be illegal, since GMO restrictions should be based on attributes of specific GMOs. Concurrently, three biotech companies (Monsanto, Syngenta, and Pioneer) challenged

Italy's ban on food products containing authorized GM maize before the Italian courts. In September 2003, the ECJ ruled that Italy must conduct 'a risk assessment which is complete as possible . . . from which it is apparent that, in light of the precautionary principle, the implementation of such measure is necessary in order to ensure that novel foods do not present a danger', which Italy had so far failed to demonstrate.[4]

With the 'completion' of the new regulatory framework, the EU tentatively resumed approvals of new GM varieties in May 2004. By early 2004, the Commission had received twenty-two notifications for approvals of GM varieties (Commission 2004*f*). In November 2003, it proposed to approve the importation of a variety of GM maize (Bt-11 maize), for which EFSA had delivered a favourable opinion. This was the first time that the Commission had initiated a GM approval since 1998. The regulatory committee, however, refused approval, and the matter was referred to the Council, which was given until the end of April to act. In April, a divided Agriculture Council failed to reach agreement. In the absence of a decision by the Council, the Commission was free to adopt the proposal—the first new approval of a GM variety in almost six years. Despite this apparent breakthrough, US officials noted that the Commission's decision—greeted by a chorus of condemnation from European environmentalists and consumer groups—was taken over the objections of a bloc of implacably hostile member governments, with no guarantee that additional approvals were to follow, or that EU risk managers would continue to be guided by the scientific risk assessments carried out by the EFSA. In addition, the Commission's approval applied only to importation and not cultivation, and was subject to the full range of EU regulations regarding traceability and labelling, with all their attendant costs. Under the circumstances, Syngenta, the crop's manufacturer, indicated that it had no immediate intention of marketing Bt-11 maize in Europe (*European Report* 2004).

Subsequent approval procedures appeared to support this cautious interpretation of the 'end' of the moratorium. One month following the approval of Bt-11 maize, a regulatory committee of member-state representatives from the now-enlarged EU failed to agree on the Commission's proposed approval of a GM rapeseed (canola). Significantly, six of the ten new member states (Cyprus, Estonia, Hungary, Malta, Lithuania, and Poland) joined six old members (Austria, Denmark, Greece, Italy, Luxembourg, and the UK) in voting against the approval, which was then scheduled for decision by the Council of Ministers. A similar pattern emerged later that month when the Environment Council met to consider the Commission's recommendation to approve another Monsanto variety, the NK603 GM corn. Here again, the Council was divided, with nine member governments (including four new members) voting against, nine in favour, and seven abstaining. Although the Commission approved the variety in July 2004 in the absence of Council agreement, this case once more demonstrated the persistent divisions in the Council on new approvals. Significantly, these cases also seemed to dispel some initial concerns that the new member states— most of which were already engaged in the cultivation of GM crops, often without adequate controls—might serve as a 'Trojan horse' for the US and the biotech industry. Ensuring adequate testing facilities in the new member states remains a challenge, but the ambivalence toward agricultural biotechnology in the 'old' EU is also reflected in public opinion and the governmental positions of the new members.[5]

The future of biotech regulation in the EU thus appears unclear. The Commission has underlined the 'completion' of the EU regulatory framework and the resumption of approvals as major steps forward, yet a careful examination reveals continuing opposition to GMOs among EU member governments as well as in the EP and in European public opinion. Some member governments are now calling for the establishment of an EU liability regime and EU rules on the coexistence of GM and non-GM crops, to protect against the risk of contamination. The Commission held a round-table on the issue in April 2003 with a range of 'stakeholders'. In July 2003, it issued guidelines on coexistence, but left rule-making to the member governments on the grounds of 'subsidiarity'. Despite these efforts, the continuing approval of new GM varieties—and, even more so, the cultivation and marketing of these varieties within the Union—remain in doubt.

The international context

EU regulatory policy for GMOs also faces external challenges, in particular from the US which has exercised bilateral pressure in the shadow of the rules of the WTO. The WTO Agreement on Sanitary and Phytosanitary Measures (SPS Agreement) places the onus on the EU to demonstrate that its regulatory measures for GM products are based on scientific risk assessments and are not disguised restrictions on trade. In the earlier US–EU dispute over the EU's ban on hormone-treated beef, the WTO Appellate Body held that the EU had violated the SPS, because it had failed to base its ban on a scientific risk assessment. When the EU did not comply with the ruling, the WTO Dispute Settlement Body authorized the US and Canada to prescribe retaliatory tariffs against EU products.

Starting in 1997–8—when the EU tightened labelling requirements for GM foods, stopped approving new GM varieties, and effectively shut down the marketing of varieties that had been approved—the US threatened to lodge a complaint with the WTO. It nonetheless hesitated to initiate legal proceedings for years (Pollack and Shaffer 2001b; Shaffer and Pollack 2005). In part, the US government was preoccupied with the EU's ability to retaliate against its own non-compliance with other WTO rulings. In part, it was concerned with larger systemic challenges to the international trade regime that such a controversial case could trigger. In part, it hoped that the dispute would subside once Europeans learned to accept GM products under a reformed European food safety regime. Yet, because the EU moratorium continued, and because affected US commercial interests became increasingly frustrated, the US finally stepped up the pressure by filing a WTO complaint in May 2003 against the EU moratorium and the member-state 'safeguard' bans. The US also appeared poised to challenge new EU labelling rules under another WTO agreement, the Agreement on Technical Barriers to Trade. If the US proceeds with the lawsuit, and if the WTO judicial bodies rule against any of the EU's restrictions and the EU does not comply with the ruling, the US and other complainants could retaliate by raising tariffs on EU products.

WTO rules, and the threat of an adverse WTO judicial ruling, have influenced EU decision-making in two primary ways. First, EU authorities would like to tailor their regime so as to survive a challenge under WTO rules. In order to fend off a US challenge, European public officials have been pressed to set up a system where they do not simply ban GMOs without justification, but rather conduct risk assessments on a case-by-case basis, explicitly justify their decisions on the basis of these assessments, and take account of alternative measures that could accomplish the same regulatory goals in a less trade-restrictive manner (Scott 2003; Young and Holmes 2005). Secondly, many European constituents, and, in particular, the European biotech sector, favour a more flexible European legal regime. They have allies at different levels of government who wish to facilitate the EU's development of this technology. WTO rules offer these advocates a further rationale to press for a more conducive legal regime.

The EU has not accepted passively the influence of WTO rules on its regulatory system. Instead, it has sought actively to *export* its precautionary approach to the international trade, environmental, and food safety regimes, and thus help shield the EU from a WTO legal challenge (Skogstad 2001; Shaffer and Pollack 2005). During the late 1990s, the EU and its members worked with other countries to press for a new international environmental treaty governing GMOs. The treaty was eventually signed in January 2000 as a protocol to the 1992 Convention on Biodiversity, after the US failed to block it. The protocol, known as the 'Biosafety Protocol' or 'Cartagena Protocol', entered into force in June 2003. It expressly incorporates the precautionary principle, providing that a country may reject the importation of a GMO for release into the environment where there is 'lack of scientific certainty regarding the extent of the potential adverse effects . . . on biological diversity in the Party of import, taking also into account risks to human health'. The EU can now cite the protocol as evidence of international consensus (involving over 130 signatory countries) regarding the application of the precautionary principle.

In the light of the multi-sectoral, multi-level nature of GM risk regulation, international rules have both constrained and offered opportunities for EU authorities. The Commission, in particular, can refer to WTO rules to further its policy goals in EU internal debates so as to end member-state safeguard bans and the moratorium on new approvals of GM products. The Commission has also acted as an international policy entrepreneur by working to export the EU's precautionary regulatory approach for GM products to the rest of the world. The EU's regulation of GM foods and crops is intimately bound up, not only with that of its member states, but with regulatory standards and practices at the international level.

Conclusions

The regulation of biotechnology has presented the Union with a number of challenges. Many of these are common to all EU regulations, but others relate specifically to the nature of biotechnology as a highly politicized case of risk regulation, a multi-sectoral challenge requiring cross-sectoral coordination, and a multi-level concern in which EU regulations must respond to both national fears and international disciplines. The policy process most closely approximates the 'regulatory mode' of governance set out in Chapter 3. We find all of its five features in the case of biotech regulation, albeit to differing degrees, and with some policy-specific exceptions.

The Commission has acted as the primary entrepreneur in the development and implementation of EU policies. However, member governments retain important prerogatives, including the power to regulate trial releases of GMOs in the environment, to determine liability and coexistence rules, and to impose safeguard bans on GM seed, feed, and food. The creation of the EFSA in 2002, in addition, has resulted in a separation of executive functions at the EU level, with the EFSA taking primary responsibility for risk assessment, while risk management continues to be shared between the Commission and the member states.

The Council of Ministers has played the dominant role in the adoption of framework directives and regulations, with an increasing role for the EP. In the implementation of EU regulations, and the approval (or blockage) of new GM varieties, regulatory committees of officials representing member states have played at least as important a role as the Council meeting at ministerial level. The Parliament has been essentially an onlooker regarding the implementation of EU legislation—albeit an approving one since the moratorium on new varieties has dragged on from year to year. The ECJ, by contrast, has not yet been a major player in the enforcement (or the challenging) of EU agricultural biotech regulation, which would involve the Court in some of the most sensitive and politically charged areas of EU policy. There are signs, however, that the Court may play a greater role insofar as citizens, interest groups, grain traders, and biotech companies seek to challenge, clarify, and enforce the growing corpus of EU biotech regulation in the courts.

Although the EU has been a pioneer and a laboratory for international regulatory harmonization, it is joined in this endeavour by other international organizations, such as the WTO, to the disciplines of which EU regulation is increasingly subject. Indeed, we suggest that a central lesson of the biotech case is that EU policy-making is no longer simply above the nation-state, but instead lies *between* the nation-state and the growing imperatives of global governance.

Finally, we re-emphasize the special challenges posed to the EU by biotechnology as a question of risk regulation. As we have seen, national governments and publics have repeatedly questioned the legitimacy of EU regulations in this area, prompting root-and-branch reform of the policy in the early 2000s. In addition to these reforms, the Commission has experimented with two alternative modes of governance. First, and in common with other areas of EU regulation, it has moved toward a system of 'structured transgovernmentalism' in which EU regulatory committees and the new EFSA bring together a community of scientists from throughout the Union that specialize in GMOs. Many EU authorities hope that this 'epistemic' community can reach common accord and help structure European political and social understandings of GM products. Secondly, the EU has also moved toward 'new governance' mechanisms with the holding of numerous 'stakeholder forums' on GMO-related issues, and Commission officials speak of the need to 'democratize expertise' and to 'expertise democracy' (Christophorou 2003). The adoption of these governance modes, however, has been quite limited, with the EFSA providing only risk assessment and stakeholder forums having only a limited impact on EU decision-making. References to these governance modes appear primarily as responses to legitimacy challenges to EU decisions about risk management, as opposed to genuine alternative modes of governance.

Most importantly, the case of agricultural biotech regulation in the EU points to the limitations of EU supranational policy-making when regulatory issues become highly politicized. Neither the adoption of a more centralized regulatory model, nor attempts to complement it with transgovernmental and stakeholder modes of policy-making, have shielded EU risk-management decisions on GMO approvals from public challenge. Disputes over risk regulation in this domain risk becoming disputes over the legitimacy of EU law itself.

Notes

1 This chapter, like previous collaborations, represents an ongoing and equal intellectual partnership. The authors would like to thank Timo Weishaupt for invaluable research assistance, and the Center for World Affairs and the Global Economy at the University of Wisconsin-Madison for financial support. Earlier versions of this chapter were presented at the 2004 Conference on Europeanists, 11–13 March, Chicago, IL, and at the 2004 annual meeting of the Law and Society Association, 27–30 May, Chicago, IL. We thank Daniel Wincott, and other conference participants for their comments and suggestions.

2 This section draws liberally from Lee Ann Patterson's (2000: 319–32) analysis of the early history of EU biotech regulation, as well as from Cantley's (1995) detailed study.

3 In 2002, the Council and EP adopted EC Regulation 178/2002 pursuant to which the new agency, EFSA, was created. While member states lobbied over its location, the EFSA was temporarily housed in Brussels.

The European Council finally determined in December 2003 that its headquarters would be established in Parma, Italy. See EFSA press release (*www.efsa.eu.int/*). When fully operational, the EFSA is expected to employ 250 people with a budget of €40 mn., a tiny agency compared to the US Food and Drug Administration that employs over 9,000 people and has 2,100 scientists working for it (Buonanno 2005).

4 See Case C-236/01 on a reference for a preliminary ruling from the Tribunale amministrativo e regionale dei Ministri: *Monsanto Agricoltura Italia Spa and Others v. Presidenza del Consiglio dei Ministri and Others* (9 Sept. 2003).

5 A second major change in the Union, the Constitutional Treaty signed in Rome in October 2004, does not alter the substance of EU policy or policy-making with regard to agricultural biotechnology, and is therefore unlikely to affect policy toward GMOs if and when it is ratified and comes into force.

Further reading

The literature on agricultural biotechnology has mushroomed in recent years. Cantley (1995) provides the definitive early history of EU policy-making in this area, while Majone (2003), Vogel (2001), Wiener and Rogers (2002), and Young (2003) all provide useful analyses of EU risk regulation in comparative and international perspective. On the precautionary principle in risk regulation, see, for example, Bodansky (1991), Commission (2000c), Wiener and Rogers (2002), and Majone (2002). On risk regulation and EU governance, see Neyer (2000), Vos (2000), Joerges (2001b), Vogel (2001), Chalmers (2003), and Majone (2003).

Bodansky, D. (1991), 'Scientific Uncertainty and the Precautionary Principle', *Environment*, 33/4–5: 43–4.

Cantley, M. (1995), 'The Regulation of Modern Biotechnology: A Historical and European Perspective: A Case Study in How Societies Cope with New Knowledge in the Last Quarter of the Twentieth Century', in Rehm and Reed (eds.), *Biotechnology, xii, Legal, Economic and Ethical Dimensions* (Weinheim: VCH), 506–681.

Chalmers, D. (2003), 'Food for Thought: Reconciling European Risks and Traditional Ways of Life', *Modern Law Review*, 66/4: 532–64.

Commission (2000c), Commission Communication on the Precautionary Principle, COM (2000) 1 final.

Joerges, C. (2001b), 'Law, Science and the Management of Risks to Health at the National, European and International Level: Stories on Baby Dummies, Mad Cows and Hormones in Beef', *Columbia Journal of European Law*, 7: 1–19.

Majone, G. (2002), 'What Price Safety? The Precautionary Principle and its Policy Implications', *Journal of Common Market Studies*, 40/1: 18–109.

Majone, G. (2003), 'Foundations of Risk Regulation: Science, Decision-Making, Policy Learning and Institutional Reform', in Majone (ed.), *Risk Regulation in the European Union: Between Enlargement and Internationalization* (Florence: European University Institute).

Neyer, J. (2000), 'The Regulation of Risks and the Power of the People: Lessons from the BSE Crisis', European Integration online Papers (EIOP), 4/6, *http://eiop.or.at/eiop/texte/*.

Vogel, D. (2001), *Ships Passing in the Night: GMOs and the Contemporary Politics of Risk Regulation in Europe* (San Domenico di Fiesole: EUI-Robert Schuman Centre for Advanced Studies), RSC Working Paper No. 2001/16.

Vos, E. (2001), 'EU Food Safety Regulation in the Aftermath of the BSE Crisis', *Journal of Consumer Policy*, 23: 227–55.

Wiener, J. B., and Rogers, M. D. (2002), 'Comparing Precaution in the United States and Europe', *Journal of Risk Research*, 5/4: 317–49.

Young, A. R. (2003), 'Political Transfer and "Trading Up"? Transatlantic Trade in Genetically Modified Food and US Politics', *World Politics*, 55: 457–84.

Chapter 14

Fisheries Policy

Letting the Little Ones Go?

Christian Lequesne

Contents

Summary

Technological changes, extensions of territorial waters, and successive enlargements of the European Union (EU) have transformed the context since the common fisheries policy (CFP) was first formulated in 1970. Although this is not a particularly economically significant sector, employing only approximately 260,000 people throughout the EU25, its political and social salience is high. There are sharp differences of interest, and of approach, not only among member governments, but also within the major fishing countries. In addition to political, social, and economic factors, conservation of fish stocks has become a major concern, articulated by an expert policy community of biologists and economists. The diversity of distinct and geographically-concentrated fishing communities has made it difficult for an EU-wide lobby to emerge; instead interests are mobilized locally. As a result a nominally common policy has been implemented in very different ways within different member countries and regions. Challenges to national fisheries regulation have accounted for a rising number of cases presented to the European Court of Justice (ECJ). Negotiations with third countries over access to fishing grounds have also become a significant aspect of the EU's external relations, and eastern enlargement, bringing in Polish and Baltic fishing fleets, presents a further challenge for the CFP.

Introduction

A common fisheries policy (CFP) has been on the agenda of the European Union (EU) since 1970. Although it appears at first hand to be a technical area which affects few European citizens, this policy has not met the predictions of neo-functionalist theorists, who envisaged the process of European integration as a matter of experts pooling policy problems in order to produce rational compromises. Instead, the CFP reveals that the EU has not enabled expertise to supplant politics and politicians. Alongside the Commission officials, who endeavour to preserve fish stocks on the basis of scientific opinion, the CFP illustrates, above all, that the EU is an arena for negotiating compromises between governments and social actors. These actors comprise not only fishermen, but also manufacturers in the fish-processing industry, consumers, and environmentalists, who occasionally obtain additional resources from the EU for representing their interests. Moreover, the CFP demonstrates how European integration cannot be studied and understood without taking into account a series of factors, such as: the implementation of the CFP in areas where market forces have not erased the idiosyncrasies of the sector; the globalization of trade; the role of borders (both terrestrial and maritime); and the importance of history and of symbols in the European context.

The CFP operates not through a transnational process in which experts regulate problems in a rational way; instead it is based on negotiations between diverse political and social actors who defend interests which are anchored in national and local territories. This chapter identifies the conditions and results of this permanent negotiation, using four axes of analysis. First, the historical conditions leading to the inclusion of fisheries on the agenda of the EU are examined. Secondly, the interests at stake are described, and, as we shall see, the European arena supplements, but does not replace, the national and local arenas. Thirdly, we asked why the conservation of fish stocks constitutes simultaneously a cornerstone of the CFP and the domain where implementation varies widely between member states. Finally, we argue that the EU, as a new arena for reaching a social compromise, has developed a redistributive function with regard to the different social actors involved in the fisheries sector, while having to evolve to respond to the forces of globalization.

How fisheries policy came onto the EU agenda

Although Article 38 of the Treaty of Rome of 1957 (now Art. 32 TEC) stated that the rules of the common market would apply to fisheries products, under the same heading as agricultural products, it was not until 1970 that Regulation 2141/70 and Regulation 2142/70 introduced the first specific measures for the sector. Three measures were decided: (i) the creation of a common market organization for fisheries' products; (ii) structural aids for the modernization of the sector; and, (iii) guarantees of free access for fishing vessels to the waters of all member states, subject to certain conditions.

An additional step was taken in January 1983 with the adoption of Regulation 170/83, which established a Community regime for the conservation and the management of fisheries resources. This constitutes the cornerstone of the current CFP which has subsequently been amended (in particular to deal with successive enlargements), but not fundamentally altered. Following a report on the CFP compiled by the Commission in 1991 (Commission 1991), Regulation 3760/92, adopted by the Council in December 1992, established a common regime for fisheries and aquaculture. This applies the rules until 2002, where a new Regulation 2371/2002 on the conservation of fisheries resources under the CFP has been adopted, fixing most of the previous arrangements. As is typical of many EU policies, the inclusion of fisheries on the agenda has not been a linear process, but an incremental one, marked not only by developments within the evolution of the EU and its member states, but also by the wider international context (see Box 14.1).

The impact of enlargements

Successive enlargements of the EU have been a key factor in, first, promoting the inclusion of the CFP on the agenda of the EU, and, later, in shaping its evolution. At the end of the 1960s, the applications of the UK, Ireland, Denmark, and Norway (where the negative referendum on accession in September 1972 was largely due to the opposition of its farmers and fishermen) led to predictions of a quadrupling of fish production within the EU, in comparison with that of the six founding members. In 1970 the French government, which was the primary producing country, forced the adoption of two important measures. The first created a common market organization for fisheries products, governed by price stabilization mechanisms, even though the German and Dutch governments were unhappy about the budgetary costs. The second established the principle of free access for member states' vessels to all Community waters. The imminent extension of the exclusive economic zones (EEZ) to 200 nautical miles from the coasts of the applicant countries in the North Sea, was perceived as a threat by the French deep-sea fishermen who, in 1970, caught almost 65 per cent of their fish in what would become the British EEZ, and 20 per cent in the Norwegian and Faroese EEZ (Shackleton 1986).

The enlargement to include Spain and Portugal in 1986 was a second step which shaped the evolution of the CFP. It led to a doubling of the number of fishermen,

Box 14.1	Key dates in the common fisheries policy
1970	Adoption of the first regulations establishing the CFP; free access for vessels, common market organization, structural aid.
1973	Accession of Denmark, Ireland, and the UK to the CFP; Norway does not join, following a negative referendum in which fisheries play an important role.
1976	The foreign ministers of the EU agree at The Hague to create a 200-mile EEZ from 1 January 1977, to which member state vessels would have free access; establishmentof the principle of *relative stability*, but failure to introduce an EU regime of TACs and quotas.
1983	Adoption of a regulation setting a common regime for fisheries resources: introduction of TACs and quotas; a system of 12-mile coastal zones, reserved for the exclusive use of each coastal state; the sole exceptions being 'historical [fishing] rights'.
1991	Publication of a half-term review on the CFP by the Commission.
1992	Adoption of a regulation establishing a Community regime for fisheries and aquaculture: continuation until 2002 of rules of access set in 1983; introduction of a policy to limit catches (licences).
1995	Accession of Austria (no maritime border), Finland, and Sweden to the CFP; following another negative referendum (in which fisheries are less important than in 1972) Norway does not join the EU.
1998	Exercise in consulting the professionals on reforms to the CFP (effective as of 31 December 2002).
2002	Adoption of new regulation on the conservation and sustainable exploitation of fisheries resources under the CFP (effective as of 1 January 2003).

an increase of 65 per cent in fleet tonnage and of 45 per cent in production. Moreover, the rule of free access to all Community waters had to accommodate the fact that two-thirds of Spanish fishing activity and a quarter of Portuguese fishing activity was traditionally practised outside their national waters. The governments of these two applicant countries agreed in the Acts of Accession of 1985 to adopt the *acquis communautaire* in the domain of the CFP, although with a transitional regime until 2002. Their arrival forced a rethinking of policy. The need to modernize the Spanish and Portuguese fleets—older than the Community average—encouraged a stronger emphasis on the structural aspect of the CFP from 1986. Thus, enlargement also enhanced the external dimension of the CFP, since the EU had to assume the obligations—including budgetary obligations—of the bilateral fisheries agreements which linked Spain and Portugal with many third countries.

The accession of the three EFTA countries in 1995 did not, in the event, have a significant impact on the CFP. Had the 1994 referendum in Norway produced a positive result, the situation would have been different, with an increase of 17 per cent in the tonnage of the EU fishing fleet, and 10 per cent in the number of fishermen, as well as the impact of Norway's strict policy on the conservation of resources.

The enlargement of 2004 has been still more marginal than the previous one. None of the ten new member states has a substantial deep-sea fishing fleet. In 2004, Poland, as the country most affected, had only three deep-sea vessels. The majority of Polish fishing takes place in Baltic sea. Some 400 cutters (15–50 metres), and 860 boats (less than 15 metres) fish in Polish waters, mainly for sprat, herring, and cod. The average age of the fleet is thirty years old. For the period 2004–6, €200 million have been earmarked from the structural funds to help restructure the Polish fisheries sector. The same situation applies in the Baltic countries, Cyprus, and Malta. An obvious consequence would be to simply divide structural aid into a greater number of slices.

The issue of conservation

Since the 1970s the debate on dwindling stocks has gained weight through the impetus of the UN institutions and environmental NGOs. The debate has been propelled by the technological changes to fishing vessels and equipment in most producing countries between 1950 and 1960. The development of vessels with deep-freeze facilities, and of techniques such as deep-sea trawling, significantly increased the volume of catches, as well as making them more indiscriminate (Antoine 1995; Revéret and Weber 1997).

The fishery departments of EU member governments, and some Commission officials, considered that the non-binding recommendations made by scientists in the International Council for the Exploration of the Sea (ICES) and in intergovernmental fishery commissions, such as the North East Atlantic Fisheries Commission (NEAFC), were not sufficiently stringent to control overfishing. It became accepted that the EU would need a new regime to manage fishery resources. The expertise of the Commission, which had a 'small' fisheries unit within the Directorate-General for Agriculture (DG AGRI), and the constraints of Community law provided the discipline which the NEAFC could never achieve, in particular measures such as Total Allowable Catches (TACs) (Shackleton 1983).

Extended national territorial waters

Efforts to control over-fishing at a global level had another result which influenced the EU policy, namely widespread pressure on states to exercise stronger national control over the seas. In 1971, the Icelandic government unilaterally declared that it was henceforth sovereign over the waters up to fifty nautical miles from its coasts. This triggered a 'cod war' with British fishermen who were excluded, without further ado, from what had been a traditional fishing area. In 1975, Iceland, this time followed by Norway and Canada, extended its national fishing control up to 200 nautical miles, just as the Third Conference of the United Nations on the Law of the Sea, launched in 1973, seemed to legitimize this measure. The impact of this 'nationalization' of the seas on the UK, Ireland, and Denmark, the new members of the EU, was considerable. Accustomed to operating in Norwegian and Icelandic waters for generations, British fishermen in particular suffered from this exclusion, which was exacerbated by the severe increase in oil prices, and made it more expensive to redeploy vessels to new fishing grounds.

This pervasive ideology of sovereignty, prompted by the new international law of the sea, encouraged these new member states to press for a collective response which would limit the access of third countries to Community waters. Meeting at The Hague in November 1976, the foreign ministers of the EU decided to create an EEZ of

200 nautical miles for all member states as of January 1977. As part of a larger package, the European Commission was also authorized to conclude fisheries agreements with third countries and to negotiate with relevant international organizations, thus signifying a withdrawal of EU members from the NEAFC (Thom 1993). On the other hand, the proposal of the European Commission to introduce a system of TACs in the new EEZs of the member states was not accepted by the governments, and similarly a proposal to establish a common regime of coastal zones under the control of each member state was also shelved. The reservations of the Irish and, above all, of the British governments had a major influence on this failure at The Hague—these two states having 'already accepted' the imposition of the principle of free access as a *fait accompli* during their enlargement negotiations, although the Community fish stocks were concentrated in their EEZs. It was necessary to wait until 25 January 1983, after six long years of negotiation, for an agreement on a common regime, which endorsed the principle of free access for all EU vessels within the 200-mile zone, but reserved a coastal zone of twelve miles for the exclusive use of each coastal state. Only a limited number of vessels from other countries, those which had operated in the twelve-mile zone before the establishment of the CFP, could fish in these coastal zones on the basis of what were termed 'historical rights'. No EEZ was established in the Mediterranean and thus the CFP did not originally apply in this area.

The issue of free access heated up with the accession of Spain and Portugal on 1 January 1986. The strong interest of Spanish fishermen in gaining access to the French, Irish, and British EEZs led the governments of these three countries to insist on strict limits on catches and on the number of vessels authorized to operate during the transitional period. While the conditions for access to the Atlantic became more or less the same after 1 January 1996 for Spanish and Portuguese fishermen as those for fishermen from other member states, the North Sea and the Irish Sea remained still closed to them.

The reform of 2002 has not changed the basic principles of free access. In November 2003, however, the Council adopted a regulation (1954/2003) for a limitation scheme in the Western Waters which includes the end of restrictions for Spanish and Portuguese vessels.

Between Brussels and national and local territories: opposing interests

In the fisheries sector political salience appears to be inversely related to the real economic weight of the sector. In 2004, in no member state of the EU, even Spain, did the value of catches exceed 1 per cent of gross domestic product (GDP). Compared with the total labour force of the EU, fishermen constitute a tiny social group: barely 260,000 people (see Table 14.1).

This political salience derives from a series of factors which have little to do with the statistical indicators. Fishing remains an occupation that, in most European countries, appeals to images that belong to the maritime past of the nation, to the hardships of fishermen seeking to provide food for the population, and to a harsh occupation which bureaucrats—yesterday national, today European—fail to understand.

Table 14.1 Employment in the catching sector, full and part-time, 2000

Member state	1990	1995	2000
Belgium	845	624	540
Cyprus	n.a.	n.a.	5,400
Denmark	6,945	5,055	6,500
Estonia	n.a.	n.a.	5,400
Finland	3,046	2,792	5,600
France	32,622	26,879	21,000
Germany	4,812	4,979	4,300
Greece	39,124	40,164	19,800
Ireland	7,905	5,500	8,400
Italy	41,429	45,000	48,770
Latvia	n.a.	n.a.	n.a.
Lituania	n.a.	n.a.	2,400
Malta	n.a.	n.a.	2,000
Netherlands	3,502	2,752	3,700
Poland	n.a.	n.a.	5,400
Portugal	40,610	30, 937	25,000
Slovenia	n.a.	n.a.	130
Spain	87,351	75,009	85,000
Sweden	3,823	3,400	2,780
UK	24,230	19,928	18,600
EU15	295,399	263,019	n.r.
EU25	n.r.	n.r.	270,720

Source: Commission, DG FISH.

The territorial dimension

Another political dimension is the strong regional concentration of the sector, even if it concerns a limited number of population. In some ports in west Galicia, a significant part of the local population is active in fishing and ancillary activities: canning factories, unloading and fish handling facilities, and shipyards. This is also the case in some Scottish ports such as Lerwick and Scalloway and in some coastal areas of southern Brittany such as the *Pays Bigouden*. This concentration helps to forge strong local identities which, if provoked, can mobilize political activity around the defence of the occupation. In 1993–4, the fall in the price of fish in France led to the setting-up of a 'Committee for Survival' in southern Brittany, which was strongly supported by the local population, despite some violent attacks on public buildings (Couliou 1998). In the UK, 'Save Britain's Fish' (SBF) can also be considered a political movement. Born in the English port of Grimsby, since 1990 the SBF has organized regular demonstrations with the elected representatives of both the Conservative Party and the Labour Party, and the most radical fishermen have called for the UK to opt out of the CFP altogether. SBF has, however, never resorted to violent action.

Fishing, like agriculture, is a heterogeneous sector in the member states of the EU where it is present. In Spain the fishing techniques, income levels, and professional opportunities of the Basque coastal fishermen have little in common with those of the Galician deep-sea fleet which fishes for hake off the coast of Ireland. These in turn differ from the concerns of the shipowners of Vigo, who fish for tropical tuna off the African coast. This social diversity, combined with geographical concentration, fragments the interests of fishermen even within their own national professional organizations. In France, the Union des Armateurs à la Pêche de France (UAPF) traditionally represents industrial fishing, while the Coopération Maritime defends the interests of small-scale fishermen. In Spain, the Federación Nacional de Cofradías de Pescadores primarily represents the inshore fishing sector, while the Confederación Española de Asociaciones Pesqueras and the Federación Española de Armadores de Buques de Pesca defend the interests of the deep-sea fleets. This fragmentation of national representation is sometimes due also to differences which are territorial rather than functional. In the UK, the National Federation of Fishermen's Organizations (NFFO) represents English and Welsh fishermen, whereas the Scottish Fishermen's Federation (SFF) represents most of Scotland's fishermen. Although the NFFO and the SFF produced a joint document on the general approach of the 2002 reform of the CFP (NFFO and SFF 1998), their positions are not identical. The Scottish organization has always been more moderate than its Anglo–Welsh counterpart in its criticism of the CFP and, in particular, has never advocated a renationalization of fisheries policy. The more open position of Scottish fishermen can be explained by their privileged access to the stocks protected by the 'Shetland Box', an area off Northern Scotland where fishing activity is restricted to a limited number of vessels. Indeed, the EU has often been seen by Scottish fishermen as an additional means for protecting themselves against their main competitors, the Norwegian fishermen.

The fragmentation of interests at the national level needs to be seen in context, since corporatist traditions, which link the state to socio-economic groups, vary between countries. A Comité national des pêches maritimes et des élevages marins (CNPEM) has existed in France since 1945. It is sub-divided into regional and local committees, which the various professions linked to fisheries are legally obliged to join (Thom 1993). Similarly, in the Netherlands, a country strongly imbued with the corporatist model, the *Produktschap Vis*, registered in public law, has represented the interests of all producers and processors of fish since the 1930s. This position is quite different in the UK where the state has not provided any channels for fishermen to express their economic and political objectives.

In the EU member states, the central authorities responsible for fisheries often continue to consider themselves as sovereign in their domain, even though their administrative and budgetary resources are rather weak, and despite the fact that the bulk of the legislation which they have to enforce is of Community origin. In some countries, decentralization of government has added an extra level of local or regional administration. In Spain, the Autonomous Communities are responsible for fisheries—including controls—within territorial waters and for aquaculture (Criado Alonso 1996). The officials from the regions most affected, such as Galicia (which has its own Ministry for Fisheries at Santiago de Compostela), or the Basque country, therefore tend to be more involved in EU negotiations on the CFP, a situation which the central governments in Madrid have always resisted. The Spanish Autonomous Communities have never hesitated to exploit EU institutions and law at every possible opportunity in order to involve themselves to a greater extent in the formulation of the CFP. In July 1996, the autonomous government of Galicia obtained the right to intervene directly on behalf of Galician shipowners in the proceedings which the latter had brought before the Court of First Instance (CFI) (T-194/95 and T-12/96 against the Council of the EU. The shipowners wanted to have a Community regulation annulled which, following pressure from Canada, had reduced the European fishing quota for black halibut in international waters off the coast of Newfoundland. This was the first time that the regional government of a member state had succeeded in arguing that an economic and social interest justified its recognition in the EU legal process.

In England and Wales, all controls over a coastal zone of six miles are the responsibility not of the Ministry of Agriculture, Fisheries and Food (MAFF), but of the twelve Sea Fisheries Committees (SFC), linked to local authorities, for example the Cornwall Sea Fishery Committee. The SFC issue bylaws which, once vetted by MAFF, establish measures for conservation which are sometimes more severe than national laws. In Scotland, the process of devolution directly involves the Scottish Rural Affairs Minister in preparing British positions at EU Councils, keeping in mind that fisheries is one of the functions devoted to Scottish Parliament by the Scotland Act and that the Scottish vessels account for two-thirds of the landings in the UK.

This fragmentation in the way the sector is represented at the national level goes a long way to explaining the weak organization of fishermen at the European level. The EU-level lobbying group Europêche, created in the 1970s, is a federation of national associations of producers, but has only limited resources at its disposal in comparison with those of European groups in the agricultural sector. National contributions from national associations provide funds for only a modest secretariat, composed of a part-time secretary general and an assistant. Certain national fishermen's organizations (such as the Portuguese or the Finnish) have been unable to join Europêche, because they cannot pay the subscription. More fundamentally, Europêche has found it difficult to define common positions with regard to the CFP, and the search for consensus has been made more difficult, as successive enlargements have added to the diversity of its membership. Europêche brings little by way of added value to national fishermen's organizations in terms of information flows in comparison with what the latter obtain directly from their governments or from the Commission. Europêche thus mainly operates as a vehicle through which the national fishermen's organizations agree their official representation vis-à-vis the Commission.

The Commission has an official Consultative Committee on Fisheries, established in 1971 on the model of the agricultural committees instituted in the late 1960s for the management of the CAP. These committees reflect the ambitions of the Commission in the 1960s to establish itself as the future government of Europe, and in retrospect they can be seen as milestones in the effort to construct a European corporatist model. In July 1999, the Commission proposed a reform of the Consultative Committee which was less and less considered as a forum for dialogue with the industry. The number of members of the Consultative Committee on Fisheries and Aquaculture has been reduced—from forty-five to twenty—and other actors involved in the CFP, like representatives of consumers' organizations or of green NGOs, have been invited to join the Committee. The reform of the CFP in 2002 created the Regional Advisory Councils. They allow fishermen, scientists, and other stakeholders (e.g. representatives of NGOs) to work together and to have an input on issues relevant to specific areas and fisheries.

The Commission as a promoter of expertise

The Commission is the best-placed European institution to gather expertise on fisheries issues. Created in 1976, DG FISH is composed of officials who see themselves as the guardians of expertise in contrast to member governments under clientelist pressure from fishermen. Their role is to construct a public policy based on a scientific rationale. The cornerstone of this is to work towards a policy of surveillance. Its staff includes marine biologists who direct national oceanographic institutes—such as the Institut français de recherche pour l'exploitation de la mer (IFREMER) in France, or the Centre for Environment, Fisheries and Aquaculture Science (CEFAS) in the UK— among which ICES is by traditional a sort of 'Vatican'. These officials, together with their colleagues in the national oceanographic institutes, form a scientific community with a common creed. This has three core beliefs: (i) that fish stocks are threatened by the natural tendency of fishermen to over-fish; (ii) that the mission of scientists is to encourage governments to counter this threat with regulatory measures (TACs and quotas); (iii) and that it is consequently necessary to devise statistical models to evaluate stocks, so as to demonstrate to politicians the extent of this threat.

This resilient paradigm carries support from meetings of the Scientific, Technical and Economic Committee for Fisheries (STECF) which has, since 1979, brought together most of the marine biologists who are responsible for submitting advice on fish stocks in the ICES. Since 1993, economists have also been involved in the work of the ICES, as DG FISH has become concerned to increase expertise on questions such as over-investment, competition between fishermen, or rates of return. Fewer in number than the biologists, these economists (drawn from institutes of applied research, but also from universities) have however never won the same place as the biologists who study fish stocks in the EU decision-making process.

A parallel can be drawn with the environmental policy community. In the fisheries domain, the opinions of scientists, even if a source of controversy within the scientific community, provide DG FISH and the successive Commissioners responsible for fisheries with rational arguments for passing unpopular regulatory measures, such as the establishment of new TACs or reductions in fleet capacity, for which it is necessary to convince fishermen and national ministers.

Council negotiations

The Council of the Ministers of Agriculture and Fisheries is the place where the main decisions over the CFP are discussed, argued over, and finally adopted. This Council has powers at its disposal which, in contrast to most other sectors, virtually amount to direct administration. The Council legislates mainly through regulations, directly binding on the member states, and not directives. In contrast to many other policy areas, Article 37 (TEC) (ex Art. 43 EEC), which also covers the CAP, requires no stronger role for the European Parliament (EP) than the right to be consulted. The Council may take its decisions by qualified majority voting (QMV), and this sometimes poses problems for those ministers who must return to their capitals and explain to the fishermen that they found themselves in the minority. This was the case in June 1998, when the Irish and French ministers were over-ruled by a majority of their colleagues who favoured the ban of drift nets in the Atlantic and the Mediterranean.

Most configurations of the Council now comprise agriculture and fisheries questions. It has reduced the identity of the fishery sector in the negotiation compared to what existed since 2002. However, the agenda relating to fisheries is still prepared by a network of high-level national officials who are responsible for fisheries in the capitals, and the fisheries counsellors from the Permanent Representations in Brussels, who attend the fisheries working groups of the Council and accompany Deputy Permanent Representatives to the meetings of Coreper I.

Parliamentary scrutiny

Article 43 (EEC) (now Art. 37 TEC) does not allow the EP to exercise much influence on legislation in the area of the CFP, in contrast to most other policy areas. However, the EP looks for ways of intervening through other routes, such as in the annual budgetary process or in debates on the structural funds and their reform.

In 1979 the EP had only a working group covering fisheries, then from 1984 a subcommittee of the Agriculture Committee, and a full committee since 1994. The involvement of British and Spanish MEPs, and—since 2004—of Polish MEPS, in this committee has been particularly active.

The Fisheries Committee holds one or two public meetings a month. It is the sole EU institution which uses its reports and hearings to bring an alternative expertise to bear on the proposals of DG FISH. What is striking about the way the Fisheries Committee operates is its deliberate cultivation of expertise as the basis of its efforts to influence the Commission. This approach is quite a contrast to the political rhetoric which tends to excite national parliamentarians on the same subject during debates in their own chambers. The lyrical flights of fancy on fishing or fishermen, observable, for example, in the debates of the House of Commons, are seldom reproduced in the EP, since they appeal to a national symbolism which cannot rally support in a transnational assembly (Lequesne 2004). The professional organizations in the fisheries sector nonetheless find some MEPs to act as advocates of specific interest, regions, or occupational groups. One such MEP, originating from Cuxhaven, has been the regular spokesperson for the processing industry in the north of Germany which favours a liberal import regime for fisheries products. The report on the CFP after 2002, drafted in 1997 by the Committee's President, Carmen Fraga Estévez, reflected the position of Galician shipowners, who favoured complete liberalization of access to community waters by 2002 (Fraga Estévez 1997). In 1999 the Irish MEP, Pat 'the Cope' Gallagher, wrote a report on the extension of national coastal zones from twelve to twenty-four miles and on decentralizing the management of fisheries to regional units. Its recommendations corresponded quite closely to the views of the Irish Fishermen's Organization.

The EP also provides an arena where environmental NGOs, such as Greenpeace, the World-Wide Fund for Nature (WWF), or the Eurogroup for Animal Welfare can regularly intervene on the CFP. After having long directed their lobbying at the Environment Committee, these NGOs, all with offices in Brussels, understood over the course of the 1990s that it was equally necessary to 'invest' in lobbying other committees of the EP. Indeed they even encouraged the creation of 'intergroups' or informal bodies for MEPs who share a particular idea or interest on the fringes of the EP's legislative function. Often the secretariats are provided by NGOs, as is the case for the Eurogroup for Animal Welfare. The Fisheries Committee became the target of regular approaches from environmental NGOs, not only on the question of the conservation of stocks, but also on the impact of certain fishing techniques on marine flora and fauna (dolphins, turtles, etc.). Since 1990 the Fisheries Committee has been opposed to the use of drift nets; this stance is not unconnected to the lobbying from environmental NGOs. It has not so much been fishermen themselves, as the European fish processing and distribution industries, that have recognized the implications for their commercial activities of the efforts by NGOs to promulgate environmental standards (precautionary principle or sustainable development). This explains the initiative taken by Unilever to associate the WWF with the creation of the Marine Stewardship Council (MSC). Based in London, this is an NGO working to develop an approach to product-labelling that will promote the marketing of those marine products which take account of the goal of 'sustainable development' (Marine Stewardship Council 1997).

Operating through the courts

Finally, the European Court of Justice (ECJ) and the CFI have played a crucial role in the evolution of the CFP. Prompted by both cases brought directly by institutions and individuals, and those referred for preliminary rulings by national courts, the ECJ has since 1970 pronounced regularly on questions concerning quotas, the free movement of capital in the sector, and the external competence of the EU. In his study of which substantive issues came before the ECJ between 1980 and 1989, Christopher Harding (1992) demonstrated that fisheries came in fourth place, after agriculture, competition, and the free movement of goods, with the majority of cases being prompted by complaints originating from one member state: Spain. Some defining points of Community jurisprudence resulted from disputes related to the CFP. Thus, the judgment on the 1976 *Kramer* case reinforced the concept that the definition of an internal EU policy implied parallel external competences for the EU; and the series of *Factortame* cases, notably that in 1991 established that provisions of national laws which infringed European law could be struck down to prevent discrimination. These were UK cases in relation to the 1998 British Merchant Shipping Act.

Common management of resources and differences in implementation

The regime for conserving and managing resources forms the cornerstone of the CFP. The risk of depleting stocks is real, and the way in which marine biologists have become influential actors in the Commission helped to make conservation a priority issue on the EU agenda.

Setting limits on catches

Conservation policy appeared first as a system of TACs and quotas to regulate the fishing of some 120 stocks in the Atlantic, the North Sea, and the Baltic (Karagiannakos 1997; for the system of zones see Fig. 14.1). Because the Mediterranean was not covered by an EEZ, the fisheries ministers decided in 1983 that it could be exempted from the system of TACs. However, a recommendation from the International Commission for the Conservation of Atlantic Tuna (ICCAT) revealed the extent of the threat to blue-fin tuna, and the fisheries ministers of the EU then decided, in December 1998, to establish a TAC for this species, including the catches in the Mediterranean.

In December each year TACs are set for the following year by EU fisheries ministers in a ritual exercise where scientific reasoning confronts political reasoning. The point of departure for the process is scientific advice. A report from the marine biologists on the Advisory Committee on Fishery Management (ACFM) of the ICES is forwarded to DG FISH in October-November. This suggests the TACs by species and by geographical division concerning both EU stocks and those shared with third countries, such as Norway or the Faroe Islands (Guegen, Laurec, and Maucorps 1990). A majority of these TACs are precautionary, that is to say they are designed to protect a resource estimated by scientists to be at risk, but for which the specific data allowing for an accurate analysis are missing. The opinion is then transmitted to the EU's STECF, a body which often includes the same biologists who work at ACFM, where it is usually

Figure 14.1 Maritime zones

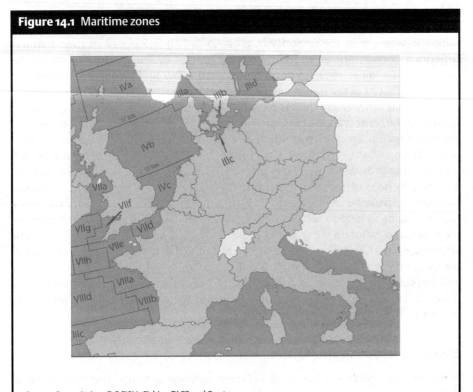

Source: Commission, DG FISH, *Fishing TACS and Quotas 2004.*

agreed without any significant modifications. This forms the basis from which the conservation unit of DG FISH makes its proposal to member governments.

The officials in the conservation unit of DG FISH regard themselves as 'guardians of stocks'. They see it as their job to ratify the choices made by the scientists, knowing that national officials and ministers will rely quite heavily on the scientific advice and tend to revise downwards their negotiating targets. Ministers also draw on the terms of the proposal of the Commission as a means of adjusting downwards the demands of their own fishermen. Once the Commission issues its proposal to member governments each November, the negotiations move into a political mode, shifting from an emphasis on the protection of stocks to the balance between different geographical areas and the preservation of socio-economic peace.

This double imperative has developed from the principle of *relative stability* established at The Hague in 1976 and later formalized by Community Regulations and by the jurisprudence of the ECJ. A key is fixed for the allocations of TACs between states, based on three criteria which have little to do with biology: the preservation of traditional fishing activities within each member state; the particular needs of those regions most dependent on fisheries; and the loss of catches in the waters of third countries, as they have extended their own fishing zones. The autumn meetings of the Council working groups and the December session of the Agriculture and Fisheries Council provide the arena for defining what relative stability means. At this stage governments engage in intensive bargaining over the levels of the TACs. As in most EU negotiations, the confrontation between many different interests usually ends in a compromise which neither the Commission nor the member governments can totally control. QMV may make arriving at a decision easier, but it sometimes puts ministers who are in the minority in an awkward situation *vis-à-vis* their national fishermen's organizations, which are usually present in Brussels for this event. The Council of December 1998, for example, adopted a TAC on blue-fin tuna against the minority opinions of the Italian and Greek delegations.

The system of TACs and quotas has often been criticized for not making a strong impact on the conservation of resources (Oliver 1998). However, the CFP, like most EU policies, depends on implementation at a national level, which involves different constellations of actors from one state to another. TACs mean a short-term approach which fails to provide the necessary protection for a number of fish stocks which are currently in need of recovery measures. The 2002 reform allows a more long-term approach to fisheries management. It introduced two types of multi-annual plans: recovery plans to help to rebuild stocks that are in danger of collapse and management plans to maintain other stocks of safe biological levels. If TACs continue to be set annually, the Commission will also ask the Council to take into account the objectives set in the multiannual plan. It is difficult to know yet whether these measures will improve the situation of fish stocks. CFP, as other international regimes for fisheries, has not produced an outcome linked to sustainability of fish resources. In this sense, it is an example of policy failure.

Efforts to make controls effective

Whatever the individual merits of different national systems, their effectiveness depends essentially on what controls the national administrations are able to exercise over catches, as well as on how far fishermen are able to regulate themselves through their own producers' organizations (POs). The British and Irish administrations have proved stricter than their Spanish and French counterparts in compelling vessels over a given size to record their catches in a logbook. The fact that the vast majority of vessels over ten metres in length belong to a PO facilitates the work of British and Irish inspectors. Strict administration can, however, have an inverse effect, by encouraging the practice of illegal landings. The problem of 'black fish' is a burning issue in the UK, to the extent that the Anglo–Welsh and Scottish fisheries authorities have required all vessels over twenty metres long to land their catches solely at thirty-one designated ports and at designated times (*Fishing News*, 20 November 1998).

The historical relationship between a state and its fishermen is a factor which has a deciding influence on the capacity of administrations to control the sector, and which creates distinctive 'policy styles'. In France, a trade-off of 'impunity from fraud in exchange for the preservation of social peace' has historically structured the relationship between fishermen and the state, which makes it hard to establish the idea of 'co-management' with the government in operating the TACs. The Dutch system, which obliges the POs themselves to impose fines on members who exceed their allocated quota, could not be reproduced in France (Dubbink and van Vliet 1996).

The policy of the conservation of stocks is not limited to the system of TACs and quotas. It also involves a series of other measures established by the EU. A licensing system governs the access of vessels to certain large breeding grounds of species, which are called 'boxes' (Shetland Box, Irish Box). Numerous measures specifying permitted fishing techniques (engine types, size of nets and meshes, and so forth).

From 1983 to 2002, there were four Multi-annual Guidance Programmes (MAGPs) which fixed the rate of multiannual reductions in fleet capacity by country and by sector, with a view to achieving a more appropriate level for managing resources (see Table 14.2).

The MAGPs were much disliked by fishermen, as they represented the regulatory power of the EU over national fleets which have been decreasing in size in all EU member states since the late 1980s. These programmes never succeeded in meeting expectations and proved impossible to manage. For example, MAGP IV, which came to an end in December 2002, was replaced by a simpler scheme. The 2002 reform achieved two things in this area: it simplified the fleet management policy by giving more responsibility to the member states in ensuring a balance between their national fleets and their fishing potential; and it brought to an end the development of national or regional subsidies for fleet renewal. This last measure has been the most controversial issue of the reform. The strict control of aids gave rise to a coalition of member states around France, Spain, Ireland, Greece, Italy, and Portugal, calling itself 'The Friends of the Fishermen' (Flaesch-Mougin, Le Bihan, and Lequesne 2003).

Limits to the common regime

Although DG FISH has had its own corps of fishing inspectors since 1983, EU regulations allow them only to accompany national authorities in their land and sea investigations, and not to carry out autonomous controls. In a domain which touches the sovereignty of national fleets, the member governments have not been keen to delegate responsibility for these controls to the EU level. Following the 2002 reform,

Table 14.2 The Community fleet in 2002

	Number of vessels	Tonnage	Fleet in kW (engine power)
Belgium	130	24,276	66,699
Denmark	3,874	99, 339	347,476
Germany	2,247	69,490	163,912
Greece	19,747	104,255	606,188
Spain	14,887	519,878	1,257,221
France	8,088	229,749	1,111,330
Ireland	1,448	72,661	210,624
Italy	16,045	215,242	1,289,681
Netherlands	932	200,068	470,031
Portugal	10,427	116,734	401,186
Finland	3,571	19,883	188,800
Sweden	1,820	45,373	224,450
UK	7,379	246,589	924,218
EU15	90,595	1,963,537	7,261,816

Source: Commission 2004t, *Facts and Figures of CFP.*

in spring 2003 the Commission presented proposals for setting up a Joint Inspection Structure at the EU pooling national and EU monitoring and inspection resources.

Controls such as these vary greatly in their effectiveness across the member states. As a general rule, the increased cost of controls at sea is never welcomed by national budgetary authorities, in the light of the modest contribution which fishing makes to national GDP. In England and Wales, the Treasury regularly expresses its reservations about the cost of inspections undertaken by the Royal Navy on behalf of MAFF. Nonetheless this British system of controls at sea is regarded as 'an example of the way in which the CFP ought to be applied' (Commission 1996a: 112). Far less strict controls operate in Belgium, Spain, and Portugal, which are underequipped in terms of surveillance vessels and aeroplanes. Secondly, the fines which punish infringements of the CFP are much more severe in the UK and Ireland than in Italy or France. Thirdly, not all governments give the same emphasis to the exercise of controls. In France, the priority of preserving the social peace makes the responsible national agency reluctant to appear too coercive in dealing with offenders. For example, in one southern Breton port undersized hake were landed for many years in full view and knowledge of the Administration for Maritime Affairs, which refused to take any action. Finally, the national inspectorates do not form a powerful transnational network, despite regular calls from the Commission (1998b), and from some governments such as the Irish one, for closer cooperation. In this sense the fisheries administrations are very different from the customs authorities, where the mechanisms of control are now largely transnational. This difference is partly explained by the strong historical association of the sea with sovereignty and national borders, and with the survival of local communities. The development of new inspection technologies, such as satellites, is used progressively in the EU to monitor vessels. It concerns since July 1998 vessels of twenty-four metres in length; it was extended to vessels over eighteen metres from 1 January 2004, and to those over fifteen metres as of 1 January 2005.

The way in which controls are operated within the EEZs also raises the interesting question of how fairly the EU regime is applied. Actual practice reveals, in effect, a tendency for national administrations to be rather stricter in dealing with non-national fishermen than with their own nationals. This is the case in France as regards Spanish vessels, and in Ireland as regards French vessels, and even more so for Franco–Spanish vessels. This state of affairs explains why Spanish deep-sea fishermen, the most active in the EEZs of other member states, generally support giving the Commission its own control powers, judging that they will be less discriminated against than by the current national systems. A positive step of the 2002 reform is that the Commission now has the power to penalize member states which do not take the necessary measures to prevent fishing by deducting quotas from their allocation. A compliance scoreboard showing the enforcement record of member states in relation to the CFP is also published and regularly updated by the Commission. The aim is to raise public awareness of the situation in each member state thus putting pressure to improve on those with unsatisfactory records—a means of regulation and compliance through publicity.

The CFP between redistribution and globalization

The EU is often described as a polity whose characteristics are derived from the fact that its main successes are in regulation rather than in the distribution of resources (Majone 1995). The modest scale of the EU budget seems to support this view, but it is more complex than it appears. Even without pointing out the strong redistributive logic driving the agricultural and regional policies of the EU over many years, we can still observe that the fisheries sector is marked by similar intensive lobbying and claims for financial intervention, albeit from a smaller pot of money.

In practice, a kind of triad of the Commission, governments, and fishermen has established a compromise around a regime of structural aids, conceived as compensation for the social costs of each successive reform. When Emma Bonino, the Fisheries Commissioner in 1995–9, attempted to justify the decision to ban drift nets, she automatically used the argument that reconversion did not pose any problems as 'the structural funds can intervene' (Bonino 1998). The fishermen's organizations got the message, and continue to press Brussels, and at the national and regional level, for financial aid as a condition of accepting social change.

Financial support for the fishing industry

It was not until the reform of the structural funds in 1993 (see Chapter 9), applicable for the period 1994–9, that the fisheries sector was granted its own Financial Instrument for Fisheries Guidance (FIFG). With €2.9 billion (almost 1.9 per cent of the total structural funds), the FIFG was intended to help achieve Objective 5a, which promoted structural adaptation of the cohesion policy in agriculture and fisheries. Between 1994 and 1999, the main beneficiaries of these structural operations were Spain (40 per cent of the total), Italy, Portugal, and France. However, these financial contributions, accumulated from different levels of government (EU, national, and local), have not always favoured the selection of appropriate projects. Structural aids also contradicted the policy to reduce the fleet imposed by the MAGPs.

Following the Agenda 2000 exercise by the Commission, the Council approved in June 1999 the Regulations 1260/1999 and 1263/1999 for the revision of the Community structural funds, including the new FIFG. Regarding the renewal and modernization of fleets, it introduced an explicit link between the aid from the funds and the monitoring of fleets. For the period 2000–6, any financial support must be compensated by the withdrawal of at least equal capacity without public aid. Penalty measures can be introduced towards member states which do not observe the reduction of fleets. Structural policy in the fishery sector is increasingly becoming an instrumental addition to conservation policy. For this reason it has been criticized by the fishermen of the member states which received much support from EU aids in the previous period 1994–9.

International trade and Community preference

In contrast to agricultural products, fisheries products have since 1962 been subject to the rules of the GATT/WTO, which have strictly limited the fixing of tariffs in the Common Commercial Tariff (CCT), and have prevented quantitative restrictions and measures having an equivalent effect'. Moreover, 60 per cent of EU imports of fish products are governed by preferential agreements with groups of third countries which involve derogations from the CCT: Mediterranean countries; African, Caribbean, and Pacific (ACP) countries; countries benefiting from the GSP; and Norway and Iceland under the European Economic Area (EEA) (see Chapter 15). These trade arrangements facilitate imports of third-country products to the EU, and have contributed to the deficit in the EU's trade balance (see Tables 14.3 and 14.4).

The marked gap between EU production and consumption has led to a constant pendulum movement within the CFP between defence of the principle of Community preference, on the one hand, and the need to guarantee imports at low prices for the distribution and processing industries which provide most of the employment in the sector, on the other. Managing these two requirements is all the more complicated because the main producing countries (Denmark, Spain, the UK, France, Italy, and the Netherlands) are generally also the main importers of third-country products. The only exception is Germany which has a relatively low output, but has a processing industry, and specializes in deep-frozen products, which is overwhelmingly supplied from outside the EU.

The CFP operates several trade instruments designed to support Community preferences, the main one being the common market organization for aquaculture and fisheries products, created in 1970 along the lines of the market organizations used in the CAP. This is a support mechanism for the prices of fresh and frozen products,

Table 14.3 Foreign trade of EU countries in fishery products, 1995 and 2000 (in 1,000 €)

	1995			2000		
	Imports	Exports	Balance	Imports	Exports	Balance
Belgium-Luxembourg	796,77	283,708	−513,062	1,214,952	570,831	−644,121
Denmark	1,215,572	2,050,241	834,670	1,942,067	2,842,463	900,396
Germany	1,928,019	644,604	−1,283,416	2,560,486	1,126,043	−1,434,442
Austria	144,049	13,310	−130,739	179,275	9,391	−169,884
Greece	176,564	135,879	−40,684	322,983	252,743	−70,240
Spain	2,343,833	936,413	−1,407,419	3,830,794	1,857,120	−1,973,674
Finland	86,738	17,150	−69,588	131,564	17,498	−114,066
France	2,468,560	766,466	−1,701,794	3,328,602	1,230,771	−2,097,831
Ireland	69,131	264,424	195,293	123,672	382,422	208,750
Italy	1,894,468	272,556	−1,621,912	2,812,034	421,524	−2,390,511
Netherlands	942,254	1,179,747	237,492	1,872,455	1,897, 479	325,025
Portugal	602,775	222,272	−380,503	963,123	319,310	−643,814
Sweden	414,611	195,925	218,685	771,191	510,927	−260,283
UK	1,496,495	865,600	−630,895	2,381,537	1,180,131	−120,408
EU15	14,579,539	7,848,296	−6,731,243	23,149,685	12,939,485	−10,210,200

Sources: Eurostat, *La pêche européenne en chiffres*, Luxembourg OPOCE, 1998; *Fisheries Yearbook 2002*.

financed from the EU budget, and which comes into play when prices reach a threshold level at which they would have to be withdrawn from the market. Aid may be provided for storage and for re-launching products on the market, or indeed for their destruction. One species—tuna—benefits from a specific compensatory payment, paid to producers at the moment when a fall in prices significantly affects the Community market. The operation of these market organizations in the member states is not the responsibility of national governments, but of the producers' organizations (POs), the creation and extension of which has been much encouraged by the EU.

These 150 POs, all located in the member states, are based on the principle of free membership for fishermen, and marketed approximately 80 per cent of the production of those species subjected to price regimes. Although the figures vary a good deal depending on the year, country, and species, less of the production of the fisheries sector is withdrawn from the market than in the agricultural sector (see Chapter 7). Financing from the EU budget nevertheless forms part of the redistributive compromise which was established between fishermen and European governments when the CFP was set up in 1970 (Commission 1997*b*).

The second type of measures which support Community production involves regularly imposing quotas on imports and, in the case of disturbances to the market, using safeguard clauses. The latter is rarely applied, however, since it requires the Commission to conduct an investigation and to consult the contracting parties of the WTO. It is not surprising that in some of the EU producer countries the fishermen regularly criticize the CFP as ill-adapted to international trade and ask for increased protection of external borders. Whatever the real facts of the case, during a crisis in 1993–4 one of the demands of Breton fishermen was that imports from third countries should be blocked. Their opposition to the CFP became all the more violent when the Commission refused the French government's request for the introduction of a safeguard clause, because, so the Commission judged, not all European markets were affected; instead the Commission proposed a system of minimum pricing for imports of seven species which were particularly vulnerable to competition (du Guerny and Bauer 1994). The EU can, in contrast, operate forms of protection welcomed by producers, when it moves to prevent unfair practices such as dumping. In April 1998, Scottish and Irish producers thus welcomed the decision of the Council to make definitive the anti-dumping measures taken by the Commission against Norwegian salmon exporters. On these matters of trade, it has quite suited national ministers that the Commission had been delegated so many powers to intervene, since the interests of fishermen and those of processors are often at variance inside each member state.

This difficult trade relationship between the EU and the rest of the world as a result of the CFP is mirrored in the arrangements for access to resources. It is estimated nowadays that 35 per cent of the world's seas and oceans are under the jurisdiction of individual states, through the establishment of both EEZs and exclusive fishing zones. Thus, EU fleets find themselves excluded from many areas where they operated freely until the 1970s (Del Vecchio 1995).

Negotiating with third countries

In 1976 the governments of the member states entrusted the EU with the power to conclude fishing agreements with third countries concerning access to resources, assuming that their negotiating capacity would be strengthened as a result. The arrival of Spain and Portugal, whose deep-sea shipowners had a specific interest in fishing third-country waters, strengthened this side of the CFP, and there are now some thirty agreements in force. They rest on three main forms of reciprocity (European Parliament 1996a):

- access to resources/access to resources (Norway, the Faroe Islands, Iceland, and the Baltic states);
- access to resources/financial compensation and access to markets, through the device of joint-ventures, the 'second generation' agreements (Argentina); and
- access to resources/financial compensation and developmental measures, such as the training of local fishermen, landing of a certain quota of captures in local ports, the 'third generation' agreements with ACP countries, such as Senegal, Guinea-Bissau, and the Seychelles.

With the exception of purely reciprocal agreements, which apply to European countries, the other types of agreement thus involve the costs of financial compensation. These are sometimes borne by European shipowners themselves, and sometimes by the EU budget which is supposed to contribute to the development of local fisheries networks (for example, port management or canning factories). The budgetary cost is the subject of argument within the EU, because these essentially serve the interests of one category of shipowners from some member states (those who practise deep-sea fishing in the southern seas).

The fleets which benefit from negotiated access to African and Latin-American waters, are mainly from the southern parts of the EU: Spain, Portugal, Italy, and France. British, Danish, and Irish fleets are less concerned and thus have a tendency to consider that these agreements exist to the detriment of the financing of other aspects of the CFP. In its response to the Commission questionnaire on the 2002 reform, the Irish Fishermen's Organization, for example, stressed that 'the cost and consequently the percentage of the EU fisheries budget committed to supporting third-country agreements has risen enormously over the years. It now has to be questioned whether financial support should be continued' (Irish Fishermen's Organization 1998). In contrast, the Union des Armateurs à la Pêche de France, which includes among its members the Breton tuna fleet which fishes off the African coast and in the Indian Ocean, observed in its response to the Commission that the EU should pursue 'an aggressive, dynamic and expansionist policy in the matter of fishing agreements. It no longer suffices to safeguard what already exists, [the EU] should develop what could be!' (Union des Armateurs à la Pêche de France 1998). The difference in interests is so marked that in Spain, the main country which benefits from these agreements, some politicians and representatives of the fishing and processing industries have called for powers to be granted to individual member states to negotiate bilateral agreements with third countries in those cases where the EU does not wish to take on the necessary financial obligations (Fraga Estévez 1997).

The decision of Morocco in 1999, for example, not to renew its agreement with the EU affected the regular activities of some 600 Spanish and (to a lesser extent) Portuguese deep-sea fishing vessels. A total of 150 vessels, employing 1,400 fishermen who mainly catch cephalopods (such as cuttle-fish and squid) had to find other waters to fish. The consequence has been dramatic for the cephalopodian stocks of Mauritania where Spanish boats decided to move. The Iberian countries attach all the more importance to the international agreements in Africa and Latin America, as their fleets have progressively been excluded from the territorial waters of some coastal states of the Northern Atlantic. The decision of the Canadian government in 1995 to reduce the TAC for cod came as a severe blow to the Portuguese deep-sea fishing fleet and necessitated its redeployment to other areas and fishing grounds (de Jesus 1998). Similarly, the creation of joint ventures and the transfer of flags of convenience to Argentina or to Namibia has provided certain sections of the Spanish fleet (such as the forty deep-freeze trawlers from Vigo, which carry 1,800 sailors) with a way of meeting the requirements of MAGP III. This stratagem has become all the more attractive, because aid from the EU budget has covered the costs of transferring the vessels, and the production of joint ventures can be exported to the EU market.

The durability of such agreements with third countries cannot be taken for granted, as the example of Morocco showed. To take another example, in December 1998 the Argentine Senate insisted that in future all officers and 75 per cent of ordinary seamen employed on vessels of joint-venture companies should be Argentinian; this is also part of a political strategy aimed at tough negotiation of the terms of trade with the EU (Arocena 1998).

The strong trend towards extending territorial control over fisheries resources indicates that EU agreements with third countries over access to fishing resources are not immutable. If eroded, there are severe consequences for the EU; fleets will have to be redeployed and there will be pressure for increased financing for decommissioning.

But none of this would rule out new agreements with third countries in the future, focusing on technological or industrial matters relating to the processing of fish products (Chaumette 1998).

Conclusions

This survey of the CFP highlights several distinctive features of the EU policy process in this domain. First, the CFP is one of the few EU policies designed to be implemented by direct administration. The reliance on regulations rather than directives to make legislation is one indication of this, although this formal characteristic should not blind us to the conspicuous variations between member states in their methods of implementation. Secondly, the formulation of the CFP in its early years rested mainly on the political interaction between two institutions: the Commission on the one hand, and the Council on the other. This duopoly has been gradually eroded, as the EP has progressively and pragmatically inserted itself into the decision-making process, and by the interventions of the ECJ, in response to cases brought by social actors. Thirdly, the CFP is a policy in which there is very weak representation of interests at the transnational level. Fishermen still prefer to lobby mainly at the national state level. However, other social groups which are becoming increasingly concerned by the CFP, such as the environmental NGOs, have, in contrast, developed lobbying practices and, indeed, policies, which are primarily transnational and directed at the Commission and the European Parliament.

The CFP also illustrates a typical feature of European integration, namely the temporal dimension (Abélès 1996). Every major development since 1970 has been accompanied by a timetable, causing those involved in the sector to face up to the next reform. Regulation 3760/92 of December 1992 established a common regime for fisheries and aquaculture, and defined the terms for its own revision: on the basis of a proposal of the Commission, the Council had to decide before 31 December 2002 on the adjustments to be made in many areas, of which access is the most important. The new regulation of December 2002 states again that 'the Commission shall report to the European Parliament and the Council on operation of the Common Fisheries Policy [. . .] before the end of 2012'.

The Commission has held to its primary function as the mobilizer of expertise, a role which it has always known better how to accomplish than that of managing its programmes. The Commission prepared for reform of the CFP in 2002, by initiating a process of consultation with the social groups concerned. This consultation, conducted by DG FISH, took the classic path: a request for an opinion from the Consultative Committee on Fisheries, and the organization of public meetings with representatives of the sector in member states. It also involved the preparation and dispatching of a questionnaire to a deliberately wide-range of recipients (professional fishermen's organizations, but also scientific institutes, environmental NGOs, and such like). DG FISH asked these organizations also to give their opinions on certain other aspects of the CFP, which were not formally envisaged by the 2002 reform, such as the market organization for fisheries products or the agreements with third countries. This effort to broaden out policy issues is an excellent illustration of the way in which the DGs of the Commission use the work of experts in order to shape the political agenda for future reforms. This tactic did not escape criticism from some national fishermen's organizations.

Forced to position themselves in the debate on reform, the national organizations of shipowners and fishermen have indicated that access to resources remains, as at the beginning of the CFP, the vital issue for all concerned, despite their often opposing interests. The professional organizations from the countries possessing the deep-sea fleets which are most mobile in EU waters (Spain, the Netherlands, and France) argued in favour of maintaining free access to the 200-mile zone after 2002, as well as the twelve-mile coastal zone which guarantees the protection of their inshore fishermen. In contrast, the professional organizations of some other member states are in favour of renationalizing some of the current EEZs and, if need be, of suppressing certain historical rights that can still be exercised within the twelve-mile coastal zones. A resolution was voted by the Portuguese parliament in March 1998, and then endorsed by the organization of Portuguese fishermen which advocated the extension of the coastal zone to fifty nautical miles (de Jesus 1998). The Irish Fishermen's Organization proposed thirty nautical miles (Irish Fishermen's Organization 1998). The UK National Federation of Fishermen's Organizations and of the Scottish Fishermen's Federation jointly called for the management of the CFP to be decentralized by transferring to the coastal states the responsibility for applying the rules for conserving stock within the 200-mile zone. Such a step could be tantamount to a form of renationalization of fisheries (NFFO–SFF 1998). But at the end, the status quo remained for access rules, as it remained for the principle of *relative stability*. Only regional advisory councils have been set up, with a discursive rather than decision-making power.

The reform of 2002 has raised a debate in all member states about the individual responsibility of fishermen regarding fish stocks, even though it is hard to discern concrete suggestions for reform on this subject. With the exception of Dutch fishermen, to whom it already applies, and of some representatives of the deep-sea fishing industry (for example, Galicians or French), most European fishermen remain resistant to the idea of TACs being replaced by individual transferable quotas (ITQs), which would mark the emergence of individual property rights over fisheries resources. The main argument against ITQs is that these favour the concentration of resources around the large ship-owning companies to the detriment of the traditional fishing industry. It is, however, important to note that the phenomenon of concentration has started to occur without ITQs. Boosted by the free movement of capital, the consolidation of the large European ship-owning groups has been underway since the 1980s (Pescanova in Spain, Jaczon in the Netherlands). These buy up firms in the EU and the rest of the world. The same trend towards concentration can be observed in the deep-sea fishing sector at the national level (Intermarché in France, and Stevenson in the UK).

In a sector which needs significant investment competitiveness depends on the search for economies of scale. In the majority of producing countries, however, concentration poses a political problem, namely the image which both the state and society at large have of an occupation which is historically constructed around the figure of the traditional fisherman as an artisan. This question in turn is generating a debate over what the priority objectives of the CFP should be. Should they be to help particular countries preserve the historical model of the traditional fishing industry by means of redistributive programmes—the traditional option? Or should they, on the contrary, be to accompany the march towards concentration and the demand for competitiveness, despite the price of financing the social costs of transition—the liberal option? Or should they do both at once—the syncretic option (i.e. reconciling different traditions), which would fit with the European social model?

Finally, the CFP cannot escape from the dynamic of the changes which followed new enlargements of the EU to include new maritime states situated this time in the East: Poland, Latvia, Estonia, and Lithuania. In Poland, which is the main country concerned, the fisheries sector employs 40,000 people (Commission 1997c). The Polish fishing fleet is composed of around thirty factory-ships operating principally in the Bering Sea, and of many ageing, small, and under-powered boats which fish in the Baltic. At the time of its accession, the Polish fleet has necessarily found itself confronted with the requirements of the EU to reduce capacity. This implies subjecting Polish fishing vessels to a restructuring plan, which would have to be financed primarily from the EU budget. Such a change will imply social and political costs for Poland. It will also carry costs for the current EU member states and for the Community institutions, by modifying the terms of redistribution once more.

Further reading

On the governance of fisheries in general, Crean and Symes (1999), and Symes (1999), offer useful analysis and bibliographic information. On the politics of fishing in the UK and northern Europe, see also Gray (1998), with interesting chapters by academics and practitioners. On the CFP see Lequesne (2004). On the reform of CFP in 2002, see Flaesch-Mougin, Le Bihan, and Lequesne (2003), and Shackleton (1983). Articles on the CFP are regularly published in the academic journal *Marine Policy*, published by Elsevier Science Ltd in the UK. The professional press is also a relevant source of information on the national debates: *Fishing News* (UK), *Le Marin* (France), *Industrias Pesqueras,* and *Europa Azul* (Spain).

Crean, K., and Symes, D. (1996) (eds.), *Fisheries Management in Crisis: A Social Science Perspective* (Oxford: Fishing News Books).

Fishing News (1998), article of 20 November.

Flaesch-Mougin, C., Le Bihan, D., and Lequesne, C. (2003) (eds.), *La politique européenne de la pêche: vers un développement durable?* (Rennes: Éditions Apogée).

Gray, T. S. (1998) (ed.), *The Politics of Fishing* (London: Macmillan).

Lequesne, C. (2004), *The Politics of Fisheries in the European Union* (Manchester: Manchester University Press, European Policy Research Unit Series).

Shackleton, M. (1983), 'Fishing for a Policy? The Common Fisheries Policy of the Community', in Wallace, Wallace and Webb (eds.), *Policy-Making in the European Community* (Chichester: Wiley), 349–72.

Symes, D. (1999) (ed.), *Alternative Management Systems for Fisheries* (Oxford: Fishing News Books).

Chapter 15

Trade Policy

From Uruguay to Doha and Beyond

Stephen Woolcock

Contents

Summary

As one of the major areas of Community competence established in the original Treaty of Rome (EEC), European Union (EU) trade policy has to reconcile national policy objectives, and national and sectoral interests pushing for protection and regulatory provisions with the broader, external aims of the EU, and with the international forces and multi-level negotiating arena and regulatory environments. Article 133 (TEC) grants exclusive powers for common commercial policy to the EU. EU trade policy has evolved in response to national and international developments, and in particular to successive rounds of negotiations in the GATT/WTO, from a customs union and common policies, to responding to US initiatives that favour multilateral trade liberalization, especially in agriculture, and multilateral negotiations as opposed to agreements with individual states in the developed or developing world. The European Commission established itself as the negotiator for the European Union (EU) on trade issues, but always under the watchful eyes of the member governments. The role of civil society, particularly non-governmental organizations (NGOs) and parliaments, both European and national, has increased and the deepening of the trade agenda requires changes in the *acquis communautaire* on agricultural policy, liberalization of services, environmental protection, and food safety. Despite growing pressures to make EU trade policy more transparent and directly accountable, the decision-making model remains essentially the classic Community method supported by a strong functionalist logic. The process of 'globalization' has raised expectations of a greater role for parliaments and NGOs in the policy process, but the modest reforms introduced have been mostly aimed at increased transparency, leaving the traditional Community method for trade policy largely intact.

Introduction

The trade policy of the European Union (EU) is about reconciling domestic aims, sectoral interests, and regulatory provisions with the external aims of the EU and with the forces and multiple levels of negotiation and rules that constitute the international environment within which EU trade policy operates. The EU negotiates bilateral or region-to-region agreements under Article 310 (TEC) (ex Art. 238 EEC), as well as plurilateral[1] or multilateral agreements under Article 133 (TEC) (ex Art. 113 EEC). The pressures to reconcile these 'domestic' and international interests and rules have increased with globalization. Trade policy is no longer simply about tariffs and quotas on cross-border trading, but now includes services and investment and touches on a range of what trade economists call 'non-trade issues', such as the regulation of food and product safety, the environment, competition, ethical, and labour issues.

When trade policy was mostly about tariffs and market access it was played out in a fairly narrow policy community made up of national and EU trade officials and lobbies from the major sectoral interests in agriculture and manufacturing. Trade officials generally made judgments about national interests under the influence of sectoral lobbying without much close scrutiny by any national—let alone the European—parliament. As trade policy has become more extensive and more intrusive into domestic preferences, pressure has grown to make it more inclusive and transparent. International pressures on EU policy have also grown. EU trade policy has significant implications for the international trading system, and for other countries which look to the EU to provide leadership, as in the Doha Development Agenda (DDA) negotiations in the World Trade Organization (WTO). How the EU balances these domestic and international pressures is therefore the central question with regard to EU trade policy.

After summarizing the treaty provisions related to trade, the chapter shows how the EU has moved progressively from a trade policy preoccupied with building domestic policies towards a more outward oriented, multilateral posture. It describes the EU policy process and the key players in trade, and illustrates these with reference to the central issues in the DDA. It argues that the classic 'Community method' (see Chapter 3 in this volume) still most accurately describes the policy process in trade.

The treaty provisions

Article 133 (TEC) (ex Art. 113 EEC) grants exclusive powers for common commercial policy to the EU. Together with agriculture and competition policy, the common commercial policy (henceforth EU trade policy), was one of the major areas of Community competence granted in the original Treaty of Rome (EEC). The treaty provisions set out how member governments should cooperate in reaching common positions on trade. These provide for the Council of Ministers to authorize the European Commission, in consultation with the member states, to negotiate trade agreements, which the Council then adopts under a qualified majority voting rule (QMV). For bilateral association agreements Article 310 (TEC) (ex. Art. 238 EEC) requires unanimity in the Council to adopt the results of any negotiation and the European Parliament must give its assent. Examples are the Economic Partnership Agreements (EPAs) being negotiated between the EU and the regional groups of African, Caribbean, and Pacific (ACP) states which replace Lomé. These basic provisions on trade policy are confirmed in Article III 315(3) of the Constitutional Treaty (CT).

The reality is a little more complicated. The EU has competence, but what constitutes 'common commercial policy', and how we define European trade policy are more open to question. When the Treaty of Rome (EEC) was drafted trade policy was basically a question of cross-border tariffs. The decision to create a customs union required the original member states jointly to set tariffs and to develop a collective trade policy. The 1965-6 Kennedy Round of the General Agreement on Tariffs and Trade (GATT) was a first test of collective capability. As the trade agenda expanded the EU was called on to negotiate an ever wider range of policy issues. The subsequent Tokyo Round of the GATT (1973-9) included negotiations on technical barriers to trade (TBTs), subsidies and countervailing duties (SCVs), and public procurement, which were partly EU and partly national competence (Winham 1986). In the GATT Uruguay Round (1986-94) the EU negotiated on services in the General Agreement on Trade in Services (GATS), investment in the Trade-Related Investment Measures (TRIMs), and intellectual property rights in the Trade-Related Intellectual Property Rights (TRIPs). More recently the EU has pushed for, and pragmatically negotiated on, the inclusion of competition (see Chapter 5), and the environment in WTO negotiations (Paemen and Bensch 1995; Woolcock and Hodges 1996). Member governments have accepted that the Commission should act as the negotiator for the EU as a whole, but have also been at pains to ensure that such *de facto* authority for the Commission in negotiations does not lead to an increase in the acquired powers of the EU in trade. The European Court of Justice (ECJ) has therefore been called on to adjudicate on the scope of Article 133 (TEC) (ex Art. 113 EEC) in particular, in cases such as 1/94 on the issues of services and intellectual property rights following the Uruguay Round (ECJ Opinion 1/94).

Intergovernmental conferences (IGCs) dealing with treaty revisions have addressed the scope of EU competence in trade, with the Commission typically arguing for more collective powers in the fields of services, investment issues, and intellectual property. In the IGC that led to the 1992 Treaty on European Union (TEU), most member governments defended the retention of national competences and blocked any extensions of EU competence. By the time of the Treaty of Amsterdam (ToA), member governments recognized the need for some flexibility by adopting the 'enabling clause' in Article 133(5) (TEC). This allows the member states, acting unanimously, to extend EU competence to any issue at any time without the need for a treaty revision. In the ICG leading to the Treaty of Nice (ToN), some member governments, most determinedly the Finnish, called for a significant broadening of EU trade competences. The eventually agreed text clarified that EC competence applied to cross-border services, but acceded to French pressure for a general cultural exclusion on goods and services (Art. 133(5) TEC, and Art. 133(6) TEC). This means member governments have a *de jure* veto over any liberalization of, for example, audio-visual services. Finally, Article III-315(1) of the CT should, when ratified, bring foreign direct investment (FDI) more under EU competence by requiring 'uniform principles' for EU policy.

The Treaty of Rome (EEC) provided no role in trade policy for the then European Assembly, or its successor the European Parliament (EP). The EP has however, acquired some trade policy powers under Article 310 TEC (ex. Art. 238 EEC) to ratify, by a simple majority vote, any (mostly bilateral) association agreement. The TEU went out of its way to limit the role of the EP under Article 133 in multilateral negotiations, although when a trade negotiation requires modifications to 'internal' EU legislation adopted by co-decision under Article 251 TEC (ex Art. 189b EEC) the EP must give its assent by a simple majority. This gives the EP the power to block an agreement after it has been accepted by all EU governments, and by the relevant trading partners. Less formally, consultations take place regularly between the Council and Commission and the EP on trade negotiations, and hence the Commission and Council have, in recent years, made an effort to consult the EP during GATT/WTO rounds. During the 2000–4 Parliament this consultation took place within a sub-committee of the Committee on Industry, Trade, Research and Energy. In July 2004 a new Committee on International Trade (INTA) was set up by the new Parliament. The CT will, when ratified, help anchor these arrangements by establishing 'a special committee' of the EP on trade policy.

The evolution of policy: towards a more proactive and outward orientation

European trade policy has evolved in response to domestic and international developments, and in particular to a succession of rounds of negotiations in the GATT/WTO. Initially the EU's domestic priorities were to build a customs union and common policies, such as the common agricultural policy (CAP; see Chapter 7). The then EEC was obliged to respond to US initiatives favouring multilateral trade liberalization. The Dillon Round was underway when the Treaty of Rome was signed, but the US pressed for further negotiations in what became the Kennedy Round (1964–9), with the aim of limiting trade diversion resulting from the EEC tariff preference and bringing the CAP under multilateral discipline (Preeg 1970). Faced with what appeared to be a threat to the foundations of the new European initiative, the EEC adopted a defensive position.

Trade policy in the 1970s was also shaped by the US initiative to launch the Tokyo Round (1973–9), with the aim of 'updating the trading system'. For the US this also meant disciplining what was perceived as 'unfair competition' from Europe and Japan, by pressuring for GATT rules on agriculture, TBTs, procurement, and subsidies. At the time many European governments were still pursuing national champion strategies that made considerable use of these policy instruments. Thus, the EU was again on the defensive, given the desire of its member governments to retain scope for such discretionary intervention.

Another systemic factor shaping EU trade policy was the need to regulate commercial relations with former colonies. The primary mechanism for this was a series of non-reciprocal preferential arrangements with what came to be known as the African, Caribbean, and Pacific (ACP) countries under a series of agreements, first Yaoundé, then Lomé, and most recently Cotonou. These were non-reciprocal because the EC offered tariff-free access to the EC market for many products from these countries without requesting reciprocal liberalization on the part of the ACP states. Paradoxically, it was the generosity of the EU in offering non-reciprocal concessions to the ACP states that was deemed contrary to the 'most favoured nation' provisions of the GATT/WTO. Other EU preferential agreements, in what some call the EU's 'preference pyramid', have been criticized as being contrary to the spirit of the GATT. However, the wording of Article XXIV (GATT) and Article 5 (GATS), is so loose that the EU (and other GATT members that have been criticized) have avoided any real challenge to their other preferential agreements under the GATT/WTO.

In the 1980s another US initiative tried to extend the scope of the GATT to include services, investment, and trade in high technology. The 1982 GATT ministerial meeting failed, however, to launch a new round and the US shifted towards greater reliance on unilateral and regional/bilateral trade measures. The 1988 US Omnibus Trade and Competitiveness Act provided for the unilateral definition of 'fair trade'. Although this was mainly directed at Japan and the newly industrializing countries, there was concern in the EU that it would threaten European interests.

The US also began to actively pursue bilateral or regional initiatives in the form of the Canada–US Free Trade Agreement of 1988 and negotiations on the North American Free Trade Agreement (NAFTA), which began in 1991. This threat of US unilateralism and/or preferential agreements provided an important incentive for the EU to push for a stronger multilateral trade regime. Domestically the EU shifted away from following national champions towards more liberal policies, as reflected in the single European market initiative (see Chapter 4). The acceptance of stronger EU discipline over discretionary national policies also facilitated a shift in EU policy towards accepting the new rules-based trading system of the WTO rather than the looser, less binding GATT regime. By the end of the Uruguay Round in 1994 the EU was matching the US on liberalization, with the important exception of agriculture (see Chapter 7).

During the second half of the 1990s the EU became much more proactive in its approach to multilateral trade negotiations. If successful, these would satisfy two EU aims by anchoring the US in the multilateral system, and by integrating the developing countries.[2] As a down payment, to demonstrate that the EU was serious about helping to integrate developing countries into the international trading system and to promote their development, the EU introduced its Everything But Arms (EBA) policy of liberalizing exports from least developed countries.

During the 1990s the EU developed its own approach for balancing the forces of liberalization/globalization with other legitimate social objectives. The developing *acquis communautaire* covered a wide range of issues relevant to trade, as the single market process moved forward within the EU and associated policy developments occurred. The *acquis* provided a common starting point for a more offensive approach to trade. The EU therefore had a strong interest in ensuring that the *acquis* was compatible with the international trade and investment regime that was emerging in the WTO. This helps explain why the EU favoured comprehensive agenda negotiations, that included efforts to shape new rules as well as the traditional market access issues.

The EU pressed for a comprehensive work programme in the WTO to include investment, competition, public procurement, and labour standards at the Singapore Ministerial Meeting in 1996, now known as the 'Singapore issues'. To win support from developing countries for a comprehensive new WTO round, Leon Brittan, then Trade Commissioner (1998), proposed that the new round should have a development focus. At the Geneva Ministerial Meeting in 1998 the EU persuaded President Clinton to support a new millennium round, only to discover that there was not sufficient backing in the US for a comprehensive round, as revealed by the failure of the Seattle Ministerial Meeting in December 1999 (Odell 2003). The EU continued to press for a new round, which was launched in Doha in December 2001 and entitled the Doha Development Agenda (DDA).

Since the early 1990s the EU has progressively emerged as the major proponent of multilateralism in global discussions. Today's climate is, however, very different from that of the late 1940s to the mid-1970s, when the US was the world's leading multilateralist. The trading system is now more complex, with 148 WTO members, compared to thirty or so (counting all EU member states) as active contracting parties to the old version of the GATT. India, Brazil, South Africa, and China are now major players, while many developing and least developed WTO members wish to have a say in the outcomes. This poses a challenge for the EU. Whilst multilateralism is the policy of preference, plurilateral agreements among countries willing to sign up to obligations that bind national policies may still be an option for the EU in the future.

The EU has also continued to negotiate regional and bilateral trade agreements, but these have tended to be the result of political events rather than a conscious strategy. Preferential trade agreements (Europe Agreements) were negotiated with individual central and east European countries as part of the post cold-war settlement, and then as a precursor to eastern enlargement (see Chapter 16). Political or security objectives were also largely responsible for the series of bilateral association agreements developed over a longer period with countries in the Middle East and North Africa. The bilateral agreement with South Africa had as a primary political motive the promotion of economic and political stability in the newly democratic South Africa, although this did not prevent some tough arguments on the EU side to protect west European products (Stevens 2000).[3] Bilateral agreements with Mexico and Chile were negotiated largely in order to limit trade diversion as a result of the NAFTA and US–Chile Agreement. Similarly, continuing negotiations between the EU and Mercosur, a grouping of Argentina, Brazil, Paraguay, and Uruguay, were in part a response to the US initiative to promote the Free Trade Agreement of the Americas (FTAA).

In recent years the EU has refined and redefined its relationships with erstwhile colonies in the less-developed world by promoting regional groupings among the ACP countries (Stevens 2000). The Economic Partnership Agreements (EPAs), which the EU began to negotiate in 2004 were necessary because the EU and ACP states did not obtain an indefinite waiver from the WTO for a continuation of the discriminatory, non-reciprocal trade provisions in the Lomé Agreement. The EU opted to negotiate reciprocal, region-to-region agreements with each of the ACP 'regions', although these regions are in many cases not natural economic groupings. Thus, the EU negotiates with the Economic Community of West African States (ECOWAS), rather than the ACP states of west Africa, or with the Caribbean Community and Common Market (CARICOM), rather than with the individual Caribbean states. EU free trade agreements with other regions are also presented as a way to promote regional integration and thus development in the partner regions.

Trade relations are also intended to play an important role in the European Neighbourhood Policy to promote economic growth and stability in countries bordering the EU. These include the Mediterranean partners, the western Balkans, the EU's eastern neighbours, Russia, Ukraine, Belarus, and Moldova and some of the countries in the Caucasus. During the period 2000–4 when Pascal Lamy was the Trade Commissioner, the Commission resisted other new regional or bilateral initiatives. The EU argued that, unlike the US, it maintained a moratorium on bilateral agreements. However, with such a large number of negotiations 'in the pipeline' the EU continued to be an active player in regional and bilateral negotiations.

The policy process

Multilateral negotiations

In multilateral negotiations, notably within the WTO, the Commission produces a draft mandate, drawing on the positions of the member governments, and the views of business, and increasingly civil society, and resolutions or reports from the European or national parliaments. The Commission rarely works from a blank sheet. The agenda for multilateral trade policy is an iterative process, so that the EU position on the DDA was shaped by positions in previous rounds and continuing work in the WTO working groups. Indeed, the EU negotiated in the early stages of the DDA within a formal mandate adopted before the Seattle WTO Ministerial Meeting in 1999. The Commission's draft mandate is discussed in the Article 133 Committee, which consists of senior trade officials from each member government, and is chaired by the rotating Council presidency. The final text is adopted by the General Affairs and External Relations Council (GAERC), the renamed configuration of the Council (see Fig. 15.1).

The Commission then negotiates on behalf of the EU in consultation with the member governments, mostly through the regular weekly meetings of the Article 133 Committee. In negotiations with the EU's trading partners the Commission is the only member of the EU delegation to speak, although national officials from member

Figure 15.1 EU decision-making process for multilateral trade negotiations

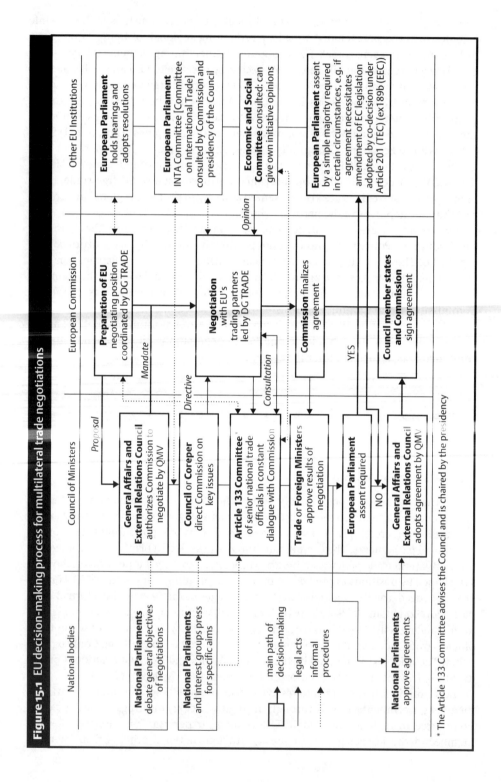

* The Article 133 Committee advises the Council and is chaired by the presidency

governments are present in formal negotiations. This is the case for topics on which the EU has competence, as well as in trade negotiations in which there is mixed or national competence. The Commission is also expected to report to the member governments on important informal contacts with the EU's trading partners, for example, to exchange information. There is a grey area here in the sense that there is no clear dividing line between exchanging information and negotiations. If the negotiations are in Geneva, where the WTO has its headquarters, national officials are drawn from the national delegations to the WTO, or from experts travelling from national capitals. At key junctures in negotiations or at WTO Ministerial Meetings, member governments are represented at ministerial level.

Member governments can direct the Commission on any issue during negotiations, but in most cases new initiatives or changes in the EU's position are raised by the Commission and discussed in the Article 133 Committee. If the position proposed by the Commission does not have sufficient support, the chair will refer the matter back to the Commission. Although QMV is provided for in the treaty, the Article 133 Committee hardly ever takes a formal vote. Trade practitioners prefer a more pragmatic and consensual approach, and, although there is always the chance that a vote will be called, member governments go to great lengths to avoid being so isolated that they risk being outvoted.

The Commission and Council consult the EP, and this has become more formal with the establishment of the INTA Committee in 2004. Although the EP has only an indirect role *vis-à-vis* the negotiation process, its ability to block both bilateral, and ultimately refuse to grant its assent to multilateral, agreements means that the Commission and Council are keen to maintain good relations with the EP. The Economic and Social Committee (ESC) of the EU has a formal, albeit purely consultative, role and may produce its own opinions on negotiations.

The EU policy process has generally allowed opportunities for pressure groups to feed in their views. Latterly, in the trade field this now tends to mean engaging with 'civil society'. An increased sensitivity to civil society has resulted in the Commission establishing semi-formal consultative processes. These include business groups, sectoral interests, and consumers, as well as a wide range of non-governmental organizations (NGOs) in a broad forum. Although these semi-formal consultations may have helped improve transparency, they probably have little direct impact on policy. A smaller Contact Group of about twelve key groups prepares for the larger consultations. This includes representatives of business, farming, trade union, and consumer interests, as well as developmental or environmental NGOs. The more important lobbying takes place bilaterally between the Commission and interest groups. Unlike the statutory provision for Trade Advisory Committees in the US, EU trade policy consultations are informal, in that they are not based on any formal or legislative provision. This leads to criticism, especially from the US, that they are opaque.

The Council adopts the eventual results of each negotiation. As noted, the members of the Council are normally present at key stages and at the end of a major negotiation, so as to provide final instructions and to endorse last minute deals. Formal adoption then follows in the GAERC under the QMV rule on issues within EU competence, although in practice the Council operates by consensus at least as far as major issues affecting major member governments are concerned. Smaller member states may be bought-off with side payments. For example, in the Uruguay Round France did not allowed itself to be outvoted on agricultural trade issues, but it is claimed that the opposition of Portugal to the liberalization of textile and clothing trade, was 'bought off' with additional structural funding (Woolcock and Hodges 1996: 320).

The EP must then give its assent, by a simple majority, if the agreement negotiated requires changes in EU internal legislation. Given the nature of trade policy today, it is likely that the EP will have to vote on the outcome of any major WTO agreement. Unanimity in the Council is required to adopt the results of negotiations on issues within national competence or mixed competence, which are then subject to national ratification processes, including national parliaments.

Negotiating bilateral agreements

The policy process for bilateral association agreements (see Fig. 15.2) is similar. However, the formal basis for decision-making in the Council is the unanimity rule. The EP must give its assent to any such agreement with a simple majority vote, so the threat of an EP rejection is also more credible, and the EP generally has more say in the course of bilateral negotiations than in multilateral negotiations. The issues in bilateral negotiations are also more straightforward, so that parliamentarians find it easier to make judgments on the merits.

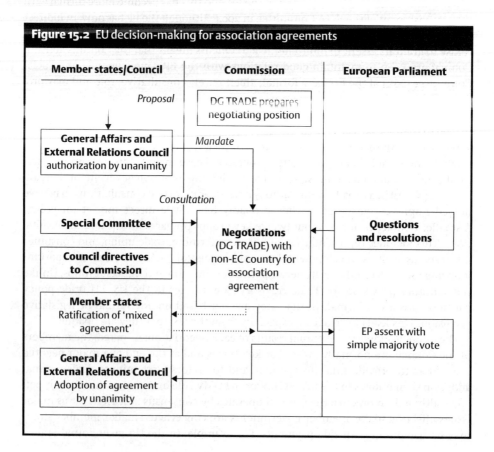

Figure 15.2 EU decision-making for association agreements

Member states/Council	Commission	European Parliament
Proposal	DG TRADE prepares negotiating position	
General Affairs and External Relations Council authorization by unanimity	*Mandate*	
Consultation		
Special Committee	**Negotiations** (DG TRADE) with non-EC country for association agreement	**Questions and resolutions**
Council directives to Commission		
Member states Ratification of 'mixed agreement'		EP assent with simple majority vote
General Affairs and External Relations Council Adoption of agreement by unanimity		

Instruments of commercial defence

The use of instruments of commercial defence is the third pillar of EU trade policy. These are the measures that are used on a day-to-day basis to protect EU industries from 'unfair' trade practices or to ensure that the EU's trading partners comply with WTO obligations. Countervailing duties are tariffs that can be applied under GATT rules when foreign suppliers of goods into the EU market benefit from public subsidies in their country of origin; and anti-dumping duties can be imposed when exporters 'dump' products on the EU market, for example, at prices below the cost of production. When EU exporters face 'unfair' barriers to market access in other markets, they have recourse to the Trade Barriers Regulation (TBR) (Council Regulation (EC) No. 3286/94), which in 1995 replaced the earlier New Commercial Policy Instrument (NCI).

Anti-dumping has been by far the most important commercial instrument used by the EU, and since the late 1960s implemented at European level. The GATT Article VI, which lays down rules on anti-dumping, provides some discretion for WTO members on how these rules are interpreted. The Commission leads on anti-dumping, and can thus exploit this discretion (see Fig. 15.3). An anti-dumping complaint is generally triggered by a claim from EU manufacturers that an exporter has caused them damage. The Commission has to establish, after consulting the member governments, if dumping has occurred, whether the industry concerned has been injured, and where the 'Community interest' lies. The Community interest test requires an assessment of the costs to consumers and other industries, and benefits—for the injured industry of imposing anti-dumping duties. The Commission can impose preliminary anti-dumping duties, to prevent injury to an industry, while the Council considers whether to impose definitive duties, which now means that a Commission proposal is upheld, unless there is a negative vote in the Council by simple majority.

The Council must approve definitive duties, which can run for up to five years. In the early 1990s the French government led a group of governments pressing for changes to the rules to make it easier to use anti-dumping duties and other instruments of commercial defence. As a *quid pro quo* for their support for the implementation of the Uruguay Round member governments agreed to lower the threshold for adopting definitive duties from QMV to a simple majority (Council Regulation 522/94).

The paradox was that a lower threshold for a protectionist position was also a lower threshold for a liberal position. The 1995 enlargement brought in liberal Sweden and Finland which made it easier to obtain a (simple) negative majority against adopting definitive duties. Abstentions are also a problem, since they count as negative votes where a 'positive' vote is needed (see Molyneux 1999). Concerns that the enlargement to twenty-five members would increase the likelihood of abstentions, led in 2004 to a further rule change which now means that a Commission proposal is upheld, unless there is a negative vote in the Council by simple majority. Notwithstanding these changes, explicitly contested votes in the Council on anti-dumping are rare, and the voting rules are operated more implicitly in the Council Committee (Council Regulation 461/2004).

Day-to-day trade policy also consists of implementation of bilateral or multilateral agreements. Here the relevant dispute settlement procedures are used. Most disputes are resolved through consultations between the Commission and the relevant trading

Figure 15.3 EU decision-making for anti-dumping measures

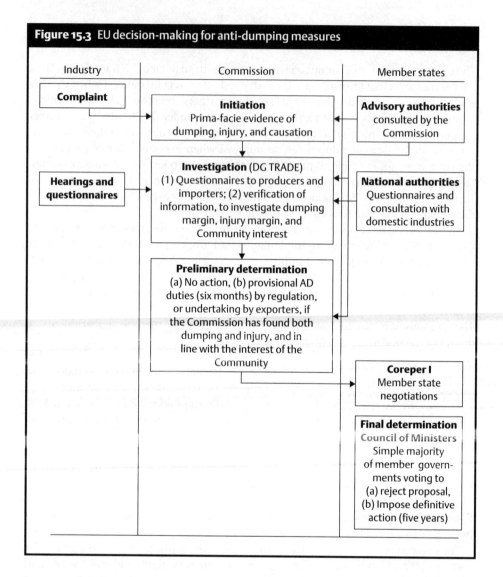

partners. However, there is a greater use of adjudication mechanisms for dispute settlement, especially in the WTO. The EU has won several important WTO cases, such as on US safeguard actions on steel, and the US Foreign Sales Corporation Tax (FSC), but it also lost some, such as the beef hormones case (see Chapter 13). Decisions on whether to bring a case in the WTO are generally taken by the Commission, but with the backing of the Article 133 Committee. Challenging another WTO member under the Dispute Settlement Understanding (DSU) can be seen as an aggressive step, especially when losing the case carries major costs or requires changes in policy or legislation, such as in the FSC case; in these instances decisions are taken by the Council (Petersmann 2002, 2004).

The key players

At the end of the 1990s the increased scope of trade policy, together with enlarged membership of the EU, significantly increased the number and range of actors in the EU policy process. The key players remain the Commission and national trade officials, and—despite pressure for more transparency, more involvement from civil society, and more parliamentary accountability—important judgments on the balance between different sectoral interests, between different policy objectives, and between different points of view, are still made within a fairly small policy élite comprising the Commission and member-government trade officials and ministers. Increased NGO activity has generated a much higher public awareness of the impact and importance of trade policy, which may in turn have generated more debate in the European and national parliaments, in the sense that NGOs shape public opinion which leads to more response from parliamentarians, but not much more direct influence over decision-making. Direct lobbying of the Commission and member governments by leading environmental and developmental NGOs has been reflected in EU positions on such topics as trade and the environment. However, this lobbying, with that of business groups, has been largely channelled through the European and national trade administrations. This has left European trade officials in more control of the process than, for example, the case of the US, where lobbies are more powerful, and have much greater ability to shape and mobilize Congressional opinion.

As one moves away from trade policy *per se* to look at policies that shape the 'domestic' regulatory framework in the EU, so the role of pressure groups and parliaments, both European and national, increases. The deepening of the trade agenda means that the *acquis communautaire* on agricultural policy (see Chapter 7), liberalization of services (see Chapter 4), the protection of the environment (see Chapter 12), or food safety (see Chapter 13), shapes the EU's starting position in trade negotiations that touch upon these topics. Therefore, in these issue areas a much wider policy community is evident at all stages in the process, thus involving not only the trade policy élites.

The central dynamic of EU trade policy lies in the interaction between the Commission and the Council/Article 133 Committee. This is probably best captured by the principal-agent approach to the delegation of authority (see Chapter 2). In this analysis the Council consists of a group of principals who delegate to the Commission, their agent, the task of taking forward a collective trade policy. This seems to capture what happens better than the executive/legislative model of the US. The Council does not really behave like a legislature, authorizing the executive Commission to negotiate, since the member governments do not only set the objectives and ratify the results, but also want to have a say in every nuance of the package that emerges from trade negotiations.

The US story is slightly different. Under the Trade Promotion Authority (TPA), formerly 'fast track', procedure the US Congress grants negotiating authority to the President and sets out specific objectives. Constitutionally Congress must ratify what the executive branch negotiates; it can either accept or reject, but cannot amend. Hence the office of the United States Trade Representative (USTR) is very sensitive to

Congressional opinion, because it must have majority support for the final package, but, despite this constraint, it probably has more negotiating flexibility or 'agency slack' than the Commission *vis-à-vis* member governments. This is because the latter intervene directly over negotiating tactics and the composition of the final package deal. The fact that consensus is the norm for adopting the results of negotiations in the EU also reduces agency slack. The EU system works well when communication between the Commission and the member governments is effective and when the Commission is seen as a credible negotiator by its principals, the member governments.

Some caution is called for when categorizing member governments as liberal or protectionist, because positions will vary from one topic to another and domestic political factors with each country, such as the electoral cycle. For example, Ireland is liberal on trade in manufacturing, investment, and services, but protectionist on agriculture. France is protectionist on agriculture, but liberal on services, except audio-visual services. Germany is liberal on trade in goods, but less so on the liberalization of agriculture or services. Generally speaking, Sweden has tended to occupy the liberal end of the spectrum, at least until Estonia joined the EU, and France is at the other protectionist end. The UK, the Netherlands, Denmark, Finland, and Germany tend to adopt liberal positions, whereas Italy, Spain, and Portugal are more protectionist, with the other member states in swing positions. France also tends to see itself as providing the backbone for the EU trade policy in the sense of holding out against pressure from other countries, especially the US. Successive enlargements of the EU have influenced this pattern. UK accession meant that EU policy would in future be shaped by a state that has deep liberal traditions. Portuguese and Spanish accession tipped the balance towards protectionism, especially in sectors such as steel and textiles, whereas Nordic enlargement shifted the centre of gravity towards a more liberal position. The 2004 enlargement will probably prove to be relatively neutral. Whilst Poland and Slovakia have sectors they will wish to protect, there are liberal countervailing forces in Estonia, the Czech Republic, Slovenia, and Hungary.

Enlargement increases the number of players and thus the complexity of decision-making, with some countervailing factors. More members in the Article 133 Committee will mean a greater diversity of interests. But smaller member states may well look to the Commission to reflect their interests in draft proposals, rather than rely on Article 133 Committee discussions which could strengthen the role of the Commission. After the 1995 enlargement, new members were integrated smoothly into EU trade policy but it is still rather early to say how the 2004 enlargement will play out in terms of the dynamics of the Article 133 Committee.

Sectoral interests are also key players in EU trade policy and sectoral interests shape the structure of EU trade policy, as in other countries. EU policy is, however, less immediately influenced by focused coalitions of private sector interests than is the case in the US. Sectoral lobbies press their positions on national and Commission officials. This lobbying is mainly channelled through the administrative process rather than in more open, pluralist debate in parliament, which leaves the bureaucracy more in control. European business interests are strongly organized in sectoral or national federations, which tends to result in an aggregation of aggressive and defensive positions, which helps offset narrower protectionist interests. The exception is agriculture, where sectoral interests dominate EU policy.

Civil society has not become the sort of influential player in trade policy that some expected in the wake of demands to open-up EU trade policy (see Woolcock 2000). The Commission and member-state delegations to major trade negotiations generally include representatives from business groups and NGOs. The Commission also includes a representative from the EP, who during the 2000–4 parliament was the chair of the relevant committee. These representatives are present in plenary sessions of important trade negotiations, where ministers make speeches. This enhances transparency considerably, because these representatives observe what goes on. This is quite different from having an impact on the core of the EU's negotiating position or bottom line, which is determined in the Article 133 Committee or Council of Ministers, where only member governments and the Commission are present. Nor do these representatives of wider society participate in 'Green Room' meetings in the WTO, where a group of leading WTO members come together to thrash out solutions.

EU trade policy and the Doha Development Agenda

The EU has been the main protagonist of a new, comprehensive round of trade negotiations. The Uruguay Round (1986–94) left an inbuilt agenda that required, among other things, further negotiations on services and agriculture by 2000. The origins of the Doha Development Agenda (DDA) were therefore in the previous rounds of the GATT. The WTO Ministerial Meetings held every two years also invited proposals for further negotiations. In Singapore in 1996 WTO Working Groups were established for investment, competition, government/public procurement and trade facilitation, now known as the 'Singapore issues'. But developing country members resisted any commitment to include these in future WTO negotiations, succeeded in blocking any discussion of labour standards, and held back progress on environmental policy links with trade.

In Geneva in 1998 the US agreed to a new 'millennium' round, but not with the EU proposal for a comprehensive round, which the Seattle Ministerial Meeting of December 1999 was supposed to discuss further. However, bad judgments in the conduct of the negotiations, poor preparation, vocal developing countries, and NGO opposition resulted in the failure to launch the round in Seattle. It was only after 9/11 and more political support from the US that the DDA round was launched at the Doha Ministerial Meeting in December 2001, with the goal of concluding the negotiations by the end of 2004. Agreement in Doha was also facilitated by a more ambiguously worded text, that left scope for different interpretations of the agenda for negotiations was in contrast to Seattle. In Cancún in September 2003 efforts to reach agreement on the agenda failed, and it was not until July 2004 in Geneva that a framework was finally established for the DDA.[4]

Agriculture

There are three types of issues in the agricultural trade negotiations in the DDA: market access; subsidies; and other issues, such as sanitary and phytosanitary measures and geographic indicators.[5] The market access heading includes efforts to reduce the tariffs on agricultural products. In the Uruguay Round quotas once widely used in agricultural trade were replaced by tariff protection (tariffication), but the resulting tariffs were in many cases prohibitive, ranging up to and over 100 per cent. Consequently, those agricultural exporting countries that were competitive wished to see reductions in tariffs, using a formula that would produce the biggest cuts in the highest tariffs. The EU favoured product-by-product tariff reduction on agricultural products, because this would provide sufficient flexibility to protect sensitive sectors.

Agricultural subsidies in the OECD countries totalled some $360 billion, or $1 billion a day, in the first years of the new millennium. These consisted of export subsidies, on the one hand, used to enable surplus production resulting from price support schemes to be exported, and domestic subsidies, such as income support schemes for farmers that distort trade less, on the other. In the Uruguay Round GATT disciplines were applied to both export and domestic support schemes. A distinction was also made between domestic support programmes that distorted trade ('amber box'), and income support type schemes that were less distorting of trade ('blue box'). Schemes that did not distort trade but promoted environmental goals or rural development were put into the 'green box'.

Major agricultural exporting countries, such as Australia, Brazil, Argentina, and Canada, wished to see significant reductions leading to the elimination of all subsidies; they saw the boxes as a means of re-labelling rather than removing subsidies. The US switched its domestic policy from price support to income support in the 1960s and 1970s and had therefore wanted to see elimination of export subsidies. However, in the Farm Act of 2002 it had increased agricultural support spending. Some poor developing countries also wanted the elimination of subsidies, arguing that they could never compete with the level of support of the OECD countries. Others, concerned with food security, wished to retain scope for their own domestic agricultural support programmes.

The EU began the switch from price to income support with the MacSharry reform of the CAP in 1992. The Agenda 2000 programme for the CAP resulted in a further shift that was presented as the 'decoupling' of support from trade. The EU was therefore ready to accept reductions in (and even elimination of) export subsidies. However, in order to sell reform to the European farming interests, it had to retain scope for sizeable subsidies in the 'blue box', as well as scope for developing the 'multifunctional' role of agriculture in promoting environmental protection and rural development through 'green box' subsidies.

The EU had been isolated on the agricultural issue in much of the Uruguay Round, at least after the 1988 Mid-Term Review (Woolcock and Hodges 1996). This created major problems for EU trade diplomacy. In order to avoid a similar position in the DDA, the Commission, led by Franz Fischler, Commissioner for Agriculture, and Pascal Lamy, Trade Commissioner, pressed for further decoupling reform. This was endorsed by the British, Swedish, and Dutch governments with support from consumer groups, but resisted by the farm lobby supported by the French, Irish, and Belgian governments, which argued that this would devalue the EU's negotiating coinage. In a rather surprising turn of events the Commission succeeded in pushing through significant further decoupling at the July 2003 Mid-Term Review of the Agenda 2000 reforms. This was possible because farmers in member states such as Ireland opted to 'take the money and run', accepting the inevitability of further reform, but cushioning this with increased income support. Isolated within the EU Agricultural Council, the French were unable to block further reforms. These EU reforms, together with increases in US farm spending, facilitated convergence between the EU and US policies sufficient that an unprecedented joint paper was produced in advance of the Cancún WTO Ministerial Meeting in September 2003.[6]

At the WTO Ministerial Meeting in Cancún the EU came under pressure to eliminate export subsidies within a specified period, to make significant reductions in domestic support programmes, and to open their markets to developing country agricultural products. The EU's position was that it was ready to negotiate elimination of export support for those products of most interest to least developed countries, but on the condition that all forms of export support were also included in the negotiations, including the export credits and the *de facto* support for US food exports provided by US food aid programmes. The EU was not ready to set a date for the abolition of such support, and was not ready to make commitments on this until some major developing countries, such as Brazil and India, opened their markets. As regards domestic support measures the EU's position was that it needed to retain the blue box support measures, on which its domestic reform was based. The EU made few commitments on market access.

The issue for the EU at Cancún on agriculture was whether it should show leadership and make further concessions in order to get negotiations going again, or make further concessions conditional on movement by others. European farmers' organizations, supported by the French government and some other member states, had argued against further concessions. European business, in the shape of the Union of Industrial and Employers' Confederations of Europe (UNICE), which wished to see further CAP reform, was split on tactics. Those sectoral interests seeking greater market opening in manufacturing and services in the major developing country markets (especially Brazil and India) argued that the EU should not make further unilateral moves, but negotiate further concessions on agriculture only in return for lower bound tariffs in the major developing country markets. Civil society groups generally favoured a new improved offer by the EU. Consumers and trade unions favoured CAP reform, development NGOs and others concerned about developing countries favoured lower EU subsidies and better market access for developing country exporters, and environmental NGOs saw reform of the CAP and the CFP as a way to make agriculture and fishing more sustainable. In 2003 talks in Cancún broke down on the 'Singapore issues' before the Ministerial Meeting got to agriculture. However, the EU did move further, on export support at least, as part of the Framework Agreement in July 2004, which helped bring the DDA back to some semblance of life.

Non-agricultural market access

Non-agricultural market access (NAMA) was essentially concerned with tariff reductions. For historical reasons the EU has had a higher average tariff, but fewer tariff peaks, than the US. As a result the EU continued to favour a formula approach, called compression, that would reduce peaks, whereas the US favoured sector-by-sector tariff reductions. This was the reverse of the situation for agricultural market access. With regard to tariff protection in developing countries, the EU differentiated between the major developing country markets, such as Brazil and India, where it sought reductions in the still high bound tariff rates, and the least developed countries, to which it offered non-reciprocal tariff-free access to the EU market under the banner of its EBA proposal.

Services

The DDA negotiations on services involved a mixture of concessions for reciprocal market access and rule-making. Market access negotiations in services involved negotiating reciprocal increases in commitments, as regards service sectors covered by the national treatment and most favoured nation (MFN) obligations of the GATS. These basic provisions require non-discrimination between foreign and national service providers to achieve 'national treatment', so that service providers in all WTO member states are treated in the same way as those with 'most favoured nation' status. Because non-discriminatory policies that comply with national treatment and MFN can still represent barriers to markets, the rule-making aspect of negotiations touched on aspects of regulatory policy, such as the promotion of best practices and transparency in the regulation of service industries.

The EU has favoured liberalization of services since the Uruguay Round because it is a leading exporter of services. Sectoral interests, led by the European Services Forum (ESF), therefore pressed for further liberalization during the DDA. This was relatively uncontroversial among member states, so the EU made fairly extensive offers to liberalize more services activities, especially in sectors which had already been substantially liberalized, such as financial services and telecoms, in order to gain reciprocal access to other markets. The only controversy in the service sector concerned proposals to liberalize sectors, such as education and health services, in which there was a tradition of public service provision in Europe and strong opposition from civil society and public sector trade unions. As a result the EU offer made no reference to such sectors. Another area of some debate was in what is known in GATS terminology as 'mode four'. This concerns the supply of services by the movement of labour from one country to provide a service, such as consultancy services or more controversially health services, in the consuming country. Immigration authorities in the EU member states opposed such liberalization, while the private sector, with some support from economic and trade ministries, favoured modest liberalization, on the grounds that the EU needed skilled workers in a number of professions. Development economists have argued that 'mode four' liberalization would contribute significantly to development and the reduction of poverty, but opposition to significant inflows of foreign workers resulted in only modest scope for EU liberalization.

The Singapore issues

The Singapore issues of the WTO Working Groups established at the 1996 WTO Ministerial Meeting in Singapore were investment, competition, government procurement (or transparency in government procurement), and trade facilitation. On these issues the EU was the main *demandeur* in the DDA. In Doha the EU continued to press for the inclusion of all four Singapore issues in the face of opposition from the leading developing countries, such as India, and the decision was put off until the 2003

Ministerial Meeting in Cancún. After some debate the EU offered to withdraw investment and competition from the DDA and was willing to talk about government procurement. In a rather confused negotiation this shift in the EU position was not enough to save the Ministerial Meeting from collapse, ostensibly on the Singapore issues. Subsequently, the EU confirmed its willingness to drop two or three of the issues from the agenda, although it retained the option of seeking plurilateral agreements within the WTO on these issues.

In 1996 there was broad consensus among OECD countries in favour of stronger WTO discipline on investment. The EU sought this discipline on investment on the grounds that trade and investment were intrinsically linked in a globalized economy, and that the WTO required a comprehensive set of principles covering investment rather than the patchwork of GATT and GATS rules that currently applied (Woolcock 2000). Stronger disciplines were supported by medium-sized manufacturing companies and the European services sector. The large European multinationals could rely either on bilateral investment agreements between the EU member states and host countries, or on their own negotiating leverage *vis-à-vis* host governments. The relatively uncommitted lobbying from the business community, contrasted with determined opposition to investment in the WTO from labour, environmental, and development NGOs, which saw such rules as undermining national policy autonomy in developed and developing countries. This NGO coalition opposed to investment rules had been formed in opposition to a previous proposal within the OECD to develop a Multilateral Agreement on Investment (MAI), and helped block negotiations in 1998. The coalition was easily reconstructed to counter plans to bring investment rules into the WTO.[7]

The aim to include closer cooperation in competition policies within the WTO appears to have been almost exclusively shaped on the EU side by a belief in the validity of the EU model, which had been fully assimilated by the EU member states in the 1980s (see Chapter 5). The argument was that more active cooperation was needed to replace territorially distinct national competition policies, with their limited application. As globalization is in no small part driven by the cross-border operations of companies, as well as mergers, acquisitions, and strategic alliances between companies, the EU argued that this made a compelling case for greater international cooperation in competition policy. There were no strong sectoral interests pushing this approach, and indeed, many large companies were sceptical or opposed to such efforts. Among the active European lobbies only the European Bureau of Consumer Unions (BEUC) strongly favoured the inclusion of competition in the DDA.

As regards government procurement and especially trade facilitation measures there were more clear-cut sectoral interests at stake. On the EU side there was a desire to improve the chances for European suppliers to access government procurement markets in all WTO countries, through the introduction of more transparent and less discriminatory purchasing practices. As for trade facilitation measures European exporters wished to see a reduction in the costs of customs and other administrative procedures, especially inefficient customs services in developing countries. As tariffs came down, the administrative costs tended to rise in importance, as had long been recognized within the EU.

The EU motives for promoting the Singapore issues were therefore mixed. It has been suggested that the Singapore issues represented a 'poisoned chalice', that would obstruct the WTO negotiations and thus prevent or slow down further liberalization of agriculture. This view presupposes that the complex EU policy process could sustain so coherent a tactical strategy. Moreover, all of these issues had, to a greater or lesser degree, been on the trade agenda since the Havana negotiations over the International Trade Organization in 1948. The EU push to include the Singapore issues in the DDA can be better understood as a desire to promote rule-making in the WTO in order to provide a regulatory framework for liberal markets, on the one hand, and the interests of exporters and investors in reduced costs and a predictable environment for investment, on the other. Paradoxically, the two issues on which there was the strongest push from EU lobbies, procurement and trade facilitation, are the ones to which the developing countries were least opposed.

The main criticisms of EU policy

A common criticism of EU trade policy is that the EU has not shown enough leadership in liberalizing its agricultural markets. Despite the recent reforms the EU continues to provide considerable support for its farming sector. Even if export subsidies are negotiated away, there is persistent remaining tariff protection and, above all, domestic support schemes under the blue box. In developing countries these are seen as simply the continuation of huge subsidies that distort trade and which poor developing countries can never match. The Cairns Group (a group of agricultural exporters formed in 1986 in Cairns in Northern Australia to influence agricultural trade negations), and the G20 are most vocal in this criticism. Agricultural support remains high and is likely to continue, even if there is a shifting of support to less directly trade distorting forms of support.

The EU is also criticized for not providing effective market access for products from developing countries. Despite offers such as the EBA and the commitment to remove protection for the textile and clothing sector by the end of 2004, the EU is criticized for continued exceptions to this liberalization, generally judged to be in sectors of particular interest to the developing countries. This criticism is less well founded, although EU negotiators often manage to find ways of limiting the impact of liberalization on sectors that are sensitive for European producers.

The EU is also criticized by liberal trade economists and developing countries for overburdening the trade agenda by seeking to include 'non-trade' issues. These are seen either as inappropriate for developing countries, or even as a tactic to frustrate progress in negotiations, thus further delaying liberalization of agriculture. Yet, the trading system is constantly evolving and there is in practice not so clear a distinction between trade and non-trade issues. EU policy is evidently seeking to shape the wider multilateral system, so that it is compatible with its own internal policies, although in a less aggressive fashion than the US sought to do in the past. US initiatives on new trade rules have by and large served those sectoral interests that seek greater market access. In contrast, the EU approach to rules is based on agreed common preferences on how to strike a balance between liberalization and other policy objectives.

Finally, EU policy is criticized by European NGOs as well as other countries, in particular the US, for being opaque or lacking in transparency. The NGOs argue that key decisions in the Article 133 Committee or Council of Ministers are not open to effective public scrutiny. The US criticism is instead based on a frustration that EU trade policy is not conducted in the way to which US actors are accustomed at home.

Factors shaping EU trade policy

The focus in this chapter on institutions should not lead the student into believing that these are the sole determinants of policy. Other domestic factors, such as sectoral lobbies and, to an increasing degree, the nature of the EU domestic regulatory system or *acquis* are important determining factors and trade policy outcomes are also dependent on the specific characteristics of the sector, whether this is agriculture or services.

EU trade policy is also shaped by external factors. For many years the main focus was on responding to US initiatives in multilateral trade negotiations. Indeed, EU policy and some policy-makers in DG TRADE are still preoccupied with US policy. As for the EU's bilateral trade agreements, the initiatives for, if not the substance of, the resulting agreements, have been significantly driven by foreign policy and security considerations. The Europe Agreements with the central and east European countries in the 1990s, the agreements with the EU's Mediterranean partners, and those with countries such as Russia and South Africa are all examples. Relations with the ACP states have always been a feature of EU trade policy. However, as the importance of the EU in the international trading system has grown, so development issues *per se* and the EU's responsibility for maintaining a trading system that benefits all, have become a bigger factor. This is reflected in initiatives such as the EBA, and in the promotion of regional integration among developing countries, both among the ACP states and in Latin America.

Trade policy in general, and EU trade policy in particular, are also influenced by precedent, that is, 'path dependence'. International trade negotiations are an iterative process, with advances and modifications made from round to round of the WTO. Moreover, the somewhat technocratic way in which EU trade policy is managed helps to ensure that the EU has a strong institutional memory.

Finally, EU trade policy, and every round of multilateral negotiations, is partly shaped by events or political developments unrelated to trade. For example, de Gaulle's veto of the British application to the EEC came with the onset of the Kennedy Round, which might have had a different outcome had the UK then been an EEC member. In October 1973, the Tokyo Round started during the Yom Kippur war and the oil crisis. During the Uruguay Round negotiators had to contend with the consequences of the end of the cold war and two IGCs on EU treaty reform, just as negotiations reached a critical juncture. The DDA has not been helped by the focus of international relations on the bundle of post-9/11 issues.

Conclusions

Despite growing pressures to make EU trade policy more transparent and directly accountable, the decision-making model remains essentially the classic Community method. The Commission initiates and drafts proposals on the basis of consultations with sectoral interests, NGOs, and the European Parliament. The Council then decides on the mandate and adopts the final agreement negotiated by the Commission. This is not surprising since the Treaty of Rome gave the European Economic Community exclusive competence for common commercial policy (i.e. external trade policy).

EU trade policy also exhibits a strong functionalist logic. There has been policy spill-over as the trade agenda, initially driven by the US, has deepened to include technical barriers to trade, subsidies, public procurement, services, and investment. Hence the number of trade issues to which the Community method is applied has increased. There has also been political spill-over in the sense that national trade administrations, sectoral lobbies, and NGOs have now shifted their focus to EU decision-making. National lobbying continues, but it is recognized that key policy decisions are taken in Brussels. Other features of EU trade policy-making fit with the functionalist model, such as the remoteness of parliamentary scrutiny, whether national or European, of EU policy decisions. Increased public awareness resulting from 'globalization' has raised expectations of a greater role for parliaments and NGOs in the policy process. But the modest reforms introduced have been mostly aimed at increased transparency and have left largely intact the essence of the Community method for trade policy.

Notes

1 Plurilateral agreements are functional agreements negotiated with a number of countries from different regions, such as the 1994 Government Purchasing Agreement within the WTO.

2 In the 1990s and early 2000s, the US has sought leverage in negotiations by embarking on a strategy of 'competitive liberalization' that entails pressing ahead with bilateral liberalization with willing partners (Bergsten 1996; Zoellick 2003).

3 See, Council Decision of 29 July 1999 on the provisional application of the Agreement on Trade, Development and Cooperation between the European Community and its Member States, of the one part, and the Republic of South Africa, on the other (1999/753/EC).

4 See, text of Decision adopted by the General Council (of the WTO) on 1 August 2004, World Trade Organization WT/L/579.

5 Geographical indicators are names of products such as 'Parma ham', which indicate production in a specific area of origin. As part of the restructuring of European agriculture there is a desire to promote the use of high-quality, high value-added products, and a desire to ban the use of such names by products not made in the specific area of origin.

6 See joint initiative by EU and US presented to trade partners in Geneva

(WTO) to advance negotiations in the Doha Round towards a successful conclusion in Cancún as requested by our trading partners (13 August 2003), available on-line at *www.europa.eu.int/comm/agriculture*.

7 The EU also favoured negotiations on investment in the WTO with developing countries. This contrasted with the US approach, which was to seek a 'strong' agreement in the OECD modelled on the NAFTA investment provisions.

Further reading

For an overview of earlier GATT and WTO rounds see Preeg (1970), Winham (1986), and Paemen and Bensch (1995). For EU trade policy in earlier periods see Woolcock and Hodges (1996) and Woolcock (2000). Stevens (2000) gives an account of EU trade policy towards developing countries. Molyneux (1999) gives a useful account of one episode of EU trade policy-making, with particular reference to the legal dimension. Odell (2003) looks at negotiating behaviour in the Doha Development Round.

Molyneux, C. G. (1999), 'The Trade Barriers Regulation: The European Union as a Player in the Globalization Game', *European Law Journal*, 5/4: 375–418.

Odell, J. S. (2003), *Making and Breaking Impasses in International Regimes: The WTO, Seattle and Doha* (San Domenico di Fiesole: EUI–Robert Schuman Centre), RSC Working Paper No. 2003/2.

Paemen, H., and Bensch, A. (1995), *From GATT to WTO: The European Community in the Uruguay Round* (Leuven: Leuven University Press).

Preeg, E. H. (1970), *Traders and Diplomats: An Analysis of the Kennedy Round of Negotiations under the General Agreement on Tariffs and Trade* (Washington: Brookings Institution).

Stevens, C. (2000), 'Trade with Developing Countries: Banana Skins and Turf Wars', in Wallace and Wallace (eds.), *Policy-Making in the European Union*, 4th edn. (Oxford: Oxford University Press), 401–26.

Winham, G. (1986), *International Trade and the Tokyo Round Negotiation* (Princeton: Princeton University Press).

Woolcock, S. (2000), 'European Trade Policy: Global Pressures and Domestic Constraints', in Wallace and Wallace (eds.), *Policy-Making in the European Union*, 4th edn. (Oxford: Oxford University Press), 373–99.

Woolcock, S., and Hodges, M. (1996), 'EU Policy in the Uruguay Round: The Story Behind the Headlines', in Wallace and Wallace (eds.), *Policy-Making in the European Union*, 3rd edn. (Oxford: Oxford University Press), 301–24.

Chapter 16

Eastern Enlargement

Towards a European EU?

Ulrich Sedelmeier

Contents

Summary

The end of the cold war necessitated a radical reorientation of the EU's policy towards the central and east European countries (CEECs). The CEEC governments were swift in stating their goal of eventually joining the EU, but most member governments were reluctant even to discuss this prospect and possible adjustments to the EU's integration model. Furthermore, the characteristics of enlargement as a 'composite policy' created obstacles to matching political rhetoric with substantive policy. However, after the conclusion of Europe Agreements, policy entrepreneurs in the Commission successfully shifted the perspective of policy to eastern enlargement. The Commission developed a 'pre-accession' strategy to prepare the CEECs for membership and began to address the key challenges of enlargement in Agenda 2000. Accession negotiations opened with the first five CEECs in 1998, while some internal EU policy reform was settled in March 1999, and partial institutional reform in the Treaty of Nice (ToN) in December 2000. Ten new members joined in May 2004, but further enlargement and the challenge of a 'European policy' remain key items on the EU's agenda.

Introduction

Enlargement was always an integral part of the integration process and policy-making in the EU (H. Wallace 2000: 150), even if for much of its history, it appeared limited to a succession of discrete episodes (see Box 16.1; Nugent 2004a; Preston 1997). The EU Treaty specifies the basic procedures for enlargement, and the EU developed the specific rules to conduct accession negotiations in the context of its first enlargement (see Box 16.2; Friis 2003). The procedures remained in place, despite the changing circumstances and characteristics of the candidate countries (Ruano 2002). The pattern of earlier enlargement rounds allows us to identify key characteristics of a 'classical method of enlargement' (Preston 1997; see Box 16.3).

The end of the cold war made enlargement a permanent item at the top of the EU's agenda. Several members of the European Free Trade Association (EFTA), with traditions of neutrality, had started to envisage EU membership. The new democratic governments in the CEECs early on declared membership as a central foreign policy goal, as part of their 'return to Europe'. These expectations confronted the EU not only with an unprecedentedly long list of applicants, but also with countries at very different stages of socio-economic development (EU v. CEEC, and among the CEECs themselves).

One challenge for the EU was to find an agreement on whether to enlarge, given the strongly diverging preferences of the member governments. Enlargement threatened vested interests in the EU, the existing balance of power between member states, the functioning of EU institutions that were originally designed for six members, and future steps to 'deepen' integration. As even the proponents of enlargement acknowledged that accession would take some time, an additional challenge was which policies to adopt for the interim period. These questions included how to prepare for membership countries emerging from a non-market system and how to make most effective use of the incentive of accession to support the consolidation of political reforms.

Enlargement as a composite policy

On the surface, EU enlargement sits somewhat uneasily among the other chapters in this volume. It is not a policy area in its own right, it is not a single-issue policy, and it does not have a single location in the policy process. Despite this, enlargement affects literally all of the EU's policy areas, as most of the chapters in this volume demonstrate. It also has strong elements of a constitutive policy, as it has profound effects on the EU's institutional set-up.

The EU's enlargement policy has very particular characteristics. These characteristics affect both the policy process through which it is produced and the shape of substantive policy outcomes. Enlargement is a 'composite policy', that is, a broad policy framework that draws on policies in a broad range of issue areas (Sedelmeier 1998, 2002). A composite policy has two distinctive dimensions: a 'macro-policy', and

Box 16.1 A chronology of eastern enlargement

January 1973	Accession of the UK, Denmark, Ireland
January 1981	Accession of Greece
January 1986	Accession of Spain, Portugal
April 1987	Application of Turkey
December 1990	Negotiation on Europe Agreements (EAs) opened with Hungary, Poland, Czechoslovakia
December 1991	EAs signed with Hungary, Poland, Czechoslovakia
February 1993	EA with Romania
March 1993	EA with Bulgaria
June 1993	Copenhagen European Council (endorsement of membership perspective)
October 1993	EAs with Czech Republic and Slovakia
December 1994	Essen European Council (agreement on pre-accession strategy)
June 1995	EAs with Estonia, Latvia, Lithuania
December 1995	Madrid European Council (indicative date for accession negotiations)
June 1996	EA with Slovenia
July 1996	Start of 1996/97 IGC (failed attempt at institutional reform)
June 1997	Treaty of Amsterdam (ToA) signed
July 1997	Commission's Agenda 2000 published
December 1997	Luxembourg European Council (decision on candidates for accession negotiations)
March 1998	Start of accession negotiations with first five CEECs and Cyprus
March 1999	Berlin European Council (agreement on budget for 2000–6)
December 1999	Helsinki European Council (decision to start negotiations with three more CEECs and Malta)
December 2000	Treaty of Nice (ToN) (decision on institutional reforms)
April 2001	Stabilization and Association Agreement (SAA) with Macedonia
October 2001	SAA with Croatia
December 2002	End of accession negotiations for ten countries

---

Box 16.1 *(Continued)*

April 2004	Commission recommends opening accession negotiations with Croatia
May 2004	Accession of Poland, Hungary, Czech Republic, Slovakia, Estonia, Latvia, Lithuania, Slovenia, Cyprus, Malta
May 2004	Council requests the Commission to prepare an Opinion on Macedonia's application
June 2004	Brussels European Council decides to open accession negotiations with Croatia in early 2005
December 2004	European Council agreed to open accession negotiations with Turkey on 3 October 2005; accession negotiations completed with Bulgaria and Romania and membership planned for January 2007; accession negotiations with Croatia to open in March.

Box 16.2 Enlargement: rules and procedures

- Application submitted to Council of Ministers
- Commission Opinion on candidate
- Unanimous Council decision to start accession negotiations
- First phase of accession negotiations (conducted by the Commission): screening of the candidates' ability to apply the *acquis* and identifying potentially controversial issues for negotiations
- Council presidency conducts bilateral accession negotiations on the basis of common position by Council and Commission
- Endorsement of accession treaties by Council (unanimity), Commission, and EP (simple majority)
- Ratification of accession treaties by applicant and member states

---

Box 16.3 The 'classical method' of enlargement (Preston 1997)

- Candidates accept the *acquis communautaire* in full (no permanent opt-outs); negotiations only focus on practicalities of candidates' adoption of the *acquis*
- Only incremental adaptation of EU's institutional structure and no fundamental reform of existing policies and instruments to address increased diversity in enlarged EU
- EU preference for parallel negotiations with groups of applicants
- Member states pursue their own interests and collectively externalize internal problems

a range of distinctive 'meso-policies'. The macro-policy concerns the overall objectives and parameters of policy. In the case of eastern enlargement, this dimension concerns decisions about the broad framework for policy and which instruments to use. The choice of framework relates to the direction in which the relationship with particular candidates will evolve (such as 'standard' external relations, some form of a 'special relationship', or eventual membership).

The meso-policies translate these broader objectives into substantive policy outputs. This dimension concerns specific decisions about the 'setting' of the policy instruments in the various policy areas that are part of the composite policy. In the case of eastern enlargement, these decisions set, for example, the extent and speed of trade liberalization in particular sectors, or, during accession negotiations, the length of transition periods granted to new members in specific areas.

A key characteristic of a composite policy is that different groups of policy-makers have the lead for its different components. For eastern enlargement, the policy-makers responsible for the macro-policy include officials in the Commission's Directorate-General for Enlargement (DG ELARG),[1] and its Commissioner, as well as officials of the member states' foreign ministries. However, decision-making competences for the various meso-policies rest with sectoral policy-makers who also have the relevant technical expertise. The 'macro-policy-makers' thus cannot take decisions in the various meso-policies autonomously; they have to engage in horizontal policy-coordination with, or even delegate these decisions to, sectoral policy-makers.

A key challenge for horizontal coordination—and, by extension, for devising a coherent policy—is that the meso-policies that constitute EU policy towards the CEECs are simultaneously parts of other policy areas. The instruments that the enlargement policy employs are at the same time instruments in other policy areas—where they often serve quite different purposes. The more enlargement policy attempts to change relations with the candidate countries, the more it will have to challenge the status quo in other policy areas. It will thus clash with vested interests and prevailing strategies for achieving the objectives of these policy areas. The result is a conservative bias against changes that are favourable to non-members. It presents an obstacle to devising a new policy that is not only ambitious but also coherent in matching declared goals and policy practice. It also reinforces the classical enlargement method's inclination to shift adjustment burdens on to the new members.

One key factor that affects the likelihood of achieving both ambitious and coherent policy is the extent to which the preferences of the macro-policy-makers converge or diverge. In the case of eastern enlargement, the reluctance of a majority of governments to start contemplating enlargement and the fragility of the agreement to enlarge were a significant handicap. On the other hand, despite divergent material interest constellations, the macro-policy-makers did demonstrate a considerable shared sense of purpose, and collectively were much more receptive to the demands of the CEECs than the meso-policy-makers either in the member states or the Commission.

Another key factor relates to the structure of the policy-coordination process, that is the extent to which it is fragmented or centrally coordinated. A fragmented policy process allows the meso-policy-makers to veto policy decisions that affect their area of competence, resulting in 'negative coordination' (Scharpf 1997: 132–3). Conversely, hierarchical coordination and a centralized policy process are more likely to produce policies that reflect the collective preferences of the macro-policy-makers, who—in the case of enlargement—occupy positions at the top of the decision-making hierarchy. The flipside is that whilst centralized policy-making may generate more coherence in an ambitious policy towards the CEECs, it may also cause dysfunctionalities and incoherence within the other policy areas that enlargement affects.

The main implication for the policy process is that enlargement as such is unlikely to fit clearly with any one of the policy modes outlined in Chapter 2. Policy modes may differ across individual meso-policies and phases of the policy process. For example, trade liberalization in particular sectors as part of the association agreements may resemble more closely the policy modes more generally associated with trade policy (see Chapter 15). Intra-EU bargaining during accession negotiations, where the Commission plays an informal, but significant role as a policy-broker, reflects elements of the traditional Community method. The Commission's monitoring and regular reporting on the CEECs' accession preparations exhibit elements of benchmarking. In this case, it is less a form of decision-making and cooperation than a form of governance relying on singling out good performance and shaming the laggards—a method that has been re-imported into the EU through the internal market scoreboards.

One feature of the policy process was the important role of policy entrepreneurship from within the Commission, which kept policy moving towards a commitment to enlargement, despite resistance among the member states and from other parts of the Commission. Another feature was the recurrent prominence of transgovernmental cleavages, which reflected the macro/meso tensions in a composite policy. Although interstate bargaining played an important role, the debates repeatedly pitched the macro-policy-makers against meso-policy-makers, irrespective of their nationality.

The EU's reactions to the political changes in the CEECs

The challenge of devising a new relationship with the CEECs suddenly shot onto the EU's agenda in the late 1980s, prompted by dramatic political changes taking place in the Soviet Union. Previously, relations between the EU and the CEECs were virtually non-existent (Pinder and Pinder 1975; Pinder 1991: 8–23). Cold-war antagonism precluded formal relations with the Council for Mutual Economic Assistance (CMEA), or its individual members. The centrally planned economies did not engage much in foreign trade, and EU activities were limited to sectoral agreements designed to protect the 'sensitive' sectors of agriculture, coal, steel, and textiles (Maresceau 1989). EU governments also used trade policy to encourage individual CEECs to take more independent positions from the Soviet Union, such as Yugoslavia in the early 1970s, or Romania in 1980.

The new *détente* under Gorbachev led to tentative attempts to establish 'more normal' relations, cumulating in a joint EC–CMEA declaration in June 1988 that established official relations between the two sides (Lippert 1990). Such cautious unfreezing of relations was overtaken by the rapid political changes—utterly unexpected for both analysts and policy-makers alike—that brought down the communist regimes in the CEECs and the Soviet Union in a matter of months. Suddenly, the EU could radically redefine the relationship with the CEECs, but had no mental map with which to define the new relationship, no contingency planning, and no precedents to build on. Amidst enthusiastic pledges of support for the political changes, the EU swiftly responded with a number of initiatives. The Commission provided leadership, backed by a broad consensus among the member states that the EU should play a central role.

At the level of discourse, EU integration always sought to end the division of the continent, and to promote liberal democracy and market economies. Once the political changes in the CEECs unfolded, scripts for public speeches and statements were thus readily available for national and EU policy-makers. The Rhodes European Council in December 1988 reaffirmed the EU's 'determination to act with renewed hope to overcome the division of the continent' (Council of the European Union 1988: 19), and the Strasbourg European Council in December 1989 declared that the EU and its members were:

fully conscious of the common responsibility which devolves on them in this decisive phase in the history of Europe. . . . They are prepared to develop . . . closer and more substantive relations . . . in all areas. . . . The Community is at the present time the European identity which serves as the point of reference for the countries of Central and Eastern Europe. . . . The Community has taken and will take the decisions necessary to strengthen its cooperation with peoples desiring liberty, democracy and progress, and with states which demonstrate their commitment to the principles of democracy, pluralism, and the rule of law. The Community will encourage, by all the means at its disposal, the necessary economic reforms. (Council of the European Union 1989: 9, 15)

Despite the collective rhetoric of the macro-policy-makers, which asserted a special role of the EU in supporting the CEECs' transformations and re-integration, it was not self-evident that they would assign to the EU the key role in responding to the changes in the CEECs. Although the member governments shared an interest in geopolitical stabilization of the region and the long-term economic opportunities, the intensity of these interests varied considerably, particularly among the larger member states (Niblett 1995). The West German government was keen to re-establish historical ties in the region, particularly with the German Democratic Republic (GDR). The French and British governments were concerned about growing German influence in the CEECs, and German unification in particular. The smaller member states feared that unilateral activities of the larger member states would create tensions within the EU. EU coordination was thus a reassuring way forward. The Germans saw it as a way to reassure the other member states and to share the burden of stabilizing the CEECs. The French and British governments, albeit reluctant to curtail their capacity for unilateral action, preferred it to unilateral German initiatives.

External demands and expectations brought the EU's role into sharper focus. The new CEEC governments framed their goals of reforms with explicit references to the core values of European integration and presented 'joining Europe' by entering the EU as a principal foreign policy objective. The US administration repeatedly encouraged a leading role of the EU as it prepared to become less present in European affairs. Once German unification was under way it also appeared that the Soviet Union could live with an EU enlarged eastwards.

The Commission's activism and leadership were crucial elements in establishing the EU's central role in supporting the CEECs' transformations (Pelkmans and Murphy 1991). At the same time, the EU's policy response was necessarily characterized by a short-term logic; it focused primarily on 'normalizing' relations and technical aid for the economic transition. The Commission developed bilateral Trade and Cooperation Agreements (TCAs) with individual countries, as they embarked on political and economic reform (Lequesne 1991). Following a suggestion by the then US president George Bush at the G7 summit in July 1989, Jacques Delors accepted that the Commission would coordinate aid from the so-called G24 (western industrialized countries), with which other international organizations and agencies (OECD, World Bank, International Monetary Fund, and the Paris Club) were associated. In addition, the Commission developed an Action Plan for EU aid, including emergency humanitarian aid, improved market access, and macro-economic assistance. Its most innovative element was a technical assistance programme for economic restructuring: Phare (*Pologne, Hongrie: aide à la restructuration économique*; 'phare' being the French word for 'lighthouse'), which presented a curious mix of ambition and caution (Bailey and De Propris 2004; Mayhew 1998: 138–50).

The overall thrust of policy was still rather conventional. The principal focus of EU policy on 'normalizing' (trade) relations eliminated previous discriminations erected against the communist regimes, but did not give the CEECs a preferential position, and concrete concessions remained limited (Lequesne 1991: 364). The focus on assistance revealed a perception of transition as a predominantly technical problem, solvable through a transfer of expertise and financial resources. This emphasis was also reflected in the EU's initiative to establish the European Bank for Reconstruction and Development (EBRD), set up to provide public loans for investment until private capital became available (Dunnet 1991; Weber 1994). Therefore, although the EU emphasized the political dimension of economic cooperation and assistance (de La Serre 1994: 24), the policy had somewhat mixed results.

Phare came to depend on an army of consultants from western Europe under contract to the Commission, which led to a disturbing bias in actual expenditure away from the intended CEEC beneficiaries. Efficiency of aid was also hampered by the relative lack of resources allocated to the management of the programme, and by the considerable pressure that the coordination of programmes put on the overstretched staff in DG External Relations (DG RELEX), subsequently assisted by the Commission delegations in the CEECs. At the same time, Phare turned the Commission into a patron *vis-à-vis* the CEECs, locking it into direct bilateral and contractual relationships with individual recipient countries. The Commission channelled wide-ranging advice about economic transformation—initially deliberately confined to market-developing measures, until the establishment of the Phare 'democracy programme' upon an initiative of the European Parliament (EP)—and imposed demanding conditions on the clients of its policy. From early on this approach established an asymmetrical relationship, in which the EU set the conditionality for assistance, and ultimately for accession. Similar elements of political and economic conditionality determined eligibility of individual CEECs for TCAs (and assistance from the EBRD) (Pinder 1991: 32–4), which was hardened through the inclusion of an explicit suspension clause.

It is perhaps not surprising that policy responses were *ad hoc*. The EU had been unprepared for these unexpected changes and was operating under time pressure and uncertainty about the speed and the nature of the political changes. There was a lack of clear-cut prescriptions or policy blueprints for appropriate support for the transformation to a market economy and democracy. Shortages of staff and of expertise were another complication. Both EU and national agencies had to construct policy machinery, as staff were rapidly redeployed from other tasks, often from teams experienced in development assistance programmes for the third world (Pinder 1991: 91). Policy was invented with little clarity about how short-term action might relate to more long-term goals. The resulting mix of tradition and innovation reflected a sense that 'something had to be done', but not a policy. Not surprisingly, therefore, difficulties emerged once the focus shifted from the symbolic dimension of the relationship to the substance and the need to deliver economic results.[2] To reach consensus on the longer term objectives for policy towards the CEECs and a durable framework for the relationship proved just as difficult.

Towards a longer term policy framework: the Europe Agreements

Attempts to move towards a more long-term framework for relations with the CEECs were supported notably by the UK and German governments and parts of the Commission. The difficulty of devising a coherent strategic policy was not reflected in open controversies, but rather in the striking absence of thorough debate. Policymakers were busy with other issues, but they were also nervous about opening up a potentially divisive debate about the future of the EU integration model. To the extent that a discussion did take place it was mainly framed by the conventional antithesis of 'widening versus deepening' and the new geopolitical balance within Europe (Sedelmeier 1994: 7–20). Neither of the two more innovative ideas—French President Mitterrand's suggestion of a 'European Confederation' (Vernet 1992), and the proposal for a 'European Political Area', by Frans Andriessen (1991), the Commissioner for External Relations—enjoyed much support.

A consensus emerged around association agreements as the appropriate framework for relations with the CEECs, as first suggested by the UK government in November 1989 (Kramer 1993). In December 1989 the Strasbourg European Council agreed to devise 'an appropriate form of association' and the Commission's DG External Relations quickly sketched a broad framework (Commission 1990a). In April 1990 the Dublin European Council agreed without much discussion to create 'Europe Agreements' (EAs), as a 'new type of association agreement as a part of the new pattern of relationships in Europe', to be offered to the leading reformers, Hungary, Poland, and Czechoslovakia.

This decision reflected the preference of most member states for 'deepening' rather than 'widening'. EU policy-makers found it convenient to separate the CEECs from their internal agenda (Rollo and Wallace 1991). The Commission presented further proposals on the contents of the EAs. They would consist mainly of the establishment of a free trade area for industrial products, supplemented by a 'political dialogue' on foreign policy, and backed by technical and financial assistance and economic cooperation (Commission 1990b).

The concrete substance of trade liberalization, however, had to be negotiated with sectoral policy-makers within both the Commission and the member governments. The trade-off between trade opportunities for the CEECs and the vested interests of particular domestic groups in the incumbent member states shaped the drafting of the negotiation directives, on the basis of which the Commission negotiated on behalf of the member states with the CEECs. The initial framework presented by DG I-E was fairly generous to the CEECs. The concessions in the directives finally adopted by the Council were much more limited, after the Commission's specialist services filled in the detail, and sectoral experts in the member states became more involved in the intra-EU negotiations, often functioning as channels for domestic interest groups.

The EA negotiations, which opened in December 1990 with Poland, Hungary, and Czechoslovakia, brought into sharp focus the gap between CEEC expectations and the EU's offers. The dissatisfaction of the three governments from the CEECs (often referred to as the 'Visegrád group') led to two periods of deadlock in late March 1991 and culminating in the refusal of the Polish government in July 1991 to send a high-level delegation to the negotiations. On each occasion, the Commission successfully persuaded the Council to amend the negotiation directives in order to take better account of CEEC demands (Sedelmeier and Wallace 1996: 370–2). Despite some improvements, the CEECs were still far from enthusiastic about the final outcome of the negotiations (see Box 16.4).

A key criticism was that the EAs did not establish a clear link to future membership of the EU. The Commission had attempted to pre-empt argument by stating that there was 'no link either explicit or implicit' between association and accession, and while 'membership is not excluded when the time comes', it was 'a totally separate question' (Commission 1990b). The revised negotiation directives allowed the preamble of the EAs to note that 'this association, in the view of the parties, will help to achieve [the CEECs'] objective [of eventual membership]', but this concession still fell short of the firm commitment that the CEECs had hoped for.

Another key area of contestation concerned trade liberalization. While the EU offered to open its market to industrial products over a period of five years, special protocols and annexes covering 'sensitive' sectors—notably agriculture, textiles, coal, and steel—offered slower and more limited liberalization. These sectors accounted precisely for the bulk of CEEC exports and their medium-term comparative advantages. Furthermore, provisions for contingent protection provided EU producers with instruments to limit competition from CEEC exporters (Hindley 1992), and deterred potential foreign investors.

Thus, in their general design, the EAs were undoubtedly the most wide-ranging agreements ever concluded by the EU with third countries, but their effectiveness was reduced by the EU's inability to deliver generous concessions. However generous their economic content relative to other trade agreements, they were seen by the CEECs as grudging.

Although the EA negotiations did involve bargaining between EU member governments, the debate over policy substance was often not simply a confrontation between different national positions (Niblett 1995; Sedelmeier 1994; Torreblanca 2001). Much of the debate—also within individual governments and the Commission—was polarized

---

Box 16.4 Main elements of the Europe Agreements

Political dialogue: regular bilateral meetings between EU and CEEC officials for consultations on foreign policy.

Free trade in industrial goods:

- Progressive and asymmetrical trade liberalization (EU: elimination of tariffs over up to five years, immediate elimination of quantitative restrictions, exceptions for coal and textiles; CEECs: ten-year transition period);
- special provisions for rules of origin (at least 60 per cent 'local content' required);
- safeguards: anti-dumping provisions; special and general safeguard clauses; unilateral measures possible.

Agricultural products: consolidation of previous concessions and some reciprocal concessions.

Free movement of labour, services, capital:

- equal treatment for workers legally established in the EU;
- right of establishment: national treatment for establishment and operation of new economic and professional activities; transitional periods for application by the associates; restriction on freedom of movement through limitation to 'key personnel';
- progressive allowance of cross-border supply of services; special rules for transport;
- freedom of financial transfers for commercial transactions, provision of services and investment operations; repatriation of capital or investment benefits.

Approximation of legislation with EU: long list of 'priority areas', more concrete for competition policy.

Cooperation: *economic* cooperation in sectors of mutual interest; extension of EU *cultural* cooperation programmes to associates; *financial* cooperation: Phare grants, EIB loans; possibility of macroeconomic assistance through G24; but no financial protocol.

Source: compiled from [1993] OJ L348 (EA with Poland).

---

between macro-policy-makers, emphasizing longer term political objectives, and various groups of meso-policy-makers, under the pressures from short-term economic problems. Within the Commission this manifested itself in the rivalry between DG External Relations on the one hand, and DG Industry (ex DG III, now DG Enterprise, ENTR), and DG Agriculture (ex DG VI, now DG AGRI) on the other, as well as inside DG External Relations, between the units dealing respectively with the CEECs and those responsible for trade defence instruments. Within most member governments, the foreign ministry competed with the ministries of industry and agriculture, which were pressured by producer lobbies. The fragmentation of the policy process and lack of close oversight by the macro-policy-makers in the national foreign ministries allowed a sectoral logic to dominate the agreements. Defensive sectoral interests were able to insulate specific aspects of the EAs from political pressures for a more generous approach to the CEECs.

At times, the context of the negotiations allowed the Commission negotiators to manipulate the policy process in such a way as to force greater involvement of foreign ministers in the General Affairs Council to adjudicate in disputes over national nego-tiation positions. On occasion, this strategy facilitated more generosity towards the CEECs, such as on the question of voluntary restraints on steel trading (Sedelmeier 2005, ch. 6; Torreblanca 2001: 250–68).

An accession perspective for the CEECs

Policy advocacy and political leadership from the Commission played a key part in improving the economic substance and overall perspective of EU policy, which cul-minated in the endorsement of the CEECs' membership objective by the Copenhagen European Council in June 1993. DG External Relations and the Andriessen *cabinet* were able to reopen the debate within the Commission. The result was reflected in the Commission's report to the Lisbon European Council. In strongly normative language, it claimed that 'enlargement is a challenge that the EU cannot refuse' (Commission 1992*b*: 167). The Commission considered the EFTA applicants as immediately eligible for membership. It also suggested that the EU might develop a special 'partnership' for the CEECs, going beyond the EAs, but at this stage there was not sufficient consensus to give details on what this might entail (Michalski and Wallace 1992). However, in a further report, the Commission elaborated on such a 'reinforced asso-ciation' and proposed that the EU should endorse the general principle of an eventual membership of the CEEC (Commission 1992*c*). In December 1992 the Edinburgh European Council did not discuss the Commission's report in detail, but committed itself to take at its next meeting 'decisions on the various components of the Commission's report in order to prepare the associate countries for accession to the Union' (*Bulletin of the European Communities*, December 1992: 37), the first official indication that the CEECs might be considered as candidates for membership of the EU.

The Commission's initiative gathered momentum in early 1993, in particular with the appointment of Leon Brittan as Commissioner for External Economic Relations, and of Hans van den Broek as Commissioner for External Political Relations. The Commission team worked closely with the British and Danish Council presidencies and with the German government to build a sustainable coalition against the erosion of this new approach. The careful formulation of the qualitative criteria for member-ship minimized the ground for opposition against a general endorsement of the CEECs' membership perspective from the macro-policy-makers in the more hesitant member governments.

An important factor that strengthened the policy advocates was the acknowledgement by the macro-policy-makers that their collective rhetoric regarding the EU's special role in its relationship with the CEECs could not rely on a 'take it or leave it' approach (Schimmelfennig 2003*d*; Sedelmeier 1998, 2005). The macro-policy-makers clearly appeared vulnerable to criticism from the CEECs, as well as academic commentators and the media, who were largely unanimous in denouncing the shortcomings of EU policy (Winters 1992; Messerlin 1993; Rollo and Smith 1993; Baldwin 1994; Smith and Wallace 1994).

The criticism of the EAs was exacerbated by clear evidence of shortcomings in their implementation. While the difficulties of the transformation process in the CEECs and decreasing public support for painful reforms become more apparent, the EU seemed unable to resist interest group pressures to use trade defence instruments,[3] while running a trade surplus with the CEECs. These matters were politically highly sensitive within the CEECs and contributed to some cooling off of support for EU membership. Meanwhile the conflict in the former Yugoslavia was a salutary reminder of the costs of failed transition to liberal democracy (see Chapter 17). Thus, it became harder to dismiss criticisms of the gap between EU rhetoric and substance. The two Visegrád memoranda (September 1992 and June 1993) were important signals and showed the glimmerings of a collective response from several of the associates.

A re-engagement of the macro-policy-makers in the member states facilitated substantive concessions. After the Commission (1993b) set out its concrete proposals for deepening association and further concessions on market accession, a high-level group of senior officials took on the task of obtaining comprehensive concessions horizontally across the range of sectors. This was mostly endorsed by the General Affairs Council, thus sidelining the technical experts at the working group level. The Copenhagen European Council thus marked an important qualitative change in the evolution of policy: it endorsed the eventual membership of the CEECs as a shared goal, backed up with accelerating market access (see Box 16.5).

Box 16.5 The Declaration of the Copenhagen European Council

Conditional endorsement of the CEECs' eventual membership

Membership conditions ('Copenhagen criteria'):

- stable institutions (guarantee of democracy, rule of law, human rights, minority rights);
- functioning market economy and capacity to cope with competitive pressures inside the EU;
- ability to adopt the *acquis*; shared goals of political, economic, and monetary union;
- *capacity of the EU* to absorb new members without endangering the momentum of European integration.

Improved market access to the EU: acceleration of EA provisions for market liberalization, including (although to a more limited degree) the sensitive sectors.

Structured relationship with the EU institutions:

- *political dialogue* (second pillar): shift from bilateral towards multilateral framework; reinforced through additional meetings at expert level and greater frequency;
- extension to *other EU policy areas* (multilateral meetings at ministerial level and heads of state/government); particularly energy, environment, transport, science/ technology and JHA.

Reorientation of Phare: up to 15 per cent of Phare budget available for infrastructure projects.

Sketching the path towards enlargement

The pre-accession strategy

The Copenhagen declaration rested on a fragile compromise, which left open how the new policy would be achieved. Most member states remained sceptical about the prospect of enlargement and consented to the Copenhagen declaration in the belief that it would lay the enlargement debate to rest for the foreseeable future. The policy advocates in DG External Relations, and the Brittan *cabinet* were keen to use the momentum for a follow-up initiative that placed accession preparations on a concrete working footing without which the process might stall.

The policy advocates envisaged a strategy to prepare the CEECs for accession that focused on their alignment with EU legislation—the *acquis communautaire*. Progress with alignment would dispel fears that the CEECs were insufficiently prepared for membership and make it difficult for the EU to justify dragging its feet on accession. Alignment could be also beneficial in its own right. As long as the CEECs remained sufficiently flexible to set their own priorities, it could bolster the broader process of economic restructuring and internationalizing the CEEC economies. Alignment with EU competition and state aids policies could reduce the threat from the EU's trade defence instruments.

Although a significant body of opinion in the Commission, shared by Delors, urged a consolidation of existing policy, rather than new initiatives, Brittan and van den Broek gained support for their proposals to prepare the CEECs for accession. In addition to regulatory alignment, this included: improved trade opportunities through liberalization in agriculture; limiting the use of commercial defence instruments; an accumulation of rules of origin; more effective use of Phare (following the structural funds model); and making the 'structured dialogue' more operational.

Some member states were also in favour of further reinforcing relations with the CEECs, such as a proposal by the British and Italian foreign ministers for a more direct participation by CEEC representatives in CFSP and Justice and Home Affairs (*Agence Europe*, 22 December 1993: 6). Other governments were more hesitant. The French and Spanish governments wanted a comparable investment in an active Mediterranean policy. The tensions about enlargement surfaced briefly during the closing phase of the accession negotiations with the EFTA applicants. A bargain was nevertheless struck in which the French and Spanish accepted eastern enlargement as a goal, as well as immediate EFTA enlargement, in return for German support for what became the Barcelona process to develop a new Mediterranean policy.

Informal cooperation between the Commission team and the German government resulted in the call of the Corfu European Council in June 1994 for the Commission to report on 'the strategy to be followed with a view to preparing for accession' (Council of the European Union 1994: 19). This mandate gave the policy advocates a crucial advantage inside the Commission. The Commission agreed the outline of the 'pre-accession' strategy in July 1994 (Commission 1994a). The substantive follow-up paper (Commission 1994c) was more contested and the college of Commissioners watered down the original proposals on commercial defence, agricultural subsidies, rules of origin, and financial transfers. The two surviving cornerstones were the 'structured dialogue'—extending regular ministerial meetings between EU and CEEC officials into the first and third pillars—and the progressive integration of the CEECs into the single market through regulatory alignment. The Commission promised a White Paper on those parts of the *acquis* essential for the CEECs to transpose into their national legislation, as well as the legal and institutional framework required for implementation.

During the early stages of the German presidency in July 1994, the Council largely endorsed the Commission's approach. Regulatory alignment through a Commission White Paper proved largely uncontroversial, despite persistent differences of emphasis. The 'structured dialogue' proved more difficult, as some member states feared that it would lead to some sort of membership through the backdoor. These difficulties were reflected in an embarrassing row over the reluctant endorsement of the planned invitation of the CEECs' heads of government to attend part of the European Council meeting in Essen.

Arguments also continued over the concrete accompanying measures on trade and financial aid, which divided most EU governments internally, including the German presidency. The German Council Presidency averted further weakening of the proposals by centralizing negotiations at the level of the Committee of Permanent Representatives (Coreper); a 'Coreper *restreint*' adopted the final text. The results of the Essen European Council (see Box 16.6) may appear undramatic compared with some expectations, but nonetheless sketched a roadmap to membership that presented accession preparations as a feasible task.

Box 16.6 The Essen European Council's 'pre-accession' strategy

Structured relationship: making the agreement at Copenhagen more operational (e.g. concrete decisions on issue areas and frequency of meetings connected to corresponding Council; schedule for joint meetings at the beginning of each year in agreement between the two presidencies; stronger emphasis on meetings of 'the fifteen' with CEEC counterparts after Council meetings).

Preparing the CEECs for integration into the single market

- *Commission White Paper*: identification of key *acquis* essential for the creation and maintenance of the internal market in each sector; suggested sequencing for legal approximation, but not priorities between sectors; specification of administrative and organizational structures for effective implementation and enforcement;

- creation of *Technical Assistance Information Exchange Office* (TAEIX) in Commission: database on alignment with internal market; clearing-house to match requests for assistance with expertise available in Commission, member states, and private bodies;

- Commission *monitoring* of implementation of recommendations with regular reports;

- *CEECs*: establishment of national work programmes to identify sectoral priorities and timetables for alignment; phased adoption of legislation, regulatory systems, standards, and certification methods compatible with EU.

Supporting policies: including infrastructure development, cooperation in Trans-European Networks (TENs), intra-regional cooperation.

The White Paper on regulatory alignment

The White Paper on regulatory alignment was published in May 1995 and agreed without much discussion at the Cannes European Council in June of the same year (Commission 1995). It used a similar approach as the 1985 Commission White Paper on the single market (see Chapter 4), identifying the EU's core market regulations which the CEECs would have to adopt. It stressed the importance of the legal and administrative infrastructure to enforce legislation, as opposed to mere formal transposition into national law. By presenting the White Paper predominantly as a technical exercise, the Commission reduced the opportunities for veto groups on the EU side to intervene and to block progress.

Yet the approach of the White Paper was profoundly political. It touched on the question of what level of convergence would be required for full accession, what could be left for post-accession transition, and the scope for the CEEC governments to express regulatory preferences of their own. The White Paper distinguished regulations of *product* characteristics, which could constitute non-tariff barriers to trade, from regulations concerning the *processes* for making products and generating services (e.g. standards of social and environmental protection), and excluded the latter from its menu. This distinction remained a persistently important issue until the accession negotiations. High process standards are costly, and more easily achieved by advanced than by developing economies (McGowan and Wallace 1996; Smith *et al.* 1996; see Rouam 1994 for a critical view), but they are embedded in the dominant policy paradigm underpinning the EU's internal market (Sedelmeier 1998, 2002).

DG Internal Market (ex DG XV, now DG MARKT) drafted the White Paper, working closely with DG IA. Its strong coordinating role and the support of DG Economic and Financial Affairs (ex DG II, now DG ECFIN), and DG Competition (ex DG IV, now DG COMP) secured general acquiescence to the selective approach. The White Paper largely excluded process regulations—notably in environmental policy—but DG Social Affairs (ex DG V, now DG Employment and Social Affairs, EMPL) insisted on the inclusion of social policy *acquis*. The exception of social policy notwithstanding, the implicit suggestion that some parts of the *acquis* were more important than others breached an important taboo. The newly created Technical Assistance Information Exchange Office (TAIEX) in the Commission supported the efforts for regulatory convergence, including through organizing the seconding of administrators from the member states to advise their counterparts in the CEECs.

Towards an enlargement policy

The Madrid European Council in December 1995 shifted EU policy firmly towards enlargement. The prompt came mainly from member governments, which now started to assume the central role in the policy process previously occupied by the Commission after Leon Brittan lost responsibility for relations with the CEECs in the Santer Commission. The German government in particular lobbied to set a date for opening accession negotiations in order to complete them around the year 2000. Chancellor Kohl was widely reported to favour opening negotiations initially with only Poland, the Czech Republic, and Hungary, starting a debate about whether or not to 'differentiate' between the applicants, and, if so, at what stage in the accession process. Early differentiation could weaken the incentives for reform (both in the 'ins' and 'outs'), but negotiations with too many candidates at once could make the process unmanageable. In addition, individual EU members had their own favourites among the applicants, based on geographical and historical ties.

The Spanish presidency brokered an agreement on an indicative timetable for starting accession negotiations. In the context of the agreement on the customs union with Turkey in April 1995, the Greek government had obtained a commitment that negotiations with Cyprus would begin six months after the end of the Intergovernmental Council (IGC) scheduled to start in July 1996.[4] The Madrid European Council declared its hope 'that the preliminary stage of negotiations [with the CEECs] will coincide with the start of negotiations with Cyprus and Malta' (Council of the European Union 1995: 23). The precondition that the IGC would need to agree the institutional reforms necessary for the effective functioning of the EU after enlargement reassured those member states reluctant about enlargement, but at the same time made it difficult to refuse agreement to such a conditional date for accession negotiations. Otherwise, the European Council set no priorities among applicants and underlined that the EU would treat them all on an equal basis. Furthermore, it agreed that after conclusion of the IGC, the Commission should present certain key documents to take the enlargement process forward: the opinions on the candidates, an evaluation of the effects of enlargement on the EU's policies, and proposals for the EU budget from 2000.

The focus of EU policy thus shifted from association and pre-accession towards an eastern enlargement policy, though the follow-through would have to await the end of the IGC. Significantly, although the 1996–7 IGC failed to agree on the key questions of institutional reform, the member states nonetheless agreed to conclude the IGC in June 1997, enabling the Commission to publish its documents on enlargement that were necessary for the process to go ahead.

The Commission's collection of reports, ambitiously titled Agenda 2000 (Commission 1997a), presented an opportunity to reinsert itself at the centre of the enlargement debate. Agenda 2000 sketched an incremental pathway for addressing the key challenges of the enlargement policy, which thus proceeded on four tracks in parallel: institutional reform, internal policy reform (especially the CAP and structural funds), accession negotiations (including the selection of candidates), and accession preparations of the CEECs (on the basis of the assumption of a full adoption of the acquis by the CEECs). Such a sequencing of parallel, but separate, tracks disentangled difficult issues that could otherwise cause mutual blockages, but lacked a more strategic view of the character of a much larger Union. However, the start of accession negotiations prior to an agreement on internal reforms clearly signalled the EU's commitment to enlargement, and conversely that all the incumbents accepted that they could not allow enlargement to break down through a failure to do their homework.

Institutional reform

The initial reason for convening an IGC in 1996 was a commitment in the TEU to review the workings of the pillar structure. However, the link with enlargement was made early on, given the emphasis at successive European Councils on the need to strengthen the institutional capacity to handle enlargement. The Reflection Group of member state representatives, responsible for preparing for the IGC, and the Commission presented enlargement as a main rationale for the IGC (Sedelmeier 2000).

The debate centred primarily on how to improve the efficiency of EU decision-making after enlargement, while ensuring a 'fair' representation for each member state. The accession of a large number of new members put pressure on the capacity of the EU's decision-making structures to produce collective agreements. Calls for an extension of QMV, to be balanced by a reinforced weight for the larger member states, became common place (Kerremans 1998; Edwards 1998). As most of the candidates were small countries, politicians from the larger member states increasingly objected to the inherited formula for QMV, which had been deliberately generous to smaller member states. Hence the issue crystallized around a re-weighting of votes, on which numerous proposals and models were put forward. The debate was politically charged, although in practice the Council operates mostly by consensus and rarely resorts to explicit voting, and smaller members do not gang up on the larger states (Hayes-Renshaw and Wallace 2005).

Discussions about efficient decision-making also concerned the other key institutions, such as limiting the number of commissioners (Dinan 1998) and MEPs. Much to the displeasure of the Commission, this discussion became caught up in the question of a re-weighting of votes in the Council, with a proposed trade-off that larger member states would nominate only one commissioner.

The other key issue at the IGC purported to be about enlargement was the question of 'flexible integration' (Stubb 1997, 2002; Wallace and Wallace 1995). The assumption was that on an increasing number of issues not all member states would favour further integration, and the question was whether a formula could be agreed to allow issue-specific closer cooperation among more limited groups of member states.

However, the IGC reached only limited decisions on these issues (see Box 16.7). Enlargement did not provide the lever for compromises on reform. The early date of the IGC did not make credible the link between the outcome of the IGC and the EU's commitment to enlargement. The Belgian, French, and Italian governments immediately recorded their insistence that enlargement could not take place without a settlement on the institutional issues. Yet, although the Madrid European Council in 1995 had made agreement on institutional reform in the IGC a precondition for proceeding with enlargement, the negotiators agreed to defer decisions on institutional reform to an IGC to be convened at a later date. The decision to conclude the 1996–7 IGC, despite its limited success, paved the way to go ahead with the accession process.

The IGC dealing with the outstanding questions of institutional reform took place in 2000, culminating in the Treaty of Nice. The debates were no less controversial than at the 1996–7 IGC. Moreover, the French presidency was perceived as blatantly promoting its own interests, both as a large member state and in pressing for parity with Germany. Increasingly bitter arguments brought the Nice European Council in December 2000 to the brink of failure, as some governments from smaller member states—notably Belgium and Portugal—considered walking out. Nonetheless, the IGC agreed on institutional reform (see Box 16.7; Phinnemore 2004). All member governments were conscious that the credibility of their commitment to enlargement hinged on their ability to deliver an agreement. The governments from the CEECs were mere observers in the process, but welcomed the agreement with much relief,

Box 16.7 Enlargement-related provisions under the ToA of 1997, and under the ToN of 2000

	Treaty of Amsterdam (ToA)	Treaty of Nice (ToN)	
Extension of QMV	very limited	re-weighting of votes	more favourable to large member states, but small members still receive more votes relative to population; parity between France and Germany
Weighting of votes	no decision, but indication of an eventual re-weighting of votes, or introduction of a 'dual majority' (of votes in the Council, and share of population)	double majority	qualified majority requires 74.6 per cent of weighted votes plus the backing of countries representing 62 per cent of EU population
Number of commissioners	one commissioner per member state from the next enlargement *if* the weighting of votes has been modified	number of commissioners	large states give up second commissioner from 2005; size of Commission may be capped at twenty from 2007
Number of MEPs	capped at 700 (now 732, ToN)	extension of QMV	moderate, e.g. into trade in services
'Flexible integration'	enabling clause, but circumscribed as a 'last resort' (conditions: involving majority of members; respecting rights and obligations of non-participants; veto possible if 'important national interests' at stake)	'flexible integration'	eight countries or more required to pursue closer cooperation that does not include all EU members in certain areas
Institutional review	comprehensive review at least one year before EU membership exceeds twenty		
Schengen	new members have to apply Schengen *acquis* in full		

despite some criticism, especially from the Hungarian and Czech governments, of the inequitable allocation of seats in the EP (which they subsequently managed to redress in accession negotiations).[5] The question of allocating votes resurfaced during the 2003 IGC on the Constitution (Cameron 2004).

Internal policy reforms

The documents in Agenda 2000 concerning policy reforms were an impact study of the effects of enlargement on the Union's policies and a proposal for the EU's financial perspective from 2000–6. Agricultural policy and the structural funds were the two areas of EU expenditure most under pressure from enlargement (see Chapters 7–9), as the CEECs have large agricultural sectors and a GDP per capita well below the EU average. The prevailing arrangements would have made the CEECs eligible for significant budgetary transfers on both counts. In the case of the CAP, this would require an overall increase in the budget. For the structural funds, maintaining the status quo meant a loss of receipts for existing beneficiaries in the EU15 (or an even larger budgetary increase).

The Commission's proposals in Agenda 2000 presented enlargement as acceptable to the incumbents in terms of budgetary receipts or contributions. Agenda 2000 suggested that enlargement could be financed within the current budget limit at 1.27 of EU GNP, with any increases in real terms resulting from growth in EU GNP (see Chapter 8). The key political message was that the reforms needed for enlargement were far less dramatic than most calculations over the past five years had suggested. However, this approach was distinctively more cautious than in previous enlargements, e.g. the Mediterranean enlargement for which the Delors-1 package increased the EU budget.

Agenda 2000 took the enlargement discussion onto new ground; new actors and interests now moved to the centre of the debate, and different alliances started to emerge. The question of budgetary contributions and reform of the structural funds pitched the beneficiaries of EU funding against the main contributors, typically through interstate bargaining. A transgovernmental cleavage characterized the debate on agriculture. Agriculture ministries defended the status quo, while finance ministries advocated reform of the costly CAP and foreign ministries attempted to prevent the CAP from complicating the enlargement process.

The Berlin European Council in March 1999 hammered out an agreement on the financial perspective from 2000–6, which many observers had considered impossible only a few months earlier. In an attempt to centralize the policy process, the foreign ministers in the General Affairs Council were asked to negotiate a deal to be put before the heads of state or government. However, the final agreement was less generous than either the Commission's proposals or the foreign ministers' package. At the European Council, President Chirac in particular pressed the case of sectoral interests for more moderate agricultural reform. Most member states obtained generous transition deals for their poor regions, and the cohesion fund was continued (see Chapters 7–9 for details). The agreement reserved for the CEECs an amount rising from €6.45 billion in 2002 to €16.78 billion in 2006, which the Commission judged adequate for both pre-accession aid and post-accession receipts. In any case, these figures presumed that allocations to the new CEEC members would be more modest than for the incumbents. However, the European Council's ability to strike a deal at all was vital for the enlargement process to proceed. Final decisions about the CEECs' receipts from the CAP and structural funds would have to wait until the final stages of the accession negotiations.

Towards accession

Following Agenda 2000, and thus in parallel, and to a large extent prior, to settling the outstanding issues of institutional and policy reforms, the EU started to tackle the key decisions on accession negotiations. The Commission's Opinions on the various applicants' injected some realism into the speculations about the timetable for eastern enlargement. In contrast to previous Opinions, which assessed candidates' *current* preparedness for membership, the Commission assessed (except for the political criteria) the candidates' *prospective* ability to meet the conditions in the medium term—with 2002 as the reference date. This date began to gain acceptance within the EU as a realistic, even optimistic, reference point. Previously both Chancellor Kohl and President Chirac had voiced the year 2000 as a possible date, but this was beginning to look increasingly implausible.

The queue for EU membership included ten CEEC candidates, plus Cyprus and Malta, with Turkey waiting in the wings as an applicant. Choosing which to engage in negotiation was necessarily a tough challenge. The Opinions assessed in separate sections the ability of the applicants to meet the three Copenhagen criteria (Avery and Cameron 1998; Grabbe and Hughes 1998: 41–54). This seemingly technical assessment was tied up in a profoundly political debate. While few doubted that Poland, Hungary, and the Czech Republic would meet the conditions, some member states lobbied for the inclusion of particular countries. The Nordic EU countries supported Estonia, and Austria favoured Slovenia. The US government put pressure on the EU to 'compensate' the Baltic states for missing out on early membership of the North Atlantic Treaty Organization (Nato). In part, the candidate selection reflected a broader debate about the merits of the differential treatment of candidates. A strong minority both within the Commission and among member governments argued for a 'regatta' option to keep up both encouragement and pressures for reform: all candidates should start the accession race, but might row at different speeds towards the finishing line, depending on the pace of their alignment with the *acquis* and the success of their domestic reforms. The politically charged debate made some observers doubt that the Commission would grasp the nettle and make clear recommendations, not least to avoid a situation similar to that of the Greek accession, where the Commission's Opinion had urged caution, only to be overruled by the Council. However, the Commission recommended a differentiated approach, with accession negotiations to open first with the Czech Republic, Hungary, Poland, Estonia, and Slovenia, plus Cyprus (see Box 16.8).

Box 16.8 The Commission's Opinions on the CEEC applicants in 1997

Country	Political criteria	Economic criteria	Adoption of *acquis*[a]
Bulgaria	+	—	—
Czech Republic	+	fairly close to meeting the criteria	+ provided more progress in specific sectors
Estonia	+	functioning market economy, but not yet adapted to competitive pressures	substantial efforts necessary
Hungary	+	very close to meeting the criteria	+ provided more progress in specific sectors
Latvia	+	—	very substantial efforts necessary
Lithuania	+	—	very substantial efforts necessary
Poland	+	very close to meeting the criteria	+ provided more progress in specific sectors
Romania	+	—	—
Slovakia	—	adapted to competitive pressures, but not fully functioning market economy	provided efforts are strengthened and more progress made in specific sectors
Slovenia	+	fairly close to meeting the criteria	considerable efforts necessary

Notes: + condition fulfilled; — conditions not fulfilled.

[a] Ability to adopt the *acquis* in the medium term, including effective implementation of the measures in the White Paper and other parts of the *acquis*; administrative and judicial capacity to apply the *acquis*.

In December 1997 the Luxembourg European Council essentially endorsed the Commission's recommendations. It somewhat blurred the distinction between the two groups, as the Swedish, Danish, and Italian governments in particular argued successfully for an inclusive process so as not to create new divisive boundaries (Friis 1998). The European Council decided that the screening process—the first step in accession negotiations—would cover all candidates, but would be carried out individually for the first five CEECs and Cyprus, and in a less detailed and multilateral form for the remainder. The Commission would provide annual 'regular reports' on the progress of individual candidates' accession preparations, and might recommend a country's promotion into accession negotiations (thus creating a language of 'ins' and 'pre-ins', rather than 'ins' and 'outs').

The decision to link accession negotiations closely with individual CEECs' accession preparations bestowed on the Commission a crucial role in the accession process. In Agenda 2000, the Commission had already insisted that accession preparations had to ensure the CEECs' capacity to apply the *acquis* fully upon accession (although some transitional arrangements might be agreed in accession negotiations). This goal was supported through a 'reinforced pre-accession strategy', which targeted pre-accession aid more directly at investment necessary to adopt the *acquis* through a revamping of Phare. The progress of accession negotiations was organized through bilateral Accession Partnerships, which set clear timetables for regulatory alignment in various areas of the *acquis*, closely monitored by the Commission. The more rigid approach of the Accession Partnerships compared to the original pre-accession strategy left little scope for the candidates themselves to shape their pace and content, causing considerable criticism that the language of partnership disguises rather thinly the imposition of EU priorities (Grabbe 1999).

The Commission developed a fairly hands-on approach in the domestic politics of the CEECs, far exceeding its role in previous enlargements or in member states, as the progress reports allowed it to shape both the pace of the accession process and the selection of participants. Furthermore, although the Commission does not play a formal role in accession negotiations, it plays a crucial role as a facilitator (Avery 1995). Especially after the establishment of a separate DG Enlargement in the Prodi Commission from 2000, the Commission successfully reinserted itself in the process.

Accession negotiations with the five CEECs and Cyprus opened formally in March 1998. After the Commission's 'screening', the negotiations in parallel bilateral accession conferences focused on the granting (and length) of transition periods, either for the candidates to comply with certain obligations of membership, or obtain certain benefits (see Box 16.2). The Helsinki European Council in December 1999 followed the Commission's recommendation to start accession negotiations also with the remaining candidates, made in the regular reports in October 1999, which confirmed the progress in Latvia and Lithuania, while the political obstacles in Slovakia were removed after Prime Minister Meciar left office.[6] Although progress with accession preparations in Bulgaria and Romania had been more limited, they were rewarded for their support of Nato action in Kosovo and compensated for the economic difficulties that the conflict had created for them.

In November 2000, the Commission recommended a 'roadmap' for completing the negotiations by the end of 2002. The roadmap, which the Council adopted, considerably accelerated the negotiations by setting a timetable for the formulation of EU positions and by committing successive presidencies to concluding negotiations on particular issues. In the light of the progress of the various candidates with accession negotiations and parallel preparations for accession, a consensus started to emerge around a 'big bang' enlargement: the simultaneous accession of all candidates, except for Bulgaria and Romania. The Laeken European Council in December 2001 confirmed that negotiations with these ten countries could be concluded by the end of 2002, 'if the present rate of progress of the negotiations and reforms . . . is maintained' (Council of the European Union 2001: 3).

Box 16.9 Accession referenda in candidate countries			
	yes (%)	no (%)	turnout (%)
Hungary	83.76	16.24	45.62
Poland	77.45	22.55	58.85
Czech Republic	77.33	22.67	55.21
Slovakia	92.46	6.20	52.15
Estonia	66.92	33.08	64.00
Latvia	67.00	32.3	72.53
Lithuania	91.04	8.96	63.3
Slovenia	89.61	10.39	60.29
Malta	53.65	46.35	91.00
Cyprus		No referendum	

In the first half of 2001, the environmental chapter was closed (on accession negotiations, see Avery 2004; Mayhew 2000, 2002). Despite initial opposition from certain member states and parts of the Commission, the CEECs obtained long transition periods of ten years or more for certain investment-intensive regulations that did not affect product standards—thus confirming the selective approach adopted in the Commission's 1995 White Paper. The other controversial issues were settled in the final phase of the negotiations. The CEECs had to accept transition periods of up to seven years for their workers to enjoy the full freedom of movement, while in return, the CEECs were allowed to maintain restrictions on the sale of land for up to twelve years. Negotiations on the CAP and structural funds were—unsurprisingly—most controversial. The final agreement reflected victories of meso-policy-makers over macro-policy-makers in the EU, and deeply disappointed the CEEC negotiators. Receipts from the structural funds per capita would be much lower than for the incumbents. Direct payments from the CAP to their farmers would be initially only 25 per cent and rise to 100 per cent only after a ten-year transition period. Initially, some officials in member states and the Commission even wanted to prevent any payment of direct income support, originally intended to compensate EU farmers for decreasing price support. The agreement allowed the negotiations to be concluded in December 2002. After ratification of the accession treaties by the member states, by the EP, and through referenda in most candidate countries (see Box 16.9), the new members joined on 1 May 2004, in time to participate in the EP elections.

Wider Europe

Although the Commissioner for Enlargement, Verheugen, stated in May 2004 that 'the enlargement process is finished for the time being' (*www.euractiv.com*, accessed 21 May 2004), the challenge of a 'European policy', and a long queue for accession, remain on the EU agenda. Bulgaria and Romania have been given 2007 as their date of accession. The European Council has approved the opening of accession negotiations with Turkey for 2005, but the country continues to present the EU with difficult dilemmas and to receive a mix of ambivalent signals from the EU's member governments. Progress with democratic reforms and human rights, and a rapprochement with Greece, including a constructive role in the debate on a Cyprus settlement triggered recognition as an 'official candidate' for accession at the Helsinki European Council (1999). In December 2002 the Copenhagen European Council announced that it would assess whether Turkey met the Copenhagen political criteria in December 2004, in which case the EU would open accession negotiations 'without delay' (Council of the European Union 2002: 5). The Commission's report in October 2004 gave cautious support to opening negotiations (Commission 2004e). Not all thirty commissioners backed the recommendation and President Prodi emphasized that the approval implied no guarantees that the negotiations would succeed. However, in December 2004, the European Council agreed to open accession agreements with Turkey in October 2005.

Following Nato intervention in Kosovo, the EU developed a specific 'Stabilization and Association Process' for the countries of south-east Europe (Friis and Murphy 2000). The Feira European Council in June 2000 affirmed their status as 'potential candidates' (Council of the European Union 2000: 13). The first step towards membership consists of Stabilization and Association Agreements (SAAs), largely modelled on the EAs, but with a much more detailed political conditionality (Phinnemore 2003; Pippan 2004). As of March 2005, Macedonia and Croatia have signed SAAs and applied for membership. Following a positive Opinion from the Commission (Commission 2004c), accession negotiations with Croatia were scheduled to start in March 2005, but postponed due to the country's apparent failure to extradite General Ante Gotovina to the International Criminal Tribunal for the Former Yugoslavia.

Beyond the declared accession candidates, EU policy-makers have started to address the questions of how to manage the impact of the accession of some CEECs on those for whom this is not an immediate prospect, as well as how to square it with relations with the more extended neighbourhood. In 2004 the Commission proposed a 'European Neighbourhood Policy', including not only Russia, Ukraine, Belarus, and Moldova, together with Armenia, Azerbaijan, and Georgia, but also all the non-EU participants in the Euro-Mediterranean Partnership (Commission 2004d). The main components appear familiar—trade liberalization, regulatory alignment, cooperation on JHA, and foreign policy—but its contours are still vague; crucially, cooperation is not geared towards accession.

Conclusions

The unexpected political changes of 1989 presented the EU with the challenge to invent from scratch a framework for relations with the CEECs and indeed a 'European policy'. Policy was driven by EU policy-makers' own perception of the EU's special role in reintegrating the continent and supporting the political and economic transformations, and by a notion, not always well-defined, of the opportunities arising from successful transformation, and the risks entailed by failure.

The challenge was not only to devise a rounded and long-term policy for a very different set of partners, and to do so in a context that had changed considerably—internally and externally—but also to confront many of the paradoxes and idiosyncrasies of the west European integration process. The challenge was not just about what policy to adopt. To deliver whatever policy was agreed tested the EU policy process and its political capacities to the limits.

With the accession of the first eight CEECs achieved, in retrospect the process appears almost deceptively conventional and it might seem as if enlargement was always inevitable. Yet only the Commission's skilful and determined entrepreneurship forged agreement on placing enlargement firmly on the agenda and prevented it from stalling in the face of widespread reluctance from inside the EU, given the complexity of the challenges involved. The main pattern of policy was the incremental nature of its overall development and the difficulty of matching declared broader goals with substantive policy practice. This chapter has suggested that these difficulties relate to the specific characteristics of a 'composite policy'.

The lack of a clear consensus among the member states and within the Commission about the desirability of enlargement, let alone its speed and terms, meant that policy could be constructed only incrementally in fits and starts. Yet the collective sense of purpose among the macro-policy-makers was sufficiently strong to accept that the EU's credibility was at stake in delivering on their collective commitment to enlargement. The policy advocacy from inside the Commission was crucially important for policy to evolve, and for obtaining compromises on the many awkward questions that enlargement raised for the incumbents. Allies were to varying degrees certain member states, notably the German government, and the UK, Austria, and the Nordic members, especially during their Council presidencies. Although some national macro-policy-makers occasionally played an important part in this process, none, not even those in the German government, have sustained a role of leadership.

The fragility of the consensus between the macro-policy-makers on the core question of enlargement compounded the structural obstacles that a composite policy poses for devising coherent policy through horizontal coordination. The macro-policy-makers had difficulties in obtaining the support of their sectoral colleagues. The general fragmentation of the policy process at the level of detail made it easier for sectoral policy-makers to insulate issues from broader political objectives and to prevent a more far-reaching accommodation of the concerns of the CEECs. In certain episodes, the macro-policy-makers centralized the policy process and limited the veto power of the meso-level through hierarchical coordination. On certain aspects of the EA negotiations or Agenda 2000 it thus proved possible to disentangle decisions on concrete substance from their narrower sectoral logic. European Councils have played a very important part in this process, both by setting credible deadlines for agreements and by making the General Affairs Council, rather than sectoral ministers, responsible for preparing agreements. On balance, however, the policies towards the CEECs and the accession treaties bear witness to the limits of any attempts to accommodate the preferences of the new members. It remains to be seen whether they will spend much of the initial membership period attempting to redress these bargains, as was the case for Britain and Spain following their accession.

Notes

1 Before the creation of DG Enlargement
in 1999, responsibility in the
Commission for policy regarding the
CEECs changed repeatedly between
DGs with successive reorganizations of
the external relations portfolio. Until
1993, it was DG External Relations
(DG I), specifically unit DG I-E. From
1993 to 1995, responsibility was split
between DG External Political
Relations (DG IA), and DG External
Economic Relations (DG I). From 1995
to 1999, it was DG External Relations
(Europe and CIS, and CFSP; DG IA)
(see also, Chapter 3, Table 3.1).

2 This is in stark contrast to the EU's
unusual and highly adaptive policy of
accepting the transformation of
the eastern German *Länder*, not
covered here, as an intra-EU task
(Spence 1991).

3 With the entry into force of the
Interim Agreements, the EU used
anti-dumping measures against:
pig-iron and ferro-silicum imports
from Poland; seamless steel and
iron tubes from Poland,
Czechoslovakia, and Hungary; urea
ammonium nitrate from Bulgaria
and Poland, etc. Among the most
publicized restriction was the
temporary ban on live animal
and dairy imports of April 1993
(*Euro-East*, Apr. 1993: 26).

4 Malta was included until the
incoming Labour government
suspended the membership
application.

5 Allegedly, the French presidency
also initially intended allocating
fewer weighted council votes to Poland
than to Spain, despite similarly-sized
populations.

6 After its electoral victory, the
Nationalist Party revived the Maltese
application in September 1998.

Further reading

Mayhew (1998) presents an overview of the
evolution of enlargement and discusses the
key issues. Baun (2000), and Torreblanca
(2001) provide detailed accounts of policy
developments for the earlier period.
Preston (1997), and Michalski and
Wallace (1992) set eastern enlargement
in the context of earlier enlargements.
Schimmelfennig and Sedelmeier
(2002, 2005) present a state-of-the-art
collection of theoretically-informed
studies of enlargement. For recent
discussions and overviews of key issues,
see the *Kok Report* (Kok 2004), and the
edited volumes by Cremona (2003) and
Nugent (2004*b*). For overviews,
developments, and key documents,
see DG Enlargement's website at
europa.eu.int/comm/enlargement.
For regular news, dossiers, and links,
see the EurActiv.com website at
www.euractiv.com.

Baun, M. (2000), *A Wider Europe: The Process
and Politics of EU Enlargement* (Lanham:
Rowman & Littlefield).

Cremona, M. (2003) (ed.), *The Enlargement of
the European Union* (Oxford: Oxford
University Press).

Kok, W. (2004), *Facing the Challenge*, Report
by Wim Kok to the European
Commission (Brussels).

Mayhew, A. (1998), *Recreating Europe: The European Union's Policy towards Central and Eastern Europe* (Cambridge: Cambridge University Press).

Michalski, A., and Wallace, H. (1992), *The European Community: The Challenge of Enlargement* (London: Royal Institute of International Affairs).

Nugent, N. (2004a) (ed.), *European Union Enlargement* (London: Palgrave).

Preston, C. (1997), *Enlargement and Integration in the European Union* (London: Routledge).

Schimmelfennig, F., and Sedelmeier, U. (2002), 'Theorising EU Enlargement: Research Focus, Hypotheses, and the State of Research', *Journal of European Public Policy*, 9/4: 500–28.

Torreblanca, J. (2001), *The Reuniting of Europe: Promises, Negotiations and Compromises* (Aldershot: Ashgate).

Chapter 17

Foreign and Security Policy

The Painful Path from Shadow to Substance

William Wallace

Contents

Summary

Defence and diplomacy are part of the core of state sovereignty, around which practitioners of functional integration tiptoed throughout the formative years of the European Union (EU). Transfer of effective authority (and budgetary responsibility) over foreign policy and defence would require a European federation. Policy cooperation in this field has therefore operated under contradictory pressures. The EU developed as a self-consciously 'civilian' power, with European security provided through Nato under a US guarantee. Nevertheless, since the mid-1990s significant steps have been taken towards more effective structures for the common foreign and security policy (CFSP), including elements of defence integration. The 1997 Treaty of Amsterdam (ToA) established the post of 'High Representative' for CFSP. The Franco–British Declaration at St Malo, in December 1998, unblocked long-standing differences over defence cooperation. The Helsinki European Council, in December 1999, set 'headline goals' for defence. Defence ministers began meeting within the EU framework, and a Military Committee and military staff were set up. In 2003–4 the EU took over civil police and military operations in Bosnia and Macedonia, and conducted its first autonomous operation outside

Europe, despatching 1,800 troops to Eastern Congo. In December 2003, EU heads of government agreed their first common security strategy, *A Secure Europe in a Better World*. The winter of 2002–3, however, also witnessed the most bitter dispute over foreign policy since 1973–4, as member governments fell out over the US intervention in Iraq.

CFSP has developed through a cycle of crises, followed by limited moves forward: moderate successes building on major failures. At the conclusion of each cycle, patterns of European cooperation have been re-established on a rather firmer basis, institutional mechanisms reinforced; but underlying contradictions remain. Ratification of the Constitutional Treaty, which establishes a 'European Foreign Minister', and an EU External Action Service, would mark a further significant advance, but still leave key instruments in the hands of member states.

The Atlantic context for European foreign and security policy[1]

Foreign policy and defence have been coordinated among most west European states since 1949 within the broader framework of the North Atlantic Treaty, under US leadership. For as long as the cold war lasted, maintenance of the US commitment seemed to most west European governments vital to their security. Behind concerns about the Soviet threat lay parallel concerns about Europe's 'alternative hegemon', Germany, as a truncated West German state, re-emerged as the dynamo of the west European economy. Proposals to develop an autonomous capability to coordinate foreign and defence policies among European Community members thus opened up fundamental questions: about the transatlantic relationship; about the balance of influence and power within Europe itself; and about 'the Atlantic idea and its European rivals', including the Gaullist challenge to US security leadership (van Cleveland 1966; Grosser 1980).

None of the three founding treaties touched on foreign policy, let alone defence. The Treaty of Rome (EEC) included only limited competences to conduct external relations, under Articles 113–16 (EEC) (now Arts. 131–4 TEC) (common commercial policy), Articles 228–31 (EEC) (now Arts. 300–4 TEC) (relations with third states and international organizations), and Article 238 (EEC) (now Art. 310 TEC) ('. . . agreements establishing an association involving reciprocal rights and obligations, common action and special procedures' with 'a third State, a union of States or an international organization'). In the distinction made by Gaullists between 'high' and 'low' politics the EEC was clearly limited to the low politics of commercial diplomacy, leaving the high politics of foreign policy and defence to sovereign states—and to Nato.

Yet issues of national security and foreign policy were fundamental to the development of west European integration. The Schuman Plan for a European Coal and Steel Community was launched in 1950 by the French government in response to intense US pressure to accept the full reconstruction of German heavy industry, in a divided Germany facing apparent internal and external communist threats. US pressure to accept West German rearmament, after the outbreak of the Korean War, led a reluctant

French government to advance the Pleven Plan for a European Defence Community (EDC), into which German units might be integrated. The European Defence Treaty, signed in Paris in May 1952, committed its signatories (under Art. 38) to examine the form of the political superstructure needed to give the EDC direction and legitimacy. The resulting de Gasperi Plan for a European Political Community would have transformed the Six into an effective federation, with a European Executive accountable to a directly-elected European Parliament (see Table 17.1).

After the death of Stalin and the Korean armistice, however, so direct an attack on the core of national sovereignty was rejected in 1954 by the French National Assembly. An intergovernmental compromise, promoted by the British, transformed the 1948 Treaty of Western Union (signed by Britain, France, the Netherlands, Belgium, and Luxembourg, as a preliminary commitment in the negotiations which led to the Atlantic Alliance), into the seven-member Western European Union (WEU), bringing in West Germany and Italy. The WEU had a ministerial council, a small secretariat, a consultative assembly, and a defence agency (primarily to control German arms production); but its military functions were integrated into Nato. The collapse of more ambitious proposals for defence and political communities was a defeat for European federalists, who concluded that future developments could only be gradual and indirect, through economic and social integration. It was also a defeat for US policy-makers, who looked to the development of an integrated Europe as a future partner with the US, able to shoulder a larger share of the burden of Western international order which the US had carried since 1947 (Fursdon 1980; Lundestad 1998).

Five years later, President de Gaulle chose foreign policy cooperation as the ground on which to make his double challenge to US hegemony and to the supranational ambitions of the infant EEC. A 'conference of heads of state and government and foreign ministers' of the Six met, at French invitation, in Paris in February 1961 'to discover suitable means of organizing closer political cooperation' as a basis for 'a progressively developing union'. This Fouchet Plan was vigorously opposed by the Dutch, and found little support even within the German government. With Britain applying to join the EEC, and the Kennedy administration calling for a new 'Atlantic partnership', this was an evident challenge to US leadership and to Nato as such. De Gaulle subsequently withdrew French forces from Nato's integrated structure, pursuing bilateral consultations with Bonn under the 1963 Franco–German Treaty. Foreign policy and defence consultations among other EEC members remained firmly within the Nato framework.

The Commission's competences under the Treaties of Paris and Rome for external trade and for assisting development in former colonial territories nevertheless formed the basis for limited authority in external relations (see Chapter 15). Walter Hallstein, the first president of the EEC Commission, set out to establish its international status through active external relations, by, for example, negotiating association agreements with third countries: most significantly agreements with Greece in 1960, and Turkey in 1963. Commission delegations were established in major third countries and the associated developing states, with a Directorate-General for External Relations (DGI) to support them. His ambitions to claim international legal personality for the EEC, by formally accrediting ambassadors from third countries, were, however, blocked by de Gaulle, as a direct challenge to national sovereignty.

Table 17.1 Cycles of crises: major developments of foreign and security policy

Phases	Initiatives among EC/EU governments	Aims of EC/EU initiatives	External events
1950–1954	▪ Negotiation of European Defence Community and European Political Community Treaties	▪ Recreate German armed forces within an integrated framework ▪ Contain restored German sovereignty	▪ Korean War, 1950–3 ▪ Death of Stalin, 1953
1961–1966	▪ Fouchet Plans for 'Political Union'	▪ French challenge to American leadership through Nato ▪ Franco–German partnership as core	▪ Berlin Crises, 1958–62 ▪ Kennedy Administration's 'Atlantic Community' initiative, 1961–2
1970–1974	▪ Launch of European Political Cooperation (EPC) ▪ Luxembourg Report ▪ Copenhagen Report	▪ Foreign policy cooperation among EC governments ▪ Exclusion of EC Commission ▪ Separation of 'foreign policy' from 'external relations'	▪ Launch of Conference on Security and Cooperation in Europe (CSCE), 1972–4 ▪ US 'Year of Europe', 1973 ▪ Arab–Israeli War, October 1973
1981–1983	▪ London Report ▪ Solemn Declaration on European Union ▪ Single European Act	▪ EPC secretariat, joint action ▪ Increasing coordination between EC and EPC	▪ Coup in Poland, revolution in Iran, 1979 ▪ Soviet invasion of Afghanistan, 1979 ▪ New cold war, US/USSR; Reagan Administration in US, 1981–3
1990–1992	▪ Negotiation of the Treaty on European Union	▪ Launch of Common Foreign and Security Policy ▪ Closer association of WEU and EU	▪ German unification, 1989–90 ▪ Collapse of Soviet Union, 1990–1 ▪ First Gulf War, 1991 ▪ Disintegration of Yugoslavia, 1991
1998–2003	▪ Launch of European Security and Defence Policy ▪ First military and civilian missions led by EU	▪ Make EU a comprehensive security actor by strengthening defence cooperation ▪ Give EU autonomous civilian and military crisis management capacity ▪ Improve European military capabilities	▪ Kosovo War 1998–99 ▪ 9/11 terrorist attacks on US, 2001 ▪ Intervention in Afghanistan, 2001– ▪ Intervention in Iraq, 2003–

European political cooperation: 1970–90

The 'relaunch' of European integration at the summit meeting in The Hague in December 1969, which followed de Gaulle's departure, was a carefully-crafted package deal. French acceptance of 'widening' with negotiations for British accession was balanced by insistence on 'completion' of the system of agricultural finance within the Community budget, by commitments to 'deepen' economic and monetary union (EMU), and by renewed efforts at 'political cooperation'. Yet European political cooperation (EPC), which began with quarterly meetings of foreign ministers and officials in 1970, more clearly served German international interests than French in its early years. It provided multilateral support for West Germany's *Ostpolitik* (towards East Germany, Poland, and the Soviet Union), through the Conference on Security and Cooperation in Europe (CSCE), in a period when US policy-makers were preoccupied with Vietnam; and it provided a caucus within which to operate when the two German states were admitted into the UN in 1973.

The initial scepticism of other governments lessened as foreign ministers discovered the utility of informal consultations, and as their diplomats learned to appreciate this private framework for multilateral diplomacy. EPC was an entirely intergovernmental process, outside the treaties, agreed among governments and managed by diplomats. Foreign ministers' meetings were prepared by the Political Committee, consisting of 'political directors' from foreign ministries, under which developed a network of working groups. The Commission was rigorously excluded in the early years, though the overlap between foreign policy and economic relations in the CSCE soon gave European Commission officials a limited role. In sharp contrast to the leaky policy-making processes of the EEC, EPC was managed confidentially, with infrequent reporting to national parliaments and little coverage in the press. Coreu, a secure telex link managed by the Dutch foreign ministry, provided direct communications; working groups, joint reporting from EPC embassies in third countries, and later exchanges of personnel, slowly transformed working practices within national diplomatic services.

The evolution of EPC can be seen as a cycle of hesitant steps to strengthen the framework, followed by periods of increasing frustration at the meagre results achieved, culminating in further reluctant reinforcement of the rules and procedures. Relations with the US were a significant factor in this cycle; the Middle East was the most frequent and difficult focus for transatlantic dispute. Henry Kissinger, US Secretary of State, provoked a debate on the links between European and Atlantic political cooperation in his 'Year of Europe' speech of April 1973. Divergent reactions to the Arab–Israeli War of October 1973 escalated this debate into a bitter Franco–US confrontation, with other west European governments caught in between. The dispute was resolved in the 'Ottawa Declaration' of June 1974, in the context of a Nato summit; this set up an additional consultative mechanism between the rotating presidency of EPC and the US State Department before and after each EPC ministerial meeting (H. Wallace 1983). The French, who in 1973 had proposed to use WEU as the vehicle for a more autonomous European defence, remained formally outside Nato's integrated structure, though in the years which followed they attached informal 'liaison missions' to Nato headquarters. Extensive military cooperation among other EU members developed during the 1970s and 1980s within the Nato framework, largely without French participation; the lightly-armed Franco–German Brigade, which was formed in 1983, was little more than a symbolic alternative (W. Wallace 1989).

European dismay at the drift of US policy in 1979–81, over the coup in Poland and over the revolution in Iran, as well as at their own failure to concert their response to the Soviet invasion of Afghanistan, led to renewed efforts to promote cooperation: first, the London Report, under the 1981 British presidency, which provided for a small travelling secretariat to assist the presidency and ended restrictions on Commission participation in EPC; and then the much more ambitious 1992 Genscher–Colombo Plan for a 'single' European Union. But other governments, in particular the Danish, the neutral Irish, and the Greeks (who joined the EC and the EPC procedures in 1981), retained strong reservations over sharing sovereignty in such a sensitive area, where the views of the larger member governments were likely to prevail. The 1986 Single European Act (SEA), formally brought EPC together with the EC under the framework of the European Council, but provided for only limited reinforcement of foreign policy consultations among member governments (de Schoutheete 1986; Nuttall 1992).

Western Europe's self-image as a 'civilian power' in the 1970s and 1980s partly reflected the exclusion of security and defence issues which followed from the unresolved Gaullist challenge to the US security leadership (Bull 1982). It took accumulated dissatisfaction with the quality of US leadership at the end of the 1970s to weaken the taboo. A Franco–German defence dialogue was re-launched in 1982, and then extended through a trilateral meeting with the British into a revival of six-monthly WEU ministerial meetings (of foreign and defence ministers) in 1983 (W. Wallace 1984). WEU membership expanded to nine with the accession of Spain and Portugal in 1987, following their accession to the EC, although not without a sharp debate on the merits of expansion. But warnings from Washington continued to accompany every gesture towards closer European cooperation, with the German, Dutch, and British governments in particular anxious to reassure the Atlantic hegemon of their prior loyalty to the Atlantic Alliance (Menon, Forster, and Wallace 1992).

By the end of the 1980s the procedures of EPC had evolved into an extensive network, drawing in some thousands of diplomats in the foreign ministries of the member states, in their embassies outside the EU and in missions to international organizations. The rotating Council presidency acted as convenor and coordinator until the SEA was signed. The development of the Council presidency into a key EU mechanism, indeed, was partly due to the development of EPC. But the discontinuities created by the six-monthly rotation led, first, to the development of the 'rolling troika' (three representatives, of the previous presidency and the next in line as well as the current office-holder, named after the Russian three-horse sleigh), and then to the slow emergence of a secretariat, a mixed group of seconded officials who moved with each presidency from capital to capital. The SEA settled the EPC Secretariat in Brussels.

Looking back over twenty years, the transformation of diplomatic working practices was evident. Traffic around the Coreu telex network had grown from an initial 2–3,000 telegrams a year to some 9,000 in 1989. Desk officers in foreign ministries now dealt directly with their opposite numbers, in working groups, by telephone, and through Coreu. Cooperation and joint reporting among embassies in third countries was of particular value to smaller member governments. The habits and assumptions of a generation of national diplomats were thus reshaped, reinforced by joint training courses, exchanges of personnel, even sharing of embassy facilities in some third countries (Nuttall 1994). Commission officials, who had at first been rigorously excluded on French insistence from participation, had been accepted as observers into working group after working group. The small EPC office within the Commission Secretariat-General grew after the SEA into a Directorate (Nuttall 1994).

For its defenders, in Paris and London, EPC in 1989 represented a working model of intergovernmental cooperation without formal integration. The model had indeed been extended to justice and home affairs (JHA), a similarly sensitive area in terms of sovereignty. Foreign ministers, and foreign ministries, now spent much of their working life within this multilateral context, moving from EC Councils of Ministers to EPC ministerial meetings to WEU, each with their subordinate committee structures, meeting with each other more often than they met with their colleagues in national cabinets. But it was entirely self-contained within this circle of foreign ministries. Defence ministries remained entirely outside EPC; nine EU defence ministries and armed forces (all except those of France, Spain, and Ireland) worked together instead within Nato's integrated military structure. The structure resembled a diplomatic game, providing work for officials without engaging or informing parliaments, or press, let alone public opinion. It thus failed to promote any substantial convergence of national attitudes. There was little evidence that EPC had exerted any direct influence on Arab–Israeli relations, for example, or on events in sub-Saharan Africa or in the Persian–Arabian Gulf (Redmond 1992). US arms and US diplomacy still determined the course of western interests throughout the regions to Europe's immediate south.

European transformation and political union: 1990–2

The IGC planned for 1990–1 was initially intended to focus on monetary union and its institutional consequences, not directly on political union defined in terms of foreign and defence policy. The revolutions in central and eastern Europe in the course of 1989, and the rapid moves towards German unification which followed in 1990, forced foreign and security policy up the IGC agenda. One of the underlying purposes of west European integration since the Schuman Plan had, after all, been to constrain the sovereignty of a reconstructed Germany (Soetendorp 1990: 103); the end of the cold war brought Germany back to the centre of a potentially reunited continent. Washington was, however, the first to respond. James Baker, US Secretary of State, in his Brussels speech of 12 December 1989, proposed a reshaping of the Atlantic political community, with an agenda extending across the full range of politico-military, economic, and environmental issues. West European governments resisted the idea of incorporating this redefined relationship into a formal new treaty. The Transatlantic Declaration, which was signed in the autumn of 1990, more modestly formalized and extended the network of contacts between the EC, the EPC presidency, and the US administration (Peterson 1994), and did not touch the defence relationship.

European governments moved much more slowly. In March 1990 the Belgian government proposed a second IGC on 'political union'. Paris and Bonn jointly endorsed the Belgian initiative, proposing that the IGC formulate a common foreign and security policy as a central feature of the European Union (Laursen and Vanhoonacker 1992). There were, however, significant differences over the link between economic and political union, and much reluctance to recognize that rhetorical commitments implied real resources and practical obligations. Chancellor Kohl and the German political élite saw their acceptance of monetary union as part of a package which should include the development of common foreign policy within an integrated (and democratically accountable) Community framework. The Benelux states shared this perspective. The French and British governments, however, resisted the transfer of authority over foreign policy from a confidential intergovernmental framework to the Community proper. On security policy and defence there was a different dividing line between Atlanticists (in Britain, the Netherlands, and Portugal), resisting any substantial weakening of the Nato framework, and Europeanists (in France, Belgium, and Italy), with the German government in the middle (Gnesotto 1990). Negotiations over preferred policy outputs were thus entangled with ideological and constitutional questions throughout the IGC.

As important a dividing line, less willingly recognized by many delegations, lay between those states with the capacity and the domestic support for active foreign policies and those for which an engaged foreign policy (let alone defence) was surrounded by political inhibitions. Here France and Britain lay at one end of the spectrum, with Germany, the government most determinedly pushing for a CFSP, at the other. When Iraq invaded Kuwait in August 1990 Britain responded to US calls for military support by sending an armoured division; France (to the embarrassment of its military and political leaders, who wished to demonstrate a comparable commitment) could assemble and despatch from its depleted conventional forces only an under-strength and lightly-armed division, which the US considered of marginal utility. Italian ships and planes provided support; Germany contributed (substantially) to the financial costs of the military operation, without any military involvement. This reflected historical and constitutional inhibitions about the projection of military power beyond German borders, an inhibition to which public opinion and the opposition parties within the Bundestag remained firmly committed. Belgium turned down a British request for ammunition to supply its forces in the Gulf, mainly, it was rumoured, because the ammunition was unreliable.

It was impossible to contemplate options for European defence integration without first establishing how these might affect the relationship between the Atlantic Alliance and the EU (Foster 1992). The US was thus an active player throughout the IGC, across the whole common foreign and security policy dossier, determined to maintain the primacy of Nato in post-cold war Europe. Successful agreement on the conclusions of the Alliance Strategic Review, launched in April 1990 and running in parallel with the EU deliberations, was a precondition for successful agreement among the Twelve (Menon, Forster, and Wallace 1992). Negotiations thus proceeded in 1990–1 in three parallel fora: Nato, WEU, and EU–IGC, with overlapping but non-identical memberships.

If the negotiators had been able to focus on the issues at stake undistracted by extraneous developments, the Maastricht package on CFSP might conceivably have been tied up more neatly. But external developments intruded from beginning to end. New regimes to the EU's east were pressing for trade concessions and the promise of membership (see Chapter 16). US forces transferred from Germany to the Gulf returned direct to the US in 1991, accelerating a rundown of US troops in Europe from 350,000 in 1989 to 150,000 by 1994. The disappearance of the Soviet threat encouraged finance ministries across western Europe to take the 'peace dividend' through cuts in defence spending, far deeper than Washington's post-cold war retrenchment.

Foreign ministers were also preoccupied by the fraught atmosphere of US–EC negotiations (and intra-EC differences) in the final stages of the Uruguay Round. When the Yugoslav crisis broke in June 1991, many of the most sensitive issues in the IGC remained unresolved. Ministers assembled to discuss the principles of future common policy, but found themselves disagreeing over immediate actions. The Luxembourg foreign minister, as President of the Council for the first six months of 1991, unwisely declared that: 'This is the hour of Europe, not of the United States'. The attempt to establish a cease-fire in Croatia quickly moved beyond diplomacy to the deployment of EC peace monitors, and then, reluctantly, to the dispatch of peace-keeping forces under the auspices of the UN. The attempted *putsch* of 19 August in Moscow, and the progressive disintegration of the Soviet Union from then until the declarations of independence in its constituent states in December 1991, accompanied the final stages of the IGC negotiations. Foreign ministers and their representatives were thus caught up in negotiating the terms under which they might act together, while under acute external pressures to take common action in a rapidly-changing international environment. As the IGC reached its end game the German government, which had been pressing for a binding commitment to a CFSP, was threatening to recognize Croatia unilaterally, in defiance of the consensus among its partners not to do so.

Negotiations within the IGC focused instead on institutional issues. The German and Benelux governments were in favour of bringing foreign policy—and in time defence—within the integrated framework of the EC. The French and British argued against this that an effective foreign policy, which included the 'hard' issues of security and defence, could rest only on the commitments of governments representing states. The Luxembourg Presidency's first 'non-paper', circulated in April, sketched out a 'pillar' model, with CFSP and justice and home affairs (JHA) remaining outside the EC proper. The succeeding Dutch presidency was more determinedly *communautaire*; but the radical nature of its proposals to integrate foreign and security policy fully within the EC attracted support only from the Belgians (Cloos *et al.* 1994; Buchan 1993). Negotiations on the appropriate link between the EU and WEU proceeded in parallel. On this the French and Dutch governments exchanged positions, with the Dutch (and the British) visualizing WEU as a permanent 'bridge', linking the EU and Nato, and the French (supported by the Belgian, Italian, and Spanish delegations) envisaging a 'ferry' which would gradually transfer defence functions from Nato to the Union. The British and Italians proposed to re-define WEU as the European pillar of Nato, with a WEU Rapid Reaction Force based on 'double-hatted' Nato and national contributions. The French and German governments countered by proposing to transform the Franco–German Brigade into a 'Eurocorps', as the basis for an integrated European military structure (Menon, Forster, and Wallace 1992; A. Forster 1994). A compromise was struck at the Nato summit in Rome of 7–8 November 1991, after some sharp exchanges between French and US leaders, from Presidents down. The new Nato 'Strategic Concept', which heads of government agreed, approved the development of European multinational forces, but also reaffirmed the primacy of Nato as the forum for defence cooperation.

The confident opening statement of Article J of the Maastricht Treaty on European Union (TEU)[2]—'A common foreign and security policy is hereby established'—was thus qualified by carefully-crafted subsequent clauses, which registered unresolved differences. Heads of government arrived in Maastricht to find square brackets and alternative drafts scattered throughout the CFSP text. They devoted much of their time to other politically-sensitive chapters, leaving to foreign ministers and political directors the task of negotiating mutually acceptable language. The outcome represented a modification of existing institutional arrangements, rather than the major change that the opening language of the treaty implied.

Policy initiative, representation, and implementation were explicitly reserved to the Council presidency, 'assisted if need be by the previous and next member states to hold the Presidency' (thus institutionalizing the existing *troika*). The Commission was to be 'fully associated' with discussions in this intergovernmental pillar, and 'the views of the European Parliament . . . duly taken into consideration' (Arts. J.5, J.9, J.7 TEU; now Arts. 18 and 21 CTEU). The WEU was designated 'an integral part of the development of the Union', with its secretariat strengthened and moved from London and Paris to Brussels (Art. J.4.(2) TEU; now Art. 17(1) CTEU); Declaration on Western European Union). Ambiguous language allowed for 'joint actions' in pursuit of agreed common aims, and referred to 'the eventual framing of a common defence policy, which might in time lead to a common defence' (Arts. J.3, and J.4.(1) TEU; now Arts. 14 and 17(1) CTEU). An unresolved dispute between the British and the French over further enlargement of WEU was overtaken by the Greek government's last-minute declaration that it would veto the entire TEU unless it was allowed to join the WEU. This forced negotiators to offer associated status to Turkey and to other European (but not EU) Nato members as well.

The most remarkable aspect of the CFSP negotiations in 1990–1 was how successfully they were contained within the network of foreign ministries established through EPC, and how little attention was paid to them by the press, by politicians outside government, by national parliaments, or by the wider public. Even defence ministries in Paris and Bonn were excluded from consultation on Franco–German policy initiatives, a factor which explained the absence of detail in successive French proposals. If negotiators had addressed the resources and capabilities required to fulfil the expectations raised by their ambitious rhetoric, then finance ministries and parliaments would have had to be drawn in, with press and public following (Hill 1998). But much of the CFSP negotiations at Maastricht amounted to shadow-boxing behind the security cover which the US provided, while monetary union and social policy preoccupied heads of government. Article J.4 (TEU) (now Art. 17(5) CTEU) committed the signatories to report on the operation of CFSP to a further IGC, to be convened (under Art. N TEU; now Art. 48 CTEU) in 1996, linking this to the fifty-year review of the WEU Treaty due in 1998.

Learning by doing: 1992-6

Subsequent developments, however, resolved some of Maastricht's unfinished business, without waiting for ratification. Partly under the pressure of events in eastern and south-eastern Europe, partly thanks to the excellent personal relations between Nato's German Secretary-General and his Dutch counterpart at WEU, the WEU ministerial meeting in Bonn in June 1992 was able in the 'Petersberg Declaration' (see Box 17.1) to outline a distinctive role for WEU in undertaking peace-keeping and peacemaking operations (WEU 1992). Franco–British rivalry over European joint forces abated; the expanded Franco–German Brigade, now as the Eurocorps to be joined by double-hatted Spanish and Belgian contingents, was in future to be 'assigned' to WEU alongside other double-hatted 'European' forces in Nato (most importantly the British-led Rapid Reaction Corps), and 'made available' for possible WEU use (A. Forster 1992).

It was the evolution of the Yugoslav crisis, however, that was the key learning process for European governments. West Europeans had instinctively looked to the USA to provide leadership, while the US administration had firmly signalled that the west Europeans should take responsibility. WEU lacked the command and control structures required to mount the complex intervention needed in Croatia and Bosnia. The French commander of the United Nations Peacekeeping Force (Unprofor), the initial peacekeeping force, based his headquarters on a Nato structure, with US and German officers taken out and French brought in. The US was sharply critical of the hesitant and incoherent west European policies in former Yugoslavia; but there were also conflicting policies within Washington. The French and the British provided the largest single forces on the ground; the Spanish and Dutch also contributed substantial contingents. Five of the other eleven EU member states had troops in Bosnia or Croatia in early 1995, Danes, Finns, and Swedes with Norwegians and Finns in a joint Nordic battalion. French attitudes both to Nato and to Britain shifted further under the experience of cooperation with British forces in the field, and closer appreciation of the utility of Nato military assets, now partly under French command. An active, though confidential, Franco–British defence dialogue was under way by the end of 1993; the two foreign ministers publicly announced its existence in November 1994, setting up a joint air wing (van Eekelen 1993; Gnesotto 1994).

Despite the permissive conclusions of the Nato summit in Rome, both the US State Department and the Pentagon continued to assume that Nato would define European security and foreign policy. They regarded WEU's creation of a consultative forum with the foreign and defence ministers of eight central and east European states as a competitor to Nato's then recently created Advisory Council for Cooperation (NACC). While west European governments collectively and individually provided by far the largest proportion of economic assistance to the former socialist states, including Russia, the US defined East-West political strategy. The Clinton administration proposed yet another reformulation of the Atlantic politico-military partnership at the Nato summit in Brussels of January 1994, now to include enlargement of Nato to Poland, Hungary, and the Czech Republic. The EU's approach to eastern enlargement was a slower and more deliberate process. In the Middle East, the EU and its members were providing the largest share of economic assistance to the Palestinians, but without any significant influence over Israeli–Palestinian relations. The EU's southern members pressed for Mediterranean programmes, oriented particularly towards the Maghreb, to parallel the eastern-oriented Phare and TACIS, and with a comparable share of the EU budget; the Spanish presidency convened a Euro–Mediterranean Conference in Barcelona in November 1995, which committed the EU in principle to a generous long-term programme (Barbé 1998).

The machinery, activity, and personnel involved in CFSP nevertheless expanded. The EPC Secretariat, now with twenty staff, became part of the Council Secretariat. It had, however, little contact with the WEU Secretariat and almost none with the Nato Secretariat, both less than three kilometres away. For the European Commission, external relations were fast becoming one of its most thickly-staffed fields. The rapid expansion of Community activities in central and eastern Europe and in the former Soviet Union led to the creation of Commission representations in those states. With over 100 missions in third countries, it had a wider network than many member states, with significant funds to distribute in developing countries and in the former socialist states. In the allocation of portfolios for the new Commission in January 1992, Jacques Delors as Commission President expanded the EPC directorate into a full Directorate-General: DG IA External Political Relations, alongside (and partly duplicating the work of) DG I External Economic Relations. This tactical move provided prestigious posts for two rival Commissioners, at the cost of institutionalizing competition among Commissioners and officials. Two other directorates-general, each reporting to different Commissioners, were responsible for relations with Mediterranean states and with the African, Caribbean, and Pacific states (associated through the Lomé Convention). This scarcely made for an integrated approach to economic and political issues, or for a global approach to the EU's external relations.

There were also institutional obstacles within national governments to integrating the political, security, and economic strands of foreign policy. Most foreign ministries had separate political and economic directorates, the former relating to CFSP and Nato, the latter to the EU, with separate national missions in Brussels to Nato and to the EU. Coordination of this unwieldy machinery depended heavily on foreign ministers, most of whom attended Nato Councils and WEU ministerial meetings, as well as General Affairs Councils and formal and informal CFSP meetings. But foreign ministers were often distracted by immediate issues or domestic politics, and had limited time or inclination either to ensure that different organizations dovetailed neatly or to think strategically.

The Bosnian conflict was not the only issue on which EU member governments, constrained by different domestic assumptions about foreign policy and national interests, found it difficult to agree on a common approach. French engagement in the linked conflicts in Zaire and Rwanda embarrassed other member states. The Greek government's sustained veto over recognition of the former Yugoslav Republic of Macedonia infuriated its partners. The accession in 1995 of three more non-aligned states (Austria, Finland, and Sweden) further complicated attempts to add defence to EU responsibilities. The emergence of a northern perspective among a strengthened Nordic group also shifted the focus of concerns towards the Baltic and Barents Seas and to problems of stability and nuclear safety in north-western Russia, and generated vigorous support for the Baltic states in their approach to EU membership.

Geographical diversity created unavoidable differences of priorities in national capitals. The German government was most directly concerned about its eastern neighbours, and about Ukraine and Russia; France reserved relations with Algeria to itself; while Spain was preoccupied with Morocco, and with the stability of North Africa as a whole.

France, Germany, and Britain were the key players in moves towards a more effective CFSP. Painful reassessment of post-cold war German responsibilities was leading to a gradual 'normalization' of German foreign and defence policy, starting with the deployment of German aircrew in multinational AWACS aircraft over Bosnia in 1992. Nevertheless continuing support for the principle of a citizen army, based on conscription, left its armed forces poorly structured and ill-equipped for the different demands of peacekeeping and peacemaking. Attitudes in the French and British governments, antagonists in the debate about European versus Atlantic frameworks for foreign policy and defence over the previous forty years, were converging. The French government had explicitly modelled its post-Gulf War defence review on the British, ending conscription to focus on a smaller, better-equipped and more deployable military force. Cooperation on the ground in Bosnia was building mutual respect between the French and British military. At the political level the British and French shared similar frustrations over the reassertion of US leadership in the Balkans, with its assumption that the European allies would support the imposition of the Dayton Agreement in December 1995—a settlement less generous to the Bosnians than earlier EU proposals which the US had refused to support. All this contributed to a convergence of attitudes between London and Paris, though the strength of Euroscepticism within the Conservative party and within the British press meant that its implications did not become evident until well after the election of a Labour government in May 1997 (Neville-Jones 1997).

The Amsterdam Review

There was little enthusiasm among member governments for the major review of progress towards CFSP which they were committed by the TEU to conduct in 1996. With ratification of the TEU completed only in 1993, there was little useful experience to draw on; nor was there any consensus about whether to strengthen, transform, or abolish WEU when the treaty reached its fiftieth anniversary (Deighton 1997). Proposals from member governments revived the debate of five years before. The French government pressed for the appointment of a High Representative for CFSP, to provide for the continuity and leadership which—French ministers claimed—the rotating presidency and the *troika* were unable to ensure. Governments from the smaller states suspected this was an attempt to consolidate large-state dominance of CFSP, already evident in the Bosnian Contact Group, within which the British, French, Germans, and Italians worked with Russia and the USA. There was broader agreement on the appointment of a policy planning unit within the Council Secretariat, to strengthen central support for the intergovernmental structure of CFSP. Several preliminary papers reopened the question of qualified majority voting (QMV); the

French, in mid-IGC, proposed to move on from the TEU's 'joint actions' to 'common strategies' (B. Smith 1999). The British Conservative government, determinedly focusing on 'practical' measures, saw the High Representative post as suitable for a senior official rather than a political figure, integrated into the Council Secretariat and reporting to the Council and Presidency; the German government agreed, not wishing to create competition in status with national foreign ministers.

As in 1990–1, intra-European negotiations on security policy and defence moved in parallel with developments within Nato. The French and US governments had been attempting to find a compromise between their formerly entrenched positions since their agreement on the new Nato Strategic Concept in November 1991. At the Brussels Nato summit in January 1994, the US delegation launched the concept of Combined Joint Task Forces (CJTFs), intended to enable European governments to launch operations without direct US commitment, but also with the right to request the use of Nato's headquarters, command facilities, communications systems, and logistical support—assets disproportionately provided by the US. France in its turn had been edging back towards participation in the Nato integrated military structure. The concept of a European Security and Defence Identity (ESDI), on which the alliance had now agreed, expressed US willingness to accommodate French sensitivities, as well as US insistence that the European allies should play a larger role in maintaining the security of their own region. In December 1995 the French government announced a formal return to some parts of the Nato structure, although President Chirac made clear, in a speech to the US Congress the following February, that France expected a genuine 'Europeanization' of the alliance in return. But President Chirac (much to the dismay of his defence ministry) then publicly demanded that a French officer should take over Nato's southern command, directly challenging US strategic priorities in the eastern Mediterranean. Washington's refusal dashed hopes in several capitals that French re-entry into Nato's integrated military structure would permit the emergence of a stronger European pillar within the alliance, closely integrated with the EU.

Paradoxically, Franco–British convergence on defence was not reflected in the formal outcome of the 1996–7 IGC. Both governments were inhibited by commitment to sovereignty within their own parliaments and public from admitting how far they had moved; both therefore stressed practical cooperation, an approach with much more content but much less symbolism than that which characterized Franco–German defence cooperation. The lengthy IGC had moved from Italian to Irish presidency in the second semester of 1996, a neutral with little interest in pressing this dossier forward. The Dutch government, which took over the presidency in January 1997, was internally divided between different coalition parties and different ministries over how far Atlantic defence integration should be modified by Europeanization. The German foreign ministry was enthusiastic for greater defence integration, the German defence ministry much more hesitant. The Finnish and Swedish governments, new members and neutrals, were nevertheless strong proponents of closer association between the WEU and EU in crisis management, conflict prevention, and peace-keeping—the Petersberg tasks (see Box 7.1). Confusion in Paris, after the blocking of moves towards full French re-entry into Nato's military structure, left the Italians, Luxembourgers, Belgians, and Spanish as the strongest protagonists of a full merger of WEU and EU in the IGC endgame.

Box 17.1 The Petersberg tasks

Petersberg Declaration, June 1992, Section II, *On Strengthening WEU's Operational Role*, para. 4:

'Apart from contributing to the common defence in accordance with Article 5 of the Washington Treaty and Article V of the modified Brussels Treaty respectively, military units of WEU member states, acting under the authority of WEU, could be employed for:

- humanitarian and rescue tasks;
- peacekeeping tasks;
- tasks of combat forces in crisis management, including peacemaking.'

Western European Union Council of Ministers, Bonn, 19 June 1992, available at: *www.weu.int.*

The Treaty of Amsterdam's substantial revisions of the Maastricht Treaty provisions in Title V (TEU) on CFSP incorporated this list, as Article 17(2) (CTEU). The Constitutional Treaty would replace the Petersberg Tasks with the following (Art. I–41(1) CT):

'The common security and defence policy shall be an integral part of the common foreign and security policy. It shall provide the Union with an operational capacity drawing on civil and military assets. The Union may use them on missions outside the Union for peace-keeping, conflict prevention and strengthening international security in accordance with the principles of the United Nations Charter. The performance of these tasks shall be undertaken using capabilities provided by the Member States.'

Hardly surprisingly, the language of Article 17 CTEU (ex Art. J.4 TEU) was thus opaque. The European Council could now 'avail itself' of WEU action, with the possibility of a merger 'should the European Council so decide'. Article 13 CTEU (ex Art. J.3 TEU) declared that the European Council 'shall define the principles and general guidelines' for CFSP, 'including for matters with defence implications', leaving for future negotiation what matters might be agreed. It also allowed for agreement on 'common strategies . . . to be implemented by the Union in areas where the Member States have important interests in common . . . in particular by adopting joint actions and common positions'. But there was no common understanding as to what this implied. Irritation at the way in which the Greeks had blocked common policies on Macedonia and Turkey had however led to some movement away from insistence on unanimity, registered in Article 23 (CTEU). Decisions could be taken on the basis of 'constructive abstention', where abstention by up to three member governments would not prevent the Union adopting a position.

The ToA commitment (Arts. 18 and 26, CTEU) to a High Representative marked potentially a larger step forward: the post was to be combined with that of Secretary-General of the Council, with a post of Deputy Secretary General to manage the Council Secretariat. Article 18(5) (CTEU) empowered the Council to appoint 'a special representative' with a mandate in relation to particular policy issues—generalizing the experiment adopted (with Lord Carrington, David Owen, and Carl Bildt) in the

Bosnian conflict. Creation of a new policy planning unit, alongside the existing CFSP secretariat, registered the continuing increase in the size and influence of the Council Secretariat.

Distracted heads of government, among them newly-elected prime ministers from both Britain and France, did not wish to move further on this difficult dossier when they met at Amsterdam to settle the final terms of the treaty. Agreement at official level as the IGC progressed had produced texts which registered marginal strengthening of the positions of the Commission and the European Parliament (EP) in the second pillar. The Commission was now to be 'fully associated' (Art. 18.4, CTEU), but the Council and presidency retained the initiative; the presidency 'shall consult the European Parliament on the main aspects and basic choices' of the CFSP (Art. 21, CTEU). Expenditure on CFSP had been a contentious issue in the Maastricht IGC, because of French and British resistance to the EP acquiring an oversight of spending which might give it future leverage over CFSP. Article 28 (CTEU) charged administrative expenditure and non-military operational expenditure to the EU budget, leaving 'operations having military or defence implications' to be funded by those states which have not exercised their right of constructive abstention. Modest improvements in machinery thus left for post-IGC negotiation many of the most contentious issues which governments had been reluctant to address at Amsterdam.

After Amsterdam: Britain and France as leaders

A key factor in the unblocking of the defence dimension in the eighteen months after the end of the IGC, and in acceptance of Javier Solana, a political figure, as High Representative, was the continuing learning experience of managing conflict in south-eastern Europe. European–US differences were again evident as conflict developed in Kosovo in late 1998. The US administration favoured the use of air power alone, in which its contribution was also dominant; the French and British were willing to use ground forces. The new British government had conducted its own strategic defence review in the course of 1997–8, with the European dimension only a background factor. Tony Blair, the British prime minister, was now shocked to discover how limited a force the European allies were able to mobilize in an emergency, and how dependent they were on US transport and communications; the mantra that European governments spent two-thirds as much as the US on defence, but could deploy only 10 per cent as many troops, was thereafter repeated in prime ministerial speeches and government statements. Contingency planning for a ground invasion of Kosovo, too late to prevent Serbian expulsion of a substantial proportion of its ethnic Albanian population, depended heavily on the professional forces provided by the British and French. The unilateral style of US policy, as refugees poured into Macedonia and Albania and from there into Italy, Germany, and other EU member states, shifted opinion in London, The Hague, and Berlin further towards accepting the principle of a European pillar within the Atlantic Alliance. German willingness to deploy ground troops, with over a thousand posted to Macedonia in 1998, met another necessary precondition for an autonomous European defence capability.

In parallel with developments in Kosovo, the British government was now moving from laggard to leader in promoting European defence integration. At the Pörtschach informal European Council in October 1998, Tony Blair introduced a number of proposals on closer defence cooperation. This was followed by the Franco–British St Malo Declaration of December 1998 (see Box 17.2), which robustly stated that 'the Union must have the capacity for autonomous action, backed up by credible military forces', with member governments operating 'within the institutional framework of the European Union', including 'meetings of defence ministers'. Intensive Franco–British consultations between political directors and senior defence officials expanded bilaterally to other key EU governments, and then to the US, the Norwegians, and the Turks. Within the EU the Germans and Dutch were most closely drawn in, although the new coalition government in Berlin, with a social democrat defence minister and a green foreign minister, found it hard to formulate a coherent response.

Initial reactions in Washington were mixed; like its predecessors, the Clinton administration publicly supported the greater Europeanization of Nato, but warned of the danger of such an initiative being misconceived, or mishandled. The North Atlantic Council which met in Washington in April 1999 to celebrate the fiftieth anniversary of the Atlantic Alliance and to welcome three new members—Poland, the Czech Republic, and Hungary—declared in its carefully-balanced communiqué that 'we reaffirm our commitment to preserve the transatlantic link', but also 'welcome the new impetus given to the strengthening of a common European policy in security and defence'. Discussions then moved forward, under the German presidency of both the EU and WEU, through the WEU Council of foreign and defence ministers and through EU foreign ministers in the Council of Ministers, to the Cologne European Council in early June. Its communiqué stated that 'we are now determined to launch a new step in the construction of the European Union . . . our aim is to take the necessary decisions by the end of the year 2000. In that event, the WEU as an organization would have completed its purpose'.

Franco–British partnership, with the support of the German presidency, had pushed through other significant innovations. At an informal foreign affairs Council in March 1999, the presidency's proposal to establish an EU military committee met with some initial resistance, most strongly from the neutral Irish; but the British proposal to create a permanent committee of deputy political directors in Brussels (in parallel with Coreper), to improve coordination of CFSP, was accepted. After the meeting the Spanish foreign minister told the press that he had the impression he was 'seeing the beginning of a process similar to that which marked the beginning of reflection leading to the single currency' (*Agence Europe*, 15 March 1999). In June the German government proposed a broader EU 'stability pact' for south-eastern Europe. At the Cologne European Council in June 1999 member governments adopted their first 'Common Strategy', a lengthy statement of principles for future relations between the EU and Russia. There was now general agreement that the new secretary-general should be a senior political figure, rather than an official. The nomination of Javier Solana, former Spanish foreign minister and current Nato Secretary-General, was both appropriate and symbolic. Secretaries-General of Nato had always been Europeans, accepted by the US as an *interlocuteur* on behalf of its allies; Solana was already well-known, and well-trusted, in Washington. George Robertson, the British defence minister, who had played a leading role in promoting the Franco–British initiative, succeeded Solana as Nato Secretary-General.

Box 17.2 Developments in ESDP since St Malo, 1998–2004

3–4 December 1998: France and the UK issue the *St Malo Declaration* which stated that 'the Union (EU) must be given appropriate structures and a capacity for analysis of situations, sources of intelligence, and a capability for relevant strategic planning, without unnecessary duplication, taking account of the existing assets of the WEU and the evolution of its relations with the EU. In this regard, the EU will also need to have recourse to suitable military means (European capabilities pre-designated within Nato's European pillar or national or multinational European means outside the Nato framework).'

10–11 December 1999: The European Council in Helsinki defines the EU *Headline Goal* of creating a military capacity by 2003 to deploy within 60 days and sustain for at least one year a force of 50–60,000 personnel, with support elements, capable of the full range of Petersberg tasks. The European Council further decides to set up the necessary political and military bodies to manage ESDP. Interim bodies begin operating in the spring of 2000.

20–1 November 2000: At the *Capabilities Commitment Conference*, EU defence ministers pledge initial national contributions to the Rapid Reaction Force envisioned in the Headline Goal. The voluntary national contributions added up to a pool of more than 100,000 personnel, approximately 400 combat aircraft and 100 vessels.

7–9 December 2000: At the European Council in Nice, the Political and Security Committee (COPS, from its French title), the Military Committee of the EU (EUMC), and the Military Staff of the EU (EUMS), are incorporated into the treaties.

19–20 November 2001: EU foreign and defence ministers make additional pledges to the Headline Goal at the *Capabilities Improvement Conference* and launch the *European Capability Action Plan* (ECAP).

1 January 2002: The *WEU subsidiary bodies*, the Torrejon Satellite Centre and the Paris-based Institute for Security Studies, become EU agencies.

12–13 December 2002: The European Council in Copenhagen approves terms for EU access to Nato planning, logistics, and intelligence for missions in which Nato is not involved; after three years of negotiations over implementing the 'Berlin Plus' Nato–EU agreement, in which the status of Turkey as a non-EU Nato member has proved the most difficult issue.

1 January 2003: The *EU Police Mission* takes over from the UN International Police Task Force in Bosnia and Herzegovina, as the first ESDP mission, with a three-year mandate. The initial contingent has 530 police officers from EU members and third states.

31 March 2003: The EU launches *Operation Concordia* in the Former Yugoslav Republic of Macedonia (FYROM), taking over from Nato, and with access to Nato assets under the 'Berlin Plus' agreement. This is the first military ESDP mission: 350 lightly armed soldiers from 13 EU member states and 14 non-member states. Concordia was requested by the government of FYROM, was backed by a UN Security Council resolution, and contributed to the implementation of the 2001 Ohrid Framework Agreement.

Box 17.2 (*Continued*)

5 June 2003: Responding to an appeal by the UN Secretary General, *Operation Artemis*, a military mission, is despatched to the Democratic Republic of Congo (DRC). The force, 1,800 strong, begins to deploy within seven days of the UN request. Stationed in the eastern DRC until September, Artemis handed responsibility over to a larger but slowly-assembled UN force. Artemis was the first ESDP mission outside Europe and the first military mission not to involve Nato assets and capabilities.

12 December 2003: The European Council approves the first-ever *European Security Strategy*, 'A Secure Europe in a Better World', prepared by the EU High Representative Javier Solana and his secretariat.

15 December 2003: The EU police *Operation Proxima* replaces the military operation Concordia in FYROM. At the invitation of the Prime Minister of FYROM, the 200-strong police force trains local law enforcement agencies, focusing particularly on the fight against organized crime.

17 May 2004: The General Affairs and External Relations Council defines the *Headline Goal 2010* which is endorsed by the European Council of 17–18 June 2004. Building on the 1999 Headline Goal, member states decide 'to commit themselves to be able by 2010 to respond with rapid and decisive action applying a fully coherent approach to the whole spectrum of crisis management operations covered by the Treaty on the European Union' (Headline Goal 2010). The Headline Goal 2010 puts special emphasis on high readiness joint force packages (battle groups) which would be capable of implementing a mission no later than 10 days from the EU decision to launch an operation.

12 July 2004: The Council of the European Union establishes the *European Defence Agency*. The agency is given four principal tasks: to develop defence capabilities in the field of crisis management; to promote and enhance European armaments cooperation; to strengthen the European defence technological and industrial base; and to enhance European defence research and technology.

16 July 2004: Launch of the first EU Rule of Law mission *EUJUST Themis* to Georgia. A group of approximately ten senior civilian experts backed by local staff support and advise ministers, senior officials, and appropriate bodies at the level of the central government. They are located in ministries and governmental bodies in the Georgian capital. This mission falls under the rule of law priority area of the civilian side of ESDP and is foreseen to last 12 months.

2 December 2004: The EU *Operation Althea* replaces the Nato-led SFOR mission in Bosnia and Herzegovina—with recourse to Nato assets and capabilities. It starts with the same force levels as Nato-led SFOR (7,000 troops), drawn from the same states. Althea's primary mission is to ensure continued compliance with the Dayton/Paris Agreement and to contribute to a safe and secure environment in Bosnia and Herzegovina.

From CFSP to ESDP

The impact of the Kosovo conflict was a crucial element in this post-Amsterdam surge towards an effective European Security and Defence Policy (ESDP). As after earlier crises, however, it proved difficult to maintain the momentum once memories of Kosovo began to fade. In the summer of 1999 there were already signs of backtracking on com- mitments made to south-eastern Europe, as EU governments considered the costs to the EU, and to national budgets, of implementing the stability pact and of preparing all states in the region for the long-term prospect of EU membership. Nevertheless, it had

Figure 17.1 Structures for CFSP/ESDP, 2004

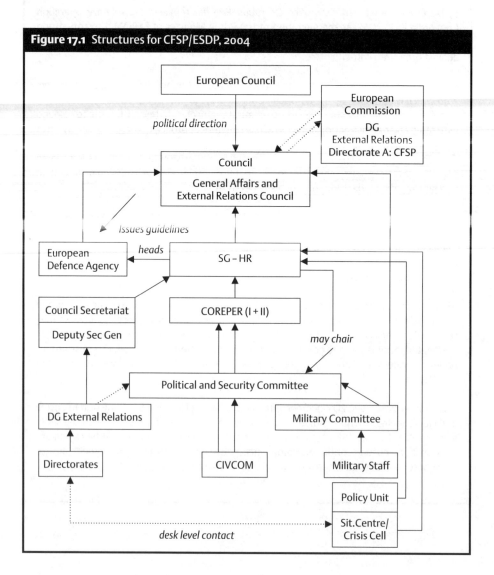

again spurred member governments to improve their institutional framework—this time, very substantially (see Fig. 17.1). The Political and Security Committee (COPS), began operating, on an 'interim' basis pending a further revision of the Treaty, in March 2000; so did the Military Committee, with representatives of national chiefs of staff. Expansion of the Council Secretariat to include a military staff (some 130 officers by 2004, with a further twenty civilian officials, all on secondment from national governments) required a sharp adjustment in traditionally open EU working practices, with a 'secure' area established within the Council Secretariat building.

The Franco–British strategy was to focus first on capabilities, and only later on institutional reform. They challenged their European partners to reshape their armed forces, and in some cases to increase their defence spending, in order to enable European states to manage conflicts in their own region, and to contribute to peace-keeping operations outside their region, without depending on the US for crucial equipment and reinforcement. Their intention, outlined in the Cologne communiqué, was to gain stronger commitments from their partners to build deployable European forces, and then to merge WEU into the EU in the negotiations on revision of the treaties at the IGC planned to conclude in December 2000. They achieved the first of these aims at the December 1999 European Council, which adopted the 'Helsinki headline goals', pledging EU governments collectively to constitute a European Rapid Reaction Force of up to fifteen brigades (60,000 troops), 'militarily self-sustaining with the necessary command, control and intelligence capabilities, logistics, other combat support services and additionally, as appropriate, air and naval elements on operations beyond their borders'—and to achieve this aim 'by 2003'.

A follow-up Capabilities Commitment Conference, in November 2000, identified the major shortcomings in weapons and transport systems, and drew up a list of pledges and priorities. The working method was similar to that of the Lisbon process, intended to spread 'best practice' from the most advanced to the laggards, and to shame the most deficient governments into improving their performance. Nineteen working groups were set up to consider each target and shortfall in more detail, and to report back. As so often before, the US was sponsoring a parallel process through Nato, the Defence Capabilities Initiative, which focused on a similar agenda. Neither process, however, made much impact on most governments. Meetings of EU defence ministers received almost no attention in parliaments or press. Competing pressures on national budgets blocked any reversal in the reduction of defence spending. Hesitation in many member states over the domestic acceptability of planning to project power outside Europe blocked explicit discussion of where such a force might be deployed. The German government, which had only recently persuaded the Bundestag to deploy troops to Kosovo, discouraged discussion of whether the Rapid Reaction Force might be sent beyond Europe to Africa or the Middle East.

In south-eastern Europe, however, the succession of crises had left behind a much higher level of European political and military engagement. The Pentagon pressed for European forces to take over its share of the task of maintaining and reconstructing order, within the Nato framework. In Washington, however, policy-makers remained deeply ambivalent about allowing their European allies to take over political and military responsibility as well. Meanwhile, the proportion of US troops declined, and the number of contributing European countries rose: Latvians and Estonians within a Baltic battalion, Swiss support troops with the Austrian contingent, Poles, Czechs, and others from EU candidate states. The prominent, and professional, role that German forces played in Kosovo and Macedonia was an important stage in accustoming Germans to a 'normal' international role; it was a learning process also for many other participating states.

Beyond Europe, only the British and French governments were prepared to project military forces for more than UN peacekeeping operations. A small British force re-established order in Sierra Leone in 2001, after a UN force of over 17,000 had failed to contain civil conflict. French forces intervened in Côte d'Ivoire in 2002. In a gesture of shared commitment to the stability of a continent where Franco–British rivalry had persisted into the 1990s, the British and French foreign ministers travelled round Africa together the same year. Nordic governments, the Irish and Austrians had long contributed to UN peacekeeping operations, in Africa and the Middle East. The Germans were maintaining a chemical warfare battalion in Kuwait in support of the sanctions regime against Iraq. The dominance of US power across the Middle East, however, left European governments able only to issue diplomatic declarations, to provide core financial assistance to the Palestinian Authority—or to pursue commercial interests. After the collapse of the Palestinian–Israeli Peace Process at the end of 2000, Israeli aircraft destroyed much of the infrastructure which the EU had financed.

The implications of the EU's forthcoming eastern enlargement for the European region preoccupied European governments much more directly. If enlargement is seen as a part of the EU's foreign policy, the extension of security, prosperity, and democracy within a strong international framework across eastern Europe must be counted as a major achievement. The Helsinki European Council of December 1999 also saw reluctant heads of state and government accept Turkey as a formal candidate, under intense US pressure—justified on the grounds of Turkey's strategic importance to western interests across the Middle East. Negotiations with Russia—managed in unwieldy fashion by representatives of the Commission, the High Representative, and the rotating Council Presidency—ranged from relations with Belarus to energy security to the future of Kaliningrad to cross-border criminal networks. Nato enlargement, which passed another milestone with the Prague summit of 2002, was relatively straightforward in institutional terms. EU enlargement necessitated delicate adjustments of common policies, financial flows, institutional representation, and voting weights.

Failure to agree these at Amsterdam led to a further IGC, ending with President Chirac's mismanaged late-night compromises at Nice in December 2000. This, in turn, set the framework for the ambitious proposal for a Convention on the Future of Europe, with representatives of thirteen applicant states (including Bulgaria, Romania, and Turkey) as participating observers, which met from mid-2002 to July 2003. Meanwhile the European Commission was attempting to focus the attention of member governments on the implications of enlargement for the wider European periphery, east and south. In early 2003 it floated proposals for a broader 'Neighbourhood Policy', aimed at providing a framework for economic association, and political consultation, for the states around the EU's eastern and southern borders.

Unity over Afghanistan, discord over Iraq

The change of administration in Washington in January 2001 brought in a foreign policy team resistant to transatlantic partnership, focused instead on the geopolitics of the 'greater Middle East' and East Asia, and determined to leave nation building and peacekeeping to others. President Bush's first visit to Europe, for an EU–US summit in Gothenburg in June 2001, was a disastrous exchange of misunderstandings, and a demonstration of the unwillingness of national leaders to subordinate domestic concerns to shared European interests. Fifteen heads of government repeated similar criticisms of US policy on climate change, to report back to their domestic audiences, rather than seizing the opportunity to convey agreed messages to their most important external partner.

In 2001 the terrorist attacks of 9/11 transformed the context, both for European foreign and security policy and for transatlantic relations—and the rapid move of US attention from armed intervention in Afghanistan to preparations for the invasion of Iraq transformed the context again. European solidarity with the USA over the attacks on New York and Washington led to the first-ever invocation of Article 5 of the North Atlantic Treaty, that 'an armed attack against one . . . shall be considered an attack against them all and consequently . . . each of them . . . shall assist the party or parties so attacked'. But the Bush administration, far less committed to Nato as a political alliance than its predecessors, refused—at that stage—the suggestion that Nato should provide the multilateral framework for a shared response. Nevertheless, under US command, French, German, and Spanish ships patrolled the Indian Ocean, British air tankers refuelled US planes, German and Danish special forces operated inside Afghanistan—marking a further point of transition in the gradual adjustment of European governments to global commitments. In April 2002 the alternative *troika* of Javier Solana, the (Danish) foreign minister in the Presidency, and the External Relations Commissioner, Chris Patten, joined US Secretary of State, Colin Powell, the UN Secretary-General and the Russian Foreign Minister, in forming 'the Quartet' to relaunch efforts at a negotiated solution for the Israeli–Palestinian conflict.

In moving rapidly on from Afghanistan to Iraq, however, US policy-makers made little effort to carry their European allies with them. The flimsy structures of CFSP, weakened further by poor personal relations between British and French leaders and by the domestic politics of a German election campaign, buckled under the strain. The British and French governments reverted to their divergent approaches to transatlantic relations: the British offered full public support, in the hope of influencing the direction of US policy, and British troops entered Iraq with the US; the French refused support without US concessions, and undermined the British–US efforts to gain authorization from the UN Security Council for military action. The Franco–German claim to represent 'European' opposition to the invasion provoked competing statements by other groups of governments. In April 2003 the Belgian government worsened divisions by convening a 'summit' to establish an independent European defence headquarters, in Tervuren, which was attended only by the French, German, and Luxembourg heads of government. Washington policy-makers celebrated the division between 'old Europe' and 'new Europe', as Donald Rumsfeld dubbed them.

Disintegration of European common foreign policy over the invasion of Iraq, in the winter of 2002–3, demonstrated the fragility of the consensus established among EU governments. It revealed the wide gap between a 'common' policy, created out of political negotiations among heads of government and foreign ministries, and a 'single' policy built on integrated institutions and expenditure and on a Europe-wide public debate. CFSP had remained a field in which ministers and officials controlled the agenda, assisted by increasing numbers of staff within the Commission and the Council Secretariat. A few scrutiny committees of national parliaments were beginning to examine its declarations and joint actions by the end of the 1990s. The European Parliament (EP) was too preoccupied with its own detailed legislative responsibilities to address the EU's international priorities, and lacked the authority to scrutinize CFSP. Europe's national media reported common European actions (if they thought them significant enough) in terms of different domestic preconceptions; convergence among national approaches to foreign policy, filtered through each government's interpretation of its European commitments to parliament and public, had a long way to go. The arrival of ten new EU members—active players in the disagreements of 2002–3, provoking an ill-tempered outburst from President Chirac—widened the diversity of national perspectives.

The US-led intervention in Iraq was, however, a peculiarly difficult test for European common policy, in such a sensitive area. The United States had been a major external player in European foreign policy cooperation from the outset; the Bush administration was demanding European support, without consultation, for a military intervention about which most European governments harboured doubts, and to which their publics were largely opposed. Policy towards the Middle East had become, since the end of the cold war, the most contested area in the transatlantic relationship. The war in Iraq divided America as well as Europe: it was the authority of the federal government, and the shared sense of patriotism among US citizens, that nevertheless enabled Washington to act.

After Iraq

The intervention in Iraq constituted the sharpest crisis in transatlantic relations since 1973–4. The underlying issue for common foreign and security policy remained how far European governments should converge towards an autonomous international role, as opposed to one rooted within the Atlantic framework; on this the EU25 in 2004 were still far from any consensus. Bitter words among Europe's political leaders, and across the Atlantic, did not however prevent a rapid return to cooperation among EU governments. Here, as after previous crises, the European response to failure was to re-establish collaboration, on a firmer base where possible. The British, French, and German foreign ministers continued to pursue joint negotiations with the Iranian government over its contested nuclear programme, in spite of Washington's preference for confrontation. The British and French governments were pushing the ESDP agenda forward together only months after the invasion of Iraq (Menon 2004). Frustrated with the failure of other governments in the multilateral capabilities-pledging process to achieve the Helsinki goals, they declared in February 2004 that they would advance in defence through 'enhanced cooperation'; they announced that they would provide 'battle groups' of 1,500 troops, at fifteen days' readiness, in response to international crises, and invited other members (or groups of members) which could demonstrate a comparable capability to join them. The German government announced its commitment to join them the following day. The Swedes and the Finns announced a joint battle group in the autumn of 2004, while negotiating with Norway to contribute a contingent; a Benelux joint force was also under negotiation.

Under the pressures of US determination to remove its forces from south-eastern Europe, while expecting their Nato allies to share the burden across the greater Middle East, inhibitions over long-range military deployment were giving way. Every EU member government (and candidate states Turkey and Bulgaria) had contributed troops to Afghanistan since the end of 2001: the International Stabilization Assistance Force in Kabul, Operation Enduring Freedom in other provinces, or both. Most EU25 governments contributed troops to post-conflict reconstruction in Iraq: recognizing their shared interest in successful reconstruction, whatever their views of the conflict itself. The EU as a security organization formally took over command of the modest civil and military operations in Macedonia in 2003, and took over military responsibility from Nato in Bosnia in December 2004. In Eastern Congo, in the summer of 2003, the EU mounted its first rapid deployment, *Operation Artemis*, in response to a UN request, with the first troops arriving within seven days. European governments sustained 60–70,000 troops on operations outside the boundaries of the EU and Nato throughout 2003—thus meeting the level of the Headline Goals even as they missed their formal deadline (Giegerich and Wallace 2004).

The structures for supporting common policy in Brussels had been transformed since the mid-1990s. Javier Solana had proved a hyper-active High Representative, in and out of Belgrade, Moscow, Washington, and across the Middle East—operating in the Quartet and elsewhere as part of the new (and sometimes unwieldy) *troika* with the External Relations Commissioner, Chris Patten, and the foreign minister of the Council Presidency. The location of COPS, of the Military Committee and a parallel Committee on Civilian Aspects of Crisis Management, together with supporting staffs in the Council Secretariat, had shifted the balance of CFSP to Brussels. Alongside this the Commission now had some 5,000 staff in its external relations and development DGs, including external representations. Duplication of functions between the Commission and the now-substantial external Directorate-General of the Council Secretariat had been moderated by the easy personal relations between Solana and Patten, although bureaucratic rivalry was a constant problem, in particular from those within the Commission who viewed the expansion of the Council Secretariat as a threat to its powers and privileges. There were turf battles, too, over funding CFSP activities; the Commission and the European Parliament were seeking to use the 1 per cent of external action expenditure (€60 million) allocated to the CFSP to introduce Community procedures and oversight, while governments were torn between seeking additional common funding and defending the intergovernmental approach.

The Constitutional Convention of 2002–3 included federalists who wanted to establish the primacy of the Commission over European foreign policy, as well as others who recognized the unavoidable tensions between these parallel structures.

Their proposals, incorporated in the Constitutional Treaty, therefore included a single EU 'foreign minister', who would be both a vice-president of the Commission and chair of the external relations Council of Ministers. They also recommended a common 'EU External Action Service', to staff upgraded representations in third countries, to be constituted from staff seconded from national governments as well as from the Commission and the Council Secretariat. A European Defence Agency, to promote and develop defence capabilities, shared procurement, and defence industrial research, had been agreed by governments responding to a proposal in the Convention; it was already recruiting staff in late 2004. Two other agencies supported aspects of CFSP: the European Satellite Centre near Madrid, inherited from the WEU and dedicated to the interpretation of available satellite images; and the Global Navigation Satellite System Supervisory Authority, established in mid–2004 to oversee the security aspects of the European *Galileo* satellite system.

Conclusions

The EU is now a civilian power, which is making some progress towards shared military capabilities—and towards shared civilian capabilities, building on police missions, and police training missions, in south-eastern Europe. A rising proportion (now approaching 10 per cent) of its common budget is spent on external relations, including nation-building in south-east Europe; further development of neighbourhood policy would increase this further. But authority remains disaggregated, even over financial transfers. The EU15 in 2003 collectively provided over 40 per cent of the UN regular budget, and 55 per cent of global development assistance; but most of the latter came through national budgets, from governments with distinctive priorities, distrustful of the Commission's cumbersome procedures. EU member governments take common positions in over 90 per cent of votes in international organizations, with an effective caucus at the UN and a Commission UN representation. Solidarity has, however, proved most difficult within the UN Security Council, where Britain and France are permanent members, and other EU states alternate in two elected seats, while Germany in 2004 was campaigning, alongside Japan, to gain an additional permanent seat.

The absence of a European public space—of a shared public debate, communicating through shared media, think tanks, political parties, responding to and criticizing authoritative policy-makers—remains the greatest inhibitor of further subordination of sovereignty, national traditions, and national expenditure to common policy. A transnational expert community has gradually developed across the EU, communicating through specialist journals and think tanks, such as the EU Institute for Security Studies (the transformed WEU Institute). National parliaments and mass media, however, were only intermittently interested. In June 2003 Solana's Secretariat produced a draft European Security Strategy, *A Secure Europe in a Better World*, partly as a response to the Bush administration's National Security Strategy, but also as a means of stimulating an EU-wide debate. A revised version was adopted by heads of government at the December 2003 European Council, declaring *inter alia* that 'the European Union is inevitably a global actor . . . it should be ready to share in the responsibility for global security and in building a better world'. In the intervening six months, however, it had received scarcely any mention in the EU's national media, and had been briefly debated only in the Bundestag and the Finnish Parliament's scrutiny committee. National governments, in spite of approving the document, had not wanted to encourage an open debate.

At the end of another cycle of crisis and reconstruction, European cooperation in foreign policy has gone far beyond the framework of sovereign state diplomacy, but still remains far short of an integrated single policy, with integrated diplomatic, financial and military instruments. The dominant modes of policy-making (see Chapter 3) are to be found in policy coordination, underpinned by intensive transgovernmentalism among foreign ministries within the EU and among embassies in third countries. Within its restricted fields of competence for external relations the European Commission pursues the Community method, with national representatives monitoring its ambitions to extend its authority. Variable geometry is a frequent characteristic: both in closer cooperation between Britain and France, often also with Germany in an informal leadership group of states with active international interests, and across the EU's external boundaries, with Turkey, Norway, and even Switzerland contributing to external actions. There remain evident tensions between national autonomy and common policy, and (particularly for the smaller member states) between national passivity and the acceptance of the 'global . . . responsibilities' which the European Security Strategy spelled out. Acceptance of shared responsibilities and institutions, since 1970, had been driven as much by a succession of external demands and crises as by competing Gaullist and federalist grand designs. It seemed likely that further development would similarly be driven by external pressures, but with the significant path dependence of established structures and procedures through which to respond.

Notes

1 This chapter draws on Forster and Wallace, Chapter 17, in Wallace and Wallace (2000), *Policy-Making in the European Union*, 4th edn., and sections have been reproduced with the kind permission of Anthony Forster.

2 This foundational statement of the CFSP is no longer found in subsequent treaties, ToA or ToN.

Further reading

There is a substantial and growing literature on European foreign and defence policy, and EU external relations. Hill and K. E. Smith (2000), provides a useful guide to the accumulation of

declarations, joint actions, and common strategies. Among the more recent publications, see K. E. Smith (2003) Carlsnaes *et. al.* (2004), and C. J. Hill and M. H. Smith (2005). For the security dimension see M. E. Smith (2004) and Howorth and Keeler (2003).

Carlsnaes, W., Sjursen, H., and White, B. (2004) (eds.), *Contemporary European Foreign Policy* (London: Sage).

Hill, C. J., and Smith, K. E. (2000), *European Foreign Policy: Key Documents* (London: Routledge).

Hill, C. J., and Smith, M. H. (2005) (eds.), *International Relations and the European Union* (Oxford: Oxford University Press).

Howorth, J., and Keeler, J. (2003) (eds.), *Defending Europe: The EU, Nato, and the Quest for European Autonomy* (London: Palgrave Macmillan).

Smith, K. E. (2003), *European Union Foreign Policy in a Changing World* (Cambridge: Polity Press).

Smith, M. E. (2004), *Europe's Foreign and Security Policy: The Institutions of Cooperation* (Cambridge: Cambridge University Press).

Chapter 18

Justice and Home Affairs

Towards a 'European Public Order'?

Sandra Lavenex and William Wallace

Contents

Summary

The control of, entry to, and residence within national territory, citizenship, civil liberties, law, justice and order, lie very close to the core of the nation-state. Nevertheless, the permeability of borders in Europe necessitated cooperation among governments, in combating illegal trade and cross-border terrorism. The Maastricht Treaty on European Union (TEU) regularized this intergovernmental network into the EU's 'third pillar'. The Treaty of Amsterdam (ToA) transformed justice and home affairs (JHA) from a peripheral aspect to a focal point of European integration; the Tampere European Council in 1999 followed this with a five-year programme to establish an area of 'freedom, security and justice'. Cooperation among national agencies concerned with combating crime, managing borders, immigration and asylum, and with the judicial and legal implications of rising cross-border movement, has thus been gradually moved from loose intergovernmental cooperation to more systematic collaboration within the European Union (EU). Eastern and southern enlargement has been an important motor of integration. These develop-ments, however, continue to be marked by reservations about the role of EU institutions, resulting in a hybrid institutional structure, and policy measures which are riddled with delicate compromises and flexible arrangements between the member governments.

Introduction

The ambition involved in creating an 'area of freedom, security and justice' (AFSJ) within the EU may be compared with that which propelled the single market and generated its dynamics. In contrast to economic integration, however, which had been at the core of the European integration project, JHA touches on many issues which are deeply entrenched in national political and juridical systems and have a strong affinity to questions of state sovereignty. In this context, the preparatory work on the Convention drafting the Constitutional Treaty speaks of an emerging 'European public order' which shall respond to the desire of citizens for security and reflect the values of freedom and justice to which the Union is committed. This discourse resonates with modern theories of the state, which, since the seventeenth century, have drawn on its capacity to provide security to its inhabitants (Mitsilegas, Monar, and Rees 2003: 7). The development of a common response to immigration and asylum-seekers, the joint management of the external borders, the increasing coordination of national police forces in the fight against crime, the approximation of national criminal and civil law, and the creation of specialized Union bodies such as Europol or Eurojust to deal with these matters thus constitute a new stage in the trajectory of European integration. These processes reflect the increasing involvement of EU institutions in core functions of statehood and, concomitantly, the transformation of traditional notions of sovereignty in the member states.

The dynamics of this new area of European integration reside both within and outside the EU and its member states. One important motor has been the learning process within the Schengen 'laboratory' among its five initial members, and later most member states. The decision to abolish controls on persons at the internal borders spurred concern about safeguarding internal security and prompted closer cooperation on questions relating to cross-border phenomena such as immigration, organized crime, or drug trafficking. The surge of asylum-seekers from outside western Europe in the 1980s, and the end of the cold war, which opened the EU's previously closed eastern border to hopeful immigrants and criminal networks, generated external pressures for closer cooperation. The subsequent opening of cooperation with the CEECs, which then became candidates for EU membership, provided an important further impetus, and promoted their gradual integration into the structures of the EU.

Notwithstanding the strong symbolism inherent in the creation of a European area of freedom, security, and justice, the Union is far from having unified, integrated common policies in JHA. As in other areas of EU policy, integration has been incremental, riddled with delicate compromises and reservations by member governments. Reservations about transfers of responsibilities to the EU, and the domestic sensitivity of issues such as immigration or organized crime in national political debates and electoral campaigns, have sustained transgovernmental governance as the dominant mode in JHA. Transgovernmentalism combines elements of the traditional 'Community method' with more intergovernmental ones and has generated a peculiar pattern of shared competences between subnational, national, and European levels of governance, with the continuity of some level of cooperation outside the formal institutions of the Union.

This chapter starts with a short review of the emergence and evolution of cooperation in JHA, before going on to examine the Treaties of Amsterdam and Nice, presenting its key actors and institutional set-up, and discussing the main policy developments in related fields and recent proposals for reform.

How justice and home affairs moved onto the EU agenda

The development of international cooperation was linked to the challenges posed by cross-border phenomena, such as international organized crime and terrorism, to nationally-bounded police systems and jurisdictions on the one hand, and the economic aim of promoting free movement of persons across borders, on the other. This was relevant not only to the original EC6, but to all west European democracies that were progressively opening their borders. Free movement of labour was included as one of the four basic freedoms set out in the 1957 Treaty of Rome (EEC). Article 3c (EEC) (now Art. 3c TEC) listed among the Community's intended 'activities . . . the abolition, as between member states, of obstacles to the free movement of persons, services and capital', and Article 48 (EEC) (now Art. 39 TEC) provided for the free movement of workers (see Chapter 10). The Single European Act (SEA) reaffirmed this, and the Maastricht Treaty on European Union (TEU) inserted provisions on citizenship, giving extra emphasis in Article 8a (now Art. 18 TEC) to the rights to free movement of citizens from the member states. Easier travel and liberalization of border controls led to a radical increase in cross-border movements by both citizens of the member states and third-country nationals. The parallel increase in cross-border crime and terrorism pushed west European governments into informal cooperation among security services and law enforcement agencies: first through the Pompidou Group on drugs, set up in 1972 within the wider Council of Europe, and then in the EU within the framework of European Political Cooperation (EPC) (Edwards and Nuttall 1994: 84; Anderson *et al.* 1995: 113). The Trevi Group was created in December 1975 by the Rome European Council, to coordinate anti-terrorist work among EU governments faced with Irish, Italian, German, and Palestinian groups operating within and across their borders. In 1985, Trevi's mandate was widened from the fight against terrorism to take in other issues of cross-border public order and serious international crime such as drug trafficking, bank robbery, and arms trafficking. A rising number of working groups were added, Trevi 1992, the Mutual Assistance Group 1992 (MAG'92, customs), and a Judicial Cooperation Group, reflecting the rise in activities which accompanied the single market programme. Faced with this proliferation of consultations and proposals, the 1988 European Council in Rhodes established a Group of Coordinators. This group then presented the Palma Document to the Madrid European Council in June 1989, setting out a programme of 'compensatory measures' to maintain internal security within the completed single market.

In parallel, and originally for quite different reasons, five governments signed the Schengen Agreement to remove border controls among their countries. This complemented three pre-existing common travel areas, within which frontiers were opened, and which overlapped with the expanded EC: Benelux, UK–Ireland, and the Nordic Area, which linked Denmark to four non-member states. The Schengen Agreement of 1985 brought France and Germany together with the Benelux, partly in response to pressures from business and transport interests, frustrated with delays at borders, and partly to promote the idea of a Single European Space. The Maastricht Treaty on European Union (TEU) added a 'third pillar' of cooperation on JHA on an initially loose intergovernmental framework. From then until the ratification of the Treaty of Amsterdam (ToA), negotiations among the Schengen Group and developments within Trevi and the third pillar overlapped, with a gradually expanding core group setting the pace for other EU governments to follow in response to increasing substantive pressures for policy cooperation.

By 1990 two important international treaties had been negotiated which set the guidelines for future cooperation. The Schengen Implementing Convention (SIC) signed in June 1990 set out 'compensatory measures' for the removal of frontier controls, covering asylum, a common visa regime, illegal immigration, cross-border police competences, and a common computerized system for the exchange of personal data (Schengen Information System, SIS). The Dublin Convention on Asylum of 1990, concluded among all EU member states, incorporated the asylum rules also included in the SIC, and established the responsibility of the state in the territory of which an asylum-seeker first enters for the examination of an asylum claim.

In the period before the TEU, an extensive network had already developed which operated both outside and under the overall authority of the European Council on several political and executive levels, ranging from the responsible ministers through directors-general of the relevant ministries to middle-ranking civil servants and representatives of police forces and other agencies. There were several overlapping rationales for developing common policies within the EU, emerging both from functionalist spill-over from other EU policies, and from new challenges faced by the member states. The rhetoric of European integration was based on the Preamble to the Treaty of Rome (EEC) that its signatories are 'determined to lay the foundations of an ever closer union among the *peoples* of Europe' (authors' italics). The requirements of the single market included 'free movement of persons'. Cross-border movements intensified among geographically compact, densely populated countries, as prosperity rose and communication links improved. The success of the 1992 internal market programme in removing controls on goods crossing internal frontiers focused on the remaining controls on people at the EU's internal frontiers. The further surge in border-crossing which the internal market programme encouraged also alerted law enforcement agencies to the need to agree on 'compensatory measures' to maintain public order across the EU for the movement of both the lawful and the unlawful, legal and illegal.

Apart from these functionalist dynamics, new domestic priorities shaped the agenda of evolving cooperation. These included concern about cross-border crime and the international mobility of criminals as well as changing patterns of migration. Tightened controls on immigration from the mid-1970s onwards coincided with increasing flows from outside Europe and a global rise in the number of refugees, leading to a surge of asylum-seekers arriving in western Europe. Figures provided by the United Nations High Commission for Refugees (UNHCR) estimated that the number of asylum-seekers arriving in western Europe had averaged 100,000 a year from the early 1970s, with some 70 per cent of these originating from eastern Europe. Larger numbers from other continents began to arrive in the early 1980s. In 1986, 200,000 sought asylum; by 1989 this figure was 300,000, peaking in 1992 when almost 700,000, including Kurds from Turkey and Iraq, Tamils from Sri Lanka, Somalis, Sudanese, and Sierra Leoneans arrived in western Europe, fleeing violence and unrest.

German concerns and anxieties were a driving force in the development of common policies. West Germany had a particularly sensitive history and geographical position, a citizenship law based on ethnic descent rather than birth within the national territory, a liberal asylum law drafted in the aftermath of the Third Reich as the cold war divided Europe, a large *Gastarbeiter* population attracted by its strong economy, and a structural ambivalence about sovereignty and nationhood. Experience of terrorism on German soil, from the Baader-Meinhof gang and from radical Middle Eastern groups, combined with the threat of subversion from across the eastern border, created a climate of insecurity. Chancellor Kohl's call in 1988 for a 'European FBI', was reportedly triggered by police reports that the Italian Mafia had infiltrated the restaurant trade in German cities. Demolition of the Berlin Wall in November 1989 increased anxieties that millions of migrants and asylum-seekers, some of them linked to criminal networks, would pour into Germany. In addition, in the early 1990s nearly two and a half million people from former socialist countries arrived in Germany as *Aussiedler*, claiming German citizenship by virtue of their descent. External security and internal security concerns thus merged into a 'security continuum', in which migration and crime across Europe's eastern and southern borders increasingly preoccupied politicians, press, and public opinion (den Boer 1994b; Bigo and Leveau 1992).

Maastricht's 'third pillar'

In line with these preoccupations, the German government was committed in principle to full integration of JHA into the EU during the 1991 intergovernmental conference (IGC) leading to the TEU. The British government was firmly opposed. The French government was ambivalent, declaring its support for common action, while protective of state sovereignty. The Dutch presidency draft, which proposed to bring both the common foreign and security policy (CFSP) and JHA into a single integrated structure, was dismissed, and instead, foreign policy and internal security remained primarily intergovernmental, in separate 'pillars'. Asylum policy, rules and controls on external border-crossing, immigration policy, and police and judicial cooperation in civil and criminal matters were included as 'matters of common interest' in the third pillar of the TEU. In this way the existing network of committees was formalized, without transforming the framework of authority and accountability (see Figure 18.1). This compromise exemplifies the intense tensions between sovereignty and integration in this field, and the sensitivity of questions of social order and national tradition for the member states.

The greatest innovation of the TEU was to transfer the preparation and management of meetings to a new Directorate-General of the Council Secretariat, under the direction

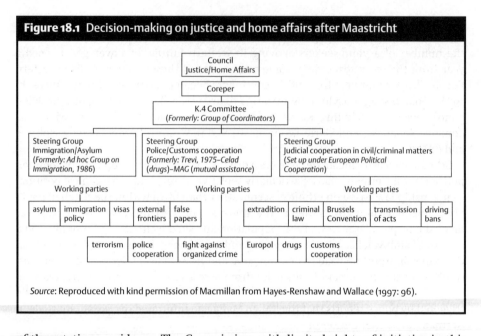

Figure 18.1 Decision-making on justice and home affairs after Maastricht

Source: Reproduced with kind permission of Macmillan from Hayes-Renshaw and Wallace (1997: 96).

of the rotating presidency. The Commission, with limited rights of initiative in this field, maintained a small 'task force' within the Secretariat-General to represent its interests and to manage the overlap between Community competences and third-pillar issues. DG XV, responsible for the internal market, also monitored the development of policy. The European Parliament (EP) made less effort to monitor the flow of proposals than in the second pillar, though its Civil Liberties Committee came to develop an interest in the years which followed. Irrespective of whether or not the jurisdiction of the European Court of Justice (ECJ) might extend to the interpretation of JHA, the subject became a topic for contentious debate.

In contrast to the second pillar, which brought together officials from national foreign ministries, with a shared professional approach and the common experience (and personal links) of diplomatic postings in third countries, participants in the extended network of Council committees which constituted the third pillar were drawn from diverse national ministries, forces, and agencies, rooted in distinctive state traditions. The division of functions between ministries of the interior and of justice differed from state to state. Germany's federal structures, and the UK's separate system of Scots law, tended to create particular complexities in national representation and policy preparation. The policing of internal order was organized along national lines in France and Italy, with both paramilitary (*gendarmerie* and *carabinieri*) and civil forces. The philosophy of policing in the UK, on the contrary, was that of single forces locally recruited and accountable.

Different national traditions (and geographical circumstances) were also evident in the non-congruence of national agencies combating financial fraud, smuggling, and border control, as for example, Germany's Bundesgrenzschutz, Italy's guardia di finanza, and the UK's Customs and Excise, Immigration Service, and Civilian Coastguards. Legal traditions, judicial training, court procedures, even concepts of crime and of the appropriated hierarchy of penalties, were also deeply distinctively embedded in each state structure and society. Each national professional community tended to assume that their tried and tested rules were best, and that foreign laws and foreign practices were deficient. Each professional grouping nevertheless shared a certain mutual respect and a certain style, which set police apart from lawyers and judges, and both from the *fonctionnaires* who attempted to coordinate their activities (Anderson *et al.* 1995). Ministry of interior officials had remained among the least internationally-minded within national governments throughout the first forty years of western European integration, working within an ideological framework which clearly separated domestic law and order from events beyond national boundaries. To learn the habit of transgovernmental cooperation therefore required a substantial reorientation of working assumptions.

The loose intergovernmental structure did not prevent JHA from becoming the most active field for meetings convened under the Council of Ministers in the late 1990s. The frequency and intensity of interaction, especially in the area of police cooperation and organized crime, induced a transformation of the working practices of interior ministries and of police forces and led to the emergence of an intensive transgovernmental network (see Chapter 2). After five years of operation, by the time of the 1996–7 IGC, the third pillar had developed an extensive set of instruments and institutions. Europol was taking shape as a coordinating agency for cooperation among national forces, even though the Europol Convention had not yet been ratified by all member states. The Customs Information System was being computerized, to be managed by the Commission with respect to both its first-pillar and third-pillar usage. Two other databases were being developed: a Europol Information System; and Eurodac, the finger-print database for asylum-seekers, accompanying the implementation of the Dublin Convention determining the responsibility of the member states in asylum matters. The SIS was already up and running, with fourteen million entries relating to banned entrants to the Schengen Area, and a parallel database on stolen property and related cross-border crime. Ministries of justice were drawn in more slowly; and it was not until the revival of the concept of a European Judicial Area, after the Treaty of Amsterdam, that justice ministries began to be drawn into a similar European network.

Uneasy communitarization: the Treaties of Amsterdam and Nice

The current framework of cooperation in JHA was shaped by the treaties of Amsterdam and Nice. This framework, which shifted parts of JHA to the Community pillar while maintaining a 'streamlined' third pillar on police and judicial cooperation in criminal matters (PJCCM), reflects the delicate compromise between intensive transgovernmental cooperation, on the one hand, and the incremental consolidation of supranational structures, on the other (see Box 18.1). More radical changes are foreseen in the Treaty establishing a Constitution for Europe signed by heads of state or government on 29 October 2004 (see section, 'The agenda for reform' below).

The 'Amsterdam' reforms were motivated by widespread dissatisfaction with the working of the intergovernmental procedures. Three weaknesses, in particular, stood out: ambiguity about the legal and constitutional framework, evident in the frequency with which institutional issues were entangled with policy proposals; the low political visibility and accountability of this essentially bureaucratic framework for policy, which allowed the practice of cooperation to develop far beyond what was reported to parliaments or to national publics; and the absence of mechanisms for ensuring national ratification or implementation.

The issue of democracy and legitimacy was (and still is) particularly pertinent in the area of JHA which, whilst touching sensitive issues of domestic politics and civil liberties, was characterized by a clear dominance of executive policy-making, secretive modes of operation and the by-passing of the European and national parliaments. At the same time, intensifying domestic politicization of problems of undocumented migration, asylum, organized crime, and drug trafficking, increased the pressure for European solutions and their implementation. Accordingly, the Westendorp Reflection Group preparing the 1996 IGC agenda identified JHA reform as one aspect of 'making Europe more relevant for its citizens' (McDonagh 1998; Monar 1997). The Reflection Group (1995) made a link (paras. 24–9) between 'serving the citizens' interests', and the asserted 'demand on the part of the public for greater security', extending to 'the citizens calling for better handling of the challenge posed to the Union by the growing migratory pressures'. This led to the rationale for the particularly encouraging phraseology written into the Treaty, when it talks of 'establishing an area of freedom, security and justice'. For outside observers, internal security cooperation and its connection with the achievement of freedom of movement offered 'a means of locking in popular support for the Union' (Twomey 1999: 358).

The positions of member governments on such reforms were divided. Only the Dutch and German governments were actively canvassing such changes. A majority of eight member states (the Dutch, Belgian, Luxembourg, German, French, Italian, Portuguese, and Austrian governments) called for external frontier issues to be transferred from the third pillar into the regular Community structure: 'communitarization', in the jargon of Brussels negotiators. Germany and Austria also proposed that matters relating to crime, terrorism, and drug trafficking 'should be dealt with on the basis of supranational coordination of legal and police authorities'. The UK government, on the contrary, opposed any such transfer; while the French government was in favour of partial communitarization, but considered that police cooperation should remain intergovernmental. Six member governments suggested that the incorporation of the Schengen system into the EU proper should be on the agenda: the three Benelux countries, Italy, Spain, and Austria (B. Smith 1999).

The ToA contained substantial changes to the framework for JHA, more substantial than for CFSP (see Box 18.1). A new Title IV transferred migration and other related policies to the first pillar. Police cooperation and judicial cooperation in criminal matters remained in a revised and lengthened Title VI TEU. The greatest surprise was the incorporation of the Schengen conventions and *acquis* into the ToA, since it had not been actively under negotiation during the Italian and Irish presidencies in 1996. The Dutch presidency in the first semester of 1997, however, drove this, together with the other changes to the framework of JHA, through the final stages of the IGC, succeeding in part because of internal divisions in both the French and German positions, and in particular because of French distractions during their election campaign and unexpected change of government (B. Smith 1999: 173–213). A major impetus for Schengen's incorporation was the decision that the candidate countries of central and eastern Europe would have to implement this *acquis* in full (Art. 8, Schengen Protocol of the TEU; Lavenex 1999, 2001*b*). At the time when the ToA was signed, however, there was no definitive or agreed text of the Schengen *acquis*. Such as there was consisted—in addition to the conventions and accession agreements—of an uncatalogued miscellany of decisions and agreed working practices, a sort of disjointed incrementalism *par excellence*. The member governments had thus signed, and ratified, a treaty without having agreed the text of one of its most sovereignty-sensitive subordinate documents (House of Lords 1998*b*).

Box 18.1 Changes to JHA in the Treaty of Amsterdam and the Treaty of Nice

Title IV, Arts. 61–9 TEC

- 'visas, asylum, immigration and other policies related to the free movement of persons' and 'judicial cooperation in civil matters having cross-border implications' (Art. 61 TEC) were transferred from the third to the first pillar.
- 'flanking measures' (Arts. 62–3 TEC) to compensate for free movement within the EU, including common procedures for controls on persons at the EU's external borders, common visa policy, common measures on asylum seekers, 'temporary protection' of refugees, and immigration policy. The target for adoption of these common measures is set for five years after the entry into force of the ToA (May 2004).
- A series of reservations, first largely at French, but then, at the European Council in Nice in 2000, also at German insistence, limiting the Commission's powers of initiative until the end of the transitional period in 2004, offering the EP only 'consultation', maintaining unanimity voting in the Council, and setting strict limits of reference to the ECJ (Arts. 64, 67–8 TEC).
- Different opt-outs for Denmark, the UK, and Ireland.

Title VI, Arts. 29–42 TEU

- Arts. 29–34 (TEU) provide more detail on 'common action' in police and judicial cooperation in criminal matters, including references to 'operational cooperation' among law enforcement agencies, and collection and storage of data. The ToN specified in Art. 31 (TEU) the functions of Eurojust.
- The opaque legal instruments of the TEU were replaced by well-established, legally binding legal instruments, but some of these, the framework decisions, are excluded from direct effect.
- Arts. 35–9 (TEU) reflect parallel unresolved disputes on the involvement of the EU institutions (Commission, EP, ECJ) in this field; lengthy section on ECJ reflects sensitivity of extending cooperation in legal administration and law enforcement without providing for judicial review. Article 40 (TEU) extends provision for 'closer cooperation' among smaller groups of member states, which were facilitated under the ToN. In addition, the Article registers the integration of the Schengen *acquis* 'into the framework of the European Union' (set out in more detail in an attached protocol).

While preparing the ground for a greater involvement of supranational actors in JHA, the ToA also broke with the traditional doctrine of the Community method by introducing important intergovernmental elements into the first pillar. For the communitarized issues, that is, asylum, immigration, and judicial cooperation in civil matters, a transitional period of five years (that is, until 2004) was adopted during which the Maastricht rules of interaction were maintained. The Treaty of Nice (ToN) included only limited changes to this delicate balance. Intergovernmental procedures persisted in the third pillar, though the Commission was now given a right of initiative shared with the member states.

National sensitivities on sovereignty encouraged a high degree of flexibility in the application of common rules. Denmark, for example, participates in the free movement area and may adopt relevant European provisions as international law (avoiding the direct effect of EU law and ECJ jurisdiction). Ireland and the UK maintain their opt-out from lifting internal frontier controls, but adhere, on a selective basis, to the flanking measures of the JHA *acquis* such as asylum, police, and judicial cooperation in criminal matters (PJCCM), and the SIS (Kuijper 2000: 354). Another element of flexibility accompanies the 'rolling ratification' of conventions in the third pillar, according to which conventions shall, once adopted by at least half of the member states, enter into force for those member states. Another *à la carte* solution was found for the ECJ's role under the third pillar: it is up to the member governments to decide on the viability of preliminary ruling procedures. At present, the UK, Ireland, and Denmark have an opt-out and Spain permits only final courts to refer cases. Procedures to permit enhanced cooperation further add to the fragmented institutional framework of JHA cooperation.

Yet, even in the light of these generous provisions, the formalization of flexibility has not prevented individual member states from engaging in selective forms of intergovernmental cooperation outside the provisions of the treaties. This was demonstrated in May 2003 with the creation of the so-called G5, an intergovernmental group bringing together the five interior ministers from France, Italy, Spain, Germany, and the UK. The creation of this group followed an unsuccessful German attempt to launch a sort of 'Schengen II'. Seeking to speed up the move towards operational goals and to circumvent the lengthy decision-making processes of the Council of Ministers, the group is working to conclude a series of bilateral agreements which should then form the basis of future EU-wide laws and measures. Among the issues on the table are cooperation to combat terrorism, illegal immigration, establishing a list of 'safe' countries of origin whose citizens would not be entitled to make refugee applications, establishing financial criteria for issuing visas for entry to the EU, making it compulsory for airlines to communicate passenger data to the law enforcement agencies, and EU biometric passports.

The association of non-member states exacerbates the variable geometry of the 'area of freedom, security and justice'. Norway and Iceland, as members of the pre-existing Nordic common travel area, have been included within the Schengen area, and are fully associated with the Schengen and Dublin Conventions. Switzerland, entirely surrounded by Schengen members, but not (like Norway and Iceland) a member of the wider European Economic Area, has negotiated a provisional bilateral agreement which is due for ratification including a possible popular referendum in 2005. The US was actively pursuing access to shared data and networks of cooperation from the early 1990s; the terrorist attacks of September 2001 led to a redoubling of its efforts, leading to a series of agreements on transatlantic association in this field, some of them very controversial.

Key actors

Organization and capacities of EU institutions

With the new powers attributed under the ToA, the Commission gradually expanded its organizational basis in JHA. One of the first moves of the new President of the Commission, Romano Prodi, was the transformation of the small Task Force which had been established within the Secretariat of the Commission under the TEU into a new Directorate-General on Justice and Home Affairs (DG JAI). It was widely recognized that the task force, with only forty-six full-time employees in 1998, had been desperately overworked and understaffed, and therefore had had little impact on third pillar developments. With the creation of the new DG under the lead of the Portuguese Commissioner, António Vitorino, the number of personnel was significantly increased, and by 2002 it had 283 employees. Its budget also saw a steep increase, from €42 million in 1999 to €124 million in 2002 (see European Union Financial Reports 1999–2003). Nevertheless, compared to older DGs dealing tangentially with related issues, such as Social Affairs or Internal Market, DG JAI remains one of the smallest units in the Commission, both in terms of staff and money (see also Table 3.2 in Chapter 3).

With its limited resources, the Commission was challenged *vis-à-vis* its counterparts in the Council Secretariat. The responsible unit there, DG H, was more generously staffed than the Commission Task Force on JHA during the 1990s, with additional staff recruited in 1998–9. The Treaty of Amsterdam (ToA) furthermore provided for the separate Schengen Secretariat, which had been co-located with the Benelux Secretariat in Brussels, to be integrated into DG H (provoking strong protests from staff unions in the Council Secretariat). Permanent representations of the member states in Brussels were also drawn in, adding legal advisors and officials seconded from interior ministries to their staff.

The JHA Council inherited from Trevi and from the TEU's third pillar a heavily hierarchical structure of policy-making. It is one of the few areas in the Council that has four decision-making layers. Agendas for JHA Councils are prepared by Coreper 2 which meets weekly, at ambassadorial level. Between Coreper and the working groups, the JHA structure has an additional intermediary level composed of special coordinating committees which bring together in Brussels senior officials from national ministries, meeting normally once a month. The lowest level is composed of working groups of specialists from national ministries and operational bodies (see Fig. 18.2).

Under the ToA, the former 'Coordinating Committee' (the K4 Committee) was renamed the Article 36 Committee, after the new treaty text. At the same time, its mandate was narrowed to cover only the remaining third pillar issues, while two new

Figure 18.2 Decision-making on justice and home affairs after Treaties of Amsterdam and Nice

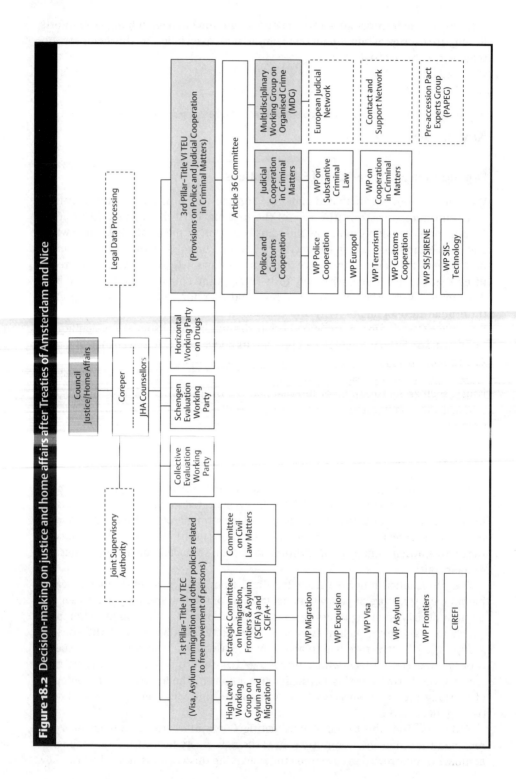

committees were created for those issues falling under the Community pillar: the Strategic Committee on Immigration, Frontiers and Asylum (SCIFA); and the Committee on Civil Law Matters. Set up initially for a five-year transitional period, these new committees of senior national officials were another sign of the intergovernmental legacy of JHA cooperation, and an anomaly under first pillar procedures. Rather than phasing out this additional layer of consultation, in summer 2002 a new 'external borders practitioners' common unit', the 'SCIFA+', regrouped the members of the SCIFA with the heads of national border control authorities.

From a procedural point of view, these committees of senior officials share a certain rivalry with their colleagues from foreign ministries in Coreper, who monitor the cycle of working group meetings week by week, and prepare agendas for the JHA Council. This allows them to act as a gateway between the collective gathering of senior officials and ministerial council sessions at which all the strands of policy are supposed to be brought together. The coordinating committees have often been slower to clear dossiers because of their less frequent meetings and their close ties to their national ministries which limits their room for manoeuvre in negotiations. The secondment of staff from interior and justice ministries to the permanent representations in Brussels has mitigated this rivalry.

In practice, two additional levels of policy-making levels are relevant, and have even been gaining importance. The first is composed of various 'horizontal' or 'high level' groups linking together relevant negotiations within the different working groups in asylum and migration matters, drugs, or organized crime. These groups are the (informal) successors of the former steering groups developed under Maastricht's third pillar which had been abolished in an attempt to streamline the cumbersome decision-making structure in JHA. The second level is the European Council, which has been the formal pinnacle of the policy-making hierarchy since cooperation emerged in the 1970s. In recent years, the European Council has played an increasingly influential political role, and this has been very evident in the field of JHA. The ground was laid with the first European Council focused specifically on JHA held under the Finnish presidency in Tampere in 1999, which set out far-reaching objectives. The Seville and Thessaloniki European Council sessions in 2002 and 2003 took these further.

The role of the European Parliament (EP) has remained limited. Even in those issues falling under the first pillar, the EP has not been granted any powers to amend or block legislation by the Council—either during or after the transitional period. The Council has only to consult the EP prior to adopting a measure. The exception to this rule are measures concerning visas and judicial cooperation in civil law matters, for which the ToN introduced the co-decision procedure. For matters under the third pillar, a deadline of at least three months was introduced for the consultation of the EP in order to allow it a real opportunity to examine, and, where necessary, to propose, amendments to proposed measures. Despite its limited legislative powers, the EP, especially through its Committee on Citizens' Freedoms and Rights, Justice and Home Affairs (LIBE), has intensified its engagement with JHA. Since the Portuguese Council presidency in 2000, the President of LIBE has regularly been invited to attend part of the informal meetings of the JHA ministers. In addition, Council representatives regularly visit the EP in the framework of the interinstitutional dialogue. Nevertheless, relations between the EP and the Council continue to be contentious. This is reflected not only in the frequent criticisms made of Council initiatives, but also in repeated complaints about lack of information during the consultation procedure or the Council's failure to take due account of its proposed amendments.

The proliferation of semi-autonomous agencies and bodies

A special characteristic of the governance of the JHA is the proliferation of semi-autonomous special agencies and bodies. The multiplication of actors over the past five years has been impressive, and illustrates the dynamism of this field of cooperation. Some of the earliest were agencies established on the basis of first pillar secondary legislation: the European Monitoring Centre on Drugs and Drug Addiction (EMCDDA) set up in 1993 in Lisbon, and the European Monitoring Centre on Racism and Xeno-phobia (EUMC) established in 1997 in Vienna. Most developments, however, took place in the framework of the third pillar. Here the earliest was UCLAF, the predecessor of OLAF, the now communitarized European Anti-Fraud Office (see Chapter 8). The Europol Convention had been adopted in 1995, but it was not until 1998 that it entered into force, after lengthy national ratification procedures, and Europol became operational only one year later. In 1998, the European Judicial Network was launched, an initiative pushed forward by the Belgian presidency, supporting the proposal of Élisabeth Guigou, then the French Minister of Justice, for the creation of a European Judicial Area. Following the model of the European Judicial Network in Criminal Matters, a network on civil and commercial matters was set up in 2001.

The European Council in Tampere in 1999 proposed the creation of three new bodies. The Tampere Conclusions provided for the creation of: the European Police College (CEPOL), initially established in Denmark in 2000 and later based in the UK, to develop cooperation between the national training institutes for senior police officers in the member states; the European Police Chiefs' Task Force (PCOTF), created the same year, to develop personal and informal links among the heads of the various law-enforcement agencies across the EU and to promote information exchange; and Eurojust, the 'college' of senior magistrates, prosecutors, and judges, to coordinate cross-border prosecutions, which became operational in 2002. The immediate reaction of the urgent European Council on Terrorism meeting after the terrorist attacks in Madrid in March 2004 was the creation of an additional post: the EU Anti-Terrorism Coordinator. Acting under the EU High Representative for Foreign and Security Policy, the coordinator was intended to promote effective counter-terror coordination and intelligence sharing; Gijs de Vries, a former Dutch minister and MEP, was appointed. Lacking its own operational or police powers, however, this new post will remain dependent on cooperation from member states and national agencies. In addition, the Commission has proposed the creation of two more agencies: the office of a European Public Prosecutor, proposed without success at the Nice European Council in December 2001; and a Border Management Agency to take over the work of the 'Common Unit' of external border practitioners created in June 2002 (see Box 18.2). The Commission envisages this agency as the core of a future European Border Guard. With these new common bodies, the number of common databases has also proliferated; the data of EU and third-country nationals are stored and scrutinized partly under Commission supervision (Eurodac, Customs Information System), but mostly monitored by a special joint supervisory authority within the Council Secretariat (Europol and Eurojust databases SIS). The most recent developments are the establishment of a Visa Information System (VIS), a database with personal information

Box 18.2 JHA agencies and bodies

- European Monitoring Centre on Drugs and Drug Addiction (EMCDDA), set up in 1993 in Lisbon, *www.emcdda.eu.int*
- European Monitoring Centre on Racism and Xenophobia (EUMC), set up in 1997 in Vienna, *www.eumc.eu.int*
- European Police Office (Europol), set up in 1999 in The Hague, *www.europol.eu.int*
- European Police College (CEPOL), set up in 2000 with a provisory secretariat in Brøndby, Denmark pending a Council Decision on the location of its permanent secretariat, *www.cepol.net*
- European Police Chiefs Task Force (PCOTF), set up in 2000 without headquarters and web page
- Eurojust, set up in 2002 in The Hague, *www.eurojust.eu.int*

Planned or envisaged agencies and bodies:

- European Border Management Agency
- European Public Prosecutor

(including biometrics) on every visa application and a revamped SIS II which, in the words of the European Commission, will transform the SIS 'from a reporting system to a reporting and investigation system' (Commission 2001e).

This proliferation of actors indicates the strong impetus for more intensive cooperation in internal security, but it also reflects the tension, between, on the one hand, the case for tighter collective policy management by the EU institutions and, on the other, the persistence of looser transgovernmental coordination. It also shows the interplay between practitioners' preference for flexibility and the pressures for greater transparency and accountability. For instance, most of these agencies created since the end of the 1990s lack a clear legal base in the treaties. PCOTF remains an *ad hoc* forum with no legal base, no formal rules of procedure, and no mechanism for scrutiny. Now that they are institutionalized, both Europol and Eurojust have seen a rapid expansion of their mandates. Europol was originally set up to put pressure on the national agencies responsible for combating terrorism, and its objectives were to improve the effectiveness of, and cooperation among, the competent authorities in the member states. However, its mandate was expanded—even before the agency became operational in 1998—to include 'crimes committed or likely to be committed in the course of terrorist activities'. After 9/11 the Council added a long list of serious international crimes requiring collective action, such as murder, kidnapping, hostage-taking, racism, corruption, unlawful drug trafficking, smuggling illegal immigrants, trafficking in human beings, motor vehicle crime, and so forth. In 2002, Europol's budget was increased by almost 50 per cent in order to address these additional tasks. Originally conceived of exclusively as coordinating bodies, both Europol and Eurojust have also gradually gained operational powers. Representatives of both agencies are allowed to participate in a 'supporting capacity' in joint investigation teams. Furthermore, Europol and Eurojust have been granted the right to request EU member states to start or to abstain from an investigation or prosecution in specific cases, a request which can only be turned down by giving good reasons.

Overall, therefore, JHA is based on a complex pattern of governance. The problem is not only this proliferation of agencies and bodies, which poses an increasing challenge of coordination, but also deficits regarding transparency or democratic and judicial accountability. Thus, for example, based as it is on an intergovernmental convention, Europol's activities are subject neither to the supervision of the EP nor to judicial control by the ECJ. Under the present system, the Council acts not only as initiator and legislator, but also as executive and supervisor (in the form of the Article 36 Committee), thereby defying the principle of separation of powers.

The flow of policy

The main innovation of the ToA was not so much the cautious institutional reforms introduced in the decision-making procedure, as the enumeration of a detailed set of measures to be introduced under the first pillar before the deadline of May 2004. This list was further specified and widened at the 1999 Tampere European Council, which also added path-breaking measures in the area of judicial cooperation in criminal matters. Subsequent European Councils in Seville, Thessaloniki, and Brussels have further widened the policy agenda. Interacting with this impetus from the heads of state and government, the Commission's shared right of initiative with the JHA Council, and alternating European presidencies, have maintained member states' influence on the JHA agenda, with short-term national priorities jostling with long-term common objectives.

Substantive policy developments

External events and domestic preoccupations have played an important role in the trajectory of JHA policies, as expressed in the respective priorities of the Council presidencies and various European Councils. Since 2000, progress in implementing the goals laid down in the ToA and by the subsequent European Councils has been monitored by the European Commission, in the form of a bi-annual scoreboard which is published on DG JAI's website.

These scoreboards give a mixed picture of progress towards the completion of the first stage of the creation of an area of freedom, security, and justice. According to the ToA, this was to be accomplished within five years, and before enlargement in May 2004. While some areas have remained contentious, new issues have come onto the agenda which have evolved much more rapidly. The main emphasis has been on the fight against organized crime and illegal immigration, while judicial cooperation in criminal matters has seen real progress since 2001. The impact of 9/11 sharply increased the salience of the external dimension of JHA, with a growing emphasis on cooperation with third countries in the neighbouring regions and across the Atlantic.

Refugee policy remains one of the most controversial issues in domestic political debates. Progress towards a 'European asylum system', called for at the Tampere European Council, however, has been mixed. Substantive harmonization of refugee law has been much more difficult to achieve than agreement on the allocation of responsibility for the examination of asylum claims (see Box 18.3; Lavenex 2001a).

Box 18.3 Common European asylum system

■ The cornerstone of EU asylum policy is the system of exclusive responsibility for the examination of asylum claims. The regulation (343/2003) determining the member state responsible for examining an asylum application replaced the 1990 Dublin Convention by a Community instrument. Its implementation is linked to the Eurodac database which became operational in January 2003. Eurodac is a computerized system for the comparison of fingerprints in order to assist the member states in the identification of asylum applicants.

■ Another measure that should prevent secondary movements of asylum seekers in the EU is the approximation of the standards on reception conditions for asylum seekers. Common minimum standards were also adopted for temporary protection in situations of mass influxes.

■ A more symbolic measure was the creation of the European Refugee Fund to support reception, integration, and voluntary return measures in the member states plus a financial reserve for the implementation of emergency measures to provide temporary protection in the event of a mass influx of refugees. With its budget of €216 million for the period 2000–4, the fund is little more than a drop in the ocean. It was decided in the 'The Hague Programme' adopted in November 2004 to significantly expand the fund.

■ The Programme also notes that from 2005, all decisions in the Justice and Home Affairs area will be taken by majority voting. Legal immigration will remain as an exception to this rule. Majority voting in this area will not start until the new EU Constitution comes into place—where it is foreseen anyway—following strong opposition by Germany, Austria, Estonia, and Slovakia. The programme also iterates the goal of a Common European Asylum System. The aims of the Common European Asylum System in its second phase will be the establishment of a common asylum procedure and a uniform status for those who are granted asylum or subsidiary protection.

■ The realization of these goals would put an end to the diversity of national practices, expressed in the difficulties to agree on common standards. Notwithstanding acknowledgement of the principle of mutual recognition of asylum determination outcomes, agreement on a common definition of the term refugee and on common minimum standards on asylum procedures was repeatedly postponed until the very last moment, a few days before expiry of the deadline for accomplishing the first phase of the European asylum system and before accession of the ten new member states.

■ These delays show not only the reluctance to accept supranational rules in a sensitive field of domestic policy, but also the fundamental confusion about what constitutes a refugee today, what persecution means, and where the responsibility of the international community comes in. Instead of finding a new consensus on these difficult questions, JHA ministers have shifted their attention outside the EU towards the countries of transit and origin of asylum-seekers. 'Partnership' with countries of origin and transit includes preventive activities in the areas of foreign and development policies and, with growing emphasis, control-oriented measures aimed at the transfer of border control technology and the conclusion of readmission agreements to ensure the effective return of rejected asylum-seekers and irregular migrants to their countries of origin. This external policy agenda reached its preliminary peak with the British, and, later, German and Italian proposals to create asylum processing centres at the EU's external borders to alleviate immigration pressure on the EU.

Agreement on which forms of immigration to classify as legal has proved as difficult, if not even more controversial. The main achievements were the adoption of two directives, 2003/86 on family reunification, and 2003/109 on long-term resident status for third-country nationals. The latter subject had been contentious since freedom of movement of workers became effective in the 1960s. After several revisions, the directive was finally adopted in 2003, and extends free movement rights to long-term residents in the member states. A third Commission proposal on the admission of immigrants for the purpose of work and self-employment has met little support in the Council. From the onset of cooperation in the mid-1980s, the emphasis has instead been on the fight against illegal immigration. This trend was reinforced in the aftermath of 9/11 with the adoption of a 'Comprehensive Action Plan to Combat Illegal Immigration and Trafficking in Human Beings' in 2002, and by the Conclusions of the Seville European Council in the same year. The British and Spanish initiative for putting stronger pressure on countries of origin which did not cooperate through potential cuts in economic and financial aid from the programmes failed, due to the opposition of countries such as France and Sweden. The Presidency Conclusions opened the door for the use of negative sanctions available under both first and second pillars in both the CFSP and EC context, if a country of origin showed an 'unjustified lack of cooperation'. The most significant developments in terms of changes to member states' territorial sovereignty, however, concern the emergence of collective supranational instruments for the management of external borders. Two factors have been decisive for member governments' increasing support for an External Border Management Agency: pressure of the southern member states, with their very porous borders, for greater financial solidarity in sharing the burden of controlling external borders; and concern as to whether the new member states would be able to uphold EU and Schengen standards at their eastern borders by the time of their accession in 2004.

Evolution in police cooperation has been reflected in the expansion of Europol's mandate. However, negotiations in the Council have not always been easy, and the wish to circumvent lengthy parliamentary ratification procedures for any amendment of the Europol Convention has spurred interest in working instead via the mechanism of Council decisions. This measure would increase flexibility, as Europol's legal framework could then be amended by QMV and without the assent of the national parliaments. However, most member governments are at the same time committed to maintain Europol's special status as an intergovernmental agency. This became clear in 2002 when several of them rejected a Commission proposal which would have established a legal base for funding Europol out of the EU budget: national representatives feared that this would gradually transform Europol into a Community agency, giving the EP and the Commission some degree of control over its development and priority-setting. Despite these developments, and the adoption of two ambitious Action Plans against organized crime in 1997 and 1999, cooperation between national police forces and Europol has fallen short of the expectations of most JHA ministers. Furthermore, the newly created European Police Chiefs Task Force (PCOTF) has been criticized for failing to provide leadership and continuity on the further development of European police cooperation. The main impediments to more effective cooperation between national police forces are not only the short history of transnational cooperation, and the need to build mutual trust in the exchange of data and information, but also the wide diversity in their organization (Occhipinti 2003). With enlargement, both issues—the need for trust and problems associated with diversity—have clearly increased, prompting concern about how to invigorate the operational aspects of police cooperation.

In comparison, cooperation in the judicial sphere was initially slower to develop, but in recent years has turned into one of the most dynamic aspects of JHA cooperation (de Kerchove and Weyembergh 2002). The European Council in Tampere was also a turning point in this field, with agreement being reached on four basic principles for establishing a common European judicial space: mutual recognition of judicial decisions; approximation of national substantive and procedural laws; the creation of integrated actors of cooperation; and the development of the external dimension of criminal law. Spurred by the events of 9/11, the speed with which these principles were translated into concrete measures in the sphere of criminal law has been formidable. Indeed, the adoption of the European Arrest Warrant has been described as a 'revolution' by criminal lawyers (see Box 18.4).

Box 18.4 Judicial cooperation in criminal law

- Judicial cooperation in criminal law is a response to the increasingly transnational character of crime and a complement to intensifying cooperation between national police forces. Touching central pillars of national jurisdictions, these developments have direct implications for the citizens, their fundamental rights and civil liberties. Since the Tampere European Council in 1999, the principle of mutual recognition, well-known from the single market, has become the cornerstone of judicial cooperation in criminal matters. The most important measure incorporating this principle was the adoption in 2002 of the Framework Decision 2002/584/JHA on the European Arrest Warrant. This instrument replaces former extradition procedures and means that a decision by the judicial authority of a member state to require the arrest and return of a person should be recognized and executed as quickly and as easily as possible in the other member states. For a number of serious offences (terrorism, trafficking in human beings, corruption, participation in a criminal organization, counterfeiting currency, murder, racism and xenophobia, rape, trafficking in stolen vehicles, fraud), the Decision also abolishes the requirement of double criminality. The basis for this incisive step is confidence in the equivalence of national standards of criminal law.

- The principle of mutual recognition is complemented by the approximation of criminal laws with regard to the definition of certain crimes and the sentences. Even before the ToA provided the legal basis, common measures were adopted on financial fraud against the financial interests of the Community, corruption, paedophilia, participation in a criminal organization, and racism and xenophobia. The ToA provided for legal approximation concerning organized crime, terrorism, and drugs trafficking. The approximation of procedural laws has faced more obstacles but the Commission's Green Paper on procedural guarantees will make it more important in the years to come.

- The third element in the consolidation of criminal justice cooperation is the proliferation of European level bodies such as the European Judicial Network and Eurojust.

- Finally, like the other fields of JHA, also the judicial sphere has developed a strong external dimension. Two agreements on extradition and mutual legal assistance were signed in 2003 with the US after thorny negotiations on the inclusion of data protection standards compatible with EU norms.

This short review of the most important developments in JHA shows the remarkable progress made in this field. The institutional set-up, as well as policy development and implementation, confirm the importance of transgovernmentalism as a mode of governance, despite pressure for greater use of more tightly integrated EU policy modes. Attempts by the Commission to prepare the ground for greater integration through introduction of the 'open method of coordination' (OMC) in asylum and immigration policy have met opposition in the Council. An informal consultative committee on asylum and immigration was nevertheless created by the Commission, whose work has been referred to as 'OMC minus'. In addition, drawing together the approximation of national approaches and the exchange of best practices has been supported by a large number of specialized programmes, some managed by the Commission and others through the Council Secretariat: ARGO for administrative cooperation at EU level in the fields of asylum, immigration, and crossing of external borders; INTI for the integration of third-country nationals in the EU member states; and OISIN, STOP II, Falcone, Octopus, and Agis in various fields of police and judicial cooperation in criminal matters. Most of these programmes have concentrated on administrative and policy adaptations in what are now the new member states and other candidate countries, and have now developed an explicit external dimension.

The search for the emulation of 'best practice' and national assimilation of agreed standards has led to some experimentation with mutual inspection, both in border management and in court procedures, for which teams of police or judges drawn from at least three countries have inspected the standards of administration in a fourth member state. The widespread appointment to embassies in other member states of liaison officers between law enforcement agencies, and the more limited appointment of liaison officers for judicial cooperation, has strengthened the transgovernmental network through which information and ideas are exchanged.

The increasing emphasis on relations with third countries has contributed to a blurring of the boundaries between internal and external security, and hence between JHA and CFSP (Lavenex and Uçarer 2002). As enlargement became imminent, attention shifted to the EU's new neighbours to the east and the south, giving JHA a prominent place in relations not only with the Balkan countries and Turkey, but also with Russia, Ukraine, Moldova, and the Maghreb countries. This attempt to bind into cooperation the countries of origin and transit, which may generate internal security risks such as terrorism, organized crime, drugs, or illegal immigration, is paralleled by intensified cooperation with like-minded states in Europe (Norway, Iceland, and Switzerland), and overseas (the US and Canada). In short, this variable geometry reflects not only the transnational nature of the preoccupations which underlie the development of JHA, but also the continual need to reinforce transgovernmental mechanisms both within and beyond the circle of the member states.

The US government has been particularly concerned to establish close cooperation and information exchange since 9/11. A Europol–US Agreement was signed in December 2002, despite concerns expressed by some national parliaments in EU countries regarding safeguards for the exchange of personal data. Before it was signed in June 2003, the text of the proposed EU–US Judicial Cooperation Agreement was offered for national scrutiny only on a confidential basis, until a strong protest from the British House of Lords led the Greek Presidency to declassify it (Mitsilegas 2003). The secrecy under which negotiations with the US have been conducted, and concerns over lack of reciprocity in exchange of information and over the protection of personal data, have made transatlantic cooperation in this sphere a source of unease for civil liberties groups and parliamentarians.

The agenda for reform

Discussions in 2002–3 on the Convention drafting the Constitutional Treaty confirmed the central place that JHA occupies in the EU today. In its final report to the Convention, the Working Group on 'Freedom, Security and Justice' argued that 'if the European Union is to win a maximum support of its citizens, it must show that it can deliver concrete results on issues that really matter'. Indeed, Eurobarometer surveys suggest increasing public concern with internal security. In the 2004 Eurobarometer survey, crime figured third among the 'most important issues' identified by the respondents in their respective countries, coming after unemployment and the economic situation. Immigration and terrorism followed closely.

The Treaty establishing a Constitution for Europe (TCE), signed by heads of state or government on 29 October 2004, includes far-reaching reform proposals which centre around two basic principles: the 'reunification' of JHA into a common general legal framework, and, herewith, the abolition of the pillar structure; and, secondly, a separation between 'legislative' and 'operational' tasks. The final compromise embedded in the Constitutional Treaty is surprisingly close to the Convention proposal and reflects the successful lobbying of national governments by the Convention's Praesidium. It brings the AFSJ as an area of 'shared competence' closer to the Community method, yet maintaining transgovernmental elements. The Treaty establishes that all measures concerning border controls, immigration, and asylum would shift to a qualified majority vote in the Council. Germany's support for this shift could only be won, however, by inserting an explicit clause on the right of member states to determine numbers for the admission of economic immigrants.

With regard to the European Parliament, the Treaty provides that in all cases (with the exception of emergency asylum decisions) there would also be co-decision with the European Parliament. The same would apply to the majority of legislation concerning criminal law and policing, excluding the creation of the European Public Prosecutor, cross-border actions by police and operational police measures. In contrast to the broad mandate conferred to the Union in asylum and immigration matters, the detailed enumeration of EU powers in criminal matters circumscribes the scope for communitarization. The limitation of European competences to 'minimum standards' and the propagation of the principle of mutual recognition in criminal law also preserve a high degree of autonomy for the member states and their different legal systems and traditions. A final caveat is that if a member state claims that a rule would 'affect fundamental aspects of its criminal justice system' a 'reflection period' of up to a year is permitted, although other member states may proceed through enhanced cooperation. In those areas where the Commission does not have the exclusive right to propose legislation, the dominant role of the Council Presidency would be weakened through the rule that a proposal may only be submitted by a quarter of the member states. At the same time, the Treaty codifies the important role played by the European Council, and provides that the latter shall define the strategic guidelines for legislative and operational planning.

The Treaty also includes significant changes in the role of the ECJ and national parliaments. Judicial control would be expanded by applying the normal rules of the ECJ's jurisdiction to all JHA matters in all member states, with the exception of the validity and proportionality of policing actions, where this is a matter of national law. Democratic control would be enhanced by greater scrutiny from national parliaments, both as guardians of the principles of proportionality and subsidiarity and as participants in the evaluation of the work of the JHA bodies and agencies. Apart from general notions of judicial and democratic accountability, which are particularly important in a field touching civil liberties and fundamental rights, stronger involvement of these actors is also motivated by poor implementation, especially of decisions under the third pillar. However, the development of the necessary resources for efficient scrutiny in sensitive and time-sensitive questions will be a major institutional challenge for the Court and national parliaments.

The second axis of reform, the separation between 'operational' and 'legislative' functions, may turn out to play a pivotal role with regard to judicial as well as parliamentary scrutiny, and, more broadly, the fate of transgovernmental practices in JHA. If adopted, this separation will exclude all 'operational' activities of JHA actors, both at the European (Europol, Eurojust, PCOTF, etc.) and the national level, from the decision-making and supervision mechanisms of the Community. Instead, a revamped Article 36 Committee would be responsible for overseeing this, thereby confirming the persistence of transgovernmentalism in JHA.

The Commission's *Assessment of the Tampere Programme* in June 2004 described the creation of an area of freedom, security, and justice over the previous five years as 'one of the most outstanding expressions of the transition from an economic Europe to a political Europe at the service of its citizens'. It went on to propose an agenda for the next five years, including the development of an integrated system of border management, a common policy on 'the management of migration flows', both legal and illegal, the creation of 'a European Judicial Area' in which mutual recognition would be complemented by the establishment of shared legal principles and minimum standards, with Europol to be financed from the Community budget and given the authority to conduct its own investigations. The tension between the Commission and the member states was evident in the cautious reactions of member governments to this ambitious programme, which would extend Community policies further over domestic law and order, rights of residence, even of citizenship.

The European Council adopted the 'The Hague Programme' at its November 2004 meeting, setting out future priorities. It approved a gradual increase in the European Refugee Fund to reach €150 million per annum by 2008, agreed to finalize a European Drugs Strategy for 2005–12, and approved the Council Secretariat's (CFSP) Situation Centre providing the Council 'with strategic analysis of the terrorist threat based on intelligence from member states' intelligence and security services and, where appropriate, on information provided by Europol' from the beginning of 2005. Detailed agreement on many other issues was, however, postponed, by inviting the Commission to present to the Council an Action Plan 'in 2005', as well as a yearly report on progress with implementation of the programme.

Conclusions

The House of Lords' verdict on the first year of operation of Eurojust could be applied to the whole field of JHA: evidently 'at the crossroads between two conflicting models: one seeking increased harmonization . . . and centralized EU structures and the other based on mutual recognition of Member States' laws and procedures and enhanced cooperation between them' (House of Lords 2004b). In different ways, all member states have a contradictory stance regarding closer integration: recognizing the logic that rising cross-border movement and crime requires responses that override the boundaries between national jurisdictions, while resisting the adjustments in national practices and the public concessions of sovereignty that this entails. Even the German government, so often a leader in this area, struggles with the division of competences within its federal system, in which *Länder* governments resist the transfer of judicial and policing authority through Berlin to EU institutions.

There are limitations in what can be achieved through dependence on trans-governmental networks, mutual recognition, and initiatives by member governments. In a field where concerns about civil liberties are powerful, these methods leave major problems of scrutiny and transparency. Both Europol and Eurojust have suffered from significant differences in the quality of information provided by, and in the degree of cooperation from, member states. The quality of proposals put forward by Council presidencies, exporting their domestic agendas, has often been lower than those promoted by the Commission, which have emerged from a broader process of consultation with national experts. Even without the Constitutional Treaty, EU institutions are extending their role. The ECJ has used the references to 'citizenship' in the TEU to extend its jurisdiction over free movement and asylum cases. The EP has examined proposals—such as the EU–US Agreements—over which it lacks formal jurisdiction. Cooperation among twenty-five member governments may increase pressures for common rules and effective monitoring of their implementation; equally well, the opposite could occur. The proliferation of agencies with different legal and financial bases raises questions of duplication and overlap, even if moderated by the co-location of Europol and Eurojust in The Hague. Yet differences persist in national cultures, which underpin different approaches to law, liberty, and citizenship. The local knowledge and languages needed to manage the border between Finland and Russia are not interchangeable with those needed to patrol the Mediterranean coast. Cooperation and integration, EU institutions and agencies, and national bodies, are therefore likely to coexist, in constructive tension, for the foreseeable future.

Further reading

On the development of the third pillar, see Bieber and Monar (1995). For the development of police cooperation, see Anderson *et al.* (1995), and Occhipinti (2003). For judicial cooperation, see Barrett (1997). Geddes (2000) focuses on migration, Lavenex (2001a) on refugee policy. Mitsilegas, Monar, and Rees (2003) provide an overview of the field.

Anderson, M., den Boer, M., Cullen, P., Gilmore, W. C., Raab, C. D., and Walker, N. (1995), *Policing the European Union: Theory, Law and Practice* (Oxford: Clarendon Press).

Barrett, G. (1997) (ed.), *Justice Cooperation in the European Union* (Dublin: Institute of European Affairs).

Bieber, R., and Monar, J. (1995) (eds.), *Justice and Home Affairs in the European Union: The Development of the Third Pillar* (Brussels: European University Press).

Geddes, A. (2000), *Immigration and European Integration: Towards Fortress Europe?* (Manchester: Manchester University Press).

Lavenex, S. (2001), *The Europeanisation of Refugee Policies: Between Human Rights and Internal Security* (Aldershot: Ashgate).

Mitsilegas, V., Monar, J., and Rees, W. (2003), *The European Union and Internal Security: Guardian of the People?* (London: Palgrave).

Occhipinti, J. D. (2003), *The Politics of EU Police Cooperation: Towards a European FBI?* (Boulder: Lynne Rienner).

Part III

Conclusions

Chapter 19

Post-sovereign Governance: The EU as a Partial Polity

William Wallace

Contents

Summary

Policy-making within the EU is shaped by rules and procedures which have evolved, with successive modifications and extensions, over half a century. Yet the scope of EU policy has expanded remarkably over the past twenty years, in response to internal and external challenges, including repeated expansion of the EU itself. There is no single pattern of policy-making; the different demands of distinctive issue areas, the different actors and institutions drawn in, make for diversity. EU policy-making is a process of mutual learning and accommodation, resting on mutual trust, in which ideas as well as interests shape the search for consensus. The mutual penetration of law, regulation, even political campaigning deep into what political scientists had long characterized as the core of domestic politics, define a level of politics and of governance which is most straight-forwardly described as a political system. It is, however, a post-sovereign system, within which many of the traditional distinctions between the domestic and international have been eroded. It is, also, only a partial political system, with little popular engagement and fragile legitimacy.

   The EU represents a stable system of policy-making in an unstable environment, struggling to adapt to internal and external changes. National and sectoral interests have locked in established policies, resisting reform. Diverse modes of policy-making coexist in different sectors, reflecting distinctive patterns of coordination or delegation. European policy-making must also be situated within the broader context of global multilateralism, with governments negotiating to moderate the pressures of economic transformation, technological change, and shifting security threats on their societies and economies. The EU both imports and exports policies and policy styles, interacting with other industrial democracies, most significantly with the US.

A stable system, or one under continuous negotiation?

The European Union (EU) is at one and the same time a stable system, and in constant flux. Its core institutions, designed half a century ago, have developed extensive procedural rules and standard operating procedures, embedded in successive revisions of the treaties—the EU's proto-constitution. An extended network of committees links the Brussels institutions to those of the member states. The rules and rituals which form stable patterns of policy-making are firmly entrenched within the EU, shaping the behaviour of ministers and officials, judges and parliamentarians, lobbyists and journalists. The familiar annual cycle of meetings of the European Council, the Council of Ministers, and subordinate committees interacts with the six-monthly cycle of changing presidencies and the longer, five-year terms of office of European parliamentarians and the college of commissioners. As successive chapters in this volume have emphasized, the density and intensity of interactions among many thousands of actors set the EU apart from any other intergovernmental policy-making system or international regime. The EU dimension of policy has become part of the daily work of national officials, lobbyists, ministers, even heads of government. For the populations of the six original member states, European institutions have shaped their economic activities, and increasingly impinged on their social rights, throughout their lifetimes.

Yet the EU as a system has also been under continuous renegotiation, in terms of size, structure, and policy coverage. The ten member states which negotiated the Single European Act (SEA) in 1985, with Spain and Portugal on the verge of full membership, had grown to twenty-five in 2004, with more to follow. In December 2004 Bulgaria and Romania concluded negotiations, with accession for membership planned in January 2007. Negotiations with Turkey were scheduled to begin in October 2005, and with Croatia in March 2005, although the conditions for this date were not met. The other small states of the western Balkans are next in the queue, with the prospect that political change within other states that emerged from the Soviet Union, such as Ukraine, might produce further candidates for membership. The Constitutional Treaty (CT), that the EU25 are setting out to ratify in 2005-6, is the fifth substantial revision of the treaties since 1985, following the SEA, the 1992 Maastricht Treaty on European Union (TEU), the 1997 Treaty of Amsterdam (ToA), and the 2001 Treaty of Nice (ToN). The limited competences of the EC of 1985 have grown, to a remarkable extent: to encompass most aspects of economic regulation, including the impact of environmental and social regulation on markets; to manage the successful launch of a single currency, with an autonomous European Central Bank (ECB); to develop close patterns of cooperation among national police forces and judicial authorities; and to extend foreign policy cooperation tentatively even into defence.

This volume has gone to press too early to assess the impact of the ten new member states which joined the EU in May 2004 on EU politics and policy-making. The enlargement of 2004 represented a potentially more significant change in the balance of interests and attitudes within the EU than any of the previous enlargements. Ten new members, mostly with GDPs well below the EU average, and with far higher proportions of their workforce in agriculture, reshape the parameters of negotiations on budget packages, cohesion funds, and reform of the common agricultural policy (CAP). Most of the new members are smaller countries—Poland being the key exception—and share assumptions about the need to protect EU policy-making from domination by large states. Their insistence on each state retaining its own Commissioner had already made an impact on the Convention, in which representatives of all candidate states participated. New members from the eastern Mediterranean and central and eastern Europe have brought with them different perspectives on priorities for foreign policy and external relations. The implications for the established *acquis*, and for negotiations over new policies, of this new balance will start to become clearer in the course of 2005-6, although the full impact will take longer to discern.

This volume has described distinctive patterns of policy-making, both in long-established areas of EU competence and in new. One evident observation is the inertia of the established *acquis*. Bargains once struck are difficult to reopen; entrenched interests, both governmental and private, defend what has been achieved. The bargains at the 1969 summit in The Hague on own resources and Community access to fishing waters, struck among six member governments, have held through successive enlargements, and through the transformation of agriculture and fisheries by technological innovation and generational change. Yet successive case studies report innovation and experimentation, both in policy sectors covered by the original treaties and in fields which were beyond the imagination of negotiators in the 1950s. Competition policy in the past decade has seen major changes in practice, and in the balance of responsibility between EU and national authorities (see Chapter 5). Social regulation is both a sector contested in the courts (see Chapter 10), and one in which the open method of coordination (OMC) is promoting mutual learning (see Chapter 11), among governments which face comparable problems in maintaining national welfare systems. EU regulation of environmental (see Chapter 12) and biotechnology (see Chapter 13) policies has been reshaped by technological innovation, changing popular expectations, and external constraints.

The original European Communities represented a negotiated compromise, in which rhetorical commitment to integration, even to eventual federation, was intertwined with the promotion and protection of national interests. The CT, as agreed by member governments in October 2004, represented a far more complex series of negotiated compromises. The contested character of the EU as a polity was reflected in the length and intricate drafting of the CT, and in the inclusion (in Part Three) of detailed clauses from previous treaties on the allocation of authority and the guidelines for policy in specific sectors. The sense of a shared political community was too weak, the development of mutual trust too limited, to support a shorter and simpler constitution.

Member governments and national publics also contested some of the underlying principles around which common policies should be built. Embedded in the Lisbon Strategy of 2000 lay divergent assumptions about social market protection and free market flexibility, between welfare capitalism and 'Anglo-Saxon' capitalism (V. A. Schmidt 2002). The ECJ's willingness to extend the single market into the provision of services which had traditionally been part of the national welfare state, reported in Chapter 10, went well beyond the political consensus in most member states. The Commission's attack on state aids (see Chapter 5) has roused stubborn resistance within key member states. Slow progress in coordinating economic policies, and the reluctance of member governments to transfer economic policy issues away from the open method of coordination, with its voluntaristic pattern of consultation, to the tighter mechanisms of the Community method, reflects the continuing divergence of national preferences about the balance between public and private, between employment protection and job creation, between banks and companies as national champions and multinational enterprises. The surge in deregulation and re-regulation that marked the 1992 programme (see Chapter 4), and the move beyond that towards a single currency (see Chapter 6), exposed the divisions between, and within, national political systems on economic and social priorities more sharply.

Nevertheless, policy-makers across the EU have repeatedly used its established framework to respond to new challenges, as the record of policy innovation over the past decade illustrates. Path dependence follows from established patterns of policy-making; it is easier for policy-makers to use, and if necessary to adapt, existing channels than to negotiate to set up new structures. Thus, after the terrorist attacks on the US in September 2001, ministers turned to and extended the developing agenda of justice and home affairs (JHA) (see Chapter 18). Thus, following on from the completion of negotiations with ten candidate countries in 2003, governments approved proposals from the Commission to adapt its style of detailed negotiations with conditional benefits to neighbouring non-candidate countries (see Chapter 16). Thus successive, and increasingly frequent, European Councils have set out agendas for new fields of cooperation, though often without agreeing on how exactly these should be pursued. The robustness of the framework is to be seen in the increasing commitments, of time and of attention, that national governments have given to EU policy-making, and the further expansion of the agenda that they have brought within it. The continuing fragility of many parts of the framework, however, can be discerned in the continuing tensions between centralization of authority in Brussels and reasserted autonomy for national governments, and in the wide gap in many of the fields covered here between shared commitments and shaky implementation.

The flow of policy

The case studies in this volume have shown that there is no single pattern of policy-making in the EU. Different modes of policy-making, as Chapter 3 argues, have emerged in different policy domains. The 'classic' Community method remains characteristic of a number of established policy sectors, although often hemmed in by watchful national governments and their clients, and modified by differences in national implementation—as the agriculture (Chapter 7), and fisheries (Chapter 14) case studies show. It has not, however, become the dominant pattern, as early theorists suggested and Commission enthusiasts hoped. From the early 1980s, regulation became the dominant paradigm, with the single market programme occupying much of the Commission and preoccupying member governments, and increasingly spreading its style of policy-making to other domains. Budgetary packages and IGCs, characterized by explicitly political negotiations among member governments, have given comfort to those who see the EU as an international regime within which rational state actors bargain on the basis of long-term state preferences (see Chapter 8). The scope for distributional politics to develop has been limited by the resistance of the net payers to higher transfers; the Commission's autonomy as a designer and manager of regional, research, and educational programmes has thus been constrained. The evolution of JHA, as of common foreign and security policy (CFSP), and European security and defence policy (ESDP), has demonstrated an intensity of interaction among agencies of member states, with Community institutions only marginally involved, which we have labelled intensive transgovernmentalism. The OMC, with its emphasis on target-setting and peer review, provided a way forward in promoting policy convergence for governments unwilling to delegate authority over core economic and social decisions to the Commission, the European Parliament (EP), and the European Court of Justice (ECJ).

A number of commentators—including the editors of this volume—have attempted to categorize EU policy-making according to levels of politicization, from constitutive (or history-making) decisions to redistributive bargains, distributive politics, and regulatory adjudication (W. Wallace 1983b, 1996; Peterson 1995). Each of these levels, we argued, was characterized by distinctive actors and distinctive patterns of policy-making. As the chapters in this edition have however shown, these categories overlap and spill into each other. Both the Maastricht and Amsterdam grand bargains postponed a number of the most contentious issues on the table. The Convention on the Future of Europe and the CT focused on procedures and allocation of authority, rather than on strategic decisions on policy. Narrow sectors of regulatory and distributive politics, where limited economic interests are at stake, blow up into political confrontations which preoccupy ministers at successive Council meetings, and heads of government in European Councils; the classic example in this volume is fisheries. Environmental issues, food safety, animal welfare, issues where public passions may disrupt rational policy-making, can erupt from regulatory committees to preoccupy heads of government at European Councils—even threatening to push discussion of more strategic issues off the agenda.

The flow of policy is, nevertheless, shaped by established procedures and institutional frameworks. The case studies in this volume provide support for those who argue that institutions matter, and that governing ideas matter, in shaping agendas and formulating preferences (Pierson 1996b; Bulmer 1994a). Governments hesitate to reopen agreed policies or to question the established *acquis*, where it does not suit their immediate interests, because they have embedded interests in other policy fields, and because they are pursuing other interests through parallel negotiations which they hesitate to put at risk. But they also *define* their preferences within the context of the continuous multilateral processes which constitute the EU collective governance system. The recent development of 'social constructivism' as a self-conscious movement within political science has led researchers to pay particular attention to the role of constitutive ideas in shaping the framework for policy-making (Christiansen, Jørgensen, and Wiener 2001).

Given their commitment to the continuation of the system, actors internalize its constraints. The calendar of meetings does not allow for dispassionate calculation of state preferences in the intervals between major multilateral negotiations. Member governments are engaged in a continuous multilateral and bilateral dialogue at all levels, from heads of government to junior officials, punctuated by formal negotiations and mediated through the Commission and other EU institutions. Proposals are floated, criticized by interested organizations and parliamentarians, modified, examined in detail, before final adoption. Concepts—Community preference, solidarity, subsidiarity, flexibility, convergence, stabilization, sustainability, and the precautionary principle—interact with perceived interests in shaping acceptable options for agreement. Europeanization—the process through which EU norms and rules are internalized within national administrations, and national actors socialized into a shared discourse—is a vital element in binding national and EU-level policy-making together (Goetz and Hix 2001).

There *are*, on occasion, major turning points at which heads of government set out new priorities in the context of transformed external circumstances or reconsidered state preferences. But even here, as Chapters 6 and 17 make clear, the flow of policy development redefines the parameters of decision. Within the framework of assumptions provided by successful operation of the European Monetary System (EMS), and of substantial progress with the single market programme, the Hanover European Council in 1988 took the contingent decision to establish a committee to consider what detailed proposals for economic and monetary union (EMU) might form the basis for agreement. Achievement of a unanimous report by the Delors Committee, including the signatures of the heads of the UK and German central banks, redefined the agenda for decision. The St Malo Franco–British initiative of November 1998 launched defence as a dimension of EU cooperation. But the two sponsoring heads of government understood its long-term implications very differently. The articulation of their headline proposals through official negotiations modified, and to some extent undermined, what they had intended. Other governments formally agreed to accept these Franco–British proposals, but their degree of commitment was less firm, ebbing further as detailed negotiations followed at lower levels.

Governance in the EU is, in large part, governance by committees. The significance of the extensive substructure of Council and Commission committees and working groups which characterizes the EU system lies largely in the role they play in transmitting detailed information and ideas, and transforming disparate working assumptions into a framework for common policy (van Schendelen 1998). The Commission uses consultative groups to learn about the diversity of national working practices and the areas of potential common ground, as well as to coopt national officials into a collective endeavour. Heads of government depend upon the network of committees and working groups which sustains the flow of policy from one European Council to another in order to convert agreements in principle into detailed and practicable proposals. Identifying the policy entrepreneur in this process of mutual learning and accommodation is not easy. The chapters in this volume have shown that policy initiatives emerge from many different sources, often from more than one. Commission initiatives may be taken up by particular member governments, just as presidency proposals may be modified and developed by the Commission through extensive consultation with affected interests and national agencies. Scholars have long argued (as

Chapter 4 notes) as to whether the single market initiative was launched by the Commission, by key national governments, or by organized business interests. The successful launch of the initiative, however, reflected the convergent ideas of these different policy entrepreneurs, coming together to agree in principle, to define and then to support an ambitious programme.

It follows from this that policy outcomes are not necessarily—and never entirely—the product of deliberate bargains among strategically oriented rational actors. Deliberations move through too many *fora*, with too many players involved, for coherence to be maintained by any single political leader throughout the policy process. Heads of government must turn their attention to other issues as negotiations proceed, while those around them follow the flow of papers and the succession of proposals and counter-proposals. The outcome of multilateral negotiation is difficult to predict at the outset, partly because the definition of the issue changes as negotiations proceed, as unexpected aspects emerge, and as external actors intervene. Policies flow, through European Councils and through day-to-day discussions; political leaders may succeed in diverting or redirecting the flow, but rarely manage entirely to control the process.

Policy-making in the EU is not unique in its character. All modern governance is complex, and technical. National governments also struggle to distinguish between strategic issues for political decision and meso- or micropolitical questions, which can safely be left to individual ministers or to officials to decide. National political leaders and their advisers do not always succeed in identifying potentially explosive political issues within the daily flow of papers with which they deal, nor anticipate the long-term implications of agreements in principle or declarations of intent. Politics is politics, at whatever level. There is no case for insisting that only one interpretation of EU policy-making can be correct, any more than one can squeeze the diverse patterns of American politics—or German, or Italian—into the iron framework of a single model.

EU policy-making is, unavoidably, affected by changes in its external and internal policy environments. The end of the cold war and the subsequent re-unification of Germany altered national attitudes to integration, pushed monetary unification forward, and raised the difficult new issue of how to respond to the hopes of post-socialist regimes for early EU membership. The economic cycle within the single market affects the context for negotiation on common policies. In periods of slow growth or recession, as in the 1970s and again in the 1990s, governments find it harder to make immediate concessions with the prospect of longer term gains. When, as during the 1960s and the late 1980s, European economic confidence supports faster growth, European political confidence—and mutual generosity—rise with it. Prospects for policy innovation over the coming years may thus depend partly on whether or not the core of the European economy regains momentum (Kok 2004; Sapir *et al*. 2004). The situation across the enlarged EU is highly variegated. The German economy has been disturbingly sluggish in recent years, with marked consequences for other European countries, given the hub-and-spoke character of the broader European economy. Similar problems persist in France and Italy, although economic performance in some of the smaller countries of western Europe, notably Finland and Ireland, continues to be buoyant. This is the backdrop to the slow progress with the Lisbon Agenda, which the Barroso Commission has identified as a top priority for its period in office. It will be interesting to see whether, and how, the more rapid growth rates in the new member states serve to inject more momentum into the EU policy process.

Ideas and identities

The role of ideas in influencing the evolution of policy comes across in almost every chapter in this volume. Governing ideas—the conventional wisdom, fashionable paradigms, and the implicit ideologies of practical policy-makers—set limits to conceivable or acceptable policy options. As governing ideas change, so new ways of formulating policy open up. The shift from a dominant Keynesian economic consensus towards monetarism in the late 1970s and 1980s, as Chapter 6 makes clear, narrowed the debate on EMU, enabling policy-makers to focus on monetary policy without taking broader macroeconomic and fiscal implications into consideration. Divergent national assumptions about social policy and the future of the welfare state inhibited the formulation of EU-level rules in this field, leaving to the ECJ the task of adjudicating on difficult cases, stepping in where member governments had feared to tread (see Chapter 10). When new issue areas emerge, as with the environment or biotechnology, the pre-negotiation phase focuses on how best to define the issue: whether in terms of predominantly economic interests, or of social concerns, or of scientific expertise. Part of the complexity of EU-level policy-making is that political decisions are understood and interpreted within national political systems through the filters of distinctive received opinions. The CT, with its embedded compromises, was attacked in France as a victory of Anglo-Saxon free market principles, while in Britain it was denounced for its subservience to French social market ideas.

European policies are constructed and reconstructed through the moving consensus which limits acceptable intellectual approaches to political problems. This, we note, differs from the way in which national policies are constructed and reconstructed only in the unfocused character of the broader political debate at the EU-level. Scharpf's (1999: 187) lament of 'the lack of Europe-wide policy discourses', however, overstates the weakness of political and intellectual exchanges at European level. Compared to the focus which national parliaments, parties, and media provide for domestic political debate, the Europe-wide discourse is weak. But exchanges among élites, conducted through the many élite networks which link expert and influential groups within European societies, do shape and reshape policy assumptions. Chapter 5 notes the importance of the epistemic community of economists and lawyers which links the separate national discourses on competition policy. Meetings between political leaders from the same political families before European Council meetings, and other exchanges among political leaders and parties, search—often with limited success—for shared attitudes and campaigning themes (Hix and Lord 1997). There were elements of an EU-wide debate over reshaping social democracy at the end of the 1990s, with the British 'Third Way' and the German 'Neue Mitte' meeting with mixed responses from social democrats in France and the Nordic countries. So transnational policy discourses on such underlying issues as the relationship between the state and the market, and the appropriate boundaries between the public and the private sector, are emerging, if only among political élites.

Almost all actors in the EU policy process have multiple identities, and may play multiple roles (Peterson and Bomberg 1999: 234–5). Most commissioners are recruited from national politics, and many return after their term of office to national political life. National political leaders take their turns in the Council presidency, and play their EU-wide representative and policy roles in most respects conscientiously; they value the national prestige which they gain from being seen to act successfully on a wider stage. Ambitious national officials work for periods in Brussels, in commissioners' *cabinets*, in Commission services, or in their governments' permanent representations, learning to balance national perspectives with transnational EU roles inside EU institutions. Independent experts and interest group leaders see themselves as players on both national and European stages—and sometimes on a wider transatlantic or global stage as well. The EU system, through the intensive interactions of transnational and transgovernmental networks which now characterize it, has become a collective system of governance, resting on overlapping élites.

Governance without statehood: post-sovereign politics

The EU *is* a collective political system, not an intergovernmental regime. Almost all European scholars start from this assumption (Majone 1996; Taylor 1996; Rometsch and Wessels 1996; Cram 1997; Scharpf 1999; Jachtenfuchs 2001). Some international relations scholars, however, remain 'trapped in the supranational-intergovernmental dichotomy', insisting that the EU must conform to one overall conceptual model or another of transactions among states (Branch and Øhrgaard 1999). Moravcsik (1999: 494–501) and Mattli (1999) both placed the EU in the same category as the North American Free Trade Agreement (NAFTA) and the Asia-Pacific Economic Cooperation (APEC) as examples of complex international regimes. Comparison between NAFTA and the EU, however, demonstrates how distant the dispute settlement procedures of NAFTA are from the federal jurisdiction of European law, and how far the complex balance of multilateral negotiation and coalition-building within the EU is from the US-dominated procedures of NAFTA. The mutual penetration of law, regulation, even political campaigning deep into what political scientists had long characterized as the core of domestic politics, define a level of politics and of governance which is most straightforwardly described as a political system.

Policy-making within a stable system of transnational governance, outside the framework of the state, challenges the classical dichotomy between domestic politics, within sovereign states, and international relations among states. These were, however, two exclusive ideal types, which never entirely corresponded to the intermediate examples of untidy reality (W. Wallace 1994*b*). The monolithic centralization of republican France, a century ago, differed from the Prussian-dominated, but semi-federal, German *Reich*. Both of these differed from the loosely-integrated Italian state. Austria-Hungary, with its dual structure and its sixteen official languages, offered a still looser model. The US, until the New Deal (and the second world war) still a loose federation with a tiny federal budget within which political power in crucial domains rested with the component states, takes us still further away from the ideal type of the monolithic sovereign state. Contemporary Canada, India, and Australia offer examples of relatively loose federations, within which the component states strike intergovernmental bargains and haggle over redistributive package deals. Within the EU, as the case studies in this volume have made clear, authority, political accountability, budgetary capacity, and administrative capability all remain primarily with the component states. But these component states *share* authority and administrative capability over a significant range of policy domains.

European and American enthusiasts for a United States of Europe, 50–60 years ago, and the neo-functionalists who predicted a progressive transfer first of interests and then of loyalties from the national to the supranational frame, believed that interests, loyalty, and power must lie at one level or another: to be *retained* by states, or *transferred* to a new entity. The experience of the EU over the past two decades has, however, demonstrated how far all these three elements of politics can be shared and dispersed. Multiple identities, multiple tiers of policy-making and policy implementation, and interlocking processes of ratification and scrutiny make for a far less tidy process than that which characterized the centralized French or British states of a century ago. Some observers have seen it also as unavoidably slow-moving and resistant to change, 'interblocking' as well as interlocking (Scharpf 1988). But all modern government is slow-moving, held back by the diversity of interests at stake and the inflexibility of administrative structures. The loosely-structured government of the EU has a far more diverse group of interests to persuade or to override than any of its component state systems, and must rely for implementation on the varied quality and entrenched traditions of the different national administrations. Nevertheless, it moves: not as swiftly or as smoothly as some would like, but so far without seeing the majority of politicians or public from any of its member states jump off the juggernaut.

One demonstration of the resilience of the EU as a system of governance is that it does *not* simply serve—as Moravcsik (1998) suggested—as a forum for intergovernmental bargaining among its largest states. German and French political leaders, certainly, have most often attempted to define the terms for negotiation, and to strike strategic bargains bilaterally. British leaders, similarly, have attempted to impose their priorities on EU negotiations rather than to converge on a multilateral consensus—successfully, after years of hard bargaining, on the budget, though less successfully in fisheries, in social policy, and elsewhere. But it is impossible to explain policy outcomes within the EU without taking into account the interests, and the initiatives, of other governments as players.

The Dutch, for example, have played an active part in shaping policy and in crafting compromises across the whole range of EU policy domains, since the Treaties of Paris and Rome were negotiated; Dutch presidencies in the last stages of the 1991 and 1996–7 IGCs left their distinctive imprint on the Maastricht and Amsterdam treaties. The Danes have been significant players in the development of environmental policy, as Chapter 12 indicates. The Spanish have successfully promoted their own interests in fisheries and in north-south relations, as well as in cohesion funds. Greek political leaders have stood out against majorities in defence of national interests as determinedly, and as successfully, as the British. Only months after their entry into the EU, the Polish and Lithuanian governments were leading EU diplomacy over contested presidential elections in neighbouring Ukraine. Small states benefit disproportionately from the added voice and standing which strong institutions give them in negotiating with their larger neighbours. The EU remains a firmly supported system of collective governance because it is seen to serve the interests of *all* its members, large and small.

Students of comparative and international politics should be careful not to exaggerate the coherence of national policy-making, nor the rationality of multilateral intergovernmental negotiation. One of the oddest aspects of American international relations scholarship about the EU is that it imagines a political system so much more tidy and structured that what one may observe in Washington. US trade policy emerges out of a messy process of lobbying, log-rolling, side payments, and interinstitutional conflicts, however 'rational' the behaviour of particular actors. It should not be surprising that European trade policy emerges from a similarly political process, in which the rational calculations of different actors are bounded by the conflicting assumptions and expectations of the many other players, as well as by the institutional conventions and constraints within which they operate. US environmental diplomacy has been marked by contested understandings of the issues, internal contradictions, and inconsistent objectives; the twists and turns of European environmental diplomacy look astonishingly coherent by comparison. Multi-level and multi-issue policy-making is an inherently complex activity. States and federations, as well as this non-state system of governance, do not always manage to pursue strategic objectives as they balance among conflicting pressures and priorities.

American students of EU policy-making should also note the importance of crowded geography—and of population density—in setting the context for cooperation among EU member states, their economies, and societies. Nordrhein-Westfalen, south-east England, and Nord Holland are amongst the most densely populated areas in the world. The broad corridor that stretches from the low countries to northern Italy has a cross-border density of population, of prosperity, and of traffic greater than in any other international region. Europeans are, necessarily, city-dwellers, more dependent on the provision of public goods for their security and comfort than the scattered sub-urbanites of the US. They place a high value on their limited rural environment, and are acutely conscious that air or water pollution spill over from one population centre to another. The spread of motorways, high-speed rail, and low-cost airlines across borders has encouraged the growth of transborder second homes and of trans-state retirement—with implications for cross-border pensions and healthcare, for disputes over property and family law, and for political rights claimed by long-term residents. Cross-border shopping, commuting, and crime are easy, intergovernmental exchange and multilateral meetings simple. The centre of Brussels is 105 minutes by high-speed train from Paris, 140 minutes from London, and only a little longer from Luxembourg and The Hague. Travellers from most other national capitals within the EU25 can reach Brussels the same day by a flight of less than three hours; only Athens and Nicosia require two days away whenever ministers or officials attend EU meetings. Collective governance is thus both necessary and manageable.

Policy-making within the EU may thus be described as post-sovereign. It spills across state boundaries, penetrating deep into previously domestic aspects of national politics and administration. It embodies the principle of mutual interference in each others' internal affairs, now extending (as Chapter 18 notes) even to mutual inspection of each others' border policing and judicial procedures. It depends upon mutual trust, and on collective consent to implement European law and regulation through national administrations (W. Wallace 1999). States, as represented by national governments, remain central to the EU policy process, but they are no longer the *only* significant actors—and are not always the predominant actors. Their actions are constrained by institutional frameworks, and moderated by the intervention of institutionally autonomous actors such as the Commission, the ECJ, and the EP. More importantly, as previous chapters have shown, they are constrained by their diminished control of their own governments, administrations, and national political processes, as information on their own negotiating objectives is traded in transnational and transgovernmental interactions in return for information on the intentions of others, feeding backwards and forwards assumptions and expectations which shape possible outcomes.

The EU as a partial polity

The EU remains, however, a partial polity, without many of the features which one might expect to find within a fully-developed democratic political system. Scharpf (1999: 6, 22) characterizes it as resting on 'output-oriented legitimacy', while lacking 'input-oriented legitimacy'. He argues that it provides government for the people, but does not represent government by the people. 'In the absence of political account-ability' and of a strong sense of collective political identity, 'the legitimacy of politically salient European decisions depends on their effectiveness in achieving consensual goals'. Passive popular consent, from his perspective, rests upon the ability of this slow-moving consensual policy-making system to provide outcomes sufficiently satisfact-ory to avoid provoking active dissent. This partial polity is particularly dependent on regulatory instruments as policy outcomes—as Chapters 4, 5, 10, 11, 12, and 13 illus-trate. This makes, however, for an opaque policy process and a technical and non-trans-parent series of policy outcomes, drafted in terms accessible to expert élites, but beyond the interest or understanding of the broader public.

National governments rebuilt and maintained collective identity after the second world war through large-scale spending programmes for economic development and welfare. The small size of the EU budget has foreclosed this option for building pol-icies and polity (see Chapter 8). European policy-making thus remains an élite process, into which non-governmental organizations, the EP, and national parliaments and opposition parties intrude, without succeeding on most policy issues in attracting much wider public attention. Those issues on which wider opinion is aroused, as we have seen, are most frequently questions of taste or values—environmental protec-tion, food safety, biotechnology, immigration (see Chapters 12, 13, 18). Taylor (1996) has labelled the EU political system a 'cartel of élites', through which—as in the 'consociational' representative democracy characteristic of the postwar Netherlands and of contemporary Switzerland—popular opinion is indirectly represented, each group relying on its own participating élites to take care of its interests and to deliver satisfactory outcomes.

Collective governance moves slowly, coopting as broad a coalition of interested groups as possible into the consultative committees and hierarchy of working groups through which it operates, in order to legitimize the policy outcome. Environmental organizations, and non-governmental organizations concerned with social policy and food safety, are invited into the Brussels process in order to engage their leaders in the common enterprise, and so inhibit them from attacking the eventual compromise that may emerge. This is a costly process, involving lengthy consultations over successive draft proposals, sometimes extending over several years (van Schendelen 1998). But it is a necessary part of a policy-making process that rests on such a weak foundation for legitimacy: a post-sovereign political system in which the outcomes agreed justify the continuing collective input.

Neo-functionalist theorists of European integration hoped that the Commission, through the 'Community method', would successfully coopt nationally organized interest groups to work together at the European level. It would thus by-pass the conventional mechanisms for popular representation and interest aggregation, parties and parliaments. Several of the case studies confirm that EU-level organized interests now cluster round the Brussels institutions. The extension of EU regulation over the past twenty years, together with the extra-territorial reach of EU rules and competition policies, has drawn them in. This has not, however, created a network of functional organizations that link more than a small minority within each member state to the Brussels policy process. The Commission has done its best to encourage the emergence of supportive non-governmental organizations, providing them with useful financial subsidies out of the Community budget (*Economist*, 23 October 2004). This top-down approach to organizing civil society, however, risks alienating further those who are sceptical of transferring further authority to Brussels, and misrepresenting within the EU institutions what 'the peoples of Europe' would prefer or accept. The EU Convention's consultations with 'civil society organizations', promoted as a 'listening phase' in its deliberations, were thus in some ways a circular conversation, in which those who had already gained privileged access told the Convention members what they were happy to hear (Norman 2003).

Students who have worked their way through this volume, noting appropriate treaty articles and successive revisions of their terms, grasping the distinction between Coreper I and Coreper II, the differences between the Commission and the Council Secretariat, the subtleties of the OMC, and the extent and limits of qualified majority voting (QMV), will understand why the EU as a political system seems opaque to the mass public. They should also understand that the structure of the EU, as a partial polity, muffles political issues in technical language, and stifles partisan debate beneath multilateral negotiations among governments of different colours. The characteristic focus of MEPs on scrutinizing particular proposals for EU legislation, largely through committees—as noted in several of our chapters—plays an increasingly active role in shaping that legislation, but does little to engage a wider public. The EP appears on national television screens only when it threatens to remove the Commission, or to refuse to accept a newly-nominated Commission, thus providing the political drama that its regular business lacks.

Had the EU budget now reached the 4–5 per cent of GDP that some optimists in the 1970s envisaged, the policy-making process would attract more attention, and perhaps also more support. Cross-border transfers would be more substantial, and outcomes from EU expenditure more visible. A single currency accompanied by national autonomy in fiscal policy, and virtual autonomy in macroeconomic policy, it was assumed, would risk structural imbalance. The budget, however, was captured at an early stage by agricultural interests and their sponsoring governments, leading to a countervailing coalition of governments resisting further transfers—as Chapters 7, 8, and 9 have described. The distributive mode of EU governance is thus hobbled by the tight limit imposed on budgetary resources, leaving the Commission with a weak hand in its attempts to build constituencies of support.

The legitimacy of the system thus depends very heavily on the quality of its output for popular support. Sadly, however, the perceived efficiency of EU outputs has been declining; the feedback on implementation of EU policies has as often been negative as positive in recent years. Chapter 8 notes the rising discontent with the Commission's management of its own expenditure, which eventually led the EP to censure the college of commissioners in 1999 (thus forcing their resignation). A programme of Commission reform has been under way since then, but—as the case studies also note— it is as yet far from complete. The Commission as a college and as an administration has to a significant extent lost the respect of national administrations, and of national media, over the past decade. There is a wide gap between the Commission's self-perception of its role, as guardian of the treaties and agenda-setter, and outside perceptions of its weaknesses as policy manager.

It is national governments, moreover, that are responsible for implementing most EU policies, on a basis of mutual trust and commitment, and under the potential challenge of a case before the ECJ. Here again, as the chapters above note, the recent record has been poor, even deteriorating. The French government has never enforced EU fisheries regulations on its own fishermen. The Commission's discontent with implementation of single market regulations has led to the publication of 'league tables', with Greece, Belgium, France, and Italy at the bottom. The Stability and Growth Pact (SGP), agreed in 1997 as a pillar for the single currency, had been broken by France and Germany in 2003–4, while Greece and Italy were suspected of providing false financial statistics to demonstrate compliance. Chapter 16 notes that the Commission carefully monitored the progress of incorporation and implementation of EU legislation in the ten applicant states, in the transition to full membership. It was, however, less well empowered, or perhaps inclined, to monitor implementation within the EU15. Chapter 14 notes that member governments have furthermore resisted allowing the Commission to establish supranational inspectorates, in fisheries or in other sectors. Experimentation with mutual inspection, within the field of JHA, may offer a more acceptable way forward, although at the time of writing there is no sign that this might be extended into other areas.

The EU is also a partial polity in terms of the marginal engagement, and attentiveness, of national publics. In a political system in which ultimate authority remains with national governments, this may matter little. All politics is local, as the political cliché goes. Voters are most directly concerned about health, welfare transfers, education, law and order, fields in which EU competence is limited, and EU policy-makers only marginally involved. Yet, as we have seen, the ECJ has extended EU competence some way into welfare policies, even into the provision of health services; the development of JHA has taken the EU into aspects of law enforcement and the courts. Neo-functionalists saw the EC gaining the 'permissive' consent of the mass public through providing the legitimizing outputs of higher economic growth, wider choice, and free movement (Lindberg and Scheingold 1970). Low economic growth since the mid-1990s, and ineffective delivery of some agreed policies, risk alienating national publics from a distant policy-making system. Some argue that the key failure in maintaining the legitimacy of the system lies with national governments: that 'national leaders have bungled their communicative role' (V. A. Schmidt 2004: 978). This is, it must be said, part of the structural weakness of such a partial polity: that national leaders are primarily attuned to domestic politics, rather than to European statesmanship, while the Commission has lost much of the authority it had to set a common agenda and to communicate shared priorities to distinctive national audiences. How far that represents an underlying instability in this apparently stable political system is, however, beyond the scope of this book.

European government between national policy-making and global negotiation

Policy-making within the EU, as earlier chapters have illustrated, responds to both internal and external demands. Changes in the EU external environment force changes to embedded bargains. It was, for example, sustained pressure from successive GATT/WTO trade rounds, reinforced by surpluses on world agricultural markets and the uncertainties of Russian demand for EU exports, which (as noted in Chapter 7) pushed forward the MacSharry reforms to the CAP, and provided impetus for Commissioner Fischler's continuing efforts. The delays in pursuing the Doha Round of the WTO (see Chapter 15) have thus softened the pressures for further CAP reform. Fisheries policy has operated within the context of changing international rules on national fishery limits and on sustainable levels of fish catches. Environmental policy has been shaped within a broader worldwide debate, drawing on scientific evidence from outside the European continent as well as within. Migration policy has been intrinsically a response to pressures from outside, including the disappearance of the EU's secure eastern frontier after 1989, and the impact of ethnic conflict and state collapse to the EU's east and south.

Technological change, with global competition in emerging technologies, has also driven EU policy. The exploitation of biotechnology, both within the EU and within the US, set the framework within which European policies had to be defined and developed. US and European companies were competing to capture new patents and potential markets, as European and American scientists compared research findings and environmental NGOs exchanged their concerns. The transformation of telecommunications through the information revolution needed an altered framework for policy, as state telephone monopolies faced the challenges of rising traffic, new equipment, falling unit costs, and a rapidly-developing international market. One of the many reasons why EU policies and policy-making in the late 1990s differ in character from the patterns which prevailed some twenty years before is that the problems which they face have been transformed, and the instruments available to manage those problems are often of a different order. The information which flows through global television, radio, and now also the internet, has increased the surges of asylum-seekers which cross the external borders of the EU after successive external conflicts. On the other hand, the availability of computer networks has made it easier in turn for EU governments to monitor each surge, to record each arrival, and to inhibit 'asylum-shopping' by immigrants.

The US has been an active presence, sometimes almost a participant, in many of the policy domains we have described. Despite the increasing frictions of recent years, US and European interests overlap across a wide range of EU concerns. The US Mission to the European Communities, in Brussels, is comparably staffed to the permanent representations of major member governments (Hayes-Renshaw and Wallace 2005). It intervenes to protect and to promote American interests as early as possible in the long process of formulating and negotiating EU policies. Negotiation and consultation within the EU interact with consultation within the OECD; two-thirds of the OECD's members are EU member states. The G7 and G8, with half of their participants drawn from EU member countries, address agendas which overlap substantially with EU concerns, based on preparatory papers from groups of experts who also serve on EU committees. In trade policy, competition policy, agriculture, environment, biotechnology, and foreign and defence policy, EU policy-makers necessarily refer to US policy, and often negotiate with US policy-makers. EU policy-makers had to respond to the terrorist attacks on US targets, in September 2001, but clearly with reference to their own previous experience in combating both domestic and transborder terrorism. They also found themselves, however, responding to American demands for cooperation on a US-defined counterterrorist agenda.

The flow of EU policy, with the introduction of new concepts and information into the policy debate, thus takes place within a wider context. This is not fully global, since most developing countries (including Russia, China, and India) remain marginal players in the international system. There is, however, a widening group of advanced industrial democracies, working through the formal mechanisms of multilateral conferences and organizations, as well as the informal and semi-formal networks of expert communities and advisory groups. Much of what we have described as characterizing the transformation of intra-European policy-making—intensifying transgovernmental and transnational interactions, exchanges of information and ideas among agencies within governments, multi-level lobbying by economic interests and NGOs—has also modified patterns of national policy-making within other OECD member states. Business leaders and management experts also exchange ideas with politicians and officials from industrial democracies in meeting places such as Davos (the World Economic Forum) and Denver (the Aspen Institute), and in other seminars and conferences across the developed world. Greenpeace campaigns in North America, Australia, and New Zealand as well as in western Europe. EU policy-making takes place in constant interaction not only with national policy-making, but also with wider international regimes, and within a global context. European integration is not an autonomous phenomenon; it is nested within the liberal world economy.

Three questions follow from this. First, how far should we think of European policy-making as driven by pressures to respond to US-led global preferences? Secondly, given that the EU has so far been embedded in a wider framework of American-led institutions, how far is it dependent for further development on the assumption of continuing US support? Thirdly, how useful is it to compare European integration with other regional policy frameworks within the global economy? The way in which several member governments have approached European social and competition policies has certainly been influenced by their concern to maintain some distinctive aspects of the European social market model against the growing predominance of Anglo-American market assumptions (Scharpf 1999; V. A. Schmidt 2002). The pressure of American (and East Asian) competition has been a constant external reference point for European policy-makers over the past two decades. Modernizing élites in Russia and Turkey a century or more ago attempted to select from the cultural, political, and economic structures of their European models those aspects they regarded as most useful, while resisting other aspects they saw as harmful to their own values. Similarly, the aim of social democratic and christian democratic élites in Germany, France, the Benelux countries, and the Nordic countries since the second world war has been to learn from and copy some parts of the American model, while resisting others. Part of the underlying rationale for EU common policies is that a common European negotiating position enables European governments to bargain with the US on much more equal terms over global rules, regimes, and standards. In environmental negotiations, on genetically modified foods, on common rules affecting multinational companies and foreign investment, on domestic content rules in television and cinema transmissions, many European politicians and NGOs argue that political, social, and cultural values—not simply economic interests—are at stake. Regional integration, through the EU, thus acts to moderate the pressures of global integration. It enables governments which can aspire on their own to only minor influence over global regimes to gain greater influence through combining with their like-minded neighbours, and to set standards and regulations that extend extra-territorially across their dependent neighbours and trading partners.

Successive US administrations, from Truman and Eisenhower to Bush-1 and Clinton, have given their support to the further development of the EU. In the early years of western European institutions, policy-makers in Washington pushed for closer integration, while insisting that cooperation among their European partners must remain firmly nested within Nato. As the EU extended its scope, transatlantic differences emerged on issues such as agricultural trade, competition policy, patents and standards, airlines, and aircraft production. US administrations nevertheless remained broadly supportive of the EU as a whole, including the promotion of successive enlargements to the south and east, and beyond to include Turkey. The reaction of the second Bush administration to the further development of European autonomy, especially in foreign policy and defence, has, however, been more sceptical. As regards Iraq, in 2003 some major European governments resisted US pressure to follow the American-led intervention, even though others responded positively. Transatlantic American hegemony, institutionalized through Nato, has rested on a rhetoric of partnership and of American commitment to multilateral cooperation. It remains to be seen whether a strategic shift in US policy towards the EU is now under way, and what the impact of such a shift might be on the future development of EU policies.

Regional integration schemes are also under way in other continents. As in the 1960s, when, in the first flush of enthusiasm for regional integration, common markets were set up in East Africa, the Caribbean, and Latin America, the renewed dynamism which European institutions have displayed since the mid-1980s prompts questions about comparison between European processes and preconditions and those in other regions (Haas 1961; W. Wallace 1994a; Mattli 1999). The three-member North Atlantic Free Trade Association (NAFTA), the four-member Mercosur (the Common Market of the Southern Cone, comprising Brazil, Argentina, Uruguay, and Paraguay) and the sixteen-member Asia-Pacific Economic Cooperation (APEC) might be seen, at the end of the 1990s, as possible comparators to the EU.

We question the closeness of this comparison with such loose regional frameworks. EU policy-making, as successive chapters have made clear, depends on extensive networks of officials, experts, and activists, operating across national boundaries through common institutions, and on the basis of a relatively high degree of mutual trust and mutual understanding. These rest upon common expectations that each other member state and society is equipped not only with fully democratic government, but also with a relatively non-corrupt and efficient national administration, an independent system of justice and administrative redress, autonomous media, and a vigorous civil society of competing political movements and organized groups. Postwar American hegemony, through the Marshall Plan and other agencies, together with the social democratic compromise of corporatist consultation and welfare provision, helped to root these standards, social institutions, and habits of behaviour firmly across most of western Europe. In Spain, Portugal, and Greece (and in some respects in Ireland) the transition towards an open society was slower and later. In all of these countries, it should be noted, it is widely believed that participation within the EU has played a significant part in entrenching (and monitoring) the full development of civil institutions and democratic standards. The lengthy process of transition to EU membership within the former socialist states, as Chapter 16 notes, is partly about assisting and monitoring the development of democratic standards and civil institutions, now specifically included in the accession negotiations as a pre-condition for membership.

Outside Europe similar conditions of mutual trust, based upon extensive interaction among official and non-official élites, obtain between the US and Canada, but only in a much more limited way extend across Mexico. Within APEC they clearly obtain between Australia and New Zealand, between these two and the US, and to some extent between these three and Japan, it would, however, be premature to argue that such conditions extend between this core group and Chile, or Korea, or Indonesia, while China remains a half-closed society deeply mistrustful of many of its APEC partners. The broader interaction between governments and societies which we have described as intensive transgovernmentalism and extensive transnationalism holds the advanced industrial democracies together, and provides a foundation of mutual understanding and trust. Scholars who focus primarily on state actors, or concentrate on economic interests to the exclusion of political values and mutual trust, ignore the significance of the substructure of shared ideas and overlapping networks in providing a framework within which political leaders negotiate. Regional integration in other continents would not have the depth and complexity comparable to those of the EU political system without a comparable substructure, extending beyond governments into societies and across borders into other national societies and their domestic élites. The relationship between the US, Canada, and Mexico through NAFTA is more directly comparable to those between the EU and Switzerland, or the members of the European Economic Area (the EU plus Norway, Liechtenstein, and Iceland), or between the EU and its Mediterranean partners. These are highly asymmetrical. Formal institutions allow for consultation, but in practice the associated states have little alternative, except where clear national economic interests are threatened, but to follow the legislative lead of their dominant partner.

The persistence of the provisional

Thirty years ago it was plausible to picture the Community system as a provisional political structure, halfway between sovereignty and integration. After some fifty years of operation, the observer must remark on the persistence and adaptability of the provisional. Member governments and national publics appear more comfortable with the deliberate ambiguity of this semi-confederation, this *Staatenverbund*—as the German constitutional court has described it—than with the logical alternative of a full federation (Ress 1994). Ambiguity of objectives, agreement to disagree, the postponement of difficult but non-urgent decisions until later, are characteristic features of this relatively stable *provisorum*; but they are not unique to the EU. Canadian federal politics, American federal politics, German and Italian national politics, and the processes of constitutional devolution within the UK, France, and Spain display similar elements of deliberate imprecision.

The EU has demonstrated considerable flexibility in adapting its institutional practices to the demands of a shifting agenda over the past fifteen years. The frequency of heads of government meetings and sectoral Councils has fallen and risen as circumstances have changed. Committees and working groups have been convened to formulate proposals, following well-recognized standard procedures, and sometimes dissolved when their tasks are complete. The flexibility of this cumbersome, stateless political system appears more remarkable if one considers the counter-factual: the number of alternative outcomes which EU actors have avoided in keeping this provisional system of collective government in place. There were, for example, many within France, Germany, and the Benelux who argued in the early 1990s that neither progress towards EMU nor further enlargement would be practicable without the creation of an inner core of member states. Yet eleven of the fifteen 'old' member states participated in the launch of the single currency, in January 1999, joined later by Greece. Of these, the UK, Denmark, and Sweden remained outside the Eurozone in 2004 for reasons of domestic politics rather than inability to meet the economic conditions for entry.

As this volume went to press, the EU appeared to be successfully adapting its institutions and procedures to the participation of ten additional member states. In terms of policies, however, the EU has been slow to adapt to the challenges of a rapidly changing environment. As Pollack notes in Chapter 2, EU policy-making is sticky. Its budget still reflects the compromises of thirty years ago, leaving little to spare for more recently-identified priorities: for research and innovation, for the management of borders and asylum-seekers, and for external relations. Its agricultural regime is still struggling with reform. Its fisheries regime has failed to conserve falling stocks. The ten new members have been expected to conform to the existing *acquis*, without much willingness among the EU15 to adapt the *acquis* to the needs of an EU25. The cautious approach to GMOs has weakened the competitiveness of Europe's infant biotechnology industry. Worst of all, in a system of governance that has depended for past acceptability on its association with faster economic growth, the economies of its core member states have grown only slowly over the past decade, while their governments have resisted collective attempts to promote reform of employment and welfare policies. There remains a wide gap between the lack of progress on the Lisbon Agenda, five years after heads of government formally agreed it, and the critical conclusion of the Sapir Report, that 'what is required is a massive change in economic institutions and organizations, which has not yet occurred on a large scale in Europe' (Sapir *et al.* 2004: 2).

The case studies in this volume indicate the increasing diversity of modes of policymaking. Some members of the Convention in 2002–3 clung to the old faith that integration was a linear process, which should move from soft consultation and coordination to full delegation to the Commission, cumulatively transferring powers from national authorities to the EU level. They therefore resisted proposals to strengthen the involvement of national parliaments, or to reinforce the 'subsidiarity' clause incorporated in the TEU (Norman 2003). Yet there has, as Mark Pollack (2000) notes, been something of a backlash against centralizing tendencies within the EU since the conclusion of the 1992 programme, with member governments resisting further transfers of powers to the Commission and seeking for softer forms of policy coordination.

The case studies provide some evidence of governments continuing to delegate new responsibilities to the Commission, for want of alternative agencies to pursue common policies. The European Council's acceptance of a new five-year programme in JHA, for example, in November 2004, delegated to the Commission the task of drawing up more detailed proposals, as appropriate under the progressive transfer of competences in this sector from the third to the first pillar. Nevertheless, this volume provides plenty of evidence that alternative patterns of delegation and coordination are also developing, to display a more diverse system of policy-making and policy implementation. The Council Secretariat has grown significantly in numbers and responsibilities since 1990, and has grown further with the arrival of a military staff (Hayes-Renshaw and Wallace 2005). New agencies have been set up, from those dealing with food safety and standards for medicines to Europol and Eurojust; others are under discussion, such as perhaps an independent European Competition Office. The emerging pattern for policy-making and policy-management looks to be more diverse, and possibly more flexible, than a classical model of delegation to a Commission that is still only partially reformed.

The chapters above have also illustrated the spread of variable geometry, both within and across the EU's borders, that is to say, circles of cooperation in which only some EU members or neighbours are involved. In negotiating with candidate states, the Commission has continued to insist that there can be no opt-outs from the *acquis*. Denmark and the UK, however, as incumbent members have negotiated a number of opt-outs; Sweden has also remained outside the single currency; and Ireland is not fully included in Schengen. France and the UK reshaped their proposals for rapidly-deployable European forces, in February 2004, on a 'closer cooperation' basis of 'opting-in', challenging other EU members to prove their capacity to take part by providing the forces and equipment required. Norway and Iceland participate in the Schengen border-control regime, while not being members of the EU; the Norwegian government in late 2004 was also discussing with its Swedish and Finnish counterparts whether to participate jointly in providing a ready battle-group for ESDP. Even common policies have in practice been implemented in highly diverse ways, as Elmar Rieger has shown. It seems likely that the EU25, negotiating with various neighbours for association or membership, will accommodate even greater diversity in the future.

The conventional wisdom from many consultative groups and academic studies, from 1970 to 1990, was that monetary union was not achievable without political union, and that further movement to integrate foreign policy and defence, or internal policing and justice, would necessitate the transformation of the EU into a federation. By 2004, however, a single currency had been in place for several years, and member governments and EU institutions were moving towards closer integration of foreign policy, defence, policing, and justice, without addressing the hard choices of transferring sovereignty to federal institutions. Political logic, clarity of decision-making and accountability, administrative efficiency, and external representation all argue for stronger central institutions. Member governments, and most of their publics, prefer to live with ambiguity, accepting the costs in terms of slow-moving mechanisms for policy-making in return for the benefits of national representation and accountability which this consociational cartel of élites continues to provide.

We have not offered any single theoretical model for the EU policy process in this volume. We have preferred to allow the case studies to illustrate the complexity and diversity of EU policy-making, pointing out common features and offering a range of models which best illuminate different aspects of the political process. Single models are unavoidably reductionist, shutting out significant aspects of political interaction in order to achieve the clean lines of parsimonious simplicity. But politics is not a simple business, and political actors rarely devote their undivided attention to the pursuit of singular and well-defined strategic objectives. The EU is a partial polity, with a profoundly political process of policy-making: a stable structure of collective governance, which continues to serve the mixed purposes of its constituent member states relatively well.

References

Most EU institutions can be researched on the world wide web. The Council is on-line at *http://ue.eu.int/en/summ.htm*. The Commission at *http://europa.eu.int/comm/index-en.htm*, and its DG V at *http://europa.eu.int/comm/dg05/*, and similarly for other DGs. The European Court of Justice's decisions under *http://europa.eu.int/cj/index.htm*. The European Parliament is at *www.europarl.eu.int/* and its Committee on Employment and Social Affairs (ESOC) is available at *www.europarl.eu.int/committees/en/default.htm#ESOC*, and similarly for other committees. Other actors, such the European Trade Union Confederation (ETUC) under *www.etuc.org*, or the Union of Industrial and Employers' Confederations of Europe (UNICE), via e-mail at *main@unice.be*.

Abélès, M. (1996), *En attente d'Europe* (Hachette: Paris).

Addison, J. T., and Siebert, W. S. (1993), 'The EC Social Charter: The Nature of the Beast', *National Westminster Bank Quarterly Review*, Feb., 13–28.

Agence Europe, various issues.

Allmendinger, J., and Leibfried, S. (2003), 'Education and the Welfare State: The Four Worlds of Competence Production', *Journal of European Social Policy*, 13/1: 63–81.

Alter, K. J. (2001), *Establishing the Supremacy of European Law: The Making of an International Rule of Law in Europe* (Oxford: Oxford University Press).

Alter, K. J., and Meunier-Aitsahalia, S. (1994), 'Judicial Politics in the European Community: European Integration and the Pathbreaking Cassis de Dijon Decision', *Comparative Political Studies*, 26/4: 535–61.

Amato, G. (1997), *Antitrust and the Bounds of Power* (Oxford: Hart).

Anania, G., Carter, C. A., and McCalla, A. F. (1994) (eds.), *Agricultural Trade Conflicts and GATT: New Dimenions in US–European Agricultural Trade Relations* (Boulder: Westview).

Anderson, J. A. (1995), 'The Structural Funds and the Social Dimension of the EC Policy', in Leibfried and Pierson (1995*b*) (eds.), *European Social Policy: Between Fragmentation and Integration* (Washington: Brookings Institution), 123–58.

Anderson, K., and Hayami, Y. (1986), *The Political Economy of Agricultural Protection: East Asia in International Perspective* (Sidney: Allen & Unwin).

Anderson, M., den Boer, M., Cullen, P., Gilmore, W. C., Raab, C. D., and Walker, N. (1995), *Policing the European Union: Theory, Law and Practice* (Oxford: Clarendon Press).

Andrews, D. (2003), 'The Committee of Central Bank Governors as a Source of Rules', *Journal of European Public Policy*, 10/6: 956–73.

Andriessen, F. (1991), 'Towards a Community of Twenty-Four?', speech to the 69th Assembly of Eurochambers, Brussels, 19 Apr.

Angenendt, S. (1997) (ed.), *Migration und Flucht: Aufgaben und Strategien für Deutschland, Europa und die internationale Gemeinschaft* (Bonn and Munich: Bundeszentrale für politische Bildung/ R. Oldenbourg).

Ansell, C., Rahsaan, M., and Sicurelli, D. (2005), 'Protesting Food: NGOs and Political Mobilization in Europe', in Ansell and Vogel (eds.), *Why the Beef? The Contested Governance of European Food Safety* (Cambridge, Mass.: MIT Press), forthcoming.

Ansell, C., and Vogel, D. (2005) (eds.), *Why the Beef? The Contested Governance of European Food Safety* (Cambridge, Mass.: MIT Press), forthcoming.

Antoine, L. (1995), 'Quand la controverse tourne à l'impasse: la guerre du thon', *Natures, Sciences, Société*, 3/1: 6–15.

Arbault, F., and Suurnakki, S. (2002), 'Commission Adopts Eight New Decisions Imposing Fines on Hard-core Cartels', *Competition Policy Newsletter*, 2002/1: 29–43.

Arkleton Trust (1992), *Farm Household Adjustment in Western Europe, 1987–1991: Final Report on the Research Programme on Farm Structures and Pluriactivity* (Luxembourg: Office for Official Publications of the European Communities).

Armstrong, K., and Bulmer, S. (1998), *The Governance of the Single European Market* (Manchester: Manchester University Press).

Arnold, C. U. (2002), 'How Two-Level Entrepreneurship Works: The Influence of the Commission on the Europe-Wide Employment Strategy', paper presented at the conference of the American Political Science Association, Boston, 29 Aug.–1 Sept.

Arnold, C. U., Hosli, M. O., and Pennings, P. (2004), 'Social Policy-Making in the European Union: A New Mode of Governance?', paper presented at the Conference of Europeanists, Chicago, 11–13 March.

Arocena, J. (1998), 'Argentine: inquiétude des Espagnols', *Le Marin*, 27 Feb.

Aspinwall, M. D., and Schneider, G. (1999), 'Same Menu, Separate Tables: The Institutionalist Turn in Political Science and the Study of European Integration', *European Journal of Political Research*, 38: 1–36.

Avery, G. (1995), *The Commission's Perspective on the EFTA Accession Negotiations*, SEI Working Paper No. 12 (Falmer: Sussex European Institute).

Avery, G. (2004), 'The Enlargement Negotiations', in Cameron (ed.), *The Future of Europe: Integration and Enlargement* (London: Routledge), 35–62.

Avery, G., and Cameron, F. (1998), *The Enlargement of the European Union* (Sheffield: Sheffield Academic Press).

Bache, I. (1998), *The Politics of European Union Regional Policy: Multi-Level Governance or Flexible Gatekeeping?* (Sheffield: Sheffield Academic Press).

Bache, I. (1999), 'The Extended Gatekeeper: Central Government and the Implementation of the EC Regional Policy in the UK', *Journal of European Public Policy*, 6/1: 28–45.

Bache, I. (2004), 'Multi-Level Governance and EU Regional Policy', in Bache and Flinders (eds.), *Multi-Level Governance* (Oxford: Oxford University Press), 165–78.

Bache, I., and Bristow, G. (2003), 'Devolution and the Gatekeeping Role of the Core Executive: The Struggle for European Funds', *British Journal of Politics and International Relations*, 5/3: 405–27.

Bache, I., and Flinders, M. (2004), 'Themes and Issues in Multi-Level Governance', in Bache and Flinders (eds.), *Multi-Level Governance* (Oxford: Oxford University Press), 1–11.

Bache, I., George, S., and Rhodes, R. (1996), 'The European Union, Cohesion Policy and Sub-national Authorities in the United Kingdom', in Hooghe (ed.), *Cohesion Policy and European Integration: Building Multi-Level Governance* (Oxford: Oxford University Press), 294–319.

Bachtler, J., Wishlade, F., and Yuill, D. (2001), *Regional Policy in Europe after Enlargement*, Regional and Industrial Policy Research Paper 44, June, European Policies Research Centre, University of Strathclyde.

Bahle, T. (2003), 'The Changing Institutionalization of Social Services in England and Wales, France and Germany: Is the Welfare State on the Retreat?', *Journal of European Social Policy*, 13/1: 5–20.

Bahle, T., and Pfennig, A. (2001), *Angebotsformen und Trägerstrukturen sozialer Dienste im europäischen Vergleich* (Mannheim: Mannheimer Zentrum für Europäische Sozialforschung), MZES Working Paper 34.

Bailey, D., and De Propris, L. (2002), 'The 1988 Reform of the Structural Funds: Entitlement or Empowerment?', *Journal of European Public Policy*, 9/3: 408–28.

Bailey, D., and De Propris, L. (2004), 'A Bridge too Phare? EU Pre-Accession Aid and Capacity Building in the Candidate Countries', *Journal of Common Market Studies*, 42/1: 77–98.

Baker, S. (2003), 'The Dynamics of European Union Biodiversity Policy: Interactive, Functional and Institutional Logics', *Environmental Politics*, 12: 23–41.

Balassa, B. (1975), *European Economic Integration* (Amsterdam: North-Holland).

Balcerowicz, L. (1999), 'Europe Growing Together', in Curzon Price, Landau, and Whitman (eds.), *The Enlargement of the European Union* (London: Routledge), 3–9.

Baldwin, R. (1994), *Towards an Integrated Europe* (London: CEPR).

Barbé, E. (1998), 'Balancing Europe's Eastern and Southern Dimensions', in Zielonka (ed.), *Paradoxes of European Foreign Policy* (The Hague: Kluwer Law International), 117–30.

Barber, L. (1998), *Financial Times*, 20 March 1998.

Barbier, J.-C., and Samba Sylla, N. (2004), *La stratégie européenne pour l'emploi: genèse, coordination communautaire et diversité nationale*, Rapport de Recherche pour la DARES, Ministère de l'Emploi.

Barnard, C. (2000), 'Regulating Competitive Federalism in the European Union? The Case of EC Social Policy', in Shaw (ed.), *Social Law and Policy in an Evolving European Union* (Oxford: Hart), 49–69.

Barnard, C. (2002), 'The Social Partners and the Governance Agenda', *European Law Journal*, 8/1: 80–101.

Barnard, C. (2004), *The Substantive Law of the EU: The Four Freedoms* (Oxford: Oxford University Press).

Barrett, G. (1997) (ed.), *Justice Cooperation in the European Union* (Dublin: Institute of European Affairs).

Barry, F., and Begg, I. (2003), 'EMU and Cohesion: Introduction', *Journal of Common Market Studies*, special issue, 41/5: 781–96.

Barwig, K., and Schulte, B. (1999) (eds.), *Freizügigkeit und soziale Sicherheit: Die Durchführung der Verordnung (EWG) Nr. 1408/71 über die soziale Sicherheit der Wanderarbeitnehmer in Deutschland* (Baden-Baden: Nomos).

Baun, M. J. (2000), *A Wider Europe: The Process and Politics of EU Enlargement* (Lanham: Rowman & Littlefield).

Baun, M. J. (2002), 'EU Regional Policy and the Candidate States: Poland, the Czech Republic', *Journal of European Integration*, 24/3: 261–82.

Becker, U. (1998), 'Brillen aus Luxemburg und Zahnbehandlung in Brüssel: die Gesetzliche Krankenversicherung im Europäischen Binnenmarkt', *Neue Zeitschrift für Sozialrecht*, 7/8: 359–64.

Becker, U. (2003), 'Gesetzliche Krankenversicherung im Europäischen Binnenmarkt', *Neue Juristische Wochenschrift*, 32: 2271–7.

Becker, U. (2004a), 'Die soziale Dimension des Binnenmarktes', in Schwarze (ed.), *Der Verfassungsentwurf des Europäischen Konvents: Verfassungsrechtliche Grundstrukturen und wirtschaftsverfassungsrechtliches Konzept* (Baden-Baden: Nomos), 201–19.

Becker, U. (2004b), 'Grenzüberschreitende Versicherungsleistungen in der (gesetzlichen) Krankenversicherung—Die juristische Persektive', in Basedow et al. (eds.), *Versicherungswissenschaftliche Studien*, 26 (Baden-Baden: Nomos), 171–88.

Begg, I., and Grimwade, N. (1998), *Paying for Europe* (Sheffield: Sheffield Academic Press).

Bercusson, B. (2000), *European Labour Law* (London: Butterworths).

Berenz, C. (1994), 'Hat die betriebliche Altersvorsorge zukünftig noch eine Chance?', *Neue Zeitschrift für Arbeitsrecht*, 11/9: 385–90, 433–8.

Beyers, J., and Dierickx, G. (1998), 'The Working Groups of the Council of Ministers: Supranational or Intergovernmental Negotiations?', *Journal of Common Market Studies*, 36/3: 289–317.

Bieback, K.-J. (1993), 'Marktfreiheit in der EG und nationale Sozialpolitik vor und nach Maastricht', *Europarecht*, 28/2: 150–72.

Bieback, K.-J. (1997), *Die mittelbare Diskriminierung wegen des Geschlechts: ihre Grundlagen im Recht der EU und ihre Auswirkungen auf das Sozialrecht der Mitgliedstaaten* (Baden-Baden: Nomos).

Bieback, K.-J. (2003), 'Die Bedeutung der sozialen Grundrechte für die Entwicklung der EU', *Zeitschrift für Sozialhilfe und Sozialgesetzbuch (ZFSH/SGB)*, 42/10: 579–88.

Bieber, R., and Monar, J. (1995) (eds.), *Justice and Home Affairs in the European Union: The Development of the Third Pillar* (Brussels: European University Press).

Bigo, D., and Leaveau, R. (1992), *L'Europe de la sécurité intérieure* (Paris: Institut des hautes études de la sécurité intérieure).

Blankenburg, E. (2000), *Legal Culture in Five Central European Countries* (The Hague: Netherlands Scientific Council for Government), WRR Working Documents W 111.

Bodansky, D. (1991), 'Scientific Uncertainty and the Precautionary Principle', *Environment*, 33: 4–5, 43–4.

Bohman, J. (1998), 'Survey Article: The Coming of Age of Deliberative Democracy', *Journal of Political Philosophy*, 6/4: 400–25.

Boldrin, M., and Canova, F. (2001), 'Inequality and Convergence in Europe's Regions: Reconsidering European Regional Policies', *Economic Policy: A European Forum*, 0/32: 205–45.

Boltho, A. (1989), 'European and United States Regional Differentials: A Note', *Oxford Review of Economic Policy*, 5/2: 105–15.

Bonino, E. (1998), *Le Figaro*, 7 April.

Borrás, S., and Greve, B. (2004) (eds.), 'The Open Method of Coordination in the European Union', special issue, *Journal of European Public Policy*, 11/2: 185–208.

Borrás, S., and Jacobsson, K. (2004), 'The Open Method of Coordination and the New Governance Patterns in the EU', *Journal of European Public Policy*, 11/2: 185–208.

Börzel, T. A. (2001), 'Non-Compliance in the European Union: Pathology or Statistical Artifact?', *Journal of European Public Policy*, 8/5: 803–24.

Börzel, T. A., and Cichowski, R. (2003) (eds.), *The State of the European Union, vi, Law Politics and Society* (Oxford: Oxford University Press).

Börzel, T. A., and Hosli, M. (2003), 'Brussels between Bern and Berlin. Comparative Federalism Meets the European Union', *Governance*, 16/2: 179–202.

Börzel, T. A., and Risse, T. (2000), *When Europeanization Hits Home: Europeanization and Domestic Change* (San Domenico di Fiesole: EUI–Robert Schuman Centre for Advanced Studies), RSC Working Paper No. 2000/56.

Bowler, I. R. (1985), *Agriculture under the Common Agricultural Policy: a Geography* (Manchester: Manchester University Press).

Bradley, K. St Clair (1998), 'The GMO-Committee on Transgenic Maize: Alien Corn, or the Transgenic Procedural Maize', in van Schendelen (ed.), *EU Committees as Influential Policymakers* (Aldershot: Ashgate), 207–22.

Branch, A. P., and Øhrgaard, J. (1999), 'Trapped in the Supranational-Intergovernmental Dichotomy: A Response to Stone Sweet and Sandholz', *Journal of European Public Policy*, 6/1: 123–43.

Brunetta, R., and Trenti, L. (1995), 'Italy: The Social Consequences of Economic and Monetary Union', *Labour*, 149–201.

Buchan, D. (1993), *Europe: The Strange Superpower* (Aldershot: Dartmouth).

Buiges, P., and Sheehy, J. (1994), 'European Integration and the Internal Market Programme', paper presented at the ESRC/COST A7 conference, University of Exeter, 8–11 Sept.

Bull, H. (1982), 'Civilian Power Europe: A Contradiction in Terms?', *Journal of Common Market Studies*, 21/1: 149–65.

Bulmer, S. (1994), 'The Governance of the European Union: A New Institutionalist Approach', *Journal of Public Policy*, 13/4: 351–80.

Bulmer, S., and Burch, M. (2002), 'British Devolution and European Policy-Making: A Step Change Towards Multi-Level Governance', *Politique Europeene*, 6/2002: 114–36.

Bulmer, S., and Lequesne, C. (2005) (eds.), *Member States and the European Union* (Oxford: Oxford University Press).

Bulmer, S., and Patterson, W. (1987), *The Federal Republic of Germany and the European Community* (London: Unwin Hyman).

Buonanno, L. (2005), 'Politics versus Science: Apportioning Competency in the European Food Safety Authority and the European Commission', in Ansell and Vogel (eds.), *Why the Beef? The Contested Governance of European Food Safety* (Cambridge, Mass.: MIT Press), forthcoming.

Burgess, M. (1989), *Federalism and European Union: Political Ideas, Influences and Strategies in the European Community, 1972–1987* (London: Routledge).

Burley, A.-M., and Mattli, W. (1993), 'Europe Before the Court: A Political Theory of Legal Integration', *International Organization*, 47/1: 41–76.

Cafruny, A. W., and Rosenthal, G. G. (1993) (eds.), *The State of the European Community, II: The Maastricht Debates and Beyond* (Boulder: Lynne Rienner).

Cameron, D. (1992), 'The 1992 Initiative: Causes and Consequences', in Sbragia (ed.), *Euro-Politics: Institutions and Policymaking in the 'New' European Community* (Washington: Brookings Institution), 23–74.

Cameron, D. (1995), 'Transnational Relations and the Development of European Economic and Monetary Union', in Risse (ed.), *Bringing Transnational Relations Back In: Non-State Actors, Domestic Structures and International Institutions* (Cambridge: Cambridge University Press), 37–78.

Cameron, D. (2004), 'The Stalemate in the Constitutional IGC over the Definition of a Qualified Majority', *European Union Politics*, 5/3: 373–91.

Camm, T., and Bowles, D. (2000), 'Animal Welfare and the Treaty of Rome: Legal Analysis of the Protocol on Animal Welfare and Welfare Standards in the European Union', *Journal of Environmental Law*, 12/2: 197–205.

Cantley, M. (1995), 'The Regulation of Modern Biotechnology: A Historical and European Perspective: A Case Study in How Societies Cope with New Knowledge in the Last Quarter of the Twentieth Century', in Rehm and Reed (eds.), *Biotechnology: Legal, Economic and Ethical Dimensions*, xii (Weinheim: VCH), 506–681.

Capelletti, M., Seccombe, M., and Weiler, J. (1986) (eds.), *Integration through Law: Europe and the American Federal Experience* (New York: De Gruyter).

Caporaso, J. A. (1997), 'Across the Great Divide: Integrating Comparative and International Politics', *International Studies Quarterly*, 41/4: 563–92.

Carlsnaes, W., Sjursen, H., and White, B. (2004) (eds.), *Contemporary European Foreign Policy* (London: Sage).

Casey, B. (2003), 'Coordinating "Coordination": Beyond "Streamlining" ', in Verband Deutscher Rentenversicherungsträger (VDR) (ed.), *Offene Koordinierung in der Alterssicherung in der Europäischen Union* (Frankfurt a.M.: VDR), DRV Schriften 34, 89–97, special issue, *Deutsche Rentenversicherung*.

Cecchini, P. with Catinat, M., and Jacquemin, A. (1988), *The European Challenge 1992: The Benefits of a Single Market* (Aldershot: Wildwood House).

Chalmers, D. (2003), 'Food for Thought: Reconciling European Risks and Traditional Ways of Life', *Modern Law Review*, 66/4: 532–64.

Chalmers, D. (2004), *The Dynamics of Judicial Authority and the Constitutional Treaty* (New York: New York University School of Law, Jean Monnet Program/Woodrow Wilson School of

Government, Princeton University), Jean Monnet Working Paper 5/04, available on-line at *www.jeanmonnetprogram.org/papers/*.

Chaumette, P. (1998), 'La politique commune de pêches', in Beurier, Chaumette, and Proutiere-Maulion, *Droits maritimes: Exploitation et protection de l'Océan*, iii (Lyon: Juris-Éd.), 67–108.

Checkel, J. (1999), 'Norms, Institutions, and National Identity in Contemporary Europe', *International Studies Quarterly*, 43: 83–114.

Checkel, J. (2001), *Taking Deliberation Seriously*, ARENA Working Paper 01/14, available on-line at *www.arena.uio.no/publications/*.

Checkel, J. (2003), "Going Native" in Europe? Theorizing Social Interaction in European Institutions', *Comparative Political Studies*, 36/1–2: 209–31.

Checkel, J., and Moravcsik, A. (2001), 'A Constructivist Research Program in EU Studies?', *European Union Politics*, 2: 219–49.

Christiansen, T., Jørgensen, K. E., and Wiener, A. (1999), 'The Social Construction of Europe', special issue, *Journal of European Public Policy*, 6: 528–44.

Christiansen, T., Jørgensen, K. E., and Wiener, A. (2001) (eds.), *The Social Construction of Europe* (London: Sage).

Christoforou, T. (2003), 'The Precautionary Principle and Democratizing Expertise: A European Legal Perspective', *Science and Public Policy*, 30/3: 205–11.

Cichowski, R. (2001), 'Litigation, Compliance and European Integration: The Preliminary Ruling Procedure and EU Nature Conservation Policy', paper presented at the Annual Meeting of the European Community Studies Association, Madison, Wisconsin, 31 May–2 June.

Cini, M., and McGowan, L. (1998), *Competition Policy in the European Union* (London: Macmillan).

Cloos, J., Reinesch, G., Vignes, D., and Weyland, J. (1994), *Le Traité de Maastricht: genèse, analyse, commentaires* (Brussels: Bruylant).

Closa, C. (2004), 'The Convention Method and the Transformation of EU Constitutional Politics' in Eriksen, Fossum, and Menéndez (eds.), *Developing a Constitution for Europe* (London: Routledge), 183–206.

Cockfield, Lord (1994), *The European Union: Creating the Single Market* (London: Wiley Chancery Law).

Cohen, J., and Sabel, C. (2003), 'Sovereignty and Solidarity in the EU', in Zeitlin and Trubek (eds.), *Governing Work and Welfare in a New Economy: European and American Experiments* (Oxford: Oxford University Press), 345–75.

Collins, D. (1975), *The European Communities: The Social Policy of the First Phase*, 2 vols. (London: Martin Robertson).

Collins, K., and Earnshaw, D. (1992), 'The Implementation and Enforcement of European Community Environment Legislation', *Environmental Politics*, 1/4: 213–49.

Colwell, A., and Shutt, J. (2002), *The Future of EU Regional Policy 2006–2013: Issues and Responses* (Manchester: Centre for Local Economic Strategies).

Commission (1977–), *The Agricultural Situation in the European Union*, DG AGRI (previously *The Agricultural Situation in the Community*).

Commission (1981–), *Annual Reports on Competition Policy* (Luxembourg: Office for Official Publications of the European Communities).

Commission (1985a), *Completing the Internal Market: White Paper from the Commission to the European Council*, COM (85) 310 final.

Commission (1985b), Internal memo from DGIII to DGXI, photocopy.

Commission (1986), *A Community Framework for the Regulation of Biotechnology*, Communication from the Commission to the Council, COM (86) 573.

Commission (1987*a*), *The Single Act: A New Frontier for Europe*, COM (87) 100.

Commission (1987*b*), *Report on Financing of the Community Budget*, COM (87) 101.

Commission (1988), *Proposal for a Council Directive on the Deliberate Release to the Environment of Genetically Modified Organisms*, COM (88) 160 final.

Commission (1990*a*), *Association Agreements with the Countries of Central and Eastern Europe: A General Outline*, COM (90) 398 final.

Commission (1990*b*), *The Development of the Community's Relations with the Countries of Central and Eastern Europe*, SEC (90) 194.

Commission (1991), *Report 1991 from the Commission to the Council and the European Parliament on the Common Fisheries Policy*, SEC (91) 2288 final.

Commission (1992*a*), *From the Single Act to Maastricht and Beyond: The Means to Match our Ambitions*, COM (92) 2000.

Commission (1992*b*), *Europe and the Challenge of Enlargement*, Bulletin of the EC, supplement 3/92.

Commission (1992*c*), *Towards a Closer Association with the Countries of Central and Eastern Europe*, SEC (92) 2301 final.

Commission (1993*a*), *Towards Sustainability: A European Community Programme of Policy and Action in Relation to the Environment and Sustainable Development* (Luxembourg: Office for Official Publications of the European Communities).

Commission (1993*b*), *Towards a Closer Association with the Countries of Central and Eastern Europe*, SEC (93) 648 final.

Commission (1993*c*), *Growth, Competitiveness, Employment: The Challenges and Ways Forward into the 21st Century*, COM (93) 700 final.

Commission (1994*a*), *The Europe Agreements and Beyond: A Strategy to Prepare the Countries of Central and Eastern Europe for Accession*, COM (94) 320 final.

Commission (1994*b*), *European Social Policy: A Way Forward for the Union, A White Paper*.

Commission (1994*c*), *Follow-up to Commission Communication on 'The Europe Agreements and Beyond: A Strategy to Prepare the Countries of Central and Eastern Europe for Accession'*, COM (94) 361 final.

Commission (1995), *Preparation of the Associated Countries of Central and Eastern Europe for Integration into the Internal Market of the Union, White Paper*, COM (95) 163 final.

Commission (1996*a*), *Monitoring the Common Fisheries Policy*, COM (96) 100 final.

Commission (1996*b*), *Report on Directive 90/220/EEC on Genetically Modified Organisms*, IP/96/1148, 10 Dec.

Commission (1996*c*), *First Report on Economic and Social Cohesion* (Luxembourg: Office for Official Publications of the European Communities).

Commission (1997*a*), *Agenda 2000: For a Stronger and Wider Union*, COM (97) 2000, Bulletin of the EU, Supplement 5/97.

Commission (1997*b*), *The Future for the Market in Fisheries Products in the European Union: Responsibility, Partnership, and Competitiveness*, Communication from the Commission to the Council and the European Parliament, COM (97) 719.

Commission (1997*c*), *Commission Opinion on Poland's Application for Membership of the European Union*, COM (97) 2002.

Commission (1998*a*), *Single Market Scoreboard*, No. 3, Oct.

Commission (1998*b*), *Fisheries Monitoring under the Common Fisheries Policy*, Communication from the Commission to the Council and the European Parliament, COM (98) 92.

Commission (1999*a*), *Sixteenth Annual Report on Monitoring the Application of Community Law (1998)*, COM (1999) 301 final.

Commission (1999*b*), *Agricultural Council: Political Agreement on CAP Reform, Newsletter*, special edition, DG AGRI, 11 Mar.

Commission (1999c), *White Paper on Modernization of the Rules Implementing Articles 85 and 86 of the EC Treaty*, 28 Apr.

Commission (2000a), *Seventeenth Annual Report on Monitoring the Application of Community Law (1999)*, COM (2000) 92 final.

Commission (2000b), *White Paper on Food Safety*, COM (1999) 719 final.

Commission (2000c), *Commission Communication on the Precautionary Principle*, COM (2000) 1 final.

Commission (2000d), *Social Policy Agenda*, COM (2000) 379 final.

Commission (2000e), *Reforming the Commission: White Paper*, Part I, COM (2000) 200 final.

Commission (2000f), *The Community Budget: The Facts and Figures* (Luxembourg: Office for Official Publications of the European Communities).

Commission (2001a), *Eighteenth Annual Report on Monitoring the Application of Community Law (2000)*, COM (2001) 309 final.

Commission (2001b), *Commission proposes new Action Programme for the Environment*, Press Releases IP/01/102, 24/01/2001.

Commission (2001c), *The Challenge of Environmental Financing in the Candidate Countries*, Communication from the Commission, COM (2001) 304 final.

Commission (2001d), *European Governance: A White Paper*, COM (2001) 428 final.

Commission (2001e), *Development of the Schengen Information System II*, Communication from the Commission to the Council and the European Parliament, COM (2001) 720.

Commission (2001f), *Ninth Survey on State Aid in the European Union*, COM (2001) 403.

Commission (2001g), *Unity, Solidarity, Diversity for Europe, its People and its Territory: Second Report on Economic and Social Cohesion*, COM (2001) 24.

Commission (2002a), *Nineteenth Annual Report on Monitoring the Application of Community Law (2001)*, COM (2002) 324 final.

Commission (2002b), *Second Biennial Report on the Application of the Principle of Mutual Recognition in the Single Market*, COM (2002) 419 final.

Commission (2002c), *The Internal Market: Ten Years without Frontiers*.

Commission (2002d), *Communication from the Commission: Free Movement of Workers: Achieving the Full Benefits and Potential*, COM (2002) 694 final.

Commission (2002e), *European Union Public Finance* (Luxembourg: Office for Official Publications of the European Communities).

Commission (2002f), *Communication from the Commission: Taking Stock of Five Years of the European Employment Strategy*, COM (2002) 416 final.

Commission (2003–), *Factsheet on Rural Development in the European Union*, available on-line at *http://europa.eu.int/comm/agriculture*.

Commission (2003a), *Commission Recommendation on the Broad Guidelines of the Economic Policies of the Member States and the Community [2003–2005]*, COM (2003) 170 final.

Commission (2003b), *Communication from the Commission to the Council, Strengthening the Social Dimension of the Lisbon Strategy: Streamlining Open Coordination in the Field of Social Protection [2003–2009]*, COM (2003) 261 final.

Commission (2003c), *Communication from the European Commission: Modernising Social Protection for More and Better Jobs—A Comprehensive Approach Contributing to Making Work Pay*, COM (2003) 842 final.

Commission (2003d), *The Future of the European Employment Strategy*.

Commission (2003e), *Twentieth Annual Report on Monitoring the Application of Community Law (2002)*, COM (2003) 669 final.

Commission (2003*f*), *Financial Report 2002* (Luxembourg: Office for Official Publications of the European Communities).

Commission (2004*a*), *Report on the Implementation of the Internal Market Strategy (2003–6)*, COM (2004) 22 final.

Commission (2004*b*), *2003 Environment Policy Review: Consolidating the Environmental Pillar of Sustainable Development*, Communication from the Commission to the Council and the European Parliament, COM (2003) 745 final/2.

Commission (2004*c*), *Opinion on the Application of Croatia for Membership of the European Union*, COM (2004) 257.

Commission (2004*d*), *European Neighbourhood Policy: Strategy Paper*, COM (2004) 373.

Commission (2004*e*), *Recommendation on Turkey's Progress towards Accession*, COM (2004) 656.

Commission (2004*f*), *State of Play on GMO Authorizations under EU Law*, MEMO/04/17.

Commission (2004*g*), *Achievements in Agricultural Policy under Commissioner Franz Fischler, 1995–2004*, available on-line at *http://europa.eu.int/comm/agriculture/*.

Commission (2004*h*), *Third Report on Economic and Social Cohesion*, COM (2004) 107.

Commission (2004*i*), *Building our Common Future: Policy Challenges and Budgetary Means of the Enlarged Union 2007–2013*, COM (2004) 101.

Commission (2004*j*), *Financing the European Union*, COM (2004) 505.

Commission (2004*k*), Press Release IP/04/189, 10 Feb.

Commission (2004*l*), *Communication from the Commission concerning a European Health Insurance Card*, COM (2003) 73 final.

Commission (2004*m*), *Proposal for a Directive of the European Parliament and of the Council on Services in the Internal Market*, COM (2004) 2 final.

Commission (2004*n*), *White Paper on Services of General Interest*, COM (2004) 374 final.

Commission (2004*o*), *A Pro-active Competition Policy for a Competitive Europe*, Communication, COM (2004) 293.

Commission (2004*p*), *XXXIIIrd Report on Competition Policy–2003*, SEC (2004) 658.

Commission (2004*q*), *Commission Notice on Cooperation within the Network of Competition Authorities*, available on-line at *http://europa.eu.int/comm/competition*.

Commission (2004*r*), *General Budget of the European Union for the Financial Year 2004* (Luxembourg: Office for Official Publications of the European Communities).

Commission (2004*t*) *Facts and Figures of CFP*, Brussels.

Committee of Independent Experts (1999), *First Report on Allegations regarding Fraud, Mismanagement and Nepotism in the European Commission*, 15 March, available on-line at *www.europarl.eu.int/experts/*.

Conant, L. (2002), *Justice Contained: Law and Politics in the European Union* (Ithaca: Cornell University Press).

Cooter, R. D., and Ginsburg, T. (1996), 'Comparative Judicial Discretion: An Empirical Test of Economic Models', *International Review of Law and Economics*, 16: 295–313.

Corden, W. M. (1997), *Trade Policy and Economic Welfare*, 2nd edn. (Oxford: Clarendon Press).

Council of European Municipalities and Regions (2002), *The Added-Value of European Union Cohesion Policy* (Paris and Brussels: Council of European Municipalities and Regions).

Council of the European Union (1988), *Presidency Conclusions*, European Council in Rhodes, 2–3 Dec., SN 4443/1/88.

Council of the European Union (1989), *Presidency Conclusions*, European Council in Strasbourg, 8–9 Dec., SN 441/2/89.

Council of the European Union (1994), *Presidency Conclusions*, European Council in Corfu, 24–25 June, SN 150/94.

Council of the European Union (1995), *Presidency Conclusions*, Madrid European Council, 15–16 Dec., SN 400/95.

Council of the European Union (1999), *Presidency Conclusions*, European Council in Berlin, 24–25 Mar.

Council of the European Union (2000), *Presidency Conclusions*, Santa Maria da Feira European Council, 19–20 June, SN 200/00.

Council of the European Union (2001), *Presidency Conclusions*, Laeken European Council, 14–15 Dec., SN 300/1/01 REV 1.

Council of the European Union (2002), *Presidency Conclusions*, Copenhagen European Council, 12–13 Dec., SN 400/02.

Council of the European Union (2003), *Council Regulation No. 1/2003 of 16 December 2002 on the Implementation of the Rules on Competition laid down in Articles 81 and 82 of the Treaty (OJ, L1/1, 4.1.2003).*

Council of Ministers (2002), 2445th Council Meeting, Agriculture, Brussels, 15 July, 10747/02.

Cowles, M. G. (1994), 'The Politics of Big Business in the European Community: Setting the Agenda for a New Europe', Ph.D. dissertation, The American University, Washington, DC.

Cowles, M. G. (1997), 'Organizing Industrial Coalitions: A Challenge for the Future?', in Wallace and Young (eds.), *Participation and Policy-Making in the European Union* (Oxford: Clarendon Press), 116–40.

Cowles, M. G., Caporaso, J. A., and Risse, T. (2001) (eds.), *Transforming Europe: Europeanization and Domestic Change* (Ithaca: Cornell University Press).

Couliou, J.-R. (1998), *La pêche bretonne: les ports de Bretagne sud face à leur avenir* (Rennes: Presses Universitaires de Rennes).

Crean, K., and Symes, D. (1996) (eds.), *Fisheries Management in Crisis: A Social Science Perspective* (Oxford: Fishing News Books).

Cremona, M. (2003) (ed.), *The Enlargement of the European Union* (Oxford: Oxford University Press).

Criado Alonso, F. (1996), 'Regional Participation in Governance in the EU: The Cases of Galicia, the Basque Country, and Scotland in the Fisheries Policy Field', Bruges, thesis for the Master of European Studies, College of Europe.

Crombez, C. (1997), 'The Co-Decision Procedure in the European Union', *Legislative Studies Quarterly*, 22: 97–119.

Dalton, R. J. (1991), 'Comparative Politics in the Industrial Democracies: From the Golden Age to Island Hopping', in Crotty (ed.), *Political Science*, II (Evanston: University of Illinois Press), 15–43.

Dam, K. W. (1970), *The GATT: Law and International Economic Organization* (Chicago: University of Chicago Press).

Dashwood, A. (1977), 'Hastening Slowly: The Communities' Path Towards Harmonization' in Wallace, Wallace, and Webb (eds.), *Policy-Making in the European Communities* (Chichester: Wiley), 273–99.

Dashwood, A. (1983), 'Hastening Slowly: The Communities' Path towards Harmonization', in Wallace in Wallace, Wallace, and Webb (eds.), *Policy-Making in the European Communities*, 2nd edn. (Chichester: Wiley), 177–208.

Dehousse, R. (1998), *The European Court of Justice* (London: Macmillan).

De Grauwe, P. (2002), *Economics of Monetary Union*, 5th edn. (Oxford: Oxford University Press).

Deighton, A. (1997) (ed.), *Western European Union 1954–1977: Defence, Security, Integration* (Oxford: St Anthony's College).

de Jesus, J. A. R. (1998), 'The Portugese Fisheries Policy in the Context of European Integration: Challenges and Perspectives', College of Europe, Bruges, thesis for the Master of European Studies.

De La Porte, C., and Nanz, P. (2004), 'OMC—A Deliberative-Democratic Mode of Governance? The Cases of Employment and Pensions', *Journal of European Public Policy*, 11/2: 267–88.

De La Porte, C., and Pochet, P. (2004), 'Participation in the OMC: The Cases of Employment and Social Inclusion', Brussels, mimeo.

De La Porte, C., Pochet, P., and Room, G. (2001), 'Social Benchmarking, Policy-Making and New Governance in the EU', *Journal of European Social Policy*, 11/4: 291–301.

della Sala, V. (2004), 'Maastricht to Modernization: EMU and the Italian Social State', in Martin and Ross (eds.), *Euros and Europeans: Monetary Integration and the European Model of Society* (Cambridge: Cambridge University Press), 126–41.

de Kerchove, G., and Weyembergh, A. (2002) (eds.), *L'espace penal européen: enjeux et perspectives* (Brussels: Éditions de l'Université de Bruxelles).

de Schoutheete, P. (1986), *La Cooperation politique européene*, 2nd edn. (Brussels: Labor).

Del Vecchio, A. (1995), 'La politique de la pêche: axe de développement', *Revue du Marché Unique Européen*, 2: 27–36.

den Boer, M. (1994), 'The Quest for European Policing: Rhetoric and Justification in a Disorderly Debate', in Anderson and den Boer (eds.), *Policing Across National Boundaries* (London: Pinter), 174–96.

Denza, E. (1996), 'The Community as a Member of International Organizations', in Emiliou and O'Keeffe (eds.), *The European Union and World Trade Law: After the Uruguay Round* (Chichester: Wiley), 3–18.

De Rynck, S., and McAleavey, P. (2001), 'The Cohesion Deficit in Structural Fund Policy', *Journal of European Public Policy*, 8/4: 541–57.

de Swaan, A. (1992), 'Perspectives for Transnational Social Policy', *Government and Opposition*, 27/1: 33–52.

Devuyst, Y. (2004), *EU Decision-Making after the Treaty Establishing a Constitution for Europe*, Policy Paper No. 9 (Pittsburgh: University of Pittsburgh, European Union Center).

Dinan, D. (1998), 'The Commission and Enlargement', in Redmond and Rosenthal (eds.), *The Expanding European Union: Past, Present, Future* (Boulder: Lynne Rienner), 17–40.

Dinan, D. (2004), *Europe Recast: A History of European Union* (London: Palgrave Macmillan).

Dogan, R. (1997), 'Comitology: Little Procedures with Big Implications', *West European Politics*, 20: 31–60.

Donahue, J. D., and Pollack, M. A. (2001), 'Centralization and Its Discontents: The Rhythms of Federalism in the United States and the European Union', in Nicolaidis and Howse (eds.), *The Federal Vision: Legitimacy and Levels of Governance in the United States in the European Union* (Oxford: Oxford University Press), 73–117.

Dowding, K. (2000), 'Institutionalist Research on the European Union: A Critical Review', *European Union Politics*, 1: 125–44.

Dubbink, W., and van Vliet, M. (1996), 'Market Regulation versus Co-management', *Marine Policy*, 20/6: 499–516.

du Guerny, S., and Bauer, A. (1994), 'Bruxelles n'accordera pas de clause de sauvegarde à la pêche', *Les Échos*, 14 Feb.

Dunnet, D. (1991), 'The European Bank for Reconstruction and Development: A Legal Survey', *Common Market Law Review*, 28/3: 571–97.

Drahos, M. (2001), *Convergence of Competition Laws and Policies in the European Community* (Duventer: Kluwer).

Drake, H. (2000), *Jacques Delors: Perspectives on a European Leader* (London: Routledge).

Duchêne, F., Szczepanik, E., and Legg, W. (1985), *New Limits on European Agriculture: Politics and the Common Agricultural Policy* (London: Croom Helm).

Duisenberg, W. (1998), 'EMU: The Building of One Monetary System in the European Union', speech delivered in Tokyo, 16 Jan., available on-line at *www.ecb.int/press*.

Dyson, K. (1994), *Elusive Union: The Process of Economic and Monetary Union in Europe* (London: Longman).

Dyson, K., and Featherstone, K. (1999), *The Road to Maastricht: Negotiating Economic and Monetary Union* (Oxford: Oxford University Press).

Eberlein, B., and Kerwer, D. (2004), 'New Governance in the European Union: A Theoretical Perspective', *Journal of Common Market Studies*, 42/1: 121–42.

Ebsen, I. (2002), 'Das EG-Wettbewerbsrecht und die deutsche Sozialversicherung', in von Bogdandy (ed.), *Solidarität und europäische Integration, Kolloquium zum 65: Geburtstag von Manfred Zuleeg* (Baden-Baden: Nomos), 21–40.

Economist, various issues.

ECOTEC (2003), *Evaluation of the Added Value and Costs of the European Structural Funds in the UK*, Final Report to Department of Trade and Industry (DTI) and Office of the Deputy Prime Minister (ODPM) (London: DTI/ODPM).

EDS (Europavertretung der Deutschen Sozialversicherung, European Representation of German Social Insurance) (2004), *Europäische Sozialpolitik: Einblicke 2003/2004* (Brussels: Europavertretung der Deutschen Sozialversicherung), Aug.

Edwards, G. (1998), 'The Council of Ministers and Enlargement: A Search for Efficiency, Effectiveness, and Accountability', in Redmond and Rosenthal (eds.), *The Expanding European Union: Past, Present, Future* (Boulder: Lynne Rienner), 41–64.

Edwards, G., and Nuttall, S. (1994), 'Common Foreign and Security Policy', in Duff, Pinder and Price (eds.), *Maastricht and Beyond: Building the European Union* (London: Routledge), 84–103.

Edwards, G., and Spence, D. (1997) (eds.), *The European Commission*, 2nd edn. (London: Longman).

EEA (European Environment Agency) (1999), *Environment in the European Union at the Turn of the Century* (Copenhagen: EEA), Environmental Assessment Report No. 2, available on-line at *http://reports.eea.eu.int*.

EET (European Employment Taskforce) (2003), *Jobs, Jobs, Jobs: Creating More Employment in Europe*, EET Report, Brussels, Nov.

Egeberg, M. (1999), 'Transcending Intergovernmentalism? Identity and Role Perceptions of National Officials in EU Decision Making', *Journal of European Public Policy*, 6/3: 456–74.

Eichener, V. (1993), *Social Dumping or Innovative Regulation Processes and Outcomes of European Decision-Making in the Sector of Health and Safety at Work Harmonization* (Florence: European University Institute), EUI Working Papers in Social and Political Sciences (SPS) No. 92/28,

Eichener, V. (1997), 'Effective European Problem Solving: Lessons from the Regulation of Occupational Safety and Environmental Protection', *Journal of European Public Policy*, 4/4: 591–608.

Eichener, V. (2000), *Das Entscheidungssystem der Europäischen Union: institutionelle Analyse und demokratietheoretische Bewertung* (Opladen: Leske & Budrich).

Eichengreen, B. (1992), *Should the Maastricht Treaty be Saved?* (Princeton: Princeton University Economics Department), Princeton Studies in International Finance, No. 74.

Eichenhofer, E. (1992) (ed.), *Die Zukunft des koordinierenden Europäischen Sozialrechts* (Cologne: Carl Heymanns).

Eichenhofer, E. (2003a), *Sozialrecht der Europäischen Union* (Berlin: Erich Schmidt).

Eichenhofer, E. (2003b), Unionsbürgerschaft—Sozialbürgerschaft?, *Zeitschrift für ausländisches und internationales Arbeits- und Sozialrecht*, 17/3-4: 404–17.

Eichenhofer, E. (2004*a*), 'Europäisierung sozialer Sicherung', *Deutsche Rentenversicherung*, 4: 200–10.

Eichenhofer, E. (2004*b*), 'Diskriminierungsschutz und Privatautonomie', *Deutsches Verwaltungsblatt*, 119/17 (Sept. 1): 1078–86.

Eichhorst, W. (1998), *European Social Policy between National and Supranational Regulation: Posted Workers in the Framework of Liberalized Services Provisions* (Cologne: Max Planck Institute for the Study of Societies), MPIfG Discussion Paper 98/6.

Eichhorst, W. (2000), *Europäische Sozialpolitik zwischen nationaler Autonomie und Marktfreiheit: die Entsendung von Arbeitnehmern in der EU* (Frankfurt a.M.: Campus).

Eising, R. (1999), 'Governance in the European Union: A Comparative Assessment', in Kohler-Koch and Eising (eds.), *The Transformation of Governance in the European Union* (London: Routledge), 263–97.

Eising, R. (2003), 'Interest Groups in the European Union', in Cini (ed.), *European Union Politics* (Oxford: Oxford University Press), 192–207.

Elster, J. (1998) (ed.), *Deliberative Democracy* (Cambridge: Cambridge University Press).

EMEA (European Agency for the Evaluation of Medicinal Products), Yearly Reports (London: EMEA).

Emmert, F. (1996), *Europarecht* (Munich: C. H. Beck).

Endo, K. (1999), *The Presidency of the European Commission under Jacques Delors: The Politics of Shared Leadership* (Basingstoke: Macmillan with St. Anthony's College, Oxford).

Epstein, D., and O'Halloran, S. (1999), *Delegating Powers: A Transaction Cost Politics Approach to Policy Making under Separate Powers* (Cambridge: Cambridge University Press).

Eriksen, E. O., and Fossum, J. E. (2000), 'Post-national Integration', in Eriksen and Fossum (eds.), *Democracy in the European Union* (London: Routledge), 1–28.

Eriksen, E. O., and Fossum, J. E. (2003), *Closing the Legitimacy Gap?*, available on-line at *www.arena.uio.no/ ecsa/papers/FossumEriksen.pdf*.

Eureport, various issues.

Eureport social, various issues.

European Court of Auditors (2000), '*Greening the CAP'*, *with the Commission's replies*, Special Report No. 14/2000, OJ: Information and Notices 43 (2000/C 353/01), 1–56.

European Court of Auditors (2003), *Annual Report Concerning the Financial Year 2002*, Official Journal of the European Union, C286.

European Parliament (EP) (1984), *Draft Treaty Establishing the European Union* (Luxembourg: European Parliament).

European Parliament (EP) (1989), *Report drawn up on behalf of the Committee on the Environment, Public Health, and Consumer Protection on the Proposal from the Commission to the Council*, COM (88) 160 final, Doc. C 2-73/88.

European Parliament (EP) (1990), *Recommendation of the Committee on the Environment, Public Health and Consumer Protection on the COMMON POSITION of the Council for a Directive on the Deliberate Release to the Environment of Genetically Modified Organisms* (C3–228/89), Doc A3-0049/90 of 23 Feb.

European Parliament (EP) (1993), *The Power of the European Parliament in the European Union*, DG for Research, Working Paper Series E-1 (Luxembourg: European Parliament).

European Parliament (EP) (1996*a*), *Bilateral Agreements and International Fishing Conventions* (Luxembourg: European Parliament, DG for Research).

European Parliament (EP) (1996*b*), Committee on the Environment, Public Health and Consumer Protection, *Working Document on Implementation of Community Environmental Law* (Rapporteur: Ken Collins), PE 219, 240 (Brussels).

European Parliament (EP) (2002), *On the Impact Evaluation and Future of the European Employment Strategy—Overview of Technical Analysis*, Committee on Employment and Social Affairs, 24 June.

European Report (2004), *Biotechnology: Contrasting Reactions to Authorisation for Bt11 Transgenic Corn*, European Report, 29 May.

European Voice, 11 November 1991.

Evans, P. B., Jacobson, H. K., and Putnam, R. D. (1993) (eds.), *Double-Edged Diplomacy: International Bargaining and Domestic Politics* (Berkeley: University of California Press).

Everson, M., Majone, G., Metcalfe, L., and Schout, A. (2001), *The Role of Specialized Agencies in Decentralising EU Governance*, Report presented to the Commission Working Group on Governance, available on-line at *http://europa.eu.int/comm/governance/areas/group6/contribution_en.pdf*.

Falke, J. (2000), 'Soziale Grundrechte als Bestandteil einer Charta der Grundrechte der Europäischen Union', in Bremische Bürgerschaft (ed.), *Charta der Grundrechte der Europäischen Union: Fachtagung am 26. September 2000* (Bremen: Bremische Bürgerschaft), 27–72.

Falkner, G. (1994), 'Die Sozialpolitik der EG. Rechtgrundlagen und Entwicklung von Rom bis Maastricht', in Haller and Schachner-Blazizek (eds.), *Wirtschaftliche Integration, soziale Gerechtigkeit und Demokratie* (Graz: Leykam), 221–46.

Falkner, G. (1998), *EU Social Policy in the 1990s: Towards a Corporatist Policy Community* (London: Routledge).

Falkner, G. (2003a), 'The Interprofessional Social Dialogue at European Level: Past and Future', in Keller and Platzer (eds.), *Industrial Relations and European Integration* (Aldershot: Ashgate), 11–29.

Falkner, G. (2003b), 'The EU's Social Dimension', in Cini (ed.), *European Union Politics* (Oxford: Oxford University Press), 264–77.

Falkner, G., Treib, O., Hartlapp, M., and Leiber, S. (2005), *Complying with Europe: EU Harmonisation and Law in Member States?* (Cambridge: Cambridge University Press), forthcoming.

Farnam, A. (2001), 'Poland's Small Farms Stunt EU Aspirations', *Christian Science Monitor*, Dec. 28.

Fennell, R. (1997), *The Common Agricultural Policy: Continuity and Change* (Oxford: Clarendon Press).

Fernández, J. (2002), 'The Common Agricultural Policy and EU Enlargement: Implications for Agricultural Production in the Central and East European Countries', *Eastern European Economics*, 40/3, 28–50.

Ferrera, M., and Gualmini, E. (2000), 'Italy: Rescue from Without?', in Scharpf and Schmidt (eds.), *From Vulnerability to Competitiveness: Welfare and Work in the Open Economy* (Oxford: Oxford University Press), II, 351–98.

Ferrera, M., and Gualmini, E. (2004), *Rescued by Europe? Social and Labour Market Reforms in Italy from Maastricht to Berlusconi* (Amsterdam: Amsterdam University Press).

Ferrera, M., Hemerijck, A., and Rhodes, M. (2001), 'The Future of the European "Social Model" in the Global Economy', *Journal of Comparative Policy Analysis*, 3/2: 163–90.

Fishing News (1998), article of 20 November 1998.

Flaesch-Mougin, C., Le Bihan, D., and Lequesne, C. (2003) (eds.), *La politique européenne de la pêche: vers un développement durable?* (Rennes: Éditions Apogée).

Flora, P. (1999) (ed.), *State Formation, Nation-Building and Mass Politics in Europe: The Theory of Stein Rokkan* (Oxford: Oxford University Press).

Foden, D., and Magnusson, L. (2003) (eds.), *Five Years' Experience of the Luxembourg Employment Strategy* (Brussels: European Trade Union Institute).

Forster, A. (1994), 'The EC and the WEU' in Moens and Anstis (eds.), *Disconcerted Europe: The Search for a New Security Architecture* (Oxford: Westview), 135–58.

Foster, E. (1992), 'The Franco–German Corps: A "Theological" Debate?', *RUSI Journal*, 137/4: 63–7.

Fraga Estévez, C. (1997), *Report on the Common Fisheries Policy after the Year 2002*, European Parliament, EP 220.887 (Luxembourg).

Franchino, F. (2000), 'Control of the Commission's Executive Functions: Uncertainty, Conflict and Decision Rules', *European Union Politics*, 1: 63–92.

Franchino, F. (2001), 'Delegating Powers in the European Union', paper presented at the Seventh Biennial International Conference of the European Community Studies Association, Madison, 31 May–2 June.

Franklin, M., Marsh, M., and McLaren, L. (1994), 'Uncorking the Bottle: Popular Opposition to European Unification in the Wake of Maastricht', *Journal of Common Market Studies*, 32/4: 455–73.

Franzius, C. (2003), 'Der "Gewährleistungsstaat": ein neues Leitbild für den sich wandelnden Staat', *Der Staat*, 42/4: 493–517.

Frieden, J. (1991), 'Invested Interests: The Politics of National Economic Policies in a World of Global Finance', *International Organization* 45: 425–52.

Friedrich, C. J. (1969), *Europe: An Emergent Nation* (New York: Harper & Row).

Friis, L. (1998), *The End of the Beginning of Eastern Enlargement: Luxembourg Summit and Agenda-setting*, European Integration Online Papers 2/7.

Friis, L. (2003), 'EU Enlargement: And Then There Were 28?', in Bomberg and Stubb (eds.), *The European Union: How Does it Work?* (Oxford: Oxford University Press), 177–94.

Friis, L., and Murphy, A. (2000), 'Turbo-charged Negotiations: The EU and the Stability Pact for South Eastern Europe', *Journal of European Public Policy* 7/5: 767–86.

Fritsch, M., and Hansen, H. (1997), *Rules of Competition and East-West Integration* (Dordrecht: Kluwer).

Fuchs, M. (2003), 'Koordinierung oder Harmonisierung des europäischen Sozialrechts?', *Zeitschrift für ausländisches und internationales Arbeits- und Sozialrecht*, 17/3–4: 379–90.

Fursdon, E. (1980), *The European Defence Community: A History* (London: Macmillan).

Gabel, M., Hix, S., and Schneider, G. (2002), 'Who is Afraid of Cumulative Research? The Scarcity of EU Decision-Making Data and What Can Be Done about This', *European Union Politics*, 3/4: 481–500.

Garrett, G. (1992), 'International Cooperation and Institutional Choice: The European Community's Internal Market', *International Organization*, 46/2: 533–60.

Garrett, G. (1995), 'The Politics of Legal Integration in the European Union', *International Organization*, 49: 171–81.

Garrett, G., and Tsebelis, G. (1996), 'An Institutional Critique of Intergovernmentalism', *International Organization*, 50: 269–99.

Garrett, G., and Weingast, B. (1993), 'Ideas, Interests, and Institutions: Constructing the European Community's Internal Market', in Goldstein and Keohane (eds.), *Ideas and Foreign Policy* (Ithaca: Cornell University Press), 173–206.

Gaskell, G., Allum, N., and Stares, S. (2003), *Eurobarometer 58.0: A Report to the EC Directorate General for Research from the project 'Life Sciences in European Society'* QLG7-CT-1999-00286.

Geddes, A. (2000), *Immigration and European Integration. Towards Fortress Europe?* (Manchester: Manchester University Press).

George, S. (1991), *Politics in the European Union* (Oxford: Oxford University Press).

Gerber, D. (1998), *Law and Competition in Twentieth Century Europe* (Oxford: Clarendon Press).

Gerber, D. (2001), 'Modernising European Competition Law: A Developmental Perspective', *European Competition Law Review*, 22: 122–30.

Giegerich, B., and Wallace, W. (2004), 'Not Such a Soft Power: The External Deployment of European Forces', *Survival* 46/2 (Summer): 63–82.

Giesen, R. (1995), *Sozialversicherungsmonopol und EG-Vertrag* (Baden-Baden: Nomos).

Giesen, R. (2001), *Wettbewerb zwischen Sozialversicherungsträgern und Privatversicherungen nach europäischem Kartellrecht, Soziale Sicherheit und Wettbewerb* (Wiesbaden: Chmielorz), 123–46 (Schriftenreihe des Deutschen Sozialrechtsverbandes, Vol. 48).

Giesen, R. (2004), 'Das BSG, der EG-Vertrag und das deutsche Unfallversicherungsmonopol', *Zeitschrift für europäisches Sozial- und Arbeitsrecht*, 3/4: 151–60.

Global Competition Review (2003), *The 2003 Handbook of Competition Enforcement Agencies* (London: Global Competition Review).

Gnesotto, N. (1990), 'Défence européenne: pourquoi pas les douze?', *Politique Étrangère*, 55/4: 881–3.

Gnesotto, N. (1994), *Lessons of Yugoslavia* (Paris: WEU Institute on Security Studies), Chaillot Paper No. 14.

Goetschy, J. (2003), 'The European Employment Strategy, Multi-level Governance and Policy Coordination: Past, Present and Future', in Zeitlin and Trubek (eds.), *Governing Work and Welfare in a New Economy: European and American Experiments* (Oxford: Oxford University Press), 61–88.

Goetz, K. H., and Margetts, H. Z. (1999), 'The Solitary Center: The Core Executive in Central and Eastern Europe', *Governance* 12/4: 425–53.

Goetz, K. H., and Hix, S. (2001) (eds.), *Europeanised Politics? European Integration and National Political Systems* (London: Frank Cass).

Gohr, A. (2001), 'Der italienische Wohlfahrtsstaat: Entwicklungen, Probleme und die europäische Herausforderung', in Kraus (ed.), *Sozialstaat in Europa* (Wiesbaden: Westdeutscher Verlag), 143–69.

Goldstein, J., and Martin, L. L. (2001), 'Legalization, Trade Liberalization, and Domestic Politics: A Cautionary Note', in Goldstein, Kahler, Keohane, and Slaughter (eds.), *Legalization and World Politics* (Cambridge, Mass.: MIT Press), 219–48.

Goodman, D., and Redclift, M. (1991), *Refashioning Nature: Food, Ecology & Culture* (London: Routledge).

Goodman, D., Sorj, B., and Wilkinson, J. (1987), *From Farming to Biotechnology: A Theory of Agro-Industrial Development* (Oxford: Blackwell).

Gourevich, P. (1978), 'The Second Image Reversed,' *International Organization*, 32/4: 881–912.

Govecor (Economic Governance through Self-Coordination) (2003), *Self-Coordination at the National Level: Towards a Collective 'Gouvernement Economique'*, Final Report, April, Cologne, available on-line at *www.govecor.org*.

Goyder, D. (2003), *EC Competition Law*, 4th edn. (Oxford: Oxford University Press).

Grabbe, H. (1999), *A Partnership for Accession? The Implications of EU Conditionality for the Central and East European Applicants* (San Domenico di Fiesole: EUI–Robert Schuman Centre for Advanced Studies), RSC Working Paper No. 1999/12.

Grabbe, H., and Hughes, K. (1998), *Enlarging the EU Eastwards* (London: Pinter).

Grant, W. (1997), *The Common Agricultural Policy* (New York: St Martin's Press).

Grant, W., Matthews, D., and Newell, P. (2000), *The Effectiveness of European Union Environmental Policy* (Basingstoke: Macmillan).

Graser, A. (2004), 'Sozialrecht ohne Staat? Politik und Recht unter Beingungen der Globalisierung und Dezentralisierung', in Héritier, Stolleis, and Scharpf (eds.), *European and International Regulation after the Nation State* (Baden-Baden: Nomos), 163–84.

Gray, T. S. (1998) (ed.), *The Politics of Fishing* (London: Macmillan).

Greven, M. T. (2000), 'Can the European Union Finally Become a Democracy?', in Greven and Pauly (eds.), *Democracy Beyond the Nation-State: The European Dilemma and the Emerging World Order* (New York: Rowman & Littlefield), 35–61.

Gros, D., and Thygesen, N. (1998), *European Monetary Integration: From the European Monetary System towards Monetary Union, Power Politics*, 2nd edn. (London: Longman).

Grosser, A. (1980), *The Western Alliance: European-American Relations since 1945* (London: Macmillan).

Gruber, L. (2000), *Ruling the World: The Rise of Supranational Institutions* (Princeton: Princeton University Press).

Gualina, E. (2003), 'Challenges to Multi-level Governance: Contradictions and Conflicts in the Europeanization of Italian Regional Policy', *Journal of European Public Policy*, 10/4: 618–36.

Guegen, J., Laurec, A., Maucorps, A. (1990), 'La gestion des pêcheries communautaires et les mécanismes de décision', in Lebullenger and Le Morvan (eds.), *La Communauté européenne et la mer* (Paris: Economica), 145–61.

Guersent, O. (2003), 'The Fight Against Secret Horizontal Agreement in the EC Competition Policy', paper presented to the Fordham Corporate Law Institute.

Guillén, A. M., and Palier, B. (2004) (eds.), *EU Enlargement and Social Policy*, special issue, *Journal of European Social Policy*, 14/3: 203–349.

Haahr, J. H. (2004), 'Open Co-ordination or Advanced Liberal Government', *Journal of European Public Policy*, 11/2: 209–30.

Haas, E. B. [1958] (2004), *The Uniting of Europe* (Stanford: Stanford University Press, reprinted by Notre Dame, Indiana: University of Notre Dame Press).

Haas, E. B. (1961), 'European Integration: The European and Universal Process', *International Organization*, 4: 607–46.

Haas, E. B. (1976), 'Turbulent Fields and the Theory of Regional Integration', *International Organization*, 30 (Spring), 173–212.

Haas, R. (1992), 'Introduction: Epistemic Communities and International Policy Coordination', *International Organization* 46/1: 1–35.

Habermas, J. (1985), *The Theory of Communicative Action*, ii/ii (Boston: Beacon Press).

Habermas, J. (1998), *Between Facts and Norms: Contributions to a Discourse Theory of Law and Democracy* (Cambridge, Mass.: MIT Press).

Hagen, K. P. (1992), 'The Social Dimension: A Quest for a European Welfare State?', in Ferge and Kolberg (eds.), *Social Policy in a Changing Europe* (Boulder: Westview), 281–303.

Hagen, K. P. (1998), 'Towards a Europeanisation of Social Policies? A Scandinavian Perspective', in MIRE, *Comparing Social Welfare Systems in Nordic Countries and France* (Paris: MIRE), 405–22.

Hagen, K. P., Norrman, E., and Sørensen, P. B. (1998), 'Financing the Nordic Welfare States in an Integrating Europe', in Sørensen (ed.), *Tax Policy in the Nordic Countries* (Basingstoke: Macmillan), 138–203.

Haigh, N. (2004) (ed.), *Manual of Environmental Policy: The EU and Britain*, Institute of European Environmental Policy (IEEP) (Leeds: Maney Publishing).

Hailbronner, K. (2004), 'Die Unionsbürgerschaft und das Ende rationaler Jurisprudenz', *Neue Juristische Wochenschrift*, 57/31: 2185–9.

Hall, P. A. (1986), *Governing the Economy: The Politics of State Intervention in Britain and France* (Oxford: Oxford University Press).

Hall, P. A. (1999), 'The Political Economy of Europe in an Era of Interdependence', in Kitschelt *et al.* (eds.), *Continuity and Change in Contemporary Capitalism* (Cambridge: Cambridge University Press), 135–63.

Hall, P. A., and Soskice, D. (2000), *Varieties of Capitalism: The Institutional Foundations of Comparative Advantage* (Oxford: Oxford University Press).

Hall, P. A.. and Taylor, R. C. R. (1996), 'Political Science and the Three New Institutionalisms', *Political Studies*, 44/5: 936–57.

Hancher, L., and Moran, M. (1989), 'Introduction: Regulation and Deregulation', *European Journal of Political Research*, 17/2: 129–36.

Harding, G. (1999), 'Wallström Vows to "Name and Shame" Environmental Laggards', *European Voice* (10–17 Nov.), 2.

Harvie, C. (1994), *The Rise of Regional Europe* (London: Frank Cass).

Hauser, R. (1996), 'Sozialpolitische Optionen in der Europäischen Union', in Fricke (ed.), *Jahrbuch für Arbeit und Technik 1995* (Bonn: Dietz), 232–44.

Haverkate, G., and Huster, S. (1998), *Europäisches Sozialrecht: Eine Einführung* (Baden-Baden: Nomos).

Hayes-Renshaw, F., and Wallace, H. (1997) (eds.), *The Council of Ministers* (London: Macmillan).

Hayes-Renshaw, F., and Wallace, H. (2005) (eds.), *The Council of Ministers*, 2nd edn. (London: Palgrave Macmillan), forthcoming.

Held, D. (1991), 'Democracy, the Nations-State and the Global System', in Held (ed.), *Political Theory Today* (Stanford: Stanford University Press), 197–235.

Helleiner, E. (2003), *The Making of National Money: Territorial Currencies in Historical Perspective* (Ithaca: Cornell University Press).

Henderson, D. (1999), *The Changing Fortunes of Economic Liberalism* (London: Institute of Economic Affairs).

Héritier, A. (2002), 'New Modes of Governance in Europe: Policy-Making without Legislating?', in Héritier, *The Provision of Common Goods: Governance Across Multiple Arenas* (Boulder: Rowman & Littlefield), 185–206.

Héritier, A. (2003), 'New Modes of Governance in Europe: Increasing Political Capacity and Policy Effectiveness', in Börzel and Cichowski (eds.), *The State of the European Union, vi, Law Politics and Society* (Oxford: Oxford University Press), 105–26.

Héritier, A., Knill, C., and Mingers, S. (1996), *Ringing the Changes in Europe: Regulatory Competition and the Transformation of the State* (Berlin: DeGruyter).

Hibbs, D. A., and Madsen, H. J. (1981), 'Public Reactions in the Growth of Taxation and Government Expenditure', *World Politics*, 33/3: 413–35.

Hill, C. (1998), 'Closing the Capability–Expectations Gap', in Peterson and Sjursen (eds.), *A Common Foreign Policy for Europe? Competing Visions of the CFSP* (London: Routledge), 18–38.

Hill, C. J., and Smith, K. E. (2000), *European Foreign Policy: Key Documents* (London: Routledge).

Hill, C. J., and Smith, M. H. (2005) (eds.), International Relations and the European Union (Oxford: Oxford University Press).

Hindley, B. (1992), 'Exports from Eastern and Central Europe and Contingent Protection', in Flemming and Rollo (eds.), *Trade, Payments and Adjustment in Central and Eastern Europe* (London: RIIA/EBRD), 144–53.

Hine, D., and Kassim, H. (1998) (eds.), *Beyond the Market: The EU and National Social Policy* (London: Routledge).

Hix, S. (1994), 'The Study of the European Community: The Challenge to Comparative Politics', *West European Politics*, 17/1: 1–30.

Hix, S. (1996), 'CP, IR, and the EU! A Rejoinder to Hurrell and Menon', *West European Politics*, 19/4: 802–4.

Hix, S. (1998), 'The Study of the European Union II: The "New Governance" Agenda and its Rival', *Journal of European Public Policy*, 5: 38–65.

Hix, S. (1999), *The Political System of the European Union* (London: Palgrave Macmillan).

Hix, S. (2001), 'Legislative Behaviour and Party Competition in European Parliament: An Application of Nominate to the EU', *Journal of Common Market Studies* 39/4: 663–88.

Hix, S. (2005), *The Political System of the European Union*, 2nd edn. (London: Palgrave Macmillan).

Hix, S., and Lord, C. (1997), *Political Parties in the European Union* (New York: St Martin's Press).

Hix, S., Noury, A., and Roland, G. (2002), 'A "Normal" Parliament? Party Cohesion and Competition in the European Parliament, 1979–2001', EPRG Working Paper No. 9, available on-line at: *www.lse.ac.uk/Depts/eprg/working-papers.htm*.

HMSO (2003), *A Modern Regional Policy for the United Kingdom* (London: HMSO, HM Treasury, DTI and ODPM).

Hodson, D., and Maher, I. (2001), 'The Open Method of Coordination as a New Mode of Governance: The Case of Soft Economic Policy Co-ordination', *Journal of Common Market Studies*, 39/4, 719–46.

Hoffmann, S. (1966), 'Obstinate or Obsolete? The Fate of the Nation-State and the Case of Western Europe', *Deadalus*, 95/3: 862–915.

Hoffmann, S. (1995), *The European Sisyphus: Essays on Europe, 1964–1994* (Boulder: Westview).

Holmes. P., and McGowan, F. (1997), 'The Changing Dynamics of EU–Industry Relations: Lessons from the Liberalization of the European Car and Airline Markets', in Wallace and Young (eds.), *Participation and Policy-Making in the European Union* (Oxford: Clarendon Press), 159–84.

Holmes. P., and Young, A. R. (2000), *Emerging Regulatory Challenges to the EU's External Economic Relations*, SEI Working Paper 42 (Falmer: Sussex European Institute).

Holzinger, K. (1994), *Politik des kleinsten gemeinsamen Nenners? Umweltpolitische Entscheidungsprozesse in der EG am Beispiel des Katalysatorautos* (Berlin: Sigma).

Holzinger, K., Knill, C., and Schäfer, A. (2003), 'Steuerungswandel in der europäischen Umweltpolitik?', in Holzinger *et al.* (eds.), *Politische Steuerung im Wandel: der Einfluss von Ideen und Problemstrukturen* (Opladen: Leske & Budrich), 103–29.

Hooghe, L. (1996) (ed.), *Cohesion Policy and European Integration: Building Multi-Level Governance* (Oxford: Oxford University Press).

Hooghe, L. (2002), *The European Commission and the Integration of Europe* (Cambridge: Cambridge University Press).

Hooghe, L. (2005), 'Several Roads Lead To International Norms, But Few Via International Socialization: A Case Study of the European Commission', *International Organization*, forthcoming.

Hooghe, L., and Keating, M. (1994), 'The Politics of European Union Regional Policy', *Journal of European Public Policy*, 1/3: 367–93.

Hooghe, L., and Marks, G. (1995), ' "Europe with the Regions": Channels of Regional Representation in the European Union', *Publius*, 26: 73–91.

Hooghe, L., and Marks, G. (1999), 'The Birth of a Polity: The Struggle Over European Integration', in Kitschelt *et al.* (eds.), *Continuity and Change in Contemporary Capitalism* (Cambridge: Cambridge University Press), 70–97.

Hooghe, L., and Marks, G. (2001), *Multi-Level Governance and European Integration* (Lanham: Rowman & Littlefield).

Hoskyns, C. (1996), *Integrating Gender: Women, Law and Politics in the European Union* (London: Verso).

House of Commons (2004), Select Committee on European Scrutiny, *Twenty-First Report, Report on Commission Communication* COM (04 107), Third Report on Economic and Political Cohesion.

House of Lords (1997), Select Committee on the European Communities, *Reducing Disparities within the European Union: The Effectiveness of the Structural and Cohesion Funds*, Session 1996–7, 11th Report (London: HMSO).

House of Lords (1998), Select Committee of the European Communities, *Incorporating the Schengen Acquis into the European Union*, Session 1997–8, 31st Report (London: Stationery Office).

House of Lords (2000), European Union Committee, *Report on EU Proposals to Combat Discrimination*, 9th Report, HL Paper 68 (London: HMSO).

House of Lords (2002), Select Committee on the European Union, *The Review of the EC Merger Regulation* (London: House of Lords), HL Paper 165.

House of Lords (2004a), Sub-Committee G (Social and Consumer Affairs), *Equality in Access to Goods and Services Report* (London: House of Lords), HL Paper 165-I, available on-line at *www:publications:parliament.uk.*

House of Lords (2004b), *Judicial Cooperation in the EU: The Role of Eurojust*, 23rd Report of Lords EU Committee, 2003-4, HL 138, July 2004.

Howorth, J., and Keeler, J. (2003) (eds.), *Defending Europe: The EU, Nato, and the Quest for European Autonomy* (London: Palgrave Macmillan).

Huber, J. D., and Shipan, C. R. (2002), *Deliberate Discretion?: The Institutional Foundations of Bureaucratic Autonomy* (Cambridge: Cambridge University Press).

Hughes, J., Sasse, G., and Gordon, C. (2004), 'Conditionality and Compliance in the EU's Eastward Enlargement: Regional Policy and the Reform of Sub-national Government', *Journal of Common Market Studies*, 42/3: 523-51.

Hurrell, A., and Menon, A. (1996), 'Politics Like Any Other? Comparative Politics, International Relations and the Study of the EU', *West European Politics*, 19/2: 386-402.

Hurwitz, L., and Lequesne, C. (1991) (eds.), *The State of the European Community: Politics, Institutions and Debates in the Transition Years* (Boulder: Lynne Rienner).

Husmann, M. (1998), 'Koordinierung der Leistungen bei Arbeitslosigkeit durch EG-Recht', *Die Sozialgerichtsbarkeit*, 45/6: 245-52 (pt. 1); 7: 291-8 (pt. 2).

Ingham, M., and Ingham, H. (2003), 'Enlargement and the European Employment Strategy: Turbulent Times Ahead?', *Industrial Relations Journal*, 34/5: 379-95.

Irish Fishermen's Organization (1998), 'Response to CFP Questionnaire' (Dublin).

Iversen, T., and Wren, A. (1998), 'Equality, Employment and Budgetary Restraint: The Trilemma of the Service Economy', *World Politics*, 50: 507-46.

Jabko, N. (1999), 'In the Name of the Market: How the European Commission Paved the Way for Monetary Union', *Journal of European Public Policy*, 6: 475-95.

Jachtenfuchs, M. (1995), 'Theoretical Perspectives on European Governance', *European Law Journal*, 1/2: 115-33.

Jachtenfuchs, M. (2000), 'Die Problemlösungsfähigkeit der EU: Begriffe, Befunde, Erklärungen', in Grande and Jachtenfuchs (eds.), *Wie problemlösungsfähig ist die EU? Regieren im europäischen Mehrebenensystem* (Baden-Baden: Nomos), 345-59.

Jachtenfuchs, M. (2001), 'The Governance Approach to European Integration', *Journal of Common Market Studies*, 39/2: 245-64.

Jachtenfuchs, M., and Kohler-Koch, B. (2004), 'Governance and Institutional Development', in Wiener and Diez (eds.), *European Integration Theory* (Oxford: Oxford University Press), 97-115.

Jacobs, F., Corbett, R., and Shackleton, M. (2000), *The European Parliament*, 3rd edn. (London: John Harper).

Jacobsson, K. (2004a), 'The Methodology of the European Employment Strategy: Achievement and Problems', mimeo (SCORE, Stockholm University).

Jacobsson, K. (2004b), 'Soft Regulation and the Subtle Transformation of States: The Case of EU Employment Policy', *Journal of European Social Policy*, 44/4: 355-70.

Jacobsson, K., and Schmid, H. (2002), 'The European Employment Strategy at the Crossroads: Contributions to the Evaluation', paper presented at the Nordic Sociology Conference, Reykavic, 15-17 Aug.

Jacobsson, K., and Vifell, Å. (2003), 'Integration by Deliberation? On the Role of Committees in the Open Method of Coordination', paper presented at the workshop 'The Forging of Deliberative Surpanationalism in the EU', European University Institute, Florence, 7-8 Feb.

Jacquemin, A., and Wright, D. (1993), 'Corporate Strategies and European Challenges post-1992', *Journal of Common Market Studies*, 31/4: 525–37.

Jeffrey, C. (1997) (ed.), *The Regional Dimension of the European Union* (London: Frank Cass).

Jeffrey, C. (2002), 'Social and Regional Interests: ESC and Committee of the Regions', in Peterson and Shackleton (eds.), *The Institutions of the European Union* (Oxford: Oxford University Press), 326–46.

Jehlička, P. (2002), *Environmental Implication of Eastern Enlargement of the EU: The End of Progressive Environmental Policy* (San Domenico di Fiesole: EUI–Robert Schuman Centre for Advanced Studies), RSC Working Paper No. 2002/23.

Jobelius, S. (2003), 'Who Formulates the European Employment Guidelines?: The OMC between Deliberation and Power Games', paper presented at the ESPAnet conference, 'Changing European Societies: The Role for Social Policy', Copenhagen, 13–15 Nov.

Joerges, C. (1999), ' "Good Governance" Through Comitology?', in Joerges and Vos (eds.), *EU Committees: Social Regulation, Law and Politics* (Oxford: Hart), 311–38.

Joerges, C. (2001a), ' "Deliberative Supranationalism": A Defence', European Integration on-line Papers (EIoP) 5/8; available on-line at *http://eiop.or.at/eiop/texte/2001-008a.htm*.

Joerges, C. (2001b), 'Law, Science and the Management of Risks to Health at the National, European and International Level: Stories on Baby Dummies, Mad Cows and Hormones in Beef', *Columbia Journal of European Law*, 7: 1–19.

Joerges, C. (2003), 'Comitology and the European Model: Towards a Recht-Fertigungs-Recht in the Europeanisation Process', in Eriksen, Joerges and Neyer (eds.), *European Governance, Deliberation and the Quest for Democratisation* (Oslo: Arena Report 2/2003), 501–40.

Joerges, C., and Neyer, J. (1997a), 'From Intergovernmental Bargaining to Deliberative Political Process: The Constitutionalization of Comitology', *European Law Journal*, 3/3: 273–99.

Joerges, C., and Neyer, J. (1997b), 'Transforming Strategic Interaction into Deliberative Problem-Solving: European Comitology in the Foodstuffs Sector', *Journal of European Public Policy*, 4/4: 609–25.

Johansson, K. M. (1999), 'Tracing the Employment Title in the Amsterdam Treaty: Uncovering Transnational Coalitions', *Journal of European Public Policy*, 6/1: 85–101.

Johnson, D. G. (1991), *World Agriculture in Disarray* (London: Macmillan, for the Trade Policy Research Centre).

Johnstone, A. I. (2003), 'Security Council Deliberations: The Power of the Better Argument', *European Journal of International Law*, 14/3: 437–87.

Jones, E. (2002), *The Politics of Economic and Monetary Union: Integration and Idiosyncrasy* (Boulder: Rowman & Littlefield).

Jordan, A. (2002a) (ed.), *Environmental Policy in the European Union: Actors, Institutions and Processes* (London: Earthscan).

Jordan, A. (2002b), *The Europeanization of British Environmental Policy: A Departmental Perspective* (London: Palgrave Macmillan).

Jordan, A., and Fairbrass, J. (2002), 'EU Environmental Policy after the Nice Summit', *Environmental Politics*, 10/4: 109–14.

Jordan, A., Wurzel, R., and Zito, A. (2003), *'New' Instruments of Environmental Governance: National Experiences and Prospects* (London: Frank Cass).

Jorens, Y., and Schulte, B. (1998) (eds.), *European Social Security Law and Third Country Nationals* (Brughes: die Keure).

Jørgensen, K. E. (1997), 'Introduction: Approaching European Governance', in Jørgensen (ed.), *Reflective Approaches to European Governance* (New York: St Martin's Press), 1–12.

Josling, T. (1998), 'Can the CAP Survive Enlargement to the East?', in Redmond and Rosenthal (eds.), *The Expanding European* (Boulder: Lynne Rienner), 89–106.

Josling, T., and Tangermann, St. (2003), 'Production and Export Subsidies in Agriculture: Lessons from GATT and WTO Disputes Involving the US and the EC', in Petersmann and Pollack (eds.), *Transatlantic Economic Disputes: The EU, the US, and the WTO* (Oxford: Oxford University Press), 207–32.

Jouen, M. (2001), *How to Enhance Economic and Social Cohesion in Europe after 2006?* (Paris: Groupement d'Etudes et de Recherches, Notre Europe).

Jupille, J. (2004), *Procedural Politics: Issues, Influence, and Institutional Choice in the European Union* (New York: Cambridge University Press).

Jupille, J. (2005), 'Knowing Europe: Metatheory and Methodology in EU Studies', in Cini and Bourne (eds.), *Palgrave Advances in European Union Studies* (London: Palgrave), forthcoming.

Jupille, J., and Caporaso, J. A. (1999), 'Institutionalism and the European Union: Beyond International Relations and Comparative Politics', *Annual Review of Political Science*, 2: 429–44.

Jupille, J., Caporaso, J. A., and Checkel, J. T. (2003), 'Integrating Institutions: Rationalism, Constructivism, and the Study of the European Union', *Comparative Political Studies*, 36/1–2: 7–40.

Kaelberer, M. (2004), 'The Euro and European Identity: Symbols, Power and the Politics of European Monetary Union', *Review of International Studies* 30/2: 161–78.

Kaelble, H., and Schmid, G. (2004) (eds.), *Das europäische Sozialmodell: auf dem Weg zum transnationalen Sozialstaat* (Berlin: Sigma).

Kagan, R. (2001), *Adversarial Legalism: The American Way of Law* (Cambridge, Mass.: Harvard University Press).

Kalman, J. (2002), 'Possible Structural Fund Absorption Problems', in Marcou (ed.), *Regionalization for Development and Accession to the European Union: A Comparative Perspective* (Budapest: Local Government and Public Services Reform Initiative), 31–63, available on-line at *http://lgi.osi.hu/publications*.

Kaluza, H. (1998), *Der europäische Sozialfonds. Seine Entwicklung und Funktion in der europäischen Integration mit einem Exkurs zu seiner Bedeutung für die bundesdeutsche Arbeitsförderung* (Baden-Baden: Nomos).

Kapteyn, P. (1996), *The Stateless Market: The European Dilemma of Integration and Civilization* (London: Routledge).

Karagiannakos, A. (1997), 'Total Allowable Catch and the Quota Management System in the European Union', *Marine Policy*, 20/3: 235–48.

Karlsson, B. O. (2002), *What Price Enlargement?—Implications of an Expanded EU* (Oslo: Swedish Ministry of Finance/Expert Group on Public Finance), available on-line at *http://finans.regeringen.se/eso/PDF/ds2002_52e.pdf*.

Keating, M. (1998), 'Is there a Regional Level of Government in Europe', in Le Gales and Lequesne (eds.), *Regions in Europe* (London: Routledge), 11–30.

Keating, M., and Hughes, J. (2003) (eds.), *The Regional Challenge in Central and Eastern Europe* (Paris: PIE-Peter Lang).

Keating, M., and Loughlin, J. (1997) (eds.), *The Political Equality of Regionalism* (London: Frank Cass).

Keeler, J. T. S. (2004), 'Mapping EU Studies: The Evolution from Boutique to Boom Field, 1960-2001', paper presented at the University of Wisconsin-Madison (28 Apr.), and the European University Institute, Fiesole, Italy (5 May).

Kelemen, R. D. (2003), 'The Structure and Dynamics of EU Federalism', *Comparative Political Studies*, 36/1–2: 184–208.

Kelemen, R. D. (2004), *The Rules of Federalism: Institutions and Regulatory Politics in the EU and Beyond* (Cambridge, Mass.: Harvard University Press).

Kenner, J. (2003), *EU Employment Law: From Rome to Amsterdam and Beyond* (Oxford: Hart).

Keohane, R. O., and Milner, H. V. (1998), *Internationalization and Domestic Politics* (Cambridge: Cambridge University Press).

Kerremans, B. (1998), 'The Political and Institutional Consequences of Widening: Capacity and Control in an Enlarged Council', in Laurent and Maresceau (eds.), *The State of the European Union, iv: Deepening and Widening* (Boulder: Lynnne Rienner), 87–109.

Kiewiet, R. D., and McCubbins, M. (1991), *The Logic of Delegation: Congressional Parties and the Appropriations Process* (Chicago: University of Chicago Press).

King, S. J. (2003), 'Legal and Institutional Dynamics of New Governance in the EU: Participation and Policy Learning in the Employment OMC', mimeo, European University Institute, Florence.

Kingreen, T. (2003), *Das Sozialstaatsprinzip im europäische Verfassungsverbund: gemeinschaftsrechtliche Einflüsse auf das deutsche Recht der gesetzlichen Krankenversicherung* (Tübingen: Mohr Siebeck).

Kingreen, T. (2004), 'Wettbewerbsrechtliche Aspekte des GKV-Modernisierungsgesetzes', *Medizinrecht*, 22/4: 188–97.

Kleinman, M. (2001), *A European Welfare State? European Union Social Policy in Context* (London: Palgrave Macmillan).

Kleinman, M., and Piachaud, D. (1992*a*), 'Britain and European Social Policy', *Policy Studies*, 13/3: 13–25.

Kleinman, M., and Piachaud, D. (1992*b*), 'European Social Policy: Conceptions and Choices', *Journal of European Social Policy*, 3/1: 1–19.

Knill, C. (2002), *The Europeanisation of National Administrations: Patterns of Institutional Change and Persistence* (Cambridge: Cambridge University Press).

Knill, C. (2003), *Europäische Umweltpolitik: Steuerungsprobleme und Regulierungsmuster im Mehrebenensystem* (Opladen: Leske & Budrich).

Knill, C., and Lenschow, A. (2000) (eds.), *Implementing EU Environmental Policy: New Directions and Old Problems* (Manchester: Manchester University Press).

Kochan, T., Locke, R., Osterman, P., and Piore, M. (2001), *Working in America: Blueprint for a New Labor Market* (Cambridge, Mass.: MIT Press).

Kohler-Koch, B. (2003) (ed.), *Linking EU and National Governance* (Oxford: Oxford University Press).

Kok, W. (2004), *Facing the Challenge, Report of Wim Kok to the European Commission* (The Kok Report) (Brussels).

Kooiman, J. (1993), 'Social-Political Governance: Introduction', in Kooiman (ed.), *Modern Governance* (London: Sage), 1–6.

Koppen, I. (1993), 'The Role of the European Court of Justice', in Liefferink, Lowe, and Mol (eds.), *European Integration and Environmental Policy* (London: Belhaven Press), 126–49.

Kötter, U. (1998), 'Die Urteile des Gerichtshofs der Europäischen Gemeinschaften in den Rechtssachen Decker und Kohll: der Vorhang zu und alle Fragen offen?', *Vierteljahresschrift für Sozialrecht*, 4: 233–52.

Kotzian, P. (2002), *Stuck in the Middle: Welfare Effects of the European Pharmaceutical Markets' Incomplete Integration and a Possible Remedy* (Mannheim: Mannheimer Zentrum für Europäische Sozialforschung), MZES Working Paper 59.

Kotzian, P. (2003), *Verhandlungen im europäischen Arzneimittelsektor: Initiierung–Institutionalisierung–Ergebnisse* (Baden-Baden: Nomos).

Kramer, H. (1993), 'The European Community's Response to the "New Eastern Europe" ', *Journal of Common Market Studies*, 31/2: 213–44.

Kreher, A. (1997), 'Agencies in the European Community: A Step Towards Administrative Integration in Europe', *Journal of European Public Policy*, 4/2: 225–45.

Kreppel, A. (1999), 'The European Parliament's Influence over EU Policy Outcomes', *Journal of Common Market Studies*, 37: 521–38.

Kreppel, A. (2001), *The European Parliament and Supranational Party System: A Study in Institutional Development* (Cambridge: Cambridge University Press).

Kreppel, A. (2002), 'The Environmental Determinants of Legislative Structure: A Comparison of the US House of Representatives and the European Parliament,' paper presented at the conference, 'Exporting Congress? The Influence of the US Congress on World Legislatures,' Jack D. Gordon Institute for Public Policy and Citizenship Studies, Florida International University, 6–7 Dec.

Kreppel, A., and Hix, S. (2003), 'From "Grand Coalition" to Left-Right Confrontation: Explaining the Shifting Structure of Party Competition in the European Parliament', *Comparative Political Studies*, 36/1–2: 75–96.

Kreppel, A., and Tsebelis, G. (1999), 'Coalition Formation in the European Parliament', *Comparative Political Studies*, 32: 933–66.

Krugman, P. (1995), *Growing World Trade: Causes and Consequences* (Washington: Brookings Institution), Brookings Papers on Economic Activity, I: 327–77.

Krupp, H.-J. (1995), 'Die Rahmenbedingungen für die Sozialpolitik auf dem Weg zur europäischen Wirtschafts- und Währungsunion', in Riesche und Schmähl (eds.), *Handlungsspreilräume nationaler Sozialpolitik* (Baden-Baden: Nomos), 173–88.

Kuijper, P. J. (2000), 'Some Legal Problems Associated with the Communitarisation of Policy on Visas, Asylum and Immigration Under the Amsterdam Treaty and Incorporation of the Schengen Acquis', *Common Market Law Review*, 37: 345–66.

Laffan, B. (1996), 'The Politics of Identity and Political Order in Europe', *Journal of Common Market Studies*, 34/1: 81–102.

Laffan, B. (1997), *The Finances of the European Union* (London: Macmillan).

Laffan, B., O'Donnell, R., and Smith, M. (1999), *Europe's Experimental Union: Rethinking Integration* (London: Routledge).

Landáburu, E. (1994), 'How to Make Ill-placed Regions Fit to Compete', *European Affairs*, 4/2: 97–9.

Lange, P. (1992), 'The Politics of the Social Dimension', in Sbragia (ed.), *Euro-Politics: Institutions and Policy-Making in the 'New' European Community* (Washington: Brookings Institution), 225–56.

La Serre, F. de (1994), 'A la Recherche d'une Ostpolitik', in de La Serre *et al.* (eds.), *L'Union Européenne: Ouverture à l'Est?* (Paris: Presses Universitaires de France), 11–41.

Laudati, L. (1996), 'The European Commission as Regulator: The Uncertain Pursuit of the Competitive Market', in Majone (ed.), *Regulating Europe* (London: Routledge), 229–61.

Laursen, F., and Vanhoonacker, S. (1992) (eds.), *The Intergovernmental Conference on Political Union* (Maastricht: European Institute of Public Administration).

Lavenex, S. (1999), *Safe Third Countries: Extending EU Asylum and Immigration Policies to Central and Eastern Europe* (Budapest: Central European University Press).

Lavenex, S. (2001a), *The Europeanisation of Refugee Policies: Between Human Rights and Internal Security* (Aldershot: Ashgate).

Lavenex, S. (2001b), 'Migration and the EU's New Eastern Border: Between Realism and Liberalism', *Journal of European Public Policy*, 8/1: 24–42.

Lavenex, S., and Uçarer, E. (2002) (eds.), *Migration and the Externalities of European Integration* (Lanham: Lexington Books).

Leibfried, S. (1994), 'The Social Dimension of the European Union: En Route to a Positive Joint Sovereignty?', *Journal of European Social Policy*, 4/4: 239–62.

Leibfried, S. (2001), 'Über die Hinfälligkeit des Staates der Daseinsvorsorge: Thesen zur Zerstörung des äußeren Verteidigungsringes des Sozialstaats', in Schader-Stiftung (ed.), *Die*

Zukunft der Daseinsvorsorge: öffentliche Unternehmen im Wettbewerb (Darmstadt: Schader-Stiftung), 158–66.

Leibfried, S., and Pierson, P. (1995a), 'Semi-sovereign Welfare States: Social Policy in a Multi-tiered Europe', in Leibfried and Pierson (eds.), (1995b) *European Social Policy: Between Fragmentation and Integration* (Washington: Brookings Institution), 43–77.

Leibfried, S., and Pierson, P. (1995b), *European Social Policy: Between Fragmentation and Integration* (Washington: Brookings Institution).

Leibfried, S., and Zürn, M. (2005), 'Reconfiguring the National Constellation', in Leibfried and Zürn (eds.), *Transformations of the State?* (Cambridge: Cambridge University Press).

Lenschow, A. (2003), 'New Regulatory Approaches in Greening EU Policies', *European Law Journal*, 8/1: 19–37.

Lequesne, C. (1991), 'Les Accords de Commerce et de Coopération Communauté Européenne: Pays d'Europe de l'Est', in Gautron (ed.), *Les Relations Communauté Européenne: Europe de l'Est* (Paris: Economica), 357–71.

Lequesne, C. (2004), *The Politics of Fisheries in the European Union* (Manchester: Manchester University Press).

Lewis, J. (1998), 'Is the "Hard Bargaining" Image of the Council Misleading? The Committee of Permanent Representatives and the Local Elections Directive', *Journal of Common Market Studies*, 36/4: 479–504.

Lewis, J. (2003), 'Institutional Environments and Everyday EU Decision-Making: Rationalist or Constructivist?', *Comparative Political Studies*, 36/1–2: 97–124.

Liefferink, D., and Jordan, A. (2004) (eds.), *Environmental Policy in Europe: The Europeanisation of National Environmental Policy* (London: Routledge).

Lindberg, L. N. (1963), *The Political Dynamics of European Economic Integration* (Stanford: Stanford University Press).

Lindberg, L. N., and Scheingold, S. A. (1970), *Europe's Would-Be Polity* (Englewood Cliffs, NJ: Prentice-Hall).

Lindner, J. (2005), *Conflict and Change in EU Budgetary Politics* (London: Routledge).

Lippert, B. (1990), 'EC–CMEA Relations: Normalisation and Beyond', in Edwards and Regelsberger (eds.), *Europe's Global Links: The European Community and Inter-Regional Cooperation* (London: Pinter), 119–40.

Longo, M. (2003), 'European Integration: Between Micro-Regionalism and Globalism', *Journal of Common Market Studies*, 41/3: 475–94.

Lowi, T. (1964), 'American Business, Public Policy, Case Studies and Political Theory', *World Politics*, 16/4: 677–715.

Ludlow, P. (1982), *The Making of the European Monetary System* (London: Butterworth).

Lundestad, G. (1998), *Empire by Integration: The United States and European Integration, 1945–1997* (Oxford: Oxford University Press).

McAleavey, P. (1994), *The Political Logic of the European Community Structural Funds Budget: Lobbying Efforts by Declining Industrial Regions* (San Domenico di Fiesole: EUI-Robert Schuman Centre for Advanced Studies), RSC Working Paper No. 942.

McClintock, J. (2004), *Key Issues in the Agricultural Enlargement Negotiations*, DG AGRI Information Conference, Mar., Sofia, available on-line at *http://europa.eu.int/comm/agriculture/events/sofia/ mcclintock.pdf*.

McDonagh, B. (1998), *Original Sin in a Brave New World* (Dublin: Institute of European Affairs).

McElroy, G. (2004), 'Party Leadership and Representative Committees in the European Parliament,' paper presented at the Annual Meetings of the American Political Science Association, Chicago, 2–5 Sept.

McGowan, F., and Wallace, H. (1996), 'Towards a European Regulatory State?', *Journal of European Public Policy*, 3/4: 560–76.

McNamara, K. (1998), *The Currency of Ideas: Monetary Politics in the European Union* (Ithaca: Cornell University Press).

McNamara, K. (2001), 'Where Do Rules Come From? The Creation of the European Central Bank' in Stone Sweet, Fligstein, and Sandholtz (eds.), *The Institutionalization of Europe* (Oxford: Oxford University Press), 155–70.

McNamara, K. (2002), 'Rational Fictions: Central Bank Independence and the Social Logic of Independence', *West European Politics* 25/1: 47–76.

McNamara, K. (2003), 'Towards a Federal Europe? The Euro and Institutional Change in Historical Perspective', in Börzel and Cichowski (eds.), *The State of the European Union, VI: Law, Politics, and Society* (Oxford: Oxford University Press), 253–68.

Magnette, P. (2004), 'Deliberation or Bargaining? Coping with Constitutional Conflicts in the Convention on the Future of Europe', in Eriksen, Fossum, and Menéndez (eds.), *Developing a Constitution for Europe* (London: Routledge), 207–25.

Majone, G. (1991), 'Cross-National Sources of Regulatory Policymaking in Europe and the United States', *Journal of Public Policy*, 2/1: 79–106.

Majone, G. (1993), 'The European Community between Social Policy and Social Regulation', *Journal of Common Market Studies*, 31/2: 153–70.

Majone, G. (1994), 'The Rise of the Regulatory State in Europe', *West European Politics*, 17/3: 77–101.

Majone, G. (1995), *La Communauté européenne: un Etat régulateur* (Paris: Montchestien).

Majone, G. (1996) (ed.), *Regulating Europe* (London: Routledge).

Majone, G. (2000), 'Two Logics of Delegation: Agency and Fiduciary Relations in EU Governance', *European Union Politics*, 2/1: 103–21.

Majone, G. (2002), 'What Price Safety? The Precautionary Principle and its Policy Implications', *Journal of Common Market Studies*, 40/1: 89–109.

Majone, G. (2003), 'Foundations of Risk Regulation: Science, Decision-Making, Policy Learning and Institutional Reform', in Majone (ed.), *Risk Regulation in the European Union: Between Enlargement and Internationalization* (Florence: European University Institute), 9–32.

Majone, G. (2005), *Dilemmas of European Integration: The Ambiguities and Pitfalls of Integration by Stealth* (Oxford: Oxford University Press).

Manow, P., Schäfer, A., and Zorn, H. (2004), *European Social Policy and Europe's Party-Political Center of Gravity, 1957–2003* (Cologne: Max Planck Institute for the Study of Societies), MPIfG Discussion Paper 04/6.

March, J. G., and Olsen, J. P. (1984), 'The New Institutionalism: Organizational Factors in Political Life', *European Union Politics*, 2/1: 103–21.

March, J. G., and Olsen, J. P. (1989), *Rediscovering Institutions: The Organizational Basis of Politics* (New York: Free Press).

Maresceau, M. (1989) (ed.), *The Political and Legal Framework of Trade Relations Between the European Community and Eastern Europe* (Dordrecht: Nijhoff).

Marjolin, R. (1989), *Architect of European Unity: Memoirs 1911–1986* (London: Weidenfeld & Nicolson).

Marks, G. (1992), 'Structural Policy in the European Community', in Sbragia (ed.), *Europolitics: Institutions and Policy-Making in the 'New' European Community* (Washington, DC: Brookings Institution), 191–224.

Marks, G. (1993), 'Structural Policy and Multilevel Governance in the EC', in Cafruny and Rosenthal (eds.), *The State of the European Community, Vol. 2: The Maastricht Debates and Beyond* (Boulder: Lynne Rienner), 390–410.

Marks, G., Hooghe, L., and Blank, K. (1996), 'European Integration from the 1980s: State-Centric v. Multi-Level Governance', *Journal of Common Market Studies*, 34: 341–78.

Marks, G., Nielsen, F., Ray, L., and Salk, J. (1996), 'Competencies, Cracks and Conflicts: Regional Mobilization in the European Union', in Marks, Schmitter, and Streeck (eds.), *Governance in the European Union* (London: Sage), 40–63.

Martin, A., and Ross, G. (2004), *Euros and Europeans: Monetary Integration and the European Model of Society* (Cambridge: Cambridge University Press).

Mattila, M. (2001), *Contested Decisions: Empirical Analysis of Voting Power in the EU Council of Ministers*, University of Helsinki Working Paper.

Mattli, W. (1999), *The Logic of Regional Integration: Europe and Beyond* (Cambridge: Cambridge University Press).

Mattli, W., and Slaughter, A.-M. (1995), 'Law and Politics in the European Union: A Reply to Garrett', *International Organization*, 49: 183–90.

Mattli, W., and Slaughter, A.-M. (1998*a*), 'Revisiting the European Court of Justice', *International Organization*, 52/1: 177–210.

Mattli, W., and Slaughter, A.-M. (1998*b*), 'The ECJ, Governments, and Legal Integration in the EU', *International Organization*, 52/1: 177–210.

Maurer, A. (2003), 'Less Bargaining—More Deliberation: The Convention Method for Enhancing EU Democracy', *Internationale Politik und Gesellschaft*, 1: 167–90.

Maurer, A., and Wessels, W. (2003) (eds.), *Fifteen into One? The European Union and its Member States* (Manchester: Manchester University Press).

Maydell, B. Baron von (1991), 'Einführung in die Schlussdiskussion', in Schulte and Zacher (eds.), *Wechselwirkungen zwischen dem europäischen Sozialrecht und dem Sozialrecht der Bundesrepublik Deutschland* (Berlin: Duncker & Humblot), 229–36.

Maydell, B. Baron von (1999), 'Auf dem Weg zu einem gemeinsamen Markt für Gesundheitsleistungen in der Europäischen Gemeinschaft', *Vierteljahresschrift für Sozialrecht*, 1: 3–19.

Mayhew, A. (1998), *Recreating Europe: The European Union's Policy towards Central and Eastern Europe* (Cambridge: Cambridge University Press).

Mayhew, A. (2000), *Enlargement of the European Union: An Analysis of the Negotiations with the Central and Eastern European Candidate Countries*, SEI Working Paper 39 (Falmer: Sussex European Institute).

Mayhew, A. (2002), *The Negotiating Position of the European Union on Agriculture: The Structural Funds and the EU Budget*, SEI Working Paper 52 (Falmer: Sussex European Institute).

Mazey, S. (1998), 'The European Union and Women's Rights: From the Europeanization of National Agendas to the Nationalization of a European Agenda?', *Journal of European Public Policy*, 5/1: 131–52.

Mazey, S., and Richardson, J. (1993), 'Introduction: Transference of Power, Decision Rules, and Rules of the Game', in Mazey and Richardson (eds.), *Lobbying in the European Community* (Oxford: Oxford University Press), 3–26.

Mazower, M. (1999), *Dark Continent: Europe's Twentieth Century* (London: Penguin).

Meller, P., and Pollack, A. (2004), 'Europeans Appear Ready to Approve a Biotech Corn', *The New York Times*, 15 May, B1, B3.

Menon, A. (2004), 'From Crisis to Catharsis: ESDP after Iraq', *International Affairs*, 80/4 (July): 631–48.

Menon, A., Forster, A., and Wallace, W. (1992), 'A Common European Defence?', *Survival*, 34/3: 98–118.

Menz, G. (2003), 'Re-regulating the Single Market: National Varieties of Capitalism and their responses to Europeanization', *Journal of European Public Policy*, 10/4: 532–55.

Messerlin, P. (1993), 'The EC and Central Europe: The Missed Rendez-Vous of 1992?', *Economics of Transition*, 1/1: 89–109.

Michalski, A., and Wallace, H. (1992), *The European Community: The Challenge of Enlargement* (London: RIIA).

Midelfart-Knarvik, K., and Overman, H. (2002), 'Delocation and European Integration: Is Structural Spending Justified?', *Economic Policy*, 35: 325–59.

Milner, H. V. (1998), 'Rationalizing Politics: The Emerging Synthesis of International, American, and Comparative Politics', *International Organization*, 52: 759–86.

Milward, A. S. (1981), 'Tariffs as Constitutions', in Strange and Tooze (eds.), *The Internatinal Politics of Surplus Capacity: Competition for Market Shares in a World Recession* (London: Allen & Unwin), 57–66.

Milward, A. S. (1992), *The European Rescue of the Nation-State* (London: Routledge).

Milward, A. S. (2000), *The European Rescue of the Nation-State*, 2nd edn. (London: Routledge).

Milward, A. S., and Lynch, F. M. B. (1993) (eds.), *The Frontiers of National Sovereignty: History and Theory 1945–1992* (London: Routledge).

Mitsilegas, V. (2003), 'The New EU–USA Cooperation on Extradition, Mutual Legal Assistance and the Exchange of Police Data', *European Foreign Affairs Review* 8/4 (Winter): 515–36.

Mitsilegas, V., Monar, J., and Rees, W. (2003), *The European Union and Internal Security: Guardian of the People?* (London: Palgrave).

Moe, T. (1984), 'The New Economics of Organization', *American Journal of Political Science*, 28/4: 739–77.

Molyneux, C. G. (1999), 'The Trade Barriers Regulation: The European Union as a Player in the Globalization Game', *European Law Journal*, 5/4: 375–418.

Monar, J. (1997), 'European Union—Justice and Home Affairs: A Balance Sheet and an Agenda for Reform', in Edwards and Pijpers (eds.), *The Politics of European Treaty Reform: The 1996 Intergovernmental Conference and Beyond* (London: Pinter/Cassell), 326–39.

Monti, M. (2003), 'EU Competition Policy after May 2004', paper presented at the Fordham Corporate Law Institute.

Moravcsik, A. (1991), 'Negotiating the Single European Act: National Interests and Conventional Statecraft in the European Community', *International Organization*, 45/1: 19–56.

Moravcsik, A. (1993*a*), 'Preferences and Power in the European Community: A Liberal Intergovernmentalist Approach', *Journal of Common Market Studies*, 31: 473–524.

Moravcsik, A. (1993*b*), 'Introduction: Integrating International and Domestic Theories of International Bargaining', in Evans, Jacobson, and Putnam (eds.), *Double-Edged Diplomacy: International Bargaining and Domestic Politics* (Berkeley: University of California Press), 3–42.

Moravcsik, A. (1994), *Why the European Community Strengthens the State: Domestic Politics and International Cooperation* (Cambridge, Mass.: Harvard University), Center for European Studies, Working Paper Series 52.

Moravcsik, A. (1995), 'Liberal Intergovernmentalism and Integration: A Rejoinder', *Journal of Common Market Studies*, 33: 611–28.

Moravcsik, A. (1998), *The Choice for Europe: Social Purpose and State Power from Messina to Maastricht* (Ithaca: Cornell University Press).

Moravcsik, A. (1999), 'Is Something Rotten in the State of Denmark? Constructivism and European Integration', *Journal of European Public Policy*, 6: 669–81.

Moravcsik, A. (2001), 'Federalism in the European Union: Rhetoric and Reality', in Nicolaidis and Howse (eds.), *The Federal Vision: Legitimacy and Levels of Governance in the United States in the European Union* (Oxford: Oxford University Press), 161–87.

Morelli, P., Padoan, P. C., and Rodano, L. (2002), 'The Lisbon Strategy to the New Economy: Some Economic and Institutional Aspects', paper presented to the conference 'Institutions and Growth: The Political Economy of International Unions and the Constitution of Europe', XIV Villa Mondragone International Economic Seminar.

Morgan, R., and Bray, C. (1984) (eds.), *Partners and Rivals in Western Europe: Britain, France and Germany* (Aldershot: Gower).

Moser, P. (1996), 'The European Parliament as an Agenda-Setter: What are the Conditions? A Critique of Tsebelis', *American Political Science Review*, 90: 834–8.

Moser, P. (1997), 'The Benefits of the Conciliation Procedure for the European Parliament: Comment to George Tsebelis', *Aussenwirtschaft*, 52: 57–62.

Moser, S., Pesaresi, N., and Soukup, K. (2002), 'State Guarantees to German Public Banks: A New Step in the Enforcement of State Aid Discipline to Financial Services in the Community', *Competition Policy Newsletter*, 2002/2: 1–11.

Mosher, J. S., and Trubeck, D. (2003), 'Alternative Approaches to Governance in the EU: EU Social Policy and the European Employment Strategy', *Journal of Common Market Studies*, 41/1: 63–88.

Mossialos, E., and McKee, M. (2002), *EU Law and the Social Character of Health Care* (Brussels: P.I.E-Peter Lang).

Mossialos, E., Dixon, A., Figueras, J., and Kutzin, J. (2002) (eds.), *Funding Health Care: Options for Europe* (Buckingham: Open University Press).

Motta, M. (2004), *Competition Policy: Theory and Practice* (Cambridge: Cambridge University Press).

Müller, H. (2003), 'Interests or Ideas? The Regulation of Insurance Services and the European Single Market: Trade Liberalisation, Risk Regulation and Limits to Market Integration', D.Phil. thesis, Falmer, University of Sussex.

Myrdal, G. (1957), 'Economic Nationalism and Internationalism', *Australian Outlook*, 11/4: 3–50.

Nanetti, R. (1996), 'EU Cohesion and Territorial Restructuring in the Member States', in Hooghe (ed.), *Cohesion Policy and European Integration: Building Multilevel Governance* (Oxford: Oxford University Press), 59–88.

Network of Independent Agricultural Experts in the CEE Candidate Countries (2004), *The Future of Rural Areas in the CEE New Member States—Annex* (Halle/Saale: Institut für Agrarentwicklung in Mittel- und Osteuropa).

Neville-Jones, P. (1997), 'Dayton, IFOR and Alliance Relations', *Survival*, 38/4: 45–65.

Neyer, J. (2000), 'The Regulation of Risks and the Power of the People: Lessons from the BSE Crisis', European Integration online papers (EIOP), 4/6, http://eiop.or.at/eiop/texte/.

NFFO and SFF (National Federation of Fishermen's Organizations & Scottish Fishermen's Federation) (1998), 'European Fisheries after 2002: Decentralization of the Common Fisheries Policy'.

Niblett, R. (1995), 'The European Community and the Central European Three, 1989–92: A Study of the Community as an International Actor', Ph.D. thesis, Oxford.

Nicolaidis, K., and Howse, R. (2001), *The Federal Vision: Legitimacy and Levels of Governance in the United States in the European Union* (Oxford: Oxford University Press).

Nivola, P. S. (1998), 'American Social Regulation Meets the Global Economy', in Nivola (ed.), *Comparative Disadvantages: Social Regulations and the Global Economy* (Washington: Brookings Institution), 16–65.

Nollkaemper, A. (2002), 'Three Conceptions of the Integration Principle in International Environmental Law', in Lenschow (ed.), *Environmental Policy Integration: Greening Sectoral Policies in Europe* (London: Earthscan), 22–32.

Norman, P. (2003), *The Accidental Constitution: The Story of the EU Convention* (Brussels: Eurocomment).

North, D. C. (1990), *Institutions, Institutional Change and Economic Performance* (Cambridge: Cambridge University Press).

Notermans, T. (2001) (ed.), *Social Democracy and Monetary Union* (New York: Berghahn Books).

Nugent, N. (1997) (ed.), *At the Heart of the Union: Studies of the European Commission* (London: Macmillan).

Nugent, N. (2002), *The Government and Politics of the European Union*, 5th edn. (London: Palgrave Macmillan).

Nugent, N. (2004*a*), 'Previous Enlargement Rounds', in Nugent (ed.), *European Union Enlargement* (London: Palgrave), 22–33.

Nugent, N. (2004*b*) (ed.), *European Union Enlargement* (London: Palgrave).

Nuttall, S. J. (1992), *European Political Cooperation* (Oxford: Clarendon Press).

Nuttall, S. J. (1994), 'The Commission and Foreign Policy-Making', in Edwards and Spence (eds.), *The European Commission* (London: Longman), 287–303.

O'Leary, S. (2002), *Employment Law in the European Court of Justice: Judicial Structures, Policies and Processes* (Oxford: Hart).

Obinger, H., Leibfried, S., and Castles, F. (2005) (eds.), *Federalism and the Welfare State: New World and European Experiences* (Cambridge: Cambridge University Press).

Occhipinti, J. D. (2003), *The Politics of EU Police Cooperation: Towards a European FBI?* (Boulder: Lynne Rienner).

Odell, J. S. (2003), *Making and Breaking Impasses in International Regimes: The WTO, Seattle and Doha* (San Domenico di Fiesole: EUI–Robert Schuman Centre for Advanced Studies), RSC Working Paper No. 2003/2.

OECD (Organization for Economic Co-operation and Development) (2002), *Agricultural Policies in Transition Economies* (Paris: OECD).

OECD (Organization for Economic Co-operation and Development) (2003), *Farm Household Incomes: Issues and Policies* (Paris: OECD).

OEEC (Organisation for European Economic Co-operation) (1956), *Agricultural Policy in Europe and North America* (Paris: OEEC).

Offe, C. (2000), 'The Democratic Welfare State in an Integrating Europe', in Greven and Pauly (eds.), *Democracy Beyond the State? The European Dilemma and the Emerging Global Order* (Boston: Rowman & Littlefield), 63–89.

Offe, C. (2003), 'Demokratie und Wohlfahrtsstaat: eine europäische Regimeform unter dem Streß der europäischen Integration', in Offe (ed.), *Herausforderungen der Demokratie: zur Integrations- und Leistungsfähigkeit politischer Institutionen* (Frankfurt a.M.: Campus), 239–73.

Oliver, T. (1998), 'Can Quotas Save Stocks?', in Gray (ed.), *The Politics of Fishing* (London: Macmillan), 68–80.

Orden, D., Paarlberg, R., and Roe, T. (1999), *Policy Reform in American Agriculture: Analysis and Prognosis* (Chicago: University of Chicago Press).

Ostner, I., and Lewis, J. (1995), 'Gender and the Evolution of European Social Policy', in Leibfried and Pierson (1995*b*: 159–93).

Paemen, H., and Bensch, A. (1995), *From GATT to WTO: The European Community in the Uruguay Round* (Leuven: Leuven University Press).

Page, E. (1997), *People who Run Europe* (Oxford: Clarendon Press).

Patterson, L. A. (2000), 'Biotechnology', in Wallace and Wallace (eds.), *Policy-Making in the European Union* (Oxford: Oxford University Press), 317–43.

Pearce, J., and Sutton, J. (1985), *Protection and Industrial Policy in Europe* (London: Routledge).

Pedersen, A. W. (2004), 'The Privatization of Retirement Income? Variation and Trends in the Income Package of Old Age Pensioners', *Journal of European Social Policy*, 14/1: 5–23.

Pelkmans, J. (1984), *Market Integration in the European Community* (The Hague: Martinus Nijhoff).

Pelkmans, J., and Casey, J.-P. (2004), *Can Europe Deliver Growth? The Sapir Report and Beyond*, Centre for European Policy Studies, Policy Brief No. 45.

Pelkmans, J., and Murphy, A. (1991), 'Catapulted into Leadership: The Community's Trade and Aid Policies *vis-à-vis* Eastern Europe', *Journal of European Integration*, 14/2–3: 125–51.

Pelkmans, J., and Winters, L. A. (1988), *Europe's Domestic Market* (London: Royal Institute of International Affairs).

Pelkmans, J., Gros, D., and Núñez Ferre, J. (2000), *Long-run Economic Aspects of the European Union's Eastern Enlargement* (The Hague: Scientific Council for Government Studies—WRR), WRR Working Documents No. W109.

Petersen, J. H. (1991), 'Harmonization of Social Security in the EC Revisited', *Journal of Common Market Studies*, 29/5: 505–26.

Petersen, J. H. (1993), 'Europäischer Binnenmarkt, Wirtschafts- und Währungsunion und die Harmonisierung der Sozialpolitik', *Deutsche Rentenversicherung*, 1/2: 15–49.

Petersen, J. H. (2000), 'Financing of the Welfare State: Possibilities and Limits', in von Maydell (ed.), *Entwicklungen der Systeme sozialer Sicherheit in Japan und Europa* (Berlin: Duncker & Humblot), 289–318.

Petersmann, E.-U. (2002), *Preparing the Doha Development Round: Improvements and Clarifications of the WTO Dispute Settlement Understanding* (San Domenico di Fiesole: EUI–Robert Schuman Centre for Advanced Studies).

Petersmann, E.-U. (2004), *Preparing the Doha Development Round: Challenges to the Legitimacy and Efficiency of the World Trading System* (San Domenico di Fiesole: EUI–Robert Schuman Centre for Advanced Studies).

Peterson, J. (1994), 'Europe and America in the Clinton Era', *Journal of Common Market Studies*, 32/3: 411–26.

Peterson, J. (1995), 'Decision-Making in the European Union: Towards a Framework for Analysis', *Journal of European Public Policy*, 2/1: 69–93.

Peterson, J. (1997), 'States, Societies and the European Union', *West European Politics*, 20/4: 1–24.

Peterson, J. (2004), 'Policy Networks', in Wiener and Diez (eds.), *European Integration Theory* (Oxford: Oxford University Press), 117–35.

Peterson, J. and Bomberg, E. (1999), *Decision-Making in the European Union* (London: Palgrave Macmillan).

Peterson, J., and Shackleton, M. (2002) (eds.), *The Institutions of the European Union* (Oxford: Oxford University Press).

Peterson, J., and Shackleton, M. (2005) (eds.), *The Institutions of the European Union*, 2nd edn. (Oxford: Oxford University Press), forthcoming.

Peterson, P. E., and Rom, M. C. (1990), *Welfare Magnets: A New Case for a National Standard* (Washington: Brookings Institution).

Phinnemore, D. (2003), 'Stabilisation and Association Agreements: Europe Agreements for the Western Balkans?', *European Foreign Affairs Review*, 8: 77–103.

Phinnemore, D. (2004), 'Institutions and Governance', in Nugent (ed.), *European Union Enlargement* (London: Palgrave), 118–31.

Pielow, J. C. (2001), *Grundstrukturen der öffentlichen Versorgung. Vorgaben des euoropäischen Gemeinschaftsrechts sowie des französischen und deutschen Rechts unter besonderer Berücksichtigung der Elektrizitätswirtschaft* (Tübingen: Mohr Siebeck).

Pielow, J. C. (2002), ' "Öffentliche Daseinsvorsorge" als Herausforderung für die deutschen Länder und Kommunen: Stand und Perspektiven', *Jahrbuch des Föderalismus: Föderalismus, Subsidiarität und Regionen in Europa* (Baden-Baden: Nomos), 3: 163–81.

Pierson, P. (1995a), 'The Creeping Nationalization of Income Transfers in the United States', in Leibfried and Pierson (1995b: 301–28).

Pierson, P. (1995b), 'Federal Institutions and the Development of Social Policy', *Governance*, 8/4: 449–78.

Pierson, P. (1996a), 'The New Politics of the Welfare State', *World Politics*, 48/2: 147–79.

Pierson, P. (1996b), 'The Path to European Integration: A Historical Institutionalist Analysis', *Comparative Political Studies*, 29/2: 123–63.

Pierson, P. (1998), 'Irresistible Forces, Immovable Objects: Post-Industrial Welfare States Confront Permanent Austerity', *Journal of European Public Policy*, 5/4: 539–60.

Pierson, P. (2000), 'Increasing Returns, Path Dependence, and the Study of Politics', *American Political Science Review*, 94/ 2: 251–67.

Pierson, P. (2001) (ed.), *The New Politics of the Welfare State* (Oxford: Oxford University Press).

Pierson, P., and Leibfried, S. (1995), 'The Dynamics of Social Policy Integration', in Leibfried and Pierson (1995b), 432–65.

Pinder, J. (1968), 'Positive Integration and Negative Integration: Some Problems of Economic Union in the EEC', *World Today*, 24/3: 88–110.

Pinder, J. (1991), *The European Community and Eastern Europe* (London: Pinter).

Pinder, J., and Pinder, P. (1975), *The European Community's Policy Towards Eastern Europe*, Chatham House European Series No. 25.

Pippan, C. (2004), 'The Rocky Road to Europe: The EU's Stablisation and Association Process for the Western Balkans and the Principle of Conditionality', *European Foreign Affairs Review*, 9: 219–45.

Pochet, P. (2003), 'Pensions: The European Debate', in Clark and Whiteside (eds.), *Pension Security in the 21st Century: Redrawing the Public-Private Debate* (Oxford: Oxford University Press), 44–63.

Polanyi, K. (1994) [1944], *The Great Transformation* (New York: Rinehart)

Pollack, M. A. (1995), 'Regional Actors in an Intergovernmental Play: The Making and Implementation of EC Structural Policy', in Mazey and Rhodes (eds.), *The State of the European Union, Vol. III* (Boston: Lynne Rienner), 361–90.

Pollack, M. A. (1997), 'Delegation, Agency and Agenda Setting in the European Community', *International Organization*, 51/1: 99–134.

Pollack, M. A. (2000), 'The End of Creeping Competence? EU Policy-making since Maastricht', *Journal of Common Market Studies*, 38/3: 519–38.

Pollack, M. A. (2003), *The Engines of Integration: Delegation, Agency and Agenda Setting in the European Union* (Oxford: Oxford University Press).

Pollack, M. A. (2004), 'The New Institutionalisms and European Integration', in Wiener and Diez (eds.), *European Integration Theory* (Oxford: Oxford University Press), 137–56.

Pollack, M. A. (2005), 'Theorizing the European Union: International Organization, Domestic Polity, or Experiment in New Governance?', *Annual Review of Political Science*, 7, forthcoming.

Pollack, M. A., and Hafner-Burton, E. (2000), 'Mainstreaming Gender in the European Union', *Journal of European Public Policy*, 7/3: 432–56.

Pollack, M. A., and Shaffer, G. C. (2001a), 'Who Governs?', in Pollack and Shaffer (eds.), *Transatlantic Governance in the Global Economy* (Lanham: Rowman & Littlefield), 287–305.

Pollack, M. A., and Shaffer, G. C. (2001b), 'The Challenge of Reconciling Regulatory Differences: Food Safety and GMOs in the Transatlantic Relationship', in Pollack and Shaffer (eds.), *Transatlantic Governance in the Global Economy* (Lanham: Rowman & Littlefield), 153–78.

Porter, M. (1990), *The Competitive Advantage of Nations* (London: Macmillan).

Preeg, E. H. (1970), *Traders and Diplomats: An Analysis of the Kennedy Round of Negotiations under the General Agreement on Tariffs and Trade* (Washington: Brookings Institution).

Preeg, E. H. (1995), *Traders in a Brave New World: The Uruguay Round and the Future of the International Trading System* (Chicago: University of Chicago Press).

Preston, C. (1997), *Enlargement and Integration in the European Union* (London: Routledge).

Puchala, D. (1972), 'Of Blind Men, Elephants, and International Integration', *Journal of Common Market Studies*, 10/3: 267–84.

Putnam, R. D. (1988), 'Diplomacy and Domestic Politics: The Logic of Two-Level Games', *International Organization*, 42/3: 427–60.

Raveaud, G. (2005), 'The European Employment Strategy: From Ends to Means?', in Salais and Villeneuve (eds.), *Europe and the Politics of Capabilities* (Cambridge: Cambridge University Press).

Redmond, J. (1992) (ed.), *The External Relations of the European Community* (London: Macmillan).

Reflection Group (1995), *Reform of the European Union (Interim Report)*, Madrid, 10, Nov. SN 517/95 (REFLEX 18).

Reif, K. (1994), 'Less Legitimation through Lazy Parties? Lessons from the 1994 European Elections', paper presented at the XVIth World Congress of the International Political Science Association, Berlin, 21–25 Aug.

Rein, M., and Rainwater, L. (1986) (eds.), *Public-Private Interplay in Social Protection: A Comparative Study* (Armonk: M. E. Sharpe).

Ress, G. (1994), 'The Constitution and the Maastricht Treaty: Between Coopertion and Conflict', *German Politics*, 3/3: 47–74.

Revéret, J.-P., and Weber, J. (1997), 'L'évolution des régimes internationaux de gestion des pêches', in Godard (ed.), *Le principe de précaution dans la conduite des affaries humaines* (Paris: Éditions de l'EHESS), 245–58.

Rhodes, M. (1991), 'The Social Dimension of the Single European Market: National versus Transnational Regulation', *European Journal of Political Research*, 19: 245–80.

Rhodes, M. (1992), 'The Future of the "Social Dimension": Labour Market Regulation in Post-1992 Europe', *Journal of Common Market Studies*, 30/1: 23–51.

Rhodes, M. (1995), 'A Regulatory Conundrum: Industrial Relations and the Social Dimension', in Leibfried and Pierson (1995b) (eds.), *European Social Policy: Between Fragmentation and Integration* (Washington: Brookings Institution), 78–122.

Rhodes, M. (1999), 'An Awkward Alliance: France, Germany and Social Policy', in Webber (ed.), *The Franco-German Relationship in the European Union* (London: Routledge), 130–47.

Rhodes, R. (1996), 'The New Governance: Governing without Government', *Political Studies*, 44/3: 652–57.

Richardson, J. J. (1982) (ed.), *Policy Styles in Western Europe* (London: Allen & Unwin).

Rieger, E., and Leibfried, S. (2003), *Limits to Globalization: Welfare States in the World Economy* (Cambridge: Polity).

Riley, A. (2003), 'EC Antitrust Modernization: The Commission does very nicely, thank you!', *European Competition Law Review*, 24/11: 604–15, 24/12: 657–72.

Risse, T. (2000), 'Let's Argue!' Communicative Action and World Politics', *International Organization*, 54/1: 1–39.

Risse, T. (2004), 'Social Constructivism and European Integration', in Wiener and Diez (eds.), *European Integration Theory* (Oxford: Oxford University Press), 159–76.

Risse, T., Engelmann-Marten, D., Knopf, H.-J., and Roscher, K. (1999), 'To Euro or Not to Euro? The EMU and Identity Politics in the European Union', *European Journal of International Relations*, 5/2: 147–87.

Robertson, D. B. (1989), 'The Bias of American Federalism: The Limits of Welfare State Development in the Progressive Era', *Journal of Polity History*, 1/3: 261–91.

Rollo, J., and Smith, M. A. M. (1993), 'The Political Economy of Eastern European Trade with the European Community: Why so Sensitive?', *Economic Policy*, 16: 139–81.

Rollo, J., and Wallace, H. (1991), 'New Patterns of Partnership', in Bonvicini *et al.* (eds.), *The Community and the Emerging Democracies: A Joint Policy Report* (London: RIIA), 53–65.

Romero, F. (1993), 'Migration as an Issue in European Interdependence and Integration: The Case of Italy', in Milward *et al.* (eds.), *The Frontier of National Sovereignty: History and Theory, 1945–2991* (London: Routledge), 33–58, 205–8.

Rosenau, J. N. (1992), 'Governance, Order and Change in World Politics', in Rosenau and Czempiel (eds.), *Governance without Government: Order and Change in World Politics* (Cambridge: Cambridge University Press), 1–29.

Rosenblatt, J., Mayer, T., Bartholdy, K., Demekas, D., Gupta, S., and Lipschitz, I. (1988), *The Common Agricultural Policy: Principles and Consequences* (Washington: International Monetary Fund).

Ross, G. (1995a), *Jacques Delors and European Integration* (Cambridge: Polity).

Ross, G. (1995b), 'Assessing the Delors Era in Social Policy', in Leibfried and Pierson (1995b: 357–88).

Rouam, C. (1994), 'L'Union Européenne Face aux Pays d'Europe Centrale et Orientale: Délocalisations Industrielles ou Harmonisation des Conditions de Concurrence?', *Revue du Marché Commun et de l'Union Européenne*, 383: 643–8.

Ruano, L. (2002), *Origins and Implications of the European Union's Enlargement Negotiations Procedure* (San Domenico di Fiesole: EUI–Robert Schuman Centre for Advanced Studies) RSC Working Papers No. 2002/62.

Russell, R. (1977), 'Snakes and Sheiks: Managing Europe's Money', in Wallace, Wallace, and Webb (eds.), *Policy-Making in the European Communities* (Chichester: Wiley), 66–90.

Salais, R., and Villeneuve, R. (2005) (eds.), *Europe and the Politics of Capabilities* (Cambridge: Cambridge University Press), forthcoming.

Sandholtz, W. (1993), 'Choosing Union: Monetary Politics and Maastricht', *International Organization*, 47: 1–40.

Sandholtz, W., and Zysman, J. (1989), '1992: Recasting the European Bargain', *World Politics*, 42/1: 95–128.

Sapir, A., Aghion, P., Bertola, G., Hellwig, M., Pisani-Ferry, J., Rosati, D., Viñals, J., and Wallace, H. (2004), *An Agenda for a Growing Europe: Making the EU Economic System Deliver*, Report of an Independent High Level Study Group (Chairman: André Sapir) (Oxford: Oxford University Press) (originally published on-line by the Commission, 2003).

Sbragia, A. (1992), *Euro-Politics: Institutions and Policymaking in the 'New' European Community* (Washington: Brookings Institution).

Sbragia, A. (1993), 'The European Community: A Balancing Act', *Publius*, 23/3: 23–38.

Sbragia, A. (2000), 'Environmental Policy: Economic Constraints and External Pressures', in Wallace and Wallace (eds.), *Policy-Making in the European Union* (Oxford: Oxford University Press), 235–55.

Sbragia, A., and Damro, C. (1999), 'The Changing Role of the European Union in International Environmental Politics: Institution Building and the Politics of Climate Change', *Environment and Planning C: Government and Policy*, 17/1: 53–8.

Scharpf, F. W. (1988), 'The Joint-Decision Trap: Lessons from German Federalism and European Integration', *Public Administration*, 66: 239–78.

Scharpf, F. W. (1994a), 'Community and Autonomy: Multi-level Policy-Making in the European Union', *Journal of European Public Policy*, 1/2: 219–42.

Scharpf, F. W. (1994*b*), 'Mehrebenenpolitik im vollendeten Binnenmarkt', *Staatswissenschaft und Staatspraxis*, 5/4: 475–502.

Scharpf, F. W. (1997), *Games Real Actors Play: Actor-Centred Institutionalism in Policy Research* (Boulder: Westview).

Scharpf, F. W. (1999), *Governing in Europe: Democratic and Effective?* (Oxford: Oxford University Press).

Scharpf, F. W. (2002), *The European Social Model: Coping with the Challenges of Diversity* (Cologne: Max Planck Institute for the Study of Societies), MFIfG Working Paper 02/8, July.

Scheingate, A. D. (2001), *The Welfare State for Farmers: Institutions and Interest Group Power in the United States, France, and Japan* (Princeton: Princeton University Press).

Schiller, K. (1939), *Marktregulierung und Marktordnung in der Weltagrarwirtschaft* (Jena: Fischer).

Schmähl, W. (2003), 'Initial Experiences with the "Open Method of Coordination": Open Questions Regarding "Financial Sustainability" and "Adequacy" of Pensions in an Expanded European Union', in *VDR*, (Frankfurt a.M.: VDR), DRV Schriften 34, special issue, *Deutsche Rentenversicherung*, 98–113.

Schmähl, W. (2004), 'EU Enlargement and Social Security: Some Dimensions of a Complex Topic', *Intereconomics: Review of European Economic Policy*, 39/1 (Jan./Feb.), 21–8.

Schimmelfennig, F. (2003*a*), 'Strategic Action in a Community Environment: The Decision to Enlarge the European Union to the East', *Comparative Political Studies*, 36/1–2: 156–83.

Schimmelfennig, F. (2003*b*), *The EU, NATO, and the Integration of Europe: Rules and Rhetoric* (Cambridge: Cambridge University Press).

Schimmelfennig, F., and Sedelmeier, U. (2002), 'Theorising EU Enlargement: Research Focus, Hypotheses, and the State of Research', *Journal of European Public Policy*, 9/4: 500–28.

Schimmelfennig, F., and Sedelmeier, U. (2005) (eds.), *The Europeanization of Central and Eastern Europe* (Ithaca: Cornell University Press).

Schmidt, S. K. (1998), 'Commission Activism: Subsuming Telecommunications and Electricity under European Competition Law', *Journal of European Public Policy*, 5/1: 169–84.

Schmidt, S. K. (2004*a*), *Die Folgen der europäischen Integration für die Bundesrepublik Deutschland: Wandel durch Verflechtung* (Cologne: Max Planck Institute for the Study of Societies), MPIfG Discussion Paper 02/4.

Schmidt, S. K. (2004*b*), *Rechtsunsicherheit statt Regulierungswettbewerb: die nationalen Folgen des europäischen Binnenmarkts für Dienstleistungen* (Hagen: FernUniversität Hagen), habilitation thesis.

Schmidt, V. A. (2002), *The Futures of European Capitalism* (Oxford: Oxford University Press).

Schmidt, V. A. (2004), 'Democratic Legitimacy in a Regional State?', *Journal of Common Market Studies*, 42/5: 975–97.

Schmitter, P. C. (1996), 'Examining the Present Euro-Polity with the Help of Past Theories', in Marks, Scharpf, Schmitter, and Streeck (eds.), *Governance in the European Union* (London: Sage), 1–14.

Schneider, V., and Tenbrücken, M. (2004) (eds.), *Der Staat auf dem Rückzug: die Privatisierung öffentlicher Infrastrukturen* (Frankfurt a.M.: Campus).

Schneider, V., Fink, S., and Tenbrücken, M. (2005), 'Buying out the State: A Comparative Perspective on the Privatization of Infrastructures', *Comparative Political Studies*, 37, Aug., forthcoming.

Schreiber, K. (1991), 'The New Approach to Technical Harmonization and Standards', in Hurwitz and Lequesne (eds.), *The State of the European Community: Politics, Institutions and Debates in the Transition Years* (Boulder: Lynne Rienner), 97–112.

Schuler, R. (2002), 'Comments on Articles 9–10a of Reg. 1408/71', in Fuchs (ed.), *Nomos-Kommentar zum europäischen Sozialrecht* (Baden-Baden: Nomos), 143–58.

Schulte, B. (1994), 'Sozialrecht', in Lenz *et al.* (eds.), *EG-Handbuch: Recht im Binnenmarkt* (Berlin: Verlag Neue Wirtschaftsbriefe), 407–78.

Schulte, B. (1999), Communication to the author of Ch. 10.

Schulte, B. (2004), 'Supranationales Recht', in von Maydell and Ruland (eds.), *Sozialrechtshandbuch (SRH)* (Baden-Baden: Nomos), 1611–76.

Schultz, T. W. (1943), *Redirecting Farm Policy* (New York: Macmillan).

Schulz-Weidner, W. (1997), 'Die Konsequenzen des europäischen Binnenmarktes für die deutsche Rentenversicherung', *Deutsche Rentenversicherung*, 8: 445–73.

Schulz-Weidner, W. (2003), 'Die Öffnung der Sozialversicherung im Binnenmarkt und ihre Grenzen: zugleich eine Betrachtung zu der Entscheidung des Europäischen Gerichtshofs vom 3 Oktober 2002 in der Rechtssache "Danner" C 136/00', *Zeitschrift für europäisches Sozial- und Arbeitsrecht*, 2/2: 58–68.

Schulz-Weidner, W. (2004), 'Das europäische Beihilferecht und sein Einfluss auf die Sozialversicherung', *Deutsche Rentenversicherung*, 10: 592–613.

Schwaag Serger, S. (2001), *Negotiating CAP Reform in the European Union: Agenda 2000* (Stockholm: Swedish Institute for Food and Agricultural Economics), Report 2001/4.

Schwarze, J. (1998), 'Die Bedeutung des Territorialitätsprinzips bei mitgliedstaatlichen Preiskontrollen auf dem europäischen Arzneimittelmarkt', in Schwarze (ed.), *Unverfälschter Wettbewerb für Arzneimittel im europäischen Binnenmarkt* (Baden-Baden: Nomos), 59–74.

Schwarze, J. (2001), 'Einführung: Daseinsvorsorge im Lichte des Wettbewerbsrechts', in Schwarze (ed.), *Daseinsvorsorge im Lichte des Wettbewerbsrechts* (Baden-Baden: Nomos), 9–24.

Sciarra, S. (2001) (ed.), *Labour Law in the Courts: National Judges and the European Court of Justice* (Oxford: Hart).

Scott, J. (1995), *Development Dilemmas in the European Community* (Buckingham: Open University Press).

Scott, J. (1996), 'Tragic Triumph: Agricultural Trade, the Common Agricultural Policy and the Uruguay Round', in Emiliou and O'Keeffe (eds.), *The European Union and World Trade Law: After the Uruguay Round* (Chichester: Wiley), 165–80.

Scott, J. (2003), 'European Regulation of GMOs and the WTO', *Columbia Journal of European Law*, 9: 213–39.

Scott, J., and Trubeck, D. (2002), 'Mind the Gap: Law and New Approaches to Governance in the European Union', *European Law Journal*, 8/1: 1–18.

Scully, R. M. (1997a), 'The EP and the Co-Decision Procedure: A Reassessment', *Journal of Legislative Studies*, 3: 57–73.

Scully, R. M. (1997b), 'The EP and Co-Decision: A Rejoinder to Tsebelis and Garrett', *Journal of Legislative Studies*, 3: 93–103.

Scully, R. M. (1997c), 'Positively My Last Words on Co-Decision', *Journal of Legislative Studies*, 3: 144–6.

Sedelmeier, U. (1994), *The European Union's Association Policy Towards Central Eastern Europe: Political and Economic Rationales in Conflict*, SEI Working Paper No. 7 (Falmer: Sussex European Institute).

Sedelmeier, U. (1998), The European Union's Association Policy Towards the Countries of Central and Eastern Europe: Collective EU Identity and Policy Paradigms in a Composite Policy, Ph.D. thesis.

Sedelmeier, U. (2000), 'East of Amsterdam: The Implications of the Amsterdam Treaty for Eastern Enlargement', in Wiener and Neunreither (eds.), *European Integration after Amsterdam: Institutional Dynamics and Prospects for Democracy* (Oxford: Oxford University Press), 218–35.

Sedelmeier, U. (2002), 'Sectoral Dynamics of EU Eastern Enlargement: Advocacy, Access and Alliances in a Composite Policy', *Journal of European Public Policy*, 9/4: 627–49.

Sedelmeier, U. (2005), *The Path to Eastern Enlargement: EU Identity and Sectoral Policy Paradigms* (Manchester: Manchester University Press).

Sedelmeier, U., and Wallace, H. (1996), 'Policies towards the Countries of Central and Eastern Europe', in Wallace and Wallace (eds.), *Policy-Making in the European Union*, 3rd edn. (Oxford: Oxford University Press), 353–87.

Shackleton, M. (1983), 'Fishing for a Policy? The Common Fisheries Policy of the Community', in Wallace, Wallace, and Webb (eds.), *Policy-Making in the European Community* (Chichester: Wiley), 349–72.

Shackleton, M. (1986), *The Politics of Fishing in Britain and France* (Aldershot: Gower).

Shackleton, M. (1990), *Financing the European Community* (London: Pinter).

Shackleton, M. (1993*a*), 'The Community Budget After Maastricht', in Cafruny and Rosenthal (eds.), *The State of the European Community—The Maastricht Debates and Beyond*, II (Burnt Mill: Longman), 373–90.

Shackleton, M. (1993*b*), 'The Budget of the EC: Structure and Process', in Lodge (ed.), *The European Community and the Challenge of the Future* (London: Pinter), 89–111.

Shackleton, M. (1993*c*), 'Keynote Article: The Delors II Budget Package', *Journal of Common Market Studies*, 31, Annual Review of Activities, 11–26.

Shaffer, G., and Pollack, M. (2005), 'Dealing with Regulatory Differences: Global Markets, International Institutions and the Transatlantic Dispute over Agricultural Biotechnology', in Pollack and Shaffer (eds.), *The New Transatlantic Agenda and the Future of Transatlantic Economic Governance* (Florence: European University Institute), forthcoming.

Shepsle, K. (1979), 'Institutional Arrangements and Equilibrium in Multidimensional Voting Models', *American Journal of Political Science*, 23/1: 27–60.

Shepsle, K. (1986), 'Institutional Equilibrium and Equilibrium Institutions', in Weisberg (ed.), *Political Science: The Science of Politics* (New York: Agathon), 51–81.

Shapiro, M., and Stone, A. (1994), 'The New Constitutional Politics of Europe', *Comparative Political Studies*, 26/4: 397–420.

Shaw, J. (2000) (ed.), *Social Law and Policy in an Evolving European Union* (Oxford: Hart).

Sieveking, K. (1998) (ed.), *Soziale Sicherung bei Pflegebedürftigkeit in der Europäischen Union* (Baden-Baden: Nomos).

Sieveking, K. (2004), 'EU Agreements with the CEEC: Achievements and Problems with Special Reference to the Free Movement of Persons and Services and to Freedom of Establishment', *European Journal of Social Security*, 5/1: 38–54.

SIGMA–OECD (1998), *Preparing Public Administrations for the European Administrative Space* (Paris: OECD), SIGMA Papers No. 23.

Skogstad, G. (2001), 'The WTO and Food Safety Regulatory Policy Innovation in the European Union', *Journal of Common Market Studies*, 39/3: 485–505 (Sept.).

Skogstad, G. (2003), 'Legitimacy and/or Policy Effectiveness? Network Governance and GMO Regulation in the European Union', *Journal of European Public Policy*, 10/3: 321–38.

Slaughter, A.-M., Stone Sweet, A., and Weiler, J. H. H. (1997), *The European Court and National Courts* (Oxford: Hart).

Slaughter, A.-M. (2004), *A New World Order* (Princeton: Princeton University Press).

Slocock, B. (1996), 'The Paradox of Environmental Policy in Eastern Europe: The Dynamics of Policy-Making in the Czech Republic', *Environmental Politics*, 5/3: 501–21.

Smismans, S. (2004), *EU Employment Policy: Decentralisation or Centralisation through the Open Method of Coordination*, San Domenico di Fiesole-European University Institute, EUI Working Paper, Law 04-01.

Smith, A. (1998), 'The Sub-regional Level: Key Battleground for the Structural Funds', in Le Gales and Lequesne (eds.), *Regions in Europe* (London: Routledge), 50–66.

Smith, B. (1999), 'Politics and Policy-Making at the 1996–1997 Intergovernmental Conference', London School of Economics Ph.D. thesis.

Smith, K. E. (2003), *European Union Foreign Policy in a Changing World* (Cambridge: Polity Press).

Smith, M. E. (2004), *Europe's Foreign and Security Policy: the Institutions of Cooperation* (Cambridge: Cambridge University Press).

Smith, M. A. M., and Wallace, H. (1994), 'The European Union: Towards a Policy for Europe', *International Affairs*, 70/3: 429–44.

Smith, M. A. M., Holmes, P. M., Sedelmeier, U., Smith, E., Wallace, H., and Young, A. R. (1996), *The European Union and Central and Eastern Europe: Pre-accession Strategies*, SEI Working Paper No. 15 (Falmer: Sussex European Institute).

Snyder, F. G. (1985), *Law of the Common Agricultural Policy* (London: Sweet & Maxwell).

Soetendorp, B. (1990), 'The evolution of the EC/EU as a Single Foreign Policy Actor', in Carlsnaes, W. and Smith, S. (eds.), *European Foreign Policy* (London: Sage), 103–19.

Sommer, J. (2003), *The Open Method of Coordination: Some Remarks regarding Old Age Security within an Enlarged European Union* (Bremen: Centre for Social Policy Research), Working Paper 2/03, available on-line at *www.zes.uni-bremen.de*.

Spence, D. (1991), *Enlargement without Accession: The EC's Response to German Unification*, RIIA Discussion Paper No. 36.

Steunenberg, B., Koboldt, C., and Schmidtchen, D. (1996), 'Policymaking, Comitology, and the Balance of Power in the European Union', *International Review of Law and Economics*, 16: 329–44.

Steunenberg, B., Koboldt, C., and Schmidtchen, D. (1997), 'Beyond Comitology: A Comparative Analysis of Implementation Procedures with Parliamentary Involvement', *Aussenwirtschaft*, 52: 87–112.

Stevens, C. (2000), 'Trade with Developing Countries: Banana Skins and Turf Wars', in Wallace and Wallace (eds.), *Policy-Making in the European Union*, 4th edn. (Oxford: Oxford University Press), 401–26.

Stewart, T. P., and Johanson, D. S. (1999), 'Policy in Flux: The European Union's Laws on Agricultural Biotechnology and their Effects on International Trade', *Drake Journal of Agricultural Law*, 4: 243–95.

Stone, D. A. (1989), 'At Risk in the Welfare State', *Social Research*, 56/3: 591–633.

Stone Sweet, A., and Brunell, T. L. (1997), 'The European Court and National Courts: A Statistical Analysis of Preliminary References, 1961–95', *Journal of European Public Policy*, 5/1: 66–97.

Stone Sweet, A., and Brunell, T. L. (1998a), 'The European Courts and National Courts: A Statistical Analysis of Preliminary References 1961–95', *Journal of European Public Policy*, 5: 66–97.

Stone Sweet, A., and Brunell, T. L. (1998b), 'Constructing a Supranational Constitution: Dispute Resolution and Governance in the European Community', *American Political Science Review*, 92: 63–81.

Stone Sweet, A., and Caporaso, T. (1998), 'From Free Trade to Supranational Policy', in Sandholtz and Stone Sweet (eds.), *European Integration and Supranational Governance* (Oxford: Oxford University Press), 92–133.

Streeck, W. (1995), 'From Market Making to State Building?', in Leibfried and Pierson (1995b: 389–431).

Streeck, W. (1996), 'Neo-Voluntarism: A New European Social Policy Regime', in Marks, Scharpf, Schmitter, and Streeck (eds.), *Governance in the European Union* (London: Sage), 64–94.

Streeck, W. (1998), *The Internationalization of Industrial Relations in Europe: Prospects and* Problems (Cologne: Max Planck Institute for the Study of Societies), MPIfG Discussion Paper 98/2.

Streeck, W. (2000), 'Competitive Solidarity: Rethinking the "European Social Model" ', in Hinrichs *et al.* (eds.), *Kontingenz und Krise: Insititutionenpolitik in kapitalistischen und postsozialistischen Gesellschaften* (Frankfurt a.M.: Campus), 245–61.

Streeck, W., and Schmitter, P. C. (1991), 'From National Corporatism to Transnational Pluralism: Organized Interests in the Single European Market', *Politics and Society*, 19/2: 133–64.

Stubb, A. (1997), 'The 1996 Intergovernmental Conference and the Management of Flexible Integration', *Journal of European Public Policy*, 4/1: 37–55.

Stubb, A. (2002), *Negotiating Flexibility in the European Union: Amsterdam, Nice and Beyond* (Basingstoke: Palgrave).

Süddeutsche Zeitung (2004), 'Nationen im Übergang. Gewaltige Investitionen sind nötig für sauberes Wasser, Kläranlagen und Müllentsorgung', 8, 23 Mar.

Sufrin, B. (2000), 'The Chapter II Prohibition', in Roger and MacCulloch (eds.), *The UK Competition Act* (Oxford: Hart), 119–47.

Sutcliffe, J. B. (2000), 'The 1999 Reform of the Structural Fund Regulations: Multi-Level Governance or Renationalization?', *Journal of European Public Policy*, 7/2: 290–309.

Symes, D. (1999) (ed.), *Alternative Management Systems for Fisheries* (Oxford: Fishing News Books).

Syrpis, P. (2002), 'Legitimising European Governance: Taking Subsidiarity Seriously within the Open Method of Coordination', mimeo, European University Institute, Florence.

Tallberg, J. (2000), 'The Anatomy of Autonomy: An Institutional Account of Variation in Supranational Influence', *Journal of Common Market Studies*, 38/5: 843–64.

Tangermann, S. (2004), *Agricultural Support: How is it Measured and What does it Mean?* (Paris: OECD Observer), Policy Brief.

Tarrow, S. (1998), *Building a Composite Polity: Popular Contention in the European Union*, Institute for European Studies Working Paper 98.3, Cornell University.

Tarschys, D. (2003), *Reinventing Cohesion: The Future of European Structural Policy* (Stockholm: Swedish Institute for European Policy Studies), Report 17.

Taylor, P. (1983), *The Limits of European Integration* (New York: Columbia University Press).

Taylor, P. (1996), *The European Union in the 1990s* (Oxford: Oxford University Press).

Thatcher, M. (1984), 'Europe: The Future', paper presented to the European Council, Fontainbleu, 25–26 June.

Thelen, K., and Steinmo, S. (1992), 'Introduction', in Thelen and Steinmo (eds.), *Structuring Politics: Historical Institutionalism in Comparative Politics* (Cambridge: Cambridge University Press), 1–32.

Thielemann, E. (1988), 'EC Aid Control: Driving a Wedge between Europe and the Regions', paper presented at the Third UACES Research Conference, University of Lincolnshire and Humberside, Lincoln, 9–11 Sept.

Thom, M. (1993), 'The Governance of a Common in the European Community: The Common Fisheries Policy', University of Strathclyde Ph.D. thesis.

Tidow, S. (2003), 'The Emergence of a European Employment Policy', in Overbeck (ed.), *The Political Economy of European Employment* (London: Routledge), 77–98.

Tomka, B. (2004), 'Wohlfahrtsstaatliche Entwicklung in Ostmitteleuropa und das Europäische Sozialmodell, 1945–1990', in Kaelble and Schmid (eds.), *Das europäische Sozialmodell: auf dem Weg zum transnationalen Sozialstaat* (Berlin: Sigma), 107–39.

Torreblanca, J. (2001), *The Reuniting of Europe: Promises, Negotiations and Compromises* (Aldershot: Ashgate).

Tracy, M. (1989), *Government and Agriculture in Western Europe* (New York: Harvester Wheatsheaf).

Tranholm-Mikkelsen, J. (1991), 'Neo-functionalism: Obstinate or Obsolete? A Reappraisal in Light of the New Dynamism of the EC', *Millennium: Journal of International Studies*, 20/1: 1–21.

Treib, O. (2004), *Der EU-Verfassungsvertrag und die Zukunft des Wohlfahrtsstaates in Europa* (Vienna: Institut Für Höhere Studien (IHS)), Reihe Politikwissenschaft, No. 99, available on-line at *www.ihs.ac.at/publications/*.

Treib, O., Bähr, H., and Falkner, G. (2004), 'Modes of Governance, Old and New: A Note Towards Conceptual Clarification', paper presented at the NEWGOV workshop 'Emergence, Evolution and Evaluation', Brussels, 10 Dec.

Tsebelis, G. (1994), 'The Power of the European Parliament as a Conditional Agenda Setter', *American Political Science Review*, 88/1: 128–42.

Tsebelis, G. (1996), 'More on the European Parliament as a Conditional Agenda-Setter: Response to Moser', *American Political Science Review*, 90: 839–44.

Tsebelis, G. (1997), 'Maastricht and the Democratic Deficit', *Aussenwirtschaft*, 52: 29–56.

Tsebelis, G., and Garrett, G. (1997a), 'Agenda Setting, Vetoes, and the European Union's Co-Decision Procedure', *Journal of Legislative Studies*, 3: 74–92.

Tsebelis, G., and Garrett, G. (1997b), 'More on the Co-Decision Endgame', *Journal of Legislative Studies*, 3: 139–43.

Tsebelis, G., and Garrett, G. (2000), 'Legislative Politics in the European Union', *European Union Politics*, 1/1: 9–36.

Tsebelis, G., and Garrett, G. (2001), 'The Institutional Foundations of Intergovernmentalism and Supranationalism in the European Union', *International Organization*, 55/2: 357–90.

Tsebelis, G., Jensen, C., Kalandrakis, A., and Kreppel, A. (2001), 'Legislative Procedures in the European Union: An Empirical Analysis', *British Journal of Political Science*, 31/4: 573–99.

Tsekouras, K. (2000), 'Exploiting the Implementation Potential of Alternative Instruments: Design Options for Environmental Liability Funds', in Knill and Lenschow (eds.), *Implementing EU Environmental Policies: New Directions and Old Problems* (Manchester: Manchester University Press), 134–67.

Tsoukalis, L. (1977), *The Politics and Economics of European Monetary Integration* (London: Allen & Unwin).

Tsoukalis, L. (1997), *The New European Economy Revisited* (Oxford: Oxford University Press).

Tugendhat, C. (1985), 'How to Get Europe Moving Again', *International Affairs*, 61/3, 421–9.

Twomey, P. (1999), 'Constructing a Secure Space: The Area of Freedom, Security and Justice', in O'Keeffe and Twomey (eds.), *Legal Issues of the Amsterdam Treaty* (Oxford: Portland Oregon), 351–74.

Union des Armateurs à la Pêche de France (1998), 'Réponse de l'UAPF au questionnaire de la Commission sur la politique commune de la pêche après 2002', *La pêche maritime*, May–July: 322–34.

United Nations (2004), *Human Development Report*, United Nations Development Programme (New York: UN).

US Department of Agriculture (2004), *US–EU Food and Agriculture Comparisons, Washington, DC: USDA, Market and Trade Economics Division, Economic Research Service* (Agriculture and Trade Report, WRS-04-04).

Usher, J. A. (2001), *EC Agricultural Law* (Oxford: Oxford University Press).

van Cleveland, H. B. (1966) (ed.), *The Atlantic Idea and its European Rivals* (New York: McGraw-Hill).

van Eeckelen, W. (1993), 'WEU Prepares the Way for New Missions', *Nato Review*, 5: 19–23.

van Kersbergen, K., and Verbeek, B. (2004), 'Subsidiarity as a Principle of Governance in the European Union', *Comparative European Politics*, 2: 142–62.

van Riel, B., and van der Meer, M. (2002), 'The Advocacy Coalition for European employment policy—The European Integration Process after EMU', in Hegmann, H. and Neumaecker, B. (eds.), *Die Europäische Union aus politökonomischer Perspective* (Marburg: Metropolis Verlag), 117–37.

van Schendelen, M. P. C. M. (1998) (ed.), *EU Committees as Influential Policymakers* (Aldershot: Ashgate).

van Waarden, F., and Drahos, M. (2002), 'Courts and (Epistemic) Communities in the Convergence of Competition Policies', *Journal of European Public Policy*, 9/6: 913–34.

Vasey, M. (1988), 'Decision-Making in the Agricultural Council and the "Luxembourg Compromise" ', *Common Market Law Review*, 25/5: 725–32.

Vaubel, R. (1994), 'The Political Economy of Centralization and the European Community', *Public Choice*, 59/1: 151–85.

Vaughan-Whitehead, D. (2003), *EU Enlargement versus Social Europe? The Uncertain Future of the European Social Model*. Foreword by Jacques Delors (Cheltenham: Edward Elgar).

Veljanovski, C. (2004), 'EC Merger Policy after *GE/Honeywell* and *Airtours*', *The Antitrust Bulletin*, Spring–Summer: 153–93.

Verdun, A. (1999), 'The Role of the Delors Committee in Creating EMU: An Epistemic Community?', *Journal of European Public Policy*, 6/2: 308–28.

Verheijen, A. J. G. (2000), *Administrative Capacity Development: A Race Against Time?* (The Hague: Netherlands Scientific Council for Government), WRR Working Documents W 107.

Vernet, D. (1992), 'The Dilemma of French Foreign Policy', *International Affairs*, 68/4: 655–64.

Vickers, J. (2003), 'Competition Economics and Policy', *European Competition Law Review*, 24/3: 95–102.

Villain, C., and Arnold, R. (1990), 'New Directions for European Agricultural Policy', Report of the CEPS CAP Expert Group (Brussels: Centre for European Policy Studies).

Vogel, D. (1986), *National Styles of Regulation* (Ithaca: Cornell University Press).

Vogel, D. (1989), *Fluctuating Fortunes: The Political Power of Business in America* (New York: Basic Books).

Vogel, D. (1995), *Trading Up: Consumer and Environmental Regulation in a Global Economy* (Cambridge, Mass.: Harvard University Press).

Vogel, D. (2001), *Ships Passing in the Night: GMOs and the Contemporary Politics of Risk Regulation in Europe* (San Domenico di Fiesole: EUI–Robert Schuman Centre for Advanced Studies), RSC Working Paper No. 2001/16.

Vogel-Polsky, E., and Vogel, J. (1991), *L'Europe sociale 1993: illusion, alibi ou réalité?* (Brussels: Éditions de l'Université Libre de Bruxelles).

Vos, E. (2000), 'EU Food Safety Regulation in the Aftermath of the BSE Crisis', *Journal of Consumer Policy*, 23: 227–55.

Wallace, H. (1973), *National Governments and the European Communities* (London: Chatham House).

Wallace, H. (1977), 'The Establishment of the Regional Development Fund: Common Policy or Port Barrel?', in Wallace, Wallace, and Webb (eds.), *Policy-Making in the European Communities* (Chichester: Wiley), 136–64.

Wallace, H. (1983), 'Distributional Politics: Dividing up the Community Cake', in Wallace, Wallace, and Webb (eds.), *Policy-Making in the European Communities*, 2nd edn. (Chichester: Wiley), 81–113.

Wallace, H. (1984), 'Bilateral, Trilateral and Multilateral Negotiations in the European Community', in Morgan and Bray (eds.), *Partners and Rivals in Western Europe: Britain, France and Germany* (Aldershot: Gower), 156–74.

Wallace, H. (1999), 'Whose Europe Is It Anyway?', *European Journal of Political Research*, 35/3: 287–306.

Wallace, H. (2000), 'EU Enlargement: A Neglected Subject', in Cowles and Smith (eds.), *The State of the European Union, v: Risks, Reforms, Resistance and Revival* (Oxford: Oxford University Press), 149–63.

Wallace, H. (2001) (ed.), *Interlocking Dimensions of European Integration* (London: Palgrave Macmillan).

Wallace, H., and Wallace, W. (1995), *Flying Together in a Larger and More Diverse European Union*, Netherlands Scientific Council for Government Policy, Working Documents W87, 9–74.

Wallace, H., and Wallace, W. (1996) (eds.), *Policy-Making in the European Union*, 3rd edn. (Oxford: Oxford University Press), 439–60.

Wallace, H., and Wallace, W. (2000) (eds.), *Policy-Making in the European Union*, 4th edn. (Oxford: Oxford University Press).

Wallace, H., and Young, A. R. (1997) (eds.), *Participation and Policy-Making in the European Union* (Oxford: Clarendon Press).

Wallace, W. (1982), 'Europe as a Confederation: The Community and the Nation-State', *Journal of Common Market Studies*, 20/1–2: 57–68.

Wallace, W. (1983*b*), 'Political Cooperation: Integration through Intergovernmentalism', in Wallace, Wallace, and Webb (eds.), *Policy-Making in the European Communities*, 2nd edn. (Chichester: Wiley), 337–402.

Wallace, W. (1984), 'Bilateral, Trilateral and Multilateral Negotiations in the European Community,' in Morgan and Bray (eds.), *Partners and Rivals in Western Europe: Britain, France and Germany* (Aldershot: Gower), 156–74.

Wallace, W. (1989), 'European Security: Bilateral Steps to Multilateral Cooperation', in Boyer *et al.* (eds.), *Franco–British Defence Cooperation: Towards a New Entente Cordiale* (London: Routledge), 171–80.

Wallace, W. (1994*a*), *Regional Integration: The West European Experience* (Washington: Brookings Institution).

Wallace, W. (1994*b*), 'Rescue or Retreat? The Nation State in Western Europe, 1945–93', *Political Studies*, 42, special issue, 52–76.

Wallace, W. (1996), 'Government without Statehood: The Unstable Equilibrium', in Wallace and Wallace (eds.), *Policy-Making in the European Union*, 3rd edn. (Oxford: Oxford University Press), 439–60.

Wallace, W. (1999), 'The Sharing of Sovereignty: The European Paradox', *Political Studies*, 47/3: 502–21.

Waltz, K. N. (1979), *Theory of International Politics* (Reading, Mass.: Addison-Wesley).

Wapner, P. (1996), *Environmental Activism and World Civic Politics* (Albany: SUNY Press).

Watt, A. (2004), 'Reform of the European Employment Strategy after Five Years: A Change of Course or Merely Presentation?', *European Journal of Industrial Relations*, 10/2: 117–37.

Weale, A. (1992), *The New Politics of Pollution* (Manchester: Manchester University Press).

Weale, A., Pridham, G., Cini, M., Konstadakopolos, D., Porter, M., and Flynn, B. (2000), *Environmental Governance in Europe* (Oxford: Oxford University Press).

Weaver, R. E. (1986), 'The Politics of Blame Avoidance', *Journal of Public Policy*, 6: 371–98.

Webb, C. (1977), 'Introduction: Variations on a Theoretical Theme', in Wallace, Wallace, and Webb (eds.), *Policy-Making in the European Communities* (Chichester: Wiley), 1–32.

Weber, S. (1994), 'Origins of the European Bank for Reconstruction and Development', *International Organization*, 48/1: 1–38.

Webber, D. (1999) (ed.), *The Franco-German Relationship in the European Union* (London: Routledge).

Webster, R. (1998), 'Environmental Collective Action: Stable Patterns of Cooperation and Issue Alliances at the European Level', in Greenwood and Aspinwall (eds.), *Collective Action in the European Union: Interest and the New Politics of Associability* (London: Routledge), 176–95.

Weiler, J. H. H. (1991), 'The Transformation of Europe', *Yale Law Journal*, 100/8: 2403–83.

Weiler, J. H. H. (1994), 'A Quiet Revolution: The European Court of Justice and its Interlocutors', *Comparative Political Studies*, 24/4: 510–34.

Weiler, J. H. H. (1995), 'Does Europe Need a Constitution? Reflections on Demos, Telos, and the German Maastricht Decision', *European Law Journal*, 1/2: 219–58.

Weiler, J. H. H. (1999), *The Constitution of Europe: 'Do the New Clothes Have an Emperor'? and Other Essays on European Integration* (Cambridge: Cambridge University Press).

Weiss, F. (2003), 'Manifestly Illegal Import Restrictions and Non-compliance with WTO Dispute Settlement Rulings: Lessons from the Banana Dispute', in Petersmann and Pollack (eds.), *Transatlantic Economic Disputes: The EU, the US, and the WTO* (Oxford: Oxford University Press), 121–39.

Wendt, A. (1999), *Social Theory of International Politics* (Cambridge: Cambridge University Press).

Westlake, M., and Galloway, D. (2005) (eds.), *The Council of the European Union* (London: John Harper).

WEU (1992), *Petersberg Declaration*, WEU Council of Ministers, Bonn, 19 June (London: WEU Press and Information Service).

Whish, R. (2003), *Competition Law*, 5th edn. (London: LexisNexis).

Wiener, A., and Diez, T. (2004) (eds.), *European-Integration Theory* (Oxford: Oxford University Press).

Wiener, J. B., and Rogers, M. D. (2002), 'Comparing Precaution in the United States and Europe', *Journal of Risk Research*, 5/4: 317–49.

Wilensky, H. J. (1976), *The 'New Corporatism': Centralization and the Welfare State* (London: Sage).

Wilks, S. (1999), *In the Public Interest: Competition Policy and the Monopolies and Mergers Commission* (Manchester: Manchester University Press).

Wilks, S. (2005), 'Agency Escape: Decentralisation or Dominance of the European Commission in the Modernisation of Competition Policy?', *Governance*, forthcoming.

Wilks, S., with Bartle, I. (2002), 'The Unanticipated Consequences of Creating Independent Competition Agencies', *West European Politics*, 25/1: 148–72.

Wilks, S., with McGowan, L. (1996), 'Competition Policy in the European Union: Creating a Federal Agency?', in Doern and Wilks (eds.), *Comparative Competition Policy: National Institutions in a Global Market* (Oxford: Clarendon Press), 225–67.

Willgerodt, H. (1983), 'Die Agrarpolitik der Europäischen Gemeinschaft in der Krise', *Ordo*, 34 (Stuttgart: Fischer), 97–139.

Williams, S. (1991), 'Sovereignty and Accountability in the European Community', in Keohane and Hoffmann (eds), *The New European Community* (Boulder: Westview), 155–76.

Williamson, O. (1985), *The Economic Institutions of Capitalism: Firms, Markets, Regional Contracting* (New York: Free Press).

Wilson, J. Q. (1980), *The Politics of Regulation* (New York: Basic Books).

Winham, G. (1986), *International Trade and the Tokyo-Round Negotiation* (Princeton: Princeton University Press).

Winters, A. (1992), 'The Europe Agreements: With a Little Help from Our Friends', in CEPR (ed.), *The Association Process: Making It Work*, CEPR Occasional Paper, 11: 17–33.

Wishlade, F. (1998a), 'EC Competition Policy and Regional Aid: The Trojan Horse Approach to Regional Policy-Making', paper presented at the Third UACES Research Conference, University of Lincolnshire and Humberside, Lincoln, 9–11 Sept.

Wishlade, F. (1998b), 'Competition Policy or Cohesion Policy by the Back Door? The Commission Guidelines on National Regional Aid', *European Competition Law Review*, 6: 343–57.

Wishlade, F., Yuill, D., and Mendez, C. (2003), *Regional Policy in the EU: A Passing Phase of Europeanization or a Complex Case of Policy Transfer?*, University of Strathclyde, Regional and Industrial Policy Research Paper No. 58.

Wolf, K. D. (1997), 'Entdemokratisierung durch Selbstbindung in der Europäischen Union', in Wolf (ed.), *Projekt Europa im Übergang? Probleme, Modelle und Strategien des Regierens in der Europäischen Union* (Baden-Baden: Nomos), 271–94.

Wood, P. C. (1995), 'The Franco-German Relationship in the Post-Maastricht Era', in Rhodes and Mazey (eds.), *State of the European Union* (Boulder: Lynne Rienner), 221–43.

Woolcock, S. (1996), 'Competition among Rules in the Single European Market', in Bratton *et al.* (eds.), *International Regulatory Competition and Coordination: Perspectives on Economic Regulation in Europe and the United States* (Oxford: Clarendon Press), 289–321.

Woolcock, S. (2000), 'European Trade Policy: Global Pressures and Domestic Constraints', in Wallace and Wallace (eds.), *Policy-Making in the European Union*, 4th edn. (Oxford: Oxford University Press), 373–99.

Woolcock, S., and Hodges, M. (1996), 'EU Policy in the Uruguay Round: The Story Behind the Headlines', in Wallace and Wallace (eds.), *Policy-Making in the European Union*, 3rd edn. (Oxford: Oxford University Press), 301–24.

Wurzel, R. (2002), *Environmental Policy-making in Britain, Germany and the European Union* (Manchester: Manchester University Press).

Young, A. R. (1997), 'Consumption without Representation? Consumers in the Single Market', in Wallace and Young (1997) (eds.), *Participation and Policy-Making in the European Union* (Oxford: Clarendon Press), 206–34.

Young, A. R. (2002), *Extending European Cooperation: The European Union and the 'New' International Trade Agenda* (Manchester: Manchester University Press).

Young, A. R. (2003), 'Political Transfer and "Trading Up"? Transatlantic Trade in Genetically Modified Food and US Politics', *World Politics*, 55: 457–84.

Young, A. R. (2004), 'The Incidental Fortress: The Single European Market and World Trade', *Journal of Common Market Studies*, 42/2: 393–414.

Young, A. R., and Holmes, P. (2005), 'Protection or Protectionism? EU Food Safety Rules and the WTO', in Ansell and Vogel (eds.), *Why the Beef? The Contested Governance of European Food Safety* (Cambridge, Mass.: MIT Press), forthcoming.

Young, A. R., and Wallace, H. (2000), *Regulatory Politics in the Enlarging European Union: Balancing Civic and Producer Interests* (Manchester: Manchester University Press).

Young, O. R. (1997) (ed.), *Global Governance: Drawing Insights from the Environmental Experience* (Cambridge, Mass.: MIT Press)

Zeitlin, J. (2005), 'Social Europe and Experimental Governance: Towards a New Constitutional Compromise', in de Búrca (ed.), *EU Law and the Welfare State* (Oxford: Oxford Univesity Press), forthcoming.

Zeitlin, J., and Trubek, D. (2003) (eds.), *Governing Work and Welfare in a New Economy: European and American Experiments* (Oxford: Oxford University Press).

Zeitlin, J., and Pochet, P. with Lars Magnusson (2005) (eds.), *The Open Method of Coordination in Action: The European Employment and Social Inclusion Strategies* (Brussels: PIE-Peter Lang), forthcoming.

Zoellick, R. B. (2003), speech delivered at the Munich Economic Summit, 3 May, available on-line at *www.munich-economic-summit.com/sspeech-zoellick.htm*.

Zuleeg, M. (1993), 'Die Zahlung von Ausgleichszulagen über die Binnengrenzender europäischen Gemeinschaft', *Deutsche Rentenversicherung*, 2: 71–5.

Zürn, M. (2000), 'Democratic Governance Beyond the Nation-State', in Greven and Pauly (eds.), *Democracy Beyond the State? The European Dilemma and the Emerging Global Order* (Lanham: Rowman & Littlefield), 91–114.

Index

Policy-Making in the European Union

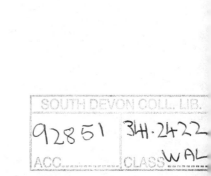

The New European Union Series

Series Editors: John Peterson and Helen Wallace

The European Union is both the most successful experiment in modern international cooperation and a daunting analytical challenge to students of politics, economics, history, law, and the social sciences. The EU of the twenty-first century will be fundamentally different from its earlier permutations, as monetary union, enlargement, a new defence role, and globalization all create pressures for a more complex, differentiated, and truly new European Union.

The New European Union series brings together the expertise of leading scholars writing on major aspects of EU politics for an international readership.

The series offers lively, accessible, reader-friendly, research-based textbooks on:

Policy-Making in the European Union

The Institutions of the European Union

The Origins and Evolution of the European Union

Theorizing the European Union

The Member States of the European Union

International Relations and the European Union

The European Union: How Does it Work